INTERNATIONAL COURTS
AND TRIBUNALS SERIES

General Editors

RUTH MACKENZIE
CESARE P. R. ROMANO
MIKAEL RASK MADSEN

Identity and Diversity on the International Bench

INTERNATIONAL COURTS AND TRIBUNALS SERIES

A distinctive feature of modern international society is the increase in the number of international judicial bodies and dispute settlement and implementation control bodies; in their case-loads; and in the range and importance of the issues they are called upon to address. These factors reflect a new stage in the delivery of international justice. *The International Courts and Tribunals series* has been established to encourage the publication of independent and scholarly works which address, in critical and analytical fashion, the legal and policy aspects of the functioning of international courts and tribunals, including their institutional, substantive, and procedural aspects.

Identity and Diversity on the International Bench

Who is the Judge?

Edited by

FREYA BAETENS

Professor of Public International Law at the PluriCourts Centre, Faculty of Law, Oslo University

OXFORD
UNIVERSITY PRESS

OXFORD
UNIVERSITY PRESS

Great Clarendon Street, Oxford, OX2 6DP,
United Kingdom

Oxford University Press is a department of the University of Oxford.
It furthers the University's objective of excellence in research, scholarship,
and education by publishing worldwide. Oxford is a registered trade mark of
Oxford University Press in the UK and in certain other countries

First Edition published in 2020

Impression: 1

Published in the United States of America by Oxford University Press
198 Madison Avenue, New York, NY 10016, United States of America

British Library Cataloguing in Publication Data
Data available

Library of Congress Control Number: 2020942398

ISBN 978–0–19–887075–3

DOI: 10.1093/oso/9780198870753.001.0001

Printed and bound by
CPI Group (UK) Ltd, Croydon, CR0 4YY

Praise for Identity and Diversity on the International Bench

The impression is often given that the interpretation and application of international laws is a matter of mechanics. It is not, as this fine collection of essays demonstrates with clarity, force and balance. The identity of our judges and arbitrators - who they are, where they come from, how they operate - is increasingly a matter of serious concern, one that goes to the very legitimacy and effectiveness of our international legal order. This work could not be more timely or significant.

Professor Philippe Sands QC, UCL; Matrix Chambers

This volume provides the most wide-ranging and thorough examination of the implications of identity and diversity of judges for the legitimacy of international courts and tribunals to date. Adopting an understanding of the notion of diversity that goes beyond gender and geographical distribution to include legal culture, religion and ethnicity, the deft and sensitive curation of the expert contributions ensures that the volume succeeds in demonstrating, rather than assuming, that increased diversity enhances the legitimacy of the institutions and processes of international adjudication.

Dr. Olufemi Elias, Mechanism for International Criminal Tribunals

The homogeneity on both sides of the bench in international courts and quasi-judicial institutions warrants that issues of diversity and equal representation of women in these institutions is given meticulous and comprehensive scrutiny. This book does that and examines, through contributions of distinguished judges, scholars and practitioners, not only the dynamics of selection of candidates for nomination and elections to these institutions but also the impact of women adjudicators on decision making. The book traverses a broad panorama of international and regional courts and tribunals and is a valuable contribution to the jurisprudence on the subject.

Judge Neeru Chadha, International Tribunal for the Law of the Sea

When law-making is perceived as a legitimate expectation of international adjudication, identity and diversity of those who compose the bench will certainly become a general concern of the international legal community. In pursuit of justice, the practice of international adjudication itself must be subjected to constant scrutiny. "Who is the Judge?" is not a simple question, as the answer to it ultimately determines the credibility of the whole institution. Discussions in this book are insightful and thought-provoking.

Vice-President Hanqin Xue, International Court of Justice

This collection draws attention to a critical, yet consistently overlooked, aspect of international courts and tribunals – the identity of the judges who serve on them. It offers a rich set of insights into how factors such as gender, geography, ethnicity, legal culture, race and religion affect adjudicators and shape international procedure and jurisprudence. The contributors' interdisciplinarity and breadth of analysis illuminates the relationship between diversity and legitimacy in international adjudication. This is a challenging and thought-provoking volume.

Professor Hilary Charlesworth, University of Melbourne

Foreword

Navanethem Pillay

Browsing through the chapters of this collection, I begin to reminisce about my own identity and how it has marked out my professional career from the beginning. Having first studied at the University of Natal in South Africa (as a student of John Dugard) and moving to the USA for my LL.M and Doctorate at Harvard Law School, my legal education has had a diverse global shaping. In 1967, I became the first non-white woman to open her own law practice in Natal Province. I had no alternative, as no law firm would employ me because they feared that white employees would not take instructions from a coloured person.

During my 28 years as a lawyer in South Africa, I defended anti-Apartheid activists and helped expose the use of torture and poor conditions of political detainees. In 1973, I won the right for political prisoners on Robben Island, including Nelson Mandela, to have access to lawyers. As a member of the Women's National Coalition, I advocated for the inclusion of an equality clause prohibiting discrimination on the grounds of race, religion, and sexual orientation in the South African Constitution. In 1992, I co-founded the international women's rights group *Equality Now*. In principle, any lawyer who had the courage to stand up against the Apartheid government could have argued these cases—but my identity as a non-white, female lawyer made the importance of obtaining and enforcing these rights all the more poignant.

In 1995, I was appointed by Mandela to become the first non-white woman judge of the South African High Court. My tenure was short as I was elected the same year to serve as a judge on the bench of the International Criminal Tribunal for Rwanda (ICTR), where for the first four years, I was the only female judge (out of six) on the bench. The case that most stands out in terms of 'identity' was the landmark trial of Jean-Paul Akayesu, in which the ICTR ruled that rape and sexual assault could constitute acts of genocide.[1] For most women, this had been evident since time immemorial—and many had been advocating an according change in international law at least since the 1915 International Congress for Women in The Hague.[2] But the first international judicial institution to formally recognize this was the ICTR in 1997 and it only did so when a woman was made responsible for

[1] *Jean Paul Akayesu* (ICTR-96-4) Appeal Judgment (1 June 2001).

[2] Baetens, Freya, 'The Forgotten Peace Conference: The 1915 International Congress for Women' in *Max Planck Encyclopedia of Public International Law* (OUP 2010, online edition).

drafting that section of the judgment. In 1999, I became the ICTR's first female president, serving for another four years.

In 2003, I was elected to the first ever panel of judges of the International Criminal Court (ICC) and assigned to the Appeals Division, but I resigned in 2008 to take up a position as UN High Commissioner for Human Rights, where I served until 2014. In my role as UN High Commissioner, I promoted the prohibition of discrimination on all grounds, and emphasized the need to focus not just on political and civil rights, but also economic, social, and cultural rights, including the right to development. This resulted, among others, in the Born Free and Equal publication on sexual orientation and gender identity.[3] In 2019, I was appointed judge ad hoc at the International Court of Justice (ICJ) in the case of *The Gambia v Myanmar*, to investigate whether genocide has been committed by Myanmar against the Rohingya.

After more than 50 years in the field, I had hoped that it would be obvious that those adjudicating at the highest courts in the world should reflect the diversity of humankind's experiences. But this is not always the case. This book identifies and analyses the benches of international adjudicatory bodies, examining these differences: how they came about, the potential effects they have on judgments and their legitimacy as a result. It highlights the obstacles many, like me, face in making it to the bench. My experiences as a victim of 54 years of South African Apartheid gave me the resilience to stay principled in my role despite political pressure. It is our experiences which forge our identity that we carry forward with us as our principles, including but not limited to justice, fairness, and impartiality.

Identity and Diversity on the International Bench: Who is the Judge? addresses the manner in which our own identity or human experiences shape the judicial bench and international adjudication. Compiled of academic analysis and personal experiences from legal practitioners each with their own identities, this book reflects the diversity of legal practitioners in international adjudication. This book reminds us that we are where we come from, and that we carry our identity with us. This collection from academics and legal practitioners is a must-read for all who work in, with, or along-side international adjudicatory bodies. It teaches us that we must not be blind to our identity, but we must recognize the benefits (and risks) that come with the experience we gain in its creation.

3 <www.ohchr.org/EN/NewsEvents/Pages/BornFreeAndEqual.aspx> accessed 23 April 2020.

Contents

List of Abbreviations

AB	Appellate Body (of the WTO)
ACHR	American Convention on Human Rights
ACtHPR	African Court on Human and Peoples' Rights
ADRIP	American Declaration on the Rights of Indigenous Peoples
ART	Arbitrator Research Tool
ASA	Swiss Arbitration Association
AU	African Union
BIT	Bilateral Investment Treaty
CARICOM	Caribbean Community
CAS	Court of Arbitration for Sport
CDDH	Council of Europe's Steering Committee for Human Rights
CEDAW	Convention on the Elimination of All forms of Discrimination against Women
CEJIL	Centro por la Justicia y el Derecho Internacional
CETA	Comprehensive Economic and Trade Agreement between the EU and Canada
CFSP	Common Foreign and Security Policy
CIDS	Center for International Dispute Settlement
CJEU	Court of Justice of the European Union
CoE	Council of Europe
CSW	UN Commission on the Status of Women
CUSMA	Canada-US-Mexico Agreement
DIAC	Dubai International Arbitration Centre
DIS	German Arbitration Institute
DG	Director-General (of the WTO)
DSB	Dispute Settlement Body (of the WTO)
DSM	Dispute Settlement Mechanism (of the WTO)
DSU	Dispute Settlement Understanding (of the WTO)
EACJ	East African Court of Justice
ECCC	Extraordinary Chambers in the Courts of Cambodia
ECHR	Convention on Human Rights
ECOSOC	UN Economic and Social Council
ECOWAS	Economic Community of West African States
ECtHR	European Court of Human Rights
EFTA	European Free Trade Association
EJTN	European Judicial Training Network
EU	European Union
FIDA	International Federation of Women Lawyers
FIFA	Fédération Internationale de Football Association

FJC	Federal Judicial Center
FPIC	Free, Prior and Informed Consent
FTA	Free Trade Agreement
GAR	Global Arbitration Review
GATT	General Agreement on Tariffs and Trade
GRULAC	Africa, Asia-Pacific, Eastern Europe, Latin America and the Caribbean
GQUAL	campaign—campaign for gender parity in international representation
HKIAC	Hong Kong International Arbitration Centre
IACtHR	Inter-American Court of Human Rights
IAI	International Arbitration Institute
IAR	Investment Arbitration Reporter
IAWJ	International Association of Women Judges
IAWL	Institute for African Women in Law
IBA	International Bar Association
ICC	International Chamber of Commerce
ICC	International Criminal Court
ICCA	International Council for Commercial Arbitration
ICCPR	International Covenant on Civil and Political Rights
ICC-RPE	ICC Rules of Procedure and Evidence
ICDR	International Centre for Dispute Resolution
ICJ	International Court of Justice
ICSID	International Centre for Settlement of Investment Disputes
ICS	Investment Court System
ICTR	International Criminal Tribunal for Rwanda
ICTY	International Criminal Tribunal for the Former Yugoslavia
ILC	International Law Commission
ILO	International Labour Organization
ISDS	investor-State dispute settlement
ITLOS	International Tribunal for the Law of the Sea
JHA	Justice and Home Affairs (Council of the EU)
LCIA	London Court of International Arbitration
MENA	Middle East and North Africa
MIC	Multilateral Investment Court
MICT	Mechanism for International Criminal Tribunals
MVR	Minimum Voting Requirements (in the context of the ICC)
NAFTA	North Atlantic Free Trade Agreement
NIEO	New International Economic Order
NJI	National Judicial Institute/Institut National de la Magistrature
OAS	Organization of American States
OLC	Office of the Legal Counsel (of the ACtHPR)
OPCV	Office of Public Counsel for Victims (of the ICC)
OSJI	Open Society Justice Initiative
PACE	Parliamentary Assembly of the Council of Europe
PCA	Permanent Court of Arbitration
PCIJ	Permanent Court of International Justice

PITAD	PluriCourts Investment Treaty Arbitration Database
SADC	Southern Africa Development Community
SCC	Stockholm Chamber of Commerce
SCSL	Special Court for Sierra Leone
SDG	Sustainable Development Goal
SDGEA	Solemn Declaration of Gender Equality in Africa
SIAC	Singapore International Arbitration Centre
SOAWR	Solidarity for African Women's Rights
STL	Special Tribunal for Lebanon
TFV	Trust Fund for Victims (of the ICC)
UDHR	Universal Declaration of Human Rights
UNAT	United Nations Appeals Tribunal
UNCITRAL	United Nations Commission on International Trade Law
UNCLOS	United Nations Convention on the Law of the Sea
UNDP	United Nations Development Program
UNDRIP	UN Declaration on the Rights of Indigenous Peoples
UNDT	United Nations Dispute Tribunal
UNGA	United Nations General Assembly
UNICO	United Nations Conference on International Organization
UNSC	United Nations Security Council
VIAC	Vienna International Arbitral Centre
WEOG	Western Europe and Others
WTO	World Trade Organization

List of Contributors

Rebecca Emiene Badejogbin, LL.B (Jos), LL.M (Jos), LL.M (Research) (Pretoria), PhD (Cape Town) is a lawyer and currently a Director of Academics at the Nigerian Law School where she has lectured since 2001. She has over the years extensively researched courts and the judiciary.

Freya Baetens (Cand. Jur. / Lic. Jur., Ghent University; LL.M, Columbia University; PhD, Cambridge University) is Professor of Public International Law at the PluriCourts Centre of Excellence (Oslo University), working on an interdisciplinary research project evaluating the legitimacy of international courts and tribunals. She is also affiliated with the Europa Institute (Leiden University). As a Member of the Brussels Bar, she regularly acts as counsel or expert in international disputes. She currently serves as the co-chair of the International Courts and Tribunals Interest Group for the American Society of International Law.

David M Bigge is an attorney-adviser at the US Department of State. He has served as U.S. Agent to the Iran–U.S. Claims Tribunal and Deputy Legal Counselor at the US Embassy in The Hague and as an attorney-adviser in the Office of International Claims and Investment Disputes. Prior to joining the State Department, Mr Bigge practised in the New York offices of two major international law firms. Mr Bigge also was an adjunct professor at Georgetown University Law Center and has guest lectured on international dispute resolution at various other universities and institutions. He currently serves as the co-chair of the International Courts and Tribunals Interest Group for the American Society of International Law.

Solomy Balungi Bossa is a judge at the International Criminal Court. She previously served as a judge at the UN International Residual Mechanism for Criminal Tribunals, the International Criminal Tribunal for Rwanda, the African Court on Human and Peoples' Rights, the East African Court of Justice, the Court of Appeal of Uganda, and the High Court of Uganda. Earlier, she worked as a lecturer at the Law Development Centre of Uganda and as a legal practitioner. She is a member of the International Commission of Jurists, the International Association of Women Judges, the East African Judges and Magistrate's Association, FIDA Uganda, the National Association of Women Judges, and the Uganda Association of Judges and Magistrates.

Myriam Christ obtained her double degree BLaw/MLaw Fribourg (Switzerland)—Paris II in 2017, after which she interned at the European Court of Human Rights.

James Crawford (BA, LL.B (Adelaide), D.Phil (Oxon.); LL.D (Cantab); SC (NSW); FBA) is a Judge at the International Court of Justice and a former Whewell Professor of International Law at Cambridge University. He was the first Australian member of the UN International Law Commission and was responsible for its work on the International Criminal Court (1994) and the second reading of the ILC Articles on State Responsibility (2001).

Cosette D Creamer is the Benjamin E Lippincott Chair in Political Economy and Assistant Professor of Political Science at the University of Minnesota, and affiliated faculty at the

University of Minnesota School of Law. Her research centres on the empirical analysis of international law and institutions, with a substantive focus on trade, human rights, and the laws of armed conflict.

J Jarpa Dawuni is Associate Professor of Political Science at Howard University, Washington DC. She is a qualified Barrister-at-Law before the Ghana Superior Courts of Judicature. She holds a Doctorate in Political Science from Georgia State University. Her primary areas of research include judicial politics, women in the legal professions, gender and the law, international human rights, women's civil society organizing, and democratization.

Teresa Doherty hails from Northern Ireland and is a judge of the Special Court of Sierra Leone. Previously she was a judge of the High Court of Sierra Leone after the civil war. She was the first and, for 11 years the only, woman judge in Papua New Guinea. She is noted for her work on women's and prisoners' rights. Her judgment on forced marriage was the first declaration that such act is a crime against humanity.

Gilles Landry Dossan is an Associate Legal Officer and Law Clerk at the International Court of Justice. Before joining the Court, he worked for the UN Office of Legal Affairs and the Office of the Legal Counsel of the African Union. He also worked as a lecturer and researcher for the University of Lyon (France).

Catherine Drummond (LL.M (Cantab); LL.B, B.A. (UQ)) is a PhD Candidate at the University of Cambridge. She was formerly an Associate in Public International Law and International Arbitration at Freshfields Bruckhaus Deringer where she advised and represented clients in relation to disputes before international courts and tribunals, including the International Court of Justice, European Court of Human Rights and arbitral tribunals.

Rolf Einar Fife is Ambassador of Norway to the European Union and Member of the Permanent Court of Arbitration. He was Director General for Legal Affairs at the Norwegian Ministry of Foreign Affairs (2002–14) and Chair of the Committee of Legal Advisers on International Law at the Council of Europe (2009–10).

Szilárd Gáspár-Szilágyi is a Lecturer in Law at Keele University and a former Postdoctoral Fellow at the PluriCourts Centre of Excellence (University of Oslo). He publishes in the fields of EU investment law, EU external relations, and international economic law. Previously, he was a postdoctoral fellow at the University of Amsterdam and a Lecturer at the Hague University of Applied Sciences and interned at the European Commission. As a visiting scholar, he conducted research at the University of Michigan, Vienna University and TMC Asser Instituut.

Zuzanna Godzimirska is Assistant Professor in International Law and Institutional Law at iCourts, Centre of Excellence for International Courts at the Faculty of Law at Copenhagen University. Her research centres on issues of legitimation and trust in international courts.

Corina Heri is a Postdoctoral Researcher focusing on international and regional human rights law at the University of Amsterdam. She has a bachelor, master's and PhD degree in law from the University of Zurich as well as an LL.M degree from King's College London.

Kristen Hessler is Associate Professor of Philosophy at the University at Albany (SUNY) in Albany, New York. Her main area of research focuses on political philosophy and human rights. She has also published articles on environmental ethics, public health ethics, and feminist philosophy. She is currently working on a book about women's human rights.

Valerie Hughes teaches international trade law at Queen's University (Canada) and is Senior Counsel with Bennett Jones LLP. She served as Director of the WTO Legal Affairs Division (2010–16), Director of the WTO Appellate Body Secretariat (2001–05), and is a WTO panellist. Valerie held various positions with the Canadian Government and has appeared as counsel before international courts and tribunals.

Helen Keller is Professor of Public International and Constitutional Law at the University of Zurich and a former Judge at the European Court of Human Rights (2011–20). Previously, she was a Member of the UN Human Rights Committee.

Laura Létourneau-Tremblay is a doctoral fellow at the PluriCourts Centre of Excellence (Oslo University). She holds an LL.M. in Public International Law (University of Oslo) and a Bachelor of Laws (Université Laval). Her doctoral project, part of the research project on the Responses to the 'legitimacy crisis' of international investment law (LEGINVEST), focuses on international investment law and environmental protection. Laura has previously collaborated with the Centre for International Sustainable Development (CISDL) and UN-Habitat.

Liesbeth Lijnzaad is a Judge at the International Tribunal for the Law of the Sea (Hamburg). She is a former Legal Adviser of the Netherlands Ministry of Foreign Affairs and head of its international law department (2006–17). She is professor of Practice of International Law at Maastricht University. She studied law and history, receiving master's degrees in international law and Dutch law from the University of Amsterdam, and holds a PhD in international law from Maastricht University.

Hemi Mistry is an Assistant Professor in Law at the University of Nottingham, where she researches in the areas of general international law theory and international criminal justice. More specifically, her research explores how formal judicial decision-making procedure and informal judicial practices on international courts and tribunals affect how these institutions discharge their functions.

Janet M Nosworthy is a judge at the Special Tribunal for Lebanon (STL). She was called to the Bar of Gray's Inn (London) in 1972 and worked until 2005, mainly in Jamaica, as a prosecutor, defence counsel and lecturer. She has also consulted in international criminal law for CARICOM. Between 2005 and 2009, before joining the STL, Judge Nosworthy served as an Ad Litem Judge at the International Criminal Tribunal for the former Yugoslavia (ICTY).

Angelika Nußberger holds a Chair at Cologne University for Public International Law, German Public Law and Comparative Constitutional Law. In 2011, she took up office as a judge in the European Court of Human Rights and served as its Vice-President from 2017–19.

Paolo Palchetti (PhD, University of Milan) is Professor of International Law at the Université Paris 1 Panthéon/Sorbonne and the University of Macerata. He is the author of books and articles on various topics of international law. He advises States on inter-State disputes and acted as counsel in several cases before the International Court of Justice.

Juan-Pablo Pérez-León-Acevedo (PhD), Åbo Akademi University; LL.M, Columbia University; LL.B, Catholic University of Peru) is a postdoc researcher/lecturer at Jyväskylä University (Finland). He is a guest researcher and was a Postdoctoral Fellow at the PluriCourts Centre (Research Council of Norway/Project 223274), University of Oslo. He held positions/visiting fellowships at Oxford University, the Max Planck Institute for Foreign and International Criminal Law, Åbo Akademi, Pretoria University, etc. He served in different capacities at the International Criminal Court, the International Criminal Tribunal for the former Yugoslavia, the International Tribunal for the Law of the Sea, and the Peruvian Ministry of Foreign Affairs.

Navanethem Pillay (BA/LL.B, Natal University; LL.M/DJS, Harvard University) is a South African jurist who served as the UN High Commissioner for Human Rights from 2008 to 2014. She was the first non-white woman judge of the High Court of South Africa, and she has also served as a judge of the International Criminal Court and President of the International Criminal Tribunal for Rwanda. In 2015, she became the 16th Commissioner of the International Commission Against the Death Penalty. She is currently serving as judge ad hoc in the *Gambia v Myanmar* case before the International Court of Justice.

Monika Prusinowska is an Assistant Professor at the China-EU School of Law at the China University of Political Science and Law. She holds a Doctorate in Law from University of Hamburg as well as a Master's Degree in Chinese Law from Tsinghua University and a Master's Degree in Polish Law from University of Lodz. She has gained work experience as a lawyer in one of the largest Chinese law firms and as a guest lecturer in the Embassy of Poland to China. Her research focuses primarily on dispute resolution in Asia and Sino-foreign business law.

Clara María López Rodríguez is a PhD Candidate at King's College London. She holds an LL.B in Law and Business from Universidad Autónoma de Madrid and an LL.M. from Queen Mary University of London. She previously worked as an arbitration lawyer in Spain and in Peru where she is admitted to practise.

Jamal Seifi has been a Judge at the Iran-United States Claims Tribunal since 2009. He has acted as arbitrator, counsel and expert in international arbitration and domestic cases for over two decades, alongside his career as a university professor at Shahid Beheshti University (Iran) and the University of Hull (UK). He is currently Distinguished Visiting Professor at Tilburg University.

SI Strong (PhD (law), Cambridge; DPhil, Oxford; JD, Duke; MPW, Southern California; BA, California, Davis) is an Associate Professor at the University of Sydney, having previously taught at the Universities of Cambridge and Oxford in the UK as well as Georgetown Law Center and the University of Missouri in the US. She is admitted to practice as an attorney in New York, Illinois, and Missouri and as a solicitor in England and Wales and in Ireland. She spent a year as a US Supreme Court Fellow working at the Federal Judicial Center, the research and education arm of the US federal judiciary, and has developed and implemented judicial education programs for domestic and international judges in Europe and North America.

Catharine Titi (Dr iur., FCIArb) is a tenured Research Associate Professor at the French National Centre for Scientific Research (CNRS)–CERSA, University Paris II Panthéon-Assas. She serves on the Steering Committee of the Academic Forum on ISDS, the Board of the European Society of International Law (ESIL), and the Academic Council of the Institute for Transnational Arbitration. Catharine sits on the panel of arbitrators of the Court of Arbitration for Art and is appointed to the roster of USMCA Annex 31-B panellists.

Mubarak Waseem is a barrister at Essex Court Chambers. He completed his LL.B (2014) and LL.M in International Dispute Resolution (2016) at King's College London. Prior to joining Essex Court Chambers, Mubarak interned at the International Tribunal for the Law of the Sea (ITLOS) in Hamburg and at the British Institute of International and Comparative Law (BIICL) in London.

1

Identity and Diversity on the International Bench

Implications for the Legitimacy of International Adjudication

*Freya Baetens**

Once we accept that who the judge is matters, then it matters who our judges are.[1]

1. Introduction

Given the recent proliferation and growing prominence of international courts and tribunals, and the increasing fear of judicial law-making,[2] it is important to pay attention to those making judicial decisions about sovereignty over territory, grave human rights violations, international crimes, or vast economic interests. The identity of judges and arbitrators, as the faces (and drivers) of the adjudicatory process has significant implications for the legitimacy—and thus the functioning—of courts and tribunals.[3]

Certain aspects of identity have received more attention than others—none more so than those set out in the requirements listed in the statutes of international courts

* Special thanks are due to Andreas Føllesdal, Geir Ulfstein, and the participants in the PluriCourts seminar on 7 November 2018 for their useful comments, as well as to my research associates, Andrea Varga and Dora Robinson. This work was partly supported by the Research Council of Norway through its Centres of Excellence funding scheme (project number 223274) and the FRIPRO Young Research Talents (project number 274946).

[1] Erika Rackley, *Women, Judging and the Judiciary* (Routledge 2013) 164.

[2] See eg Armin von Bogdandy and Ingo Venzke, 'Beyond Dispute: International Judicial Institutions as Lawmakers' in Armin von Bogdandy and Ingo Venzke (eds), *International Judicial Lawmaking* (Springer 2012) 3; Tom Ginsburg, 'Bounded Discretion in International Judicial Lawmaking' (2005) 45 Virginia Journal of International Law 631, at 635–37 on 'the inevitability of judicial lawmaking'; Hersch Lauterpacht, *The Development of International Law by the Permanent Court of International Justice* (Longmans 1934) 45: 'judicial law-making is a permanent feature of the administration of justice in every society'.

[3] But note also the role of 'unseen actors', as explored in: Freya Baetens (ed), *Legitimacy of Unseen Actors in International Adjudication* (CUP 2019).

Freya Baetens, *Identity and Diversity on the International Bench* In: *Identity and Diversity on the International Bench.* Edited by: Freya Baetens, Oxford University Press (2020). © The several contributors.
DOI: 10.1093/oso/9780198870753.003.0001.

and tribunals, pertaining not only to individual judges' qualifications, but also their moral standing, integrity, independence, and nationality.[4] Consequentially, the relationship between judicial independence and the nominating/appointing State in particular has been the subject of extensive debate. For instance, one study found that International Court of Justice (ICJ) judges 'vote for their home states about 90% of the time. When their home states are not involved, judges vote for states that are similar to their home states—along the dimensions of wealth, culture, and political regime.'[5]

Perhaps most contentiously, it has been argued that courts should be *less* independent from the State Parties appearing before them, in order to ensure their effectiveness in the absence of robust enforcement mechanisms at the international level.[6] Others have suggested that the answer is more, not less, independence;[7] and that the 'nationalist presumption' should be rejected in favour of a 'cosmopolitan approach', removing rules pertaining to the nationality of judges on international courts and tribunals.[8] Yet at the same time, States themselves appear to regard geographic representation to be an important element in the composition of such courts.[9] Furthermore, concerns relating to judicial independence may manifest not only vis-à-vis a single (nominating) State, but also more generally: recent research has found that in ICJ elections, 'professional experiences signalling a probability of independence or insensitivity to political considerations reduce a candidate's expected vote share'.[10] In fact, it has been argued that 'the states that design, and the judges that serve on, international courts confront an interlocking set of potential tradeoffs' between 'three core values':

> (1) judicial independence, the freedom of judges to decide disputes upon the facts and the law, free of outside influences such as the preferences of powerful states; (2) judicial accountability, structural checks on the exercise of individual judicial authority manifested most prominently in international courts via reappointment

[4] See eg ICJ Statute, Art 2; ECHR, Art 21; WTO DSU, Arts 8(2), 8(9), and 17(3).

[5] Eric A Posner and Miguel F P de Figueiredo, 'Is the International Court of Justice Biased?' (2005) 34 Journal of Legal Studies 599.

[6] Eric A Posner and John C Yoo, 'Judicial Independence in International Tribunals' (2005) 93 California Law Review 1. See also Laurence R Helfer and Anne-Marie Slaughter, 'Why States Create International Tribunals: A Response to Professors Posner and Yoo' (2005) 93 California Law Review 899; Eric A Posner and John C Yoo, 'Reply to Helfer and Slaughter' (2005) 93 California Law Review 957.

[7] Laurence R Helfer and Anne-Marie Slaughter, 'Toward a Theory of Effective Supranational Adjudication' (1997) 107 Yale Law Journal 273.

[8] Tom Dannenbaum, 'Nationality and the International Judge: The Nationalist Presumption Governing the International Judiciary and Why it Must Be Reversed' (2012) 45 Cornell International Law Journal 77.

[9] Ruth Mackenzie and others, *Selecting International Judges: Principle, Process, and Politics* (OUP 2010) 31.

[10] Cosette Creamer and Zuzanna Godzimirska, 'The Job Market for Justice: Screening and Selecting Candidates for the International Court of Justice' (2017) 30 Leiden Journal of International Law 947, at 949; see also ibid 963.

> processes; and (3) judicial transparency, specifically mechanisms that permit the identification of individual judicial positions, primarily through the publication of separate votes or opinions.[11]

The nature of the 'trilemma' is that only two of these values can be maximized at any given time.[12] In other words, high judicial independence will require a compromise in terms of either accountability or transparency.

A good example is the US decision to block (re-)appointment of members of the Appellate Body (AB) of the World Trade Organization (WTO).[13] Whilst the Obama administration's opposition was directed at a particular member, Chang Seung Wha (South Korea), who they accused of anti-US bias,[14] the Trump administration has objected to *any* (re)appointments in the absence of abolishing the rule allowing AB members to complete work on ongoing cases that extend beyond their four-year term.[15] This is ostensibly on the basis that the extension contravenes the terms of the WTO Dispute Settlement Understanding, but in fact appears to be due to US unhappiness with the AB's anti-dumping case law and the AB more generally.[16] Tellingly, in their complaints about the WTO system, the Trump administration chose to focus on the foreign nationality of AB members, alleging that the US was insufficiently represented on the AB bench.[17]

[11] Jeffrey L Dunoff and Mark A Pollack, 'The Judicial Trilemma' (2017) 111 American Journal of International Law 225, at 225.

[12] ibid 272.

[13] See eg Pieter Jan Kuijper, 'From the Board: The US Attack on the WTO Appellate Body' (2018) 45 Legal Issues of Economic Integration 1; Manfred Elsig, Mark Pollack, and Gregory Shaffer, 'Trump is Fighting an Open War on Trade. His Stealth War on Trade may be Even More Important' *Washington Post* (27 September 2017)<www.washingtonpost.com/news/monkey-cage/wp/2017/09/27/trump-is-fighting-an-open-war-on-trade-his-stealth-war-on-trade-may-be-even-more-important> accessed 23 April 2020.

[14] Kuijper, 'US Attack on the WTO' (n 13) 2. Statement by the United States at the Meeting of the WTO Dispute Settlement Body, Geneva, 23 May 2016 <www.wto.org/english/news_e/news16_e/us_statment_dsbmay16_e.pdf> accessed 23 April 2020.Steve Charnovitz, 'The Obama Administration's Attack on Appellate Body Independence Shows The Need for Reforms' (*International Economic Law and Policy Blog*, 22 September 2016) <https://worldtradelaw.typepad.com/ielpblog/2016/09/the-obama-administrations-attack-on-appellate-body-independence-shows-the-need-for-reforms-.html> accessed 23 April 2020; similarly, Merit Janow (AB member 2003–07) and Jennifer Hillman (AB member 2007–11) were not put forward for another term by the Office of the US Trade Representative (USTR) because they were not considered sufficiently aggressive in defending the US position and elected not to write frequent separate or dissenting opinions, see Kuijper, 'US Attack on the WTO' (n 13) 2; Jeffrey L Dunoff and Mark A Pollack, 'The Judicial Trilemma' (2017) 111 American Journal of International Law 225.

[15] Kuijper, 'US Attack on the WTO' (n 13) 3.

[16] ibid 4–8.

[17] For example, in this interview, Trump claimed that the US loses WTO disputes '[b]ecause we have fewer judges than other countries. It's set up as you can't win. In other words, the panels are set up so that we don't have majorities. It was set up for the benefit of taking advantage of the United States.' See <www.realclearpolitics.com/video/2017/10/25/full_lou_dobbs_interview_trump_asks_what_could_be_more_fake_than_cbs_nbc_abc_and_cnn.html> accessed 23 April 2020 (Real Clear Politics, 25 October 2017). In fact, ever since its inception in 1995, there has always been a US national on the WTO AB bench.

As of 10 December 2019, the terms of all but one of the AB members expired, so the AB can no longer function.[18] As a result, any Respondent in a WTO dispute who disagrees with a panel report can block the adoption of that report (and hence prevent it from becoming binding) by initiating appeal procedures—which cannot be dealt with without a functioning AB. In other words, the US has succeeded in effectively paralysing the WTO's dispute settlement system—one of international law's most successful institutions.[19] This illustrates how criticism focused on adjudicators' identity (nationality) goes to the heart of judicial integrity and independence and could significantly impact upon a court's functioning and perceived legitimacy.

Individual identity is also closely connected to the question of diversity among judges as a collective on a given bench. After all, if international law is to be truly *international*,[20] the persons deciding on the intricacies of its interpretation and application should reflect the diversity of humankind's experiences, as best a limited number of judges on any given bench can do so. A bench where judges represent multiple perspectives along different aspects of their individual identity will allow for a better understanding of arguments and aspects of a dispute. As a result, the question of diversity (or rather, the lack thereof) among international judges and arbitrators has been the subject of growing academic attention in recent years. Even so, this kind of research is generally still in its early stages, focusing mostly on uncovering the extent to which international benches are diverse, and offering some tentative explanations for why they are (almost) not.[21] In addition, most works are limited to either a particular aspect of diversity, such as gender,[22] or a particular subset of institutions, such as the ICJ or investment arbitration tribunals.[23]

[18] The AB has seven members, and operates in panels of three, but exchange views with the other four to give effect to the principle of collegiality, in order to ensure consistency, see Article 17(1) DSU and Rule 4(1) of the Working Procedures for Appellate Review; WTO Dispute Settlement System Training Module, Chapter 6: 'The process—Stages in a typical WTO dispute settlement case', Section 6.5 – Appellate review <www.wto.org/english/tratop_e/dispu_e/disp_settlement_cbt_e/c6s5p3_e.htm> accessed 23 April 2020.

[19] Kuijper, 'US Attack on the WTO' (n 13) 1, at 4. See also 11th Annual Update on WTO Dispute Settlement, Graduate Institute, Geneva, 3 May 2018 Address of Mr Ujal Singh Bhatia (Chair, Appellate Body) <www.wto.org/english/news_e/news18_e/ab_07may18_e.htm;> accessed 23 April 2020,WTO Appellate Body Annual Report for 2016, March 2017, WT/AB/27, Annex 3: Communications from Appellate Body members and former Appellate Body members concerning opposition to the reappointment of an Appellate Body member.

[20] See eg Anthea Roberts, *Is International Law International?* (OUP 2017).

[21] See eg Nienke Grossman, 'Shattering the Glass Ceiling in International Adjudication' (2016) 56 Virginia Journal of International Law 339; Susan D Franck and others, 'The Diversity Challenge: Exploring the Invisible College of International Arbitration' (2015) 53 Columbia Journal of Transnational Law 429.

[22] See eg Grossman, 'Shattering the Glass Ceiling ' (n 21) 339; Nienke Grossman, 'Achieving Sex-Representative International Court Benches' (2016) 110 American Journal of International Law 82.

[23] See eg Chittharanjan F Amerasinghe, 'Judges of the International Court of Justice – Election and Qualifications' (2001) 14 Leiden Journal of International Law 335; Mackenzie and others (n 9) particularly at 24–62 (on the ICJ and ICC); Franck and others, 'The Diversity Challenge: Exploring the Invisible College of International Arbitration' (2015) 53 Columbia Journal of Transnational Law 429.

Against this backdrop, the current volume—the result of an interdisciplinary research project carried out at the PluriCourts Centre of Excellence (Oslo University) conducted by Freya Baetens—aims to provide a more comprehensive and in-depth look at the impact of identity on (the legitimacy of) international adjudication.[24] The research project included a series of workshops held with the support of the Europa Instituut (Leiden University), exploring various characteristics—gender; geography and legal culture; and religion and ethnicity—that are relevant to the identity of adjudicators. Building on these workshops, the volume furthers existing scholarship in three main ways. First of all, the book examines a range of factors that form part of a person's identity—gender (and sex), religion, ethnicity (and race), geographical region, legal culture—several of which have so far been under-researched.[25] While studies have been published on the question of gender and geographical representation, there appears to have been little attention paid to legal culture, religion, or ethnicity.

Secondly, these factors are analysed across a broad cross-section of international adjudicatory bodies, both permanent and ad hoc. Most of the existing literature focuses on one or two specific (types of) institutions, such as the ICJ or arbitral tribunals, rather than undertaking analysis across several different types of bodies, or is only carried out with respect to a single factor (eg gender). By focusing on a wide range of factors and doing so across various types of adjudicatory bodies, this volume offers a more comprehensive picture of identity and diversity on the bench. Thirdly, and perhaps most importantly, the volume goes beyond identifying (the lack of) diversity in judicial and arbitral appointments, and offering tentative but ultimately speculative explanations. It also investigates the implications of identity in greater detail through various career stages, examining the prior experiences of judges and arbitrators leading them to (be considered for) the bench; their behaviour on the bench, including their influence on the adjudicatory process and on the court or tribunal as a collective; as well as the legacy of their appointments and their post-judicial/post-arbitral careers. By doing so, the volume provides a more in-depth analysis across the entire trajectory of adjudicators, allowing the reader to gain a greater and more holistic insight into how identity and diversity functions in international courts and tribunals.

The purpose of this introductory chapter is to set the scene, to present the scholarship, to raise relevant questions, and to explain why the topic is relevant and important. The goal is not to take firm positions on specific questions as this

[24] This work was partly supported by the Research Council of Norway through its Centres of Excellence funding scheme, project number 223274.

[25] For a handful of rare examples addressing (legal) culture, see Alison Dundes Renteln, 'Cultural Bias in International Law' (1998) 92 American Society of International Law Proceedings 232; Garry Sturgess and Philip Chubb (eds), *Judging the World: Law and Politics in the World's Leading Courts* (Butterworths 1988); Lyndel V Prott, *The Latent Power of Culture and the International Judge* (Professional Books 1979).

may pre-empt what the individual contributors argue and the topic is too broad to be comprehensively dealt with in a single chapter. In order to place the issues of identity and diversity in context, the chapter begins with outlining how they relate to legitimacy, and the justifications that are put forward when making calls for increased diversity on the bench. The chapter then provides a brief overview of the current state of affairs, including both formal or informal rules pertaining to identity and diversity, as well as the practices followed in (s)electing international judges and arbitrators. Against this backdrop, the aim and structure of the volume are laid out, including a brief summary of chapters; this is followed by a few general remarks on the methodological challenges faced in this type of research and some ways to address them.

2. Diversity's Implications for Legitimacy

International law is burdened with the legacy of a deeply Eurocentric (or at least Western-centric) history, where for centuries, much of the non-Western world was treated as falling outside the realm of 'the law of nations', and as such, excluded from the formation of the rules which govern the conduct of States. The automatic application of customary rules to newly established States, while ensuring the stability of the international legal system, has also contributed to entrenching the (real or perceived) inequalities of that system.[26] Furthermore, even where arrangements are negotiated formally between sovereign equals, the relative economic and political power of States may lead to the conclusion of treaties that could seem *prima facie* equal, but produce unequal effects.[27] Such criticism is levelled in particular at bilateral investment treaties, whose investor-State dispute settlement arrangements result predominantly in litigation brought by Western corporations against developing States.[28] The composition of investment tribunals lends itself to narratives

[26] See eg S Prakash Sinha, 'Perspective of the Newly Independent States on the Binding Quality of International Law' (1965) 14 International and Comparative Law Quarterly 121; Jorge Castañeda, 'The Underdeveloped Nations and the Development of International Law' (1961) 15 International Organization 38; F V García-Amador, 'Current Attempts to Revise International Law: A Comparative Analysis' (1983) 77 American Journal of International Law 286, especially at 289–91. The anachronistic reference to 'the general principles of law recognized by civilized nations' in Article 38 of the ICJ Statute (taken verbatim from the PCIJ Statute) may likewise be read as betraying an unsavoury distinction between States, see eg the Separate Opinion of Judge Fouad Ammoun in *North Sea Continental Shelf* (Federal Republic of Germany/Denmark and Federal Republic of Germany/Netherlands), [1969] ICJ Reports 3, at 133–35. But see also Hugh Thirlway, 'The Law and Procedure of the International Court of Justice 1960-1989: Part Two' (1991) 61 British Yearbook of International Law 1, at 123–24; and Alain Pellet, 'Article 38' in Andreas Zimmermann and others (eds), *The Statute of the International Court of Justice: A Commentary* (2nd edn, OUP 2012), 731, para 261, with the latter noting that apparently even in the drafting of the PCIJ Statute, 'the members of the 1920 Committee themselves considered "all nations" to be civilized'.

[27] See eg Andrew T Guzman, 'Why LDCs Sign Treaties That Hurt Them: Explaining the Popularity of Bilateral Investment Treaties' (1998) 38 Virginia Journal of International Law 639.

[28] See eg Olivia Chung, 'The Lopsided International Investment Law Regime and Its Effect on the Future of Investor-State Arbitration' (2007) 47 Virginia Journal of International Law 953, at

describing arbitrators as a closed club—an arbitration 'mafia'—whose members tend to hail from Western Europe and North America. This has given rise to legitimacy concerns.[29] The same countries have traditionally been overrepresented on the benches of international courts and tribunals and, in general, continue to maintain their stronghold on judicial positions, reinforcing the Western-centric control on the 'law of nations'. Thus, to increase diversity, particularly geographic, religious, and legal-cultural is to disrupt the unequal status quo between States, and from certain perspectives, to increase legitimacy.

In the context of international adjudication, legitimacy can be either *normative* (does the court have the requisite authority to issue binding decisions that merit deference by various 'deference constituencies'?) or *sociological* (is the court *seen* to have the requisite authority to do so?).[30] Diversity concerns may relate to both aspects: when people from diverse backgrounds 'think differently' on certain legal issues, then increased diversity can overcome the bias inherent in a singular viewpoint, thereby strengthening the normative legitimacy of the court.[31] Even if people with diverse backgrounds do not 'think differently', the *perception* that they are doing so is capable of enhancing the court's sociological legitimacy.[32] Inasmuch as courts' sociological legitimacy is a matter of subjective evaluation, it may be the case that some segments of their constituencies remain unconvinced; but even in such cases, legitimacy may be maximized. However, the notion of legitimacy itself is ridden with Western-centric biases.[33] The literature that scholars engage with, often despite the best intentions, suffers from and reinforces this inequality by virtue of the fact that that it is predominantly written by authors from Western

956–57; Charles N Brower and Stephen W Schill, 'Is Arbitration a Threat or a Boon to the Legitimacy of International Investment Law' (2009) 9 Chicago Journal of International Law 471, at 474–75; Umakrishnan Kollamparambil, 'Bilateral Investment Treaties and Investor State Disputes', Economic Research Southern Africa, Working Paper No. 589 (March 2016) <https://econrsa.org/system/files/publications/working_papers/working_paper_589.pdf> accessed 23 April 2020. On the trend of investors from developed States initiating most procedures against developing States, see eg UNCTAD, 'Investor-State Dispute Settlement: Review of Developments in 2017', 28 June 2018, 2.<https://unctad.org/en/PublicationsLibrary/diaepcbinf2018d2_en.pdf> accessed 23 April 2020.

[29] See eg Pia Eberhardt and Cecilia Olivet, 'Profiting from Injustice: How Law Firms, Arbitrators and Financiers are Fuelling an Investment Arbitration Boom', Corporate Europe Observatory and the Transnational Institute (November 2012) at 36–43 <https://www.tni.org/files/download/profitingfrominjustice.pdf> accessed 23 April 2020.

[30] See eg Allen Buchanan and Robert O Keohane, 'The Legitimacy of Global Governance Institutions' in Rüdiger Wolfrum and Volker Röben (eds), *Legitimacy in International Law* (Springer, 2008) 25, at 25–26, 31; Nienke Grossman, 'Sex on the Bench: Do Women Judges Matter to the Legitimacy of International Courts?' (2012) 12 Chicago Journal of International Law 647, 651.

[31] Grossman, 'Sex on the Bench' (n 30)654–60.

[32] ibid 660–68.

[33] See eg Antony Anghie, *Imperialism, Sovereignty and the Making of International Law* (CUP 2004); Martti Koskenniemi, 'Histories of International Law: Dealing with Eurocentrism' (2011) 19 Rechtsgeschichte 152–76; Nathaniel Berman, 'L'affaire des décrets de nationalité' in *Passions et ambivalences. Le colonialisme, le nationalisme et le droit international* (Pedone 2008), 279–316; Hilary Charlesworth and Jean-Marc Coicaud (eds), *Fault lines of international legitimacy* (CUP 2010).

institutions and in Western languages—primarily English—and the limited engagement between the scholarship in different languages. This volume seeks to address this problem by including a wide range of voices.

Similarly, it is important to probe other common assumptions so that efforts to increase representation does not merely uphold other biases from traditional Western-centric scholarship and thinking and so undermine its legitimacy. The distinctions between 'race and ethnicity' and 'gender and sex' are examples of this. Both broader feminist literature and that specific to international law explore what it means to be a woman and the difference between 'gender' and 'sex'. Hilary Charlesworth and Christine Chinkin write that '[t]he notion of gender captures the ascribed social nature of distinctions between women and men—the excess cultural baggage associated with biological sex [which] … is typically used to refer to biological differences between men and women.'[34] As the authors highlight, this distinction is still based upon a somewhat artificial and culturally specific distinction between nature and culture. Contributors to this volume approach the issue in various ways depending on their cultural/academic background and personal experience. The small pool of female international judges and the nature of available data sometimes necessitate taking an artificially simple approach to the notions of gender and sex.

The contested concepts of race and ethnicity are related but distinguishable: the former refers to a group of people with shared distinctive physical characteristics whereas the latter refers to shared cultural traits such as religions, language, and customs. As with the distinction between gender and sex, this volume does not impose a specific interpretation of these terms on its contributors as to do so would be to recreate colonial dynamics of Westerners imposing ideas, since the contributors are diverse—geographically, jurisdictionally, and culturally.

2.1 Justifications for Increased Diversity

Calls for increased diversity tend to be accompanied by one or both of two main justifications: deontological and consequentialist. The deontological approach, treating diversity as a good in and of itself, is commonly reflected in calls for democratic legitimacy among the international judiciary (although one may value diversity for very different reasons than its role in democratic rule).[35] This approach is perhaps best encapsulated in the statement—made by the then-President of the UK Supreme Court, Baroness Hale—that 'a diverse judiciary is an indispensable

[34] Hilary Charlesworth and Christine Chinkin, *The Boundaries of International Law: A Feminist Analysis* (Manchester University Press 2000) 3.

[35] See eg Grossman, 'Sex-Representative International Court Benches' (n 22) 88–89; Armin von Bogdandy and Ingo Venzke, 'On the Democratic Legitimation of International Judicial Lawmaking' (2011) 12 German Law Journal 1341.

requirement of any democracy'.[36] In this conceptualization, representativeness 'is a democratic value that can serve to justify the exercise of authority'.[37] Most deontological approaches also rely on consequences in justifying the rule of principle, not focusing on the consequences in specific cases, but rather on general compliance with the rule.

The consequentialist approach, meanwhile, places value not on diversity itself, but on the impact that the diverse perspectives brought by the judges and arbitrators may have on the judgments. Adjudicators' legal thinking and level of understanding of certain problems may, for instance, be influenced by identity and previous experiences.[38] This may even extend to the selection process for judges: for instance, the Council of Europe Parliamentary Assembly stated that when nominating their representatives to the Ad hoc Sub-Committee on the Election of Judges to the European Court of Human Rights, political groups of the Assembly 'should aim to include at least 40% women, which is the parity threshold deemed necessary by the Council of Europe to exclude possible gender bias in decision-making processes'.[39] In other words, the committee evaluating judicial candidates must itself be diverse in terms of gender, in order to avoid a situation where female candidates are assessed by an overwhelmingly male panel, possibly resulting in fewer female appointments due to gender bias.

Consideration of consequentialist justifications will also inevitably raise the question of descriptive *versus* substantive representation, where the first denotes the participation of members of a certain gender, legal culture, race, ethnicity, or religion on the bench, while the second refers to decision-making with the interests of a particular group taken into account (quite apart from the decision-maker's identity).[40] To what extent do the two types of representation go hand in hand? Will greater descriptive representation automatically lead to increased substantive representation? Is it possible to achieve substantive representation in the absence of descriptive representation? Although virtually no attention has been focused on these questions at the international level so far, research carried out among the US judiciary has produced some illuminating results. As regards the possible effect of descriptive representation, researchers have found that female and

[36] 'The Appointment and Removal of Judges: Independence and Diversity', International Association of Women Judges 8th Biennial Conference (3–7 May 2006).

[37] Grossman, 'Sex-Representative International Court Benches' (n 22) 88; see also Grossman, 'Sex on the Bench' (n 30) 668–69.

[38] See eg Kimi L King and Megan Greening, 'Gender Justice of Just Gender? The Role of Gender in Sexual Assault Decisions at the International Criminal Tribunal for the Former Yugoslavia' (2007) 88 Social Science Quarterly 1049; Michael Waibel and Yanhui Wu, 'Are Arbitrators Political?' American Society of International Law Research Forum (5 November 2011) 34–37<www.researchgate.net/publication/256023521_Are_Arbitrators_Political> accessed 23 April 2020.

[39] CoE Parliamentary Assembly, Resolution 1366 (2004): Candidates for the European Court of Human Rights, 30 January 2004.

[40] See generally Hanna Fenichel Pitkin, *The Concept of Representation* (University of California Press 1967).

African-American judges do decide more liberally on issues involving gender and race, respectively.[41] Nonetheless, it appears that in at least some cases, a measure of substantive representation is possible even without descriptive representation, with researchers finding that 'judges with at least one daughter vote in a more liberal fashion on gender issues than judges with sons', with the effect 'driven primarily by Republicans and, in particular, Republican men'.[42]

These two justifications—deontological and consequentialist—are of course not mutually exclusive, and are in fact often cited side by side when arguments are made to enhance legitimacy.[43] A third argument for advocating diversity on the bench—namely that it might have spillover effects, leading, for example, to increased diversity among counsel due to calls from judges[44]—in fact rests on a blend of deontological and consequentialist justifications. After all, increasingly diverse counsel would be a *consequence* of growing diversity on the bench; yet at the same time, the treatment of this result as desirable appears to rest on a presumption that diversity among counsel is a good in and of itself.

2.2 The Impact of Individual Adjudicators on Legitimacy

The legitimacy of any international court or tribunal depends on a number of factors, such as the mode of its establishment, its members, the basis of its jurisdiction, or how its judgments are reached.[45] As a result, it may be difficult to pinpoint the exact relevance and weight attached to the identity of adjudicators, either individually or as a bench. Nonetheless, one particular element may shed some light on the relative importance of individual adjudicators: whether the adjudicatory mechanism of which they form part is permanent or ad hoc. Works comparing WTO panellists' and International Centre for Settlement of Investment Disputes (ICSID)

[41] See eg Christina L Boyd, Lee Epstein, and Andrew D Martin, 'Untangling the Causal Effects of Sex on Judging' (2010) 54 American Journal of Political Science 389; Adam B Cox and Thomas J Miles, 'Judging the Voting Rights Act' (2008) 108 Columbia Law Review 1.

[42] Adam N Glynn and Maya Sen, 'Identifying Judicial Empathy: Does Having Daughters Cause Judges to Rule for Women's Issues?' (2015) 59 American Journal of Political Science 37, at 38, 50.

[43] See eg Grossman, 'Sex-Representative International Court Benches' (n 22) 88–89; Franck and others, 'The Diversity Challenge: Exploring the Invisible College of International Arbitration' (2015) 53 Columbia Journal of Transnational Law 429, at 496–99.

[44] Grossman, 'Sex-Representative International Court Benches' (n 22) 89: 'For example, more women behind the dais may result in more gender-balanced legal teams in front of it. Since the number of women on the ICJ's bench has grown from one to three out of fifteen, some of these judges have called for more diverse counsel to argue litigants' cases'. On (the lack of) diversity among counsel, see eg Shashank P Kumar and Cecily Rose, 'A Study of Lawyers Appearing before the International Court of Justice, 1999–2012' (2014) 25 European Journal of International Law 893; Kurt Taylor Gaubatz and Matthew MacArthur, 'How International Is International Law' (2001) 22 Michigan Journal of International Law 239.

[45] See eg Tullio Treves, 'Aspects of Legitimacy of Decisions of International Courts and Tribunals' in Rüdiger Wolfrum and Volker Röben (eds), *Legitimacy in International Law* (Springer 2008) 169, at 171–73.

arbitrators' profiles have noted that WTO dispute settlement is embedded in a robust institutional framework, while investment arbitration relies wholly on ad hoc tribunals constituted to adjudicate particular disputes based on specific treaties, with no permanent institutional or substantive framework in place.[46] This lack of a permanent framework means that:

> In a less regulated and institutionally weaker system . . . a strong non-formal leadership is more necessary, since legitimacy must be asserted case by case . . . Since social cohesion based on face-to-face relations or shared consensus are supposedly an inverse function of the number of members of the group, frequent arbitrators would be able to become a hard core, reinforced by high rates of social direct interactions and networks of diffusion of behavioural standards. A more institutionalized [dispute settlement system] scheme does not need such an underlying social structure.[47]

In other words, given this lack of institutionalized support, the legitimacy of investment arbitration 'must, at least in part, come from other sources—in particular, from the expertise, standing, exceptional character, and social cohesiveness of the individuals appointed on ICSID tribunals'.[48] In particular, the lack of an appeals mechanism has been singled out as a factor which:

> . . . may partly explain or justify repeat appointments of the same small pool of star ICSID arbitrators: through arbitrator selection, a certain level of centralization and consistency is thereby achieved organically. Indeed, from this perspective, the elite group of fifteen arbitrators that, according to one study, was appointed in 55 percent of all investor-state treaty disputes, can then be considered a type of de facto appellate body—not in the sense that it can directly overrule lower tribunal awards but in the sense that, through reappointments, this elite group can shape the case law and thereby inject at least some degree of consistency and authority into the investment regime.[49]

In sum, it appears that greater importance is attached to the identity (and likely the diversity) of the adjudicators where adjudicatory bodies lack a strong (permanent) institutional framework.

[46] José Augusto Fontoura Costa, 'Comparing WTO Panelists and ICSID Arbitrators: the Creation of International Legal Fields' (2011) 1(4) Oñati Socio-Legal Series 1, at 13; Joost Pauwelyn, 'The Rule of Law Without the Rule of Lawyers?: Why Investment Arbitrators are from Mars, Trade Adjudicators from Venus' (2015) 109 American Journal of International Law 761, at 794–98.

[47] Costa, 'Comparing WTO Panelists and ICSID Arbitrators' 13.

[48] Pauwelyn, 'Rule of Law Without the Rule of Lawyers' 797.

[49] ibid 794–95 (footnotes omitted).

2.3 The Debate on Quality vs. Diversity of Candidates: A False Dichotomy?

When discussing issues of diversity, one concern raised with some frequency is that the goal of diversity may be in tension with that of quality; in other words, that ensuring diversity on the bench would require a compromise to be made on the qualifications of the candidates.[50] But the goal of ensuring diversity while maintaining quality can be achieved by selecting the candidate who brings more diversity to the bench when faced with a group of candidates that are *all equally* qualified.[51]

The perceived tension between quality and diversity relies on the assertion that the reason why certain groups (eg women) are underrepresented is because there is only a 'limited pool' of suitably qualified candidates from that group. However, there are a number of factors that run counter to this narrative. First of all, the election of international judges is often based on considerations other than or *in addition to* merit (most notably, political horse-trading).[52] Secondly, the comparatively low number of available international judicial positions (a few hundred worldwide) means that only relatively few qualified candidates are required.[53] In fact, the Committee on Equal Opportunities for Women and Men of the CoE's Parliamentary Assembly described the suggestion that the requirement of including at least one woman on States' nomination lists to the European Court of Human Rights (ECtHR) could work to the detriment of other qualifications as 'untenable'.[54] It did so because the suggestion 'presupposes that a state may face a situation where there is not one single woman at least as qualified as a man – which is simply inconceivable'.[55] It may be noted that there is no citizenship requirement for serving on the Court.[56]

[50] See eg Mackenzie and others (n 9) 36: 'One interviewee put it bluntly: "Regional quotas per se are rather bad for quality." '

[51] Cf CoE Parliamentary Assembly, Resolution 1366 (2004): Candidates for the European Court of Human Rights, 30 January 2004: 'one of the criteria used by the [Ad hoc Sub-Committee on the Election of Judges to the European Court of Human Rights] should be that, in the case of equal merit, preference should be given to a candidate of the sex under-represented at the Court'.

[52] See eg Grossman, 'Shattering the Glass Ceiling' (n 21) 361–62; Mackenzie and others (n 9) 95; Cherie Booth and Philippe Sands, 'Keep Politics Out of the Global Courts' *The Guardian* (13 July 2001) <www.theguardian.com/politics/2001/jul/13/warcrimes.world> accessed 23 April 2020.

[53] Grossman, 'Shattering the Glass Ceiling'(n 21) 361.

[54] CoE Parliamentary Assembly, Committee on Equal Opportunities for Women and Men, Opinion – Candidates for the European Court of Human Rights, Doc 11243, 16 April 2007, para 10.

[55] ibid.

[56] ibid. The ECtHR, in its advisory opinion, held that States cannot be forced to nominate non-nationals, even though this is not included in the ECHR—a somewhat ironic holding, given that Malta challenged the requirement of gender-inclusive nomination lists precisely on the grounds that it went beyond what is required by Article 21 ECHR. See ECtHR, Advisory opinion on certain legal questions concerning the lists of candidates submitted with a view to the election of judges to the European Court of Human Rights, 12 February 2008, para 52: 'States must not be placed in a position where, in order to fulfil the criterion concerning the sex of candidates, they can only nominate candidates who satisfy the criteria of Article 21 § 1 if they choose non-nationals', citing concerns relating to state sovereignty and

Furthermore, research carried out on gender representativeness has shown that the 'limited pool' argument does not explain why women continue to be underrepresented on international courts even compared to the number of female lawyers both worldwide and in a given State.[57] Nor does it explain why, despite the pool ostensibly getting larger as more women turn to (international) law as a profession, there would be *fewer* female judges on international benches over time.[58] Rather, 'the data suggest that qualified women are kept off the bench and not that unqualified women are being put on it'.[59] Thirdly, beyond the minimum requirements laid down in courts' statutes, there appears to be little to no agreement on what the qualifications and professional background of an 'ideal' international judge would look like.[60] In other words, no-one has the 'perfect' experience and there will inevitably be some learning on the job involved for everyone.

3. Identity and (the Lack of) Diversity: Rules and Practice

While democratic justifications call for the international judiciary to be generally reflective of the diversity of humankind, the evidence shows that this is far from the case. To begin with, there is relatively little regulation on most aspects of diversity; and in the absence (sometimes even in the presence) of such rules, election and appointment practices reveal significant imbalances in representation.

3.1 Existing Regulation on Identity and Diversity

Existing regulation tends to relate mainly to geographical representation and legal systems, and occasionally to gender. Statutes of international courts and tribunals often provide for some form of geographic spread in order to assure 'representation', which is usually tied to representativeness among different legal systems. Perhaps the best-known example is that of the Statute of the International Court of Justice, stipulating that: '[a]t every election, the electors shall bear in mind not only that the persons to be elected should individually possess the qualifications required, but also that in the body as a whole the representation of the main forms of civilization and of the principal legal systems of the world should be assured.'[61] Similar

lack of familiarity with the particular State's domestic legal system, which is the main reason underpinning the ECtHR's system of 'national judges'.

[57] Grossman, 'Shattering the Glass Ceiling' (n 21) 358–60, 362–63.
[58] ibid 361.
[59] Grossman, 'Sex-Representative International Court Benches' (n 22) 94.
[60] Mackenzie and others (n 9) 51–60, particularly 52.
[61] ICJ Statute, Art 9.

requirements can be found elsewhere in standing courts with a worldwide reach (eg the International Criminal Court),[62] and occasionally even in regional courts. Pursuant to the Protocol on the African Court of Human and Peoples' Rights, for instance, the African Union's Assembly of Heads of State and Government is required to 'ensure that in the Court as a whole there is representation of the main regions of Africa and of their principal legal traditions', as well as 'adequate gender representation'.[63]

In effect, though, such provisions are operationalized in a way that focuses solely on geographical distribution, which in turn simply acts as a proxy for legal systems.[64] Several courts employ a quota system based on the UN's regional groups, namely: Africa, Asia-Pacific, Eastern Europe, Latin America and the Caribbean (GRULAC), and Western Europe and Others (WEOG), with a certain (minimum) number of seats assigned to each group.[65] Where there is sufficient political will, there may also be coordination within a given group: for instance, within the African group, there is a rotational system between anglophone, francophone, and Arabic-speaking countries, which broadly corresponds to the delineation between common law, civil law, and Islamic law systems.[66] However, in the absence of such coordination, legal systems *as such* are not taken into account in the selection process—and it would seem to be assumed that because someone was born in a common law country, for example, that would also be the country of their legal training. Given this state of affairs, it is little surprise that opinions diverge as to the adequacy of the geographical proxy.[67]

In the past few decades, a handful of courts have also seen the emergence of requirements relating to gender representation. The Rome Statute of the International Criminal Court, for instance, concluded in 1998, requires Member States to 'take into account the need' for a 'fair representation of female and male judges' when electing the members of the Court.[68] In 2004, the Parliamentary Assembly of the Council of Europe decided that it would no longer consider single-sex lists of nominees for the ECtHR.[69] This approach soon came to be tested, when Malta

[62] Rome Statute, Art 8(a): 'The States Parties shall, in the selection of judges, take into account the need, within the membership of the Court, for: (i) The representation of the principal legal systems of the world; (ii) Equitable geographical representation; and (iii) A fair representation of female and male judges.' Cf ITLOS Statute, Art 3(2): 'There shall be no fewer than three members from each geographical group as established by the General Assembly of the United Nations.'

[63] Protocol to the African Charter of Human and Peoples' Rights on the Establishment of an African Court of Human and Peoples' Rights, Art 14(2) and 14(3).

[64] See eg Mackenzie and others (n 9) 41.

[65] For a list of States belonging to each group, see <www.un.org/depts/DGACM/RegionalGroups.shtml;> accessed 23 April 2020 ;see eg ITLOS Statute, Art 3(2) for a reference to this system as the basis for representativeness; on the ICJ and ICC relying on this system, see Mackenzie and others (n 9) 27–31.

[66] Mackenzie and others (n 9) 34, 44.

[67] Mackenzie and others (n 9) 31–37.

[68] Rome Statute, Art 8(a)(iii).

[69] CoE Parliamentary Assembly, Resolution 1366 (2004): Candidates for the European Court of Human Rights, 30 January 2004. See also Helen Keller, Corina Heri, and Myriam Christ's chapter in

and Slovakia submitted all-male lists of nominees.[70] When challenged, Slovakia amended its list, but Malta refused to make any changes, stating that it 'did its utmost to find a female candidate with the required expertise'.[71] Interestingly, Latvia submitted an all-female list in 2005, in response to which an exception was made for cases where 'the candidates belong to the sex which is underrepresented in the Court, that is the sex to which under 40% of the total number of judges belong'.[72]

Meanwhile, as Malta refused to back down, the case of its all-male list eventually led to the ECtHR's first ever advisory opinion, in which the Court held that:

> [W]here a Contracting Party has taken all the necessary and appropriate steps with a view to ensuring that the list contains a candidate of the under-represented sex, but without success, and especially where it has followed the Assembly's recommendations advocating an open and transparent procedure involving a call for candidatures . . ., the Assembly may not reject the list in question on the sole ground that no such candidate features on it.[73]

Following the Court's advisory opinion in 2008, the Assembly decided to allow for the consideration of single-sex lists 'in exceptional circumstances where a Contracting Party has taken all the necessary and appropriate steps' to find a qualified candidate from the underrepresented sex but has not been able to do so.[74] In 2011, Belgium submitted an all-male list, noting that only one woman had applied to its open call, and maintaining that she was not suitably qualified (an assertion that has been seriously called into question).[75] In addition, Belgium argued that as 19 of the Court's 47 judges (40.42%) were female at the time of putting the list forward, there was no underrepresentation to be remedied—even though, ironically,

this volume on '50 Years of Women at the European Court of Human Rights: Success and Failure of the Council of Europe's Gender Agenda'.

[70] See Stéphanie Hennette Vauchez, 'More Women – But Which Women? The Rule and the Politics of Gender Balance at the European Court of Human Rights' (2015) 26 European Journal of International Law 195, at 203–04; for more on the history of the CoE's gender requirements for the Court, see ibid 200–09.

[71] ECtHR, Advisory opinion on certain legal questions concerning the lists of candidates submitted with a view to the election of judges to the European Court of Human Rights, 12 February 2008, para 10.

[72] CoE Parliamentary Assembly, Resolution 1426 (2005): Candidates for the European Court of Human Rights, 18 March 2005.

[73] ECtHR, Advisory opinion on certain legal questions concerning the lists of candidates submitted with a view to the election of judges to the European Court of Human Rights, 12 February 2008, para 54.

[74] CoE Parliamentary Assembly, Resolution 1627 (2008): Candidates for the European Court of Human Rights, 30 September 2008. See also CoE Parliamentary Assembly, Resolution 1841 (2005): The amendment of various provisions of the Rules of Procedure of the Parliamentary Assembly—implementation of Resolution 1822 (2011) on the reform of the Parliamentary Assembly, 7 October 2011 for the latest formulation.

[75] Françoise Tulkens, 'More Women – But Which Women? A Reply to Stéphanie Hennette Vauchez' (2015) 26 European Journal of International Law 223, at 226; see also Vauchez, 'More Women – But Which Women?'(n 70) 209.

the eventual election of a male judge for the Belgian spot was enough to bring the percentage of women below the 40% threshold.[76] This 'softening' of the gender inclusion requirement also highlights the (asserted) potential tension between individual qualification criteria and the push for greater diversity, discussed above.[77]

Furthermore, not all newer courts follow the trend of taking gender—and other diversity considerations—into account in increasing measure. The European Union's proposed investment court system, for instance, introduced in recent years' free trade agreements, does not include any provisions on diversity in terms of gender or geography.[78]

3.2 Unwritten Conventions on Representation

In addition to these written rules, some courts also have unwritten conventions regarding the representation of certain States. The best known example is that of the ICJ, where the five permanent members of the UN Security Council are customarily represented on the 15-member bench; but it is by no means the only example: prior to its current crisis, the WTO Appellate Body, for instance, has always included a member from the US and one from the EU.[79] Such conventions are particularly difficult to reconcile with geographical representativeness and with diversity more broadly, as they simply appear to reflect power relations (sometimes even frozen in time), rather than any other consideration. The conventional wisdom appears to be that representation enhances buy-in and acceptance of the regime by these powerful States;[80] but even those who note this argument point out that in the case of the ICJ, the only member of the P5 to have generally accepted the Court's jurisdiction is the UK.[81]

[76] Vauchez, 'More Women – But Which Women?'(n 70) 209.

[77] Although States are not limited to their nationals when selecting nominees, the ECtHR also held (at para 52) that 'States must not be placed in a position where, in order to fulfil the criterion concerning the sex of candidates, they can only nominate candidates who satisfy the criteria of Article 21 § 1 if they choose non-nationals', citing concerns relating to State sovereignty and lack of familiarity with the particular State's domestic legal system, which is the main reason underpinning the ECtHR's system of 'national judges'.

[78] See Freya Baetens, 'The European Union's Proposed Investment Court System: Addressing Criticisms of Investor-State Arbitration While Raising New Challenges' (2016) 43 Legal Issues of Economic Integration 367, at 373.

[79] See eg Arthur E Appleton, 'Judging the Judges or Judging the Members? Pathways and Pitfalls in the Appellate Body Appointment Process' in Leïla Choukroune (ed), *Judging the State in International Trade and Investment Law* (Springer 2016) 11, at 12, 29.

[80] See eg Mackenzie and others (n 9) 38; Antonio Remiro Brotons, 'Nomination et élection des juges à la Cour Internationale de Justice' in *Unité et diversité du droit international: écrits en l'honneur du professeur Pierre-Marie Dupuy* (Brill 2014) 639–60.

[81] Mackenzie and others (n 9) 38–39; Dapo Akande, 'ICJ Elections 2017: UN General Assembly and Security Council Elect Four Judges to the ICJ But fail to Agree on a Fifth, yet again! + Trivia Question', EJIL: *Talk!* (11 November 2017) <www.ejiltalk.org/icj-elections-2017-un-general-assembly-and-security-council-elect-four-judges-to-the-icj-but-fail-to-agree-on-a-fifth-yet-again-trivia-question> accessed 23 April 2020.

Given these concerns, it is perhaps not surprising that such conventions, once thought to be unassailable, are now facing increased pressure, as illustrated most recently by the fact that Judge Christopher Greenwood was not re-elected to the ICJ in November 2017, leading to the loss of UK representation on the Court.[82] That said, it remains to be seen whether this was merely an anomaly or if it was an event signifying a broader trend. While there have been other one-off instances at the International Law Commission (ILC) and the International Tribunal for the Law of the Sea (ITLOS),[83] a post-election analysis by the UK House of Commons Foreign Affairs Committee noted that the loss could also indicate that 'the influence of the UK within the UN is at risk', due to 'increased influence of Asian countries' and/or 'a change in the standing of, and attitudes to, the UK itself'.[84] Similarly, the Permanent Representative of India to the UN, Syed Akbaruddin, described the (re-)election of Greenwood's competitor, Judge Dalveer Bhandari 'as a "victory for emerging new India," and an "acknowledgement that the world now needs to make space for an asserting India"'.[85]

3.3 Appointment Practices and the Effect of Regulation

Beyond frequent requirements relating to the representation of geographical regions and legal systems, and occasional ones on gender, there is not much in the way of regulation requiring diversity on international benches. Furthermore, as the examples above demonstrate, even where requirements on certain aspects of diversity are laid down in the instruments governing the election process, they tend to be framed tentatively, as mere considerations to be taken into account, rather than hard rules. This may be useful inasmuch as it allows the election process to retain some flexibility, mitigating the danger of becoming paralysed; and it appears that even such aspirational statements have some effect on achieving, for instance, greater gender diversity (if not as much of an effect as quotas).[86] Nonetheless, most courts do not include gender requirements, and women continue to be

[82] See eg Owen Bowcott, 'No British Judge on World Court for First Time in its 71-Year History' *The Guardian* (20 November 2017) <www.theguardian.com/law/2017/nov/20/no-british-judge-on-world-court-for-first-time-in-its-71-year-history> accessed 23 April 2020; Akande, 'ICJ Elections 2017'.

[83] Mackenzie and others (n 9) 39–40.

[84] House of Commons Foreign Affairs Committee, '2017 elections to the International Court of Justice', Fourth Report of Session 2017–19, HC860, 28 February 2018 <https://publications.parliament.uk/pa/cm201719/cmselect/cmfaff/860/860.pdf> accessed 23 April 2020 para 22: '[i]t is possible that this failure was not a one-off but might instead be an indication that the influence of the UK within the UN is at risk. Possible reasons suggested for this were: increased influence of Asian countries; a change in the standing of, and attitudes to, the UK itself'.

[85] As reported in Sujan Dutta, 'How India Squeezed Britain Out Of the Contest, Got Justice Dalveer Bhandari Seat in International Court of Justice' *New Indian Express* (21 November 2017)<www.newindianexpress.com/nation/2017/nov/21/how-india-squeezed-britain-out-of-the-contest-got-justice-dalveer-bhandari-seat-in-international-co-1707033.html> accessed 23 April 2020.

[86] Grossman, 'Sex-Representative International Court Benches' (n 22) 92–93.

underrepresented on international courts and tribunals.[87] Furthermore, there is significant disparity regarding the participation of women on the bench across different international legal regimes.[88]

What is more, even the ostensibly most robust of diversity safeguards—geographical distribution quotas—are subject to criticism, with the Western Europe and Others Group[89] often regarded as being overrepresented.[90] Conversely, other regions, particularly Africa and Asia-Pacific, are seen as underrepresented.[91] Western influence is further compounded by the fact that even the nationals of non-Western States often receive a significant part of their (international) legal education in a Western State;[92] since the country where potential nominees studied (where their 'legal' minds were formed) may well be of far greater influence on their legal reasoning as adjudicators than where their cradle happened to stand. More generally, there appears to be some variation between different fields of law in terms of adjudicators' most common profile. In trade law, WTO panellists tend to be low-profile bureaucrats with predominantly governmental backgrounds (who have often worked in trade negotiations or representations, but do not necessarily have a law degree), while investment arbitrators tend to be high-profile and highly specialized lawyers.[93]

In arbitration, where litigants are free to appoint their own adjudicators, the diversity of arbitrators in terms of gender, geographic, legal cultural, religious, and ethnic background shows a similarly poor record.[94] As one author memorably put: '[a]rbitration is dominated by a few aging men, many of whom pioneered the field. In the words of Sarah Francois-Poncet of Salans, the usual suspects are "pale, male, and stale." '[95] While the realities may be somewhat more nuanced, empirical research on the diversity of arbitrators has indeed found 'disproportionate levels of representation by men from states in North America and Europe'.[96] For instance,

[87] See eg Grossman, 'Shattering the Glass' (n 21) 339; Grossman, 'Sex-Representative International Court Benches' (n 22) 82.

[88] Grossman, 'Shattering the Glass Ceiling' (n 21) 348–57; see also Chapter 10 by Keller et al. and Chapter 7 by Badejogbin, in the present volume exploring some of the reasons behind sex representation in particular contexts.

[89] The 'others' in WEOG refers to Northern Europe, Southern Europe, Australia, Canada, Israel, New Zealand, and the US.

[90] See eg Mackenzie and others (n 9) 31–32.

[91] ibid 32.

[92] See Kurt Taylor Gaubatz and Matthew MacArthur, 'How International Is International Law' (2001) 22 Michigan Journal of International Law 239, at 260–63. Several chapters in this volume also make this point, for example Chapter 5 by Palchetti, Chapter 8 by Prusinowska, and Chapter 15 by Gáspár-Szilági and Létourneau-Tremblay.

[93] Pauwelyn, 'Rule of Law Without the Rule of Lawyers', 768–83.

[94] See eg Franck and others 'The Diversity Challenge: Exploring the Invisible College of International Arbitration' (2015) 53 Columbia Journal of Transnational Law 429.

[95] Michael D Goldhaber, 'Madame La Présidente: A Woman Who Sits As President of a Major Arbitral Tribunal Is a Rare Creature. Why?' (2004) 1(3) Transnational Dispute Management <www.transnational-dispute-management.com/article.asp?key=158> accessed 23 April 2020.

[96] Franck and others, 'The Diversity Challenge: Exploring the Invisible College of International Arbitration' (2015) 53 Columbia Journal of Transnational Law 429, at 503. See also Jeffery Commission, 'Precedent in Investment Treaty Arbitration: A Citation Analysis of a Developing Jurisprudence' (2007) 24

ICSID statistics show that 68% of arbitrators appointed so far are nationals of Western Europe and North America, while States from these regions have been parties to arbitration in only 12% of cases.[97] That said, there is significant variation in levels of diversity depending on who makes the appointment: the parties (whose interests in the dispute at hand are arguably best served by appointing the most experienced arbitrators) or an independent appointing authority (with a view on long-term sustainability of the system).

3.4 The Identity of Appointment Authorities

Efforts to achieve diversity in international courts are further complicated by the fact that judges tend to face a two-stage selection process, consisting of a domestic and an international phase. This means that States act as gatekeepers not only through their lobbying and voting on the international stage, but also through the pre-selection for candidates, which takes place at the national level, often through relatively opaque processes.[98] Conversely, multilevel domestic systems may have their own diversity rules in place, which could come into conflict with international requirements. In any case, where conventions assign certain seats to particular States, nominees frequently go through the international stage of the process virtually unchallenged. This degree of influence by domestic selection processes—and the corresponding (relative) lack of influence of international elections—points to the need to tackle this issue partly at the national level, including through coordination between States and regional groups. In the case of arbitrators, the lack of coordination (or any incentive for it) is even more apparent, as the parties have the freedom to choose whomever they wish, and there are no diversity considerations in place for the bench as a whole. As one prominent commentator has noted, 'ICSID parties want to win the dispute at hand and are less motivated by systemic interests such as diversifying the pool of arbitrators.'[99]

Nonetheless, it appears that in general, greater emphasis is placed on such considerations by independent appointing authorities, such as the WTO, ICSID, and Permanent Court of Arbitration (PCA) secretariat. At the WTO, where panellists are proposed—and often eventually selected—by the Secretariat, appointments show greater geographical diversity than in investment arbitration, where most appointments are made by the parties.[100] But even within the latter

Journal of International Arbitration 129, at 137–41; Jeffery Commission, 'A Snapshot of ICSID Arbitrators in Pending Cases' (*Kluwer Arbitration Blog*, 4 September 2009) <http://arbitrationblog.kluwerarbitration.com/2009/09/04/a-snapshot-of-icsid-arbitrators-in-pending-cases> accessed 23 April 2020.

[97] The ICSID Caseload – Statistics (Issue 2018-2), 11 and 19 <https://icsid.worldbank.org/en/Pages/resources/ICSID-Caseload-Statistics.aspx> accessed 23 April 2020.

[98] See eg Grossman, 'Shattering the Glass Ceiling' (n 21) 363–77.

[99] Joost Pauwelyn, 'Rule of Law Without the Rule of Lawyers' 787.

[100] ibid 769–72, 784–89.

field, ICSID-appointed arbitrators show greater geographical diversity than party-appointed ones, with more arbitrators appointed from South America, Central America and the Caribbean, Middle East and North Africa, Sub-Saharan Africa, and South and East Asia and the Pacific.[101] At the Stockholm Chamber of Commerce (SCC), the gender ratio of party-appointed arbitrators was 92% male to 8% female in 2017, in stark contrast to the ratio of 63% male to 37% female among SCC-appointed arbitrators.[102] That said, there are also counterexamples to this trend: for instance, appointments to annulment committees between 2008 and 2012—made by the Chairman of ICSID's Administrative Council—showed *less* gender diversity than party appointments to arbitral panels in the same period.[103]

3.5 A Push for Greater (Gender) Diversity

In some cases, this relative lack of diversity has even prompted campaigns to remedy the situation—particularly as regards gender. One of the most notable efforts in this regard has been the development of the Equal Representation in Arbitration (ERA) Pledge, whereby signatories make a commitment 'to improving the profile and representation of women in arbitration' and consider that 'women should be appointed as arbitrators on an equal opportunity basis'.[104] Since its introduction in 2015, the Pledge has garnered significant support, with institutions such as the SCC and the International Chamber of Commerce's International Court of Arbitration among its signatories.[105] More broadly, the GQUAL campaign (campaign for gender parity in international representation) aims to achieve gender parity in international representation on tribunals and monitoring bodies (including UN special procedures), surveying 91 bodies with a total of 592 positions available.[106] As in the case of the ERA Pledge, the GQUAL campaign relies on pledges to its declaration in order to achieve this goal, as well as promoting

[101] ibid 12 (ICSID uses the World Bank's regional classifications, which are different from those used by the UN). See also Chiara Giorgetti, 'Latest Chairman Designations to the ICSID Panels Substantially Increase Diversity' (*Kluwer Arbitration Blog*, 5 November 2017) <http://arbitrationblog.kluwerarbitration.com/2017/11/05/latest-chairman-designations-icsid-panels-substantially-increases-diversity> accessed 23 April 2020. Nominations to the ICSID Panel of Arbitrators are significant, as ICSID-appointed arbitrators and annulment committee members must be selected from this list, pursuant to Articles 38, 40(1), and 52(3) ICSID Convention.

[102] SCC Statistics 2017 <https://sccinstitute.com/statistics> accessed 23 April 2020.

[103] Irene Ten Cate, 'Binders Full of Women . . . Arbitrators?' (*IntLawGrrls*, 2 November 2018) <www.intlawgrrls.com/2012/11/binders-full-of-women-arbitrators.html> accessed 23 April 2020.

[104] Equal Representation in Arbitration> Take the Pledge <www.arbitrationpledge.com/take-the-pledge> accessed 23 April 2020.

[105] Equal Representation in Arbitration> Organisation Signatories <www.arbitrationpledge.com/organisations> accessed 23 April 2020.

[106] GQUAL, for more information, see <www.gqualcampaign.org/about-gqual;>GQUAL> The Current Composition of International Tribunals and Monitoring Bodies <http://www.gqualcampaign.org/1626-2> accessed 23 April 2020.

increased transparency in selection procedures and providing information on the gender composition of existing bodies.

4. The Aim and Structure of This Volume

Against the backdrop described above, this volume seeks to promote a higher level of understanding of both current challenges and best practices in terms of assessing and promoting diversity on the international bench. In order to do so, one of its goals is to analyse when and how adjudicators' identity—in particular, features relating to legal culture, gender, nationality, religion, and ethnicity (including race, language, culture, ancestry, and membership of minority groups)—is considered in the composition of international courts and tribunals. In this context, the book considers issues such as the causes and effects of geographic representation requirements, or the prevalence of certain educational and professional backgrounds among adjudicators prior to their appointment, as well as investigating intersectionality and the interaction between different facets of diversity.

But establishing how identity and diversity are taken into account in the composition of courts and tribunals—through an examination of relevant rules and practices—is merely the first step towards the main inquiry of the volume: the effect of identity and diversity on the (perceived) legitimacy of the international adjudicatory institutions, processes, and outcomes. The underlying assumption of the book is that, with increased diversity, the (perception of) normative and social legitimacy of the international judicial process will be enhanced, for instance through the diverse perspectives brought to bear on adjudicatory processes and outcomes on the bench.

In this context, the volume aims to analyse how the identity of judges and arbitrators may affect judicial reasoning and decision-making, including not only the 'direct' effect of adjudicators on a given judgment, but also their 'indirect' effect—through engagement with other members of the court or tribunal—by examining judicial behaviour linked to the absence or presence of adjudicators with a certain background. In exploring all of these aspects, the volume goes beyond the views of adjudicators and other judicial/institutional perspectives, in order to examine the standpoints of governments and private parties as well.

In addressing these questions, the volume follows a tripartite structure, focusing on the (s)election of adjudicators and their pre-nomination career paths; the impact of judges and arbitrators from underrepresented groups during their time on the bench; and the legacy of such adjudicators, including any effect they may have on compliance with judicial decisions.

4.1 Towards the International Bench

The first part of the book focuses on the (s)election of adjudicators, through two complementary perspectives. On the one hand, it examines the path taken by (potential) judges and arbitrators that led them to be selected, or at least considered, to become part of a court or tribunal. On the other hand, it analyses the considerations of those—States, parties, and appointing authorities—who have the power to decide whether to select a particular person to serve on a court or tribunal. As regards the paths of potential adjudicators, the book first investigates whether judges from an underrepresented group tend to have a different educational or professional background as compared to their colleagues before their appointment to courts or tribunals (eg background in a particular area of international law; a career as an academic or as a legal practitioner). It then turns to examine whether there are differences between different international legal regimes in this regard, including whether prior expertise matters more for particular regimes (eg human rights, as opposed to trade law), and whether this contributes to explanations of underrepresentation.

Turning to the perspectives of those who wield the power of decision in determining the composition of courts and tribunals, the book first examines the extent to which these actors may have unfettered discretion, or conversely, the degree to which they are bound by requirements relating to factors such as geographical representation or gender balance. This includes an examination of how these requirements function; whether they are 'soft' or 'hard' law; how they are taken into account in the nomination and election of judges; any possible enforcement mechanisms of such requirements; and whether they achieve their stated (or implicit) goals. Having established the functioning of these baseline requirements, the book proceeds to scrutinize the extent to which rules on the composition of the court interact. In this context, it examines whether geographical distribution requirements, for example, can be seen to conflict with the objective of gender representativeness, and whether certain forms of representativeness should prevail over others, and if so, which ones and why. This also includes an exploration whether other aspects of social identities—not covered by the rules, eg nationality, ethnicity, or religion—have any impact on the (s)election process.

Moving beyond the framework provided by soft and hard rules and their functioning, the volume turns its attention to the behaviour of those who decide on the composition of judicial bodies, investigating whether appointing authorities, States (for standing courts), parties (for arbitration) take gender, religion, ethnicity, or requirements related to geography and legal culture into account in doing so. Where such factors are indeed taken into account, further analysis follows on how and why this takes place, and how they are weighed against other factors. In addition, the volume explores whether in the case of ad hoc bodies, this tends to happen in relation to particular types of cases; and in the case of permanent courts, whether there is variation in State practice, with different countries attaching distinctive weight to specific factors.

4.2 On the International Bench

The second part of the book turns to analysing the experiences and impact of judges and arbitrators from underrepresented groups during their time spent on courts and tribunals. In essence, this part attempts to establish whether the consequentialist justification for diversity—that adjudicators from different backgrounds bring diverse perspectives to the process, and thereby even potentially affect the outcome—is well-founded. In this regard, it examines whether being a judge from an underrepresented group affects adjudicatory 'style' and/or the behaviour of the other adjudicators on the bench, as well as counsel appearing before the court or tribunal. In terms of adjudicatory style, the volume looks into whether certain judges tend to exhibit a higher or lower level of judicial restraint in participation in oral hearings, written decisions, separate or concurring opinions, and dissenting opinions; and whether time spent on the bench leads to lower or higher restraint. Furthermore, it analyses whether identity features affect the interpretation of legal principles, facts, precedent, rules of procedure or evidence, or any other aspect of the case, asking whether judges from an underrepresented background have had a specific discernible impact on the development, application, and interpretation of different legal regimes.

As regards both adjudicatory style and impact on other members of the bench, the volume considers whether the type of decision-making process applied shifts with increased diversity. Where recourse to equity is allowed, is there significant variation between what is perceived by adjudicators from a certain background to be equitable? In light of the internal politics of international courts and tribunals, the volume examines the case allocation of underrepresented judges where the court does not always sit *en banc*; as well as the roles which such judges are allocated within the court (eg procedural rules committee, hiring committee). As for the possible impact on counsel appearing before a bench, the volume investigates whether litigation strategies and pleading styles are adjusted to the gender, geographic or legal cultural background, religious and ethnic background of the adjudicator, asking whether for instance—for female as well as male counsel—the experience of pleading before female judges is different.

4.3 Beyond the International Bench

Finally, Part 3 of the volume turns to the life and legacy of adjudicators following their time on the bench, and how their work on the bench is regarded by the parties and other actors outside the court or tribunal, as part of a comprehensive examination of legitimacy questions surrounding identity and diversity. In terms of legacy, the volume investigates whether judges' backgrounds affect which types of careers they pursue after their time on the bench or, where this is allowed, while on the bench; and how their experiences on the bench affect this choice. It also asks more broadly what type of legacy a judge may (or should) aim for; how judges with a more 'unusual' background describe their roles in interviews, speeches, articles, or other forms of interaction outside the court; and how such judges may promote, inspire, and prepare future judges (eg through mentoring).

Turning to questions of legitimacy, the volume considers whether the presence and work of judges with diverse backgrounds affects compliance with the decisions rendered and/or the authority of the international court in any way. It then analyses whether this matters to the normative or social legitimacy of the international judicial institution; and/or whether it affects the effectiveness of the international legal system more broadly. In this context, the volume explores what level of representation and diversity is required for an international court or tribunal to be perceived as legitimate; and whether requirements differ in this regard among adjudicatory systems. In particular, it asks whether certain instances of a lack of representation or diversity (eg clustering of certain backgrounds) are more problematic than others.

5. How Much Diversity is 'Enough'?

The final question is: *how much* diversity is required—or deemed sufficient—to ensure the legitimacy of the court or tribunal? This, in turn, is closely tied to the question of how diversity relates to representativeness. International courts, given the mere fact of their limited size, cannot be representative of the world's population in all its diversity, or even of all nationalities (to represent all States). Court chambers or arbitral tribunals, often composed of only three adjudicators, have even less room for such representation. In this sense, one cannot speak of representativeness. At the same time, though, there *is* an element of representation involved in matters of diversity. One way to move towards answering this question is to devote more attention to why diversity is to be desired: ensuring the presence of multiple perspectives on the bench and the perceived 'representation' of certain stakeholders etc. Some such arguments may require a 'critical mass' of certain different perspectives while others may require rough equality.

To begin with, certain statutes explicitly refer to 'the representation of the main forms of civilization and of the principal legal systems of the world' (ICJ), the 'representation of the main regions of Africa and of their principal legal traditions', or 'gender representation' (ACtHPR).[107] More generally, diversity considerations are

[107] ICJ Statute, Art 9; Protocol to the African Charter of Human and Peoples' Rights on the Establishment of an African Court of Human and Peoples' Rights, Art 14(2) and 14(3).

typically meant to ensure that courts reflect their constituencies, so to speak[108]—this is illustrated particularly when considering the composition of regional courts: after all, it would be rather odd to require seats on a regional court in the Americas to be filled from Asia or Europe, for instance. The goal is then to ensure diversity within the particular court's constituency. Depending on the court's subject-matter jurisdiction, it may also be the case to some extent that different courts require different types of diversity (eg questions of religion may come before human rights courts with some frequency in cases concerning religious freedom, but much less likely to form part of a dispute at the WTO).

Even so, it may be difficult to put a figure on diversity; nonetheless, in some cases, courts have opted for quotas on gender and geographic representation. Various courts operate long-standing processes for the cross-regional allocation of seats; and as for the more recent development of sex representation, the Council of Europe set 40% as the threshold below which a sex is considered to be under-represented; at the ICC, at least one third of the Court's 18 judges are required to be from each sex. More than these figures or quotas, the attitudes towards them may reveal underlying sentiments about diversity, at least as it relates to gender.

At one end of the spectrum, quotas or similar measures are treated not as minimum, but rather as *maximum* requirements to be fulfilled, often accompanied by the assumption that 'men are the natural occupants of such positions, that women obtain them through political manoeuvring, not merit, and that enough women have been appointed'.[109] For instance, when refusing to comply with the requirement not to present all-male lists of nominees to the ECtHR, one of the arguments advanced by Belgium was that 'since at the precise moment at which they were presenting their candidates 19 women were sitting on the Court, this was one unit in excess of the threshold of 40 per cent'—a fact that changed with the election of a male judge for the Belgian spot.[110] At the other end of the spectrum, the counterargument is centred on correcting historical gender imbalances by letting the pendulum swing the other way. In response to the question 'when will there be enough women on the court?', Ruth Bader Ginsburg, the second woman ever to serve on the nine-member US Supreme Court, famously said 'when there are nine',[111] given that for almost two centuries, all Supreme Court justices were men. Nonetheless, the practice whereby quota or thresholds for women are matched by quota or thresholds for men (as in the case of the

[108] Cf Grossman, 'Sex on the Bench' (n 30) 660–68.

[109] Sally J Kenney, 'Choosing Judges: A Bumpy Road to Women's Equality and a Long Way to Go' (2012) Michigan State Law Review 1499, at 1509.

[110] Vauchez, 'More Women – But Which Women? (n 70) 209; see also Tulkens, 'More Women – But Which Women? A Reply to Stéphanie Hennette Vauchez' (n 75) 226.

[111] See eg 'When will there be enough women on the Supreme Court? Justice Ginsburg answers that question' (*PBS NewsHour*, 5 February 2015) <www.pbs.org/newshour/show/justice-ginsburg-enough-women-supreme-court> accessed 23 April 2020.

ECtHR and the ICC) suggests that such an approach is unlikely to take hold at the international level.[112]

The question how much diversity exactly is 'enough', cannot be answered with mathematical precision—and the contributors to this volume do not claim to do so. What this book does achieve is to provide a number of building blocks for future research, not solely on identity and diversity at the international, regional, and domestic level, but also concerning independence and impartiality, legitimacy in international adjudication, and, ultimately, the pursuit of justice.

[112] Even if it did, it could end up detracting from perceived authority, see Grossman, 'Sex on the Bench'(n 30) 674.

PART I

TOWARDS THE INTERNATIONAL BENCH

2

The *Smurfette* Principle

Reflections about Gender and the Nomination of Women to the International Bench

Liesbeth Lijnzaad

1. Introduction

This chapter will discuss the appointment and election of international judges, and will stress that attention should be given to the selection and nominations process, rather than merely to the election. In preparation to the elections there are, I believe, improvements to be made with respect to the election of female judges. While parity may take some time to achieve, it is high time that more attention is given to how women are nominated for election to the international bench.

Whether a problem exists with respect to the election of women to international courts and tribunals is no matter for debate: their absence is clearly visible. To look at the Tribunal I am most familiar with, it should be noted that so far five women were ever nominated for ITLOS and one of these nominations was withdrawn prior to election. Of these four eligible women, three had been elected by 2017. This is a 75% success rate for the individual nomination, which does perhaps not sound all that bad. At the same time, it implies that by now (2020) women make up only 14% of the bench at the Law of the Sea Tribunal and that is certainly not an impressive percentage.[1]

It is fair to say that the low number of nominations demonstrates just where the issue of the participation of women is problematic: maybe not so much the elections, but to a great extent the low number of female candidates. Thus, an approach focusing on improving the nomination process may yield more results in terms of increasing the number of women on the bench, rather than merely addressing the election process itself. To follow up on the assumption that it is important to invest in the selection and nomination process for candidates to judicial positions well ahead of any election, it is necessary to look at how such

[1] For a call to action see the blog by Priya Pillai, 'Women in International Law: A Vanishing Act' (*Opinio Juris*, 3 December 2018).

Liesbeth Lijnzaad, *The* Smurfette *Principle* In: *Identity and Diversity on the International Bench.* Edited by: Freya Baetens, Oxford University Press (2020). © The several contributors. DOI: 10.1093/oso/9780198870753.003.0002.

processes function: what is required before a formal nomination takes place and who has a role to play in the nomination process?[2,3]

The so-called *Smurfette* principle refers to the (visual) role of a single woman amidst a group of men. This image has been borrowed from contemporary television and movie' critique:[4] the *Smurfette* is a single woman in the company of men. It refers to a series of comic books telling the story of a small blue people living in a mushroom village in the middle of a large forest. There are 100 *Smurfs* in the village, and only one of them is a girl: *Smurfette*, all blue, curvy, and blonde amongst her male blue Smurf pals.[5] While the spectator focuses on what happens to this group of people, the woman stands visibly alone as the odd one out. Examples would be characters like *Miss Piggy* in The Muppets, or *Princess Leia* in Star Wars. Both may have a visible role amidst their male buddies, yet in the end men control the situation.

Granted, a reference to *Smurfette* in the title of this piece may draw the attention of readers who would not otherwise be tempted to read about its subject matter but it is a recognizable shorthand term for a phenomenon seen everywhere in society, in the media and indeed on international courts and tribunals. While a single woman in a prominent role amongst men has at times been viewed as a sign of modernity (think about people such as *Margaret Thatcher* or *Benazir Bhutto*), the image in fact underlines that women in such roles are an exception rather than the norm. Her visibility underlines the normalcy of a male majority as the existing standard. Thus, the presence of that single woman identifies women as strangers in a male-dominated narrative (on television, or in the movies), and it may be suggested that this is not only the case with popular visual culture but equally so in many other parts of society. Like the single blue *Smurfette,* the few female judges tend to stand out as members of international tribunals. An example would be the attention given to writing about female judges as representatives of their gender, rather than as expert lawyers. It is striking how often authors discussing the

[2] It is not possible to address all nomination processes as they vary widely and because there are some 30 international courts and tribunals. Most significantly there is a fundamental distinction between courts and tribunals that have (at least) one seat per participating State, and courts and tribunals that have a limited amount of seat thus necessitating an election. I apologize for focusing mostly on these three international courts and tribunals: the International Court of Justice, the International Tribunal for the Law of the Sea and the International Criminal Court.

[3] For earlier discussions see amongst others: Ruth Mackenzie and others (eds), *Selecting International Judges: Principle, Process and Politics* (Oxford 2010); Nienke Grossman, 'Shattering the Glass Ceiling in International Adjudication' (2016) 56 Virginia Journal of International Law 339–406; Nienke Grossman, 'Achieving Sex-Representative International Court Benches' (2016) 110 American Journal of International Law 82–95.

[4] The term was coined by Katha Pollitt, 'Hers, The Smurfette Principle' *The New York Times* (7 April 1991) <nytimes.com/1991/04/07/magazine/hers-the-smurfette-principle.html> accessed 31 January 2020. See also: Jason Richards, 'The Problem with Smurfette, what to make of the lone female in a village of 100 Smurfs' *The Atlantic* (28 July 2011). Wikipedia tells us that '[T]he Smurfette principle is the practice in media, such as film, television series and television networks, to include only one woman in an otherwise entirely male ensemble.'

[5] *Les Schtroumpfs* (the Smurfs) is a series of Belgian comic books created by Peyo in 1958.

international judiciary specifically address the role and position of the few women who have become international judges, and elaborate on their personal careers. Essentially this is writing about the *Smurfette*: a focus on the one woman who stands out confirms that the system is essentially male-oriented.

On the one hand, such attention underlines the absence of women on the (international) bench and usefully keeps this issue under attention. Yet, it is uncomfortable that such pieces single out the perseverance and steadfast work of these few female lawyers, as though either no other women would bring such dedication (which thus clarifies the low number of women on the bench), or implying that other women are simply not up to that standard.[6] This argument is known as the 'limited pool' argument: it suggests that the low number of female judges on international courts is related to the mere absence of sufficient qualified (or sufficiently qualified?) female lawyers to choose from.[7] This, it is thought, is mostly a generational issue—in due course the availability of qualified women will supposedly improve as more women study law: it is just a matter of time.[8]

In the following I will reflect on aspects of the selection and nominations process preceding the election of international judges, and offer some suggestions as to how to improve such processes in order to enhance the number of female judges. The central proposition is that a gender balance can hardly be achieved through the election process alone but needs to be addressed at a much earlier stage—that is in the preparatory phase: at the time of selection and nomination. When looked at in greater detail, it may be that more and different steps can be taken within the existing legal system that will further the election of more female lawyers to the bench.

2. Eligibility of a Candidate

Eligibility means different things to different people, and there is no uniform view of who would be an ideal candidate for the position of judge.[9] The foundational instruments of the various courts and tribunals identify individual criteria for eligibility such as the importance of a high moral character and independence,

[6] For a particularly striking example of such an approach see Joseph Powderly and Jacob Chylinski, 'The Women Judges: Leading the Line in the Development of International Law' in William A. Schabas and Shannonbrooke Murphy (eds), *Research Handbook on International Courts and Tribunals* (Edward Elgar 2017) 143–80.

[7] Grossman's excellent research has identified the fallacy of this line of thought. See Grossman, 'Shattering the Glass' (n 3) passim; and Grossman, 'Achieving' (n 3) at 84–86. Mackenzie and others (n 3) at 165 observe that 'women are often not *seen* to be in the pool because of the exclusionary nomination processes that favour male candidates from more traditional international law backgrounds or make assumptions about career paths and candidates' motivations'.

[8] See about this idea in a domestic context, New Zealand Justice Susan Glazebrook, *It is just a matter of time and other myths*, on <www.courtsofnz.govt.nz> accessed 31 January 2020.

[9] See amongst others Mackenzie and others (n 3).

impartiality, and integrity[10], as well as broad and in-depth competence in a particular field of law. Also, overall requirements are formulated with respect to the general composition of the bench stressing the importance of the representation of major legal systems of the world and an equitable geographical distribution. These criteria will differ slightly in their formulation, but the general direction is fairly similar: international courts require experienced expert judges who are independent and impartial and will be expected to deliver quality decisions.

Given that the formal requirements for elections are clear, States may add their own wishes as they set out to look for a candidate to be elected as judge. Some States plan well ahead, and have strategies (that may describe a pathway of many years) for a candidate to be sufficiently well known in international legal circles to reach the International Court of Justice (ICJ). A good candidate has a profound knowledge of the subject matter a court is entrusted to deal with, and also understands where a State's interests lie. A candidate may be seen as a torchbearer for her State and its views on international law, and achievements will be presented as part of its commitment to international law. She should not be seen as having ideas that are too wild or creative, as States appreciate a degree of predictability and may be somewhat conservative in their views about the development of the law or the proactive role of courts.

Preferably the candidate is someone who will indeed be elected, thus making the candidacy worth the effort of the State presenting a candidate. The presentation of a candidate for the position of judge, the nomination and election campaign are expensive, not only in terms of money spent on a campaign but also in view of the bargaining chips necessary to facilitate election and the politics involved in such campaigns. Presentation of a candidate by a State implies the expectation that there is a reasonable chance the candidate will succeed. Election will be a success for the new judge, and equally so for the State who has presented the candidate.

Yet, even if the international system seems to suggest that the best international lawyers presented will be elected judges, there is no guarantee that this will be the case. It is quite clearly of great importance that the international bench consists of judges with an extensive and profound knowledge of the law, yet views on what the law is, may differ and there will invariably be nuances between interpretations. Academics and Non-Governmental Organizations (NGOs) clearly do not participate in the election of judges, but have over the years been developing their own wish lists. From an academic perspective, there is a wish to see qualified judges—so: professors with a good reputation, or indeed professors who can boast a (prior) membership of the International Law Commission (ILC). But not everyone will have been an ILC member,[11] and not all ILC members may be

[10] See for example: Article 2 ICJ Statute, Article 2 Annex VI UNCLOS, and Article 36 (3) ICC Statute.

[11] After all there are but 34 ILC members (currently 4 of whom are women), and membership is subject to regional representation.

necessarily top-notch lawyers either. Also, a good professor of international law will not necessarily make a good judge.

A great female lawyer may not be recognized as the ideal candidate for the position of judge, or would not be considered eligible for such a position. She may not participate in the social circles in which nominations are decided, and may not be perceived as a potential candidate for a judicial vacancy. There is perhaps no malice on the part of States who never nominate women, but rather the stunning absence of a reflection on the relevant legal framework and the negative impact the absence of parity has on the legitimacy of a court. That is quite apart from courts and tribunals missing out on the contribution women make, the benefits of diversity, and the importance of mixed teams as being a more effective format for performing difficult tasks. The repetition of past practice leads to the frequent re-nomination of judges or the emphasis on the judiciary as being a meritocracy (thereby not only presenting the bench as a 'closed shop', but also suggesting that male international lawyers are somehow better at this job). Such approaches ignore the applicable legal framework and do not contribute to strengthening the international bench, as they turn a blind eye to the potential of women.

The political confines of elections may have a more prominent role than is visible to the outsider. For various international courts and tribunals agreed rules on the division of seats amongst the regional groups exist, some formalized in treaties and others in political decisions.[12] Such rules are the result of political processes and are important to States. They provide a certain amount of predictability during elections: even if all States will vote[13], States putting forward a candidate will be most concerned with the direct competition within the regional group they are part of. In a way, these regional groups make the competition more transparent: the immediate competition is within the own group. However, if one considers that the election of judges should be based on an assessment of the quality of candidates, the advent of the 'agreed slate' within regional groups has sometimes thwarted the possibility of 'quality control'. Some regional groups may agree on who will be the accepted candidates for the position of judge in a particular court or tribunal and will present the exact number of candidates for the exact number of seats available, thereby obliterating any choice between candidates. Though it may appear that an agreed slate could be in favour of female candidates, on reflection this mechanism has the potential to go against the freedom of choice, and selection of the basis of merit.

[12] For ITLOS see formal rules in Article 3(2) of the Statute (Annex VI to the UN Convention on the Law of the Sea), to which further rules on the regional distribution of seats were added by the Meeting of States Parties in 2011, see doc SPLOS/201.

[13] Members of the UNGA and the UNSC for the ICJ, States Parties to UNCLOS for ITLOS and the Assembly of States Parties for the ICC.

3. The Legal Framework

When addressing the absence of women on the international bench the understanding seems to be that no legal framework exists. That is not quite correct, and it should be noted that the UN system appears to have relevant rules with respect to participation in the judiciary. These rules have become somewhat obscure and it is useful to reiterate the relevant legal framework with respect to the composition of courts and tribunals within the UN system.[14]

3.1 Article 8 UN Charter

A standard with respect to the eligibility of women to the international judiciary is clearly available with respect to the ICJ. Article 8 of the UN Charter reads: 'The United Nations shall place *no restrictions* on the eligibility of men and women to participate in *any capacity* and under conditions of equality in its *principal and subsidiary organs*'. The formulation is an unambiguous one (*no* restrictions) rather than an open-ended due diligence provision that would seek to 'promote the eligibility' or 'use all appropriate measures' similar to language found in provisions elsewhere.[15] It would seem to be a fairly straightforward obligation, also because it does not appear to be confined to formal restrictions and would seem to encompass informal restrictions (otherwise known as indirect discrimination) as well.

Strikingly, the provision has been understood as covering exclusively the employment of women by the UN, in spite of the very clear *any capacity* formula suggesting a much broader scope than only female staff at the UN Secretariat. Von Schorlemer and Papenfuß, in the Commentary on the UN Charter by Simma and others, provide some historical background, highlighting that the provision's predecessor in the League of Nations' Covenant was more forward leaning as it referred to the promotion of the full participation of women in the League (Article 7(3) of the Covenant) which had a more proactive flavour.[16] Initially the drafters of the Charter had not included any provision on equality of men and women in the draft text.[17] A consideration seems to have been the fear that a specific provision would limit the freedom to select members of delegations.[18] However, a 'feminist'

[14] Even if technically neither the Law of the Sea Tribunal nor the International Criminal Court are part of the United Nations.

[15] See the discussion of Article 8 CEDAW below.

[16] Article 7(3) League of Nations Covenant reads: 'All positions under *or in connection with* the League, including the Secretariat, shall be open equally to men and women'.

[17] Sabine von Schorlemer and Anja Papenfuß, 'Article 8' in Bruno Simma and others (eds), *The Charter of the United Nations, A Commentary*, vol. 1 (3rd edn, OUP 2012) 416–44.

[18] Putting sovereignty above equal treatment.

intervention by Eleanor Roosevelt appears to have led to the inclusion of Article 8 in the Charter.[19]

The phrase '*participate in any capacity*' has led to some initial debate about the scope of article 8. The Commission on the Status of Women (CSW) in 1948 favoured a broad interpretation[20] of *any capacity* and understood the rule to contain two different obligations: an obligation internal to the UN Secretariat with regard to staff, and an obligation with regard to Member States and how they would be represented in the UN's organs, committees, or commission. In this reading, the provision would also imply an obligation with respect to participation in the principal organs of the United Nations, the ICJ presumably included. This reading by CSW was rejected by the Economic and Social Council (ECOSOC) in favour of the more limited interpretation focusing on UN staff only.[21]

When discussing the *principal and subsidiary organs* element of the text, Von Schorlemer and Papenfuß do refer to the principal organs of the UN, but do not reflect on what this would specifically mean in terms of the composition of the ICJ bench, as opposed to the composition of the ICJ registry who are UN staff. Ubeda-Saillard, in the Commentary by Cot and others, reiterates that Article 8 is situated in Chapter III of the Charter, dealing with the principal organs of the UN (the ICJ obviously being one of them) without drawing any conclusions from that, merely referring to the Secretariat in the very same sentence.[22] The discussion then focuses on the role of the internal administrative system of the UN, and how procedures before the UN Administrative Tribunal have addressed bias in the employment conditions for UN staff referring to Article 8, followed by case law addressing harassment in the workplace. Ubeda-Saillard, however, notes that there is a certain lack of clarity in the provision which addresses the Organization but fails to provide more detail about who exactly has these obligations: while the UN General Assembly deals with staff issues at a general level it is the Human Resources department that remains responsible for setting personnel standards. Member States have retained their independence with respect to the composition of their delegations.[23] Von Schorlemer and Papenfuß equally understand the provision to be vague and conclude that the provision 'raised general awareness for gender-sensitive aspects of the UN System'. They suggest its crucial importance is with respect to UN Staff Regulations, also in relation to the work of the UN Administrative Tribunal. The

[19] See Muriel Ubeda-Saillard, 'Article 8' in Jean Pierre Cot, Alain Pellet, and Mathias Forteau (eds), *La Charte des Nations Unies, Commentaire article par article*, vol.1 (3rd edn, Economica 2005) 603–30, footnote 1 at 604; and von Schorlemer and Papenfuß (n 17) para 6, at 418. Labelling an intervention as 'feminist' will be read by many as pejorative.

[20] There is some interesting messaging taking place with respect to the reception of the views of CSW: the reading with the two different elements is not that unusual considering the text of Article 8 UN Charter. However, in discussing this debate, authors frequently consider the reading as 'expansive', suggesting this reading being too bold to be acceptable.

[21] See E/RES/154B(VII) of 20 August 1948.

[22] See Muriel Ubeda-Saillard (n 19) at 603.

[23] See paras 14–16, at 610.

provision has been understood as ensuring the equality of rights of UN staff, as opposed to other participants within the UN system. Though it is comforting that the administrative system of the Organization has a helpful standard in the Charter to address equal treatment and gender issues it is remarkable that—in spite of being located in the Chapter dedicated to the UN's Principal Organs—its scope has been understood to be quite limited. This suggests that for States the United Nations is 'them', not 'us': rules concerning equal access are for staff, not for delegations or for elected positions.[24]

The sovereignty argument is a traditional one, and it may be time for a reconsideration. Even if no obvious sanction would exist with respect to the composition of delegations to the organs of the United Nations or to not proposing candidates for the position of judge, Article 8 is a useful reminder of the desirability of a better representation of women across the UN system, the principal organs included. Without questioning sovereign authority with respect to the composition of delegations to the United Nations, or the system established with respect to nominations to the International Court, Article 8 Charter may require a fresh discussion about its implementation, given that it appears to have been last discussed in 1948. It could be envisaged that such a discussion might take place in the 6th Committee (Legal) of the General Assembly at the start of the next triannual nominations period, if only to draw attention to the importance of diversity on the Court. Alternatively, CSW could be the right forum to look back at its initial position and the contemporary relevance of that position.

3.2 Article 8 CEDAW

It may not come as a surprise that another relevant provision that may be of some use with respect to the strengthening of number of women on the international bench can be found in the Convention on the Elimination of All forms of Discrimination against Women (CEDAW). Article 8 CEDAW reads: 'States Parties shall take all appropriate measures to ensure to women, on equal terms with men and without any discrimination, the opportunity to represent their Governments at the international level and to *participate in the work of international organizations*'.

Unlike Article 8 UN Charter, this provision—as have many provisions in CEDAW—uses a due diligence formula which urges all States to use their best efforts and appropriate measures to improve the opportunities for women to participate in the work of international organizations. Unfortunately, Article 8 CEDAW has hardly had the attention it deserves and remains a bit of a sleeping provision. In the *Travaux* of the Convention, the description of the drafting of this Article

[24] NB a similar issue with respect to parity has arisen with respect to the appointments of Special Rapporteurs and similar representatives of the United Nations.

takes a mere two and a half pages, demonstrating that the authors of CEDAW at the time of drafting did perhaps not consider this a crucial right.[25] Apparently Article 8 (international representation) was a spinoff from Article 7 (participation in political and public life). Wittkopp, in the Commentary by Freeman, Chinkin, and Rudolf, notes that the provision was uncontroversial during negotiations even if this was the first time that the right to participation in the work of international organizations is mentioned in a human rights instrument.[26] The provision obliges States to take appropriate measures to ensure women have the opportunity to represent their governments at international level, and the opportunity to participate in the work of international organizations. This is the familiar dual obligation where it concerns women: both the representation of their State as well as non-discriminatory access to the work of international organizations, more or less mirroring Article 8 UN Charter.

The eligibility of women to international courts and tribunals—whether as judge, prosecutor, or indeed civil servant—seems to have escaped the attention of the supervisory Committee on the Elimination of All forms of Discrimination against Women (the Committee) so far. While the work of judges may not be considered to encompass the representation of their Governments in a diplomatic sense, it constitutes most certainly the participation in the work of international organizations. Article 8 has not been the subject of much academic research itself either, let alone from the perspective of judicial appointments more specifically.[27] It appears to have been the odd one out as well in the various commemorative publications celebrating the Convention. Here again, when the provision is addressed the attention turns to its importance for UN staff and the role of the UN Administrative System, or alternatively drifts towards the importance of the presence and participation of women in the field of peace and security and conflict resolution.

The CEDAW Committee has not drafted any specific General Recommendation so far about the composition of the international bench.[28] General Recommendations 8(1988) and 23(1997) nominally address Article 8 CEDAW, the later recommendation focusing on employment issues and to a limited extent the composition of representative organs within the United Nations. It could be suggested that the Committee focus on women in the international judiciary and take up

[25] Lars Adam Rehof, *Guide to the Travaux Préparatoires of the United Nations Convention on the Elimination of All Forms of Discrimination against Women* (Martinus Nijhoff 1993).

[26] Sarah Wittkopp, 'Article 8' in Marsha A. Freeman, Christine Chinkin, Beate Rudolf (eds), *The UN Convention on the Elimination of all Forms of Discrimination against Women, a Commentary* (OUP2012) 221–31.

[27] Art 8 CEDAW is not often discussed in legal literature either. See Claudia Martin, *Article 8 of the Convention on the Elimination of All Forms of Discrimination against Women: a Stepping Stone in Ensuring Gender Parity in International Organs and Tribunals* (posted 14 September 2015)<www.gqualcampaign.org> accessed July 2019.

[28] General recommendations are based on Article 21 CEDAW and provide a general interpretation of the Convention by its supervisory committee.

this matter by drafting either a new General Recommendation, or by reviewing Recommendation 23, to stress the importance of a gender balance in international courts and tribunals.[29] Such a strengthened General Recommendation will serve as a guide to the discussion between the Committee and States Parties in the debate about their national reports: how has your State tried to contribute towards an improved gender balance on the international bench? A strengthened General Recommendation may just take Article 8 CEDAW out of its hibernation.

4. Nomination of Candidates

Turning now to the actual selection and nomination of candidates, we must reflect on what this process entails. How are candidates selected, and what institutional guarantees exist, or could be established, in order to improve the gender balance on the bench? In a number of judicial institutions where every participating State has a national judge, the selection process will be largely regulated by domestic procedure (whether or not formalized) and the quality and inclusiveness of the selection process should be addressed at national level.[30] Sometimes pre-selection at national level is required after which an international body will provide advice or decided based upon a list of candidates presented by States.[31] Systems were all States have a 'national' judge presumably provide more clarity about how and when to address concerns with respect to the nomination of female candidates and I will not further address these here.

In other situations, States nominate candidates for election who need to fulfil the criteria for the position of judge as contained in the foundational document, but about whose selection nothing is prescribed. The Law of the Sea Tribunal is a case in point, which does provide a list of criteria but has no specific rules about the selection of a candidate. That means it is essentially a matter of picking a candidate, presenting and formally nominating her and getting that person elected. Who the 'right candidate' is, whether consultations with human resources persons takes place, who exactly makes the selection, or whether the selection is a competitive or political process, all of that will differ from State to State. Selection will clearly also depend on the type of expertise required for a particular court or tribunal. Such processes may not be transparent, yet increasingly parliaments take an interest in selection leading to more formalized and indeed published rules for the selection.[32]

[29] Or in fact, it may be helpful for an NGO to present a draft General Recommendation to the Committee in order to facilitate such debate.

[30] Such as the European Court of Justice, its Court of First Instance or the European Court of Human Rights.

[31] For example, see Article 22 European Convention on Human Rights.

[32] Thus, there may be international rules (provided in the Statute of a particular international court) as well as national rules on selection processes.

For some courts the process for the presentation of candidates is more institutionalized. The statutes of the ICJ and ITLOS speak about geographical diversity, representation of the principal legal systems of the world but not about fair gender representation, unlike the International Criminal Court (ICC) Statute's Article 36(8)(a)(iii). Perhaps a difference between courts dealing with interstate disputes as opposed to the character of international criminal proceedings is of relevance here. In the following I will first comment on the nomination process for the International Court of Justice and the International Criminal Court, before addressing the relevance of other roles and positions prior to being nominated as a candidate in the next paragraph.

Nominations to the ICJ take an unusual route, and rely mostly on an outside body. Formally it is not a State that selects and nominates, but a national group of the Permanent Court of Arbitration (PCA)[33]. The Secretary General of the United Nations will request nominations, and the national groups will respond directly to the Secretary General with a list of persons they consider to be in a position to accept the duties of member of the Court. This group has the independent authority to nominate up to four persons for election to the ICJ, as is described in Article 5 of the ICJ Statute. No more than two persons nominated may have the same nationality as the national group, and consequently the national groups may and will nominate people of a nationality other than their own. This nominations' process is detached from the State, even if the national groups tend to be composed of academics and lawyers with a certain connection to that State. It is the national group itself which sends its nominations for the ICJ elections directly to the UN Secretary-General. Though the independence of these national groups has been questioned, many of them will independently make up their own mind. Co-nomination of candidates (from other States) is common, and is seen as an expression of support for a particular candidate. In spite of the independent role of the national groups, contacts will undoubtedly be used to learn whether or not a particular candidate is likely to be supported by their own State, as national support will be necessary to ensure a successful campaign.

The nominations' process for the ICC specifically requires the participation of women on the bench as Article 36(8)(a)(iii) refers to a fair representation of female and male judges. Article 36 (4)(a) ICC presents two different manners for nominating candidates to the International Criminal Court. Either States use their domestic procedure for the nomination of candidates for appointment to highest judicial offices, or States follow the procedure used for the nomination of candidates to the ICJ. In both cases the ICC Statute seeks to take some distance from the States themselves by referring to procedures that are not strictly governmental. The scrutiny of the first option—the parallel with the appointment of the highest

[33] If no such group exists, a specific procedure is provided in Article 4(2) and (3) ICJ Statute.

judges—seems to lie with domestic authorities, while the second option takes us back to the national group of the PCA. Unlike the procedure in Articles 4 and 5 of the ICJ Statute, only one candidate may be nominated for each ICC election.

The origins of Article 36(4)(a)(ii) are not very well documented. It appears that the general sense at the time of the drafting was that the national group could be relied upon to present a suitable and qualified candidate, as their focus would be on the legal (rather than political) qualities of the person to be nominated. Writing about Article 36, Gonfrier only refers to both options in the selection process but omits a discussion of the scope of the role of the national group of the PCA.[34] Jones writing about the same subject refers to Article 36(4)(a)(ii) as implicitly including the possibility to nominate candidates from States other than the State of the national group of the PCA concerned.[35] Otherwise, most of the attention during the drafting of the ICC seems to have gone into the system with the two distinct lists created by Article 36(3)(b), which is not relevant to this chapter.

National groups may—similar to the existing practice with respect to the ICJ—also consider nominating candidates that are not their nationals. So far however, no co-nomination practice similar to that under the ICJ Statute has developed within the ICC. This may be a consequence of a lack of awareness of the ICJ nominations process in ICC circles, and it is to be regretted: co-nominations tend to reinforce the eligibility of candidates. The candidate presented by one State obtains increased credibility when there is visible support for her elsewhere—as expressed through co-nomination. Such a broader interpretation of Article 36(4)(a)(ii) ICC would be in line with the faith expressed in the national groups by the drafters of the Rome Statute, and could presumably increase the (co-)nomination of female candidates.

Even if some Commentaries consider that the procedure involving the national group of the PCA is self-evident, it should be noted though that it is somewhat unclear from the text of the Rome Statute whether these groups are independently corresponding with the Secretariat of the Assembly of the States Parties.[36] This must be presumed to be the case, given the parallel with the ICJ nominations where

[34] Olivier Gonfrier, 'Article 36' in Julian Fernandez and Xavier Pacreau (eds), *Statut de Rome de la Cour Pénale international, commentaire article par article* (Pedone 2012) 973.

[35] John R W D Jones, Chapter 4.4 *Composition of the Court*, footnote 50, at p 245 referring to discussions in the PrepCom on the use of the ICJ-system as this would 'ensure that merit would be a paramount consideration in the election of judges' (see para 37 PrepCom Report); in Antonio Cassese, Paola Gaeta, and John R W D Jones (eds), *The Rome Statute of the International Criminal Court: A Commentary*, vol 1 (OUP 2002).

[36] Even if relying on the same body, the text of Article 5 (1) ICJ Statute ('... the Secretary-General of the United Nations shall address a written request to the members of the Permanent Court of Arbitration ...') and of Article 36(4) (a) (chapeau) ('Nominations of candidates for election to the Court may be made by any State Party ...') and (ii) ('By the procedure provided for the nomination of candidates for the International Court of Justice in the Statute of that Court') Rome Statute are not strictly identical.

the Group communicates directly with the UN Secretary General. At any rate, it must be considered *contra legem* for a government to prevent, or to not submit a nomination made by a national group under Article 36(4) to the Secretariat of the Assembly of States Parties. In the run up to the elections, the Advisory Committee on Nomination, established on the basis of Article 36(4)(c) Statute will be monitoring the nominations' process, and will seek to evaluate the quality of the nominees as well as their regional spread and the gender balance.

For two important international courts, the ICJ and the ICC, the national group of the Permanent Court of Arbitration plays a crucial role. Hence, we must address our attention to this not very well-known body. The national group of the PCA finds its origin in Article 44 of the 1907 Convention for the Pacific Settlement of International Disputes,[37] which indicates that Parties may select four persons of known competency in international law and of the highest moral reputation available to accept the duties of arbitrator. These so-called 'members of the Court' are essentially people on a list who are available as arbitrator, having a renewable six years' appointment. However, apart from being available for arbitration, their most important task is the nomination of candidates for the position of judge at either the ICJ or the ICC as discussed above.[38]

In 2016, there were 121 States Parties to the 1899 and the 1907 Convention for the Pacific Settlement of International Disputes. They had nominated a total of 273 members of the Court.[39] Amongst these members were 48 women: 26 States had one woman in their national group, eight States had two women, while Norway and Romania stood out with a majority of three women in their national group. By 2018 the figures had changed somewhat: of the 121 States Parties, 37 national groups had no female members, 26 groups had one woman in their midst, and 15 had two women (and no national groups with three women remained)—so the number of female members of the Court had risen to 56.

The composition of the national groups and their role in the selection process is of crucial importance. The relevance of the participation of women in a nominations' process, as is the case with members of the Permanent Court, is not necessarily that 'women nominate women'. There may be an element of female solidarity, and a mixed selection committee is at any rate desirable if interviews are to be conducted. The importance lies also in ensuring that those responsible for selection and nomination have access to a wide variety of relevant networks, and that thus

[37] And before that, Article 23 of the 1899 Convention for the Pacific Settlement of International Disputes.

[38] See for a detailed description of these national groups: Remy Jorritsma, *National Groups: Permanent Court of Arbitration (PCA)*, Max Planck Institute Luxembourg for Procedural Law Research Paper Series | No. 2017 (8).

[39] Nominating members of the Permanent Court is a discretionary power, and not all States have nominated four people. In some cases, States fail to renew appointments when the appointment period has run out. This implies the disappearance of members from the PCA list, and thus the loss of nominating power.

a diverse group of potential candidates is considered. It is undeniable that women have other networks than men, even if these may overlap. Also, as relative outsiders in a men's world, women may take a different approach to the selection process as such: rather than starting with 'who do we know', considering first 'what kind of person are we looking for', to be followed by a search for persons fitting the profile.[40] A more open approach away from the old boys' network of senior lawyers provides the potential of opening up the selection process to unexpected candidates, and indeed to well-qualified female candidates. Mixed selection panels are likely to present a more balanced selection of candidates to the benefit of the international courts and tribunals.

5. Seniority of the Candidate

Eligibility depends on many things, but there is an understanding that a credible candidate is someone who has demonstrated over the course of her career to have obtained such relevant expertise and experience that would make her suitable for the position of judge. Academic publications alone will not be enough to convince States to vote for a candidate; a certain measure of experience in relevant positions adds to the impression of 'seniority' that is considered required for such positions. In general terms, this would refer to experience as an arbitrator, as either a judge ad hoc or as an agent in a case before an international court or tribunal, or as expert and member of a professional body (whether as member of the PCA, the ILC, or the *Institut de Droit International*). Additionally, diplomatic experience or work within the United Nations are also considered relevant in the informal list of what makes up relevant experience.

Imprecise, yet fairly well-understood informal criteria are considered by States when evaluating candidates for judicial positions. This suggests that it is interesting to explore pathways to such relevant experience, in order to address the question as to how to obtain such seniority. This is not the place to fully embark on such research, as this is an initial exploration without looking at figures and statistics (for now), yet certain questions can certainly be identified for further research. Let us gloss over the types of positions that may demonstrate a candidate's capability to take on the role of judge. One could think about courtroom experience, such as acting as a judge or judge ad hoc, as an arbitrator in interstate conflict, as Agent or Counsel for a State before an international court. Below I will explore women's participation in such positions and how this could be strengthened.

[40] This observation is based on my participation in a domestic selection panel for ICSID arbitrators.

5.1 Having Been a Judge Ad Hoc

Before the Second World War, the Permanent Court of International Justice (PCIJ) never had any female judges, and since its inception the ICJ has had only four women elected to the bench. An additional four female judges ad hoc have been appointed, all four from Western States and none of them have continued to become a full member of the Court. Yet, Van den Wyngaert went on to become a judge at the International Criminal Court and Charlesworth is currently acting as ICJ judge ad hoc for a second time. Something similar may be said about the Law of the Sea Tribunal which has so far only had three female judges, and only recently welcomed its first female judge ad hoc.[41]

Looking at the membership of women in the International Court, it does not seem bold to suggest that there appears to be a higher chance for women from the five permanent members of the UN Security Council (the so-called P5 countries) to be elected to the Court, as compared to nationals of other States.[42] This is likely related to the presumed informal understanding that the P5 States ought to be represented on the bench. If that is a broadly supported view, the nomination of a female candidate will not be perceived as risky, however, the existence of such an informal norm may also be questioned.

5.2 Having Been an Agent

Another way of demonstrating relevant prior experience is previous participation in a court case, preferably in the role of agent. Such a role implies the overall responsibility of representing a State before a court, and requires active participation in procedural strategy and knowledge of judicial work. It also implies presenting pleadings before a court, thus having experienced the procedure from the other side of the room.[43] The number of cases in which female agents have represented their States has significantly grown since 2000. In cases before the Law of the Sea Tribunal, female agents only start to appear after 2010 and indeed in its most recent case, the Law of the Sea Tribunal had two female agents before it.[44] Advisory

[41] At the ICJ: Suzanne Bastid in *Application for the Revision and Interpretation of the Judgement in Continental Shelf* (1985); Christine Van den Wyngaert in *Arrest Warrant* (2002); Louise Arbour in *Obligation to Negotiate Access to the Pacific Ocean* (preliminary objections, 2015); Hilary Charlesworth in *Whaling in the Antarctic* (2014), and *Arbitral Award of 3 October 1899* (ongoing). At ITLOS: Anna Petrig in *M/T San Padre Pio* (2019).

[42] Rosalyn Higgins (United Kingdom, 1995–2009), Hanqin Xue (China, 2010–present), Joan Donahue (United States, 2010–present). Julia Sebutinde (Uganda, 2012–present) is the odd one out.

[43] Current ITLOS judges Neeru Chadha and I have both been agents of our States before the Tribunal.

[44] Ms. Cicéron Bühler representing Switzerland, and Ms. Uwandu representing Nigeria in Case 27, *The M/T San Padre Pio* (2019).

proceedings tend to attract more female representatives in any case (including from international organizations).

5.3 Having been an Arbitrator

When looking at the election of judges to the international bench, the appointment of arbitrators may not be an obvious part of the discussion. However, this is relevant as there is often a close connection between persons acting as arbitrator and as judge: having been active as an arbitrator demonstrates the required expertise for the position of judge and appears to improve the likelihood of being elected or selected as a judge. Consequently, arbitration may be seen as useful preparatory practice for the bench.[45] If previous experience as an arbitrator is favourable to nomination for the position of judge, then how does one become arbitrator in an interstate case?

5.3.1 The appointment of arbitrators by States

Unlike a court of tribunal with a permanent composition, States enjoy a large measure of autonomy in nominating arbitrators. This offers them the possibility of determining who should be an arbitrator irrespective of the views of their opponent. Clearly, in nominating an arbitrator, States are looking to find 'the right person' who will ensure that a profound knowledge of international law, common sense, and a proper understanding of the position of the nominating State itself will be reflected around the table in the arbitral tribunal. With the focus on finding the right person, considerations such as the desirability of choosing a female lawyer become secondary, if present at all. States rarely seem to select women for such positions and that is regrettable. The number of female arbitrators is surprisingly low. Few women have risen to the top in international arbitration, yet differences may exist between commercial arbitration, investment arbitration, and 'traditional' interstate arbitration.

In this respect, reference must be made to the very clear stance taken by the International Centre for the Settlement of Investment Disputes (ICSID) secretariat and its Secretary-General Meg Kinnear on the importance of appointing female arbitrators in international investor-State dispute settlement (ISDS) and ensuring parity in arbitration. Not only does the ICSID Secretariat collect and present information about the appointment of women in order to monitor improvement, but in situations in which it is called upon to appoint arbitrators itself (essentially the role of Appointing Authority, discussed below, under 5.3.2) it focuses on the importance of appointing women. In 2017, 24% of the appointments of arbitrators made

[45] This is the case with respect to interstate cases, the role of arbitrator presumably has little relevance to nominations in the field of international criminal law.

by ICSID were women and by 2018, 50% of the new designations by the Chair of its Administrative Council were women.[46] Otherwise, a best practice of gender awareness has led to specifically including women on lists when suggestions of persons for the role of arbitrator were required.

Related to this strategy is the 2015 'Pledge' initiative agreed within international commercial arbitration circles with respect to increasing the number of women acting as counsel or arbitrator.[47] Its aim is 'to increase, on an equal opportunity basis, the number of women appointed as arbitrators in order to achieve a fair representation as soon as practically possible, with the ultimate goal of full parity' and interested law firms as well as individuals can express support for this pledge—thereby adding their voice to the importance of the issue. Clearly this is, however, not just about a pledge, but most of all about taking steps that in reality ensure the participation of more women in this field, be it as counsel or as arbitrator.

The experience and expertise of female lawyers continues to be undervalued, thereby perpetuating the image of arbitration as a male fortress. It could be suggested that States make a public commitment to appoint one-third women when appointing arbitrators—but that suggestion may be too bold. An intermediate step might be a commitment to include at least one-third women on the existing lists of arbitrators.[48] This would at least demonstrate the availability of many qualified women and will open possibilities to more diversity on arbitral tribunals.

5.3.2 The role of the Appointing Authority in appointing arbitrators

The role of the Appointing Authority is not a frequently discussed aspect of the constitution of arbitral tribunals. Yet, it is a crucial position in the sense that through the good offices of the Appointing Authority arbitrations will take place in spite of the silence of the respondent in an arbitration. This mechanism means that the lack of cooperation by the non-participating respondent Party will not hamper dispute settlement from taking place: an arbitral tribunal will be established and the dispute settlement procedure will commence without the active support of the defendant. The role of the Appointing Authority as a fall-back mechanism for the appointment of arbitrators thus implies the authority to select and appoint arbitrators.

The position of Appointing Authority is not a personal task, in the sense that it is attached to a formal position and is carried out by whoever holds that position at the time a request for the appointment of arbitrators arrives.[49] This position will

[46] See Meg Kinnear and Otylia Babiak, *International Investment Arbitration Needs Equal Representation*, Centre for International Governance Innovation, published 9 April 2018 (available at cigionline.org, last visited 31 January 2020). And Meg Kinnear, *Advancing diversity in international dispute settlement*, published 8 March 2019 <blogs.worldbank.org> accessed 31 January 2020).

[47] See <www.arbitrationpledge.com> accessed 31 January 2020 for more detail.

[48] Such as the members of the PCA, the list with ICSID arbitrators, or the lists under Annexes VII and VIII UNCLOS.

[49] Officials acting as Appointing Authority are, for example, the ICJ president, the ITLOS president, or the Secretary-General of the PCA.

ideally be established prior to a dispute in order to be effective when necessary, so it will appear in a treaty text (such as for example Article 3 of Annex VII UNCLOS) or may be included in a contract in the case of a private-public agreement. Various institutions provide for model texts to ensure a proper reference to an appointing authority.[50] The Appointing Authorities' role is an important one, as it is the security valve in the international arbitration system. It would be useful to research how arbitrators are selected in situations where an Appointing Authority is called upon to assist with the composition of an arbitral tribunal. The practice of the officials who act as Appointing Authority is not very well documented and has not been the subject of much academic reflection.[51]

Little research has been done into who are appointed in this manner and whether or not specific patterns can be discerned. It would seem that some Appointing Authorities strive for a regional spread amongst the arbitral tribunal (provided a five-person tribunal is called for), and that very few women have ever been appointed by Appointing Authorities in interstate disputes. In a recent article, Gao has looked in detail at the practice of the President of the International Tribunal for the Law of the Sea acting as Appointing Authority under Article 3 of Annex VII UNCLOS.[52] The Article clarifies that the respective ITLOS presidents have been called upon as Appointing Authority in nine cases so far. The author provides an overview that is as predictable as it is revealing: a total of 22 arbitrators were appointed by the President, and in all cases these were men (even if parties may have suggested the appointment of capable female lawyers). It is difficult to find similar aggregated information about the work of other Appointing Authorities but it would be surprising if another pattern would appear: presumably appointments by Appointing Authorities do not generally differ from appointments by States, leading to a very limited participation by female arbitrators.

The Appointing Authority may appear to be an autonomous institution, charged with the important task of ensuring that an arbitral tribunal is instituted, in spite of the lack of collaboration from the defendant in the arbitration. However, in spite of appearances, the Appointing Authority is not completely autonomous and does not exist in a vacuum. He or she will be part of some international institution where States in the end have overall responsibility for the work of the institution.

[50] See for instance model arbitration clauses referring to the Permanent Court of Arbitration, include a provision on the Secretary-General acting as Appointing Authority (see <www.pca-cpa.org> accessed 31 January 2020.

[51] Muhammad Zafrulla Khan, 'The appointment of arbitrators by the President of the International Court of Justice' Il processo international, studi in onore di Gaetano Morelli (1975) 14 Comunicazioni e studi 1021–42, at 1021 writing 'Paradoxically it is a function which is nowhere provided for in the texts governing the International Court and establishing the office of President'. Peter Tzeng, 'Appointing Authorities: Self-Appointment, Party-Appointment and Non-Appointment' in Freya Baetens (ed), *Legitimacy of unseen actors in international adjudication* (CUP 2019) 164–88.

[52] Jianjun Gao, 'Appointment of Arbitrators by the President of the ITLOS pursuant to Article 3 of Annex VII of the LOS Convention: Some Tentative Observations' (2017)16 Chinese Journal of International Law 723–49.

Consequently, such Member States will have the possibility—when discussing the work related to the role of Appointing Authority—to stress the importance of appointing female arbitrators. This does not necessarily limit the discretionary authority of the Appointing Authority, but sets a guideline for appointments to be made within existing rules.

5.4 Membership of Professional Bodies

Returning to eligibility, it is common to rely on someone's *curriculum vitae*. The candidate must be perceived as having a certain seniority, expressed in professional experience and membership of those crucial societies considered to be at the heart of the profession. International law is a conservative environment, and participation in an august body that seems to embody the core of the international legal tradition is seen as proof of eligibility to such a senior position as that of international judge. Membership of such groups seems to imply an implicit guarantee of legal quality. The aim here is to investigate participation in such fora, in view of the importance attached to such memberships. Apart from the national group of the PCA (discussed under 4 above), two bodies stand out as august and learned groupings of eminent lawyers—the non-governmental *Institut de Droit International* and the ILC.

The famous *Institut de Droit International* was founded in 1873 and was awarded the Nobel Peace Prize in 1904. As a private association, its aim is to contribute to the development of international law and to further its implementation. Over the years, the *Institut* has produced several reports on the development of international law that became influential contributions to debates about international law matters. Many of its members have been arbitrators or judges at the PCIJ or ICJ, quite apart from their individual academic contributions.[53] Thus one may safely say that the *Institut* is 'the place to be' for international lawyers, it is a judicial powerhouse. The *Institut* has rather specific membership rules and limits its membership to 132 members. Potential members need to be proposed by existing members or national groups of members—apparently, it is not possible to self-nominate as there is no open membership. Currently out of these members, only 21 are women.[54]

A somewhat similar body exists embedded in the United Nations: the International Law Commission, consisting of 34 independent members elected for a five-year term and nominated by UN Member States.[55] It is a subsidiary body of

[53] Eyffinger lists 51 IDI members acting in 134 PCA arbitrations between 1902 and 2019, and 64 members elected to the bench of either the PCIJ or the ICJ. See Arthur Eyffinger, 'Tobias Asser's Legacy: The Pertinence of the Institut de droit international to The Hague' (2019) 66 Netherlands International Law Review 313–51, footnotes 2–5, at 315.

[54] See <www.idi-iil.org> accessed 31 January 2020.

[55] See <www.legal.un.org/ilc/> accessed 31 January 2020.

the General Assembly with the mandate to codify international law and the promotion of its progressive development—which is laid down in its 1947 Statute. Since its inception, the ILC has been working on prominent issues of international law leading to drafts for treaties on a variety of issues as well as other documents bringing together the state of current law, and work on its progressive development. Not very many women are or have been members of the ILC; the first female members appeared in 2001 and currently only four women are members. Here again, women have only recently become members of the ILC but parity has by no means been reached yet.

As we have seen, membership criteria of these professional bodies are inherently restrictive and have not been favourable to women. Attaching great importance to membership of such bodies in a way implies outsourcing the selection of candidates, in as much as it means implicit reliance on their criteria for membership. What may appear to be an autonomous and sovereign selection process for candidates is in fact relegated to a different, and often less visible, process in another forum. Moreover, one look at bodies like the ILC or the *Institut* when addressing gender parity in international courts is enough to understand that these are not necessarily shining examples of parity themselves.

6. Exploring Future Steps on the Basis of Existing Rules

Starting out with the plight of *Smurfette*, who may attract attention as the only woman in the room and whose presence suggests progress without having a true impact, this chapter has focused on various aspects of the process of selecting and nominating candidates for the position of judge on an international court or tribunal. It is mostly a story about the roles of elites in the selection and nomination processes for the international judiciary, and about ways of changing this.

When considering the limited participation of women on the international bench at this time, and looking specifically at the ICJ, ITLOS, and the ICC, different steps may be suggested to improve the number of women on the bench within the existing legal system. It will be useful to mobilize various fora to agree to guidelines with respect to nominations. Such steps need not disrespect the sovereign authority to nominate candidates for judicial positions, but will be an expression of the importance attached to parity and indeed to Article 8 UN Charter. Particular attention has been given to the general legal framework governing the participation of women in the work of international organizations and how existing provisions such as Article 8 UN Charter and Article 8 CEDAW could benefit from a revised reading. Looking at the nominations process, the role of the national groups of the PCA and the gender balance amongst their members deserve attention. Building on the relationship between arbitration and courts or tribunals it is considered necessary to also address the position of women in arbitration, as this is often seen as a preparatory stage for the position of judge.

Another suggestion is to develop a public commitment in the near future on the part of those involved in selection and nomination processes to expressly address the participation of women in the international judiciary. Such a commitment (a vow? a pledge?) by those who are in a position to nominate candidates to the ICJ or the ICC would imply expressing the intention to specifically consider women in the selection process. This would in itself not pre-empt any decision about the selection, but would be a forceful reminder of the need to look wider for relevant candidates. A similar commitment by those who hold the position of Appointing Authority would be a logical pendant. As the Appointing Authority is an international official, the representative body of the international organization concerned[56] could also invite the Appointing Authority to be proactive in this respect. Again, this in itself will not determine the choices made, but it would be a clear message as to the responsibility of such authorities with the default role of selecting arbitrators.

As this chapter demonstrates, parity will not just happen. Parity requires determination and attention, as well as people in key positions being aware of their role, acting on the basis of a plan, and seizing opportunities when they present themselves. Electing female judges is a step towards balanced and adequate participation by women at all levels in the international legal system, courts and tribunals included. It is time for the *Smurfette* to disappear from the international bench, or rather for her to be joined by a multitude of other qualified female lawyers to continue carrying the torch for international law. Perhaps she could be inspired by Astrid Lindgren's character Pippi Longstocking who famously said, 'I have never tried that before, so I think I would definitely be able to do that'.

[56] The UN General Assembly, the PCA's Administrative Council or the meeting of the States Parties to the UN Law of the Sea Convention for example.

3

Generating Incentives to Appoint Women to the International Bench

Experiences with State practice

Rolf Einar Fife

1. Introduction

Feminist critiques of law have contributed to international legal analysis and political action to combat discrimination against women and promote equality of rights and representation.[1] The 1979 United Nations Convention on the Elimination of all Forms of Discrimination against Women (CEDAW) constitutes the cornerstone of human rights instruments to this end.[2] However, its application and enforcement have been uneven: it has a considerable number of reservations on the basis of religion or culture, while a relatively limited number of States have signed up to its 1999 Optional Protocol which establishes a complaints mechanism.[3] Nevertheless, CEDAW along with political road maps adopted by consensus at global levels, in particular the 1995 Beijing Platform for Action and the UN 2030 Agenda for Sustainable development, provides the international community with a common framework for policy formulation and legal reform in this field.[4]

[1] An introduction to this legal analysis is provided by Hilary Charlesworth in 'Feminist Approaches to International Law', United Nations, *Audiovisual Library of International Law*, 1 June 2012; see also Katharine T Bartlett, 'Feminist Legal Methods' (February 1990) 103(4) Harvard Law Review 829–88; Hilary Charlesworth, Christine Chinkin, and Shelley Wright, 'Feminist Approaches to International Law: Reflections from Another Century' in Doris Buss and Ambreena Manji (eds), *International Law: Modern Feminist Approaches* (Hart Publishing 2005) 17–47; Hilary Charlesworth, 'Whose Rule? Women and the International Rule of Law' in Spencer Zifcak (ed), *Globalisation and the Rule of Law* (Routledge 2005) 83–96.

[2] Convention on the Elimination of All Forms of Discrimination against Women (adopted 18 December 1979, entered into force 3 September 1981) 1249 UNTS 13 (CEDAW). The Convention had 189 States Parties as of 23 July 2019. It was preceded by the Convention on the Political Rights of Women (adopted 31 March 1953, entered into force 7 July 1954), 193 UNTS 135. Rosalyn Higgins, *Problems and Process – International Law and How We Use it* (OUP 1994) 98. Dame Higgins was the first woman elected as president of the International Court of Justice (2006–09).

[3] For reservations to CEDAW, see <www.un.org/womenwatch/daw/cedaw/reservations.htm> accessed 14 August 2020. Optional Protocol to the Convention on the Elimination of All Forms of Discrimination against Women (adopted 6 October 1999, entered into force 22 December 2000) 2131 UNTS 83. The protocol had 112 States Parties as of 23 July 2019.

[4] The Beijing Declaration and Platform for Action was adopted by the United Nations Fourth World Conference on Women on 15 September 1995 <www.un.org/womenwatch/daw/beijing/

Rolf Einar Fife, *Generating Incentives to Appoint Women to the International Bench* In: *Identity and Diversity on the International Bench.* Edited by: Freya Baetens, Oxford University Press (2020). © The several contributors.
DOI: 10.1093/oso/9780198870753.003.0003.

As a result, transnational platforms for dialogue and cooperation have emerged allowing for regular reviews and exchanges of experiences. In 2000, in the specific context of armed conflict, the (unanimously adopted) landmark UN Security Council Resolution 1325 urged Member States to 'ensure increased representation of women at all decision-making levels in national, regional and international institutions and mechanisms for the prevention, management and resolution of conflict'.[5] This exhortatory recommendation is also relevant to international judicial bodies.[6] In 2015, the Committee on the Elimination of Discrimination against Women under CEDAW adopted a general recommendation on women's access to justice, calling on States to confront and remove barriers to women's participation as professionals within all levels of judicial systems and take steps to ensure that women are equally represented in the judiciary.[7] As highlighted elsewhere in this book,[8] such exhortations at global levels have not been followed by satisfactory quantitative advances in the representation of women on the international bench.

In this chapter, I first briefly recall the criteria for the selection of judges of international judicial institutions in order to seek to identify the most effective incentives for increased gender diversity, while sketching some States' recurrent considerations around elections to the international bench. Next, I consider the obstacles in introducing a more gender-balanced approach. Finally, I suggest developing also persuasive policy arguments to surmount these obstacles at stages critical to the future recruitment of candidates by incentivizing States to effectively realize the utility of gender mainstreaming. The reader should note that my observations are coloured by my perspective as a government representative who has been involved in meetings of States Parties to relevant conventions and in the international settlement of disputes. These personal reflections do not constitute a statement of the Norwegian authorities.

platform/> accessed 14 August 2020. The 2030 Agenda for Sustainable Development was adopted at a United Nations Summit at the United Nations General Assembly on 25 September 2015, A/RES/70/1, and came into force on 1 January 2016. The 17 Sustainable Development Goals (SDGs) may be accessed at <www.un.org/sustainabledevelopment/sustainable-development-goals/> accessed 29 February 2020, Goal 5 carries the heading 'Achieve gender equality and empower all women and girls'.

[5] Operative paragraph 1, UNSC Res 1325 (31 October 2000) [on women and peace and security], UN Doc S/RES/1325 (2000) <www.refworld.org/docid/3b00f4672e.html>accessed 29 February 2020. This resolution was adopted unanimously.

[6] The resolution was adopted unanimously, 4213th meeting, Resolutions and decisions of the Security Council, 2000—UN Doc S/INF/56—(SCOR, 55th year). While not having the legally binding nature of a resolution adopted pursuant to Chapter VII of the Charter, it expresses clear unanimous directives and constitutes an important framework for the organization of UN and other initiatives in the field of peace and security.

[7] CEDAW, General Recommendation No 33 (23 July 2015), UN Doc CEDAW/C/GC/33, para 15(f).

[8] For example, see Chapters 10 (Keller et al), Chapter 2 (Lijnzaad), Chapter 13 (Mistry) and Chapter 26 (Dawuni).

2. Diversity Requirements: States' Considerations Regarding International Judicial Appointments

Despite an expansion in specific subfields of international law and specialized institutions of norm production and interpretation, there is no uniform set of formal criteria for the selection of judges to the benches of international judicial institutions.[9] Nevertheless, there are certain recurring requirements at courts such as the International Court of Justice (ICJ), the Court of Justice of the European Union (CJEU), the European Court of Human Rights (ECtHR), and the International Criminal Court (ICC). These often include requirements of predicted judicial independence, possession of the requisite qualifications in the candidates' respective countries for appointment to the highest judicial offices, or a background as a jurisconsult of recognized competence in international law.[10] The Permanent Court of Arbitration (PCA), whose members play a role in the nomination of candidates to the ICJ bench, has a requirement of 'known competency in questions of international law'.[11] Formal criteria of disciplinary specialization exist for the ICC and the International Tribunal for the Law of the Sea (ITLOS).[12] Such requirements

[9] For a thorough analysis of the selection procedures principally for the International Court of Justice and the International Criminal Court, see Ruth Mackenzie and others, *Selecting International Judges: Principle, Process, and Politics* (OUP 2010). For a critical review of this analysis, see W Michael Reisman and Ramanujan Nadadur 'Book Review: Selecting International Judges: Principle, Process, and Politics' (2012) 106(3) American Journal of International Law 704–08, Yale Law School, Faculty Scholarship Series, 4928 <https://digitalcommons.law.yale.edu/fss_papers/> accessed 14 August 2020.

[10] Art 2 of Statute of the International Court of Justice, annexed to the Charter of the United Nations, San Francisco, 26 June 1945. See also Art 2 of the predecessor institution, the Permanent Court of International Justice, Statute of the Permanent Court of International Justice, Geneva, 13 December 1920, League of Nations, Treaty Series, vol 6, p 390. The relevant provision reads in both cases '[The Court] shall be composed of a body of independent judges, elected regardless of their nationality from among persons of high moral character, who possess the qualifications required in their respective countries for appointment to the highest judicial offices, or are jurisconsults of recognized competence in international law.' For the European Court of Justice of the European Union, see Art 253 TFEU and Art 19 TEU, Consolidated versions of the Treaty on European Union and the Treaty on the Functioning of the European Union (TFEU) [2016] OJ C202/1. From Art 253 TFEU: 'The Judges and Advocates-General of the Court of Justice shall be chosen from persons whose independence is beyond doubt and who possess the qualifications required for appointment to the highest judicial offices in their respective countries or who are jurisconsults of recognised competence […]'. A similar formulation is used in Art 36(3)(a) of the Rome Statute of the International Criminal Court, Done at Rome on 17 July 1998, in force on 1 July 2002, United Nations, Treaty Series, vol 2187, No 38544. This is also the case for the European Court of Human Rights, pursuant to Art 21(1) of the European Convention on Human Rights, Convention for the Protection of Human Rights and Fundamental Freedoms, 4 November 1950, ETS 5, 213 UNTS 221.

[11] Art 44 of the Hague Convention on the Pacific Settlement of International Disputes, 18 October 1907. The relevant provision reads 'Each Contracting Power selects four persons at the most, of known competency in questions of international law, of the highest moral reputation, and disposed to accept the duties of Arbitrator.'

[12] Art 36(3)(b) of the Rome Statute for the International Criminal Court has, in addition, two alternative requirements of qualifications: '(i) Have established competence in criminal law and procedure, and the necessary relevant experience, whether as judge, prosecutor, advocate or in other similar capacity, in criminal proceedings; or (ii) Have established competence in relevant areas of international law such as international humanitarian law and the law of human rights, and extensive experience in a professional legal capacity which is of relevance to the judicial work of the Court'. Significantly, Art 36(8) of the Rome Statute also includes the need to take into account 'the need to include judges with legal

are formulated succinctly and allow for a wide margin of appreciation. However, they must also be read in the context of the relevant electoral organs' procedural requirements. These typically include the need to take account of the overall composition of the bench, regional diversity, and representation of different legal systems.

It is worth recalling not infrequent challenges relating to the reluctance of States to submit to international disputes settlement, and its impact upon judicial nominations. At the end of the 1960s, there was manifest political resistance within many States to submitting oneself to any international court's jurisdiction. The debate focused on the role of external political factors which paralysed the role of international law in international relations. Charles De Visscher referred to the '(e)xtreme political tensions' which weighed heavily upon governments that were 'already little inclined to divest themselves' of the settlement of their disputes in favour of international tribunals. They feared both 'the effect of the process and the repercussions, however distant, of the judgment'.[13] The comparative failure of States to use the ICJ in the 1970s was followed at the end of the 1980s by an upsurge in the number and scope of cases submitted to the ICJ which in turn led to an effort to enhance the standing of the Court while avoiding undue delays.[14] While the ICJ is widely regarded as having surmounted these challenges, international political conditions continue to affect international justice largely through the process of judicial appointments.

The practice of States in the nomination, campaigning, and election processes for these seats also plays an important role in the accession of women to the international bench. Over the years, States have developed competitive strategies to protect or advance their values and interests in complex multilateral settings.[15] The provisions governing the election processes will not be analysed here, save for a few

expertise on specific issues, including but not limited to violence against women and children'. Statute of the International Tribunal of the Law of the Sea, Annex VI to the Convention on the Law of the Sea, 10 December 1982, 1833 UNTS 397 Enacted as: entered into force as the 'United Nations Convention on the Law of the Sea' on 1 November 1994. Its Art 2 reads: '1. The Tribunal shall be composed of a body of 21 independent members, elected from among persons enjoying the highest reputation for fairness and integrity and of recognized competence in the field of the law of the sea. 2. In the Tribunal as a whole the representation of the principal legal systems of the world and equitable geographical distribution shall be assured.'

13 See for example Charles De Visscher, 'Reflections on the Present Prospects of International Adjudication' in Leo Gross (ed), *International Law in the Twentieth Century* (The American Society of International Law, Appleton-Century-Crofts 1969) 923, at 929.

14 For an example, see Ian Sinclair, 'The Court as an Institution: Its Role and Position in International Society' in Derek W Bowett and others (eds), *The International Court of Justice: Process, Practice and Procedure* (The British Institute of International and Comparative Law 1997) 21, at 22–26. Accordingly, discussion of the composition of tribunals centred also on the use of party-nominated members and of chambers of the ICJ, and the nature of the distinction between arbitration and judicial settlement, see Elihu Lauterpacht, *Aspects of the Administration of International Justice* (Grotius Publications Limited 1991) 77–87.

15 For a detailed description of the vigorous competition for such seats and related practices, see in particular Mackenzie and others (n 9) See also Reisman and Nadadur (n 9) 705.

examples relating to the United Nations as they represent characteristic features of such processes.[16] UN elections are decided by the votes of the 193 UN Member States whose geographical, political, and cultural diversity is considerable. UN Member States are usually organized into five regional groups. In some cases these have developed strong traditions of exchanging information and coordination, leading sometimes to the presentation of a so-called 'clean slate' for a seat, ie the entire group endorses a candidate for election to a seat allocated to the group concerned. In other cases, coordination may lead to an endorsement by a subset of group members.[17] States may also consider the broader international relations context including any elections to other bodies in the United Nations system during the same period. In such circumstances, mutual exchanges of support may take place.[18] States will include these factors in their early assessment of a potential candidate's chances of success alongside the competitiveness of other likely candidates. Overall, practice has often shown the importance of canvassing early and the need for broad support based on prior contact with other States and relevant epistemic communities. This may look like 'politicization' of the process, but it is merely a reflection of the basic constitutive features of the multilateral system. It may seem paradoxical to consider such wide-ranging concerns as relevant to the pursuit of a more balanced gender representation on the international bench but a keen assessment of all concerns is necessary to identify the best ways to promote this pursuit.

By way of example, in accordance with the ICJ Statute, ICJ judges are elected in parallel by the UN General Assembly and the UN Security Council, requiring an absolute majority in both bodies.[19] The nominations stem from proposals made by the national groups in the PCA.[20] Before making these nominations, each national

[16] Election to other judicial or arbitral bodies may differ considerably, such as the European Court of Human Rights and the European Court of Justice. Pursuant to Art 22 of the European Convention on Human Rights, judges are elected by the Parliamentary Assembly of the Council of Europe from lists of three candidates proposed by each State. As regards the European Court of Justice, it is noteworthy that the appointment procedure for judges and advocates-general pursuant to Art 253 TFEU requires, prior to achieving a common accord of the governments of the Member States, consultation of a panel responsible for assessing candidates' suitability (Art 255 TFEU). This panel set up in order to give an opinion on candidates' suitability to perform their duties comprises seven persons chosen from among former members of the Court of Justice and the General Court, members of national supreme courts, and lawyers of recognized competence, one of whom shall be proposed by the European Parliament. The decision establishing the panel's operating rules and a decision appointing its members are adopted by the European Council, acting on the initiative of the President of the Court of Justice.

[17] The following list of the Regional Groups is provided by the UN Department of General Assembly and Conference Management: African States/African Group, Asia-Pacific Group, Eastern European States Group, Group of Latin American and Caribbean States (GRULAC), and Group of Western European and Other States (WEOG) <ww.un.org/>accessed 29 February 2020. Ingo Winkelmann, Regional Groups in the UN, in A Concise Encyclopedia of the United Nations <https://doi.org/10.1163/ej.9789004180048.i-962.491>accessed 29 February 2020.

[18] Mackenzie and others (n 9) draws upon a series of interviews and is a valuable contribution to mapping actual practices particularly among UN delegations in New York.

[19] Statute of the International Court of Justice, Art 10.

[20] ibid Art 4.

group is recommended to undertake consultations with relevant national bodies.[21] Under Article 9 of the ICJ Statute, States have to bear in mind not only that the persons to be elected should individually possess the qualifications required, but also the requirement 'that in the body as a whole the representation of the main forms of civilization and of the principal legal systems of the world should be assured'.[22] In the unlikely event of more than one national of the same State obtaining an absolute majority of votes in both the General Assembly and the Security Council, 'the eldest of these only shall be considered as elected'.[23] Another example is seen in the election of ICC judges, the Assembly of States Parties to the Rome Statute must take into account a 'fair representation of female and male judges', pursuant to Article 36(8) of the Statute.[24] This provision also requires States Parties to consider the representation of the principal legal systems of the world, equitable geographical representation, and particular legal expertise, including but not limited to violence against women and children.

The substantive and procedural requirements imposed on the composition of an international judicial institution are aimed at enhancing its legitimacy and efficiency, including a sense of confidence and trust that it will competently and impartially apply the law.[25] To this end, it may be worth recalling that 'the primary work of international judges is to produce well-reasoned and timely judgments, which are seen to be so'.[26] Judges 'should remain aware that producing well-reasoned judgments, based on the applicable law, remains the central role and the lynchpin of their institution's legitimacy'.[27] This does not obviate the need to also 'give consideration to the diverse composition of international benches, including diversity by gender'.[28]

According to W Michael Reisman and Ramanujan Nadadur, one cannot exclude the fact that the process of electing judges 'simply reflects certain unyielding realities of contemporary international politics'.[29] The 'broader universe of qualities

[21] ibid Art 6.

[22] ibid Art 9.

[23] ibid Art 10(3), cf. Art 12(4). The question could *de lege ferenda* be raised whether, under equal conditions, gender should be given priority over age, where applicable.

[24] Rome Statute of the International Criminal Court (n 10) Art 36(8).

[25] For the general discussion of legitimacy in international law, and its relation to legality, see, *inter alia*, Thomas M Franck, *The Power of Legitimacy among Nations* (OUP 1990); James Crawford, The Problems of Legitimacy-Speak, 98 Proceedings of the ASIL Annual Meeting (2004), Proceedings of the ASIL Annual Meeting, 271–73 <*JSTOR*, www.jstor.org/stable/25659936> accessed 14 August 2020.

[26] The Oslo Recommendations for Enhancing the Legitimacy of International Courts, drafted on 2 June 2018 and finalized on 26 July 2018 by the participants of the Brandeis Institute for International Judges, convened in Oslo from 30 May to 2 June 2018, organized by the International Center for Ethics, Justice and Public Life (Brandeis University) and the PluriCourts Centre for the Study of the Legitimate Roles of the Judiciary in the Global Order (Faculty of Law, University of Oslo) <www.jus.uio.no/pluricourts/english/blog/geir-ulfstein/2018-08-01-biij.html>accessed 29 February 2020. See the 3rd preambular paragraph of the Recommendations <www.brandeis.edu/ethics/pdfs/Oslo%20Reccs%20Legitimacy%20of%20ICs.pdf> accessed 29 February 2020.

[27] ibid 3rd preambular paragraph and 'B. Ethics and judicial integrity', 4th paragraph.

[28] ibid 'A. Nomination and selection of international judges', 4th paragraph.

[29] Reisman and Nadadur (n 9) 705.

necessary for international courts' may not only include judges' foreign language abilities, region-specific competence, diverse legal-system proficiency, trial procedure knowledge, domestic-level trial experience, and international law expertise, but also non-judicial experience that seasoned diplomats and national politicians may bring to the bench, including their gendered experience.[30]

In sum, the demanding process of campaigning on behalf of a candidate through a gruelling number of election rounds invokes a number of considerations for States. Judicial and arbitral bodies adjudicate disputes in challenging political contexts. Trust and confidence among States that judges will produce well-reasoned and timely judgments based on the applicable law will be bolstered by the knowledge that the judges have experience, and a 'broader universe of qualities', including gender sensitivity. An important question is therefore how to promote a better gender balance whilst taking into account State considerations during the nomination process.

3. Obstacles: Culture v Strategy

A number of obstacles present themselves in creating a better gender balance, but these obstacles are not new. Women's role as active citizens in society has historically been minimized. In 1792, Mary Wollstonecraft (1759–98) wrote her appeal during the French Revolution for recognition of the role of women in society.[31] Her objective in '*A Vindication of the Rights of Woman*' was to call for a radical transformation of society for the better by including women as active citizens.[32] At the time, the concept of an 'active citizen' referred arguably more to women's rationality and to their potential societal role in education than to their independence in other matters.[33] Mary Wollstonecraft reacted to the fact that various proposals of

[30] ibid 707–08.

[31] In France, the year before, in 1791, Olympe de Gouges (1748–93) wrote her *Declaration of the Rights of Women and Citizenesses*, see Simon Schama, *Citizens – A Chronicle of the French Revolution* (Alfred A Knopf 1989) 498.

[32] Mary Wollstonecraft, *A Vindication of the Rights of Men and A Vindication of the Rights of Woman* (Cambridge Texts in the History of Political Thought, Sylvana Tomaselli ed, CUP 1995) 236 (hereinafter referred to as Tomaselli, 1995). This publication includes an introduction with a biographical and historical survey. See also Boyd Hilton, *A Mad, Bad and Dangerous People? England 1783-1846* (The New Oxford History of England, Clarendon Press 2006) 357–59; Simon Schama, 'A History of Britain 3, 1776-2000, The Fate of Empire' *BBC* (2002) 43–46, 61–64. For her stay in France and its importance for her political theory, see in particular Tom Furniss, 'Mary Wollstonecraft's French Revolution' in Claudia L Johnson (ed), *The Cambridge Companion to Mary Wollstonecraft* (CUP 2002) 59–81, at 63–65. See moreover Emily Sunstein, *A Different Face: The Life of Mary Wollstonecraft* (Harper & Row) 1975; Barbara G Taylor, *Mary Wollstonecraft and the Feminist Imagination* (CUP 2003).

[33] Tomaselli, 1995 (n 32), 'I only recreated an imagination, fatigued by contemplating the vices and follies which all proceed from a feculent stream of wealth that has muddled the pure rills of natural affection, by supposing that society will some time or other be so constituted, that man must necessarily fulfil the duties of a citizen, or be despised, and that while he was employed in any of the departments of civil life, his wife, also an active citizen, should be equally intent to manage her family, educate her children and assist her neighbours.'

fundamental societal change omitted any plans for the education of women. She dedicated her book to Charles-Maurice de Talleyrand-Périgord ('Talleyrand'), a bishop turned parliamentarian during the French Revolution, who in 1791 wrote a report for the revolutionary Constitutional Assembly on reform of the education system.[34] Wollstonecraft took him and the Constitutional Assembly to task in an attempt to improve an incomplete educational project in the spirit of the ideas of the Enlightenment.[35] While Talleyrand met with Wollstonecraft in London in 1792, there is, however, no reference in his own memoirs to her, in contrast to a number of other people he met in London, who were are all men.[36] There are also different assessments as to whether Mary Wollstonecraft's book gained much of an audience at the time, but her immediate reception, or lack thereof, was likely the effect of a phenomenon of marginalization.[37] This is mirrored in Toril Moi's later studies of Simone de Beauvoir, which focused on the difficulties women faced in trying to be taken seriously as intellectuals, including on the basis of flawed or insufficient translations of works and hostile reception.[38]

Public discourse around women's role, and indeed legal frameworks have changed, although challenges remain. The most ambitious agendas for gender equality are arguably to be found at regional levels, including in the European Union (EU) and the Council of Europe.[39] Their institutions are among those that have developed strategies of gender mainstreaming. This refers to the introduction of a gender perspective not only in initial considerations of how new policies will

[34] Charles-Maurice Talleyrand-Périgord, *Rapport sur l'Instruction Publique, fait au nom du Comité de constitution* (10 September 1791), see Tomaselli p xxvi and Emmanuel de Waresquiel (ed), *Mémoires et Correspondances du Prince de Talleyrand*, (Robert Laffont, Bouquins 2007) 197, note 1 in fine. Talleyrand had consulted the greatest scientific minds in Paris, Lagrange, Lavoisier, Monge, Condorcet, and others. Talleyrand had a remarkable political career, later becoming one of the longest-serving foreign ministers of France.

[35] 'Sir, Having read with great pleasure a pamphlet which you have lately published, I dedicate this volume to you; to induce you to reconsider the subject [...]', Dedication to M Talleyrand-Périgord, Late Bishop of Autun, in Tomaselli, 1995 (n 32) 67.

[36] de Waresquiel (n 34) 204. Wollstonecraft is not mentioned in Talleyrand's biography by former ambassador to Paris Duff Cooper, *Talleyrand*, London, 1932, Folio Society Edition 2010. There is apparently no record of Talleyrand's meeting with Wollstonecraft in London. However, the meeting took place in the time between the two first editions of *Vindication*, and the dedication was revised by Wollstonecraft without any indication that their meeting had led to her changing her mind, see Furniss (n 32) 63.

[37] Hilton (n 32) 359 ('it was not widely purchased'), contrary to Furniss (n 32) who had previously referred to it as a 'best-seller'.

[38] Toril Moi, *Simone de Beauvoir – The Making of an Intellectual Woman* (2nd edn, OUP 2008); Simone de Beauvoir, *Le deuxième sexe* (Gallimard 1949).

[39] A comprehensive updated action plan at regional levels for gender equality is provided in the Council of Europe Gender Equality Strategy 2018–23, adopted on 7 March 2018 by the Council of Europe Committee of Ministers <https://rm.coe.int/ge-strategy-2018-2023/1680791246>accessed 29 February 2020. Art 2 TEU ('The Union is founded on the values of [...], equality, [...]. These values are common to the Member States in a society in which [...] equality between women and men prevail.'). Art 153 of the Treaty on the Functioning of the European Union (TFEU) allows the EU to promote equal opportunities and equal treatment in matters of employment and occupation. Within this framework Art 157 TFEU authorizes positive action to empower women. In addition, Art 19 TFEU enables the adoption of legislation against discrimination, including on the basis of sex.

affect both women and men, but also in the actual implementation and assessment of policies. Several critics have nevertheless commented that political strategies may be constrained by structural limits imposed by patriarchal social contexts and the existence of material conditions which prevent women from exercising their rights.[40] Political uncertainties associated with increased polarization, radicalization, or populism, and economic conditions may also have a negative impact on the achievement of gender equality at national levels.[41] These influences may also play a role at the global level, although with societal divergences.[42]

It is not surprising therefore that there still is a gap between the vision expressed in the relevant international instruments and road-maps referred to at the beginning of this chapter and the reality of gender representation in international legal institutions. This is particularly the case 'up stream', ie early in the process of production of qualifying skills and experience and access to international exposure, which may in part be due to the continuing unbalanced recruitment of women to education, let alone to high office, in many States. This is compounded by the fact that elections or appointments to the international bench form the end result of a particularly lengthy process, both for an individual to progress from aspiring candidate to elected judge as well as for a State to gain representation and influence.

This process starts long before the international launch of a candidacy. Whether and how far in advance governments start thinking about potential candidates may depend on the size, resources (academic and other), and priorities of the country concerned, but also on local legal, administrative, and political cultures and traditions. All of these may have an impact on the availability of people with the relevant knowledge and experience, but also with the networking capacity at national levels.[43] Raising awareness and sensitizing decision-makers about stereotypes that result in barriers may be helped by personal accounts of role models that have identified, overcome, and mitigated practical challenges.[44] National governments rarely deem the preparation of potential future candidates to be their responsibility

[40] Emanuela Lombardo, 'EU Gender Policy, Trapped in the "Wollstonecraft Dilemma"?' (2003) 10(2) The European Journal of Women's Studies 159–80. For a seminal analysis of phenomena of patriarchy, see Sylvia Walby, *Theorizing Patriarchy* (Blackwell 1990).

[41] Various factors that may contribute to failure to implement agreed standards are seen to affect and exacerbate issues of gender equality in the Council of Europe Strategy Gender Equality Strategy 2018–2023 (n 39) 3 para 4.

[42] A member of the International Court of Justice raised in his 2007 general course at the Hague Academy of International Law the question of whether distinct feminist approaches to international law or more general approaches to international law are most appropriate when dealing with issues of discrimination, Mohamed Bennouna, *Le droit international entre la lettre et l'esprit*, Académie de Droit International de La Haye (Brill, Nijhoff 2017) 37.

[43] In some cases, candidacies are put forward for elections to the International Law Commission, maybe also with a later ICJ candidacy in mind—this may seem to point in the direction of long-term planning on the part of certain governments.

[44] A remarkable account about successfully juggling different responsibilities and practical challenges is provided by Annalisa Ciampi, 'La maternità è meravigliosa … ma quanti ostacoli per la carriera' in Giovanna Pezzuoli and Luisella Seveso (eds), *100 donne contro gli stereotipi per la politica internazionale* (Egea 2020) 37–44.

or in their interest. Instead, they consider that building the right type of *curriculum vitae* depends on the choices and priorities of interested individuals in the years, or even decades, ahead of their selection. Such apathy and myopia for the fact that many 'preparatory steps' (such as ILC or PCA membership) are not up to individual choice regardless of the motivation and ambition of the would-be candidate severely limits the available pool of judicial candidates with the requisite profile for a seat on the international bench at the time of selection. The small number of seats on the international bench may furthermore make it less likely that governments think it useful, realistic, or possible to plan long-term for the constitution of a pool of eligible candidates with the required qualifications and highly specialized experience; let alone a gender-balanced one.

The existence of any such pool of eligible candidates may also be the consequence of other phenomena. These include the degree and quality of interaction between various national institutions and relevant activities of international law. Contacts between the foreign ministry's legal adviser's office, relevant domestic institutions, particularly judicial ones, and international networks may also be useful. The identification of potential candidates may depend to some degree on the experience of the State concerned with international dispute settlement. It may also be influenced by the status, role, and position of international law in the domestic legal system. In sum, a variety of national decision-making contexts and conditions, including gender-mainstreaming, may play an early role in contributing to or, on the contrary, restricting access to opportunities for candidates.

4. Ways Ahead: Bridging Divides

The path ahead must seek to remove these obstacles, contributing to a promotion of women's access to opportunities. Making real improvement in the appointment of female judges to the international bench depends on women having the opportunities to acquire relevant previous experience and roles. This may include access to positions as government legal advisers and the highest judicial positions in a domestic system, but also the acquisition of relevant international experience. Obstacles to progress in this field may be due to conscious or unconscious resistance to change in domestic systems, preventing the creation of real equal opportunities for women to gain relevant experience through early decision-making and long-term planning at the national level. Addressing these obstacles requires asking how one can best make gender-mainstreaming part of decision-making, where, as we have seen, other considerations are concurrently being taken into account.

One way to do this is to include positive incentives by communicating the utility, in addition to the fairness of promoting such opportunities, in addition to relevant legal obligations and political commitments. Communication of these incentives will be influenced by, and in turn influence, 'culture' including societal behaviours and administrative practices. Such a broad concept may admittedly be hard to analyse, and even harder to transform. Broader patterns of behaviour may be influenced by attitudes, awareness, and the motivation of a national society. Using Roberto Mangabeira Unger's terminology, this may require generating institutional imagination, as fundamental beliefs and institutions may be decisive within a given framework of available legal institutions and process.[45] A key objective must be to destabilize entrenched resistance to change and any unconscious prejudice. This aim may be furthered by using practical and workable communication tools, such as political road maps with common terminology, that could assist various decision-makers at all levels in making gender-mainstreaming a part of decision-making.

Utility incentives are clear in the context of judicial activities pertaining to situations dealing with individual rights, procedural, or substantive issues concerning victims or witnesses, and where the legitimacy and effectiveness of the institution concerned may be particularly dependent on gender diversity of perspectives and experience. This is the case for institutions in the fields of human rights and international criminal law.[46] Such arguments might, at first blush, be less readily apparent in other international dispute settlement mechanisms at inter-State levels. However, diversity of perspectives is generally seen to increase internal quality of discussions, and external representation and trust. Such particular considerations may, however, also be relevant in other cases, for instance when dealing with intensive fact-finding adjudication in the context of armed conflict.[47]

In terms of communication tools to convey arguments of utility, the standalone goal of Sustainable Development Goal 5 (SDG 5) was approved by all UN Member States as part of the new global 2030 roadmap.[48] It sets out the need to 'achieve gender equality and empower all women and girls' by 2030, as a contribution to sustainable development, in recognition of women being underrepresented in leadership and management level positions the public and private sectors. This encapsulates the message that gender equality contributes not only to security, as stated in Security Council resolution 1325, but also to economic development.[49]

[45] Roberto Mangabeira Unger, *What Should Legal Analysis Become?* (Verso 1996) 22, 129.

[46] See references to the European Court of Human Rights and the International Criminal Court (nn 10, 12, and 14).

[47] See for example the International Court of Justice, Application of the Convention on the Prevention and Punishment of the Crime of Genocide (*Bosnia and Herzegovina v Serbia and Montenegro*), Judgment [2007] ICJ Rep 43.

[48] See n 4.

[49] Norway's Prime Minister, Ms Erna Solberg, co-chairing the Sustainable Development Goals Advocates established by the Secretary-General of the United Nations, when asked about the high number of women in key government positions in Norway, said: 'If 50% of the population does not participate in political life, 50% of our talents will be wasted'. Interview in the newspaper *Le Monde*, 13 December 2017, by Jean-Baptiste Chastand and Alexis Duval, on the occasion of the One Planet Summit convened by the French President in Paris two years after the Paris Climate accord.

Thus, such arguments of utility, and not only fairness, may stand as positive incentives for both communication networks and decision-makers.

In summary, the campaigning exigencies for States and the election process itself, in addition to the personal experience-based qualifications required of candidates, demonstrate the need to scrutinize the early obstacles candidates are likely to face before even starting to run for international judicial office. Gender-sensitivity and mainstreaming should be integrated into relevant decision-making at the domestic level. It could lead to pragmatic considerations such as the choice of language in political or administrative decision-making at the national level. In this regard, incentives to increase appointments of women on the international bench may include not only arguments about fairness, but also utility. An effort to influence the consensus among practitioners about the basic premises expressed in agreed language at the international level, regarding peace and security as well as sustainable development, may also promote dialogue to bridge cultural differences.

4

Justifications for the Promotion of Religious Diversity on the International Bench

*David M Bigge**

1. Introduction

It is unacceptable to discriminate against any person seeking to act as judge or arbitrator in international adjudication on the basis of a personal trait other than those related to the position. This is equally true of religion as it is of gender, sexuality, geographic origin, or ethnicity. No orthodox or secular religious person of any faith should be prevented on that basis from serving as judge or arbitrator, if she is otherwise qualified.

The promotion of religious diversity in appointments to the international bench, by institutions and by other stakeholders, may be a means of eliminating discrimination on the basis of religion. Such discrimination may be as opaque as it is systemic.[1] Real motivations underlying appointment decisions may be hidden or hard to unravel, even to the individuals making the decisions. Implicit bias plays an important and often underappreciated role in appointment decisions.[2] That the international bench remains woefully short on women,[3] for example, is not

* This chapter is submitted in the author's personal capacity and does not reflect the views of the US government. The author thanks Professor Freya Baetens, PluriCourts at the University of Oslo, and Leiden University for organizing and hosting the event at which this chapter was first workshopped.

[1] The phrase 'international bench' is used broadly as encompassing all adjudicative roles in international law, including but not limited to judges on interstate dispute bodies (eg ICJ, PCA), judges on international criminal tribunals or courts (eg ICC, the UN International Residual Mechanism for Criminal Tribunals (UNIRMCT), Kosovo Special Chambers), or arbitrators hearing ad hoc interstate, investor-state, or private commercial disputes. Where there are differences relevant to the subject of this chapter among judges and arbitrators serving in those different capacities, those differences are highlighted below.

[2] See Apoorva Patel, 'Implicit Bias in Arbitrator Appointments: A Report from the 15th Annual ITA-ASIL Conference on Diversity and Inclusion in International Arbitration' (*Kluwer Arbitration Blog*, 7 May 2018).

[3] See eg Priya Pillai, 'Women in International Law: A Vanishing Act?' (Opinio Juris, 3 December 2018) <http://opiniojuris.org/2018/12/03/women-in-international-law-a-vanishing-act/>accessed 10 December 2018 (reviewing the lack of women on, *inter alia*, various international courts); see also Markus Altenkirch and Jan Frohloff, 'Gender Diversity in International Arbitration – Statistics' *Global Arbitration News* (3 July 2017); Aveek Chakravarty, 'The Rationales for Diversity in Appointments in Investment Arbitration' (*EUTIP Blog*, 4 September 2018)<https://more.bham.ac.uk/eutip/

David M Bigge, *Justifications for the Promotion of Religious Diversity on the International Bench* In: *Identity and Diversity on the International Bench.* Edited by: Freya Baetens, Oxford University Press (2020). © The several contributors.
DOI: 10.1093/oso/9780198870753.003.0004.

necessarily the result of purposeful discrimination at every individual appointment. Nonetheless, the low number of female judges and arbitrators demonstrates systemic discrimination, which can only be eradicated by a determined effort to appoint more women.[4] The same holds true for non-Western judges and arbitrators, who are also inadequately represented.[5]

Discrimination on the basis of religion, too, may be difficult to eliminate without purposeful efforts to promote diversity. There are not yet statistics regarding appointments of judges from various religions similar to those for gender and geographic origin, so the promotion of religious diversity may be a solution without a problem. But the international legal community might assume that the established imbalance favouring Western Europeans and North Americans in appointments to the international bench[6] correlates with a comparative lack of, for example, Muslim, Buddhist, or Hindi arbitrators and judges. Of course, in some individual cases the discrimination may be apparent. There is, for example, the controversial case of Robert Roth, a Swiss judge on the Special Tribunal for Lebanon (STL), who (at least by his own account) was forced to resign in 2013 as a result of his wife's Jewish faith and pro-Israel writings, which some thought would predispose Judge Roth against the defendants at that tribunal.[7]

the-rationales-for-diversity-in-arbitral-appointments-in-investment-arbitration/> accessed 10 December 2018 ('[a] 2015 study [that] found that only 44 out of 785 of the arbitrators appointed in investment disputes by ICSID between 1979 and 2014 were women, accounting for 5.61% of the total appointments'), citing Greenwood and Baker, 'Is the Balance Getting Getter? An Update on the Issue of Gender Diversity in International Arbitration', (2015) 31(3) Arbitration International 413.

[4] Such promotion efforts could take the form of strict diversity requirements, like those used to appoint judges to the International Criminal Court, or movements aimed at increasing awareness of and social pressure for female candidates, eg 'The Pledge.' Compare: Procedure for the nomination and election of judges, the Prosecutor and the Deputy Prosecutor of the International Criminal Court, ICC-ASP-3-Res 6 (Sept. 10, 2004) ¶ 20, to: the Equal Representation in Arbitration Pledge <www.arbitrationpledge.com>accessed 10 December 2018. It is noteworthy that the Rome Statute establishing the International Criminal Court merely required that States Parties 'take into account' various diversity elements in selecting judges. See Rome Statute of the International Criminal Court (adopted 17 July 1998, entered into force 1 July 2002) 2187 UNTS 90 ('Rome Statute') Art. 36(8). It was only later, when specific election procedures were established, that those diversity elements were converted into requirements.

[5] See eg Courtney Dolinar-Hikawa, 'Beyond the Pale: A Proposal to Promote Ethnic Diversity Among International Arbitrators' (2015) 4 Transnational Dispute Management.

[6] See eg Chakravarty (n 3) ('in 2016 a total of 119 arbitrators from 40 different countries were appointed in ICSID cases, with 61% of the appointments originating from Western Europe or North America … In terms of appointments made directly by the parties, 67% originated from Western Europe or North America … While 22% of parties came from Eastern Europe and Central Asia, only around 2.5% of ICSID arbitrators originated from there. Similarly, 13% of ICSID parties came from the Middle East and North Africa, but only 4% of ICSID arbitrators came from those regions. 11% of ICSID parties came from Sub-Saharan Africa, but only 1.5% of ICSID arbitrators came from that region'), *citing* Lucy Greenwood, 'Tipping the Balance – Diversity and Inclusion in International Arbitration', (2017) 33(1) Arbitration International 99.

[7] See Robert Roth, 'Tribunal Special sur le Liban: Retour sur une Experience' (2017) 1 Revue Belge de Droit International 290, 306–07 (quoting letter suggesting bias by Judge Roth as a result of his wife's having edited a Jewish journal); see also Pierre Hazan, 'Swiss judge delivers harsh criticism of Lebanon Tribunal' (*JusticeInfo.net*, 17 May 2018).

There is an important difference, however, between preventing discrimination on the one hand, and promoting diversity on the other. Preventing religious discrimination in individual appointments means ensuring that qualified judges can serve *regardless* of their faith. The promotion of religious diversity necessary to overcome systemic discrimination suggests that certain judges should be appointed *because* of their faith. That difference becomes salient when we consider the justifications commonly used for the promotion of various types of diversity on the international bench. For the reasons described below, the messaging associated with the promotion of religious diversity may, at least tacitly, suggest that a religious judge should be expected to bring her religious doctrine expressly to bear on the dispute. Even in the likely event that the appointed judge does not apply religious principles to the adjudication process, the perception that the judge is expected to do so may affect stakeholder's willingness to promote religious diversity, or may affect the perceived legitimacy of the court. While the promotion of religious diversity may be useful and good, the international community should approach the *messaging* associated with that promotion with care.

The remainder of this chapter will proceed as follows: first, this chapter will address the various justifications used by those seeking to promote diversity on the international bench, focusing on what will be described as the 'value-added justification'—that a diverse bench creates additional value to the adjudication process; second, this chapter will apply the value-added justification to the promotion of religious diversity; and third, the chapter will address risks inherent in the use of the value-added justification to promote religious diversity.

2. Justifications for the Promotion of Diversity

Authors generally point to at least three reasons to promote various forms of diversity on the international bench: first, the long-overdue embrace of diversity in international adjudication;[8] second, the enhancement of normative legitimacy of international courts and tribunals;[9] and third, the benefits that a diverse bench brings to the process of adjudication itself, which this chapter will refer to as the 'value-added justification.'[10]

[8] For example, at two recent public events addressing diversity on the international bench, which were separated by six months, this author heard two different speakers cite to Canadian Prime Minister Justin Trudeau's laudable justification for his diverse cabinet—'because it's 2015'—in advocating for diversity on the international bench. See Jessica Murphy, 'Trudeau gives Canada first cabinet with equal numbers of men and women' *The Guardian* (4 November 2015). Both speakers were Canadian nationals.

[9] See Susan D Franck and others, 'The Diversity Challenge: Exploring the "Invisible College" of International Arbitrators' (2015) 53(3) Columbia Journal of International Law 429, 467–68).

[10] See generally Abhinav Chandrachud, 'Diversity and the International Criminal Court: Does Geographic Background Impact Decision Making?' (2015) 38 Brooklyn Journal of International Law 487, 491 ('Such a judge may also bring "traditionally excluded" perspectives to the cases being decided by the court.')

The first two justifications can be addressed briefly. First, the embrace of diversity and corresponding remedying of historic or current discrimination is a laudable goal in any context. The elimination of discrimination is particularly important in international adjudication, where certain categories of qualified people have historically been and are currently underrepresented.[11] Certainly, intentional discrimination may be a factor in appointment decisions. But as Lucy Reed and others have pointed out, the lack of diversity among international arbitrators (and, by extension, judges) is also the result of implicit bias;[12] conscious or subconscious views about how women and non-Western arbitrators and judges will perform on the bench informs the appointment decision. Parties and States appointing international adjudicators are also prone to be cautious in their appointments, appointing only those arbitrators with significant experience (who traditionally have been male and Western European or North American); similarly, they appoint arbitrators with whom they are familiar and comfortable.[13] The result of these factors is systemic discrimination against women and non-Western arbitrators and judges, even if such discrimination is unintentional in individual cases.

Second, the promotion of diversity enhances the legitimacy of international adjudication.[14] Various factors may affect the perceived legitimacy of an international court or tribunal, including a perception of fair process; the presence of independent and impartial adjudicators; and unbiased and professional secretaries and registries.[15] Nienke Grossman has argued that previous understandings of normative legitimacy, which focus primarily on States Parties' consent to the process, are outdated as the reach of international courts and tribunals extends beyond the litigants before it, affecting not only other States but private individuals as well.[16] Modern international courts and tribunals must reflect the diversity of

[11] See eg Kathleen Claussen, 'Keeping Up Appearances: The Diversity Dilemma' (2015) 4 Transnational Dispute Management at 3 (noting that the push for gender diversity in international arbitration is 'reflective of a general recognition of the importance of including women in spheres where they have been often excluded'). The concerted elimination of discrimination among judges and arbitrators may also have a trickle-down effect, creating norms of diversity among counsel; women remain underrepresented in partnership at many of the world's best-regarded law firms. See eg Destiny Peery, National Association of Women Lawyers, 2018 Survey on Retention and Promotion of Women at Law Firms at 7 (showing that while women comprise more than 50% of law firm graduates and almost 50% of law firm associates, they comprise only 20% of law firm equity partners).

[12] See Patel (n 2).

[13] ibid.

[14] See Dolinar-Hikawa (n 5) at 11 (arguing that a nationality diversity requirement in international arbitration would 'add legitimacy to international arbitration as a fair and unbiased dispute resolution mechanism. Critics of international arbitration could no longer point to tribunals' composition as evidence of inherent bias against non-Anglo-European countries. The addition of an arbitrator diversity requirement would increase transparency and dispel suspicions of nepotism, favoritism, and bias in arbitrator appointment.').

[15] Nienke Grossman, 'Legitimacy and International Adjudicative Bodies' (2009) 41 The George Washington International Law Review 107, at 123–24.

[16] See generally Nienke Grossman, 'The Normative Legitimacy of International Courts' (2013) 86 Temple Law Review 82.

the international community for direct and indirect stakeholders to consider them to be normatively legitimate.[17] The perception that international judges and arbitrators are 'pale, male, and stale' thus undermines the legitimacy of international adjudicative institutions.[18]

If the justifications provided for the promotion of religious diversity on the international bench ended with the elimination of discrimination and normative legitimacy, there would be little more to discuss. Both goals are of critical importance, separately and together, and both fully justify the promotion of diversity, including religious diversity.

There is, however, the third justification commonly used to promote diversity on the international bench, the value-added justification. When authors address diversity in international adjudication, they often raise the different experiences and values that diverse judges and arbitrators bring to adjudication, thereby enhancing the process. To quote Mirèze Philippe, the absence of women on the bench is:

> ... detrimental because they have their views, their experience, their talents and we would be missing this wealth of input. Gender diversity brings to the room essential components because men and women often have different approaches, views, and analyses of situations.[19]

Abhinav Chandrachaud has made the same point with respect to regional or ethnic diversity, writing of the special perspectives those diverse judges may have: '[m]inority judges might bring "special sensitivity" or "unique perspectives" to decision making.'[20] Current scholarship on group decision-making supports these arguments.[21]

[17] Gabrielle Kaufmann-Kohler and Michele Potestà, *The Composition of a Multilateral Investment Court and of an Appeal Mechanism for Investment Awards*, CIDS Supplemental Report (15 November 2017) at 31–32 (international adjudication 'should provide a "fair representation" or a "fair reflection" of those who may be affected by its decisions ... The degree of diversity on a prospective [tribunal] is likely to influence the perception of the fairness and legitimacy of the [tribunal] among all those affected by its decisions ...'); cf Chandrachud (n 10) at 488 (' ... a "rainbow court" which fairly reflects the demographic characteristics of the region in which it is sitting might be perceived as being more legitimate, but international courts are seldom honestly diverse.'). Again, one could cite to Prime Minister Trudeau, who explained, in introducing his cabinet, '[i]t's important to be here before you today to present to Canada a cabinet that looks like Canada.' See Murphy (n 8).

[18] See Franck (n 9) at 467–68.

[19] Mirèze Philippe, 'Redressing the Balance: The Path Ahead for Gender and Generational Diversity on Arbitral Tribunals' (*Kluwer Arbitration Blog*, 31 October 2016) <http://arbitrationblog.kluwerarbitration.com/2016/10/31/redressing-the-balance-the-path-ahead-for-gender-and-generational-diversity-on-arbitral-tribunals/> accessed 10 December 2018.

[20] See generally Chandrachud (n 10) at 492, citations omitted.

[21] Chakravarty (n 3) ('behavioural studies in recent years have focused on the relationship between diversity in terms of gender, ethnicity and social backgrounds and the quality of group decision-making, suggesting a positive relationship between them. With respect to adjudicatory bodies, similar research has been done in the context of domestic courts.').

Authors supporting this value-added justification argue that diversity adds value to the adjudication process particularly by preventing a too-narrow range of equitable considerations informing a judgment or award.[22] As Gabrielle Kaufmann-Kohler and Michele Potestà explain:

> ... case outcomes are not strictly mandated by the application of the law, and the law often leaves a margin of discretion to the decision-maker ... Adjudicators are human beings. Even if they are perfectly impartial as they must be for the proper exercise of their office, their judgment will inevitably be informed by who they are, to put in simple terms (by their origin, education, professional background, and more). If this is true, then diversity may play a role in counter-balancing too uniform perspective from identical or similar backgrounds.[23]

In short, according to these authors, diverse experiences and values, which we expect the judges to bring to the adjudication process, make that process richer, fairer, and more legitimate.[24] As Kaufmann-Kohler and Potestà conclude with respect to studies of diversity in US courts, 'diversity will improve the quality of justice dispensed'.[25] The value-added justification for the promotion of diversity is not without its detractors, however. Kathleen Claussen, a strong advocate for increased diversity in international arbitration, has questioned the utility of the value-added justification, writing in the context of gender diversity that:

> ... [t]he simple fact is that there is not enough data to determine how women arbitrators fare differently from men. Nor does it behove anyone to ask such questions. It does not make sense, therefore, to focus on an outcome-oriented rationale for adding more women to a pool for consideration.[26]

[22] See eg Chakravarty (n 3) ('One of the rationales that has emerged is that adjudicatory panels with more diverse composition make it likelier that a wider range of considerations will be debated in the decision-making process.')

[23] Kaufmann-Kohler (n 17) at 30-31.

[24] See eg Joseph Mamounas, 'ICCA 2014: Does 'Male, Pale, and Stale,' Threaten the Legitimacy of International Arbitration? Perhaps, but There's No Clear Path to Change' (*Kluwer Arbitration Blog*, 10 April 2014) (noting 'a general recognition that diversity could have benefits for international arbitration. Diversity spawns perspective, which, overall, may make arbitration more just and fair. Diversity counters the risk that an arbitral tribunal will look and act the same as its predecessors.').

[25] Kaufmann-Kohler (n 17) at 27–28.

[26] Claussen (n 11) at 6. The present author does not hold a view as to whether diversity by itself necessarily creates better judicial outcomes, but nonetheless, would argue that the promotion of diversity is important for redress historic and current discrimination and for the legitimacy of international judicial institutions.

3. The Value-Added Justification in the Context of the Promotion of Religious Diversity

If the international legal community relies on the value-added justification to promote religious diversity on the international bench, it raises the question of what value the religiously diverse person (in isolation of other characteristics) brings to the process of adjudication.

3.1 Religion as Culture

The value of religious diversity, similar to geographic or ethnic diversity, is likely the particular culture associated with a religion.[27] After all, when we appoint international judges based on geographical diversity, we expect them to bring their cultural experiences—including to a certain extent their diverse legal culture—to the court. But at least in terms of international courts and tribunals, religion is not a neat proxy for overall culture or values; adherents to a specific global religion may reflect a multitude of cultures and values. Simply put, religions are themselves culturally diverse. For example, if a party were seeking to appoint a Jewish person so that 'Jewish culture' would be more represented on the bench, would the party appoint someone from the United States or Israel? The cultural experience of a Jewish person in the United States may be very different from the cultural experience of a Jewish person in Israel (to say nothing of Jews in other parts of the world).[28] The same may hold true, for example, in comparing the cultures of a Muslim person from the United Kingdom and a Muslim person from Saudi Arabia.

Thus, when addressing a judge's religious 'culture,' we are more specifically addressing the underlying doctrines of the religion. Although there are doctrinal differences within religions—sometimes vast differences—elemental doctrines remain constant, and other doctrines could be regarded as accepted by the majority.

[27] This has been argued, for example, with respect to the religious backgrounds of judges in the US domestic system. See eg Donald Braman and Dan M Kahan, 'Legal Realism as Psychological and Cultural (not Political) Realism' (2009) How Law Knows ('[i]t's not that political values motivate legal actors to reach particular outcomes but rather that cultural values orient them in determining what outcome is dictated by the law and evidence at hand. Legal actors with differing values will decide culturally sensitive cases differently not because they want to impose their values on others but because the mechanisms of cultural cognition move them to view the facts and the law differently.'); see also Brian H Bornstein and Monica K Miller, 'Does a Judge's Religion Influence Decision Making?' (2009) 45(3) Court Review 112, 115 ('On the whole, there appear to be systematic differences in judges' decision making as a function of their religion. Jewish judges, on average, are consistently more liberal, arguably because of their stronger identification with the downtrodden and disenfranchised, owing to their own outsider status.').

[28] See eg 'Israel's Religiously Divided Society' (March 8, 2016) *Pew Research Center* at 46–65 (detailing various cultural and political differences between Israeli and American Jews).

Religious doctrine, even more than the cultural experiences attendant to gender or ethnicity, can provide alternate equitable considerations germane to a dispute, thus fitting the model for the value-added justification described by Kaufmann-Kohler and Potestà. In addition, religious doctrine may be used to support otherwise established and applicable legal principles, or as a basis to derogate from those principles.[29] In fact, religious doctrine could be viewed as an alternate source of law or an alternate basis of decision. Basic religious texts themselves can be quite legalistic. In addition, many religions have developed full systems of law beyond the basic texts, for example Halakha, Canon Law, Shari'a, and Dharmasāstra. These are not just vague theological concepts that can provide guidance to a decision-maker. Rather, these are substantive legal systems that may specifically address, for example, family law, laws of war, criminal law, contracts, or financial and commercial law.

3.2 Religious Doctrine in International Adjudication

The difficulty presented by applying the value-added justification to religious diversity is that there are few instances in international adjudication in which it would be appropriate to apply religious 'culture' to a dispute. In most liberal democracies, a judge's personal religious convictions cannot have any place in adjudication, because they are not a source of recognized applicable law.[30] This is the case even in disputes that could have a moral dimension, like criminal cases or cases involving international humanitarian law. As Keith Swisher explained:

> In order to apply morals in adjudication, those morals must be based in law (broadly defined). Purely personal policies and religious doctrines, then, would not qualify. Conveniently, we do not need to garner agreement in one jurisprudential view to justify this claim—they fail under virtually any conception of jurisprudence. They lack an official mooring—a birth from a recognized source of law.[31]

[29] Se eg Mubarak Waseem, *The Citation of Religious Texts in ICJ Judgements* (publication forthcoming).

[30] Cf Kent Greenawalt, 'Religion and Public Reasons: Making Laws and Evaluating Candidates' (2012) 27 Journal of Law & Politics 387, 397 (summarizing John Rawls: 'The idea is that judges within the United States and other liberal democracies must rest their rulings on existing laws and other reasons that all judges could be expected to accept. Judges are not to decide according to their own peculiar sense of what is right or desirable.')

[31] Keith A Swisher, 'The Moral Judge' (2008) 56 Drake Law Review 637; see also Howard Kislowicz, 'Judging Religion and Judges' Religions' (2018) 33(1) Journal of Law and Religion 1) ('If a judge were to justify their reasons on the basis of a particular religion, they might fairly be seen as imposing the tenets of their religion on litigants, and compromising those litigants' ability to choose for themselves a comprehensive view of the good.'); but see Scott C Idleman, 'The Role of Religious Values in Judicial Decision Making' (1993) 68(2) Indiana Law Journal 433) (arguing in favour of a role for religious values in adjudication).

Admittedly, international law in its inception was a largely religious preoccupation.[32] It has also been posited that religious law aided in the development of modern international law, including human rights law.[33] But it is indisputable that positivist theories of international law have predominated since the 19th century.[34] As former International Court of Justice (ICJ) Judge Christopher Weeramantry observed, 'in the twentieth century, international law ... so far distanced itself from religion that the latter receives scarcely a mention in the standard treatises'.[35] International law is thus currently regarded as having two primary sources: first, treaties or other agreements between States, and second, customary international law as defined by State practice and *opinio juris*.[36]

One might argue that religious concepts could be relevant to determining 'general principles' of international law, as referenced in the ICJ Statute.[37] General principles, distinct from customary international law, are 'a core of legal ideas which are common to all civilized legal systems',[38] but which extend 'beyond the limits of legal positivism'[39] outlined in the previous paragraph. Although general principles are a primary, rather than subsidiary, source of law in the ICJ Statute, 'no consensus among legal scholars exists as to the exact quality of this source'.[40] A traditional view of general principles posits that they may be derived from consistently applied domestic or municipal laws, UN resolutions, or 'expressions of other unperfected sources of international law enumerated in the statutes of the Permanent Court

[32] Hugo Grotius spilled more ink on Christian theology than he did on international law, and the international law concepts that he documented draw not only from the international practice of the time, but also from Christian doctrine. See eg Mark Weston Janis, 'A Sampler of Religious Experiences in International Law' (2003) 22 Mississippi College Law Review 233, 235) ('Another founder of international law, the Dutch protestant jurist, Hugo Grotius, relied heavily on Old and New Testament citations to demonstrate a universal law of nations in his monumental Seventeenth Century text, *The Laws of War and Peace* (1625), usually seen as the first book on international law.') Grotius and other contemporaries also relied heavily on non-Biblical Jewish sources. Shabtai Rosenne, 'The Influence of Judaism on the Development of International Law: A Preliminary Assessment', (1958) 5 Nederlands Tijdschrift Voor Internationaal Recht 119; Charles Leben, 'Hebrew Sources in the Doctrine of the Law of Nature and Nations in Early Modern Europe' (2016) 27 European Journal of International Law 79.

[33] Gad Barzilai, 'Introduction' in Gad Barzilai (ed), *Law and Religion* (Ashgate 2007) xv–xvi (noting the various ways that Halakha, Canon law, Christian concepts of natural law, and Shari'a have shaped the development of other legal systems, including 'modern human rights.')

[34] Ines Gillich, 'The Normativity of Principles within the Positive Theory of International Law' (2015) 41 North Carolina Journal of International Law 1, 2 ('The positivist legal theory, or positivism, is one of the most widely accepted theories and has even been described by some scholars as the ruling theory of law.').

[35] Christopher Weeramantry, Preface to Janis and Evans (eds), *Religion and International Law* (1999) ix.

[36] Gillich (n 34) at 3.

[37] Charter of the United Nations and Statute of the International Court of Justice, June 26, 1945, 59 Stat. 1055, Art 38(1)(c).

[38] Rudolph B Schlesinger, 'Research on the General Principles of Law Recognized by Civilized Nations' (1957) 51 American Journal of International Law 734, 739.

[39] Dissenting Opinion by Judge Tanaka, *South West African Cases (Ethiopia and Liberia v South Africa)* [1966] ICJ Rep 250, 298.

[40] Christina Voigt, 'The Role of General Principles in International Law and their Relationship to Treaty Law' (2008) RetfÆrd Årgang 31 Nr. 2/121 at 5.

of International Justice (PCIJ) and ICJ; namely, conventions, customs, writings of scholars, and decisions of the PCIJ and ICJ'.[41] Examples include the concepts of 'good faith' and 'abuse of rights'. Religious law has no place in the interpretation or application of these general principles, except to the extent that religious law is the basis of an examined domestic law.[42]

Some scholars and judges also include 'natural law' as a basis for 'general principles'.[43] To the extent that 'natural law' informs the content of general principles, one might argue that religious texts are relevant to the adjudication. For example, Hugo Grotius and John Selden based their theories of natural law at least partly on the Noahide laws, a set of universal principles found in the Jewish Talmud.[44] But there is no clear reason why religious law is necessarily determinative of 'natural law' in the modern age,[45] particularly where, assuming one accepts the concept of natural law as a component of general principles, it should be limited to principles that transcend specific cultures or religions. At best, one might assert that religious codes provide examples of the application of broader, generally accepted natural law principles.[46]

What about international commercial arbitration, where the applicable law is likely to be the domestic law of a State? Here, too, religious precepts are not relevant to the adjudicative exercise, unless the applicable law is itself premised on religious law. There are some obvious examples where that might be the case, such as an international transaction grounded in Islamic financial law. In that case, it may benefit the parties to appoint someone familiar with Islamic rules on lending.[47] But outside of such narrow examples, it is difficult to imagine a scenario where it would be appropriate for a commercial arbitrator to bring religious law to bear on a dispute otherwise governed by secular law.

41 M Cherif Bassiouni, 'A Functional Approach to "General Principles of International Law"' (1990) 11 Michigan Journal of Intermational Law 768, 768. Scholarly writings are separately included as a 'subsidiary means for determination of rules of law' under Article 38(1)(d) of the ICJ Statute.

42 As Mubarak Waseem points out, several of the citations to religious law in ICJ separate opinions were addressing a domestic (Ottoman) law in the process of establishing a general principle of international law. See Waseem (n 29). Waseem also points out that where citations to religious law appear in separate opinions in ICJ cases, it is always in addition to other sources of general principles: national laws, judicial decisions, and the like, ibid.

43 See eg Dissenting Opinion by Judge Tanaka, *South West African Cases (Ethiopia and Liberia v South Africa)* [1966] ICJ Rep. 250, 298; see also Voigt (n 40) at 8–9.

44 See Leben (n 32) at 89–91; see also Suzanne Last Stone, 'Sinaitic and Noahide Law: Legal Pluralism in Jewish Law' (1991) 12 Cardozo Law Review 1157, 1162 ('For Grotius and Selden, the Noahide laws were an early model for the Roman "law of nations."').

45 For example, many religious codes include prohibitions against murder, but that does not mean that these religions establish the prohibition against murder and provide the substantive content of the crime, as much as they are examples of a broader human understanding that murder is not acceptable.

46 Indeed, in the few instances where religious law has been cited in separate opinions at the ICJ, it is often used in this way. See Waseem (n 29).

47 Cf Abdulmajed Alrajhi, 'Islamic Finance Arbitration: Is It Possible for Non-Muslims to Arbitrate Islamic Financial Disputes?' in (2015) 4 Transnational Dispute Management (arguing that Islamic law permits non-Muslims to arbitrate Islamic financial law disputes).

4. Risks in the Promotion of Religious Diversity Based on the Value-Added Justification

Presumably, all judges appointed to the international bench understand the applicable law, and will interpret and apply only that law. Religious judges are just as capable of discerning and applying the applicable law as non-religious judges. And after all, we expect geographically diverse judges and arbitrators to bring their local legal traditions to the adjudication process, but nonetheless expect that they will not rely upon those traditions in the place of the applicable procedural and substantive law. The same should be expected of religiously diverse judges.

Nonetheless, to the extent that the push for diversity on the international bench comes to include religious diversity,[48] there are three specific reasons to avoid reliance on the value-added justification, as opposed to the other justifications for promoting diversity: first, the risk that the norm of religious diversity will be rejected because of its justification; second, the risk to the legitimacy of the court or tribunal, and related challenges against religious judges; and third, the limited bases for challenging international decisions.

4.1 Risk of Rejection of the Norm of Religious Diversity

If advocates of religious diversity rely on the value-added justification, the stakeholders in international dispute resolution—including but not limited to public and private litigants, and the broader public affected by an international decision—may understand the promotion of religious diversity to include the expectation that a judge's religious doctrine will be brought to bear on the adjudicative process. That messaging may be conveyed in a variety of ways, including through the appointment process itself. Take, for example, the International Criminal Court (ICC) election process. That process has been carefully crafted to ensure that the bench includes diverse members in terms of gender, geography, and professional background, as required by the Rome Statute.[49] The candidates running for election are expressly identified by the specific diversity requirements they meet.[50]

[48] To the author's knowledge—possibly because discrimination on the basis of religion has not been sufficiently established—there has been no real push to promote religiously diverse candidates thus far.

[49] Rome Statute, Art. 36(8); Chandrachud (n 10) at 508 (under Rome Statute, ICC judges 'must come from diverse geographic (and demographic) backgrounds—no two judges can be nationals of the same state—and in appointing judges to the court, States Parties (ie the countries that are parties to the Rome Statute of the ICC) must take account of the need for: (1) representation of the principal legal systems of the world, (2) equitable geographic representation, and (3) fair representation of female and male judges.')

[50] For example, in 2017, each ICC candidate completed a questionnaire created by the NGO Coalition for an International Criminal Court. At the very top of each questionnaire, the candidate indicated their home State, their gender, and whether they qualified under 'List A' or 'List B' of professional qualifications. See eg Questionnaire for Tomoko Akane <www.coalitionfortheicc.org/sites/default/files/

In promoting their candidacy, each judge emphasizes the value that their particular diverse characteristics might bring to the ICC, and the electors consider those characteristics.

The promotion of diverse characteristics of judges through the ICC election process has wide acceptance. It is unclear whether a process that is perceived as encouraging the application of religious law would garner the same sort of acceptance. Indeed, the value-added justification may cause some who would have otherwise accepted the new norm to reject the promotion of religious diversity.

4.2 Legitimacy of the Court or Tribunal and Challenges against Religious Judges

From the outset a judge's religion may play a role in the perceived legitimacy of an international court or tribunal, particularly if it is resolving a dispute with religious dimensions. Religious judges may be seen by affected stakeholders as voting for their 'side,' whether such a perception is warranted or not.[51]

The risk to legitimacy is increased all the more, however, by the perception that a judge will be expected to draw on her religion as a basis of decision. Concerns may be raised by litigants regarding how religious doctrine will play a role in the adjudication process. This could affect the legitimacy not only of the result, but also of the jurisprudence. Stakeholders of other religions, or more strikingly of no religion at all, may view decisions made by a judge or arbitrator appointed as a result of the promotion of religious diversity with scepticism.

Relatedly, if it is believed that a judge's religion will have some bearing on a dispute, parties may question whether those religious doctrines affect the judge's impartiality. This would lead to unjustified and time-wasting challenges to arbitrators and judges. For example, those who challenged Judge Roth on the STL, claimed that his wife's religious views and support of Israel would impact his ability to judge whether individual defendants were responsible for the murder on Lebanese Prime

cicc_documents/japan_cicc_judicial_elections_2017_candidate_questionnaires_tomoko_akane_0.pdf> accessed 17 July 2019.

[51] For example, Antonio Cassese, the first President of the ICTY, noted in an interview his satisfaction that the first ICTY prosecutor, Richard Goldstone, was Jewish and therefore an 'outsider' to the Yugoslav dispute, stating, 'a Jewish prosecutor would be excellent because we would have to deal with Catholics, the Croats, with Muslims, the Bosniacs, and with Orthodox Serbs. So a Jewish prosecutor would be an outsider. And I told [Goldstone] that, perhaps by coincidence, none of the four judges from Muslim countries were Muslims. The Pakistani judge was Zoroastrian, the Nigerian was a Protestant, the Malaysian was a Hindu, and the Egyptian was Catholic.' Heikelina Verrijn and Marlise Simons, 'The Judge: Interview with Antonio Cassese', excerpted from *The Prosecutor and the Judge* <www.press.uchicago.edu/Misc/Chicago/9789085550235.html> accessed 30 July 30 2019.

Minister Hariri.[52] There was no evidence that Judge Roth could not maintain impartiality, but he was nonetheless encouraged to step down.

4.3 Limited Bases to Challenge International Decisions

Finally, the messages the international legal community communicates to its judges and arbitrators may affect how the judges and arbitrators perceive their obligations in adjudication. Social interactions, such as the election or appointment of judges and arbitrators, may 'shape, mould or constrain' the choices ultimately made by those judges and arbitrators when deciding disputes and reinforcing (or, arguably, creating) new norms.[53] The value-added justification therefore may, on rare occasion, encourage judges and arbitrators to rely inappropriately on religious doctrine in making their decisions.

To be certain, a judge's religion may affect the outcome of a case. There are several studies showing at least a correlation between a judge's religious beliefs and that judge's rulings on particular issues.[54] In summarizing this work, Howard Kislowicz writes that '[a] modest reading of the ... empirical research supports the claim that religious affiliation and preexisting ideological commitments have some impact on judicial decision-making, though these considerations are usually not articulated in the judgments themselves'.[55] So some unconscious correlation between a judge's religion and her substantive rulings may be inevitable, even where religious tenets are nowhere addressed in the legal reasoning of the decision.

But what happens if, taking a cue from the messaging behind a push for religious diversity on the bench, the judge consciously determines that she should take the tenets of her faith into account, even expressly in the reasoning of the decision? In such instances, there may be few, if any, means for reversing the decision in the structures of international courts and tribunals.

At the ICJ, for example, there is no appellate mechanism and no basis to challenge in any other forum. Article 60 of the ICJ Statute states that an ICJ judgment 'is final and without appeal,' except that the Court may clarify the meaning or scope

[52] See (n 7). Challenges to international judges and arbitrators are becoming more common, and are succeeding for reasons hitherto uncontemplated. For example, President Theodor Meron and two other judges were successfully challenged and removed from the *Mladić* case at the UNIRMCT on the basis that they had previously heard cases involving acts of the accused's subordinates. *See Prosecutor v Mladić* (Decision on Defence Motions for Disqualification of Judges Theodor Meron, Carmel Agius and Liu Daqun) MICT-13-56-A (3 September 2018).

[53] Jutta Brunnée and Stephen J Toope, 'Constructivism and International Law' in Jeffrey L Dunoff and Mark A Pollack (eds), *Interdisciplinary Perspectives on International Law and International Relations: The State of the Art* (CUP 2012) at 8.

[54] See eg Bornstein and Miller (n 27) ('Most of the research that has been conducted on the relationship between judges' religion and their decisions focuses on appellate judges. There is a growing consensus that appellate judges' attitudes and beliefs are important predictors of their decisions.').

[55] See Kislowicz (n 31).

of the judgment upon request.[56] Article 61 permits a revision of a judgment only upon the discovery of a decisive fact that was unknown to the Court. Thus, if a judge or group of judges inappropriately relied on religious doctrine, rather than the applicable international law, there would be no basis for challenging the judgment. The ICJ is an interesting case, however, because of its unusually large bench and deliberation method. Having fifteen judges hailing from every corner of the world, deciding a case all together, would likely prevent one religious view from providing a legal basis of the decision (which may be why religious citations only appear in separate opinions).[57] Indeed, in this sense, the ICJ provides another argument for why religious diversity might be useful—to prevent a predominant religion shared by some of the judges from guiding a decision.

In contrast, commercial arbitration usually involves small panels of three arbitrators, or often sole arbitrators, deciding a case. The New York Convention, which in most countries governs the enforcement of international arbitration awards, contains no provision for challenging awards where the arbitrator relies on novel legal theories.[58] Arbitrators are generally recognized as having broad *iura novit curia* powers, or what some have termed *iura novit tribunus*. That is, the arbitrator is empowered to determine the law for herself and apply that law to the dispute even if the disputing parties did not address the particular legal doctrine serving as the basis of decision.[59] Thus, on its face, commercial arbitration raises concern about the ability of parties to challenge awards that are inappropriately based on religious doctrine.

Iura novit tribunus is not without limits, however. Where the disputing parties are surprised by the reliance on legal principles that were not addressed in pleading, in violation of their right to be heard, courts have not hesitated to vacate awards. Courts in Switzerland, Sweden, France, Canada, and the United States have all overturned arbitral awards on this basis.[60] The Swiss Federal Tribunal case involving international football player Levezinho (whose real name is Liedson da Silva Muniz) is instructive.[61] Levezinho, a Brazilian, was contracted to play for Sporting Club Lisbon, and concluded the contract himself without the assistance of his exclusive agent, who was Spanish. The agent nonetheless brought an arbitral claim to the Court of Arbitration for Sport (CAS) alleging entitlement to a fee under the agency contract, which was governed by FIFA rules.[62] CAS applied an arcane provision of

56 Statute of the International Court of Justice (adopted 26 June 1945) 33 UNTS 993.

57 See Waseem (n 29).

58 See Convention on the Recognition and Enforcement of Foreign Arbitral Awards (adopted 5 June 1958, entered into force 7 June 1959) 330 UNTS 38.

59 See Christian P Alberti and David M Bigge, 'Ascertaining the Content of the Applicable Law and Iura Novit Tribunus: Approaches in Commercial and Investment Arbitration' (2015) 70 Dispute Resolution Journal 1.

60 ibid at 14–18.

61 *José Ignacio Urquijo Goitia v Liedson da Silva Muñiz*, Swiss Federal Supreme Court (9 February 2009), Case No. 4A_400/2008, in *ASA Bulletin*, Volume 27 Issue 3, Kluwer Law International, The Hague, 2009, pp. 498–499.

62 ibid.

Swiss employment law, which had not been raised by either party, in rejecting the agent's claim.[63] The CAS arbitrator claimed that the Swiss law was mandatory, and that in any event CAS rules permitted resort to Swiss law to fill gaps. In response to a challenge of the award, the Swiss Federal Tribunal ruled that the unexpected application of Swiss law in this case had denied the agent his right to be heard:

> Whilst iura novit curia does apply, giving significant latitude to the arbitrators, resorting to a totally unexpected legal argument to decide the case is a violation of the right to be heard if the Appellant could not have reasonably expected the application of the provision relied upon by the arbitral tribunal.[64]

The story may be different, however, in a proceeding under the auspices of the International Centre for the Settlement of Investment Disputes (ICSID). At ICSID, the only basis for challenging an award is an annulment proceeding internal to the institution.[65] Once the annulment proceedings are concluded (or if they are not pursued), the arbitral award is regarded as a judgment in any enforcing State and cannot be challenged in court.[66] Unlike State courts in New York Convention cases, ICSID annulment committees have not taken kindly to challenges to *iura novit tribunus*. For example, the 2002 annulment committee in the *Vivendi* matter explained that while the reasoning adopted by the underlying tribunal 'came as a surprise to the parties, or at least to some of them . . . this would by no means be unprecedented in judicial decision-making'.[67] The challenge based on the right to be heard was thus denied in that case. Later annulment committees have consistently applied this reasoning.[68]

Finally, we should quickly examine international criminal institutions. Article 81 of the Rome Statute broadly permits ICC appellate review of decisions for any procedural error, error of fact, or error of law.[69] Both the prosecutor and the convicted person may pursue such an appeal. In addition, Article 81(1)(b)(iv) permits a convicted person to appeal on 'any other ground that affects the fairness or reliability of the proceedings or decision'.[70] The ICC decision in *Bemba* suggests that the ICC Appellate Chamber interprets these mandates broadly.[71] The UN

[63] ibid.

[64] ibid.

[65] Convention on the Settlement of Investment Disputes between States and Nationals of Other States (adopted 18 March 1965, entered into force 14 October 1966) 575 UNTS 159, Arts. 50–52, 53.

[66] ibid Art 54.

[67] *Compañia de Aguas del Aconquija S.A. and Vivendi Universal v Argentine Republic*, ICSID Case No. ARB/97/3, Decision on Annulment (3 July 3 2002), para 84.

[68] See Alberti and Bigge (n 59) at 18–19.

[69] Rome Statute (n) 4.

[70] ibid.

[71] *Prosecutor v Bemba Gombo* (Judgment on the appeal of Mr Jean-Pierre Gombo against Trial Chamber III's 'Judgment pursuant to Article 74 of the Statute'), Case No. ICC-01/05-01/08 (8 June 2018).

International Residual Mechanism for Criminal Tribunals (Mechanism), on the other hand, provides narrower bases for appeal (although both the Prosecutor and the accused may appeal): 'an error on a question of law invalidating the decision; or . . . an error of fact which has occasioned a miscarriage of justice'.[72] The STL Statute includes the same more limited bases for appeal.[73] Unlike with the ICC, the question under the Mechanism or STL systems would be not only whether there was an inappropriate application of religious law, but whether it was so egregious as to undermine the decision.

5. Conclusion

Before accepting the promotion of religious diversity on the international bench, we should be clear about motivations and messaging. No religious person should be subject to discrimination in the realm of international adjudication. And it may very well be that promoting religious diversity is the best means to curtail such discrimination. Religious diversity could also enhance the normative legitimacy of international courts and tribunals. If those are our bases for promoting religious diversity on the international bench, they are sufficient, and the endeavour is worthwhile.

Those pushing for religious diversity should avoid, however, reliance on the value-added justification. There is little room in international adjudication for the application of religious principles, but the value-added justification may communicate to stakeholders or to judges and arbitrators themselves that such an application is expected. This may, in turn, lead to the rejection of the norm of religious diversity (for fear that it will lead to the application of religious doctrine in international cases) or the questioning of the legitimacy of courts and tribunals. The value-added justification may even, in rare circumstances, encourage judges and arbitrators to apply their personal religious principles to a case. In such instances, there may be little or no recourse for the affected litigants. Thus, advocates of religious diversity on the international bench should avoid the value-added justification in their arguments.

[72] Statute of the International Residual Mechanism for Criminal Tribunals, S/RES/1966, Art 23.
[73] Statute of the Special Tribunal for Lebanon, S/RES/1757, Art 26.

5

Judges Ad Hoc at the International Court of Justice

A Means for Enhancing Regional and Legal Systemic Diversity in the Composition of the Court?

Paolo Palchetti

1. Introduction

The Statute of the International Court of Justice (ICJ or the Court) provides that, '[i]f the Court includes upon the Bench a judge of the nationality of the parties, any other party may choose a person to sit as a judge . . . .'[1] Moreover, '[i]f the Court includes upon the Bench no judge of the nationality of the parties, each of these parties may proceed to choose a judge . . . .'[2] By appointing additional judges, who exercise their function on terms of complete equality with their elected colleagues, parties can influence, though only to a limited extent, the composition of the Court in a given case.

This chapter focuses on the functions of judges ad hoc and on the selection practices of States. It does not aim to offer a systematic and complete picture of the legal problems relating to the use of judges ad hoc or of appointment practices, but it is rather intended to serve as a first look at a relatively unexplored issue: whether, and to what extent, the nomination of judges ad hoc may promote systematic regional and legal diversity on the bench of the Court. The chapter is structured as follows: after outlining the function of judges ad hoc as 'representation of the main forms of civilization' on the ICJ bench, the 'public relations' role ('to ensure that every relevant argument has been fully appreciated') and the 'representational' role ('one who lives in the region of the world with which the application deals') of judges ad hoc are discussed. Subsequently, the chapter examines trends in the selection of judges ad hoc and offers some concluding observations on the need for representativeness.

[1] Art 31(2), Statute of the International Court of Justice (ICJ Statute) 33 UNTS 993.
[2] Art 31(2), ICJ Statute.

Paolo Palchetti, *Judges Ad Hoc at the International Court of Justice* In: *Identity and Diversity on the International Bench.* Edited by: Freya Baetens, Oxford University Press (2020).
DOI: 10.1093/oso/9780198870753.003.0005.

2. Judges Ad Hoc and the 'representation of the main forms of civilization' on the ICJ Bench

The Statute of the Court does not provide much guidance on the criteria that should guide a State in the selection of a judge ad hoc. Article 31(2) establishes that States should 'preferably' select candidates from the lists of persons nominated by the national groups in the Permanent Court of Arbitration (PCA).[3] Under Article 31(6), judges ad hoc are required to satisfy the conditions of integrity and legal competence laid down in Article 2 of the Statute and, in accordance with Article 17(2), must not have taken part in the case as agent or counsel to one of the parties or in any other capacity. The 1922 Rules of the Permanent Court of International Justice (PCIJ) previously required States to appoint judges of their own nationality.[4] This stipulation was later removed in order to preserve the position of small States that might otherwise not be able to put forward a qualified candidate for that position.[5] Now, Practice Direction VII, adopted by the Court in 2002, sets another limitation that the parties 'should refrain from nominating persons who are acting as agent, counsel or advocate in another case before the Court or have acted in that capacity in the three years preceding the date of the nomination'.[6] However, the use of recommendatory language—ie 'should'—renders uncertain whether this is a mandatory requirement or whether the parties can regard this as falling within their discretion. As many commentators have pointed out, it is not clear what the consequences would be if a party decides not to follow the Court's recommendation in this respect.[7]

The general criteria guiding the selection of judges ad hoc do not differ substantially from those relating to the election of permanent judges. One notable difference, however, is that when electing permanent judges, States have to bear in mind that 'in the body as a whole the representation of the main forms of civilization and of the principal legal systems of the world should be assured', pursuant to Article 9.[8] Article 31, however, contains no such reference. In other words, a State does not need to consider the need to ensure the representativeness of the Court when

[3] It provides as follows: 'Such person shall be chosen preferably from among those persons who have been nominated as candidates as provided in Articles 4 and 5'.

[4] 1922 Rules of the Permanent Court of International Justice, Publications of the Permanent Court of International Justice, Series D. Nr. 1.

[5] See R Kolb, *The International Court of Justice* (Hart 2013) 122.

[6] On this Practice Direction, see Kolb (n 5) 121.

[7] A Pellet, 'Remarks on Proceedings before the International Court of Justice' in A Del Vecchio (ed), *New International Tribunals and New International Proceedings* (Giuffrè 2006) 99, 114; A Watts, 'New Practice Directions of the International Court of Justice' (2002) 1 The Law and Practice of International Courts and Tribunals 247, 255.

[8] Art 9 provides as follows: 'At every election, the electors shall bear in mind not only that the persons to be elected should individually possess the qualifications required, but also that in the body as a whole the representation of the main forms of civilization and of the principal legal systems of the world should be assured'.

appointing a judge ad hoc.[9] The absence of any reference to a criterion of this kind is understandable since the primary purpose of appointing a judge ad hoc is to enable a party that does not have a judge of its nationality on the bench, to appoint a person in whom it has confidence. It is a power placed at the disposal of the parties to serve their specific interests, rather than the institutional interest of preserving the representative character of the Court's composition. Given the specific function of judges ad hoc, it is unsurprising that the Statute does not limit the parties' freedom of choice in this respect. Regardless, the representativeness of the Court essentially depends on the selection of the fifteen elected judges, and not upon the geographic origin or the legal background of one or two persons who are only appointed as judges in relation to a specific case.

Yet, despite the absence in Article 31 of any reference to Article 9, there is still a link between the nomination of judges ad hoc and the Court's representativeness. The presence on the bench of one or two judges appointed by the parties may increase the geographical and cultural diversity of the bench. The next sections examine the possible representational role fulfilled by judges ad hoc and the importance that States attach to this role. I assess whether, taking into account the functions that a judge ad hoc is expected to fulfil, elements such as nationality, geographic origin, or cultural background play a role in States' selection of these judges. I then seek to identify the main trends in the selection practices, in particular relating to whether States tend to nominate nationals, non-nationals, or individuals from the same regional groups; whether States prefer individuals with specific personal and professional backgrounds; and so on. The purpose is to establish whether the institution of judges ad hoc has been used by States in a way that increases regional and legal systemic diversity of the Court's bench.

3. 'To ensure that every relevant argument has been fully appreciated': the 'Public Relations' Role of Judges Ad Hoc

There are two frequently made arguments for the existence of judges ad hoc. Albert de la Pradelle referred to them as '*la logique de l'égalité*' and '*la psychologie de la confiance*'.[10] The first, the 'logic of equality', follows that if one party's nationality is represented on the bench of the Court, it may be appropriate to establish equality between the parties by giving the other party the option to appoint a judge as well.

[9] As noted by G Hernández, *The International Court of Justice and the Judicial Function* (OUP 2014) 147, 'the "representational" element demanded of permanent judges as a whole is absent when nominating a judge *ad hoc*'.

[10] See the intervention of Albert de La Pradelle in Annuaire de l'Institut de droit international 45-I (1954), 528: 'mais ce n'est pas seulement la logique de l'égalité, c'est la psychologie de la confiance qui trouve dans le juge *ad hoc* une satisfaction d'autant plus nécessaire que l'Etat a toujours, grand ou petit, faible ou fort, une instinctive défiance de la justice internationale, défiance qui diminue lorsqu'il y participe'.

While this provides a strong reason for supporting the institution of the judge ad hoc, it is insufficient as a justification, since a State is entitled to nominate a judge even when there is no judge with the nationality of the other party already serving on the bench of the Court. The other component—'*la psychologie de la confiance*'—is harder to define and should be further examined. While the Court's lack of compulsory jurisdiction is in itself a powerful incentive for creating conditions where a State may feel reassured, it is not clear why the presence of a judge ad hoc might increase a State's trust in the Court;[11] nor is it clear to what extent the identity of the judge in question, including his or her geographic origin or the legal background, is relevant in this respect.

Different explanations are given for why States may feel reassured by the presence of a judge whom they have specifically appointed to deal with a dispute to which they are a party. Two main sets of reasons can be identified, which correspond to two different views of the function that the judge ad hoc fulfils when sitting on the bench of the Court. The first, and certainly the main, reason relates to what Alain Pellet has called 'the public relations role'.[12] States expect, and feel reassured by the fact, that the judge ad hoc 'may be able to present, in a sympathetic light within the Court, the position being asserted by his state'.[13] This view frames the judge ad hoc as a 'mediating force'.[14] This speaks to a need to reassure the appointing State that the Court will carefully consider the arguments presented during the proceedings. Several judges ad hoc have expressly subscribed to this view. Judge ad hoc Lauterpacht first articulated this, describing 'the special obligation to endeavour to ensure that, so far as is reasonable, every relevant argument in favour of the party that has appointed him has been fully appreciated in the course of collegial consideration and, ultimately, is reflected—though not necessarily accepted—in any separate or dissenting opinion that he may write'.[15] Following this, Judge ad hoc Franck stated that 'the *ad hoc* judge must always ensure that the appointing State's arguments are fully addressed by the Court, whether or not they convince the majority of the judges'.[16] According to Judge ad hoc Sur, 'for a judge *ad hoc* to ensure the proper hearing and appreciation of the arguments put forward by the party having chosen him, it is not enough for him merely to express his own

[11] For a strong criticism of the view that the appointment of a judge ad hoc may increase a state's confidence in the Court, see H Lauterpacht, *The Function of Law in the International Community* (OUP 1933) 243 et seq. See also E Lauterpacht, 'The Role of *ad hoc* Judges' in C Peck and R Lee (eds), *Increasing the Effectiveness of the International Court of Justice* (Martinus Nijhoff 1997) 371–78, at 376.

[12] See A Pellet in C Peck and R Lee (eds), *Increasing the Effectiveness* (n 11) 395 ('What judges *ad hoc* are being asked to do is a sort of public relations role').

[13] ibid.

[14] G Hernández (n 9) 151.

[15] *Application of the Convention on the Prevention and Punishment of the Crime of Genocide (Bosnia and Herzegovina v Serbia and Montenegro)* (Order of 13 September 1993, separate opinion of Judge ad hoc Lauterpacht) [1993] ICJ Rep 409.

[16] *Sovereignty over Pulau Ligitan and Pulau Sipadan (Indonesia v Malaysia)* (Merits, separate opinion of Judge ad hoc Franck) [2002] ICJ Rep 694.

opinion, be it separate or dissenting, since in this case the arguments are simply reflected in an opinion appended to the decision; he is also under a duty to do his utmost to ensure that they figure in the decision itself, even if they are not upheld'.[17]

Where the judge ad hoc is perceived as a mediating force, this perception may affect which personal qualifications appointing States seek in potential judges. Here, the ability to effectively fulfil a 'public relations' role will be the primary criterion when selecting a judge ad hoc. Therefore, a person's legal background, his or her reputation before the Court and experience within the Court will likely be among the main factors considered. A person's professional background will be more important than his or her geographic origin since an appointing State will require someone who not only knows international law but who is also familiar with the Court, its case law and its internal mechanisms. Given these criteria, it is unsurprising that States frequently choose someone coming from 'the very small microcosm of practitioners of international law'.[18]

4. 'One who lives in the region of the world with which the application deals': The 'Representational' Role

The 'public relations' role does not fully explain the institution of the judge ad hoc. There is also a second function, which emphasizes the nationality, geographic origin, and cultural background of the appointee. A State may feel reassured by the fact that, on the bench of the Court, there is at least one judge who properly understands the State's situation, including its domestic legal system, and is familiar with the historical and political background of the dispute, as well as with the sensibilities linked to the dispute. Seen from this perspective, the function of a judge ad hoc goes beyond simply ensuring that the technical legal arguments presented by the appointing party are fully appreciated by the Court, so that it amounts to fulfilling a broader 'representational' role. Because of his or her knowledge of the situation and familiarity with the background of the dispute, the judge ad hoc can help to bring a particular perspective of the dispute and of the appointing State's point of view to the Court. Seen in this light, the institution of the judge ad hoc appears to connect with the requirement, set forth in Article 9 of the Statute, that the bench of the Court reflect the main forms of civilization and the principal legal systems of the world. In this perspective, a State's ability to appoint a person who is close to it in terms of geographic origin or cultural background, becomes a means for enhancing that State's confidence in the Court and in its representativeness.

The importance for States of having someone who 'understands' their situation on the bench of the Court was forcefully stressed during the preparatory works of

[17] *Obligation to Prosecute or Extradite (Senegal v Belgium)* (order of 28 May 2009) [2009] ICJ Rep 202.
[18] A Pellet in C Peck and R Lee (eds), *Increasing the Effectiveness* (n 11) 395.

the Statute. The US member on the Advisory Committee of Jurists, Elihu Root, emphasized the fact that, to gain the 'support of masses', 'it must be possible to tell the masses that there will be at least one person upon the Court who is able to understand them'.[19] The Japanese member, Mineichiro Adatci, defended the proposal of admitting judges ad hoc on the basis that, in rendering a judgment, 'the psychology of the various people must be understood: this is important, especially in the case of a judgment given in Europe or America, but affecting States of different races'.[20] Lord Phillimore stressed that it was important 'to enable the Court to understand certain questions which require highly specialized knowledge and relate to the differences between the various legal systems'.[21] All these views appear to be based on a conception of the function of the judge ad hoc as representational, which gives importance to the judge's personal knowledge of the situation of the appointing State and his or her capacity to 'understand the masses'.

Within the practice of the Court, the clearest formulation of the 'representational' function fulfilled by a judge ad hoc is that put forward by Judge ad hoc Palmer in his dissenting opinion in the 1995 *Request for an examination* case between New Zealand and France. He observed that in the case before him, the institution of the judge ad hoc 'served a useful purpose of bringing to the Court a perspective of one who lives in the region of the world with which the application deals', adding that '[i]ts utility was in providing another perspective and some more detailed familiarity with the background'.[22]

5. Trends in the Selection of Judges Ad Hoc

If, in principle, the institution of judge ad hoc has the effect of increasing the general representative character of the Court, it still remains to be seen whether in practice States take account of this 'representational' element in their choice of a judge. As mentioned above, since the revision of the Statute in 1929, States can appoint a non-national as a judge ad hoc. At the time of the PCIJ, States rarely appointed non-nationals.[23] According to the data on the Court's website,[24] this trend continued in the first period of the ICJ's activities. For example, between

[19] Proces-Verbaux of the Proceedings of the Advisory Committee of Jurists, 24th Meeting, 14 July 1920, 538.

[20] ibid 529.

[21] ibid 528–29. Similar views were expressed by members of the Inter-Allied Committee during World War II. See S M Schwebel, 'National Judges and Judges *ad hoc*' in R-J Dupuy (ed), *Droit et Justice. Mélanges en l'honneur de Nicolas Valticos* (Pedone 1999) 319–29, at 325.

[22] *Request for an Examination of the Situation in Accordance with Paragraph 63 of the Court's Judgment of 20 December 1974 in the* Nuclear Tests *(New Zealand v France)* (order of 22 September 1995, dissenting opinion of Judge ad hoc Palmer) [1995] ICJ Rep 420.

[23] See A Oraison, 'Reflexions sur l'institution du juge ad hoc siégeant au tribunal du Palais de la Paix en séance plénière ou en chambre *ad hoc*' (1998) 31 Revue belge de droit international 272–99, at 280.

[24] <www.icj-cij.org/en/all-judges-ad-hoc> accessed 23 April 2020.

1949 and 1959, 14 judges ad hoc were appointed in nine different cases.[25] Of these 14 judges, 10 were nationals of the appointing States. They were from a wide variety of States: Colombia and Peru;[26] Iran;[27] Greece;[28] Italy;[29] Guatemala;[30] the Netherlands; Sweden;[31] Switzerland;[32] and Israel.[33]

In the cases where non-nationals had been appointed, the persons selected always had the nationality of a State that belonged to the same geographical or ideological group of the appointing State. This seems to have played a role in Albania's choice to appoint two persons of Czechoslovakian nationality.[34] The same could be said about the choice made by Bulgaria, which also appointed a person having Czechoslovakian nationality to serve as a judge ad hoc.[35] Liechtenstein appointed a jurist of Swiss nationality.[36] In all these cases, the choice of appointing a non-national may have been dictated by the difficulty of finding a national qualified for that position due to the small pool of possible candidates within these countries.[37]

If one compares the situation that prevailed during the Court's first decade to that of the current day, the difference is striking. At the time of writing, 15 judges ad hoc have been appointed in the 17 cases currently before the Court.[38] It is worth noting, incidentally, that all but two of them (Hilary Charlesworth and Navanethem Pillay)

[25] While formally distinct, the *Asylum (Colombia/Peru)*, *Request for Interpretation of the Judgment of 20 November 1950 in the Asylum Case (Colombia v Peru)*, and *Haya de la Torre (Colombia v Peru)* cases between Colombia and Peru are here counted as one.

[26] In *Asylum (Colombia/Peru)*, *Request for Interpretation of the Judgment of 20 November 1950 in the Asylum Case (Colombia v Peru)*, and *Haya de la Torre (Colombia v Peru)*, Colombia appointed Judge ad hoc José Joaquin Caicedo Castilla and Peru Judge ad hoc Luis Alayza y Paz Soldán.

[27] In *Anglo-Iranian Oil Co. (United Kingdom v Iran)* Iran appointed Judge ad hoc Karim Sandjabi.

[28] In *Ambatielos (Greece v United Kingdom)* Greece appointed Judge ad hoc Jean Spiropoulos.

[29] In *Monetary Gold Removed from Rome in 1943 (Italy v France, United Kingdom of Great Britain and Northern Ireland and United States of America)* Italy appointed judge ad hoc Gaetano Morelli.

[30] In *Nottebohm (Liechtenstein v Guatemala)* Guatemala appointed Judge ad hoc Carlos Garcia Bauer.

[31] In *Application of the Convention of 1902 Governing the Guardianship of Infants (Netherlands v Sweden)* the Netherlands appointed Judge ad hoc Johannes Offerhaus and Sweden Judge ad hoc Fredrik Julius Christian Sterzel.

[32] In *Interhandel (Switzerland v United States of America)* Switzerland appointed judge ad hoc Paul Carry.

[33] In *Aerial Incident of 27 July 1955 (Israel v Bulgaria)* Israel appointed Judge ad hoc David Goitein.

[34] In *Corfu Channel (United Kingdom of Great Britain and Northern Ireland v Albania)* Albania first appointed judge ad hoc Igor Daxner and then Judge ad hoc Bohuslav Ečer.

[35] In *Aerial Incident of 27 July 1955 (Israel v Bulgaria)* Bulgaria appointed Judge ad hoc Yaroslav Zourek.

[36] In *Nottebohm (Liechtenstein v Guatemala)* Liechtenstein appointed Judge ad hoc Paul Guggenheim.

[37] However, according to Sh Rosenne, 'Article 31 of the Statute of the International Court of Justice Revisited' in R-J Dupuy (ed), *Droit et Justice* (n 21) 301–17, at 311, 'Bulgaria probably did have competent nationals of its own for this position, although its choice still remained within the ideological group to which the country then belonged'.

[38] For these data <www.icj-cij.org/en/current-judges-ad-hoc> accessed 23 April 2020. While the survey conducted in this study is limited to cases pending before the Court on 23 April 2020 and does not cover all the cases submitted in the past, previous surveys made by other authors substantially confirm the trend signalled in this study. See, for instance, Sh Rosenne, *The Law and Practice of the International Court, 1920-2005* (Martinus Nijhoff 2006) 24, who, writing in 2005, observed that '[a]nother development is a growing tendency for litigating States to choose persons not of their nationality to serve as judge *ad hoc*'.

are male.[39] Of these 15 judges, only three have the nationality of the appointing State (two of these are sitting in two cases).[40] The number of nationals could have been even lower if one considers that in three of these cases the judges ad hoc were appointed by the United States and Russia to replace members of the Court having US and Russian nationality, who did not take part to the proceedings due to reasons flowing from Article 24(1) of the Statute.[41] Of the 12 non-nationals, only two judges ad hoc have the nationality of a State that belongs to the same geographical group of the appointing State.[42] As for the other 10 non-national judges, nine were from the Western European and Others group including three from France—with one French jurist acting as a judge ad hoc in six of the 17 cases before the Court.[43] In several cases, the judge ad hoc has the same nationality as a permanent

[39] So far, only few women have served as judges ad hoc: Louise Arbour (*Obligation to Negotiate Access to the Pacific Ocean (Bolivia v Chile)*), Suzanne Bastid (*Application for Revision and Interpretation of the Judgment of 24 February 1982 in the Case concerning the Continental Shelf (Tunisia/Libyan Arab Jamahiriya) (Tunisia v Libyan Arab Jamahiriya)*), Hilary Charlesworth (*Whaling in the Antarctic (Australia v Japan: New Zealand intervening)* and *Arbitral Award of 3 October 1899 (Guyana v Venezuela)*), Christine van den Wyngaert (*Arrest Warrant of 11 April 2000 (Democratic Republic of the Congo v Belgium)*), and Navanethem Pillay (*Application of the Convention on the Prevention and Punishment of the Crime of Genocide (The Gambia v Myanmar)*). On the paucity of women sitting on benches of international courts, N Grossman, 'Sex on the Bench: Do Women Judges Matter to the Legitimacy of International Courts?' (2012) 12 Chicago Journal of International Law 647.

[40] They are: Charles Brower and Djamchid Momtaz (*Certain Iranian Assets (Islamic Republic of Iran v United States of America)* and *Alleged violations of the 1955 Treaty of Amity, Economic Relations, and Consular Rights (Islamic Republic of Iran v United States of America)* and Leonid Skotnikov (*Application of the International Convention for the Suppression of the Financing of Terrorism and of the International Convention on the Elimination of All Forms of Racial Discrimination (Ukraine v Russian Federation*.

[41] According to Art 24(1), '[i]f, for some special reason, a member of the Court considers that he should not take part in the decision of a particular case, he shall so inform the President'. In *Certain Iranian Assets (Islamic Republic of Iran v United States of America)* and in *Alleged violations of the 1955 Treaty of Amity, Economic Relations, and Consular Rights (Islamic Republic of Iran v United States of America)* judge Donoghue decided not to take part in the decision and the United States appointed Charles Brower to serve as judge ad hoc. In *Application of the International Convention for the Suppression of the Financing of Terrorism and of the International Convention on the Elimination of All Forms of Racial Discrimination (Ukraine v Russian Federation)* Judge Gevorgian did not take part in the decision and Russia appointed Leonid Skotnikov to serve as judge ad hoc.

[42] Judge ad hoc James Kateka, of Tanzanian nationality, who was appointed by Equatorial Guinea to serve in *Immunities and Criminal Proceedings (Equatorial Guinea v France)*, and Judge ad hoc Navanethem Pillay, who was appointed by The Gambia to serve in *Application of the Convention on the Prevention and Punishment of the Crime of Genocide (The Gambia v Myanmar)*. It may be worth to clarify that the categorization used for the purposes of the present study is the UN regional group categorization, which identifies the following groups: African, Asia and the Pacific, Eastern European, Latin America and Caribbean, Western European and others.

[43] They are: judge ad hoc Yves Daudet (French) appointed, respectively, by Nicaragua, Bolivia, Qatar (three times), and the Democratic Republic of the Congo (*Alleged Violations of Sovereign Rights and Maritime Spaces in the Caribbean Sea (Nicaragua v Colombia), Dispute over the Status and Use of the Waters of the Silala (Chile v Bolivia), Application of the International Convention on the Elimination of All Forms of Racial Discrimination (Qatar v United Arab Emirates), Appeal Relating to the Jurisdiction of the ICAO Council under Article 84 of the Convention on International Civil Aviation (Bahrain, Egypt, Saudi Arabia and United Arab Emirates v Qatar), Appeal Relating to the Jurisdiction of the ICAO Council under Article II, Section 2, of the 1944 International Air Services Transit Agreement (Bahrain, Egypt and United Arab Emirates v Qatar), Armed Activities on the Territory of the Congo (Democratic Republic of the Congo v Uganda)*), Judge ad hoc Donald M. McRae (Canadian) appointed by Colombia (*Alleged Violations of Sovereign Rights and Maritime Spaces in the Caribbean Sea (Nicaragua v Colombia)*), Judge ad hoc Gilbert Guillaume (French) appointed by Kenya (*Maritime Delimitation in the Indian Ocean*

member of the Court. Thus, there are two judges of US nationality as well as two of Russian nationality in *Question of the Delimitation*,[44] two judges of French nationality in *Alleged Violations of Sovereign Rights and Maritime Spaces*, the two *ICAO Council cases* and *Silala*,[45] as well as in *Maritime Delimitation*.[46] In *CERD* there are three French judges.[47] There are two judges of Italian nationality in *Convention for the Suppression of the Financing of Terrorism*,[48] and two of Australian nationality in *Arbitral Award of 3 October 1899*.[49] Lastly, States have selected former permanent members of the ICJ bench as judges ad hoc: among the 15 judges ad hoc, there is a former President[50] and two other former members of the Court.[51]

6. No Need for Representativeness? Concluding Observations

A number of observations can be made based on this data. First, as already noted by several commentators,[52] there is a clear trend towards States appointing judges ad hoc of a different nationality. Remarkably, this includes States that should have no difficulty in finding nationals who are qualified for the position. For instance, it is surprising that South American States, which are among the most frequent 'clients' of the Court, tend to choose their judges ad hoc from amongst non-nationals despite the deeply rooted and culturally rich tradition of studies in international law in

(Somalia v Kenya)) and by Palestine (*Relocation of the United States Embassy to Jerusalem (Palestine v United States of America)*), Judge *ad hoc* Bruno Simma (German) appointed by Chile (*Dispute over the Status and Use of the Waters of the Silala (Chile v Bolivia)*), Judge ad hoc Fausto Pocar (Italian) appointed by Ukraine (*Application of the International Convention for the Suppression of the Financing of Terrorism and of the International Convention on the Elimination of All Forms of Racial Discrimination (Ukraine v Russian Federation)*), Judge ad hoc Jean-Pierre Cot (French) appointed by the United Arab Emirates (*Application of the International Convention on the Elimination of All Forms of Racial Discrimination (Qatar v United Arab Emirates)*), Judge ad hoc Sir Franklin Berman (British) appointed by Bahrain, Egypt, and the United Arab Emirates (*Appeal Relating to the Jurisdiction of the ICAO Council under Article II, Section 2, of the 1944 International Air Services Transit Agreement (Bahrain, Egypt and United Arab Emirates v Qatar)*) and by the same States including Saudi Arabia (*Appeal Relating to the Jurisdiction of the ICAO Council under Article 84 of the Convention on International Civil Aviation (Bahrain, Egypt, Saudi Arabia and United Arab Emirates v Qatar)*), Judge ad hoc Hilary Charlesworth (Australian), appointed by Guyana (*Arbitral Award of 3 October 1899 (Guyana v Venezuela)*), Judge ad hoc Couvreur (Belgian), appointed by Guatemala (*Guatemala's Territorial, Insular and Maritime Claim (Guatemala/Belize)*), and Judge ad hoc Kreß, appointed by Myanmar (*Application of the Convention on the Prevention and Punishment of the Crime of Genocide (The Gambia v Myanmar)*).

[44] Judge Donoghue and Judge ad hoc Brower, as well as judge Gevorgian and Judge ad hoc Skotnikov.
[45] Judge Abraham and Judge ad hoc Daudet.
[46] Judge Abraham and Judge ad hoc Guillaume.
[47] Judge Abraham and Judges ad hoc Daudet and Cot.
[48] Judge Gaja and Judge ad hoc Pocar.
[49] Judge Crawford and Judge ad hoc Charlesworth.
[50] Judge ad hoc Guillaume.
[51] Judges ad hoc Simma and Skotnikov. It is also notable that a former Registrar (Philippe Couvreur) is judge ad hoc in *Guatemala/Belize*.
[52] See, among others, Rosenne (n 19) 311; A Oraison, 'Réflexions sur l'institution' (n 21) 280–81. See also the authors mentioned at n 51.

the Continent.[53] Second, when non-nationals are appointed, States no longer seem to insist on appointing a person with the nationality of another State belonging to the same geographical group. States do not seem to consider the ability of judges ad hoc to bring 'a perspective of one who lives in the region of the world with which the application deals' as relevant in their selection process. Third, if one considers the provenance of judges ad hoc, there is a very high percentage of judges from Europe and the United States. Finally, there is a tendency to appoint, as judges ad hoc, persons who are familiar with the law and practice of the Court. They include, in particular, former members of the Court or persons who already acted as judge ad hoc in previous cases.

In sum, the data suggest that nowadays, in selecting a judge ad hoc, States do not attach particular importance to representation. Nationality and geographic origin appear to have lost ground in favour of other factors such as experience and familiarity with the activity and procedures of the Court. The reason may be found in the 'public relations' conception of the role of the judge ad hoc, and his/her capacity to make his/her voice heard within the Court—factors which States appearing before the Court now appear to place a particular value on. From this perspective, familiarity with the Court and its procedures as well as widely recognized standing as a legal expert are given more importance than geographic provenance. This may explain why judges ad hoc increasingly tend to be selected among a limited pool of experts and why the same persons are frequently appointed by different States.

The trend away from the appointment of nationals or persons coming from the same geographic area as the appointing State has been regarded by several authors as a positive development.[54] Some suggest that the fact that the selection appears to be based on legal competence and professional skills, rather than on nationality or geographic origin, may serve to dispel the doubts of partiality frequently associated which the institution of the judge ad hoc.[55] While there is some merit to this argument, there is also another, and in my view less positive, aspect that appears to characterize the current situation. Judges ad hoc who do not share the nationality of the appointing State tend to come from a small number of States, largely States belonging to the 'Western European and other' regional group. The best explanation for this is the fact that most judges ad hoc come from the 'small microcosm of the practitioners of international law',[56] which is largely composed of persons

[53] On this tradition see A Cançado Trindade, 'The Contribution of Latin American Legal Doctrine to the Progressive Development of International Law', (2016) 376 Recueil des cours 11–92.

[54] For this view, see G Abi Saab in *Increasing the Effectiveness*(n 8) at 394; N Valticos, 'Pratique et éthique d'un juge *ad hoc* à la Cour internationale de Justice' in N Ando and others (eds), *Liber Amicorum Judge Shigeru Oda* (Kluwer: Leiden, 2002), 107–16, at 109; J J Quintana, *Litigation at the International Court of Justice* (Brill-Nijhoff 2015) at 213.

[55] For the view that the institution of the judge ad hoc 'seems to contradict essential principles of judicial activity such as the independence of the judiciary', see, among others, I Scobbie, '"Une hérésie en matière judiciaire"? The Role of the Judge *ad hoc* in the International Court' (2005) 4 The Law & Practice of International Courts and Tribunals 421–64, at 463.

[56] A Pellet in C Peck and R Lee (eds), *Increasing the Effectiveness* (n 11).

from this regional group. As a consequence, the institution of the judge ad hoc does little nowadays to increase regional and legal systemic diversity on the bench of the Court. This is a missed opportunity—greater regional and legal diversity amongst judges ad hoc would likely benefit the Court as it could help to better understand the situation of the States in dispute and so enhance the public perception of the Court as an institution representative of the international community.[57] While the selection of judges ad hoc remains a prerogative of the appointing State, it would be in the interest of the Court, in the initial meeting with the parties or also in the public statements of its President,[58] to encourage States to take the 'representational' element into account when nominating such judges.

[57] Kolb (n 5) at 119, 122, appears to express a similar view when he notes that 'it is desirable for a judge ad hoc to understand the law and culture of the State nominating him' since the Court would thus 'be able to profit, when it came to its private deliberations, from the particular knowledge of the judge in question.'

[58] Questions concerning the nomination of judges ad hoc in cases before the Court have been sometimes addressed by the President of the Court in official speeches. For instance, in her annual speech to the General Assembly, President Higgins invited States, at least when neither party had a national on the Bench, to give very careful consideration to the possibility that the parties jointly agree not to appoint a judge ad hoc each. See Speech by H.E. Judge Rosalyn Higgins, President of the International Court of Justice, to the General Assembly of the United Nations (30 October 2008) (available at the Court's website).

6

The Party-Appointment Process

Addressing Barriers to Equal Opportunities for Women in the Appointment of Ad Hoc Adjudicators

*Catherine Drummond**

1. Introduction

Efforts to improve the representation of women in international dispute settlement continue to face significant challenges. While it is increasingly acknowledged that the lack of gender diversity needs to be addressed, this abstract concern has not translated into a meaningful increase in the number of women being appointed by parties to international courts and tribunals. For this reason, it is important to examine the selection and appointment processes in detail to determine what they reveal about the different layers of prejudice that female candidates face and their combined effect in creating and sustaining barriers to equal opportunities for women. Identifying the different layers of prejudice from a processual perspective can assist with formulating practical measures that could be taken by different stakeholders to address each of the specific barriers.

The Chapter proceeds in two sections. Section 2, which is the focus of this inquiry, examines the representation of women on international arbitral tribunals. It explains how the typical arbitrator selection and appointment process works, identifies the barriers to entry for women that derive from the way in which that process is conducted, and offers suggestions for addressing each barrier. Section 3 provides a short comparator by examining the selection and appointment of judges ad hoc to public international law courts and tribunals, such as the International Court of Justice (ICJ) and the International Tribunal for the Law of the Sea (ITLOS), the Inter-American Court of Human Rights (IACtHR), and the European Court of Human Rights (ECtHR).

What is clear, as explained below, is that to differing degrees the selection and appointment processes for both arbitrators and judges ad hoc negatively prejudice

* The views expressed herein are not the views of firms for which I have worked or any of their clients. References to the practices of law firms are not specific to the firms for which I have worked. I am grateful to Dr Kate Mitchell and Mark Lee Jin Yi for their research assistance. The statistics have been updated as of August 2019.

Catherine Drummond, *The Party-Appointment Process* In: *Identity and Diversity on the International Bench.* Edited by: Freya Baetens, Oxford University Press (2020). © The several contributors. DOI: 10.1093/oso/9780198870753.003.0006.

female candidates. Changing this system requires creating equal opportunities for women, something that counsel[1] for parties appointing arbitrators and judges ad hoc have the ability to grant, or at a minimum improve, in each individual party-appointment process. This highlights the unique role—and the special responsibility—that arbitration and public international law practitioners have in improving the number of women appointed by parties to international courts and tribunals.

2. Arbitration

This section focuses on barriers to equal opportunities for women in the arbitral appointment process. It describes the typical process for selecting and appointing arbitrators (section 2.1), identifies particular layers of prejudice can be detected at different stages of this process (section 2.2) and explores steps that could be taken to begin to address each of these layers of prejudice (section 2.3).

2.1 The Selection and Appointment Process

The first step in the standard practice for arbitrator selection and appointment is the compilation of a list of potential arbitrator candidates by the law firm engaged by the appointing party to an arbitration. This is ordinarily done by a junior lawyer under the instruction of a senior lawyer and/or partner. The list may start with one or more names that the partner or senior lawyer already has in mind as persons who would be suitable candidates. The list grows following a review of potential arbitrators profiled in various public or subscription-only arbitration databases,[2]

[1] The term 'counsel' is used in this chapter as it is used in international legal practice: to refer to persons representing parties before international courts and tribunals. This includes lawyers from law firms, barristers, professors, and other advisors. It is used interchangeably with 'practitioner' and 'lawyer'.

[2] These include: the International Arbitration Institute (IAI)'s Member Directory (646 profiles): 'Directory of Members' (*IAI*) <www.iaiparis.com/drm_search.asp> accessed 29 February 2020; ICSID's list of Arbitrators, Conciliators and Ad Hoc Committee Members (669 profiles): 'Arbitrators, Conciliators and Ad Hoc Committee Members' (*ICSID*, 2019) <https://icsid.worldbank.org/en/Pages/arbitrators/CVSearch.aspx> accessed 29 February 2020; Investment Arbitration Reporter (IAR)'s Arbitrator Profiles (187 profiles): 'Arbitrator Profiles' (*IAR*) <www.iareporter.com/arbitrator-profiles-directory/> accessed 29 February 2020; Global Arbitration Review (GAR)'s Arbitrator Research Tool (ART) (288 profiles and details of more than 5,900 other arbitrators and counsel who have worked alongside them): 'The GAR Arbitrator Research Tool (ART)' (*GAR*, 2019) <http://globalarbitrationreview.com/arbitrator-research-tool> accessed 29 February 2020; the Swiss Arbitration Association (ASA) Profiles (663 arbitrator profiles): 'ASA Profiles' (*ASA*, 2019) <https://profiles.arbitration-ch.org/> accessed 29 February 2020; Who's Who Legal's Market Insight Tool (1,695 lawyers and barristers' listed (not all of whom would be potential arbitrators)): 'Market Insight Tool – Practice Area: Arbitration' (*Who's Who Legal*, 2019) <https://whoswholegal.com/market-insight-tool?PracticeArea=46&RegionID=&CountryID=> accessed 29 February 2020; lawyers mentioned in the GAR 30 and GAR 100: 'The

in private experience databases compiled by the appointing law firm or in arbitrator lists maintained by arbitral institutions, as well as a survey of the profiles of former judges, barristers, and law firm partners with relevant arbitration experience. The candidates accessible through these resources comprise, in broad terms, the pool from which arbitrators are drawn. The junior lawyer will look, in the first instance, for: experience in the relevant type of arbitration (investment or commercial); experience relevant to the sector, industry, or particular type of legal dispute at issue in the case; experience with the applicable law or domestic legal system in question; whether the candidate comes from a legal tradition that might be expected to take a particular approach to legal questions at issue; whether the candidate has published on any topic relevant to the issues in dispute; and relevant language capabilities. The number of candidates included on the initial list can vary greatly.

After the initial list is compiled by the junior lawyer, it is reviewed and refined by the senior lawyer and/or partner involved in the case and is subject to a conflicts of interest check. Views are then sought from persons either within the firm or persons who are known through trusted external networks who have sat with, appeared before or otherwise have familiarity with the candidates. This enables counsel to gain an understanding of whether the candidates have attributes that will not be evidence from their CVs, such as an impressive intellect, that they are well-prepared, efficient, are likely to be able to influence other members of the tribunal (their perceived gravitas) and whether they have the ability and inclination to control the arbitration process and deliver an award within a reasonable period of time.

The list is then further refined on the basis of views on the candidates received from the internal and external networks, after which the law firm presents it to the client for discussion. The list proposed to the client is typically not very long. In most instances where a single arbitrator is to be appointed, the list will include no more than five names; it is easier to choose from fewer options. Often relying on the advice of counsel, the client then selects an arbitrator for appointment.[3]

GAR 30 Revealed' (*GAR*, 5 April 2019) <https://globalarbitrationreview.com/article/1189631/the-gar-30-revealed> accessed 29 February 2020 and 'GAR 100 – 12th Edition' (*GAR*, 1 January 2019) <https://globalarbitrationreview.com/edition/1001299/gar-100-12th-edition> accessed 29 February 2020; and other specific tools that might be relevant in particular cases, such as the International Centre for Dispute Resolution (ICDR)'s Energy Arbitrators List: 'Energy Arbitrators List' (*ICDR*, 2019) <www.energyarbitratorslist.com/> accessed 29 February 2020.

[3] This process broadly reflects a 2018 study of arbitration users which reported that the most common sources of information about arbitrators is drawn from 'word of mouth' (77% of participants in the study), 'from internal colleagues' (68%) and 'publicly available information' (eg legal directories or other databases) (63%): '2018 International Arbitration Survey: The Evolution of International Arbitration' (Queen Mary University of London and White & Case, 2018) 20 <www.arbitration.qmul.ac.uk/media/arbitration/docs/2018-International-Arbitration-Survey---The-Evolution-of-International-Arbitration.PDF> accessed 29 February 2020.

2.2 Identifying the Layers of Prejudice Women Face in the Selection and Appointment Process

From this brief description of the selection and appointment process, at least three layers of prejudice can be detected. The first is supply-oriented: it concerns the identification of women as potential candidates within the actual pool of potential arbitrators. The second is demand-based: it concerns the reduction of the pool as a consequence of counsel often requiring first-hand views from their trust networks on the potential candidates. The third is an implicit bias affecting all stages of the process.

The first barrier that women face concerns the means through which they are identified as potential arbitrator candidates. At the stage of initial research to compile the list of candidates, the junior lawyer should be considering qualities such as gender. This is not always simple. It is by no means correct to suggest that there are not enough qualified women in the actual pool of potential arbitrator candidates to warrant gender-balanced candidate lists, but there are certainly fewer qualified women than men in the actual pool and they are harder to find. There are, for example, fewer profiles of female arbitrators in the main databases used by law firms in arbitrator research. This is clear from a simple scroll through the profile listings, but is also demonstrated by those databases that include a gender filter in the search options, of which there are very few. The only commonly-used publicly-available arbitrator database that has a gender filter is ASA Profiles of the Swiss Arbitration Association. Of the 663 arbitrators listed on 9 August 2019, 121 are women (18.3%).[4] The only other main database with a gender filter is Global Arbitration Review (GAR)'s subscription-only service, the Arbitrator Research Tool. Of the 288 profiles listed on 9 August 2019, 56 are women (19.4%).[5]

But gender filters are the exception. The lack of such a filter on the majority of databases obscures the lack of female candidates listed and does not facilitate the conscious searching for and adding of women to candidate lists. Moreover, some services require that for a person's profile to be listed they must have had three or more appointments as an arbitrator (Investment Arbitration Reporter's Arbitrator Profiles), which rule those databases out as tools for promoting first-time female appointments and make it harder for women to gain the experience so often looked for as a criterion for appointment.[6] An attempt has been made to counter this, to

[4] ASA, 'ASA Profiles' (n 2), selecting arbitrator and using the gender filter.

[5] Email from Alexandra Palma Long (GAR Data Coordinator) to author (9 August 2019).

[6] IAR, 'Arbitrator Profiles' (n 2). It was formerly the policy of GAR's ART that a person must have sat as an arbitrator with at least three other arbitrators over the preceding three years to qualify for listing in ART. This policy has since been changed to encourage diversity among the listed arbitrators: Email from Alexandra Palma Long (GAR Data Coordinator) to author (9 August 2019).

some extent, by newer initiatives such as ArbitralWomen's female-only arbitrator database.[7]

There are also fewer women at the top end of the legal profession generally, and in arbitration specifically, from where arbitrators are commonly draw. For example, the average female partnership of the arbitration groups of the GAR 30 top arbitration law firms worldwide is approximately 17.6%.[8] This is reflective of industry-wide figures in the US that have seen only marginal improvement over the last decade: in 2006 15% of equity partners in the top 200 US law firms (by revenue) were women, and in 2018 that had risen to only 20%.[9] Similarly, there are fewer women in the ranks of judges and barristers from which arbitrators may be drawn.[10] In England and Wales, for example, only 29% of court judges in 2018 were women.[11] Notwithstanding that approximately 50% of barristers called to the English bar each year are women (and this equity at call has been maintained since 2000), in 2018 only 37.1% of practising barristers and 16.2% of QCs were women.[12] A 2015 UK Bar Council report on gender diversity concluded that, due to a lower propensity of women to convert their call into practice and a higher attrition rate, 'a 50:50 gender balance among all practising barristers is unlikely ever to be achieved' and there will be no gender balance among QCs in the foreseeable future.[13] These statistics are only slightly better in the US where 34.6% of Federal and State judgeships are held by women and 38% of practising lawyers are women.[14] This is despite

[7] 'Find Practitioners: Directory of ArbitralWomen Dispute Resolution Practitioners' (*Arbitral Women*, 2019) <www.arbitralwomen.org/Find-Practitioners> accessed 29 February 2020. As of 1 August 2019, it listed 198 profiles. This is a large increase from January 2018 when only 50 arbitrator profiles were listed.

[8] This figure is based on the author's review of the female partners in arbitration listed on the websites of the 30 law firms named in GAR 30 (see GAR, 'The GAR 30 Revealed' (n 2)).

[9] Destiny Peery, 'Report of the 2018 NAWL Survey on Retention and Promotion of Women in Law Firms' (*National Association of Women Lawyers*, 2018) 7 <www.nawl.org/p/cm/ld/fid=1163> accessed 29 February 2020.

[10] In some jurisdictions, such as the UK, sitting judges may also be appointed as arbitrators. Even in those jurisdictions where it is not permitted, judicial diversity statistics are relevant in appreciating the percentage of women who may become eligible for appointment after leaving the bench.

[11] 'Judicial Diversity Statistics 2018' (prepared by the Lord Chief Justice of England and Wales and the Senior President of Tribunals, 12 July 2018) <www.judiciary.uk/wp-content/uploads/2018/07/judicial-diversity-statistics-2018-1.pdf> accessed 29 February 2020.

[12] 'Practising Barrister Statistics' (*Bar Council*, 2019) <www.barstandardsboard.org.uk/media-centre/research-and-statistics/statistics/practising-barrister-statistics/> accessed 29 February 2020; 'Queen's Council Statistics' (*Bar Council*, 2019) <www.barstandardsboard.org.uk/media-centre/research-and-statistics/statistics/queen's-counsel-statistics/> accessed 29 February 2020; 'Momentum Measures: Creating a diverse profession. Summary of Findings' (*Bar Council*, 20 July 2015) 1 <https://www.barcouncil.org.uk/resource/momentum-measures.html> accessed 29 February 2020.

[13] Bar Council, 'Momentum Measures' (n 12) 1–2.

[14] 'A Current Glance at Women in the Law' (*American Bar Association*, April 2019) 2, 5 <www.americanbar.org/content/dam/aba/administrative/women/current_glance_2019.pdf> accessed 29 February 2020. These percentages increased from 27.1% and 35% respectively in 2018: 'A Current Glance at Women in the Law' (*American Bar Association*, January 2018) 2, 5 <www.americanbar.org/content/dam/aba/administrative/women/a-current-glance-at-women-in-the-law-jan-2018.pdf> accessed 29 February 2020.

that, for over a decade, approximately 50% of law students and entry-level lawyers in the US have been women.[15] This trend of gender parity at entry, but comparatively fewer women in senior and leadership positions has been referred to by some commentators as the 'pipeline leak'.[16] This pipeline leak to some extent explains, but also compounds, the first barrier that potential female candidates face: that there are fewer qualified women than men in the pool from which arbitrators are drawn and they are harder to find—both challenges that are not aided by entry-requirements and set-up of commonly-used databases.

Second, the practice of seeking first-hand views on arbitrator candidates from counsels' networks disproportionately prejudices female candidates. Law firms will rarely recommend to a client a candidate about whom they have not received first-hand views. In a 2016 study of arbitration practitioners, 87% regarded informal feedback from other practitioners who know the candidate as either 'very important' or 'important', and more than 90% regarded expertise and efficiency—things often not evident on CVs—as being the most important qualities when selecting an arbitrator.[17] Law firms are risk averse: they and their clients want good arbitrators. One reliable indicator of who would make a good arbitrator is someone who has been a good arbitrator in the past, judged by the subjective assessments of other practitioners. Seeking such views reduces the *actual pool* of candidates who might be suitable for appointment to the *effective pool*: the pool from which appointments are effectively made. To take a simple example, if the actual pool of qualified candidates for appointment as arbitrator is 100 people, but the personal networks of the appointing counsel can only provide first-hand knowledge on ten candidates, and the professional connections of the appointing counsel's firm can only provide first-hand knowledge on a further 15 candidates, then the actual pool of candidates has shrunk from 100 to 25 candidates—a mere 25%. This problem becomes even more pronounced when one considers that it is common practice for only a few names to be floated on personal and professional networks for feedback, rather than longer lists that might solicit more information for the appointing lawyers to work with. The reasons this occurs are unclear, however it may have to do with the assumption that busy lawyers are more likely to respond if they are being asked to comment on one or a few names, rather than a longer list of candidates

[15] Peery (n 9), 2.

[16] Lucy Greenwood and C Mark Baker, 'Is the Balance Getting Better? An Update on the Issue of Gender Diversity in International Arbitration' (2015) 31 Arbitration International 413, 418–19; Lucy Greenwood, 'Women in Disputes: What Can Be Done About the Leaky Pipeline?' (*CDR Magazine*, 6 November 2017) <www.cdr-news.com/categories/disputes/7721-women-in-disputes-what-can-be-done-about-the-leaky-pipeline> accessed 29 February 2020; Lucy Greenwood, 'Moving Beyond Diversity Towards Inclusion in International Arbitration' (2019) Stockholm Arbitration Yearbook 93, 97.

[17] 'International Arbitration Survey: Diversity on Arbitral Tribunals. Are We Getting There?' (Berwin Leighton Paisner, 10 January 2017) 8 <www-staging.bclplaw.com/images/content/1/4/v2/147241/BLP-International-Arbitration-Survey-2016.pdf> accessed 29 February 2020 (BLP, 'Are We Getting There').

many of whom they might be able to provide feedback on. This process results in what Catherine Rogers has called an 'information bottleneck':[18] the effective pool extends only so far as the appointing counsel and law firm's connections and, as a result, it limits the ability of newer and more diverse arbitrators to gain experience and a reputation. This perpetuates a system where those with more experience and who are better known among law firms' networks—ie a pool in which women have been and continue to be persistently and significantly underrepresented—are appointed more often.[19]

Some firms are so risk averse that they have a policy of not proposing any person, whether male or female, who has not previously served as an arbitrator as a candidate to clients. This kind of approach also disproportionately prejudices female candidates who are in a minority in the male-dominated pool or have not yet broken into it. Even where law firms do not take such a conservative approach, women are not being appointed as first-time arbitrators as often as their male counterparts. From July 2015 to June 2016, the International Centre for the Settlement of Investment Disputes (ICSID) reported that 23% of first-time appointees in ICSID-administered cases were women.[20] In the following year, that figure dropped to 14% despite that year having recorded the second highest number of overall appointments made in ICSID's history.[21] This climbed to 31.1% in the period between July 2017 and June 2018.[22] Interestingly, the percentage of female first-time appointees has been equal to or higher than the total percentage of female arbitrators in the last three years of ICSID reporting, but in both cases the figures fall far short of those of their male counterparts. The statistics do not reveal whether those first-time female appointees were appointed by ICSID, the parties, or co-arbitrators. The lack of gender parity in first-time appointments is in part due to the fact that there are fewer women in the effective pool, but it is also likely to be due to the third layer of prejudice female candidates face: implicit bias against women, which is likely to be heightened when considering as a candidate a woman with little or no prior experience sitting as an arbitrator.

[18] Catherine Rogers, 'The Key to Unlocking the Arbitrator Diversity Paradox? Arbitrator Intelligence' (*Kluwer Arbitration Blog*, 27 December 2017) <http://arbitrationblog.kluwerarbitration.com/2017/12/27/on-arbitrators/> accessed 29 February 2020.

[19] This is also the conclusion of Puig, who conducted a social capital network analysis and found that 'prestigious arbitrators increase in prestige and peripheral arbitrators remain peripheral as a result of preferential attachment—a process where resources are distributed among a number of individuals according to their existing share of the same resources': Sergio Puig, 'Social Capital in the Arbitration Market' (2014) 25 EJIL 387, 391.

[20] ICSID, '2016 Annual Report' (6 September 2016) 7 and 35 <https://icsid.worldbank.org/en/Documents/resources/ICSID_AR16_English_CRA_bl2_spreads.pdf> accessed 29 February 2020 (13% of all appointments were first-time appointments, 23% of which were women).

[21] ICSID, '2017 Annual Report' (6 September 2017) 35 <https://icsid.worldbank.org/en/Documents/icsiddocs/ICSID%20AR%20EN.pdf> (13% of all appointments were first-time appointments, 14% of which were women).

[22] ICSID, '2018 Annual Report' (6 September 2018) 49 <https://icsid.worldbank.org/en/Documents/resources/2018ICSIDAnnualReport.ENG.pdf> accessed 29 February 2020.

Implicit bias[23] is developed through gender stereotyping, the effects of which are evident from a young age. It is pervasive, affects men and women equally, and is often not aligned with declared beliefs. It is unconscious, automatic, and people are likely to resist acknowledging its existence.[24] At least one prominent commentator is of the view that implicit bias is 'one of the single most influential factors for the disparity between male and female representation on international arbitration tribunals'.[25] In the appointment process, implicit bias manifests itself as a perception that equally qualified women are not equally as suitable for appointment as their male counterparts; in other (Orwellian) terms, some are more equal than others. Such implicit bias can reveal itself through lawyers feeling like they require more evidence of a female candidate's experience and positive attributes before putting her on a candidate list than they would a man in the same position, particularly in respect of complex arbitrations. Women are therefore forced to work harder and prove themselves more than their male counterparts.[26] This also goes some way to explaining why the newer female arbitrators that are securing more and more repeat appointments in recent years are exceptional, an observation which is not as clearly discernible regarding their male counterparts.[27]

Anecdotal evidence suggests that implicit bias can also come through in gendered questions used by some clients in asking whether female candidates are 'good enough', 'up to the task' or 'too young' to sit as arbitrator—questions typically not asked about male candidates.[28] The suggestion that women equally as qualified as their male counterparts are not equally as suited to the task of sitting as an arbitrator is without any empirical foundation. The underlying generic assumption has been disproved by multiple blind studies in various contexts[29] and through rigorous meritorious appointment processes for other courts. One example is the United Nations Dispute Tribunal (UNDT) and its appellate bench, the United

[23] Implicit bias (or implicit social cognition), as explained by the Kirwan Institute's 2017 study on implicit bias, refers to 'the attitudes or stereotypes that affect our understanding, actions, and decisions in an unconscious manner': Cheryl Staats and others, 'State of the Science: Implicit Bias Review' (Kirwan Institute for the Study of Race and Ethnicity, Ohio State University, 2017) 10 <http://kirwaninstitute.osu.edu/wp-content/uploads/2017/11/2017-SOTS-final-draft-02.pdf> accessed 29 February 2020. Although this annual study focuses on implicit ethnic and race-related bias, as is clear from the report the science behind implicit bias generally is equally applicable to implicit gender bias.

[24] ibid 10.

[25] Lucy Greenwood, 'Could "Blind" Appointments Open Our Eyes to the Lack of Diversity in International Arbitration?' (2015) 12(4) Transnational Dispute Management <www.transnational-dispute-management.com/article.asp?key=2248> accessed 29 February 2020.

[26] See also Deborah Rothman, 'Gender Diversity in Arbitrator Selection' (Spring 2012) Dispute Resolution Magazine 21, 25.

[27] Remarks by Daniel Behn at the PluriCourts Workshop 'Identity on the International Bench', The Hague, 11–12 January 2018 in relation to joint research published in 'Glass Ceilings and Arbitral Dealings: Explaining the Gender Gap in Investment Arbitration' in this edited volume.

[28] Discussions conducted by the author with arbitration practitioners in Paris and London. See also 'Arbitration Future Leaders 2018: Women in Law Roundtable Discussion' (*Who's Who Legal*, 12 January 2018) <https://whoswholegal.com/women-in-law/arbitration-future-leaders-2018-women-in-law-roundtable-discussion> accessed 29 February 2020.

[29] See eg Greenwood, 'Could "Blind" Appointments Open Our Eyes' (n 25).

Nations Appeals Tribunal (UNAT), the appointment process for which encourages applications from female candidates and involves blind grading of written assessment. Both the UNDT and UNAT have had, from their inception, benches with equal gender representation or a majority of female judges.[30] These blind studies and tribunal experiences go some way to showing that with true equality of opportunity, gender parity is achievable. In this respect, a gender imbalance can be seen as a symptom of a problem; a manifestation of a system that does not (yet) truly provide equal opportunities for qualified women.

As a result of these barriers, a woman who might make an excellent arbitrator (including one who has not before sat as an arbitrator) may find (a) it more difficult to be identified within the actual pool and considered for inclusion on a candidate list in the first place; (b) that she is less likely to be included in the effective pool and therefore less likely to remain on the candidate list and be proposed to clients even if she is identified and added to an initial candidate list; and (c) that she is less likely to be chosen for appointment even if she were proposed to clients. How, then, can each of these layers of prejudice be addressed and what is the arbitration community already doing in this regard?

2.3 Addressing the Different Layers of Prejudice

This section explores ways to address the three layers of prejudice that have been identified. It focuses on measures that could increase the number of qualified female candidates in both the actual pool (2.3.1) and the effective pool (2.3.2), and ways to address the implicit bias that pervades all stages of the appointment process (2.3.3).

2.3.1 How should the actual pool be broadened and how can women in the pool be more easily identified?

2.3.1.1 Putting gender on the agenda (and on the minds of those identifying and selecting arbitrators)

Broadening the actual pool of arbitrator candidates is about creating equal opportunities for women. The international arbitration community has recognized the need to promote qualified women by creating networks for support, mentoring, training, and showcasing of women working in arbitration.[31] Initiatives such as

[30] Memooda Ebrahim-Carstens, 'Gender Representation on the Tribunals of the UN Internal Justice System: A Response to Nienke Grossman' (2016) 110 AJIL Unbound 98.

[31] See also '2015 International Arbitration Survey: Improvements and Innovations in International Arbitration' (Queen Mary University of London and White & Case, 2015) 10 <www.whitecase.com/sites/whitecase/files/files/download/publications/qmul-international-arbitration-survey-2015_0.pdf> accessed 29 February 2020 noting that participants expressed an interest in 'broadening the pool of arbitrators in number as well as in ethnic and gender diversity'.

ArbitralWomen,[32] a network of women in arbitration established formally in 2000, have made important progress in connecting and raising the profile of female practitioners and arbitrators.[33] Similarly, the Equal Representation in Arbitration Pledge (the Pledge), launched in 2016, aims to improve the profile and representation of women in arbitration by asking individual signatories, law firms and other organizations to pledge to take steps to ensure equal opportunities and representation for women in arbitration. One of the key steps to achieving this is to ensure that, wherever possible, 'lists of potential arbitrators or tribunal chairs provided to or considered by the parties, counsel, in-house counsel or otherwise include a fair representation of female candidates'.[34] The Pledge is often explicitly referred to by arbitral institutions in connection with the publication of gender statistics and promotion of initiatives focusing on gender diversity,[35] and is generally considered to give practitioners the confidence to raise the need for greater representation of women when the opportunity arises and to have led to an increase in female appointments.[36] Individual lawyers and law firms should sign the Pledge. Law firms should also adopt (or amend) and publicize policies on arbitrator selection and appointment processes that feature as prominent requirements respecting the

[32] See 'About AW' (*ArbitralWomen*, 2019) <www.arbitralwomen.org/aw-outline/> accessed 29 February 2020.

[33] One such initiative is the 'Women Pioneers in Dispute Resolution' publication, the second edition of which was published in September 2018 and features profiles of 78 women from nearly 50 countries: 'Women Pioneers in Dispute Resolution' (6 December 2018) <www.arbitralwomen.org/women-pioneers-in-dispute-resolution-2/> accessed 29 February 2020.

[34] 'Equal Representation in Arbitration Pledge' <http://www.arbitrationpledge.com/> accessed 29 February 2020. It was awarded 'Best Development' at the GAR 2017 Awards: Tom Jones, 'A belle note in Milan' (*GAR*, 30 March 2017) <http://globalarbitrationreview.com/article/1138773/a-bella-notte-in-milan> accessed 29 February 2020.

[35] See eg SCC 'SCC Policy: Appointment of Arbitrators' (8 September 2017) 3 <https://sccinstitute.com/media/220131/scc-policy-appointment-of-arbitrators-2017.pdf> accessed 29 February 2020; ICDR, 'Diversity and Inclusion' (2019) <www.icdr.org/diversity> accessed 29 February 2020; 'Diversity in arbitration' (*ICC*, 2019) <https://iccwbo.org/global-issues-trends/diversity/diversity-in-arbitration/> accessed 29 February 2020; Mirèze Philippe, 'How Has Female Participation at ICC Evolved? ICC Arbitrators, Court Members and Court's Secretariat' (ICC Dispute Resolution Bulletin, Issue 2017/3) <https://assets.website-files.com/58a4313f62641fda6d995826/5aa6947e739e6a0001c2e499_ICC%20Bulletin%20%20-%20How%20has%20female%20representation%20at%20the%20ICC%20evolved%20.pdf> accessed 29 February 2020; DIS (*LinkedIn*, 2017) <www.linkedin.com/feed/update/urn:li:activity:6278599362528583680> accessed 29 February 2020. See also ICC, 'Dispute Resolution Bulletin' (Issue 1, 2019) <http://store.iccwbo.org/icc-court-bulletin-individual-issues> accessed 29 February 2020, referring to the May 2018 launch of the ICC's own 'Gender Balance Pledge' which commits to increasing gender diversity at conferences and across the ICC's global network.

[36] See eg Who's Who Legal, 'Arbitration Future Leaders 2018: Women in Law Roundtable Discussion' (n 28); 'Do more on diversity, says ArbitralWomen President' (*GAR*, 23 October 2017) <https://globalarbitrationreview.com/article/1149265/do-more-on-diversity-says-arbitralwomen-president> accessed 29 February 2020 referring to the Pledge accelerating the adoption of law firm policies requiring female candidates on arbitrator lists; 'Reed's diversity equation' (*GAR*, 6 April 2018) <https://globalarbitrationreview.com/article/1167732/reed%E2%80%99s-diversity-equation> accessed 29 February 2020: 'the Pledge is working and habits are being broken'. See also Greenwood, commenting on the success of the Pledge as 'phenomenal': Greenwood, 'Women in Disputes' (n 16). See also Figure 6.1 showing an increase in the percentage of women appointed in recent years across the surveyed institutions.

Pledge and reviewing shortlists of candidates for gender diversity. As of 13 August 2019, the Pledge had 3,671 signatories.[37] Another recent initiative is the Alliance for Equality in Dispute Resolution, launched in 2018 with the aim of striving 'for equality of opportunity regardless of sex, location, nationality, ethnicity or age' through training, mentoring, and access to online discussion fora.[38]

Arbitral institutions are also taking a leading role. They are making conscious efforts to promote women by identifying it as a goal in their annual reports and other policy documents,[39] seeking to make women more visible at institution-supported conferences and in institution-affiliated publications,[40] actively searching for and including women in arbitrators lists,[41] and encouraging parties and States to consider diversity when making arbitrator appointments or designations to arbitrator lists.[42] There is also a welcome trend towards institutions such as ICSID[43] and, more recently, the International Chamber of Commerce (ICC)[44] and Vienna International Arbitral Centre (VIAC)[45] publishing the names of their arbitrator lists,[46] which can facilitate the identification of female candidates for future appointments. Arbitral institutions also appoint more women than parties or co-arbitrators do and, for the most part, do so at slow but steadily increasing rates. For example, as Table 6.1 (below) shows, 43% of the total appointments made by the London Court of International Arbitration (LCIA) in 2018 were women, compared to 23% of those made by the co-arbitrators and only 6% of appointments made by the parties. Similarly, 43.8% of the appointments made by VIAC in 2018 were women, compared to 3.4% of those made by the parties. In a welcome contrast, 30% of appointments made by ICSID in 2018 were women, compared to 35% by Respondents, but those made jointly

[37] 'Equal Representation in Arbitration Pledge' (n 34).

[38] 'Alli29 February 2020 5 August 2019.

[39] See eg VIAC, 'Annual Report 2018' (March 2019) 14 <www.viac.eu/images/documents/Jahresbericht_2018.pdf> accessed 29 February 2020; SCC 'SCC Policy: Appointment of Arbitrators' (n 35) 3; ICSID, '2018 Annual Report' (n 22) 49; ICDR, 'Diversity and Inclusion' (n 35); ICC, 'Diversity in arbitration' (n 35).

[40] See eg ICSID, '2018 Annual Report' (n 22) 49; 'Valuing Women in International Adjudication' (ICSID Newsletter, Issue 2, 2017) <https//icsid.worldbank.org/en/Pages/resources/ICSID%20NewsLetter/2017-Issue2/Valuing-Women-in-International-Adjudication.aspx> accessed 29 February 2020.

[41] See eg ICSID, '2018 Annual Report' (n 22) 49; ICDR, 'Diversity and Inclusion' (n 35).

[42] See eg ICSID, '2018 Annual Report' (n 22) 49; ICSID, 'Valuing Women in International Adjudication' (n 40).

[43] ICSID, 'Arbitrators, Conciliators and Ad Hoc Committee Members' (n 2).

[44] 'ICC Arbitral Tribunals' (*ICC*, 2019) https://iccwbo.org/dispute-resolution-services/arbitration/icc-arbitral-tribunals/ accessed 29 February 2020 (published since June 2016).

[45] See 'VIAC Arbitral Tribunals' (VIAC, 24 June 2019) <www.viac.eu/en/arbitration/viac-arbitral-tribunals> accessed 29 February 2020 (published since 2017).

[46] In contrast, other institutions such as the American Arbitration Association (AAA)'s ICDR operate closed lists and provide an 'appointment service' whereby, upon receipt of information about the dispute and a fee, the ICDR will provide a list of potential arbitrators appropriate for the case. As of August 2019, it costs US$1,500 for a list of ten arbitrators. See 'ICDR Appointment Services: Providing Access to the ICDR's Roster of Arbitrators' (2019) <www.icdr.org/sites/default/files/document_repository/ICDR_Arbitrator_Selection_Services.pdf> accessed 29 February 2020.

Table 6.1 Recent institutional statistics on gender diversity in arbitrator appointments

Arbitral Institution	Percentage of female arbitrators appointed	Percentage of total female arbitrators appointed by the institution	Percentage of total female arbitrators appointed by the parties	Percentage of total female arbitrators appointed by co-arbitrators	Percentage of appointments by the institution that were women	Percentage of appointments by the parties that were women	Percentage of appointments by the co-arbitrators that were women
DIS							
2016	13.2%	–	–	–	29.4%	9.3%	16.9%
2017	–	–	–	–	–	–	–
2018	–	–	–	–	–	–	–
HKIAC							
2015	9.7%	–	–	–	–	–	–
2016	13.1%	–	–	–	–	–	–
2017	15.8%	–	–	–	16.5%	15%	15.4%
2018	14.2%	–	–	–	17.6%	10.1%	8.3%
ICC							7.6%
2010	7.2%	50%	35.4%	14.6%	13.3%	4.3%	8.2%
2011	7.7%	40.8%	43.7%	15.5%	11.3%	5.8%	9.7%
2012	7.8%	44.1%	39.2%	16.7%	12.4%	5.2%	4.6%
2013	9%	55.5%	37%	7.6%	16.7%	5.9%	9.6%
2014	9.7%	41.9%	41.9%	16.3%	16.6%	6.9%	6.1%
2015	10.4%	53.7%	39%	7.4%	19.4%	6.9%	12.6%
2016	14.8%	46.4%	41.1%	12.4%	23.6%	10.8%	–
2017	16.7%	45.4%	41%	13.6%	–	–	–
2018	18.4%	41%	42%	17%	–	–	
ICDR							
2016	18%	–	–	–	16.5%	–	–
2017	22%	–	–	–	–	–	–
2018	–	–	–	–	–	–	–

ICSID							
2011–2012	9.6%	–	–	–	13%	–	–
2012–2013	6.2%	–	–	–	–	–	–
2013–2014	11%	–	–	–	8%	–	–
2014–2015	16%	–	–	–	9%	–	–
2015–2016	10%	–	–	–	–	–	–
2016–2017	14%	43.5%	56.5%	0%	21%	–	0%
2017–2018	23.6%	–	–	–	30%	Respondents: 35% Claimants: 6% Jointly by the parties: 24%	8%
LCIA							
2012	9.6%	78.8%	21.2%	0%	–	–	–
2013	11.5%	74.4%	25.6%	0%	19.8%	6.9%	0%
2014	11.7%	65.3%	18.4%	16.3%	19.8%	4.4%	14.5%
2015	15.8%	77.5%	19.7%	2.8%	28.2%	6.9%	4%
2016	20.6%	78.4%	8.8%	12.7%	40.6%	4.1%	16.3%
2017	23.5%	57%	17%	26%	34%	17%	17%
2018	22.7%	71%	13%	17%	43%	6%	23%
SCC							
2016	16%	–	–	–	22.5%	11%	20%
2017	18%	–	–	–	37%	8%	0%
2018	27%	–	–	–	29%	24%	55.6%
SIAC							
2015	–	–	–	–	Nearly 25%	–	–
2016	12.9%	86.4%	11.4%	2.3%	22.8%	3.4%	3.4%
2017	–	–	–	–	29.7%	–	–
2018	–	–	–	–	34.3%	–	–
VIAC							
2015	14.3%	50%	50%	0%	80%	7.8%	0%
2016	17.1%	41.7%	58.3%	0%	62.5%	11.3%	0%
2017	16.7%	42.9%	57.1%	0%	30%	12.5%	0%
2018	24.6%	93.3%	6.7%	0%	43.8%	3.4%	0%

(continued)

Table 6.1 Continued

[a] DIS, '[a]s a signatory to the Equal Representation in Arbitration Pledge', published its '2016 statistics on gender balance' on its Linkedin page, but did not include those statistics in its official statistics for 2016 published on its website. See, DIS, *LinkedIn* (n 35). DIS also did not include gender in its official 2017 or 2018 statistics.

[b] HKIAC, 'Statistics' (2019) <www.hkiac.org/about-us/statistics> accessed 29 February 2020; HKIAC, 'Annual Report: 2017 Reflections' (31 December 2017) 9, 'Annual Report: 2016 Reflections' (31 December 2016) 10, and 'Annual Report: 2015 Reflections' (31 December 2015) 11 all available from <www.hkiac.org/about-us/annual-report> accessed 29 February 2020. Note that the 'Statistics' webpage gives the figure of 11.5% for the total percentage of female arbitrators appointed in 2016, but both it and the 2016 Annual Report states that 137 appointments and confirmations were made in 2016, of which 18 were women, which equates to 13.1%.

[c] The ICC's annual statistics are published in its Dispute Resolution Bulletins: see, ICC, 'Dispute Resolution Bulletin' (Issue 1, 2019), (Issue 2, 2018), (Issue 2, 2017), (Issue 1, 2016) all available from <http://store.iccwbo.org/icc-court-bulletin-individual-issues> accessed 29 February 2020. See also Philippe (n 35); 'ICC Court sees marked progress on gender diversity' (ICC, 31 May 2017) <https://iccwbo.org/media-wall/news-speeches/icc-court-sees-marked-progress-gender-diversity/> accessed 29 February 2020. All institutional appointment figures include appointments by other appointing authorities.

[d] AAA, '2017 Annual Report & Financial Statements' (22 May 2018) 20 <www.adr.org/annual-reports> accessed 29 February 2020; ICDR, 'The ICDR International Arbitration Reporter' (Volume 5, Fall 2016) 11 <www.icdr.org/sites/default/files/document_repository/ICDR_International_Arbitration_Reporter-Vol.5.pdf> accessed 29 February 2020. No other AAA Annual Reports provide ICDR statistics on arbitrator's gender and no volumes of the ICDR International Arbitration Reporter have been published for 2017, 2018, or 2019. Unlike the statistics from other institutions, the figures of 18% and 22% were *of cases*, not the total appointments made in 2016 and 2017, respectively.

[e] Figures includes arbitrators, ad hoc Committee members and conciliators. See, ICISD, '2018 Annual Report' (n 22) 32 and 48–49, '2017 Annual Report' (n 21) 35, '2016 Annual Report' (n 20) 7 and 35, '2015 Annual Report' (6 September 2015) 27, '2014 Annual Report' (6 September 2014) 27, '2013 Annual Report' (6 September 2013) 26, and '2012 Annual Report' (6 September 2012) 30–31 all available at <https://icsid.worldbank.org/en/Pages/resources/ICSID-Annual-Report.aspx> accessed 29 February 2020. The statistics measure from 1 July to 30 June.

[f] The ICSID Annual Report rounds down to 6%: ICSID, '2013 Annual Report' (n e) 26 (referring to a total of 145 appointments, of which 9 were women).

[g] The ICSID Annual Report rounds up to 24%: ICSID, '2018 Annual Report' (n 22) 48–49 (referring to a total of 263 appointments, of which 62 were women).

[h] Appointments by Respondents account for 43.5% and appointments jointly by the parties account for 13%. The Claimants appointed no women in 2016–17.

[i] LCIA, '2018 Annual Casework Report' 14, 'Facts and Figures: 2017 Casework Report' 15, 'Facts and Figures. 2016: A Robust Caseload' 13, 'Registrar's Report 2015' 4, 'Registrar's Report 2014' 4, 'Registrar's Report 2013' 4, and 'Registrar's Report 2012' 4 all available from <www.lcia.org/LCIA/reports.aspx> accessed 29 February 2020.

[j] SCC, 'Statistics' (2018, 2017, 2016) <www.sccinstitute.com/statistics/> accessed 29 February 2020.

[k] SIAC, 'Annual Report 2018' 19, 'Annual Report 2017' 17, and 'Annual Report 2016' 16 all available at <www.siac.org.sg/2013-09-18-01-57-20/2013-09-22-00-27-02/annual-report> accessed 29 February 2020.

[l] VIAC, 'VIAC Statistics 2018', 'VIAC Statistics 2017', 'VIAC Statistics 2016', and 'VIAC Statistics 2015' all available at <www.viac.eu/en/service/statistics> accessed 29 February 2020.

by the parties (24%), co-arbitrators (8%), and Claimants (6%) remained lower.[47] Institutional appointments, however, account for a small proportion of total appointments (for example, 28% of ICC cases, 35% of ICISID cases, and 37% of LCIA cases) and, as the statistics show, the same kind of figures are not being seen with party or co-arbitrator appointments.

Even the compilation and publication of gender indicators in the annual statistics of arbitral institutions in the last few years[48] has served as a welcome catalyst for discussion and further inquiry on the issue of gender diversity in arbitration. Statistics have aided the international arbitration community's appreciation of the scale of the problem, facilitated an understanding of how it manifests in selection and appointment processes, and provided the tools with which to measure change. There is, however, still room for improvement in what statistics institutions report. ICSID appears to be the only institution that reports gender statistics for first-time appointments. The ICC and VIAC are the only institutions that report gender breakdown of arbitrator positions (president or chair/sole arbitrator/co-arbitrator). Some institutions report *either* the percentage of total appointments by each actor (institution/parties/co-arbitrator) that are women (ICSID,[49] the Hong Kong International Arbitration Centre (HKIAC), Stockholm Chamber of Commerce (SCC), and Singapore International Arbitration Centre (SIAC)) *or* what proportion of the total female appointments each actor is responsible for (ICC), but few regularly report *both* sets of statistics (LCIA and VIAC).[50] It is only with both sets of figures that the true situation can be grasped. By way of example, 43.8% of VIAC's institutional appointments in 2018 were of women, but this accounts for 93.3% of the total female appointments.[51] Concerningly, at least one institution reports fewer gender statistics in recent years as compared to earlier years (SIAC)[52] and others do not include gender in their official statistics at all (German

[47] The higher proportion of female appointments by Respondents could be driven by a few well-known female arbitrators and may not be reflective of a systematic gender preference. See a similar comment on ICSID respondents' gender preferences across a much larger timeframe in Michael Waibel and Yanui Yu, 'Are Arbitrators Political? Evidence from International Investment Arbitration' (2017) 21 <www-bcf.usc.edu/~yanhuiwu/arbitrator.pdf> accessed 29 February 2020.

[48] DIS, ICDR, and the SCC first published gender statistics in 2017 (for the preceding year). HKIAC, the ICC, SIAC, and VIAC first published overall gender statistics in 2016 (for the preceding year, but Mirèze Philippe began publishing statistics about female arbitrators in ICC proceedings from 2013 and a 2017 edition of the ICC Bulletin published comparative statistics dating back to 2010: see Philippe (n 35)). The LCIA and ICSID have published gender statistics since 2013 (for the preceding year).

[49] In 2017 (but not 2018) ICSID did report statistics on which actors were responsible for what proportion of the total female appointments made.

[50] Although the ICC official statistics do not publish both sets of figures, the comparative statistics published by Mirèze Philippe in 2017 do give both sets of figures for 2010–16: Philippe (n 35).

[51] See Table 6.1 below.

[52] In 2016 (but not subsequent years), SIAC reported the percentage of total appointments that were women and complete breakdowns of both the total appointments by each actor that were women and which actors were responsible for what proportion of the total female appointments. In 2017 and 2018, SIAC only reported the percentage of institutional appointments that were women.

Arbitration Institute (DIS),[53] Dubai International Arbitration Centre (DIAC),[54] International Centre for Dispute Resolution (ICDR)[55]).

Initiatives such as those surveyed above that raise awareness about a lack of gender diversity in arbitration and promote equal opportunities for women have put the issue on the agenda of key players in the arbitration community. They have played a part in what Lucy Greenwood and C Mark Baker have observed as the international arbitration community becoming 'less comfortable' with women only representing a minority of the arbitration population, and an increased willingness to address the issue.[56] This may explain the gradual increase in the percentage of female arbitrator appointments in recent years across various institutions (see Figure 6.1 below). This heightened visibility and openness for taking action have served as catalysts for the developments canvassed below that are specifically targeted at increasing the representation of women in the actual pool of arbitrator candidates.

2.3.1.2 Ensuring qualified women in the actual pool are easily identified

In addition to having gender diversity on the agenda, from a practical perspective it is important for law firms recommending potential arbitrators to clients to be able to identify suitable female candidates. As noted, there are already fewer women in the pool. Consciously searching for and adding female candidates to arbitrator lists could be facilitated by the introduction of gender filters on the main databases and institution-administered arbitrator lists, and by the creation of detailed and up-to-date gender-specific research tools. ArbitralWomen's database of women arbitrators is a useful start. Firms might also consider compiling their own internal databases of female candidates on whom they have first-hand views and/or have proposed before as potential candidates to clients.

Administrators of commonly-used arbitration databases should take into account in setting the eligibility guidelines for accepting and publishing profiles the need to promote first-time appointments of female arbitrators as a means of broadening the actual pool of arbitrator candidates. In this regard, GAR should be commended for changing the policy applicable to its Arbitrator Research Tool to permit the listing of candidates seeking their first appointment in order to encourage

53 It appears, however, that DIS does keep gender statistics, because they have in the past been provided to Lucy Greenwood for statistical studies: 'The Pledge turns two: how are the numbers looking' (*GAR*, 2 July 2018) <https://globalarbitrationreview.com/article/1171218/the-pledge-turns-two-how-are-the-numbers-looking> accessed 29 February 2020.

54 Basic DIAC statistics are published in the annual reports of the Dubai Chamber of Commerce and Industry available at <www.dubaichamber.com/resources/annual-reports> accessed 29 February 2020.

55 In 2016, ICDR reported the percentage of institutional appointments that were women in its 'International Arbitration Reporter' publication, but no similar statistical reports for 2017 or 2018 are available. The AAA's annual reports publish basic statistics across its different divisions, including the ICDR, but they do not include ICDR-specific gender statistics. Similar to DIS, the ICDR must keep gender statistics because they have in the past been provided to Lucy Greenwood for statistical studies: Greenwood, 'The Pledge turns two' (n 53).

56 Greenwood and Baker (n 16) 413–14.

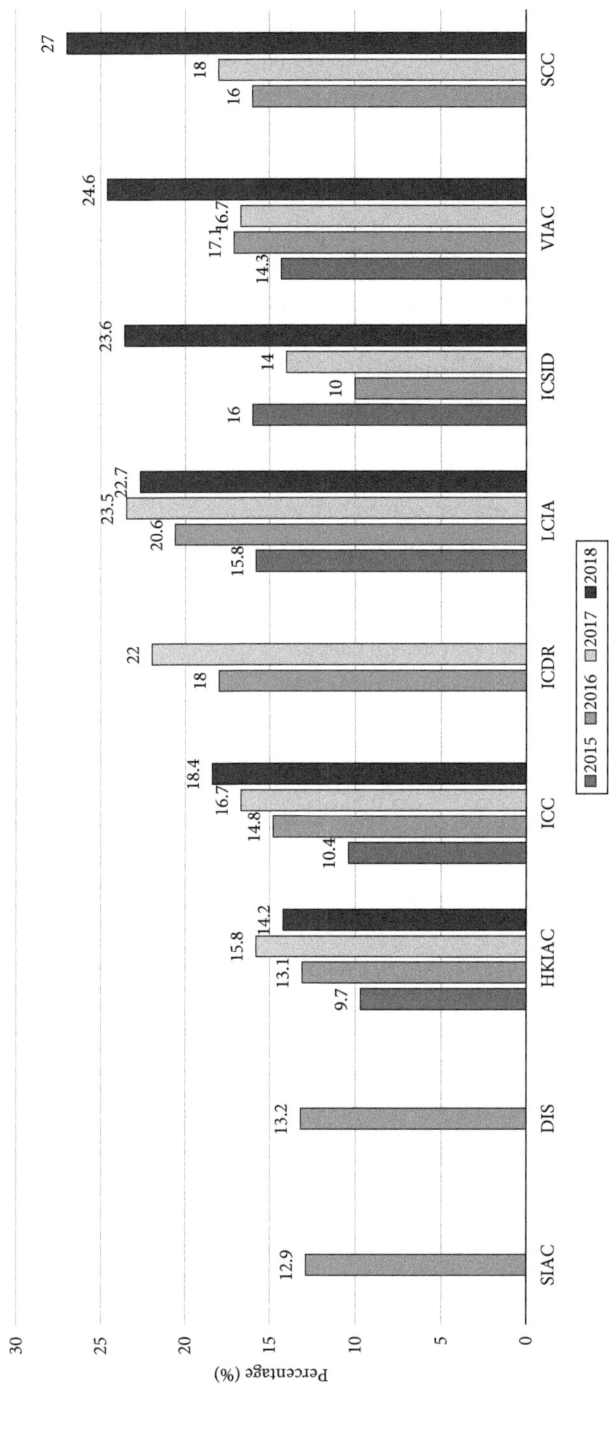

Figure 6.1 Percentage of female arbitrators appointed 2015–18 in cases administered by the identified institutions.

diversity.[57] Databases might even consider featuring experienced female counsel who would be suitable for first-time appointment as 'women to watch' as potential arbitrators in the future. The future leaders lists developed by Who's Who Legal could be a springboard for this kind of initiative, which for 2018 had a satisfying majority of women in each of the most highly regarded 'Europe-Partners' and 'Europe-Non-Partners' lists and 50% women in the 'Americas-Partners' list.[58] In an appointment culture where both the lawyers and the client have traditionally been risk averse, initiatives of this kind provide external and public support for the inclusion on a prospective arbitrator list of a candidate for first-time appointment. These kinds of initiatives may encourage women experienced in arbitration and suitable for first-time appointment to submit their profiles to databases, and in doing so go some way to addressing what has been identified as 'psycho-social barriers' that, in general, operate to prevent women from being as confident and self-promoting as their male counterparts.[59]

In addition to database listings, the Equal Representation in Arbitration Pledge offers a service to assist any person in searching for female arbitrators.[60] Persons seeking assistance are asked to provide information about the field of expertise, other relevant information about the dispute, the applicable law, the language of arbitration and potential other languages needed for the case, the place of arbitration, an estimation of the amount in dispute if possible, and any nationality that should not be considered for the given dispute. The Search Committee, comprised of members of the Pledge Steering Committee working in dispute resolution organizations (not law firms so as to avoid conflicts of interest), searches for female arbitrators based on the information provided and respond with names and profiles of potential candidates.[61] In its first seven months of operation following its launch in September 2016, the tool was used 15 times[62] and only a further 20 times in just over the subsequent two years.[63] The infrequency with which the service is used is perhaps due to a lack of awareness of its availability or concern about

[57] Email from Alexandra Palma Long (GAR Data Coordinator) to author (9 August 2019) (see also n 6).

[58] The lists showcase partners and non-partners under 45 years of age considered future leaders in the international arbitration community. 'Future Leaders 2018' (*Who's Who Legal*, 2018) <http://whoswholegal.com/news/analysis/article/34253/arbitration-future-leaders-2018-analysis/> accessed 29 February 2020. In 2019, women represented 46.6% of the Non-Partners (Global) and 11.4% of the Partners (Global) lists: 'Arbitration – Future Leaders' (*Who's Who Legal*, 2019) <https://whoswholegal.com/future-leaders/arbitration-future-leaders> accessed 29 February 2020.

[59] See Rothman (n 26) 25.

[60] 'Search for Female Arbitrators' (*Equal Representation in Arbitration*) <www.arbitrationpledge.com/arbitration-search> accessed 29 February 2020.

[61] Mirèze Philippe, 'Diversity & Transparency – ICC Gender Statistics' (2018) 15(1) Transnational Dispute Management <www.transnational-dispute-management.com/article.asp?key=2524> accessed 29 February 2020.

[62] ibid.

[63] Email from Equal Representation in Arbitration Pledge Steering Committee to author (15 August 2019), recording that the search function had been used 35 times since its introduction.

providing details about a case at an early stage to unknown persons (the members of the Search Committee remain anonymous). The search function is available to any person searching for female candidates—that includes appointing counsel compiling candidate lists, but also knowledge lawyers[64] within firms that could play a role in compiling internal databases or conducting internal training on the firm's selection and appointment policies and processes and the need to consciously consider female candidates.

2.3.1.3 Systemic progress

Addressing the pipeline leak is a larger challenge. Law firms, law societies, bar councils and other professional bodies can and should take a hard look at their own composition and membership, particularly at the senior levels, and continually ask what more could be done to implement meaningful initiatives to support and promote women to senior positions and partnership level. This includes disrupting systems that privilege characteristics that are typically 'male', investigating and addressing high attrition rates, closing the gender pay gap and offering meaningfully flexible work arrangements. Although these challenges also permeate many other professions, they have an increased significance for women in arbitration because arbitration demands more than just excellent technical skills; visibility in the field and the building of authority are essential and require considerable networking, travel, publications and participation in conferences and professional bodies (in addition to often long hours in the course of day-to-day billable work). Women wishing to start a family may find it challenging to sustain these commitments at all stages of their career.[65] Measures designed to retain and promote women have been introduced by various professional bodies that track gender statistics of their membership,[66] support the publication of studies on gender bias in the legal profession in an effort to reduce its impact,[67] and create bodies specifically dedicated to securing equal opportunities for women and addressing challenges

[64] A knowledge lawyer creates and manages the systems of collective knowledge of a law firm and its lawyers in a particular field. The role can involve keeping fee earners up to date with trends and developments in a particular field, developing and delivering internal training, assisting to produce client briefings and pitches, and managing the records of the institutional knowledge of a law firm (precedents based on prior work product, compilation of the firm's experience, internal databases of arbitrators and appointment statistics, and so forth).

[65] Who's Who Legal, 'Arbitration Future Leaders 2018: Women in Law Roundtable Discussion' (n 28).

[66] See eg Bar Council, 'Practising Barrister Statistics' (n 12); 'Legal Profession Statistics' (*ABA*, 5 August 2019) <www.americanbar.org/about_the_aba/profession_statistics/> accessed 29 February 2020.

[67] See egJoan C Williams and others, 'You Can't Change What You Can't See: Interrupting Racial & Gender Bias in the Legal Profession' (*American Bar Association's Commission for Women in the Profession and Minority Corporate Council Association*, 28 June 2018) <www.americanbar.org/content/dam/aba/administrative/women/you-cant-change-what-you-cant-see-print.pdf> accessed 29 February 2020; '2018 International Arbitration Survey' (n 3) 16–23; BLP, 'Are We Getting There?' (n 17); Bar Council, 'Momentum Measures' (n 12).

they face.[68] This is a start, but meaningful change requires commitment and perseverance over time. Progress has and can continue to be made in broadening the actual pool through initiatives to put agenda on the agenda and in the minds of those making identifying and selecting arbitrators, making it easier to find qualified female candidates for appointment and promoting systemic change to address the pipeline leak.

2.3.2 How should the effective pool be broadened?

2.3.2.1 Addressing the information bottleneck

Risk aversion and path dependence play a key role in the reduction of the actual pool to the effective pool. If counsel will not change their requirement of having first-hand information about candidates, then the information bottleneck needs to be addressed by enabling counsel to get the same information from a broader network sources, and to get more of it. In a 2016 survey of arbitration practitioners, an overwhelming 92% of participants said that they would welcome more information about new and less-well known candidates.[69] This suggests the potential for innovative research tools to make a difference in arbitrator appointments. There are two new initiatives that seek to do just this.

One is Arbitrator Intelligence,[70] launched by Catherine Rogers on 1 June 2017 as a way of making available information of the kind that is sought by law firms through their networks and which is not available on potential arbitrators' CVs. Arbitrator Intelligence's mission statement is 'to promote transparency, fairness, and accountability in the selection of international arbitrators, and to facilitate increased diversity in arbitrator appointments'.[71] The concept is based on Arbitrator Intelligence Questionnaires (AIQs), which is a feedback questionnaire designed to facilitate systematic collection of information about arbitrator case management and decision-making. Law firms, individual lawyers and parties are all asked to complete AIQs and arbitral institutions have begun undertaking to distribute the questionnaires at the end of each case they administer. The initiative is still at the data collection stage. Once sufficient information is collected, Arbitrator Intelligence Reports will be produced and made publicly available that will provide data on how prospective arbitrators compare across a range of data points. Arbitrator Intelligence acknowledges that 'more information about arbitrators will provide market-based accountability for arbitrators and allow newer and more diverse arbitrators a meaningful opportunity to build their reputations based on actual performance'.[72] One particular benefit of this kind of initiative is that the

[68] Eg in the US, 'Women in the Profession' (*ABA*, 2019) <www.americanbar.org/groups/diversity/women/> accessed 29 February 2020; 'National Association of Women Lawyers'

[69] BLP, 'Are We Getting There?' (n 17) 7.

[70] See 'Arbitrator Intelligence' <www.arbitratorintelligence.org/> 29 February 2020.

[71] ibid.

[72] ibid. See also Rogers (n 18).

information will be contained in a database and so access to it will not depend on making ad hoc telephone or email contact with individuals. Consequently, more candidates may be likely to be searched in the Arbitrator Intelligence Reports than whose names would be floated on personal and professional networks; the concern about not wanting to pepper contacts with requests for information about long lists of candidates would not apply when the information is available and searchable in a database.

A similar initiative is GAR's Arbitrator Research Tool, launched in April 2017.[73] It publishes arbitrator profiles but also gives details of who has sat with or appeared before the profiled arbitrators in the last three years. It is promoted as facilitating obtaining 'an up-to-date assessment of an arbitrator's capabilities from someone you trust'.[74] As of 9 August 2019, there are 288 arbitrator profiles, and details of more than 5,900 co-arbitrators they have worked alongside and counsel who have appeared before them.[75] It also has a gender filter. It therefore appears to have the capacity to act as a substitute for and be a larger version of the law firm/counsels' network. There is at least the potential that it will facilitate the contacting of listed persons for views on candidates even when the contacting lawyer and practitioner being contacted are not personally or professionally connected, as is the usual practice when utilizing law firm/counsels' networks. As the Arbitrator Research Tool lists persons before and alongside whom female counsel have appeared, there is also a possibility that the connections mapped out will be used in reverse, that is, used to ask arbitrators their views of how female counsel who have appeared before them might perform as an arbitrator.

Both resources could also assist co-arbitrators as well as parties in the appointment of more women. As mentioned above, there is a significant disparity between the appointment of female candidates by institutions, on the one hand, and parties and co-arbitrators, on the other. No empirical data exists that examines why co-arbitrators appoint women far less than institutions. One might assume that arbitrators also take a risk-averse approach to choosing a chairperson insofar as their future appointments depend in part on their ability to demonstrate sound judgment in choosing good chairs. That might lead them to prefer candidates with considerable experience sitting as arbitrators, thereby again privileging insiders and consequently limiting the number of women in the effective pool. Arbitrator Intelligence has the potential to provide co-arbitrators with a market-accountable basis on which to defend their judgement in selecting a chair. GAR's Arbitrator Research Tool could enable co-arbitrators to seek views on and be more comfortable with the appointment of less well-known chairs, including more women, by providing a broader network of connections.

[73] GAR ART (n 2).
[74] ibid.
[75] ibid; email from Alexandra Palma Long (GAR Data Coordinator) to author (9 August 2019).

2.3.2.2 *Arbitral rules requiring equal opportunities for women in the construction of the effective pool*

Parties in arbitral proceedings appoint arbitrators without any real restriction on how that appointment is to happen. Incorporating into arbitration rules aspirational or mandatory requirements on parties and institutions to ensure equal opportunities for women in the arbitrator appointment process may have a positive effect on the number of women in the effective pool. This could be as simple arbitral rules as directing appointing actors to take gender into account in the process of selecting and appointing an arbitrator. With respect to the appointment of permanent judges to international courts and tribunals, for example, aspirational and mandatory requirements to take gender into account in the appointment process appear to work: the courts with the highest percentage of women on the bench are those with aspirational or mandatory provisions aimed at the inclusion of more women on the bench.[76] However, in contrast to these permanent-appointment processes, what is suggested here would not operate as a quota. An aspirational or mandatory requirement to provide equal opportunities for women concerns *the conduct of the appointment process*, not its outcome (as a quota would), and should not for that reason be subject to criticism that it would impose an impermissible limitation on the freedom of parties to appoint whomever they deem to be the right arbitrator for their case. In fact, providing equal opportunities for women in the appointment process should be entirely uncontroversial and including such a requirement in arbitral rules would simply entrench it in the arbitral process in an objective manner. Articulating a formal aspirational or mandatory requirement to provide women with an equal opportunity in the appointment process would force counsel for appointing parties to turn their mind to the issue. When one recent study asked arbitration practitioners whether they considered diversity in drawing up a list of potential candidates for appointment, only 56% of participants said that they already considered diversity, including gender, and an astounding 43% responded that they either did not think about it or did not consider it relevant.[77] If the survey participants are representative of all arbitration counsel, this means that in almost half of appointments gender is not taken into account. Moreover, while 47% of participants said that they would be more likely to take into account gender in the future, a not insignificant 36% said that they would not do so.[78]

In addition to forcing the issue to the forefront of appointing counsel and clients' minds, an aspirational or mandatory equal opportunity requirement might

[76] Nienke Grossman, 'Achieving Sex-Representative International Court Benches' (2016) 110 American Journal of International Law 82, 83, and 92: 'Of the five courts with the highest percentage of women on the bench from 1999 to 2015, four had either aspirational statements for inclusion or quotas ... None of the seven courts with the lowest percentages of women on the bench had either. In mid-2015, women made up 32 percent of benches with such requirements and only 15 percent of benches without them.'

[77] BLP, 'Are We Getting There?' (n 17) 9.

[78] ibid.

prompt for law firms to disband policies that have the effect (but not the intention) of disproportionately prejudicing women, including taking the hard line that no candidate be proposed to a client without prior experience sitting as an arbitrator. It could also be articulated to apply equally to situations where co-arbitrators choose a chair. This would go some way to addressing the statistics that show that co-arbitrators generally select women as arbitrators far less than institutions and the parties.[79]

2.3.3 How should implicit bias be addressed?

Despite being unconscious and therefore difficult to address, implicit bias can be unlearned. Participating in education efforts aimed at raising awareness about implicit bias, being exposed to counter-active stereotypes, engaging in deliberative processes in which participants are encouraged to constantly self-monitor in an effort to offset implicit biases, and having a sense of accountability, that is, 'the implicit or explicit expectation that one may be called on to justify one's beliefs, feelings, and actions to others', can all assist in dismantling implicit biases.[80] This suggests that the awareness raising initiatives the international arbitration community is presently undertaking could contribute to the breakdown of implicit biases.[81] It is on this basis that new initiatives aimed at self-evaluation and recognizing gender bias are being developed and recommended.[82] It also suggests that addressing implicit bias openly within law firms and with clients could be an effective means of reducing or negating its impact in the arbitrator selection and appointment process.

It is up to the individual lawyers working in firms (at all levels), barristers and other counsel involved in arbitrator selection and appointment processes to consciously think about providing women with equal opportunities during the party-appointment arbitrator selection process. Some have suggested that the best

[79] See Table 6.1.

[80] Cheryl Staats and others, 'State of the Science: Implicit Bias Review' (Kirwan Institute for the Study of Race and Ethnicity, Ohio State University, 2015) 65–66 <http://kirwaninstitute.osu.edu/wp-content/uploads/2015/05/2015-kirwan-implicit-bias.pdf> accessed 29 February 2020. Lucy Greenwood has also explored the positive effect that blind appointment processes could have in negating implicit bias, but given the common insistence on first-hand knowledge of candidates by appointing counsel, the reception of any such proposals among the arbitration community is questionable. See: Greenwood, 'Could "Blind" Appointments Open Our Eyes' (n 25).

[81] Greenwood, 'Women in Disputes' (n 16).

[82] 'Diversity Toolkit' (*Arbitral Women*, 2019) <www.arbitralwomen.org/diversity-toolkit/> accessed 29 February 2020; 'Diversity and Inclusion Training' (*Alliance for Equality in Dispute Resolution*, 2019) <www.allianceequality.com/the-workshop> accessed 29 February 2020; Williams and others (n 67) (identifying tools for interrupting gender bias); Apoorva Patel, 'Implicit Bias in Arbitrator Appointments: A Report from the 15th Annual ITA-ASIL Conference on Diversity and Inclusion in International Arbitration' (*Kluwer Arbitration*, 7 May 2018) <http://arbitrationblog.kluwerarbitration.com/2018/05/07/implicit-bias-in-arbitrator-appointments-a-report-from-the-15th-annual-ita-asil-conference-on-diversity-and-inclusion-in-international-arbitration/> accessed 29 February 2020 (summarizing recommendations made by speakers at the 2018 ITA-ASIL Conference, including the taking of implicit bias tests and the engaging in diversity training).

way to produce more gender diverse lists of arbitrator candidates is to start with identifying desired characteristics before considering potential names and to re-think assumptions that prioritize prior appointment records.[83] But it should also be more explicit than that. As there are fewer qualified female candidates in the pool and they are harder to find, practitioners should actively search for women using all the resources available to them. This extends to expanding the number and types of 'go-to' databases practitioners typically use, actively asking colleagues and networks for suggestions for female candidates, querying shortlists that do not have women on them, and encouraging other practitioners at all levels to reflect on whether everything has really been done to give women an equal opportunity. As there are fewer and harder to find female candidates, and by virtue of the fact that many of them will have comparatively less experience as an arbitrator than their male counterparts (not least because of structural barriers to entry into the pool women face), the process of finding suitable female candidates may take more effort, more time and, therefore, more money. Lawyers and law firms should be cognisant and accepting of this additional time, effort, and cost as a product of the current state of appointment processes and resources, and work to change it. Some firms have gone so far as to introduce a policy whereby every list of potential arbitrators must include at least some female options.[84] Lucy Reed, a leading arbitrator, considers that breaking down habits in appointment processes and the bias that stems from them, and to do so with patience, persistence, and inclusiveness, is the way to improve gender diversity.[85]

It is also necessary for counsel to be conscious of the role of implicit bias when discussing arbitrator candidates with clients. Clients listen to and depend on the recommendations and advice of their counsel. Lawyers should therefore discuss the credentials of qualified candidates in gender neutral language and be open about their commitment to equality of opportunity for women. It is important, however, to be tactful. A commitment to improving equal opportunities for women should never be offered or perceived as an explanation that one or more women listed on a candidate list are token recommendations that should not be seriously considered. Lawyers should be prepared to explain and defend their recommendations of all candidates on a list presented to clients by reference to their experience, qualification, and suitability to act as arbitrator. If, however, there is a choice to be made between a male and female candidate who are equally qualified, lawyers should be willing openly to recommend the female candidate to the client on the basis that, if there is no real difference between them, it would be better to select a woman arbitrator because of the need to promote a fairer representation of women

[83] Greenwood, 'Moving Beyond Diversity' (n 16) 100; Greenwood, 'Women in Disputes' (n 16); Patel (n 82) (summarizing presentations made at the 2018 ITA-ASIL Conference).

[84] GAR, 'Do more on diversity, says ArbitralWomen President' (n 36) referring to White & Case and Allen & Overy. It is not clear whether this was an office-specific or firm-wide (ie worldwide) policy.

[85] GAR, 'Reed's diversity equation' (n 36).

in arbitration. These kinds of conscious, self-reflective and self-monitoring steps will assist in dismantling implicit bias that without concerted action would affect the appointment process.

2.4 The Responsibility of Those Making Arbitrator Appointments

Arbitration practitioners have a special responsibility to actively and openly make efforts to improve opportunities for women to be appointed as arbitrators. Parties appoint arbitrators in the majority of cases (for example, in 60% of ICSID cases and 57% of ICC cases)[86] and thus their counsel have the opportunity and capacity to effect meaningful change. It is curious, therefore, that practitioners commonly express the view that they are not best placed to take the lead on improving gender diversity. In a 2018 survey of arbitration users, almost half (45%) ranked arbitral institutions as the best placed actors to ensure greater gender diversity, highlighting a 'perception among users that arbitral institutions wield the most influence over the future of international arbitration'.[87] Only 27% of participants in the study considered the parties to be best placed to improve gender diversity.[88] Unsurprisingly, representatives of the arbitral institutions responded by pointing out that parties—or, in effect, their counsel—make most of the appointments and thus have a statistically more significant role in ensuring greater diversity among appointed arbitrators.[89]

The inclination to assign primary responsibility to arbitral institutions might be explained on the basis that institutions do not have clients. Although institutions compete to some extent to administer cases, there is, for arbitral institutions, less of a perceived tension between what is best for the client in the particular case at hand and the broader goals of promoting gender diversity in international arbitration

[86] ICSID, '2018 Annual Report' (n 22) 48; ICC, 'Dispute Resolution Bulletin' (Issue 1, 2019) (n 35 and 56).

[87] '2018 International Arbitration Survey' (n 3) 18. See also Joseph Mamounas, 'ICCA 2014. Does "Male, Pale, and Stale" Threaten the Legitimacy of International Arbitration? Perhaps, but There's No Clear Path to Change' (*Kluwer Arbitration*, 10 April 2014) <http://arbitrationblog.kluwerarbitration.com/2014/04/10/icca-2014-does-male-pale-and-stale-threaten-the-legitimacy-of-international-arbitration-perhaps-but-theres-no-clear-path-to-change/> accessed 29 February 2020; LCIA, 'Diversity; why it matters and what we can all do about it' (*LCIA*, 24 July 2015) <www.lcia.org/news/diversity-why-it-matters-and-what-we-can-all-do-about-it.aspx> accessed 29 February 2020. In contrast to the general situation in which arbitral institutions do not play the major role in appointment, the 2018 Netherlands Model BIT does away with party-appointed arbitrators and requires that all members of an arbitral tribunal be appointed by an appointing authority, and that the appointing authority 'shall strive for gender and geographic diversity': 'Netherlands Model Investment Agreement' (19 October 2018) Art 20(1)–(2) <www.rijksoverheid.nl/binaries/rijksoverheid/documenten/publicaties/2018/10/26/modeltekst-voor-bilaterale-investeringsakkoorden/modeltekst-voor-bilaterale-investeringsakkoorden.pdf> accessed 29 February 2020.

[88] '2018 International Arbitration Survey' (n 3) 19.

[89] ibid.

as a system. Institutions are accordingly less constrained from taking an approach that might be thought to privilege the latter. This apparent tension is neatly captured in the responses to a 2016 survey of arbitration practitioners. Of those that responded, 84% thought that there were too many men on arbitral tribunals, but only 50% thought that it was desirable to have a gender balance on arbitral tribunals, 41% thought that 'it makes no difference' and 6% thought it was 'not desirable'.[90] Moreover, 68% of those that responded thought that gender was 'not that important' or 'not important at all'. Only 12% considered that gender was 'very important' or 'important'.[91] The apparent tension thus manifests itself in a disconnect between, on the one hand, a recognition of the general desirability of increasing the representation of women and, on the other, a willingness to take action in individual cases. The same disconnect is reflected in the now infamous anecdotal comment posted in 2012 to a well-known arbitration discussion forum: 'when asked by a client to select an arbitrator, the desirability of promoting diversity is the last feature on anyone's mind. We are not being asked to make a statement. We are asked to pick the best person for the job.'[92] Catherine Rogers has termed this disconnect the 'arbitrator diversity paradox'.[93]

This apparent disconnect stems from a false premise. It assumes that taking steps to afford women equal opportunities in the appointment process will prevent or detract from the task of appointing the best person for the job. This is not true. It is not, as some have suggested, a zero-sum game.[94] As Greenwood and Baker note, anecdotes like the 2012 one quoted above 'perpetuate the notion that appointing diverse candidates will result in the appointment of less skilled tribunals, when, in fact, there is significant support for the belief that diverse groups produce better outcomes'.[95] They refer to studies that reveal a clear correlation between gender-balanced leadership and improved performance. This includes, in the commercial context, improved corporate governance, improved the quality and scope of decision-making, preventing group-think and increased profit margins.[96] In the legal context, while empirical data on whether women and men adjudicate differently does not yet exist, the American Bar Association and the LCIA that are of the view that a diverse legal profession and arbitration panels are more intelligent, conduct better analysis and produce better and unbiased outcomes.[97]

In the investment arbitration context, it is noteworthy that the two women who have the overwhelming majority of female appointments, Brigitte Stern and

[90] BLP, 'Are We Getting There?' (n 17) 8.
[91] ibid.
[92] Greenwood and Baker (n 16) 420, referring to a post on OGEMID 9 February 2012.
[93] Rogers (n 18).
[94] See eg Mamounas (n 87).
[95] Greenwood and Baker (n 16) 420.
[96] ibid 420–21.
[97] ibid 421. See also, SIAC, 'Annual Report 2018' (Table 6.1 n k) 11, reporting on a roundtable hosted by SIAC on whether having female arbitrators on tribunals leads to better decision-making.

Gabrielle Kaufmann-Kohler, are not just high-profile but are *at the very centre* of the investment arbitration system. According to Sergio Puig's analysis, Stern has the highest number of appointments of *any* arbitrator, male or female, and Kaufmann-Kohler is the most highly regarded figure—male or female—in investment arbitration.[98] Other women have also been singled out as the best in the entire field, such as Jean Kalicki and Domitille Baizeau, who were awarded GAR's 'Best Prepared/Most Responsive Arbitrator' in 2017 and 2018 respectively.[99] These are merely a few prominent examples, but they give a human dimension to the outcomes of the blind studies surveyed by Greenwood and demonstrate that counsel must be consciously open to the possibility that the best person for the job in any given case might actually be a woman, even one with which whom they are not personally or professionally familiar. The role of counsel to appointing parties in choosing the best person for the job requires diligently looking for and actively considering female candidates equally alongside their male counterparts to ensure that true equality of opportunity overcomes path-dependent and structural inequalities that exist in the appointment process at present.

Practitioners involved in the appointment process at all levels have a special responsibility to give women an equal opportunity. It is a personal responsibility that requires awareness of the different layers of prejudice that women face and conscious individual action during each individual appointment process. To echo one leading female arbitrator: 'We all just need to be that little bit braver'—braver at raising the need for equal representation, recommending female colleagues for various speaking and professional roles, and 'braver at selling the (possibly younger, less experienced) female candidates to our clients'.[100] This is responsibility of arbitration practitioners is not only a consequence of the opportunity and capacity for change afforded to those who appoint arbitrators, but is also as part of what James Crawford has referred to as the responsibility of international lawyers, as members of the profession of international law, to ensure 'the ongoing legitimacy, and perceived legitimacy, of our discipline'.[101] As lawyers, our internal attitudes to the daily processes in which we engage, our understanding of the role that they have in the

[98] Puig (n 19) 404, 410, 416, and 418–19.

[99] Jean Kalicki and Domitille Baizeau were the second and third women respectively to win this award, following it being awarded to Gabrielle Kaufmann-Kohler in 2012: Jones (n 34); 'Domitille Baizeau Wins GAR ART Award for Best Prepared and Most Responsive Arbitrator' (*Lalive*, 6 April 2018) <www.lalive.law/news/domitille-baizeau-wins-gar-art-award-for-best-prepared-and-most-responsive-arbitrator/> accessed 29 February 2020.

[100] Who's Who Legal, 'Arbitration Future Leaders 2018: Women in Law Roundtable Discussion' (n 28) (Ania Farren). In this respect, it is a positive thing that many of the 2019 'New Year Goals' that the Pledge encourages its signatories to adopt are focused on concrete things that individual practitioners acting for appointing parties can do, such as 'I will appoint women as arbitrators on an equal opportunity basis' and 'I will ask my firm/arbitral institution whether we have a policy in place for tracking the number of female arbitrators we appoint': see 'Equal Representation in Arbitration Pledge' (n 34).

[101] James Crawford, 'International Law as Discipline and Profession' (2012) 106 American Society of International Law Proceedings 471, 482.

broader field in which we work, and the way that we articulate priorities for change in our profession have an important role to play in preserving the legitimacy of our discipline. The persistent overrepresentation of one group—men—among arbitrators without visible and concerted action for change by the people who are appointing that one group raises questions about the normative and sociological legitimacy of the appointment process and arbitration generally.[102]

3. Public International Law Courts and Tribunals

The appointment of judges ad hoc to public (or 'general') international law courts and tribunals offers an interesting comparator for the appointment of arbitrators. Both judges ad hoc and arbitrators are appointed by parties for particular cases.[103] Judges ad hoc may be appointed to cases at the ICJ, ITLOS, IACtHR, and ECtHR. In the case of the ICJ, ITLOS, and the IACtHR, where the bench contains no judge of the nationality of a State party to an inter-State case, that party may appoint a judge ad hoc of their choosing.[104] In respect of the ECtHR, if the judge of the nationality of a State party to the proceeding is unable to sit, withdraws, is exempted, or if there is no judge of the State's nationality already on the bench, the President of the Court will appoint a judge ad hoc from a reserve list of three to five names nominated by the State in advance for renewable periods of two years.[105] The Rules of Court specifically require that reserve lists include members of both sexes.[106] When comparing the appointment of judges ad hoc to the appointment of arbitrators, five general observations can be made.

[102] See eg Rogers (n 1 8); Cecily Rose, 'Justifying Arguments about Selection Procedures for Judges at International Courts and Tribunals: A Response to Nienke Grossman' (2016) 110 AJIL Unbound 87, 89–90; Susan D Franck and others, 'The Diversity Challenge: Exploring the "Invisible College" of International Arbitration' (2015) 53 Columbia Journal of Transatlantic Law 429, 467–68; Nienke Grossman, 'Sex on the Bench: Do Women Judges Matter to the Legitimacy of International Courts' (2012) 12 Chicago Journal of International Law 647, 652.

[103] Excluding the appointment of permanent judges also avoids issues relating to the politicized and opaque nature of appointment processes for permanent judges of international courts and tribunals: See generally, Grossman, 'Achieving Sex-Representative International Court Benches' (n 76) and responses to this article in (2016) 110 AJIL Unbound 87–104.

[104] Statute of the ICJ, 24 October 1945, Arts 31(2)–(3); Statute of ITLOS, Annex VI to the UN Convention on the Law of the Sea (opened for signature 10 December 1982, entered into force 16 November 1994) 1833 UNTS 3, Arts 17(2)–(3); Statute of the IACtHR (adopted 1 October 1979), Arts 10(2)–(3).

[105] Convention for the Protection of Human Rights and Fundamental Freedoms (European Convention on Human Rights, as amended) (ECHR), Art 26(4); ECtHR Rules of Court, 3 June 2019, rules 26 and 29. This procedure came into force with the adoption of Protocol No. 14 to the ECHR in 2010. Prior to 2010, State parties could appoint as judge ad hoc any person they chose after the case in question had commenced. This led to legitimacy concerns and ultimately, Protocol No. 14: see Council of Europe, 'Information report: Ad hoc judges at the European Court of Human Rights: an overview' (Parliamentary Assembly, Committee on Legal Affairs and Human Rights, 23 January 2012), paras 2–4 and 9–11. Judges on the reserve list do not have to be nationals of the appointing State.

[106] ECtHR Rules of Court (n 105), rule 29(1)(a).

First, appointments of judges ad hoc can only be made by States. Cases before the ICJ and ITLOS are limited to inter-State cases. The right to appoint a judge ad hoc at the IACtHR arises only in inter-State cases.[107] The right to have a judge ad hoc appointed at the ECtHR applies only in respect of the State party to the proceeding. It is likely that for all courts and tribunals other than the ECtHR (where candidates are nominated on reserve lists in advance of a dispute arising) the appointing State relies on the advice of its counsel as to whom to appoint as judge ad hoc in the particular case, as is also the case in arbitration.

Second, there are comparatively fewer appointments of judges ad hoc than appointments of arbitrators. This is because there are far fewer international courts and tribunals that permit the appointment of judges ad hoc as compared to arbitral tribunals, and the rate at which new cases calling for appointments arise is far slower than the number of new arbitration cases instituted.[108]

Third, continuing (and worsening) the trend from arbitration, there is a significant disparity between the men and women appointed as judges ad hoc. From its first contentious case in 1947 to August 2019, there have been 216 appointments of judges ad hoc to the ICJ[109] only five of which have been women (2.3%): Suzanne Bastid (a French national, appointed by Tunisia in *Application for Revision and Interpretation of the Tunisian/Libyan Continental Shelf* case), Christine Van den Wyngaert (a Belgian national, appointed by Belgium in the *Arrest Warrant* case), Hilary Charlesworth (an Australian national, appointed by Australia in the *Whaling* case and Guyana in *Arbitral Award of 3 October 1899*) and Louise Arbour (a Canadian national, appointed by Chile in *Obligation to Negotiation Access to the Pacific Ocean*).[110] There does, however, appear to be a slow improvement in these figures: the percentage of female judges ad hoc appointed in cases instituted in the last 10 years alone is 5.4%.[111] Since the first ITLOS case in 1997, 20 appointments of

[107] Statute of the IACtHR (n 104), Arts 10(2)–(3). See also Rules of Procedure of the IACtHR, 28 November 2009, rule 20.

[108] Eg in 2018, 57 new cases were registered with ICSID alone compared to six new cases instituted at the ICJ cases (up from one single case instituted at the ICJ in 2017). Compare ICSID, '2018 Annual Report' (n 22) 25 to the dates of institutions of proceedings in the ICJ's pending case list: 'Pending cases' (*ICJ*, 2019) <www.icj-cij.org/en/pending-cases> accessed 29 February 2020.

[109] This figure does not double-count joined or identical cases where the same judge ad hoc was appointed by the same party in the related cases. This figure also takes into account that in some cases, more than one judge ad hoc was appointed due to the resignation of an earlier-appointed judge ad hoc. In terms of individuals, there have been 120 judges ad hoc in total, of which four (3.3%) were women.

[110] See the list of all judges ad hoc on the ICJ's website: 'All Judges *ad hoc*' (ICJ, 2019) <www.icj-cij.org/en/all-judges-ad-hoc> accessed 29 February 2020. *Application for Revision and Interpretation of the Judgment of 24 February 1982 in the Case concerning the Continental Shelf (Tunisia/Libyan Arab Jamahiriya)* [1985] ICJ Rep 192; *Arrest Warrant of 11 April 2000 (Democratic Republic of Congo v Belgium)* [2002] ICJ Rep 3; *Whaling in the Antarctic (Australia v Japan; New Zealand intervening)* [2014] ICJ Rep 226; *Obligation to Negotiate Access to the Pacific Ocean (Bolivia v Chile)* (Preliminary Objection) [2015] ICJ Rep 592; *Arbitral Award of 3 October 1899 (Guyana v. Venezuela)* (Pending) <www.icj-cij.org/en/case/171> accessed 29 February 2020.

[111] There have been 55 appointments of judges ad hoc in cases instituted from 2009 to August 2019, three of which have been women.

judges ad hoc have been made, only one of which has been a women: Anna Petrig (a Swiss national, appointed by Switzerland in *The M/T 'San Padre Pio' Case* in May 2019).[112] The low numbers of female judges ad hoc at the ICJ and ITLOS is reflective of a stark gender disparity among the permanent membership of most international courts and tribunals more generally.[113] At the ECtHR, by contrast, where reserve lists must contain judges of both sex, 44.9% of the reserve judges are women.[114]

Fourth, the appointment process for judges ad hoc and arbitrators is similar, although different skills are prioritized. Candidate lists will often start with soliciting recommendations from within the counsel team of suitable persons for appointment. Unlike arbitration, there are no databases of persons suitably experienced for appointment as a judge ad hoc to international courts and tribunals. This is in large part due to the lack of a demand—the appointments are few and the prospective candidates are likely to be high-profile and well-known. From the author's experience in being involved in or observing the appointment of two ICJ judges ad hoc and one ITLOS judge ad hoc, the most important qualities looked for are expertise in public international law (and the specific subject area to which the dispute relates),[115] whether the candidate has expressed substantive views on issues that arise in the case, standing in the public international law community and consequent ability to influence other members of the bench (gravitas). Experience having sat on international courts and tribunals[116] in the past or having engaged in large deliberative processes conducted in bodies such as the UN International Law Commission will also be an asset. Also relevant is whether a candidate will ensure that the appointee's position is properly understood, presented, and considered in deliberations. This is judged not from the relationship between the appointing State and the candidate, but from ascertaining what the candidate's published views are on the legal issues in question, assessing the strength of the candidate's conviction in those views, and considering whether the candidate would be likely to speak up and actively engage in deliberations with large numbers of other (permanent) judges. At the ICJ, for example, the judges ad hoc speak

[112] See the list of all judges ad hoc on ITLOS' website: 'Judges *ad hoc*' (*ITLOS*, 2019) <www.itlos.org/en/the-tribunal/judges-ad-hoc/> accessed 29 February 2020.

[113] See Ruth Mackenzie and others, *Selecting International Judges* (OUP 2010) 161–62; Grossman, 'Achieving Sex-Representative International Court Benches' (n 76) 82–84.

[114] See, 'List of *Ad hoc* judges for the year 2019' (ECtHR, 2019) <http://echr.coe.int/Documents/List_adhoc_judges_BIL.pdf> accessed 29 February 2020. No statistics on female judges ad hoc appointed to the IACtHR are available.

[115] Appointments to each of the ICJ, ITLOS, IACtHR, and ECtHR require minimum standards of competency to be met: Statute of the ICJ (n 104), Arts 2 and 31(6); Statute of ITLOS (n 104), Arts 2(1) and 17(6); Statute of the IACtHR (n 104), Arts 4 and 10(5); ECHR (n 105), Art 21; ECtHR Rules of Court (n 105), rule 29(1)(c).

[116] In theory, therefore, the more female judges that occupy permanent positions, the more likely that after their term has ended they will broaden the pool of female candidates for the appointment of judges ad hoc (if they choose to continue to be available for appointment).

first in plenary deliberations.[117] Having a well-respected and eloquent judge ad hoc that can with clarity and persuasion frame the issues can be of great benefit to an appointing State.

There may be a perception that gender should play no real role in the appointment of judges ad hoc: if women are qualified to make it into the pool, then they are considered equally.[118] The same logic has been expressed in relation to arbitral appointments. But this belies the role that lawyers have in the construction of the pool in the first place. Where there are no databases or institutionally compiled lists of suitable candidates, the pool is a fictional construct created by the view of counsel representing the appointing State. Traditionally, the people constructing that pool are men[119] and the well-known and highly respected practitioners, professors, and former judges that comprise it are primarily men.[120] Like arbitration, this is a form of information bottleneck and barrier to entry for female candidates. Unlike arbitration, however, prior experience sitting as judge is not an essential pre-requisite, and female candidates can therefore become well-known and highly influential international lawyers through a variety of other roles. Counsel should therefore consciously and actively turn their mind to whether any women meet the criteria for inclusion in the pool—searching in a variety of places other than merely former judges of the relevant courts or professors at a few notable academic institutions. The slow increase in the numbers of women being appointed at the ICJ and ITLOS in recent times—may suggest that counsel for appointing States are more conscious of the need to take gender into account in recommending candidates for judges ad hoc to clients. The increasing visibility of the need to address the lack of gender disparity on the international bench, as well as the rising numbers of female graduates and practitioners in international law, provides hope that the trend will continue in a positive direction.

Finally, as in arbitration, there is a general recognition of the desirability of improving the representation of women on the benches of international courts and tribunals. This has led to some practical measures, including the adoption of aspirational or mandatory requirements to have regard to gender in appointment processes for permanent judges of international courts and tribunals.[121] These institutionalized initiatives for permanent positions largely bypass the appointment of judges ad hoc, leaving it to the counsel for the appointing States to ensure

[117] 'Resolution Concerning the Internal Judicial Practice of the Court' (*International Court of Justice*, 12 April 1976) Art 5 <www.icj-cij.org/en/other-texts/resolution-concerning-judicial-practice> accessed 29 February 2020.

[118] See eg one response to this effect in Mackenzie and others (n 113) 48.

[119] Shashank Kumar and Cecily Rose, 'A Study of Lawyers Appearing Before the International Court of Justice' (2014) 25 European Journal of International Law 893, 904.

[120] Mackenzie and others (n 113) 162.

[121] See also other initiatives that promote gender parity in international representation, such as GQUAL: 'About GQUAL' (*GQUAL*, 2015) <www.gqualcampaign.org/home/> accessed 29 February 2020.

equality of opportunity in any individual appointment process. In this respect, lawyers involved in the appointment of judges ad hoc, like those involved in appointing arbitrators, need to be cognisant of their unique role and responsibility.

Somewhat unsurprisingly, the disconnect evident in arbitration between, on the one hand, the general desirability of increasing female appointments and, on the other, a willingness to take action in individual cases, is also evident in anecdotal comments regarding to the appointment of women to international courts and tribunals. Ruth Mackenzie, Kate Malleson, Penny Martin, and Philippe Sands QC concluded, after conducting interviews of users of international courts and tribunals, that '[o]f those who were in favour of a greater representation of women ... there were few who could attest to taking concrete steps towards identifying and nominating women candidates' and noted a number of responses that suggested efforts to increase opportunities for women would 'compromise standards'.[122] Although those interviews were conducted almost a decade ago, the painfully slow rate at which female appointments to judge ad hoc roles are made—including the first female appointment to ITLOS as late as May 2019—suggests that meaningful progress in tackling implicit bias has likely not been made in this field in the past decade. In the absence of rules-based requirements to take gender into account in the appointment of judges ad hoc, it again falls to international law practitioners involved in the selection and appointment process to make a conscious effort to afford female candidates an equal opportunity.

4. Conclusion

The party-appointment of ad hoc adjudicators is a self-regulating process. Counsel representing the appointing parties are themselves the gatekeepers of equality of opportunity and, in many respects, the regulators of its effects in the international dispute settlement system. In arbitration, female candidates face different layers of prejudice at each stage of the appointment process that together combine to create and sustain serious barriers to equal opportunities and a fairer representation of the sexes on arbitral tribunals. Each layer of prejudice is created and driven by different factors. There is value in considering these layers from a processual perspective, in separating them out, and in taking steps to address them individually, to form what Puig called a 'coordinated attack' on the 'very resistant' structure of the arbitrator appointment process.[123] The international arbitration community has made gains in doing so already. Diversity and transparency are at the centre of debates about priorities for change. International practitioners can and should capitalize on this momentum, consolidate the efforts that are being made towards achieving

[122] See Mackenzie and others (n 113) 48–49.
[123] Puig (n 19) 422.

a better representation of women in arbitration and recognize the responsibility that their unique role entails. Female candidates seeking an equal opportunity to be considered for ad hoc positions face similar challenges in terms of access to the pool and implicit bias, and lessons learned from progress in the arbitration domain should be applied in the appointment of judges ad hoc to public international law courts and tribunals. The special role that lawyers have in ensuring equality of opportunity in every individual appointment process should not be understated and the recognition and conscious embracing of the attendant responsibility will serve to better the international legal profession as a whole.

7

African Women's Paths to the International Bench

How to Overcome the Hurdles

*Rebecca Emiene Badejogbin**

1. Introduction

Increasing the number of African women forms a crucial part of achieving adequate overall female representation on the international bench. The appointment of African women judges falls under two broad categories. The first category encompasses regional and sub-regional courts such as the African Court on Human and Peoples' Rights (ACtHPR), the East African Court of Justice (EACJ), the Economic Community of West African States Court (ECOWAS Court), and the Southern Africa Development Community Tribunal (SADC Tribunal). The second category is composed of non-African international courts such as the International Court of Justice (ICJ), the International Criminal Court (ICC), and other special international courts. The challenges posed by the lack of gender diversity on the benches of international courts are global and it is in the interest of *all* women to address this deficit, even though this chapter focuses on African women.[1] Female appointments to international courts improve legitimacy,[2] as they bring a unique perspective shaped by women's experiences and perceptions.[3] African women, in addition, bring their own specific regional understanding. This may also imply that they face double discrimination when pursuing their career ambitions: because

* This research was conducted during my doctoral studies under Professor Chuma Himonga, DST/NRF Chair in Customary Law, Indigenous Values and Human Rights, Private Law Department, University of Cape Town South Africa. This chapter was presented at the Conference organized by PluriCourts, University of Oslo on 'Gender on the International Bench', held at The Hague, The Netherlands, on 11–12 January 2018. I acknowledge the comments and suggestions of the participants at the Conference and the insightful comments of Dr J Jarpa Dawuni.

[1] N Grossman, 'Sex on the Bench: Do Women Judges Matter to the Legitimacy of International Courts?' (2012) 12 (2) Chicago Journal of International Law 647.

[2] J Resnik, 'Judicial Selection and Democratic Theory: Demand, Supply, and Life Tenure' (2005) 26 (2) Cardozo Law Review 579. See also Grossman (n 1).

[3] That is, a perspective peculiar to a woman's nature and the circumstances of her experiences as a woman. K Bartlett, 'Feminist Legal Methods' (1990) 103 (4) Harvard Law Review 829. See also D Feenan, 'Editorial Introduction: Women and Judging' (2009) 17 Feminist Legal Studies 1.

Rebecca Emiene Badejogbin, *African Women's Paths to the International Bench* In: *Identity and Diversity on the International Bench.* Edited by: Freya Baetens, Oxford University Press (2020). © The several contributors.
DOI: 10.1093/oso/9780198870753.003.0007.

they are women and because they are Africans. The ratio of African female judges to African male judges on the international bench is higher than that of female judges to male judges generally, except for a few courts where there are more female than male judges overall.[4] This raises the question whether African women face fewer obstacles than non-African women.

This chapter analyses pathways to the bench by examining various factors that determine the appointment of women judges, with particular reference to African women at both international and regional courts. It uses Josephine Dawuni's definition of an African woman as 'one who self-identifies as an African and is placed in a category that qualifies her for judicial selection as an "African" '.[5] This definition acknowledges the similarities in the shared history and culture of African countries, more particularly sub-Saharan States, without intending to trivialize the diverse identities of the various countries within this region. This chapter applies historical institutionalist theory,[6] which is based on 'historical orientation and its attention to the ways in which institutions structure and shape political behaviour and outcomes'.[7] It examines the influence of 'pre-existing institutions'[8] in answering 'real world empirical questions'.[9] The present analysis also engages theories concerning the effect of institutional structures as well as cultural, socio-economic, and political factors affecting women gaining political appointments in a post-colonial context.[10] As such, this chapter is located within the existing scholarship on challenges to the accession of women to the international bench. It commences by making a case for African women's appointment to international courts and analyses the extent of accessibility by reference to both 'legal' and 'non-legal' factors of influence. The chapter then considers how these factors have played out in the experiences of African women, discusses hurdles that impede access and identifies possible

[4] See the Court of the Eurasian Economic Union which has a 50/50 gender representation among the judges. Also, recent appointments into regional institutions such as the Sanctions Appeal Board of the African Development Bank indicate a deliberate policy of gender parity in their appointments. In July 2019, two substantive members (Oluremilekun Ademola Adegoke and Marie-Andrée Ngwe) and two alternate members (Catherine O'Regan and Julius Nkafu) were appointed to the Board, ie one man and one woman in each category: African Development Bank Group '2019 Annual Report of the Bank Group's Sanctions Appeals Board' March 2020, 2–3 <www.afdb.org/en/documents/2019-annual-report-bank-groups-sanctions-appeals-board>accessed 29 February 2020.

[5] J Dawuni 'African Women Judges on International Courts: Symbolic or Substantive gains?' iCourts Working Paper Series, No. 60, 2016.

[6] As adopted by Dawuni and Bauer in their analysis of gender in African judiciaries. See G Bauer, J Dawuni (ed), *Gender and the Judiciary in Africa: From Obscurity to Parity?* (Routledge 2015).

[7] S Steinmo, 'What is Historical Institutionalism?' in Della Porta, D and Keating M (eds), *Approaches and Methodologies in the Social Sciences* (CUP, 2008) 118.

[8] E Immergut, 'Historical-Institutionalism in Political Science and the Problem of Change'<www.researchgate.net/publication/304689198_Historical-Institutionalism_in_Political_Science_and_the_Problem_of_Change>accessed 29 February 2020, p 242.

[9] Steinmo (n 7) at 136.

[10] This was extensively discussed in Akua Kuenyehia and J J Dawuni, *African Women Judges on International Courts: Untold Stories* (Routledge 2017). See also R. Mishra, 'Postcolonial Feminism: Looking into Within-Beyond-To Difference' (2013) 4 (4) International Journal of English and Literature 129.

solutions. Finally, it promotes adequate gender representation rather than gender parity *stricto sensu.*

2. Making a Case for African Women's Appointment to International Courts

Women have been appointed as judges of, and have even presided over, international courts. For example, Judge Julia Sebutinde (Uganda) is currently one of only three African members[11] and the first African woman to sit on the ICJ bench. Gabrielle Kirk McDonald (USA) was the first woman to preside over an international criminal tribunal at the International Criminal Tribunal for the former Yugoslavia (ICTY), Navanethem Pillay (South Africa) presided over the International Criminal Tribunal for Rwanda (ICTR), and Dame Rosalyn Higgins (UK) presided over the ICJ.[12] In 2015, the ICC simultaneously had a female President (Judge Silvia Fernandez de Gurmendi of Argentina), a female First Vice-President (Judge Akua Kuenyehia of Ghana), a female Second Vice-President (Judge Kuniko Ozaki of Japan), and a female Presiding Judge of the Trial Chamber (Judge Joyce Aluoch of Kenya).[13] Hansine N. Donli (Nigeria) was the President of the ECOWAS Community Court of Justice from 2012 to 2014, while Judge Elsie Nwanwuri Thompson (Nigeria) served as the Vice-President of the ACtHPR.

The number of African women appointed to the international bench is particularly impressive: for example, five of the 15 women who have served on the ICC bench are Africans.[14] Of the six women judges at the ICC in 2003, three were Africans.[15] In 2020, only three (out of 15) ICJ judges are women—one of them, as said above, is African. Six women sit as judges of the ACtHPR (which has 11 judges in total).[16] The higher rate of appointment of African women demands an

[11] The other African judges are from Somalia (President Abdulqawi Yusuf) and Morocco (Judge Mohamed Bennouna)<www.icj-cij.org/en/current-members>accessed 29 February 2020.

[12] C Steer, 'Four Women at the Top of the International Criminal Court – an International First' (*Intlawgrrls*, 18 March 2015) <https://ilg2.org/2015/03/18/four-women-at-the-top-of-the-international-criminal-court-an-international-first/>accessed 29 February 2020.

[13] K Askin, 'For the First Time, a Woman Judge Heads the International Criminal Court' Open society <www.opensocietyfoundations.org/voices/first-time-woman-judge-heads-international-criminal-court>accessed 29 February 2020.

[14] With the 10 spread across Asia, Europe and South America. J Dawuni, 'Race to the Top? African Women Judges and International Courts' (*Intlawgrrls*, 1 July 2016) <https://ilg2.org/2016/07/01/race-to-the-top-african-women-judges-and-international-courts/>accessed 29 February 2020.

[15] They are Elizabeth Odio Benito (Costa Rica), Maureen Harding Clark (Ireland), Fatoumata Diarra (Mali), Akua Kuenyehia (Ghana), Navanethem Pillay (South Africa) and Sylvia Steiner (Brazil). See Stephen, C 'Women judges dominate world's new war crimes court' (2003) <www.theguardian.com/world/2003/feb/09/warcrimes>accessed 29 February 2020.

[16] <www.african-court.org/en/index.php/judges/current-judges>accessed 29 February 2020. As the Statute of the ITLOS requires that equitable geographical distribution be assured among the Members and that there should be at least three Judges from each geographical group as established by the General Assembly of the United Nations [Statute of the International Tribunal for the Law of the Sea, 1982 U.N.

examination of their specific contextual narratives to discover which factors account for their ascendancy to transnational courts. This is vital since clarifying the relevant factors may aid the ascendancy of (African) women despite the challenges faced by their predecessors.[17]

Reasons to include women on the international bench relate to their right to be considered for appointment on an equal basis with their male counterparts and the wider benefits that result from their appointment. This is illustrated by the contributions of women judges to international criminal law jurisprudence on gender-based issues, such as rape.[18] As she explains in her Foreword to this book, Judge Pillay helped to develop ICTR jurisprudence that categorized rape as genocide while at the ICTY, Judge Odio-Benito was part of the bench when sexual assault and rape were included in the definition of torture.[19] These contributions could have 'far-reaching implications for ending impunity and providing justice and reparation for victims'.[20] Moreover, decisions made by international courts impact the lives of women globally so women should not be excluded from these decision-making processes.

Despite this, only four out of 108 judges appointed through the more than 70 years of the ICJ's existence have been women. Achieving more representation would create greater institutional sustainability.[21] The Statute of the ICJ provides that the composition of the Court must reflect 'the main forms of civilization and ... the principal legal systems of the world'.[22] Similarly, Article 2(2) of the Statute of the International Tribunal for the Law on the Sea (ITLOS) stipulates the representation of the principal legal systems of the world and equitable geographical distribution. The requirement found in the Statutes of the ICJ, the ICC, ITLOS, the Inter-American Court of Human Rights (IACtHR), and even the

Convention on the Law of the Sea, 1833 UNTS 3 Arts 2(2) and 3(2). Akande 'Election of Judges to the International Tribunal for the Law of the Sea' Blog of EJIL <www.ejiltalk.org/election-of-judges-to-the-international-tribunal-for-the-law-of-the-sea/>accessed 29 February 2020.

[17] Dawuni 'Race to the Top?' (n 14). For example, Stella Jane Marke (née Thomas) West Africa's first female lawyer, and the first female magistrate in the British Commonwealth in West Africa in 1945, did not ascend the higher bench due to challenges of colonialism, racism, and gender discrimination.

[18] Dawuni 'African Women Judges on International Courts' (n 5) 18 and 19. C Stephen, 'Women Judges Dominate World's New War Crimes Court' 2003) *The Guardian*, February 9, 2003 <www.theguardian.com/world/2003/feb/09/warcrimes>accessed 29 February 2020.

[19] V Krsticevic, 'Let's Talk About Gender Parity in International Justice' 2016 <www.huffingtonpost.com/viviana-krsticevic/lets-talk-about-gender-pa_b_9400860.html>accessed 29 February 2020. See also V Suhr, 'Feminism and the International Criminal Court – Still an Issue?' 19 April 2017 <https://voelkerrechtsblog.org/feminism-and-the-international-criminal-court-still-an-issue/>accessed 29 February 2020.

[20] Josephine J Dawuni 'African Women Judges on International Courts' (n 5) 6.

[21] That is a better functionality of the institution due to its policies, systems and procedures. ibid.

[22] The Statute of the ICJ (adopted 26 June 1945, in force 24 October 1945) 1 UNTS xvi, Art 91. Antônio Augusto Cançado Trindade 'Statute of the International Court of Justice' United Nations Audiovisual Library of International Law p 2. Grossman (n 1) at 668. See also R Abraham, 'How are Judges Elected to the International Court of Justice?' <www.thehindu.com/news/international/how-are-judges-elected-to-the-international-court-of-justice/article20619816.ece>accessed 29 February 2020.

ACtHPR, that there be no more than one judge of the same nationality exists to ensure widespread representation.[23] The influence of female judges' life experiences, 'cultural background, academic education, [and] personal challenges' on the judicial process does not undermine judicial impartiality but rather helps ensure that decisions reflect the diversity of the legal subjects of the courts, thus enhancing their legitimacy.[24] The female judges Patricia Wald, Akua Kuenyehia, Navanethem Pillay, Julia Sebutinde, Sophia Akuffo, and Cecilia Medina Quiroga[25] have asserted that, in addition to contributing to the jurisprudence of the courts in their areas of expertise,[26] as their male counterparts do, their perspectives are shaped by their experiences and perceptions as women, which may impact on the judicial decisions they make, such as their 'sensitivity and understanding' in cases involving sexual crimes.[27]

However, Rosalyn Higgins refutes the idea that a woman's gender influences her decisions but accepts that other female judges may have had different experiences, stating: 'I cannot stand in their shoes and disagree with them'.[28] Higgins' position that the female judge's competence is not based on her intuition but on her knowledge of the law, just as that of her male counterparts, is not in dispute.[29] Neither is the idea that male judges can also be sensitive when dealing with these issues.[30] However, there have been instances where female judges have played a significant role in ensuring that the sensitivities of victims of sexual crimes were not disregarded.[31] Dana Schmalz sums this up by stating that '[t]he diverse composition

[23] Art 10(3) Statute of the ICJ; Art 36(7) and (8) Rome Statute of the International Criminal Court (adopted 17 July 1998, entered into force 1 July 2002) 2187 UNTS 3; Art 3(1) Statute of the International Tribunal for the Law of the Sea, (adopted 10 December 1982) 1833 UNTS 3; Art 4(2) Statutes of the Inter-American Court of Human Rights (adopted 1 October 1979, entered into force 1 January 1980) 443 IACHR; Art 11(1)–(2) the African Charter on Human and Peoples' Rights (adopted 10 June 1998, entered into force 25 January 2004). D Schmalz, 'Judgment and Diversity Thinking with Hannah Arendt about the Composition of International Court Benches' (*Voelkerrechtsblog*, 3 May 2017) <http://voelkerrechtsblog.org/judgment-and-diversity/>accessed 29 February 2020.

[24] ibid at 5th paragraph. R Badejogbin, 'Elsie Nwanuri Thompson The Trajectory of a Noble Passion' in A Kuenyehia and J Dawuni, *International Courts and the African Woman Judge: Unveiled Narratives* (Routledge 2017) 124 and 131. See also Mishra (n 10); J Dawuni 'Introduction' in A Kuenyehia and J Dawuni, *International Courts and the African Woman Judge: Unveiled Narratives.*

[25] Wald was a judge at the International Criminal Tribunal for the Former Yugoslavia. She was also the first female Chief Judge of the federal appeals court in Washington DC from 1986 to 1991. Akuffo is the current Chief Justice of Ghana. She was a judge of the ACtHPR and served as its vice president for two terms from 2008 to 2012 and as its first female President in 2012. Quiroga served in the United Nations Human Rights Committee from 1995 to 2002 and as its chair in 1999–2000. She also served on the Inter-American Court of Human Rights from 2004 to 2009; she was its Vice-President in 2007 and became its President from 2008 to 2009.

[26] N Grossman, 'Sex on the Bench: Do Women Judges Matter to the Legitimacy of International Courts?' 658–659.

[27] ibid 658.

[28] Gleider I Henandez *The International Court of Justice and the Judicial Function* (OUP 2014) 136 footnote 60.

[29] ibid.

[30] ibid.

[31] Grossman 'Julia Sebutinde 'An Unbreakable' in Kuenyehia and Dawuni, (n 10) 41.

of international courts is important for tackling inequalities and blind spots'.[32] Women may give particular attention to the plight of female victims of sexual assault simply for the reason that they more readily understand its impact on women.[33] In the words of Judge Sebutinde:

> I recall a woman aged 70 years old who was gang-raped and had to testify before us about it ... She couldn't even look at the judges or anybody because her husband and grown children were sitting in the front row. These are gender sensitivities that our male colleagues may not even be aware of during the trial.[34]

She further explained the likely effect of her sensitivity when she elaborated:

> Am I not allowed to read that woman's language? If she's not able to raise her eyes because of the feeling of shame? If all she can do is to mumble with her eyes downcast and narrate her story the best way she can, should we disbelieve her testimony?[35]

The representation of women in international courts facilitates access to justice for women and children.[36] The efforts of Judge Thompson, Judge Sophia Akuffo, and Judge Solomy Bossa at the ACtHPR support this point: they were concerned that women were unaware that the jurisdiction of the ACtHPR extended to women's rights and therefore did not utilize the courts for the protection of their rights. In 2012[37] and in 2016,[38] they organized a series of seminars for women and women-related NGOs in Africa to educate them on how women could seek redress from the Court.[39]

[32] D Schmalz, 'Judgment and Diversity: Thinking with Hannah Arendt about the Composition of International Court Benches' (*Voelkerrechtsblog*, 3 May 2017) p 3.

[33] 'Women and the Judiciary' ICJ Geneva Forum Series no. 1 p 21. This point was reiterated in the First West African Sub-Regional Women Judges' Conference convened by the International Association of Women Judges in collaboration with the National Association of Women Judges, Nigeria, where the women judges committed to 'make their courtrooms a safe environment, especially for victims of child abuse, child neglect, spousal abuse, rape victims and victims of other heinous crimes' C Oloyede, 'S/ Court justice charges women judges on integrity of judiciary' Daily Trust July 18 2017 <www.dailytrust.com.ng/s-court-justice-charges-women-judges-on-integrity-of-judiciary.html>accessed 29 February 2020. See also M Williams and F Thames, 'Women's Representation on High Courts in Advanced Industrialized Countries' (2008) 4 PG 451, 456.

[34] Grossman, 'Julia Sebutinde 'An Unbreakable Cloth' in Kuenyehia and Dawuni (n 10) 43.

[35] ibid.

[36] Ellett, 'Justina Kelello Mafoso-Guni The Gendering of Judicial Appointment Processes in African Courts' in Kuenyehi and Dawuni (n 10) at 108.

[37] A seminar on the 'Overview of the Human Rights System with Special Emphasis on the African Court and Access for Women' which was held at Yaounde, Cameroun. See Badejogbin (n 24) 134 at footnote 2.

[38] International Women's Day Seminar on 'Enhancing Access to the African Court for Women under the Maputo Protocol' as part of the 10-year anniversary commemoration of the Court. See Badejogbin (n 24) 134.

[39] ibid.

African women, in particular, have made significant contributions within global institutions including international courts and tribunals. They have 'influenced international law, doctrines, norms, jurisprudence, public policy, public discourse, and global governance'.[40] As with their counterparts from other continents, African female judges bring their diverse perspectives and experiences to enhance debate within international tribunals.[41] In addition to the example of Judge Navanethem Pillay, mentioned above, one could refer to Judge Sebutinde, who helped to draw the distinction between arranged marriages and forced marriages in the context of armed conflict so as to reinforce the rights of female victims.[42] Her contributions demonstrate how cultural and gender-specific experiences can influence jurisprudence, particularly where a case concerns African women.[43] These judges have assisted the clarification and application of public international law in general as well as women's rights more specifically.[44]

The rising number of African women in international courts may also reflect a trend at the domestic level, which is unsurprising since domestic judges are sometimes appointed to the international bench.[45] Dawuni and Bauer have highlighted the benefits of African women judges sitting on domestic courts: they have set important precedents, particularly with regard to women's rights.[46] Likewise they have something to offer to international courts.[47] Further research should explore how the specific ethnic backgrounds of African women influence judicial decisions.[48]

3. Paths to International Courts: a Conundrum or Smooth Sailing?

The path to the international bench for African women, as with their female counterparts from other continents, is determined by a number of factors including

[40] J Levitt (ed), *Black Women and International Law deliberate interactions, movements, and actions* (CUP 2015) xi and 15.

[41] Krsticevic, 2016 'Let's Talk About Gender Parity in International Justice' (n 19) at line 2 para 8.

[42] Grossman, 'Julia Sebutinde 'An Unbreakable Cloth' in Kuenyehia and Dawuni (n 10) 51.

[43] ibid.

[44] See Kuenyehia and Dawuni (n 10).

[45] Dawuni, 'African Women Judges on International Courts' (n 10). Some examples are Judge Bossa, Judge Thompson, Judge Sebutinde, and Judge Akuffo who were judges of domestic courts before their appointments to transnational courts.

[46] Bauer and Dawuni (eds), *Gender and the Judiciary in Africa* (n 6) at 11.

[47] The bureaucratic judicial appointment process of civil law countries may favour the appointment of well qualified women more than in common law countries where the process is less transparent and involves a greater degree of discretion exercised by gatekeepers. Hence in common law countries, women must successfully undertake political manoeuvres as well as be suitably qualified. See J Dawuni and A. Kang, 'Her Ladyship the Chief Justice: The Rise of Female Leaders in the Judiciary in Africa' (2015) 62 (2) AT 45–69. See also Bauer and Dawuni (n 6). See also Dawuni 'Race to the Top?' (n 14).

[48] Ellett (n 36) 51. The narratives of the various chapters in Dawuni and Kuenyehia's book on the background and ethnicity of African women on the international courts give some insight.

qualification, election processes, socio-economic factors, political manoeuvres, mentoring, gatekeeping, geo-cultural politics, and a mixture of 'contextual experiences, institutional opportunities and personal agency', all against the background of a wider need for the political will to nominate women.[49] These factors are examined here under the two broad categories of (1) legal requirements and (2) non-legal factors.

3.1 Legal Requirements

GQUAL, 'a global campaign that seeks to promote gender parity in international tribunals and monitoring bodies',[50] has suggested three approaches to achieving gender parity that directly affect the appointment process of international judges. They are: persuading governments to commit to gender parity when selecting candidates for international vacancies; getting international bodies to promote gender parity in the selection process through their policies and criteria; and promoting 'research and global advocacy' on this issue.[51] There have been concerted efforts to achieve these goals.

Commonly, candidates for an international judicial position have to 'survive' three hurdles in order to be successfully appointed: meeting the qualification requirements, receiving a nomination, and getting (s)elected. The first hurdle usually includes moral, academic, experiential, and competence requirements, as well as considerations concerning the candidate's gender, nationality, and geographical origin.[52] Some courts' statutes do not refer to gender,[53] while a few others include gender but do not impose an obligation of parity.[54] Such a requirement is not strictly legal, but rather an aspirational target. The second hurdle entails the nomination of the candidate by the relevant body, as part of a country's internal nomination process.[55] The third hurdle involves a selection process which varies between courts, and the election itself.[56]

3.1.1 The first appointment hurdle: the qualifications requirement

Many qualified African women meet the relevant criteria through their careers in national judiciaries, academia, diplomatic services, professional organizations,

[49] Badejogbin (n 24).
[50] <www.gqualcampaign.org/about-gqual/>accessed 29 February 2020.
[51] Krsticevic (n 19).
[52] D Terris, C Romano, and L Swigart, '*The International Judge: An Introduction to the Men and Women who Decide the World's Cases*' (OUP, 2007).
[53] ICJ and ITLOS (n 23).
[54] ICC (n 23).
[55] N Grossman, 'Achieving Sex-Representative International Court Bench' (2016) 110 (1) American Journal of International Law 84.
[56] ibid.

and legal practice.[57] If appointments to the international bench were based only on these benchmarks, the pathway for African women would be easier. The moral standards, a criterion which the courts' statutes do not define,[58] of serving African women judges have never been questioned. With respect to professional and experiential criteria, Dawuni states that 'among the elite group of women judges serving on international courts are prominent African women judges drawn from across the continent with a wide variety of judicial and professional experience'.[59] These candidates have exhibited leadership skills prior to their appointments to the international bench, often gained through advocating the rights of women, children, and other vulnerable members of society.[60]

Charlesworth's, Chinkin's and Wright's 'thesis of institutionalized male privilege in relation to international courts' asserts that 'low numbers of qualified female candidates in the pool of candidates' presented for appointment are responsible for 'low numbers on international court benches'.[61] Grossman refutes this finding,[62] arguing that appointments to international benches are not necessarily merit-based: countries with a higher percentage of women lawyers are not represented by more women on the international bench.[63] Two issues arise here. The first is whether a high number of female lawyers generally results in a larger pool of female candidates since international judges are sourced from the highest-ranking diplomats, lawyers, academics, and judges. Even in countries with a high percentage of female lawyers, women more often than not occupy the lower echelons of the bar, bench, and government offices.[64] This is, however, changing. There are an increasing number of African women who have advanced through the legal profession and should now be in the pool of eligible candidates for the international bench.

The second issue pertains to whether appointments to international judgeship are based on merit. Grossman asserts that:

> the limited-pool argument assumes that judicial selection procedures aim to choose the most meritorious candidates. Yet, international judgeships are often used to reward political loyalty or to advance political agendas rather than to select the most qualified or meritorious candidates.[65]

[57] Dawuni, 'African Women Judges on International Court' (n 10).

[58] Terris, Romano, and Swigart (n 52).

[59] Dawuni 'African Women Judges on International Court', (n 10) at 5.

[60] ibid.

[61] H Charlesworth, C Chinkin, and S Wright, *Feminist Approaches to International Law* (1991) 85 American Journal of International Law 613.

[62] Grossman, 'Achieving Sex-Representative International Court' (n 55) .

[63] ibid.

[64] OECD 'Women in the Judiciary: working towards a legal system reflective of society' <www.oecd.org/>accessed 29 February 2020.

[65] Grossman, 'Achieving Sex-Representative International Court' (n 55).

Grossman's assertion is supported by Lesothan Judge Mafoso-Guni's experience at the ACtHPR.[66] During her first tenure at the court, she tried to convince the Lesothan government to acknowledge the right of individuals to sue their government before the ACtHPR.[67] She stated that her government considered her actions unpatriotic,[68] and therefore did not re-nominate her for a further term.[69] Rose also considers that 'non-meritorious selection procedures [are] the main problem, and the gender imbalance that we see across international courts and tribunals is a manifestation of it'.[70] Meritorious selection would open the way for both the best male and female candidates.[71] The path to an international judgeship would then be smoother for women generally and in particular for African women. Equal gender representation should not be at the expense of ensuring that candidates are suitably qualified but Grossman argues that increasing female nominations will enhance institutional legitimacy whilst maintaining qualification standards.[72]

One proposed solution, the creation of legal obligations for gender parity, would entail risks if there were insufficiently qualified female candidates for the positions and could detract from standards of competence. The whole purpose of gender representation provisions is to ensure that *suitably qualified* women are not overlooked. Aspirational statements can be upgraded to legal obligations,[73] thereby improving access for women whilst not undermining qualification requirements. Where creating a legal obligation is not feasible, clear-cut aspirational statements are better than not having any guide at all. Grossman's suggestion that States incorporate 'aspirational statements ... into court statutes or selection procedures, or through temporary special measures or quotas',[74] would help to create opportunities for suitably qualified women. Earlier statutes establishing international courts, such as the ICJ and the ITLOS, are silent on gender diversity.[75] In contrast, the Statute of the ICC requires States parties to consider 'a fair representation of female and male judges'.[76] This statutory requirement may explain the greater representation of women judges at the ICC compared to either ITLOS or the ICJ.[77]

[66] The first female judge of the High Court of Lesotho and also the first female judge of the ACtHPR.
[67] Ellett in Justina Kelello Mafoso-Guni (n 36).
[68] ibid.
[69] ibid.
[70] C Rose, 'Justifying Arguments about Selection Procedures for Judges at International Courts and Tribunals: A Response to Nienke Grossman' (2016) 110 American Journal of International Law 2.
[71] ibid.
[72] Grossman, 'Achieving Sex-Representative International Court' (n 55). See also D Schmalz and N Grossman, 'It's not About "Women's Issues" An Interview with Nienke Grossman About Parity on International Court Benches' (*Voelkerrechtsblog*, 17 April 2017) <http://voelkerrechtsblog.org/its-not-about-women-issues/>accessed 29 February 2020.
[73] This will create a basis for accountability.
[74] Grossman, N 'Achieving Sex-Representative International Court' (n 55) at 84.
[75] R Mackenzie and others, *Selecting International Judges: Principles Process, & Politics* (OUP 2010) 47.
[76] Art 36(8)(a)(iii); Akande (n 16).
[77] ibid.

3.1.2 The second appointment hurdle: the nomination stage

The second appointment hurdle for candidates is getting through the nomination process: the potential for female candidates' success here is affected by whether the institution expressly aspires to better gender representation and the extent to which the process is transparent. As discussed under the rubric of qualification, candidates are nominated by States, who may sometimes be required to consider gender representation. The specifics and scope of these obligations vary between different international bodies. Some statutes such as those of the ACtHPR and the ICC provide guidance on the nomination and selection processes,[78] as well as on gender representation.[79] Other statutes, such as that of the ICJ, stipulate little or nothing in this regard. This lack of transparency enables nominators to favour candidates from their personal networks, which will often consist mostly of men.[80] Articles 12(2) and 14(2) of the ACtHPR, for instance, provide that 'due consideration' should be given to 'adequate gender representation' both at the nomination and election stages. The ambiguity of the term 'adequate gender representation' allows for political manoeuvring,[81] which may have influenced the initially low appointment of female judges at the ACtHPR. Article 36(8)(iii) of the ICC Statute uses a more appropriate phrase, 'a fair representation of female and male judges', which has resulted in a good representation of female judges, currently standing at 47%.

These requirements for gender representation have aided female appointments. Grossman notes that fewer women judges have been appointed to courts where the establishing instruments contained no statutory requirement or even statement of goals on gender parity.[82] In mid-2015, only 15% of judges in these courts were women, compared to 32% in courts with statutes that included legal requirements or goals.[83] Dawuni asserts that the inclusion of an aspirational statement is important for improving gender representation.[84] This may partly explain why 55% of judges are women at the ACtHPR, whose statute contains an aspirational statement, while at the ECOWAS Court and the EACJ, whose statutes have no such statement, only five out of 17 judges (29%) and four out of 25 (16%) are women respectively.[85] Nonetheless, aspirational statements alone do not lead to gender

[78] Art 9 Statute of the International Court of Justice; Art 36(7) and (8) Rome Statute of the International Criminal Court; and Art 11(1) and (2) Protocol to the African Charter on Human and Peoples' Rights on the Establishment of an African Court on Human and Peoples' Rights.

[79] Art 12(2) Protocol to the African Charter on Human and Peoples' Rights on the Establishment of an African Court on Human and Peoples' Rights; Art 36(8)(a)(iii) of Rome Statute of the International Criminal Court.

[80] Grossman, 'Achieving Sex-Representative International Court', (n 55) 90.

[81] Dawuni 'African Women Judges on International Courts', (n 10).

[82] Grossman, 'Achieving Sex-Representative International Court', (n 55) 82–95.

[83] ibid.

[84] J Dawuni, 'Vive la diversité! A Roadmap to Gender Parity on African Regional Courts?' (*Völkerrechtsblog*, 15 May 2017), doi: 10.17176/20170515-101207 <https://voelkerrechtsblog.org/vive-la-diversite/>accessed 29 February 2020.

[85] ibid.

parity.[86] Transparency in the nomination process is crucial for achieving adequate representation, partly because the nomination criteria and their application are open to public scrutiny. Grossman states that 'institutional screening after nomination may increase' female appointments.[87] She draws attention to the fact that international courts which have 'institutionalised screening [i.e. a mechanism for screening] after nomination' have a higher proportion of women judges: from 1999 to mid-2015, 29% of judges serving on the ECtHR were female, compared to 47% of ICC judges.[88] The percentage of female judges at the ECtHR was improved by the Council of Europe's requirement that States put forward at least one person from 'the underrepresented sex' amongst three ECtHR judicial candidates.[89] The nomination process for the ACtHPR is unknown: this lack of transparency prevents public accountability and may have narrowed the path prior to 2017 for African women.[90] Additional factors that may have improved the percentage of women appointed to the ACtHPR from 2017 are discussed below. Overall, it seems that institutionalised screening after nomination promotes better transparency because it fosters a form of accountability for compliance.

Other instruments that are indirectly linked to international courts could also enhance gender representation. Grossman asserts that various international, regional, sub-regional, and domestic legal instruments prohibiting gender discrimination impose an obligation on States to consider the appointment of women.[91] In contrast, Rose argues that Article 8 of the UN Charter, which provides that '[t]he United Nations shall place no restrictions on the eligibility of men and women to participate in any capacity and under conditions of equality in its principal and subsidiary organs',[92] cannot be used as a legal basis for States to nominate women since it only refers to the UN and its organizations and not to Member States.[93]

[86] O Ojigho, 'Africa: In pursuit of gender parity at the African court' (2012) <https://allafrica.com/stories/201209140816.html>accessed 13 August 2020.

[87] Grossman, 'Achieving Sex-Representative International Court' (n 55) 84.

[88] ibid. Both have institutionalized screening.

[89] Council of Europe Parliamentary Assembly <http://assembly.coe.int/nw/xml/RoP/RoP-XML2HTML-EN.asp?id=ENtoc_N0A29C3B0N13FFB248>accessed 13 August 2020.

[90] The ACtHPR saw improved appointment of women judges from 2017.

[91] These include the International Covenant on Civil and Political Rights (adopted 16 December 1966, entered into force 23 March 1976) 999 UNTS 171, Art 3; the Convention on the Elimination of All Forms of Discrimination Against Women (adopted 18 December 1979, entered into force 3 September 1981) 1249 UNTS 1, Art 8; Discrimination (Employment and Occupation) Convention (adopted 25 June 1958, in force 15 June 1960 (ILO Convention No.111), Art 1 (1); African Charter on Human and Peoples' Rights (adopted 27 June 1981, entered into force 21 October 1986) 1520 UNTS 217 OAU Doc CAB/LEG/67/3/Rev 5; Protocol to the African Charter on Human and Peoples' Rights On The Rights Of Women In Africa (adopted 11 July 2003, entered into force 25 November 2005); African Charter on Human Peoples Rights, Arts 13 and 18(3); (Art 9(2) 11 July 2003); Protocol to the African Charter on Human and Peoples' Rights; Protocol No. 12 to the Convention for the Protection of Human Rights and Fundamental Freedoms, National Constitutions and other laws (adopted 4 November 2000, entered into force 1 April 2005) ETS 177 (Art 12(2)). See Grossman, (n 42).

[92] C Rose, 'Justifying Arguments About Selection Procedures for Judges at International Courts and Tribunals: A Response to Nienke Grossman' (2016) 110 AJILUnbound 86.

[93] ibid.

Article 8 alone is insufficient because, while it prohibits gender restrictions, it does not impose an obligation to promote gender representation. Moreover, other judicial institutions such as the World Trade Organization's Appellate Body, the Court of Justice of the European Union (CJEU), and the ECtHR are outside the ambit of the UN.[94] The solution instead lies in the inclusion of provisions in the statutes of international courts and tribunals that impose clear obligations on Member States to ensure a fair gender representation amongst their nominees for judicial positions.

3.1.3 The third appointment hurdle: the (s)election process

The (s)election process that follows nomination brings its own difficulties for female candidates even when States are obliged to consider gender representation. It is often difficult for women to gain the necessary support amidst political manoeuvring: they often have weaker political connections and informal networks than men, which may be due to deliberate exclusion.[95] These assets are necessary when attempting to gain States' votes. There are also geographical quotas that must be observed at this stage,[96] such as the three seats informally marked for Africans at the ICJ.[97]

Greater transparency throughout election processes would engender better female representation on the international bench.[98] This could be done through further monitoring and advocacy at national, regional, and international levels by non-governmental organizations, experts, and coalitions, who would ensure that suitably qualified women are nominated at the national level and sustained at the regional/international level.[99] This can only be achieved if the nomination and selection process guarantees public accountability, and if there is ongoing advocacy to promote and enforce statutory provisions dealing with gender equity. At the ECtHR, a special parliamentary committee carries out an evaluation of nominees by assessing their qualifications and seeking to confirm that national nomination processes were conducted in a fair manner before elections take place.[100] At the ACtHPR, the Office of the Legal Counsel of the African Union, the Assembly of

[94] ibid at 4.

[95] Additional factors are due to lack of adequate opportunities to participate in politics and interact in public spheres: Ellet (n 36) 112. See also S Kalantry, 'Women in Robes' (2012) 6(3) Americans Quarterly 82 <www.lawschool. cornell.edu/womenandjustice/Featured-Articles-and-Reports/upload/Women-in-Robes-Final.pdf>; S J Kenney, 'Choosing Judges: A Bumpy Road to Women's Equality' (2012) Mich St L Rev 1499 at 1505.

[96] Art 36 (a)(ii) Rome Statute of the ICC; Art 9 Statute of the ICJ.

[97] United Nations Conference on Trade and Development 'Dispute Settlement International Court of Justice' 2003 p 7 footnote 4.

[98] Grossman, 'Achieving Sex-Representative International Court' (n 55).

[99] This however is not foolproof because NGOs, experts, and coalitions might also have their own political agenda and push for women who are not necessarily better qualified but who they think might further their objectives.

[100] Council of Europe Parliamentary Assembly <http://website-pace.net/web/as-cdh> accessed 29 February 2020.

Heads of State and Government, the Solidarity for African Women's Rights, the Pan-African Lawyers Union, as well as bar associations and law societies at the national level play a crucial role.[101] Dawuni argues that the high proportion of female judges at the ACtHPR is a result of a 'combined result of a number of factors' which include:

> the decision by the Office of the Legal Counsel of the African Union to ensure that women candidates were on the list of nominees, and secondly, the decision by the Assembly of Heads of State and Government to postpone further elections for filling the last two vacancies until there were women nominees on the ballot. Another factor that appears to have contributed to this pay-off can be linked to the advocacy for enforcing the gender equity provisions, specifically Article 9 of the Maputo Protocol by civil society organizations such as the Solidarity for African Women's Rights (SOAWR). Lastly, we can pay some credit to the activities of the Pan-African Lawyers Union (PALU) and national Bar Associations and Law Societies across the continent for advocating for open and transparent nomination processes.[102]

This could not have been achieved without the political will of the bodies responsible for holding elections, prompted by non-governmental organizations, experts, and coalitions.[103] Even where there are African women who meet the relevant criteria and where statutes contain clear-cut legal obligations or aspirational statements, adequate gender representation may not be achieved where political will is absent. Reaching 55% female representation at the ACtHPR was possible because of additional factors which include 'the actualisation of political will by the electing bodies'.[104] Pressure groups contributed to this success in three ways. Firstly, they strengthened existing political will towards gender representation in appointments. Secondly, they ignited previously non-existent political will towards gender representation. Thirdly, they enhanced transparency and accountability in the appointing process through scrutinizing compliance with legal obligations/aspirational targets, advocacy to promote gender representation, and ensuring compliance by the appointing bodies.[105] The role of NGOs, experts, and coalitions of national bar associations and law societies in improving female judicial representation at the ACtHPR could be replicated in other courts.[106]

In sum, the hurdles that obstruct African women's aspirations with respect to qualifications, nomination, and (s)election can be overcome. If action is taken, the

101 Dawuni, 'Vive la diversité! A Roadmap to Gender Parity on African Regional Courts?' (n 84).
102 ibid at para 6 lines 3–13.
103 ibid.
104 ibid.
105 ibid.
106 ibid.

growing number of African women who have the requisite qualifications will stand a greater chance of appointment. Selection processes based on merit will also improve their chances for appointment as well as open and transparent processes, guaranteed through pressure by activist groups with the ability to change political mindsets towards fair gender representation.

3.2 Non-legal Factors

Alongside legal requirements, numerous political and socio-economic factors affect a woman's ability to reach the international bench. These include geo-cultural politics, mentoring, gatekeeping, and the deliberate mobilization of women by other women.[107] This last factor differs from mentoring in that it could involve the enlistment of women to fill vacancies. Other elements that determine a woman's career progression include institutional opportunities, and the personal experiences and choices of the woman.[108] This section examines the role these factors have played in the experiences of female African judges.

Political and socio-economic factors are inherent to formal appointing processes but also operate through informal structures. Thus, reforming appointment instruments without taking other measures will not achieve fair gender representation. At the domestic level, relevant informal structures, as identified by Williams and Thames, include 'the prestige of the courts, selection methods utilised and the importance attributed to women's role in the society'.[109] Since domestic appointment is sometimes a prerequisite for the international bench,[110] this has a knock-on effect at the international level. A clear example is the experience of the first female judge of the ACtHPR and of the Lesotho High Court, Judge Kellelo Mafoso-Guni. The constitution of Lesotho prohibits gender discrimination but informal discrimination still prevails through social norms that operate through 'informal institutional disadvantages in terms of access to the labour market',[111] and customary law.[112] The appointment of Judge Mafoso-Guni in 1995 as a High Court judge was met with strong resistance because she was a woman and no woman had ever been appointed to occupy the position: students protested and the male Justice Minister and members of the Law Society called for a boycott of her court.[113]

[107] Kuenyehia and Dawuni (n 10) at 124 and 132.

[108] ibid.

[109] Bauer and Dawuni (n 6) at 7. See also Williams and Thames (n 33).

[110] Judge Sebutinde, Jude Thompson, Judge Mafoso-Guni, Judge Akuffo, Judge Bossa to mention a few.

[111] Even though the women according to the UNDP National Report, are more educated than the men. Ellett (n 36) at 110.

[112] United Nations Development Programme, (2015) Lesotho National Human Development Report: Leveraging the Power of Youth to Promote Human Development <http://hdr.undp.org/sites/default/files/final_lesotho_high_res_single_pages.pdf> accessed 29 February 2020, p 8.

[113] Ellett (n 36) at 113.

She was forced to go underground for her safety during this period.[114] The Lesotho branch of the International Federation of Women Lawyers (FIDA) conducted a successful media campaign to support Mafoso-Guni's appointment. As Ellett writes, this 'speaks to the positive and critical support women can give other women as they gain entry to more politicized, high-power positions'.[115] Following this success, women now comprise 65% of High Court judges in Lesotho.[116] Mafoso-Guni's experience demonstrates both the insufficiency of formal legal equality and the power of civil society to change social norms and thus improve female representation.

At the international level, potential female candidates to the international bench may be unaware of their suitability and/or of vacancies. To address this problem, the Institute for African Women in Law (IAWL) and the Ghana chapter of the International Association of Women Judges (IAWJ) organized the conference 'Women Judges Demystifying International Courts'.[117] Most female African judges discovered the vacancies for judicial positions at the international courts by chance or through connections with gatekeepers. For example, Julia Sebutinde found out about the Special Court of Sierra Leone (SCSL) opening through a domestic diplomat in Uganda the day before the application submission deadline.[118] Later on, she discovered that an African judge would be retiring from the ICJ, because she was already living in The Hague.[119] Judge Elsie Thompson, formerly of the ACtHPR, was unaware of the Court's existence before her nomination was initiated by the (female) Nigerian Ambassador to Ethiopia, Nkoyo Toyo.[120] Judge Mafoso-Guni became aware she was being nominated by her government when she was asked by the Chief Justice to submit her curriculum vitae to the Ministry of Foreign Affairs.[121] These examples show that a lack of awareness of vacancies can inhibit the appointment of African women to the international bench. Some of these women may not have previously aspired to the international bench for a number of reasons: because they were content with their existing achievements, because they were intimidated and felt unqualified, or because they were genuinely unaware of the vacancies. These women were unlikely to search actively for international opportunities.[122]

114 ibid.
115 ibid at 115.
116 ibid.
117 The 2016 conference featured Justice Akua Kuenyehia, a former judge of the International Criminal Court (ICC), Justice Sophia Akuffo, a current Supreme Court judge of Ghana and former judge and President of the African Court on Human and Peoples' Rights, and Dr. Josephine Dawuni. See 'Female Judges Fired Up' Daily Guide 13 July 2016 available at <http://dailyguideafrica.com/female-judges-fired-up/>accessed 29 February 2020.
118 Grossman, 'Julia Sebutinde 'An Unbreakable Cloth' in Kuenyehia and Dawuni (n 10) at 40.
119 ibid at 46. The information was however available on the ICJ website.
120 Badejogbin (n 24) at 132.
121 Ellett (n 36) at 116.
122 Kuukuwa Andam and Sena Dei-Tutu Akuffo at 105.

Even when potential female candidates are aware of a vacancy, they may find it difficult to be nominated and gain sufficient support for election due to their weaker network links compared to their male counterparts. ICJ Judge Sebutinde had to travel to her home country Uganda, to seek and receive the nomination from the national group of her country,[123] and approval from the President and his cabinet.[124] She then spent two years campaigning to receive endorsements from the East African Community, the African Union and the Organisation of the Islamic Conference.[125] During this time, she also made over 200 visits to different embassies at her own expense.[126] Some women may not be willing to make such a commitment for the sake of gaining an international judicial appointment. Sital Kalantry argues that a lack of these connections impedes female appointments.[127] He states that 'women are typically less connected to these appointment and selection mechanisms than are their male colleagues'.[128] The experienced and qualified women who succeeded either vigorously pursued nominations and support, or were just fortunate.[129]

Circumstances and early life choices affect a woman's chance at a career on the international bench.[130] Relevant factors include family values that do not undermine female children, personal determination, hard work, exposure to opportunities, available resources, accessibility of institutions as well as personal choices made by the women themselves.[131] Access to education is particularly important. Navanethem Pillay, Julia Sebutinde, Elsie Thompson, Fatoumata Diarra, Sophia Akuffo, and Kellelo Mafoso-Guni were all able to enrol in schools and eventually universities. Some obtained academic scholarships, and some studied abroad.[132] As Ellett writes, 'public funding and support for girls' education is critical, and these early interventions can steer girls down certain pathways'.[133] Mentorship can also play an important role in obtaining a university education, excelling in legal practice and seeking judicial appointment. This was the case for Judge Thompson, who was mentored by Justice Mary Odili, the third woman to be appointed to the Nigerian Supreme Court.[134] Deliberate mobilization of women by other women

[123] Grossman, 'Julia Sebutinde An Unbreakable Cloth' in Kuenyehia and Dawuni, (n 10) 45.

[124] ibid at 46.

[125] ibid.

[126] ibid.

[127] S Kalantry, 'Women in Robes' (2012) Summer Americas Quarterly 85.

[128] ibid.

[129] Examples such as Mafoso-Guni and Thompson, as discussed earlier. Thompson sums it as Divine providence.

[130] Kuenyehia and Dawuni (n 10). See also K Adem and Dei S Tutu, 'Sophia Akuffo Balancing the Equities' in Kuenyehia and Dawuni (eds) (n 10) at 98 and 99.

[131] Judge Thompson includes divine providence as the main reason for her ascension to an international judicial position. See Badejogbin (n 24) at 125.

[132] Badejogbin (n 24) at 124. See also S Dezalay, 'Fatoumata Dembélé Diarra Trajectory of a Malian Magistrate and Civil Society Advocate to the International Criminal Court' in Kuenyehia and Dawuni (n 10) 81.

[133] Ellett (n 36) at 111.

[134] Badejogbin (n 24) at 125.

also helps, as seen with Judge Thompson who was recommended for a judicial position at the ACtHPR by Ambassador Nkoyo Toyo, who wanted the position to be occupied by another woman.[135]

Many African women judges on the international bench were committed to promoting the rights of women and children before their appointment. They exhibited this through their work with NGOs, governments, international organizations, and civil society—experiences which helped them meet position requirements for international judgeships. Often, they consider their ascension to international courts to be a way to continue to champion the cause of vulnerable victims of war, oppression, and abuse.[136] There have also been instances where women have been appointed based on their prior exposure to international court systems. The Malian government nominated Judge Fatoumata Diarra for an ICTY appointment because of her judicial and human rights work, as well as her UN training.[137] Her ICC appointment built upon her ICTY experience. As already mentioned, Judge Sebutinde had served as a judge at the SCSL before her appointment to the ICJ.

Many female judges are not merely motivated by personal ambition but strongly believe in the power of international courts to dispense justice to States and their subjects.[138] Judge Julia Sebutinde, for example, aspired to become an ICJ judge so she could contribute her personal knowledge of conflicts, involving war crimes and State-sponsored violence from her home country of Uganda, as well as from her experience at the SCSL.[139] Even though these motivations are not the exclusive preserve of women, they add to the reasons why women should be given the opportunity to serve on international benches. As shown by these examples, political and socio-economic factors, as well as legal ones, must be addressed to increase the number of women on the international bench. Reforming the applicable statutes alone is not enough. Consideration must be given to practical measures that address other informal factors affecting such appointments as set out in the next section.

4. A Proposal for Gender Parity?

There have been many efforts to improve female representation in public life, including on the international bench.[140] International instruments such as the Charter of the United Nations and the Convention on the Elimination of all Forms

[135] Badejogbin (n 24) 132.
[136] Kuenyehia and Dawuni (n 10).
[137] Dezalay (n 10) 87.
[138] Examples are Judge Thompson, Judge Sebutinde and Judge Diarra. S Allison, 'Africa's Most Senior Female Judge: "Would These Men Even Listen To Me?"' *Daily Maverick* (27 November 2016).
[139] ibid para 9.
[140] Krsticevic (n 19).

of Discrimination against Women (CEDAW) support this.[141] GQUAL, for example, calls for gender parity in international tribunals.[142] Similarly to GQUAL, scholars such as Grossman advocate a 50:50 gender representation so as to enhance the legitimacy of institutions whose exercise of jurisdiction affects both men and women.[143] Dawuni states that 'equity among the sexes is simply the right thing to do',[144] warning, however, against the alienation of men who are gender sensitive and seek to uphold the rights of women.[145] To ensure institutional legitimacy with respect to the courts' constituents, representation cannot only be a matter of numerical representation. Following this argument to the extreme would mean that the most populous countries in the world could demand proportionate representation of their citizens on the ICJ bench.

Is a 50:50 gender split the only way to ensure 'adequate' representation? 'Adequate' in this context means a sufficient, satisfactory, and acceptable number of female and male judges to maintain a court's legitimacy. While 50:50 gender parity enhances legitimacy, it should not be the benchmark per se where there are no mechanisms of exclusion i.e. the deliberate exclusion of women. The number of female and male judges has to be sufficient to preserve the legitimacy of the institution without compromising the quality of the decision-making. Therefore, what 'adequate' means, should be determined within the context of each court, acknowledging the complexities and the various factors involved in each appointment. To use an 'adequate' number rather than 'parity' as a benchmark ensures sufficient representation of both genders in situations where there is either a male or female majority on the bench. While in most domestic and international courts, men make up the majority on the bench, there are a few where women judges are in the majority, such as the ACtHPR with about 55% women, the Lesothan High Court where 65% of judges are women and the Lagos High Court where about 70% of the judges, as well as the high level administrative staff are women.[146] What should be required is a sufficient number of either gender, whereby there may be other reasons that determine the appointment of women to international courts.

A position on the international bench involves significant personal sacrifices which some women are willing to make,[147] but others are not, for understandable reasons. Appointment requirements should include provisions that would foster balanced environments that are welcoming to women; this allows courts and tribunals to benefit fully from women's valuable contributions. For instance, attention

[141] ibid. Art 8 Charter of the United Nations (adopted 26 June 1945, in force 24 October 1945) 1 UNTS xvi; Art 8 Convention on the Elimination of All Forms of Discrimination Against Women.

[142] Krsticevic (n 19). See also <www.gqualcampaign.org/about-gqual/>accessed 29 February 2020.

[143] Grossman 'Achieving Sex-Representative International Court' (n 55).

[144] Dawuni (n 5) 27.

[145] She was however silent about men who are not particularly sensitive towards gender.

[146] Currently, they are about 35 female judges and 20 male judges at the Court.

[147] Kuenyehia and Dawuni (n 10) at 154–55.

must be given to the working environments of the courts, their compatibility with family life, the working hours, whether there is flexibility to accommodate the schedules of a working mother and whether there are childcare provisions, etc. The ICJ, for example, has no scheme for parental leave system for judges, even though at least two babies were born while their fathers were serving on its bench. Further research could explore the effect of the demands of the job on female participation.

5. Conclusion

This chapter has explored the selection of African women judges to the international bench and examined factors that affect their appointments as they may unfortunately fall victim to double discrimination, for being female and African. The analysis was supported with insights into the challenges and opportunities of African women who seek to serve as international judges. The chapter identified a variety of factors that determine the ease of access for women to the international bench, covering the qualification, nomination, and (s)election stages, as well as socio-economic factors and geo-cultural politics. These elements should needfully be addressed. Accounts of how these factors played out in the experiences of African women judges provide useful guidance. Possible solutions may lie in the creation of legal obligations or at least, aspirational statements; transparency in the nomination process; institutionalized screening after nomination to ensure accountability regarding compliance; and ongoing advocacy by stakeholders and interested groups to promote and enforce statutory provisions dealing with gender equity. Finally, it is important to have activist groups who apply pressure to change political mindsets concerning adequate gender representation.

8

Analysing Appointments in International Arbitration

Nationality, Ethnicity, Race, and Legal Training of Arbitrators

Monika Prusinowska

1. Introduction

International arbitration[1] has become a popular method of resolving transnational disputes due to the neutrality of the process, the level of party autonomy, the flexibility of the arbitration proceedings, as well as the efficient enforcement of arbitral awards.[2] As a result, the caseload of arbitration institutions has been growing steadily,[3] but there has been criticism among international arbitration practitioners[4] of the lack of diversity among arbitrators.[5] So far, most attention has been devoted to gender diversity, leading to numerous steps to promote the appointment of female arbitrators. These include actions taken by arbitration

[1] The chapter's discussion pertains to both international commercial arbitration and international investment arbitration.

[2] See School of International Arbitration Queen Mary University of London and White and Case, '2015 International Arbitration Survey: Improvements and Innovations in International Arbitration' (2015) 2, 5.; School of International Arbitration Queen Mary University of London, '2018 International Arbitration Survey: The-Evolution of International Arbitration' (2018) 5–8.

[3] See the caseload comparison of the leading arbitration institutions in Gary Born, *International Commercial Arbitration* (2nd edn, Kluwer Law International 2014) 94–95.

[4] It is challenging to identify the 'international arbitration community'. For the discussions of this chapter, it includes international arbitration counsels, arbitrators, arbitration institutions' staff, in-house counsels involved in arbitration, as well as academics. See also Susan D Franck and others, 'The Diversity Challenge: Exploring the "Invisible College" of International Arbitration' (2015) 53(3) Columbia Journal of Transnational Law 430.

[5] See, for example, ibid; Berwin Leighton Paisner International Arbitration Group, 'Diversity on Arbitral Tribunals: Are We Getting There?' (2016).; Jacomijn J van Haersolte-Van Hof, 'Diversity in Diversity' in Albert Jan van den Berg (ed), *Legitimacy: Myths, Realities, Challenges* (Kluwer Law International 2015).; Christophe Seraglini, 'Who Are the Arbitrators? Myths, Reality and Challenges' in Albert Jan Van den Berg (ed), *Legitimacy: Myths, Realities, Challenges* (Kluwer Law International 2015).; Lucy Greenwood and Mark Baker, 'Getting a Better Balance on International Arbitration Tribunals' (2012) 28(4) Journal of the London Court of International Arbitration.; African Association of International Law, 'Tribunals Need Africans, Says His Excellency Judge Abdulqawi Ahmed Yusuf, Vice-President of the International Court of Justice,' (1 December 2015),<www.aail-aadi.org/single-post/2015/12/01/"Tribunals-need-Africans"-says-His-Excellency-Judge-Abdulqawi-Ahmed-Yusuf-vicepresident-of-the-International-Court-of-Justice> accessed 29 February 2020.

Monika Prusinowska, *Analysing Appointments in International Arbitration* In: *Identity and Diversity on the International Bench.* Edited by: Freya Baetens, Oxford University Press (2020). © The several contributors.
DOI: 10.1093/oso/9780198870753.003.0008.

institutions,[6] as well as less formal initiatives. The latter include the Pledge for Equal Representation in Arbitration, signed by over 3,600 individuals and organizations,[7] and ArbitralWomen, an international non-governmental organization bringing together female practitioners in international dispute resolution.[8] As a result, the number of female appointments has increased, yet it is still far from the number of male appointments.[9]

Yet, diversity aspects, other than gender, such as nationality, race/ethnicity, and age, as well as their intersectionality,[10] are still waiting to be more fully addressed. Certain voices within the international arbitration community have taken steps to promote more diversity along these lines.[11] Initiatives include the Alliance for Equality, a non-profit organization advocating increased inclusivity in dispute resolution and equal opportunities 'regardless of location, nationality, ethnicity, sexual orientation, gender or age'.[12] However, further progress needs to be made particularly with regard to non-Western arbitrators. The respondents to the *2016 Berwin Leighton Paisner International Arbitration Group Survey on Diversity in Arbitration* showed significant dissatisfaction with the current pool of adjudicators in this respect. For example, 80% expressed the view that arbitral tribunals contained too many white arbitrators and 64% agreed that there were too many arbitrators from Western Europe or North America.[13] Furthermore, 54% thought it would be desirable for arbitrators to come

[6] See, for example, the International Court of Arbitration at the International Chamber of Commerce ('ICC') reporting on the progress in 'ICC Court Sees Marked Progress on Gender Diversity' <https://iccwbo.org/media-wall/news-speeches/icc-court-sees-marked-progress-gender-diversity/> accessed 29 February 2020.

[7] The Pledge for Equal Representation in Arbitration seeks to increase, on an equal opportunity basis, the number of women appointed as arbitrators in order to achieve a fair representation as soon practically possible, with the ultimate goal of full parity. (see the official website <www.arbitrationpledge.com>accessed 29 February 2020.

[8] The ArbitralWomen is an organisation providing a platform for female dispute resolution practitioners. Among the purposes of the ArbitralWomen are advancing the interest of female dispute resolution practitioners, promoting diversity, providing professional development opportunities and mentoring. See the official website <www.arbitralwomen.org/>accessed 29 February 2020.

[9] To illustrate, the ICC reported that in 2018 were 32% of women were appointed as a president and 30% as a sole arbitrator. See the ICC's official website <https://iccwbo.org/media-wall/news-speeches/icc-arbitration-figures-reveal-new-record-cases-awards-2018/>accessed 29 February 2020.

[10] See more about the intersectionality in Joshua Karton and Ksenia Polonskaya, 'True Diversity Is Intersectional: Escaping the One-Dimensional Discourse on Arbitrator Diversity' (*Kluwer Arbitration Blog*, 10 July 2018) <http://arbitrationblog.kluwerarbitration.com/2018/07/10/true-diversity-is-intersectional-escaping-the-one-dimensional-discourse-on-arbitrator-diversity/> accessed 29 February 2020.

[11] See, for example, the ICC reporting on the increased participation of arbitrators from growing economic regions, like Asia and North Africa, as well as on the rising number of younger arbitrators: the ICC's official website <https://iccwbo.org/media-wall/news-speeches/icc-arbitration-figures-reveal-new-record-cases-awards-2018/>accessed 29 February 2020.

[12] The Alliance for Equality focuses specifically on addressing the lack of diversity in relation to ethnicity and geography in international arbitration. It provides trainings on diversity and inclusion and networking opportunities. See the official website <www.allianceequality.com/> accessed 29 February 2020.

[13] Berwin Leighton Paisner International Arbitration Group, 8, see <www.bclplaw.com/en-US/thought-leadership/diversity-on-arbitral-tribunals-are-we-getting-there.html>accessed 29 February 2020.

from more diverse ethnic and national backgrounds.[14] Fewer than a third of the participants of the 2018 survey conducted by the School of International Arbitration of Queen Mary University (London) believed that any progress had been made in the previous five years in terms of tribunal members' diversity in terms of geographic origin, age, or cultural/ethnic background.[15]

This chapter first demonstrates that the current pool of international arbitrators is close to homogenous in terms of adjudicators' nationality, race/ethnicity, and place of legal training (common or civil law system). Subsequently, it discusses why diversity matters in international arbitration and why it is important to promote diversity. Further, the chapter examines the factors that parties and arbitration institutions take into account in the selection process in order to better understand what is expected of a potential appointee. This analysis is informed by the findings of the author's Survey of Arbitrators concerning appointment incentives. This Survey focused on non-Western arbitrators, and Chinese arbitrators in particular, to explore why they are seldom appointed, despite the substantial involvement of Chinese parties in international arbitral cases. The final section of the chapter draws on these findings to discuss possible strategies to promote diversity.

2. The Current Pool of International Arbitrators

The international arbitration system is often described as being dominated by 'male, pale and stale' arbitrators.[16] This perception is supported by empirical investigations. For example, in 2016 Susan D. Franck surveyed nearly 400 participants at the biannual meeting of the International Council for Commercial Arbitration (ICCA).[17] The survey findings confirm that international tribunals are dominated by male, senior arbitrators from developed countries. More specifically, according to Franck's study, the median international arbitrator is a 53-year-old man, who is a national of a developed State with approximately ten previous arbitral appointments. This section presents the (2.1) nationality, (2.2) race/ethnicity, and (2.3)

[14] See ibid.

[15] School of International Arbitration Queen Mary University of London (2018) 16–18.

[16] See Samaa A F Haridi, 'Towards Greater Gender and Ethnic Diversity in International Arbitration,' (2015) 2 (2) *Bahrain Chamber for Dispute Resolution* International Arbitration Review 307. See also Yves Dezalay and Bryant Garth (eds), *Dealing in Virtue: International Commercial Arbitration and the Construction of a Transnational Legal Order* (The University of Chicago Press 1996), 34–36.; James Crawford, 'The Ideal Arbitrator: Does One Size Fit All?' (2017) 32(5) American University International Law Review. for the description of evolution of a 'typical' arbitrator from 'Grand Old Men' through 'Technocrats' proficient in the art of arbitration to 'Managers' effectively directing the proceedings.; Susan D Franck and others, 'International Arbitration: Demographics, Precision and Justice' in Albert Jan van den Berg (ed), *Legitimacy: Myths, Realities, Challenges* (ICCA Congress Series 2015).; also Franck and others referring to the 'invisible college' of arbitrators.

[17] Franck and others (n 4) 466. See also another study of Malcolm Langford, Daniel Behn, and Runar Hilleren Lie, 'The Revolving Door in International Investment Arbitration' (2017) 20 (2) Journal of International Economic Law.

legal training (common law/civil law system) of arbitrators, showing that the diversity of arbitrators, in particular regarding their nationality and race/ethnicity, is limited.

2.1 Nationality

The charts below compare the nationality of arbitrators to that of the parties involved in international arbitral proceedings.[18] These comparisons show that parties originate from Western (in particular the US, the UK, Switzerland, France, and Germany) as well as non-Western countries (in particular China, Russia, India, and Brazil), while arbitrators originate predominantly from Western countries (including UK, US, Switzerland, and Germany) and the involvement of non-Western arbitrators is very limited.

2.1.1 Arbitrators

Table 8.1 below presents the nationality of arbitrators appointed by five arbitration institutions (who were named as the preferred choice of parties in international commercial arbitration) in 2018.[19]

Moreover, in the field of investor-State arbitration, the International Centre for Settlement of Investment Disputes (ICSID) data is a good example of the situation in investment arbitration.[20] By the end of 2018, ICSID arbitrator, conciliator, and ad hoc committee member appointees in cases registered under the ICSID Convention and the Additional Facility Rules came from: Western Europe (47%), North America (Canada, Mexico, and US) (20%), South America (11%), South and East Asia and the Pacific (11%), Middle East and North Africa (4%), Eastern Europe and Central Asia (3%), Central America and the Caribbean (2%), and Sub-Saharan Africa (2%).[21] The top five nationalities were: France, USA, UK, Canada, and Switzerland.[22]

[18] For the case of China, the concept of 'nationality' was broken down to China Mainland and Hong Kong, for the purposes of the discussion on the Arbitrators' Appointment Survey. See section 5 below.

[19] These five arbitration institutions have been named as the preferred choice of parties in international commercial arbitration. See School of International Arbitration Queen Mary University of London (2018) 13.

[20] ICSID was selected for a number of reasons. One, the ICSID Convention, the basis for ICSID arbitration, has been so far ratified by 155 Contracting States (see the official website of ICSID <https://icsid.worldbank.org/resources/rules-and-regulations/convention/overview> accessed 31 July 2020.

Two, ICSID has accumulated significant amount of experience with 706 involving parties from all over the world as of the end of December 2018. See International Centre for Settlement of Investment Disputes, 'The ICSID Caseload – Statistics (Issue 2019-1),' (2019): 7. Three, ICSID offers the considerable public access to data important for the discussion in the context of this chapter.

[21] ibid 19.

[22] ibid 22. When looking further at the list of top appointees in the ICSID cases, it can be observed that among the top 25 arbitrators (measured by the number of appointments) only four were not nationals of Western states. However, even these four do not seem to be representative of the rest of the

Table 8.1 Nationality of arbitrators appointed by five leading arbitration institutions in 2018

Institution[a]	Top nationality	2nd nationality	3rd nationality	4th nationality	5th nationality
ICC[b]	UK	Switzerland	USA	France	Germany
SIAC[c]	Singapore	UK	Australia	USA	Malaysia
HKIAC[d]	UK	Hong Kong	Dual nationals	Singapore	China Mainland
LCIA[e]	UK	USA	France/ Ireland	Australia	Germany
SCC[f]	Specific nationalities not available	Specific nationalities not available	Specific nationalities not available	Specific nationalities not available	Specific nationalities not available

[a] Top five preferred arbitration institutions according to the 2018 International Arbitration Survey: The Evolution of International Arbitration.

[b] International Court of Arbitration at the International Chamber of Commerce (ICC)

[c] Singapore International Arbitration Centre (SIAC)

[d] Hong Kong International Arbitration Centre (HKIAC)

[e] London Court of International Arbitration (LCIA)

[f] Arbitration Institute of the Stockholm Chamber of Commerce (SCC); the specific nationalities of arbitrators were not made available; only the regional representation is given: 210 of arbitrators from Europe, 5 from North America, 5 from Asia, and 3 from Australasia in 2018.

2.1.2 Parties

Table 8.2 below presents the nationality of the parties in cases handled by the same five arbitral institutions in 2018.

Furthermore, in terms of the geographic distribution of State parties involved in ICSID cases, the landscape has been dominated by Eastern Europe and Central Asia (26% of cases), South America (23% of cases), and Sub-Saharan Africa (15%). This is followed by the Middle East and North Africa (11%), Western Europe (8%), South and East Asia and the Pacific (7%), Central America and the Caribbean (6%), and North America (Canada, Mexico, and US) (4%).[23] The PluriCourts Investment Treaty Arbitration Database (PITAD), which collects and analyses information about investment arbitration cases, provides more information on the participation of parties from specific States in ICSID and other investment arbitration

world. For example, the representative of Bulgaria (the only arbitrator from Eastern Europe on the list), Stanimir Alexandrov has been a US resident for nearly three decades and conducted a significant part of his education and practice in the US. See more in Langford, Behn, and Lie (n 17) 309–10.

[23] International Centre for Settlement of Investment Disputes, 11.

Table 8.2 Nationality of parties in cases handled by five leading arbitration institutions in 2018.

Institution & percentage of international cases[a]	Top user	Top foreign user	2nd top foreign user	3rd top foreign user	4th top foreign user	5th top foreign user
ICC[b]	N/A	USA	France	Brazil	Spain	Germany
SIAC 84%[c]	Singapore	USA	India	Malaysia	China Mainland	Indonesia
HKIAC 71.7%[d]	Hong Kong	China Mainland	British Virgin Islands	USA	Cayman Islands	Singapore
LCIA 80%[e]	UK	India	Russia	Cyprus	USA	UAE/British Virgin Islands
SCC 48%[f]	Sweden	Russia	Germany/ Ukraine	Azerbaijan	Finland/ USA/UK	Cyprus/ Norway

[a] Top five preferred arbitration institutions and percentage of international cases handled by them in 2018.

[b] No distinction of types of cases; most frequent nationalities among parties

[c] 84% of new cases filed with the SIAC were international (ie at least one party was not from Singapore)

[d] 71,7% of all arbitration cases submitted to the HKIAC were international (ie at least one party was not from Hong Kong)

[e] 79% of parties to LCIA cases were international (ie at least one party was not from the UK)

[f] 50% of SCC cases were international (ie at least one party was not from Sweden)

cases.[24] According to PITAD, private investors from the US, the Netherlands, UK, Germany, and Spain have appeared most frequently as claimants, while Argentina, Venezuela, Spain, Canada, the Czech Republic, and Mexico have appeared most often as respondents.[25]

2.2 Race/Ethnicity

Generally, 'race' is defined as 'one of the groups that people are divided into according to their physical characteristics, such as skin colour', while ethnicity should

[24] See <www.jus.uio.no/pluricourts/english/topics/investment/research-projects/database.html> accessed 29 February 2020.

[25] Daniel Behn, Malcolm Langford, Ole Kristian Fauchald, Runar Lie, Maxim Usynin, Taylor St John, Laura Letourneau-Tremblay, Tarald Berge, and Tori Loven Kirkebø, 'PITAD Investment Law and Arbitration Database: Version 1.0, Pluricourts Centre of Excellence', University of Oslo (31 January 2019) <https://pitad.org/index#welcome>accessed 29 February 2020.

be understood as 'a large group of people who have the same national, racial, or cultural origins, or the state of belonging to such a group'.[26] These divisions need to be approached cautiously since there are no universally accepted classifications.[27]

The lack of ethnic and/or racial diversity was for example brought to the fore in November 2018 when the popular African-American rap star Jay-Z halted an arbitration between his company, Roc Nation, and the clothing company, Iconix, after arguing that the lack of African-American arbitrators in the case left him vulnerable to unconscious bias.[28] Jay-Z's representatives had been asked to identify four arbitrators from the American Arbitration Association (AAA)'s Large and Complex Cases roster. When reviewing a list of more than 200 potential candidates based in New York, they found that the list had no African-American arbitrators who possessed the necessary expertise. Jay-Z's representatives alleged that the arbitration agreement was void for the reason of violating New York's public policy against racial discrimination.[29] The case was resumed in January 2019, when the AAA allowed the dispute to be heard by a three-arbitrator panel instead of a single arbitrator, and offered five African-American candidates.[30]

This lack of diversity is also apparent in investment arbitration. None of the ten most-appointed ICSID arbitrators, as of 2017,[31] were Asian or black. The only

[26] According to the Cambridge Dictionary (online edition).

[27] See more in Ann Morning, 'Ethnic Classification in Global Perspective: A Cross-National Survey of the 2000 Census Round' (2008) 27(2) Population Research and Policy Review. See also the official website of the United Nations in which the fluidity of the concepts is pointed out: 'The specific ethnic and/or national groups of the population which are of interest in each country are dependent upon individual national circumstances. Some of the criteria by which ethnic groups are identified are ethnic nationality (i.e., country or area of origin, as distinct from citizenship or country of legal nationality), race, colour, language, religion, customs of dress or eating, tribe, or various combinations of these characteristics. In addition, some of the terms used, such as "race", "origin", or "tribe", have a number of different connotations. The definitions and criteria applied by each country investigating ethnic characteristics of the population must, therefore, be determined carefully and with the involvement of or consultation with representatives of the groups which it desires to categorize. By the nature of this topic, these categories and their definitions will vary widely from country to country; therefore, no internationally accepted criteria are possible.' https://unstats.un.org/unsd/demographic/sconcerns/popchar/popcharmethods.htm> accessed 29 February 2020. For the sake of discussion of this chapter, the five categories of race and ethnicity follow the American Revisions to the Standards for the Classification of Federal Data on Race and Ethnicity by the Office of Management and Budget defining racial and ethnic categories as follows: American Indian or Alaska Native, Asian, Black or African American, Hispanic or Latino, Native Hawaiian or Other Pacific Islander, and White. See more specific explanations of particular categories on the official website of the Office of Management and Budget <https://obamawhitehouse.archives.gov/omb/fedreg_1997standards>accessed 29 February 2020.

[28] See <www.theguardian.com/music/2018/nov/29/jay-z-logo-lawsuit-racial-bias>accessed 29 February 2020.

[29] See Joshua Karton, 'Can I Get A ... Diverse Tribunal?' (*Kluwer Arbitration Blog*, 7 December 2018) (accessed 29 February 2020).

[30] See <www.reuters.com/article/us-people-jayz-lawsuit/jay-z-wins-fight-for-african-american-arbitrators-in-trademark-case-idUSKCN1PO32T>accessed 29 February 2020.

[31] Brigitte Stern (France), Gabrielle Kaufmann-Kohler (Switzerland), L Yves Fortier (Canada), Charles Brower (US), Francisco Orrego Vicuña (Chile), Albert Jan van den Berg (the Netherlands), J Christopher Thomas (Canada), Bernard Hanotiau (Belgium), Karl-Heinz Böckstiegel (Germany), VV Veeder (UK), Bernardo Cremades (Spain), Piero Bernardini (Italy). Twelve names are listed because two arbitrators with the same number of appointments shared the eighth position, for the same reason two others shared the ninth position. See more in Langford, Behn, and Lie (n 17) 309–10.

'diverse element' in this white-dominated group was the Chilean Francisco Orrego Vicuña, who passed away in 2018.

2.3 Legal Training

Another aspect of diversity is the legal training of arbitrators. In the context of this chapter, this should be understood as a division between common law and civil law legal backgrounds. The differences between the two systems are not particularly significant in international arbitration since tribunals do not apply national court procedural rules unless parties agree otherwise. Furthermore, international arbitration aspires to build bridges for parties with different legal backgrounds, so there has been a convergence of civil and common law practices.[32] For example, soft law instruments have been produced with the aim of bridging the differences between various legal cultures such as the 2010 International Bar Association (IBA) Rules on the Taking of Evidence in International Commercial Arbitration. The foreword to these Rules states: '[t]he IBA Rules of Evidence reflect procedures in use in many different legal systems, and they may be particularly useful when the parties come from different legal cultures'.[33] Nonetheless, differences between common and civil law systems should not be disregarded since, firstly, parties and their counsel may have different expectations toward procedure and, secondly, arbitrators' backgrounds can affect their shaping of proceedings.

A new soft law instrument, the Rules on the Efficient Conduct of Proceedings in International Arbitration (Prague Rules), created in response to dissatisfaction with evidence-taking practices, observes that the IBA Rules are closer to the common law practice, resulting in procedural inefficiencies.[34] The Prague Rules propose an alternative set of rules which are closer to a civil law approach.[35] Franck's 2016 study of ICCA subjects (primarily acting as counsel in international arbitration, arbitrators, or both) revealed the variety of their legal training.[36] The dominant legal training was in common law: 46% of all participants were exclusively trained in common law jurisdictions, while only 30% were exclusively trained in civil law jurisdictions. A quarter (24%) of all participants were trained in both civil and common law jurisdictions. Amongst participating arbitrators, 38.5% were trained exclusively in common law, 33.8% in civil law, and 27.7% in both.

32 See, for example, Born (n 3) 2207–10.; Tom Ginsburg, 'The Culture of Arbitration' (2003) 36 Vanderbilt Journal of Transnational Law; and Gabrielle Kaufmann-Kohler, 'Globalization of Arbitral Procedure,' (2003) 36 Vanderbilt Journal of Transnational Law.

33 See <www.ibanet.org/ENews_Archive/IBA_30June_2010_Enews_Taking_of_Evidence_new_rules.aspx>accessed 29 February 2020.

34 The Working Group of the Prague Rules was made mainly of civil law background practitioners (see the official website:<http://praguerules.com/working_group/>accessed 29 February 2020.

35 See the Note from the Working Group on p 2 of the Prague Rules.

36 Franck and others (n 4) 455.

3. Why Diversity in International Arbitration Matters

International arbitration should be an inclusive system since its goal is to address transnational disputes involving parties from all over the world. As aptly summarized by the authors the 2018 School of International Arbitration Queen Mary University of London survey:

> Arbitration has evolved to become a profoundly international practice: an ever-larger number of high-stakes disputes are being resolved across multiple jurisdictions, in virtually all existing legal systems, and involving parties from all over the world. It should therefore follow that the group of decision-makers called to resolve these disputes reflects the colourful fabric of the community of arbitration users. However, statistics on arbitral appointments seem to bear out the general sentiment within this community that this is hardly the case.[37]

The limited diversity of international arbitration adjudicators can produce a number of undesired consequences. Three of them are discussed below: section 3.1 the threat to the legitimacy of the system, section 3.2 the negative impact on procedural efficiency, and section 3.3 the lower effectiveness of non-diversified teams and the problem of 'group think'.

3.1 Lack of Diversity Threatens the Legitimacy of International Arbitration

If the pool of arbitrators is not (or barely) diverse, this risks undermining the legitimacy of the entire system of international arbitration.[38] In this chapter, 'legitimacy' should be understood as perceiving the authority of international arbitration as justified.[39] Generally, adjudicators should reflect the society in which they operate, as representativeness enhances a sense of fairness and public trust in the system,[40] which in turn increases the acceptance of arbitral decisions.[41] The range of parties resolving their disputes by means of arbitration has become more diverse, but the same cannot be said about international arbitration adjudicators.[42] Participants

[37] School of International Arbitration Queen Mary University of London (2018) 16.

[38] See, for example, Cesare Romano, Karen Alter, and Yuval Shany, *The Oxford Handbook of International Adjudication* (OUP 2014) 16–18.; also Haridi, (n 16) 307–08.; Franck and others, (n 4) 467–70, 96.; Hof in *Legitimacy: Myths, Realities, Challenges*, (n 5) 639.

[39] See Nienke Grossmann, 'Legitimacy and International Adjudicative Bodies' (2009) 41 George Washington International Law Review 115.

[40] This been stressed, for example, in the context of juries, see Christina S. Carbone and Victoria C. Plaut, 'Diversity and the Civil Jury' (2014) 55 William & Mary Law Review.

[41] See more in Franck and others (n 4) 496–97.

[42] See also section 2.1.1 above.

of the 2018 Queen Mary survey stressed that fairness is one of the main motives behind choosing international arbitration as a method of resolving disputes,[43] as it is connected with the perception of being represented and sufficiently 'heard' as a party.[44] Given the variety of parties involved in international cases, fairness can be better secured by a diverse panel of arbitrators. Introducing culturally diverse adjudicators would allow for a better understanding of non-Western parties' perspectives.[45]

As pointed out by Salim Moollan in his speech at the 2016 ICCA Meeting in Mauritius, the lack of diversity can lead to the risk of arbitration being perceived as a 'foreign process imposed from abroad, as an unwanted but inevitable corollary of trade and investment flow'.[46] In a similar spirit, the then Vice-President of the International Court of Justice, Judge Abdulqawi Ahmed Yusuf from Somalia observed that there is significant pressure on African countries to participate in international investment arbitration, yet, if the community will not welcome African arbitrators in tribunals, there is a risk that Africans will reject the system.[47] Concerns about legitimacy are particularly relevant in investment arbitration, where arbitrators' decisions may affect State policy matters and have an impact on all citizens of a particular country.

3.2 Lack of Diversity Negatively Impacts Procedural Efficiency

If the pool of arbitrators is not (or barely) diverse, this may have a negative impact on procedural efficiency because of the continuously growing caseload of arbitration institutions[48] and the time needed to render quality decisions. Paired with a limited number of available arbitrators, this can lead to difficulties in the efficient delivery of quality outcomes.[49] In fact, arbitration has been criticized by users for being too slow (and too expensive).[50] Where there is a small and uniform

[43] School of International Arbitration Queen Mary University of London, '2013 International Arbitration Survey: Corporate Choices in International Arbitration - Industry Perspectives' (2013) 7.

[44] See Haridi, 307–08.; Darius J. Kambata, 'Tensions between Party Autonomy and Diversity' in Albert Jan van den Berg (ed), *Legitimacy: Myths, Realities, Challenges* (ICCA Congress Series 2015), 615–16.

[45] Christopher Seraglini, 'Who Are the Arbitrators? Myths, Reality and Challenges' in Albert Jan van den Berg (ed) *Legitimacy: Myths, Realities, Challenges* (ICCA Congress Series 2015) 597.

[46] Salim Moollan, 'Invitation to ICCA Mauritius 2016 Presented by Mr. Salim Moollan' (*ICCA Official Website*, 9 April 2014)<www.arbitration-icca.org/AV_Library/ICCA_Mauritius_2016_by_Salim_Moollan.html>accessed 29 February 2020, 1.59–3.17 min <www.arbitration-icca.org/AV_Library/ICCA_Mauritius_2016_by_Salim_Moollan.html>accessed 29 February 2020.

[47] African Association of International Law. available at <www.aail-aadi.org/single-post/2015/12/01/>'Tribunals-need-Africans'-says-His-Excellency-Judge-Abdulqawi-Ahmed-Yusuf-vicepresident-of-the-International-Court-of-Justice (accessed 29 February 2020).

[48] See the comparison of caseload of international arbitral institutions in Born (n 3) 94–95.

[49] Franck and others 505.

[50] According to the survey conducted by the School of International Arbitration, Queen Mary University of London in 2015, cost and lack of speed were named as some of the worst features of

circle of arbitrators deciding disputes, there is also an increased risk of conflicts of interests, which in turn can lead to problems with constituting arbitral tribunals ready to hear cases impartially and independently.[51] As pointed out by the LCIA Director, Jacomijn van Haersolte-Van Hof, new arbitrators need to enter the system in order to ensure the system's sustainability for future disputes, as well as its competitiveness.[52]

3.3 Lower Effectiveness of Non-diversified Teams and the Problem of 'Group Think'

Homogenous teams perform less effectively than diverse ones and face the problem of 'group think', a phenomenon where a group of people make non-optimal or even irrational decisions due to an urge to conform, a desire for group consensus, and a wish to avoid alternative or critical positions. Diverse teams generally perform more efficiently and do not suffer from the 'group think' syndrome.[53] Diversity's positive impact on team performance has recently been discussed in the context of the need to diversify companies' boardrooms.[54] The main reasons for the better performance of diverse teams include: (1) improving the decision-making process by being able to draw upon a wider array of knowledge; (2) being more innovative, as well as overcoming tendencies toward 'group thinking'; and (3) an ability to see alternative solutions when making decisions together.[55]

international arbitration. See School of International Arbitration Queen Mary University of London and White and Case (n 2) 2, 7 (2015)

[51] Adriana Braghetta, 'Diversity and Regionalism in International Commercial Arbitration,' (2015) 46(4) Victoria University of Wellington Law review 1256–57.

[52] See Hof in *Legitimacy: Myths, Realities, Challenges*, 648.; Jacomijn van Haersolte-van Hof, 'LCIA's Director General Jackie Van Haersolte-Van Hof on Diversity; Why It Matters and What We Can All Do About It,' *Scottish Arbitration Centre Newsletter* (2015) <https://us2.campaign-archive.com/?u=6f57b2ebaad804398b0bf50db&id=425cb9b5e8> accessed 29 February 2020. See also Haridi, 309.

[53] See, for example, David Rock and Heidi Grant, 'Why Diverse Teams Are Smarter' *Harvard Business Review* (4 November 2016); see also Max Nathan and Neil Lee, 'Cultural Diversity, Innovation, and Entrepreneurship: Firm-Level Evidence from London,' (2015) 4 Economic Geography 89.; Scott E Page, *The Difference: How the Power of Diversity Creates Better Groups, Firms, Schools, and Societies* (Princeton University Press 2007).

[54] See, for example, Niclas L Erhardt, James D Werbel, and Charles B. Shrader, 'Board of Director Diversity and Firm Financial Performance. Corporate Governance: An International Review' (2003) 11 Corporate Governance: An International Review and Renee B Adams and Daniel Ferreira, 'Women in the Boardroom and Their Impact on Governance and Performance' (2009) 94 Journal of Financial Economics.

[55] See Rock and Grant.; Nathan and Lee; Irving L Janis, 'Groupthink,' in Harold J Leavitt, Louis R Pondy, and David M Boje (eds), *Readings in Managerial Psychology* (The University of Chicago Press 1980).

4. Factors Taken into Account in Making Appointments

This section explores the factors that are taken into account when appointment decisions are made by parties and arbitration institutions, in order to better understand what is expected of a potential appointee and how this can affect diversity.

4.1 General Issues

Parties play a key role in deciding who will resolve their dispute. They are largely free to design the procedure through specifying the number of arbitrators, mode of appointment, and required characteristics such as language abilities, nationality, or area of expertise. Arbitrators have to be impartial and independent, and where this is not the case, parties can seek to challenge and remove them, as reflected in arbitration rules, like the UNCITRAL Model Law on International Commercial Arbitration (UNCITRAL Model Law),[56] as well as institutional rules.[57] Arbitrator also have to act without undue delays, and can be removed if they do not perform their duties timely.[58] On the question of nationality, the UNCITRAL Model Law provides that no person should be precluded from acting as an arbitrator by reason of his or her nationality, unless otherwise agreed by the parties.[59] Some institutions provide for the 'nationality exclusion rule'. This means that an arbitrator either sitting alone or presiding over a panel should not have the same nationality as either of the parties involved, unless the parties decide otherwise.[60] In ICSID, the majority of arbitrators must be nationals of States other than a State party to the dispute or a State whose national is a party.[61]

4.2 Factors Relevant for Parties

According to the 2010 Queen Mary survey, the top attributes considered by counsels representing the parties are: open-mindedness and fairness of an arbitrator, prior experience of arbitration, quality of awards, availability, reputation, and

[56] Art 12 of the 2006 UNCITRAL Model Law.

[57] See, for example, Art 14 of the 2017 ICC Rules.

[58] See, for example, Art 14 of the 2006 UNCITRAL Model Law and Arts 13(3) and 17(2)(3) of the 2016 SIAC Rules.

[59] Art 11(1) of the 2006 UNCITRAL Model Law.

[60] See, for example, Art 13(5) of the 2017 International Court of Arbitration at the International Chamber of Commerce ('ICC') Rules, also Art 11(2)(3) of the 2013 Hong Kong International Arbitration Centre ('HKIAC') Rules, Art 6(1) of the 2014 London Court of International Arbitration ('LCIA') Rules, and Art 17 of the 2017 Arbitration Institute of the Stockholm Chamber of Commerce ('SCC') Rules.

[61] Art 39 of the ICSID Convention and Rule 1(3) of the ICSID Arbitration Rules.

knowledge of applicable law.[62] Gender, religion/faith, and nationality were considered least important. According to survey conducted by the Berwin Leighton Paisner International Arbitration Group, the most important attributes of arbitrators include: expertise, efficiency, informal feedback from other practitioners, as well as perceived gravitas/ability to influence other members of the tribunal.[63] In addition, this survey also sought to explore whether the factor of ethnicity/nationality was important: almost two-thirds of the participants found this factor to be of low relevance. The least important one was gender.[64] In sum, parties seek to have an experienced, efficient, and fair arbitrator with good reputation. They are not concerned (or less) about factors such as nationality, race/ethnicity or gender.

4.3 Factors Relevant for Arbitration Institutions

An examination of the rules of the leading arbitration institutions leads to similar conclusions. Beyond the requirement of impartiality and independence, the nationality exclusion rule (if applicable), as well as criteria prescribed by the parties, arbitration rules stress that the availability of an arbitrator to efficiently conduct the arbitral proceedings is the main factor.[65] Possessing experience in arbitration is another attribute generally considered relevant.[66] In addition, dependent on the circumstances of a specific case, other factors may include, for example, subject matter expertise or language abilities.[67] ICSID arbitrators must be persons of high moral character with recognized competency in the fields of law, commerce, industry, or finance, who may be relied upon to exercise an independent judgment.[68] Further, both ICSID and parties may additionally take account of an arbitrator's knowledge of relevant law and other areas of expertise, experience, language

[62] See School of International Arbitration Queen Mary University of London, '2010 International Arbitration Survey: Choices in International Arbitration' (2010) 25–26 and 34. The survey participants included general counsels, heads of legal departments, specialist legal counsels, and regional legal counsels from various jurisdictions.

[63] The survey participants included arbitrators, corporate counsels, external lawyers, arbitration institutions' staff working across diversified geographical regions in the world. See more Berwin Leighton Paisner International Arbitration Group>, 5.

[64] More specifically, the factor of nationality/ethnicity was found to be 'neither important nor unimportant' or 'not important at all' by respectively 30% of survey respondents (60% in total) and 14% found it to be 'not that important'. 22% of the participants considered it 'important'. See ibid 8.

[65] See Art 13(1) of the 2017 ICC Rules, Art 13(2) of the 2016 SIAC Rules, Art 5(4) of the 2014 LCIA Rules, Art 11(6) of the 2018 HKIAC Rules, Art 17(7) of the 2017 SCC Rules.

[66] See, for example, the SIAC Standards for Admission to SIAC Panel mentioning an appropriate level of expertise and experience in international arbitration (see <http://siac.org.sg/our-arbitrators/standards-for-admission-to-siac-panel>accessed 29 February 2020) or the Criteria for HKIAC's List of Arbitrators (see <http://hkiac.org/arbitration/arbitrators/criteria-application>accessed 29 February 2020.

[67] See, for example, Art 5(9) of the 2014 LCIA Rules.

[68] According to Art 14(1) and Art 40(2) of the ICSID Convention.

capabilities, availability, as well as possible conflicts of interest, and the overall cohesiveness of the tribunal.

5. Arbitrators' Appointment Survey

The author of the present chapter conducted a survey of 95 global arbitration practitioners asking about their preferences when appointing arbitrators in international disputes (see Annex).[69] The objective was to focus specifically on the nationality of arbitrators. Further, the survey asked a number of questions relating specifically to the appointment of Chinese arbitrators, because non-western and/or non-white candidates are seldom selected to resolve transnational disputes, even though non-western and/or non-white parties (and in particular Chinese parties) frequently use international arbitration and have the concomitant power of selection. The online survey contained 15 questions, was launched on 19 April 2018 and closed on 9 May 2018.[70] There were multiple choice questions and open questions.[71] Admittedly, there are several limitations to this type of survey, one of which pertains to the narrow sample of responses. Nonetheless, given the fact that the pool of survey participants was diverse in terms of nationality, amount of international arbitration experience and region of practice, it is submitted that the data generated by the survey can assist to better understand the factors influencing the selection of arbitrators.

5.1 Methodology and Profile of Survey Participants

The survey was completed by 95 arbitration practitioners coming from various jurisdictions: 8.3% (8) of participants were from mainland China, also 8.3% (8) from Hong Kong, while the remaining 83.6% (79) came from other countries and regions.[72] The participants reported to practice primarily in the region of Europe and Asia, with a lesser amount of practice in other regions, including North America,

[69] For the purposes of this survey, this should be understood as disputes in which the parties are from different jurisdictions, or disputes where the parties are from the same jurisdiction, but an international element is involved.

[70] The Smart Survey program was used to collect the answers and was announced via the LinkedIn portal and through personalized emails.

[71] In some questions, the participant could choose only one and in some a few/all answers that applied; in one question, they were asked to rank according to preferences. The participants did not have to respond to all questions (question 5 was skipped by one participant, question 9 by five, question 10 by one, question 13 by 10, question 14 by 13 participants).

[72] The other countries and regions included Switzerland, Singapore, Austria, Taiwan, UAE, USA, UK, Russia, Poland, Ireland, Germany, Mexico, India, Malaysia, Brazil, France, Australia, South Korea, Kenya, Turkey, Italy, Belgium, Greece, the Netherlands, Israel, and Czech Republic.

the Middle East, Latin America, Africa, and Oceania.[73] In the five years preceding the survey, the biggest group was primarily involved in international arbitration as arbitration counsel (68.4%). This was followed by 19% who were mainly involved as arbitrators, 6.3% as the staff of arbitration institutions, 1% as an in-house counsel. 5.3% chose the answer 'other'.[74] Survey participants were also asked about the number of cases in which they had been personally involved in the five years preceding the survey. The biggest group reported to be involved in over 20 cases (38%), followed by the involvement in 11 to20 cases (25.6%), five to 10 cases (20%), and one to five cases (16%).

5.2 Key Findings

Survey participants were asked about their practices when appointing arbitrators in international cases. The most common sources for obtaining information on a prospective arbitrator were 'colleagues' (selected by 87.4% of the participants) and 'arbitrator's profiles available on the internet' (72.6%). This was followed by 'industry reviews and rankings' (36.8%), information provided by arbitration institutions' (35.8%), 'external counsel' (13.7%). 14.7% of the participants chose the answer 'other'.[75] Among 'other' factors listed by the participants were: counsel/firms have appointed the arbitrator before, internal information available in the law firm, the institution's know-how, personal knowledge, awards, publications, conference attendance, members of the institution's board (in case of the institution's staff), databases such as the ArbitralWomen, the Energy Arbitrators List, the Newton, the Global Arbitration Review etc. Reputation in the arbitration community, previous experience with an arbitrator and legal background were selected as the most important factors when appointing an arbitrator (selected 62, 53, and 53 times respectively).[76] This was followed by the availability of an arbitrator, technical expertise, efficiency, neutrality, and language capabilities (selected 38, 37, 29, 23, and 18 times respectively). The least important factors among those listed in the question were education and age of a prospective arbitrator (selected respectively 8 and 3 times). A number of the participants (13) used the option of 'other' factors, including personality traits, motivation, predicted sensitivity to certain arguments, soft skills and likely procedural preferences, focus on diversity in terms

[73] The participants could choose a few regions. Europe (chosen 59 times) and Asia (chosen 53 times) were the most common choices; the participants practiced also in other regions, including North America (chosen 14 times), the Middle East (chosen 12 times), Latin America (chosen 11 times), Africa (chosen 9 times), and Oceania (chosen 7 times).

[74] In case of choosing the 'other' option, the participants described their primary involvement as: 'all of the above', 'arbitration counsel as well as arbitrator', 'administrative secretary', 'tribunal secretary', and 'expert witness'.

[75] Participants could select up to three factors.

[76] The survey participants could choose up to three answers.

of gender, personal recommendations of colleagues and friends previously dealing with a prospective arbitrator, quality of previous awards, and clarity of presentations made during industry seminars.

One set of questions aimed to explore whether participants preferred any particular nationalities. For example, respondents were asked about their preferences concerning an arbitrator's nationality, assuming that the parties to the dispute would not involve any of these nationalities. The participants were asked to rank: France, Hong Kong, Mainland China, Switzerland, UK, and USA.[77] Overall, the participants ranked them in the following order: UK, Switzerland, France, Hong Kong, USA, and Mainland China. Notably, however, eight participants stressed in the subsequent open questions[78] that an arbitrator's nationality as such is not important to them. To illustrate, one of the participants stated: '[t]o me, nationality is a relatively unimportant criterium in selecting an arbitrator. If I am satisfied that a mainland Chinese arbitrator is independent, impartial and he/she has experience as an arbitrator as well as industry-specific experience, I would not hesitate to recommend such arbitrator'.[79]

The survey explored whether survey participants would prefer an arbitrator from Mainland China or Hong Kong, highlighting the differences between Mainland China and Hong Kong arbitrators, such as their legal background (Mainland China has a civil law system, while Hong Kong has a common law system) and English language capabilities (English is one of Hong Kong's official languages, while it is not commonly used in Mainland China).[80] In response to this question, 61.7% of participants indicated they would prefer an arbitrator from Hong Kong; almost 30% of the participants expressed no preference while the remaining group (8.3%) would prefer a Mainland China arbitrator. When asked about the reasons underlying their choice, participants who had indicated their preference for Hong Kong arbitrators listed the following reasons: their experience with international arbitration (mentioned 24 times),[81] familiarity with the common law system (mentioned

[77] Mainland China and Hong Kong were combined with four commonly selected nationalities of arbitrators.

[78] In particular, in the last question 'Is there anything you would like to add to your answers in this survey (including any general remarks regarding the survey)?' There were also six suggestions (in question 9) that the question to rank the nationalities ranking was too narrow (or had limited answer options) and more details about a particular case would need to be known in order to consider the nationality factor.

[79] Answer to question 14: 'What are the factors that could encourage you to appoint a mainland Chinese arbitrator for international arbitration cases in the future?'

[80] When discussing the case of China, it is important to note the distinction between Mainland China and Hong Kong Special Administrative Region ('SAR'). Between 1898 and 1997 Hong Kong was a British colony, but in 1997, it was transferred to mainland China. Since then, Mainland China and Hong Kong have functioned under the doctrine of 'one country, two systems', which means that until 2047, Mainland China will allow Hong Kong to continue to govern itself and maintain an independent legal system.

[81] Related to that was mentioning that the perception of Hong Kong as being more 'international' and therefore arbitrators generally having more 'international' approach (mentioned 8 times)

17 times),[82] the perceived independence/neutrality of an arbitrator (mentioned 10 times), and English language abilities (mentioned 9 times).

This was consistent with responses to another question where participants who had indicated that, generally, they do not appoint Chinese arbitrators,[83] were asked to explain why. The main reasons were: their legal background, language capabilities, and experience in international arbitration (selected 38, 35, and 34 times respectively).[84] The responses to the survey's open questions showed a lack of familiarity with Chinese arbitrators by 19 survey participants. Unsurprisingly participants highlighted they might potentially appoint more Chinese arbitrators, if they had more international experience (the answer appearing 28 times), English language capabilities (18 times), and exposure to the common law system (5 times), or if participants had cases with Chinese elements (5 times).

To summarize, the survey results show that the most important factors for appointing an arbitrator are reputation, experience, availability, technical expertise, efficiency, neutrality, and language capabilities. This largely confirms previous studies. An apparent desire for common law exposure, however, was a new discovery. An arbitrator's nationality does not matter, as long as they are qualified. One survey participant stressed: '[i]n choosing an arbitrator my preference is to identify a competent person from my region (Eastern and Central Europe). Too many Swiss, French, British and American arbitrators have been appointed in the cases coming from the regions these arbitrators have no idea about, no understanding of and no experience at all. Some nations are overestimated in their capacity to understand others and it doesn't help arbitration'. Another problem voiced by the survey participants was the lack of familiarity with arbitrators, in particular Chinese arbitrators.

6. Ways to Improve the Diversity among International Arbitrators

Enhancing the diversity of the arbitral system could prove to be challenging. Lucy Reed in her keynote address at the 15th Annual ITA-ASIL Conference on 'Diversity and Inclusion in International Arbitration' explained the problem as follows:

> The math is not hard: the numbers readily prove that international arbitration is not diverse. [...] Harder is to quantify the impact (if any) on arbitral justice.

[82] Some participants added that if an arbitrator is familiar with the common law procedure, then she or he is also more familiar with international arbitration procedure.

[83] 85% of the participants stated that they never appointed a Chinese arbitrator in a case not involving China; 10.5% have never been involved in cases not involving China; 3.1% appointed a Chinese, but only in a minority of cases; and 1 participant (1%) appointed a Chinese arbitrator in a majority of cases.

[84] The participants were asked to choose as many answers as applied.

> Harder still is to identify, confront and accept our role in the causes, which is the first step in finding workable solutions. Long experience suggests that it is caution, habit and, yes, bias that underlie our non-diverse practice.[85]

One critical problem lies in the parties' choices. As mentioned in the survey analysis by the Berwin Leighton Paisner International Arbitration Group: '[f]or the most part, parties have one opportunity to have a dispute determined in their favour and, for wholly legitimate reasons, they will have a very short-term self-interested view of the appointment process'.[86] That means that parties and their counsel may prefer to appoint the same arbitrators repeatedly, not only because of their expertise and experience, but also as a kind of 'insurance policy': if the case is lost, those who appointed the arbitrator are less likely to be blamed for taking a risk in their choice of appointment.[87] Nevertheless, parties and their representatives also express their concerns about the limited diversity among arbitrators. Rogers calls this the 'diversity paradox'.[88]

One important question is, therefore, how to address parties' autonomy and apparent lack of incentive to consider diversity when it comes to specific appointment decisions. Abolishing party autonomy is not the solution. Rather, it is important to show that their current choices are not necessarily the best policy, especially in the longer run. Fostering diversity should not happen at any cost: experience and quality will always remain critical, particularly because arbitral awards cannot be appealed against, so there is no 'second chance'.[89] Common efforts are needed in order to promote awareness of diversity, to support less obvious choices of arbitrators, and to work on diversity going hand in hand with quality. A few possible suggestions on how to improve diversity are explored below.

First, arbitration institutions are well-placed to play an important role in fostering diversity. Numerous institutions compile the list of arbitrators that parties can refer to when selecting arbitrators;[90] they also deal with default appointments and publish data on appointments. For example, since 2015, the ICC has published the names and nationalities of arbitrators in specific cases, as well as whether they were appointed by the parties or the institution.[91] This improves transparent

[85] See the website <www.cailaw.org/Institute-for-Transnational-Arbitration/Events/2018/ita-asil.html>accessed 29 February 2020. For more about the reasons for a limited diversity in the context of gender, see Greenwood and Baker, 658–63.

[86] Berwin Leighton Paisner International Arbitration Group, 2.

[87] Braghetta, 1256.

[88] Catherine A. Rogers, 'The Key to Unlocking the Arbitrator Diversity Paradox?: Arbitrator Intelligence' (*Kluwer Arbitration Blog*, 27 December 2017)<http://arbitrationblog.kluwerarbitration.com/2017/12/27/on-arbitrators/> accessed 29 February 2020.

[89] See Kambata in *Legitimacy: Myths, Realities, Challenges*, 636.; Seraglini in *Legitimacy: Myths, Realities, Challenges*, 605–06.

[90] This is the case, for example, for SIAC and HKIAC.

[91] See the official website of the ICC <https://iccwbo.org/dispute-resolution-services/arbitration/icc-arbitral-tribunals/>accessed 29 February 2020.

decision-making and motivates other institutions to do so as well. The institutions also have a chance to facilitate the creation of a more diverse pool of prospective arbitrators through professional training in less developed jurisdictions, more diverse tribunal secretaries, and inviting potential arbitrators as speakers to their conferences. Second, since appointment decisions are initially made by parties, legal counsel could include more diverse candidates in the lists of potential arbitrators they present to their clients. Counsel could also make an effort to become more familiar with a wider range of potential candidates, for example through consulting arbitration institutions. Developments on the side of parties and in-house counsel are particularly desirable, since, as illustrated by the 2018 Queen Mary survey, this is where there is fiercest resistance to improving diversity.[92]

Third, aspiring international arbitrators can themselves take action to promote more diversity by increasing their own visibility through networking, participation in industry organizations and events, and publishing on international arbitration and related matters. In the case of China, many international arbitration stakeholders are simply not familiar with Chinese arbitrators. It is essential for Chinese practitioners (and other underrepresented groups) to build their expertise, which includes improving their foreign language abilities, familiarity with international arbitration procedures and exposure to the common law system. Reputation can be seen also in a broader context, eg the reputation of a particular country in the international arbitration arena. For example, China is not perceived as a particularly arbitration-friendly place. The respondents to the 2010 Queen Mary University Survey perceived the country (together with Russia) as one of the least favoured venues for international arbitration.[93] Chinese arbitration has been criticized by commentators for, among other, the high level of governmental influence and the limited powers of arbitrators to decide on their own jurisdiction and interim measures.[94] This in turn influences perceptions of Chinese arbitrators. Therefore, it is up to China to adjust its arbitration law and practice, which would in turn help to improve the image of Chinese arbitrators and lead to more appointments.

Fourth, law schools and academic societies can assist in promoting diversity. For example, students (and practitioners) should be exposed to international arbitration practice through curricula, open lectures, and international arbitration

[92] School of International Arbitration Queen Mary University of London, '2018 International Arbitration Survey: The Evolution of International Arbitration,' 19.

[93] School of International Arbitration Queen Mary University of London, '2010 International Arbitration Survey: Choices in International Arbitration,' 17 and 20. For more on the perception of arbitration in China, see also John Savage, 'Navigating the Pitfalls of Arbitration with Chinese Parties' (December 2010) The Metropolitan Corporate Counsel.

[94] See, for example, Manjiao Chi, 'Are We "Paper-Tigers": The Limited Procedural Power of Arbitrators under Chinese Law' (2011) 2 Journal of Dispute Resolution.; Peter Thorp, 'The PRC Arbitration Law: Problems and Prospects for Amendment' (2007) 24(6) Journal of International Arbitration.; Jingzhou Tao, 'Salient Issues in Arbitration in China' (2012) 27(4) American University International Law Review.

skills training. Arbitration moot competitions, such as the Vis Moot,[95] give students a chance not only to train for a couple of months, but also to meet arbitration practitioners and have them assess their abilities. Other possible initiatives include improving students' foreign language capabilities and cooperation between academic and arbitration institutions. Academic research into diversity, such as that conducted in this volume, is also important for raising awareness. For example, one of the participants to the author's survey stated that the survey made them 'reflect on why [they] do not consider arbitrators from mainland China'. Fifth, non-profit organizations, such as the Alliance for Equality,[96] can help build awareness among stakeholders of international arbitration, and in particular parties and their representatives who primarily decide on appointments. For example, these non-profit organizations could offer unconscious bias training.

7. Conclusion

A significant diversity deficit exists in international arbitration including with respect to the nationality of arbitrators and their race/ethnicity. Increased diversity will enhance the system's legitimacy and its effectiveness. However, in order to achieve this, efforts need to be made by all stakeholders, including parties and their representatives, who have been particularly resistant to promoting diversity, as well as arbitration institutions, prospective arbitrators, and academia.

Annex Arbitrators' Appointment Survey: Instructions and Questions

Thank you for agreeing to participate in this survey concerning the appointment of arbitrators in international arbitration. It aims to deepen the available research and, in part, to concentrate on the appointment of Chinese arbitrators. The survey should take approximately 10 minutes to complete. Your participation will be kept fully confidential and your name will not appear in any materials related to the survey. The closing date for responses is 9 May 2018 and the results will be published in an academic article in summer 2018. It would be of great help to this research project if you would please forward this survey to other potentially interested respondents. Further information can be obtained from Monika Prusinowska: prusinowska.monika_cesl@cupl.edu.cn

All questions are concerned with international disputes ONLY. For the purposes of this survey, this should be understood as disputes in which the parties are from different jurisdictions, or disputes where the parties are from the same jurisdiction, but an international element is involved.

95 See the official website of the Vis Moot <https://vismoot.pace.edu/>accessed 29 February 2020.

96 See the official website of the Alliance for Equality <www.allianceequality.com/> accessed 29 February 2020.

1. **Your name:**
2. **Your email address:**
3. **You are from:**
   Mainland China
   Hong Kong
   Other (please specify):
4. **In which region(s) do you principally practice? (Please choose all that apply)**
   Africa
   Asia
   Europe
   Latin America
   North America
   Middle East
   Oceania
5. **In how many international arbitration cases have you been personally involved during the past 5 years? (Please also include on-going cases)**
   None
   1–5 cases
   5–10 cases
   11–20 cases
   Over 20 cases
6. **What has been your primary involvement in international arbitration during the past 5 years?**
   Arbitration counsel
   In-house counsel
   Arbitrator
   Staff of the arbitration institution
   Other (please specify):
7. **What sources do you primarily refer to when obtaining information about arbitrators? (Please choose up to 3)**
   Information provided by arbitration institutions
   Arbitrator's own profile available online
   Industry reviews and rankings
   Colleagues
   External counsels
   Other (please specify):
8. **What factors regarding an arbitrator do you usually take into consideration when making an appointment in international arbitration cases? (Please choose up to 3)**
   Age
   Availability of an arbitrator
   Education
   Efficiency
   Language capabilities
   Legal background
   Neutrality
   Previous experience with an arbitrator
   Reputation in the arbitration community
   Technical expertise
   Other (please specify):

9. **In choosing an arbitrator, what would be your preference regarding the arbitrator's nationality (assume a dispute does not involve any of the nationalities listed below). When ranking please consider the nationality factor only.**
   France
   Hong Kong
   Mainland China
   Switzerland
   United Kingdom
   USA
10. **Assume a dispute does not involve either a mainland Chinese or a Hong Kong party. Which would be your preference, if you had to choose between a mainland China and a Hong Kong arbitrator?**
    An arbitrator from mainland China
    An arbitrator from Hong Kong
    No special preference between the two
11. **If you answered 1) 'An arbitrator from mainland China' or 2) 'An arbitrator from Hong Kong' in the preceding question, what would be the factors influencing your preference?**
12. **Have you appointed a mainland Chinese arbitrator for a case NOT involving a mainland Chinese party in the past 5 years?**
    Yes, in a majority of cases
    Yes, in a minority of cases
    No
    I have never been involved in a case not involving a mainland Chinese party
13. **If you answered 2) 'Yes, in a minority of cases' or 3) 'No' in the preceding question, what were the factors that influenced your decision not to appoint more arbitrators from mainland China in international arbitration cases? (Please choose all that apply)**
    Education
    Experience
    Language capabilities
    Legal background
    Technical expertise
    Other (please specify):
14. **What are the factors that could encourage you to appoint a mainland Chinese arbitrator for international arbitration cases in the future?**
15. **Is there anything you would like to add to your answers in this survey (including any general remarks regarding the survey)?**

9
Legitimacy of Investor-State Arbitration
Addressing Development Bias Among International Arbitrators

*Jamal Seifi**

1. Introduction

For an arbitrator from the 'Global South', the issue which lies at the heart of the diversity debate is the question of inclusiveness. This chapter argues that, due to insufficient concretization of international norms,[1] it is of vital importance to have broadly representative international courts and tribunals. Commentators have noted that since the end of the Cold War, 'the most significant divisions among states are those between developing and developed states, whose economic and other interests differ greatly, and, in some respects, between Islamic states and the West'.[2] In this context, any debate concerning the normative or social legitimacy of international adjudication inevitably has a development focus. This chapter aims to stress the continuing importance of the (perceived) development bias of international arbitrators.[3]

Waibel and Wu found that decisions in investor-State arbitration cases were strongly correlated with arbitrators' policy preferences and that among the bias factors, 'an arbitrator's developing status was most prominent'.[4] The predominantly

* I acknowledge the assistance of and contribution by Dr Kamal Javadi (Legal adviser to the Iran-United States Claims Tribunal) in the preparation of this chapter.

1 For instance, in the area of international investment law, the fair and equitable treatment standard may be mentioned as a broadly formulated normative standard with insufficient concretization. Some commentators use the term 'Downstream Production of International Law' to capture the creation of international law by the law applier at the time of application, see Paul B Stephan, 'Privatizing International Law' (2011) 97 Virginia Law Review 1573–664.

2 See D. J. Harris, *Cases and Materials on International Law* (Sweet and Maxwell 2004) 5–6.

3 See eg Thomas Schultz and Cedric Dupont, 'Investment Arbitration: Promoting the Rule of Law or Over-empowering Investors? A Quantitative Empirical Study' (2014) 25(4) European Journal of International Law 1147–68, at 1168: 'Since the mid-to-late 1990s, investment arbitration has seemed more oriented towards serving the function for which most international courts and tribunals are created—that is, to strengthen the international rule of law. However, it still serves this function to a relatively limited extent, given that it favours the "haves" over the "have-nots", allowing or making the international investment regime to be harder on poorer countries than on richer countries.'

4 See Michael Waibel and Yanhui Wu, *Are Arbitrators Political? Evidence from International Investment Arbitration* (January 2017) 1<www-bcf.usc.edu/~yanhuiwu/arbitrator.pdf>accessed 20 July 2020. Waibel and Wu identified 633 ICSID cases from 1972 to 2016. Applying the relevant exclusions (pending cases, annulment, interpretation, and discontinued cases) and further excluding

Jamal Seifi, *Legitimacy of Investor-State Arbitration* In: *Identity and Diversity on the International Bench*. Edited by: Freya Baetens, Oxford University Press (2020). © The several contributors. DOI: 10.1093/oso/9780198870753.003.0009.

commercial backgrounds and outlook of most international arbitrators have resulted in expansionist trends in interpreting both the jurisdictional and substantive protection provisions of Bilateral Investment Treaties (BITs). This makes them ill-equipped to decide regulatory disputes involving public law matters and ultimately undermines the legitimacy of the investment arbitration system.[5] As observed by Crawford, '[t]he criticism levelled against arbitrators in investor-State disputes are not made against arbitrators in international commercial arbitration, or at least not with the same frequency and vigor'.[6] Also, the Diversity Section of the Second Report (CIDS Supplemental Report)[7] on issues relating to the composition of a Multilateral Investment Court, written by Kaufman-Kohler and Potestà, recognizes that the need for diversity is nowadays considered 'as a value in itself'.[8] The present chapter focuses on investment treaty arbitration but many of the observations are equally relevant to international commercial arbitration. Before turning to the discussion of normative and social legitimacy of north-south arbitration (section 3) and the importance of striving for, to the extent practicable, collective cultural neutrality in international courts and tribunals (section 4), it is useful to set out the general premises of the debate (section 2).

2. General Premises of the Debate

The first observation is that the diversity debate is not aimed at undermining meritocracy: the focus of diversity initiatives must be on how best to expand the pool without lowering professional standards. The predominant consideration remains the selection of the most competent and able decision-makers. In this regard, Meg Kinnear, the Secretary-General of the International Centre for the Settlement of Investment Disputes (ICSID), stressed that the first and foremost consideration is to choose arbitrators based on merit. She added:

approximately 40 cases in which the arbitral awards remain confidential, they reviewed a sample of 231 cases.

[5] M Sornarajah, *The Retreat of Neo-Liberalism in Investment Treaty Arbitration* in by Catherine A Rogers and Roger P Alford (eds), The Future of Investment Arbitration (OUP 2009) 273, at 276–78. In addition, and in the context of the 'retreat of the State' debate, in the words of Gus Van Harten 'investment treaty arbitration is a much clearer instance of the State's retreat from adjudication because it replaces courts with a private model of adjudication in matters of public law'. See Gus Van Harten, 'The Public-Private Distinction in the International Arbitration of Individual Claims Against the State' (2007) 56 International and Comparative Law Quarterly 371–93, at 372.

[6] James Crawford, 'The Ideal Arbitrator: Does One Size Fit All?' (2018) 32(5) American University International Law Review 1003–22, at 1003.

[7] CIDS stands for the Geneva Center for International Dispute Settlement. CIDS Supplemental Report is entitled 'The Composition of a Multilateral Investment Court and of an Appeal Mechanism for Investment Awards', 15 November 2017.

[8] ibid 27.

> That said, we're very conscious that there's a need for more arbitrators. In appointing them, we have the opportunity to get new people on board, and in some respects, not always going off the roster is actually an opportunity to put forward some new names, the chance to bring some new people to the attention of parties. If they're selected, that's terrific. I have to say that we're very aware that, because in most cases we're appointing presiding arbitrators, it's helpful to know that the person has had some experience as a party-nominated arbitrator first, that they know the process and are ready to jump up to that next additional role as a presiding arbitrator. So the short answer is, number one, foremost and always, it's merit. But yes, I certainly hope and look to see if there are candidates from other regions, including women. There are some fabulous candidates who may meet that primary requirement. So yes, it's important to expand the pools, but obviously never just for the sake of diversification.[9]

The 2018 Dutch Model BIT specifies that the relevant appointing authority, ie the Secretary-General of ICSID (for arbitrations under the ICSID Convention or the Additional Facility Rules) or the Secretary-General of the Permanent Court of Arbitration (PCA) (for arbitrations under the UN Commission on International Trade Law (UNCITRAL) Arbitration Rules), in appointing tribunal members 'shall strive for gender and geographic diversity'.[10] The 2018 Dutch Model BIT further clarifies that when making appointments, the ICSID Secretary-General is not limited to the ICSID Panel of Arbitrators.

The second observation concerns the need for caution against diluting the traditional development-based foundation of the concept of diversity. Traditionally, and particularly in the context of investment arbitration tribunals, the main diversity concern has been the development status of the arbitrator's home State. For instance, a perceived development bias was among the main driving forces behind the arbitration-limiting initiative contained in the new Iranian Constitution after the 1979 Iranian Revolution. As established by the drafting history of Article 139 of the Iranian Constitution, the inclusion of the parliamentary approval requirement for foreign arbitrations with respect to public contracts was aimed at protecting the exercise of sovereign powers against the backdrop of the perceived influence of Western-dominated foreign arbitral institutions.[11] In one of its concept papers entitled 'The Diversity Deficit', the Academic Forum of the UNCITRAL Working Group III on Investor-State Dispute Settlement (ISDS)

[9] See 'ICSID in the Twenty-First Century: An Interview with Meg Kinnear' (2010) 104 American Society of International Law Proceedings 413, at 431–32.

[10] Art 20(2) Dutch Model BIT, see <https://www.rijksoverheid.nl/ministeries/ministerie-van-buitenlandse-zaken/documenten/publicaties/2018/10/26/modeltekst-voor-bilaterale-investeringsakkoorden>accessed 29 February 2020.

[11] See Mohammad-Taghi Abedi, 'Judicial Jurisdiction and Arbitral Jurisdiction' (2010) 41 International Law Review (in Persian) 132–35.

reform stated the following about the continuing importance of the perceived development bias:

> There has been a great deal of concern that tribunals are biased against developing states, and even though some empirical work casts doubt on those perceptions, they nonetheless remain and are exacerbated by the extent to which arbitrators are perceived as outsiders.[12]

More recently, additional diversity indicators and in particular, gender diversity, as well as other elements such as age, legal training or legal culture, ethnicity, and religion, are also being considered. This is mainly as a result of the emergence of the north-north strand of investment disputes in the second half of the 1990s, which was added to the first strand of north-south arbitration. While this development is undoubtedly a welcome addition, it is important to recognize that, for instance, adding Western female arbitrators to the pool would still leave the perceived development bias intact, thus diluting the concept of diversity. Thus, it is imperative to move beyond symbolic steps merely focusing on one diversity indicator. In this regard, commentators have pointed out that in order to take diversity seriously, 'we must move beyond the kind of token diversity that sees only white women from developed Western countries added to the pool of arbitrators'.[13] In other words, it would be antithetical to the development-based diversity concerns if we were to consider the increased gender diversity in isolation as an improvement without considering the intersection of these two main indicators of diversity. At the same time, the intersectionality outlook must not be considered as a one-way road. Thus, 'potential arbitrators with intersectional backgrounds – for instance, Asian female lawyers from developing states – can experience a distinctive mix of obstacles in seeking arbitral appointments'.[14] This point certainly resonates with me, having observed that, despite a significant increase in the proportion of women at the Iranian Bar, there still is a far greater number of male arbitrators compared to female arbitrators.

A third observation relates to the possible correlation between national government involvement and the risk of politicization in various current selection procedures for international adjudicative institutions, which raises legitimacy concerns. In this context, Brooks Daly (the Deputy Secretary-General of the PCA) pointed out that, '[a]ppointments should not be the product of a system of political

[12] UNCITRAL Working Group III, Academic Forum on ISDS, Concept Paper Project: Matching Concerns and Solutions, Item 5: Lack of diversity among adjudicators, The Diversity Deficit, Preliminary Draft, 30 March 2019, p 7 <https://www.cids.ch/academic-forum-concept-papers> accessed 20 July 2020 (footnotes omitted).

[13] Joshua Karton and Ksenia Polonskaya, 'True Diversity is Intersectional: Escaping the One-Dimensional Discourse on Arbitrator Diversity' (*Kluwer Arbitration Blog*, 10 July 2018).

[14] ibid.

patronage or cronyism if the public is to trust these tribunals'.[15] While acknowledging that some degree of politics in the selection process is unavoidable, the CIDS Supplemental Report has articulated this problem as follows:

> As the practice at existing permanent international courts and tribunals shows, the involvement of States ... may lead to risks of politicization of the selection process. This is true in both full representation and selective representation courts, although politics may come into play in different ways and at different levels in the two models. Appointment on the basis of political considerations rather than competence and merit may undermine the quality of the decisions and, ultimately, the perception of the adjudicatory body's independence, credibility and legitimacy.[16]

Particular features and complexities of the process of judicial selection within the UN system may add a further dimension to the diversity debate. In this regard, Patrick Robinson, the former President of the International Criminal Tribunal for the former Yugoslavia (ICTY) and currently serving as a judge at the International Court of Justice (ICJ), observed that the principal factor in a UN election 'is not the profile of the candidate; it is the political profile of his country'.[17] Robinson went on to note that equally importantly, if a highly placed and influential country makes a political appointment (ie nominates a candidate who is not a very highly qualified individual), that candidate would still be elected due to the political weight of the nominating country.[18]

My fourth observation relates to concerns raised regarding the impartiality and independence of party-appointed arbitrators. These are sometimes expressed in the context of the legitimacy debates, implying that the legitimacy of arbitral tribunals is negatively affected due to the unilateral character of their appointment.[19] In other words, the perception of selection bias would undermine the move towards greater diversity and inclusiveness. In fact, particularly in north-south arbitration, the appointment of party-appointed arbitrators could be the most efficient mechanism for ensuring that a minimum level of cultural diversity is maintained. I say

[15] Brooks Daly, 'International Courts and Tribunals Interest Group: Judicial Selection' (2011) 105 American Society of International Law Proceedings 67.

[16] CIDS Supplemental Report (n 7) 61–62 (footnotes omitted).

[17] Brooks Daly, 'International Courts and Tribunals Interest Group: Judicial Selection' (2011) 105 American Society of International Law Proceedings 67, Remarks by Patrick Lipton Robinson, p 69.

[18] ibid.

[19] See eg Jan Paulson, 'Moral Hazard in International Dispute Resolution' (2011) 8(2) Transnational Dispute Management 3 (identifying the concept of party-appointed arbitrators as one of the 'moral hazards' in the process of international adjudication, stating that 'we could remove the moral hazards'). Professor Paulson goes on to argue that the only decent solution is that any arbitrator 'should be chosen jointly or selected by a neutral body', ibid., p. 16. See also, Albert Jan van den Berg, *Dissenting Opinions by Party-Appointed Arbitrators in Investment Arbitration* in Mahnoush H. Arsanjani and others (eds), *Looking to the Future: Essays on International Law in Honor of W. Michael Reisman* (Brill-Nijhoff 2010) 821–43 ('That nearly 100 percent of the dissents favor the party that appointed the dissenter raises concerns about neutrality').

the 'perception' of selection bias, because any such perception may stem from a shared background and legal culture, and be part of the problem, not its solution. It is necessary in this context to stress the function of party-appointed arbitrators as cultural intermediaries:

> Too often, party-appointed arbitrators are *seen* as partisans, simply because they have a background similar to that of the party who appointed them. They are expected to have certain views and ways of thinking and reasoning, and are therefore often actually perceived to have these, even when this is not the case.[20]

Two further points can be noted. Article 20 (1) of the 2018 Dutch Model BIT provides that '[a]ll Members of the Tribunal under this Agreement shall be appointed by an appointing authority'[21] who is either the ICSID Secretary-General or the PCA Secretary-General. This novel provision would seem to be an attempt to respond to the criticism of the investor-State arbitration system, levelled particularly by Paulson against 'the unprincipled tradition of unilateral appointment of arbitrators'.[22] While the rule that, in appointing arbitrators, the appointing authority 'shall strive for gender and geographic diversity' is a proper initiative to address diversity concerns, its effect may be overshadowed by the current push to eliminate the concept of ad hoc appointed arbitrators from the adjudicatory process altogether. The establishment of investment courts as envisaged under the EU-Canadian Comprehensive Economic and Trade Agreement (CETA) and the EU-Vietnam Free Trade Agreement (FTA) would signify a shift from ad hoc arbitral tribunals to standing adjudicative bodies. For example, the CETA Tribunal will have 15 members, with Canada and the EU appointing five members each, which means, however, that the concept of party-appointed adjudicators insofar as States are concerned would not be wholly removed from the adjudicative system.

The party-appointment process effectively cements the dominance of arbitrators from North America and Europe,[23] possibly due to the fact that when investment disputes gained momentum in the 1990s and early 2000s, well-known arbitrators from the Global North secured multiple appointments. Over time, the non-diverse origins of the system were reinforced given the disputing parties' natural tendency to choose the most experienced arbitrators.[24] In this sense, the party appointment process 'tends to perpetuate a lack of diversity'.[25] One suggested remedy would be

[20] Rosabel Goodman-Everard, 'Cultural Diversity in International Arbitration – A Challenge for Decision-Makers and Decision-Making' (1991) 7(2) Arbitration International 155–164, at 158.

[21] See Art 20(1) of the 2018 Dutch Model.

[22] Jan Paulson (n 19).

[23] The Diversity Deficit (n 12) 6.

[24] ibid.

[25] ibid 9. As to how the party appointment process would normally unfold, the report explains: 'If the claimant has chosen a well-known, "big-name" arbitrator, the respondent is very likely to respond in kind. If the claimant has chosen a less well-known arbitrator, the respondent will often see that as an

to abolish the party-appointment process,[26] which, however, disregards the fact that non-Western arbitrators are being appointed by respondent States.[27] With these preliminary observations in mind, this chapter now turns to the discussion of normative and social legitimacy of the international judicial appointment process.

3. Normative Legitimacy: the Importance of Collective Cultural Neutrality

The 'average' arbitrator is typically a national of a developed Western country. Ibrahim Shihata, then ICSID Secretary-General, observed in 1985:

> It is no secret that developing countries often see international arbitration as a facility administered, to a large extent, by nationals of the developed countries. This is not a phenomenon which is unique to ICSID arbitration. It applies as well, if not more, to other types of institutional arbitration.[28]

In 1996, Dezalay and Garth conducted a sociological study, *Dealing in Virtue,* in which they examined the field of international arbitration and the emerging transnational legal order, focusing on the key players.[29] In this study, they developed the concept of 'symbolic capital', comprising elements such as the social class, education, career, and expertise of a person. They noted that international lawyers, in order to be selected as arbitrators, must earn 'recognized power': '[o]nly a very select and elite group of individuals is able to serve as international arbitrators. They are purportedly selected for their 'virtue' – judgment, neutrality, expertise – yet rewarded as if they are participants in international deal-making'.[30]

At the same time, the study identified two sets of competing value systems (or two forms of symbolic capital): whereas for the traditional international arbitrators or the generation of the 'grand old men' of arbitration, the symbolic capital was their standing as impeccable professionals (such as a retired lord justice of appeal)

opportunity to appoint a "big name" who will likely be more influential than the other party-appointed arbitrator. The disputing parties or their arbitral appointees usually choose the presiding arbitrator. They are very likely to then want an arbitrator of similar experience to preside.'

26 ibid 17.

27 ibid 4.

28 Remarks delivered by Mr. Ibrahim Shihata on the 'Obstacles Facing ICSID's Proceedings and International Arbitration in General' (24 October 1985), News from ICSID, Vol 3, No 1, Winter 1986, p 9.

29 Yves Dezalay and Bryant G. Garth, *Dealing in Virtue* (University of Chicago Press 1996).

30 ibid 8 and 18. In Bourdieu's words, 'the weight of different agents depends on their symbolic capital, ie on the *recognition*, institutionalized or not, that they receive from a group. Educational degrees and formal positions in the legal, economic, or political system have a certain value as capital, depending upon the purpose and audience for which they are assessed. Particular experiences, expertise, and connections likewise have a capital value to the extent that they are recognized as having such a value.'

with their rivals, the new generation of international arbitration professionals trained at large Anglo-American law firms. The constituent elements of their symbolic capital also comprised a more technical set of skills. Crawford used the notion of an 'ideal arbitrator' to capture these two types of international arbitrators:

> The notion of the 'ideal arbitrator' draws inspiration from Yves Dezalay and Bryant Garth's historical conception of commercial arbitrators as a closed group of 'Grand Old Men' – lawyers of distinction, trusted for their wisdom and judgment, although not arbitration specialists. Dezalay and Garth pinpointed a second generation of arbitrators, who they rather unhappily labelled the 'Technocrats.' These were expert arbitration practitioners who had spent their entire careers working in the field.[31]

In developing their sociological description of the field, Dezalay and Garth's discussion focused on Western international arbitrators, noting that it was difficult to contest the dominance of Western lawyers on the north-south arbitration market. They did acknowledge, however, that occasionally, lawyers of the Global South such as Ahmed El-Kosheri or Mohammed Bedjaoui, who had profiles similar to the 'grand old men', may leave the periphery and become well-established international arbitrators.[32]

In their 2015 paper, 'The Diversity Challenge: Exploring the "Invisible College" of International Arbitration',[33] Franck and others used empirical data collected at the 2014 biennial ICCA Congress to make a significant contribution to the diversity debate. All congress participants were offered an opportunity to complete the survey confidentially, which resulted in a response rate of 54.3%. The survey focused on the demographics of the international arbitration community relating to gender, nationality, age, linguistic capacity, legal training, and professional experience. As to the developed/developing countries dichotomy, the survey revealed that 48.2% of the arbitrators were European nationals, followed by 27.9% from North America. By contrast, Asian arbitrators were the second least represented (10%). The authors concluded that 'the data confirmed narratives regarding a lack of diversity in the field of international arbitration'.[34]

Moreover, the subjects were asked whether, in their experience as arbitrators, they had served on a tribunal with at least one arbitrator from a developing country.

[31] James Crawford (n 6) 1005. Crawford also approvingly mentions the 'Managers' as a third type of international arbitrators as suggested by Thomas Schultz and Rebert Kovacs: 'In 2012, Schultz and Kovacs revisited Dezalay and Garth's sociological study and added a third generation of arbitrators, whom they called the "Managers." These were arbitrators highly skilled at managing proceedings, deliberations and the organisation of tribunal work.', ibid. (footnotes omitted).

[32] Dezalay and Garth (n 29) 25.

[33] Susan Frank and others, 'The Diversity Challenge: Exploring the "Invisible College" of International Arbitration' (2015) 53 Columbia Journal of Transnational Law 429–505.

[34] ibid 466.

Table 9.1 Percentages and Frequency of Responses of ICCA Subjects Serving as Arbitrators, Describing the Frequency of Having at Least One Developing World Arbitrator on a Tribunal (including Subjects' Self-Reported Appointments using their OECD Status)

Response Type	Response Percentage	Frequency
No tribunal with a developing world arbitrator	40.2	102
1-5 tribunals with a developing world arbitrator	38.6	98
6-10 tribunals with a developing world arbitrator	9.8	25
10+ tribunals with a developing world arbitrator	11.4	29
Total	**100**	**254**

Specifically, they had to respond by ticking a box indicating that they had: (1) never sat on such a tribunal; (2) sat on such a tribunal one to five times; (3) sat on such a tribunal six to ten times; or (4) sat on such a tribunal more than ten times. Table 9.1 shows the responses to this question.[35]

The authors' inclusion of the term 'invisible college' in the title of their article, a term first coined by Oscar Schachter, signifies the enduring relevance of the concept. In his article 'The Invisible College of International Lawyers' (1977) Schachter used the term to highlight how diversity could improve the quality of decision-making. In his view, the professional community of international lawyers, notably including professors, government officials, international civil servants, and even international law students constituted 'a kind of invisible college dedicated to a common intellectual enterprise'.[36] At the ASIL annual meeting which adopted the theme,[37] Schachter explained that there was 'a sense of mission with international lawyers around the world'.[38] In an interview, he further elaborated on the use of the term 'college':

> The college used to be a fairly small community made up almost entirely of upper-class, European, French-speaking, male lawyers who knew or were related to each

[35] ibid 491.

[36] Oscar Schachter, 'The Invisible College of International Lawyers' (1977) 72 Northwestern University Law Review 217–26, at 217.

[37] However, the organizers explained that while 'at the center of this process of self-reflection' was Professor Schachter's famous 'invisible college' observation, in recognition of the extraordinary changes that had occurred in the nature of international law and its practice in the intervening period, the theme was chosen as the 'visible' college of international law. See David J Bederman and Lucy Reed, 'The Visible College of International Law: An Introduction' (2001) 95 American Society of International Law Proceedings ix.

[38] Micke J Clincy, 'An Interview with Oscar Schachter' 95 (2001) American Society of International Law Proceedings 18.

> other. This was one reason people could call it a college […]; you could see the people who comprise the college – there were not that many.[39]

Nevertheless, he acknowledged that international law is not value-free and that international lawyers are likely to reflect their value systems.[40] Schachter referred to the general phenomenon of internalization of shared social values, concluding that to enhance objectivity in international judicial decision-making, it was necessary to increase diversity and broad representation:

> A corollary of this inherent parochialism is the recognition that a less biased (and therefore more credible) judgment on controversial issues of international law would more likely be made by a broadly representative international body than by persons from a single country or by persons sharing a particular political outlook, however expert they may be.[41]

Such an analysis may be extended to include the internalization of a shared value system among nationals of developed States in the context of north-south arbitrations. Although expressed as an aspiration, Schachter believed that the essential advantage of the invisible college was to be found in its diversity. The legitimizing function of a broadly representative international body in delivering a less biased judgment correlates with his objectivity concerns. General statements as to the main 'sources' of international law give a wide scope of discretion to international decision-making bodies, thus producing 'an impression of indeterminacy and relativism'.[42] Increasing diversity would lead to more objective judgments, because a more heterogeneous and representative body would balance out national or otherwise particularistic influences.[43]

A decade later, Koskenniemi in *From Apology to Utopia* echoed the 'objectivity' concerns in respect of the structure of international legal argument. He sought to explain how international law could simultaneously possess a high degree of 'formal coherence' while remaining 'substantively indeterminate', at least as to controversial issues. Thus, while wide powers of discretion would result in an impression of indeterminacy and thus would be impermissible, 'there is no consensus on the extent of permissible discretion'.[44] As to the objectivity concerns, Koskenniemi referred to the problem of conflicting principles, explaining that, '[e]ach general principle seems capable of being opposed with an equally valid counter-principle'.[45]

[39] ibid.
[40] Schachter 218.
[41] ibid 219.
[42] ibid 220.
[43] ibid 223.
[44] Martti Koskenniemi, *From Apology to Utopia: The Structure of International Legal Argument (Reissue with a new Epilogue)* (CUP 2005) 35.
[45] ibid 3.

At any rate, it is axiomatic that sharing a particular political or economic outlook, or cultural endowments, would create preferences that might steer judicial decision-making.[46] The existence of broadly formulated normative standards (for example, the fair and equitable treatment standard), combined with an insufficient degree of concretization (which is an inherent feature of international law as a normative system), provided the international bench with a wide degree of discretion.[47] As Schwebel observed, '[o]ne of the satisfactions of working in the field of international law is that it is such an inchoate field so that the individual can make an impact, which is disproportionate to that which he or she is likely to make in a career confined to national law'.[48] As is apparent from the description of international law as an 'inchoate field', there exists a wider degree of freedom enjoyed by international arbitrators and judges compared to their domestic counterparts. This, in turn, requires the use of broadly representative decision-making bodies to function as a built-in control mechanism. In fact, in addition to the difference in terms of the level of concretization of legal norms, the international system typically lacks mechanisms ensuring the consistency of case law and a rigorous system of control.

An additional consideration is the need to address what is sometimes referred to as an unconscious or unintended ethnocentrism on the part of arbitral tribunals predominantly composed of Western legal scholars dealing with north-south disputes. In the context of the 'Globalization and Law' debate, ethnocentrism has been defined as:

> the projection of ideas derived from one's own culture and background onto others – because these ideas are assumed to be universal, or essentially the same as, or more advanced than, or superior to those of others. Ethnocentrism may often be based more on ignorance than arrogance. Our Western traditions of academic law and legal practice, parochially focused on the municipal laws of our own societies, have exhibited very little interest in non-Western legal traditions and cultures.[49]

[46] See, for example, Tom Ginsburg, 'The Culture of Arbitration' (2003) 36 Vanderbilt Journal of Transnational Law 1337.

[47] Waibel and Wu share this diagnosis in their analysis of international investment arbitration, stating that 'investment law is traditionally more open-ended than most national law, leaving even more room for the policy preferences of arbitrators and incentives to influence outcomes', (n 4) 4. As already noted, they also found that '[a]rbitrators may fill ambiguities and gaps in such an evolving field as international investment law based in part on their policy preferences' (n 4) 23.

[48] See *Judge Stephen M. Schwebel Addresses International Arbitration Issues* (15 April 2015) <https://www.law.miami.edu/news/2015/april/judge-stephen-m-schwebel-addresses-international-arbitration-issues> accessed 29 February 2020.

[49] William Twining, *Globalisation and Law: Ten Theses* in Sam Muller and others (eds), *The Law of the Future and the Future of Law*, vol II (TOAEP: Torkel Opsahl Academic EPublisher 2012) 35–36.

In dealing with concrete cases, culturally diverse international arbitral tribunals would be able to gain insights into non-Western legal traditions which could serve as an efficient means to counter unintended ethnocentrism. In this regard, the results of the 2014 ICCA survey show another aspect of the correlation between greater diversity and improving normative legitimacy: '[h]aving greater representation of different perspectives during deliberation could aid a more comprehensive appreciation of parties' positions and underlying evidence. This, in turn, could generate higher quality awards.'[50]

4. Diversity as a Key Aspect of the Social Legitimacy of North-South Arbitration

The social legitimacy of north-south arbitration is of particular importance in the area of investment arbitration due to its origins. Schultz and Dupont pointed out that, viewed in this light, the functional effects of investment arbitration as a field may be referred to as neo-colonialism.[51] Likewise, as M Sornarajah stated, the ICSID Convention of 1966 'was based on the neo-liberal assumption, stated in its Preamble, that the existence of a secure, external system of settlement of disputes would facilitate the flow of investments into developing countries, which would otherwise be seen as risky for the reason that their judicial systems do not offer impartial justice to the alien investors'.[52] Noting that north-south conflicts made up most of the best-known arbitrations of the 1970s, Dezalay and Garth refer to the problem of legitimacy deficit, ie a lack of trust in Western-dominated institutions, stating that,

> How was the law – or more precisely, the law that developed along with the field of international commercial arbitration – able to extend authority over countries that had no developed legal traditions, no trust in Western-dominated institutions, and in particular no faith in some new form of transnational law?[53]

Referring to the Libyan petroleum arbitrations as the prime example of the north-south arbitration in the 1970s, Paulson noted that Libya did not participate in the proceedings so in this context, 'the very legitimacy of the arbitral process had been challenged by the defendant'.[54] At any rate, countering perceived

[50] Susan Frank and others (n 33) 498.
[51] Thomas Schultz and Cedric Dupont (n 3) 1151.
[52] M Sornarajah (n 5) 274.
[53] Yves Dezalay and Bryant G. Garth (n 29) 64.
[54] Jan Paulson, 'Third World Participation in International Investment Arbitration' (1987) 2 (1) ICSID Review – Foreign Investment Law Journal 19–65, at 56. At the same time, Jan Paulson in his article argued against the perception that 'arbitration is designed to serve the interests of industrialized countries', ibid 20.

bias in north-south arbitration, resulting from the hegemony of Western lawyers as dominant decision-makers, was one important aspect of the legal initiatives introduced by the South in the 1970s. The backlash against north-south arbitration contributed to the momentum that lead to the New International Economic Order (NIEO).[55] As is well-known, the NIEO failed both in terms of its anti-arbitration stance and in bringing about a new approach to the law governing nationalization. Some commentators such as Shalakany argue that the unrealistic aspirations embodied in the NIEO agenda for redistribution of wealth from north to south have since been replaced by the Third World demands for cultural recognition.[56]

In the 1990s, a second strand of international arbitration emerged as a result of several NAFTA-based claims by US and Canadian investors against Canada and the US, respectively: the era of the north-north investor-State arbitration.[57] As Pauwelyn has put it, ISDS became widely used as a vehicle for bringing claims against developed States with a firmly established rule of law.[58] This new dimension, in turn, meant that the traditional debate regarding the social legitimacy of north-south arbitration was overshadowed by a backlash against investment arbitration in general. In other words, the traditional legitimacy concerns of developing countries were surpassed by wider concerns as to how best to protect the public interest and the right to regulate. Schultz and Dupont have described this development as follows:

> The position of developed and developing countries in the arbitration system veered in fact in the mid-to-late 1990s. Until then, investment arbitration was indeed a 'rich vs poor', 'developed vs developing' instrument, therefore arguably serviceable for neocolonial purposes. Since the mid-to-late 1990s, however, investment arbitration has been a mixed 'developed vs developed' and 'developed vs developing' instrument, with a slight preponderance of 'developed vs developed' claims. This shift in geometry tends to undermine the neo-colonial argument for the period after the mid-to-late 1990s.[59]

[55] UN General Assembly, Res A/RES/S-6/3201, *Declaration for the Establishment of a New International Economic Order* (1 May 1974).

[56] See Amr A Shalakany, 'Arbitration and the Third World: A Plea for Reassessing Bias under the Specter of Neo- liberalism' (2000) 41 Harvard International Law Journal 419–68, at 420.

[57] *Ethyl Corporation v Canada* (NAFTA/UNCITRAL, 1997); *SD Myers v Canada* (NAFTA/UNCITRAL, 1998); *The Loewen Group, Inc v United States of America* (Case No. ARB(AF)/98/3); *Pope & Talbot v Canada* (NAFTA/UNCITRAL, 1999); *Methanex Corporation . United States of America* (NAFTA/UNCITRAL, 1999); *United Parcel Service of America (UPS) v Canada* (NAFTA/UNCITRAL, 2000).

[58] See Joost Pauwelyn, 'The Rule of Law without the Rule of Lawyers: Why Investment Arbitrators Are from Mars, Trade Adjudicators from Venus' (2015) 109 American Journal of International Law 761–805, at 764.

[59] Thomas Schultz and Cedric Dupont (n 3) 1156.

Investment claims are now being filed roughly equally against developing and developed States. Schultz and Dupont went on to conclude that 'the neo-colonial flavour of the system started to fade'.[60] While it is understandable that in order to protect the regulatory sovereignty of host States all concerns regarding international arbitration may be considered collectively, it must be borne in mind that it is the traditional north-south divide that gives rise to the perceived development bias. It follows that for the purposes of focusing on the social legitimacy aspects of north-south arbitration in the context of the diversity debate, it is important to maintain the traditional conceptual distinction between the two strands.

5. Conclusion

Against the backdrop of the perceived legitimacy deficit, the renewed focus on the diversity of international adjudicative bodies as a necessary means to enhance legitimacy is a welcome development. A more representative international adjudicative body could achieve a more satisfactory level of objectivity, producing more credible results. Equally importantly, more heterogeneous adjudicative bodies could help to resolve the long overdue legitimacy concerns in respect of perceived bias in north-south arbitration. No doubt regulatory sovereignty concerns must also be dealt with adequately. However, as this new dimension focuses on such issues as the concerns ensuing from the claims of powerful corporations against host States exercising legitimate regulatory authority, it is important to remember that the traditional legitimacy concerns relating to cultural diversity have yet to be addressed.

In fact, the most recent confirmation of the continued relevance of this analysis may be found in the recently amended NAFTA (also referred to as the US-Mexico-Canada Agreement or USMCA) which is more limited in three ways. First, it includes a separate ISDS mechanism for the benefit of US and Mexican investors, while excluding Canadian investors.[61] Second, it only applies in relation to denial of post-establishment national treatment, most-favoured-nation treatment or direct expropriation. Third, it restricts arbitral access to certain sectors ('covered government contracts' in a number of key sectors such as oil and gas production, power generation, and telecommunications).[62] This is reminiscent of the 1988

[60] ibid 1159.

[61] See Luke Eric Peterson, *NAFTA parties unveil text of new agreement; Canada opts out of investor-state arbitration entirely, and U.S. and Mexico agree a more limited version of such dispute settlement*, Investment Arbitration Reporter (Oct 01, 2018). It is worth reminding that the TPP's dispute settlement model remains in the text now being ratified by the remaining 11 countries (the CPTPP), including Canada and Mexico, which have already ratified the CPTPP. Also, the current ISDS mechanism under NAFTA would continue to apply to the claims covered by Annex 14-C (Legacy Investment Claims and Pending Claims).

[62] See Chapter 14 of the USMCA, Annex 14-E <https://www.international.gc.ca/trade-commerce/assets/pdfs/agreements-accords/cusma-aceum/r2-cusma-14.pdf> accessed 20 July 2019.

Canada-US FTA which included an investment chapter, but did not provide for ISDS. Commentators have noted that the inclusion of the ISDS mechanism in 1994 NAFTA was 'largely because of perceptions about Mexico's potential volatility as a destination for foreign investment'.[63] In sum, the NAFTA reform reinforces the old perception that the institution of investment arbitration is predominantly designed to address north-south disputes. This development reaffirms the continued relevance of development-based concerns and reinforces the need to strive for more inclusiveness.

[63] Andrea K Bjorklund, 'NAFTA Chapter 11' in Chester Brown (ed), *Commentaries on Selected Model Investment Treaties* (OUP 2013) 465.

10

Fifty Years of Women at the European Court of Human Rights

Successes and Failures of the Council of Europe's Gender Agenda

*Helen Keller, Corina Heri, and Myriam Christ**

1. Introduction

Gender representation on the Strasbourg bench has been a priority of the Council of Europe for some time. Indeed, for more than a decade now, the Parliamentary Assembly of the Council of Europe (PACE) has required States' three-candidate lists of potential judges to the European Court of Human Rights (ECtHR) to contain at least one candidate from the sex that is underrepresented on the Court at the time.[1] In 2017, the Council of Europe's Steering Committee for Human Rights (CDDHR) considered that 'the goal of achieving a gender balance on the Court is already adequately addressed and no additional measures need to be proposed'.[2] With this in mind, it is striking that there are still far fewer women than men on the Strasbourg bench today, with 15 female and 32 male judges on the bench as of early January 2018 (and thus a Court made up of 31.9% women). The statistics concerning the number of women on the bench, including by region, indicate that the struggle to achieve equal gender representation amongst the Strasbourg judges is far from over. The present chapter provides a perspective on this topic that is grounded in data on the number of female judges at the Court over time, and builds on existing literature by adding a comparison across the various regions of Europe. The chapter is based on this data and on the personal experience of the first author, Helen Keller, and does not purport to provide a sociological account

* The authors wish to thank Andrew Drzemczewski and Françoise Tulkens for their comments on an earlier version of this chapter, as well as Andreas Føllesdal and the participants of the workshop on 'Gender on the International Bench' held in The Hague on 11 and 12 January 2018. All views expressed herein are the authors' own.

[1] PACE, 'Candidates for the European Court of Human Rights', Resolution 1366 (2004), as modified by Resolutions 1426 (2005), 1627 (2008), 1841 (2011), and 2002 (2014).

[2] CDDH, 'Report on the Process of Selection and Election of Judges of the European Court of Human Rights' (11 December 2017) CDDH(2017)R88addI, 5, para 10; see also at 10, para 75.

Helen Keller, Corina Heri, and Myriam Christ, *Fifty Years of Women at the European Court of Human Rights* In: *Identity and Diversity on the International Bench.* Edited by: Freya Baetens, Oxford University Press (2020). © The several contributors.
DOI: 10.1093/oso/9780198870753.003.0010.

of gender representation in Strasbourg. Instead, it provides an interpretation of the matter from the personal perspective of the authors, the first of whom is a (female) judge at the Court, and advances certain conclusions and recommendations from this perspective. The chapter thus attempts to provide some explanations that are, by their very nature, speculative, and must be understood as such.

A few further caveats are in order. First, the chapter will operate on the understanding that, while judges are expected to be impartial in interpreting the law, diversity among them—in respect of gender and other attributes—still adds value in other respects. This includes the legitimacy of the institution and the perceived fairness of proceedings before it, as well as of the outcomes of these proceedings. To some extent, and in specific contexts, adequate gender representation may also arguably inform the ways in which victims of certain rights violations are considered. In addition, while the chapter concerns the representation of women at the Court, which relevant Council of Europe documents seem to equate with the female sex (the Court's standardized judicial *curriculum vitae* forms, for example, require candidates for election to the Court to state their sex, not their gender),[3] the chapter should be read with the understanding that sex and gender are two different matters, that gender is socially constructed, and that there are many equally valid ways to experience and perform gender. The chapter will examine how the Court has dealt with the underrepresentation of women, as a group with a continuing history of discrimination, but lacks the space to engage more deeply with the Court's concept of sex and gender. However, nothing herein should be understood as intended to reinforce the gender binary or exclude transgender, gender non-binary, or intersex people, among others.

2. The Council of Europe's Approach to Gender

The idea of ensuring a gender balance among the Strasbourg judges was explored even before the 'permanent' Court was established in 1998.[4] In 1997, the Ministers' Deputies encouraged States to submit more gender-balanced candidate lists and ensure 'that the qualifications and experience of all the candidates put forward, whether men or women, allow their candidatures to be taken into consideration on an equal footing'.[5] Andrew Drzemczewski, in his article on the approach to (and trials of) judicial election at the time of the establishment of the 'new' Court,

[3] Appendix to PACE, 'Nomination of Candidates and Election of Judges to the European Court of Human Rights' (27 January 2009) Resolution 1646 (2009).

[4] On judicial elections at the Strasbourg Court more generally, see Andrew Drzemczewski, 'Election of Judges (European Court of Human Rights)', *Max Planck Encyclopedia of International Procedural Law*, 2018.

[5] PACE, 'Declaration Adopted by the Ministers' Deputies at their 593rd Meeting' (28 May 1997), as cited in Andrew Drzemczewski, 'The European Human Rights Convention: A New Court of Human Rights in Strasbourg as of November 1, 1998' (1998) 55 Washington and Lee Law Review 697, 730.

traced this to the initiative of Lydie Err, who at the time was a PACE representative from Luxembourg, and later went on to chair the PACE Committee on Equal Opportunities for Women and Men's Sub-Committee on Equal Participation of Women and Men in Decision-making.[6]

In 2004, PACE turned this guidance into a rule, and resolved that it would not consider lists of candidates put forth by the States Parties where the listed candidates had restricted areas of competence, had insufficient knowledge of one of the Court's two official languages, did not appear to be of the stature required under Article 21(1) of the European Convention on Human Rights (ECHR), or where 'the list does not include at least one candidate of each sex, except when the candidates belong to the sex which is under-represented in the Court, that is the sex to which under 40% of the total number of judges belong'.[7] PACE has also resolved that, as far as the selection procedure in its Committee on the Election of Judges is concerned, 'in the case of equal merit, preference should be given to a candidate of the sex under-represented at the Court'.[8] These efforts are quite innovative and PACE has taken the role of a forerunner when compared to other international courts, where similar policies are conspicuously absent.

These PACE resolutions formed part of several attempts to improve judicial selection.[9] They were also to some extent focused on protecting male candidates: the gender parity requirements were issued in light of arguments that the absence of female candidates from most candidate lists meant that those men on lists that included women who were less qualified were foregone in the context of a selection procedure desperate for female appointees.[10]

These Council of Europe developments do not stand alone, however. For example, the Convention on the Elimination of Discrimination against Women, which was adopted in 1979, states in its Article 8 that 'States Parties shall take all appropriate measures to ensure to women, on equal terms with men and without any discrimination, the opportunity to represent their Governments at the international level and to participate in the work of international organizations'.[11]

At the time of its introduction, PACE's gender policy for judicial appointees was almost immediately tested by all-male State candidate lists submitted by

[6] Drzemczewski (n 5) at 704.

[7] PACE, Resolution 1366 (2004) (n 1).

[8] ibid.

[9] On other attempts in this context, not specifically related to gender, see for example the Resolution on a standardized *curriculum vitae* (PACE Resolution 1646 (2009) (n 3)) or the recommendations on the national selection procedure (PACE, 'National procedures for nominating candidates for election to the European Court of Human Rights' (24 September 1999), Recommendation 1429 (1999)).

[10] See Renate Wohlwend, 'National Procedures for Nominating Candidates for Election to the ECtHR', COE/PACE Doc 8505, September 1999, as discussed in Stéphanie Hennette Vauchez, 'More Women – But Which Women? The Rule and the Politics of Gender Balance at the European Court of Human Rights' (2015) 26 The European Journal of International Law 195.

[11] Convention on the Elimination of All Forms of Discrimination against Women (adopted 18 December 1979, entered into force 3 September 1981) 1249 UNTS 13.

the Slovak Republic and Malta, and by an all-female Latvian list. While the Slovak list was amended and PACE changed its requirements to accommodate the Latvian list,[12] the Maltese government rallied opposition to the gender balance rule among other States.[13] This led to a request for an advisory opinion on the topic by the Committee of Ministers in 2007. That opinion, which was issued by the Court in 2008, *inter alia* concerned the question of whether lists of candidates can be rejected purely on the basis of gender-related requirements. In its opinion, the Court noted the importance of and general agreement on the need to promote gender equality, also within the courts, but held that—when talking about small countries especially—PACE's requirements are contrary to the Convention if and when they force States to include non-nationals on their list because a qualified candidate of the underrepresented gender cannot be found despite following PACE's guidance as concerns the publicity of the search for candidates.[14]

Almost a decade after that advisory opinion was issued, PACE's gender policy remains in place. Its Judicial Selection Committee may reject single-sex lists of candidates, and must in fact vote by a two-thirds majority to accept such a list.[15] The following section will seek to shed some light on the policy's effect to date on the basis of data about judges elected to the Court since its inception.

3. The Gender of ECtHR Judges by Numbers

3.1 A Timeline of Gender Representation at the Court

In 2015, Stephanie Hennette Vauchez, in an article concerning gender on the Strasbourg bench, analysed the curricula vitae (CVs) of all female candidates ever proposed for that position since the Court's inception in 1959 until 2012.[16] She noted that, until the gender parity rule was introduced in 2004, many States had

[12] PACE, Resolution 1366 (2004) (n 1), specifying in para 4 that single-sex lists will only be considered if the candidates belong to the underrepresented gender (according to the 40% threshold) or there are 'exceptional circumstances', which are deemed to exist 'where a Contracting Party has taken all the necessary and appropriate steps to ensure that the list contains candidates of both sexes meeting the requirements of Article 21 § 1 [ECHR].' Such exceptional circumstances must be established by a two-thirds majority of the Committee on the Election of Judges to the ECtHR and endorsed by PACE (see PACE, 'Procedure for Electing Judges to the European Court of Human Rights' (19 December 2017) AS/Cdh/Inf (2018) 01).

[13] For more detail, see Hennette Vauchez (n 10).

[14] ECtHR, 'Advisory opinion on certain legal questions concerning the lists of candidates submitted with a view to the election of judges to the European Court of Human Rights' (12 February 2008).

[15] PACE, 'Rules of Procedure of the Assembly (October 2017)' (4 November 1999) Resolution 1202 (1999), with subsequent modifications, at VII (4) (1). See also Andrew Drzemczewski, 'The Parliamentary Assembly's Committee on the Election of Judges to the European Court of Human Rights, Council of Europe' (2015) 35 Human Rights Law Journal 269.

[16] Hennette Vauchez (n 10).

never even included any women on their lists, much less sent a female judge to Strasbourg,[17] but that many other States had proposed female candidates long before that date.[18] In other words, she argued, the PACE gender rule is not the only factor determining whether women are elected to judicial positions at the ECtHR: gender politics also play a role.[19] On the basis of the CVs of the female judicial candidates, she argued that two types of female candidates are presented to the Court. Some, with impressive CVs and a wealth of international experience and language skills, seem to be '*des hommes comme des autres*': their CVs are basically indistinguishable from those of successful male candidates.[20] The other category are outliers as compared to the archetype of the international judge in light of their youth, lack of experience, or some other factor, and this group seems to be proposed precisely in light of their comparatively weaker CVs—because they have little chance of success.[21]

Hennette Vauchez concluded that the world of judicial appointments on the international level is far from neutral. To follow up on her research, update, and complement it, the following paragraphs provide data from the official list of judges of the Court since 1959,[22] and look systematically at judges elected between the establishment of the permanent Court in 1998 and the beginning of 2018, as well as the official CVs of the judges. We disaggregate the number of female judges who have been elected to the Court over the years into their regions of origin and also examine the age of the judges at the time of their election as well as the number and age of the children of the female judges at the time of their appointment. We chose the first two factors so as to interrogate, in light of the available information, whether female judges tend to come from specific regions or belong to a certain age category. The last factor, concerning the number and age of children, interests us because of anecdotal evidence presenting a judicial role at the Court to be, at least until recently, difficult to reconcile with care obligations, and because this relates to the stereotyped model of male breadwinners and female caregivers.[23]

[17] ibid 211. The States that had never even included a woman on their list are Andorra, Bosnia and Herzegovina, Cyprus, Georgia, Hungary, Ireland, Iceland, Italy, Liechtenstein, Lithuania, Luxemburg, the Republic of Moldova, Monaco, Montenegro, Portugal, Russia, Serbia, Turkey, and Ukraine, although Hennette Vauchez notes that some of these States joined the Council of Europe later and therefore had fewer opportunities to submit candidate lists.

[18] Hennette Vauchez (n 10) 211–12 and 215, naming, *inter alia*, the examples of Alexandra Mantzoulinos, who was presented as a candidate by Greece in 1968, Helga Pedersen, the first woman elected to the Court in 1971, in respect of Denmark, and Denise Bindschedler-Robert, who was elected in 1975 in respect of Switzerland.

[19] Hennette Vauchez (n 10) 212.

[20] ibid 216–17.

[21] Hennette Vauchez (n 10) 219–20.

[22] ECtHR, 'Judges of the Court Since 1959', <www.echr.coe.int/Documents/List_judges_since_1959_BIL.pdf> accessed 5 December 2017.

[23] On this model and the idea of a 'motherhood penalty', see Michelle J Budig, Joya Misra, and Irene Boeckmann, 'The Motherhood Penalty in Cross-National Perspective: The Importance of Work–Family Policies and Cultural Attitudes' (2012) 19 Social Politics: International Studies in Gender, State & Society 163.

The data allows us to calculate the percentage of female judges at the permanent Court—since its establishment by Protocol 11 in 1994[24] and the beginning of its work in 1998—over the 20 years of its existence.[25] The mean average proportion of women sitting on the bench from 1998 until the election of the judge in respect of Georgia on 10 October 2017 is 30.8%. As the figure below shows, the percentage as disaggregated by year steadily increased until 2011, when it peaked at 42.6%. This therefore briefly put the number of female judges over the 40% threshold, meaning that women temporarily no longer constituted an underrepresented gender, as noted by the Belgian government in defence of its all-male 2012 list.[26] Since that time, the percentage of female judges on the Court has sunk to 32% in 2018, and—as far as we are aware—the Belgian argument has not been repeated.

As Figure 10.1 shows, at the time of the entry into force of Protocol 11 and the creation of the new, permanent Court to replace the temporary Court and the European Commission of Human Rights in 1998, only 20% of the judges were women. Given that there was no requirement of continuity of judges and Commission members,[27] the Contracting Parties were free to choose new

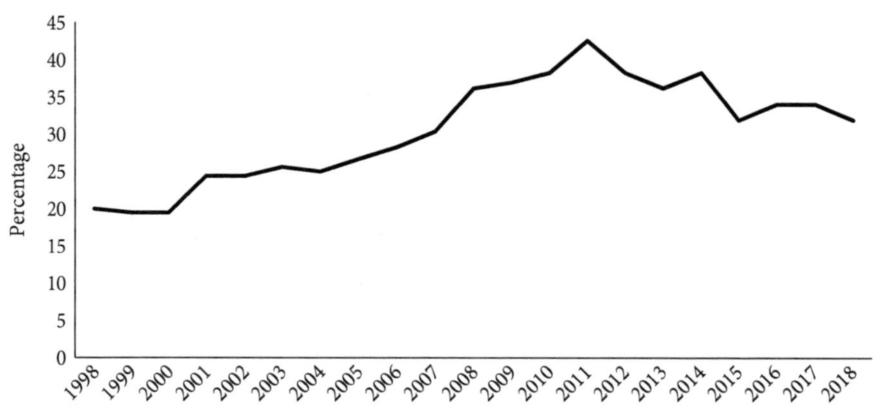

Figure 10.1 Percentage of female judges at the ECHR (1998–beginning of 2018)

[24] Council of Europe, Protocol 11 to the Convention for the Protection of Human Rights and Fundamental Freedoms, restructuring the control machinery established thereby (adopted 11 May 1994, entered into force 1 November 1998) Council of Europe Treaty Series 155.

[25] These percentages were obtained by adding up the total number of female judges serving on 31 December of each year since the permanent ECtHR was established. This number was then divided by the total number of both male and female judges serving every year since establishment and multiplied by 100.

[26] On this list, compare Hennette Vauchez (n 10) 209; Adelaide Remiche, 'Election of the New Belgian Judge to the ECtHR: An All-Male Short List Demonstrates Questionable Commitment to Gender Equality' (*Oxford Human Rights Hub*, 12 August 2012) <http://ohrh.law.ox.ac.uk/election-of-the-new-belgian-judge-to-the-ecthr-an-all-male-short-list-demonstrates-questionable-commitment-to-gender-equality> accessed 7 December 2017.

[27] Protocol 11 to the ECtHR (n 24) at Art. 5(1).

candidates for the permanent Court. Upon creation of the permanent Court, 10 former judges and 10 former members of the Commission sat on the new bench; of these, only one was a woman.[28] None of the three female members of the Commission became judges on the permanent Court. This very low percentage of women among the old members of the Court sitting on the bench of the permanent Court is perhaps a corollary of the fact that the women had only made up 2.7% of the 'old' Court—with Elisabeth Palm sitting as the lone female judge alongside 36 men—and 9%[29] at the Commission. Of the 20 other newly-elected judges of the permanent Court, seven were women. They mostly came from small countries, countries historically open to gender equality and 'new democracies'.[30] In this way, with the establishment of the new Court, the percentage of female judges jumped from 2.7% in 1997 to 20% in 1998.

This percentage jumped once more, from 19.5% in 1999 to 24.4% in 2001, after PACE invited the Committee of Ministers to encourage States to apply certain criteria to national nominations, including urging the States to 'select candidates of both sexes in every case'.[31] Then, when PACE decided no longer to consider unisex lists of candidates in 2004, the percentage of female judges rose from 25% in 2004 to 42.6% in 2011, seven years later.[32] Of course, it can take time for the effects of measures like these to be noticeable given that it might take years from the moment of their introduction before a given judge's term expires and his or her home State is called to present new candidates.[33] However, it would seem from these figures that gender balancing measures do have some effect on the number of women at the Court. Interestingly enough, however, there has been a significant decrease in the number of female ECtHR judges since the end of 2011.[34] This finding will be discussed and placed in a broader context below, in section 5.

[28] This was Elisabeth Palm from Sweden, who was elected in 1988.

[29] Three out of 33 members of the Commission were women: Mai Hion (Estonia), Jane Liddy (Ireland), and Gro Hillestad Thune (Norway).

[30] Françoise Tulkens (Belgium), Snejana Botoucharova (Bulgaria), Nina Vajic (Croatia), Wilhelmina Thomassen (the Netherlands), Hanne Sophie Greve (Norway), Viera Straznicka (the Slovak Republic), and Margarita Tsatsa-Nikolovska (North Macedonia).

[31] PACE, Recommendation 1429 (1999) (n 9) para 6.3, as discussed in Nienke Grossman, 'Shattering the Glass Ceiling in International Adjudication' (2016) 56 Virginia Journal of International Law 213.

[32] ibid 44 et seq.

[33] All ECtHR judges are elected for a single term of nine years (see Protocol 14 to the Convention for the Protection of Human Rights and Fundamental Freedoms, amending the control system of the Convention (adopted 13 May 2004, entered into force 1 June 2010) Council of Europe Treaty Series 194), and the elections of judges to the permanent Court were originally staggered take place every three years (cf Protocol 11 to the ECtHR (n 24)). However, judicial elections at the Court no longer follow a regular timetable given early retirements and the intermittent election of judges for new member States (cf Council of Europe, 'Elections of Judges to the European Court of Human Rights: Table of Progress by Contracting Party' <www.assembly.coe.int/LifeRay/CDH/Pdf/TableForthcomingJudgesElections-EN.pdf> accessed 17 August 2020).

[34] To better understand this development, it would of course be relevant to examine the national selection procedures more in depth. Unfortunately, this is beyond the scope of the present analysis.

3.2 Gender and Regional Origin

In order to evaluate whether there were obvious differences between regions, we grouped the 47 member States into Scandinavian countries,[35] Western European countries,[36] South Eastern European countries,[37] and Eastern and Central European countries[38]. The results show clear regional patterns—specifically, the Scandinavian countries had a distinctly different track-record than other countries, and so we decided to group the findings by region as well as discussing some countries individually. The findings are represented visually below.

The regional analysis of the data provided in Figure 10.2 indicates that there is quite some variation between the various regions of Europe as concerns the number of women who have effectively served on the Court to date. Specifically, the results for the Scandinavian States are much closer to gender parity, at 42.9% female judges, than the overall average of 30.8%.

In this regard, some interesting observations can be made regarding certain countries. First, it is notable that all of the judges elected in respect of three countries, namely Croatia,[39] Monaco,[40] and Sweden,[41] have been women. By contrast, the judges elected in respect of 23 other countries have been exclusively male.

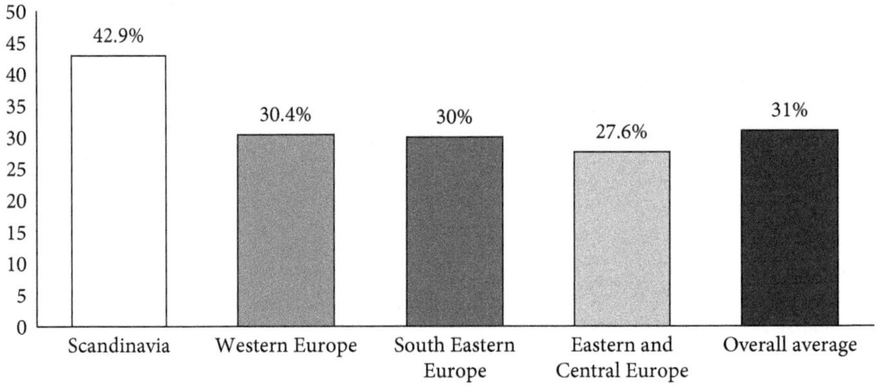

Figure 10.2 Percentage of women among all elected judges (on a regional basis)

[35] Denmark, Finland, Iceland, Norway, and Sweden.

[36] Andorra, Austria, Belgium, France, Germany, Ireland, Italy, Lichtenstein, Luxembourg, Malta, Monaco, the Netherlands, Portugal, San Marino, Spain, Switzerland, and the United Kingdom.

[37] Albania, Bosnia and Herzegovina, Bulgaria, Croatia, Cyprus, Greece, the Republic of Moldova, Montenegro, Romania, Serbia, Slovenia, North Macedonia, and Turkey.

[38] Armenia, Azerbaijan, the Czech Republic, Estonia, Georgia, Hungary, Latvia, Lithuania, Poland, the Russian Federation, the Slovak Republic, and Ukraine.

[39] Nina Vajic (1998–2012), Ksenija Turkovic (2013–).

[40] Isabelle Berro (2006–15), Stéphanie Mourou-Vikström (2015–).

[41] Elisabeth Palm (1998–2003), Elisabet Fura (2003–12), Helena Jäderblom (2012–18).

Theses judges have come from Albania,[42] Andorra,[43] Azerbaijan,[44] Cyprus,[45] the Czech Republic,[46] Denmark,[47] Italy,[48] Liechtenstein,[49] Luxembourg,[50] Malta,[51] the Republic of Moldova,[52] France,[53] Greece,[54] Hungary,[55] Iceland,[56] Montenegro,[57] Poland,[58] Portugal,[59] the Russian Federation,[60] Serbia,[61] Slovenia,[62] Spain,[63] and the United Kingdom.[64]

This includes four of the founding members of the Council of Europe, namely France, Italy, Luxembourg, and the United Kingdom. However, to be fair, it should also be noted that Greece, in respect of whom there has never been a female ECtHR judge, was in fact the first State to put forth a female candidate, presenting Alexandra Mantzoulinos in 1968. The first woman actually elected to the Court was Helga Pedersen, who was the judge in respect of Denmark from 1971 to 1980. Furthermore, a number of these States have included women in their lists of potential ad hoc judges to the ECtHR.[65] From these lists, the Court's President can choose an ad hoc judge to take the place of the judge elected in respect of the country concerned when he or she cannot sit.[66]

42 Kristaq Traja (1998–2008), Ledi Bianku (2008–19).

43 Josep Casadevall (1998–2015), Pere Pastor Vilanova (2015–).

44 Khanlar Hajiyev (2003–16), Letif Hüseynov (2017–).

45 Loukis Loucaides (1998–2008), George Nicolaou (2008–16), Georgios Serghides (2016–).

46 Karel Jungwiert (1998–2012), Ales Pejchal (2012–).

47 In respect of which no female judge has been elected since 1998. The two elected judges have been Peer Lorenzen (1998–2014), Jon Fridrik Kjolbro (2014–).

48 Benedetto Conforti (1998–2001), Vladimiro Zagrebelsky (2001–10), Guido Raimondi (2010–19).

49 Lucius Caflisch (1998–2006), Mark Villiger (2006–15), Carlo Ranzoni (2015–).

50 Marc Fischbach (1998–2004), Dean Spielmann (2004–15), Georges Ravarani (2015–).

51 Giovanni Bonello (1998–2010), Vincent De Gaetano (2010–19).

52 Tudor Pantiru (1998–2001), Stanislav Pavlovschi (2001–08), Mihai Poalelungi (2008–12), Valeriu Gritco (2012–).

53 Jean-Paul Costa (1998–2011), André Potocki (2011–20).

54 Christos Rozakis (1998–2011), Linos-Alexandre Sicilianos (2011–).

55 Andras Baka (1998–2008), Andras Sajo (2008–17), Peter Paczolay (2017–).

56 Gaukur Jörundsson (1998–2004), David Thor Björgvinsson (2004–13), Robert Spano (2013–).

57 Nebojsa Vucinic (2008–18). It should however be noted that, in 2018, after the end of the time period considered in the present chapter, Nebojsa Vucinic was replaced by a female judge, Ivana Jelić.

58 Jerzy Makarczyk (1998–2002), Lech Garlicki (2002–12), Krzysztof Wojtyczek (2012–).

59 Ireneu Cabral Barreto (1998–2011), Paulo Pinto de Albuquerque (2011–20).

60 Vladimir Toumanov (1998), Anatoly Kovler (1999–2012), Dmitry Dedov (2013–).

61 Dragoljub Popovic (2005–15), Branko Lubarda (2015–).

62 Bostjan Zupancic (1998–2016), Marko Bosnjak (2016–).

63 Antonio Pastor Ridruejo (1998–2003), Javier Borrego Borrego (2003–08), Luis López Guerra (2008–18).

64 Sir Nicolas Bratza (1998–2012), Paul Mahoney (2012–16), Tim Eicke (2016–).

65 For the current List of Ad hoc Judges see <www.echr.coe.int/Documents/List_adhoc_judges_BIL.pdf> accessed 17 August 2020.

66 See Protocol 14 to the ECHR (n 33).

3.3. Gender and Age

The data also shows that on average female judges are quite a bit younger than male judges—by an average of 6.2 years at the time of their election. We calculated the mean averages by adding up the ages of all female judges sitting on the bench in 1998, 2001, 2004, 2007, 2010, 2014, and 2017, respectively, and dividing these sums by the total number of women sitting on the Strasbourg bench in those years. We then took the same steps for male judges. The results are shown in Figure 10.3.

These numbers can be further disaggregated by region. This permits a determination of whether certain regions tend to have younger (male or female, or both) judges.[67] These findings are represented graphically below, in Figure 10.4. Overall, the average age of all (male and female) judges at their respective elections was 50.1 years.

The data shows that while Scandinavian countries tend to propose somewhat older female than male judges, women from Western European and Eastern and Central European countries are, on average, ten years younger than their male counterparts. The female judges elected from the Eastern and Central European region are by far the youngest group, at an average age of 41.6 years at the time of election.

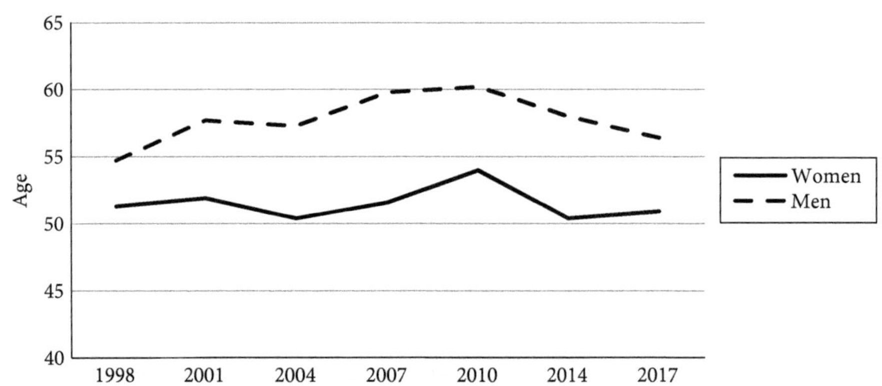

Figure 10.3 Average age of male and female judges at regular intervals between 1998 and 2017

[67] These averages were obtained by adding up the ages of all female judges from a certain European region when they were elected, and then dividing this number by the total number of women elected from that region. The same approach was then followed in respect to male judges. The overall average was obtained by adding up the age of all judges when they were appointed and dividing it by the number of judges appointed since 1998.

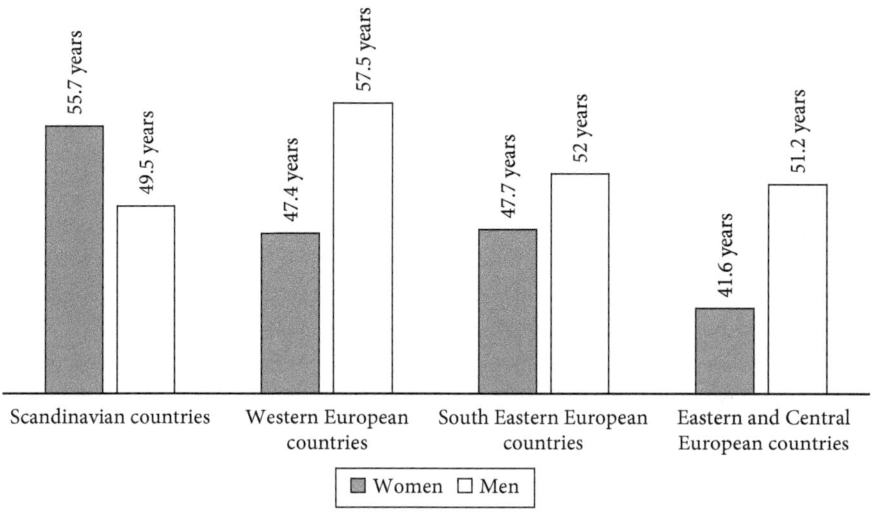

Figure 10.4 Average age of the judges when elected

The youngest woman to be elected to date was 33,[68] and the oldest was 64.[69] The youngest man to be elected was 37,[70] and the oldest was 68.[71] Twenty out of 82 male judges were 60 years old or older when they were elected (24.4%),[72] and four[73] out of 37 female judges were 60 years old or older when they were elected (10.8%). Nine[74] out of 37 female judges were 40 or younger when they were elected (24.3%); this only applies to one[75] out of the 81 male judges (1.2%). These nine female judges all either came from a very small country (Monaco and San Marino) or from 'new democracies' (Bosnia and Herzegovina, Estonia, Georgia, Latvia, Lithuania, Ukraine).[76] These countries not only sent the youngest judges to Strasbourg, but also the most women. This pattern applied even before 1998. Indeed, the three female judges who were elected before the permanent Court

[68] This was the judge in respect of Lithuania, Danute Jociene, who served from 2004 to 2013.

[69] This was the judge in respect of Germany, Renate Jaeger, who served from 2004 to 2010.

[70] This was the judge in respect of Albania, Ledi Bianku, who began his term in 2008.

[71] This was the judge in respect of Italy, Benedetto Conforti, who served from 1998 to 2001.

[72] Giovanni Bonello, Lucius Caflisch, Benedetto Conforti, Luigi Ferrari Bravo, Luis Lopez Guerra, Loukis Loucaides, Branko Lubarda, Paul Mahoney, Giorgio Malinverni, Erik Mose, George Nicolaou, Peter Paczolay, Antonio Pastor Ridruejo, Ales Pejchal, André Potocki, Georges Ravarani, Georg Ress, Georgios Serghides, Luzius Wildhaber, Vladimiro Zagrebelsky.

[73] Renate Jaeger, Pauliine Koskelo, Gabriele Kucsko-Stadlmayer, Elisabeth Palm.

[74] Danute Jociene (Lithuania), Julia Laffranque (Estonia), Ljiljana Mijovic (Bosnia and Herzegovina), Stéphanie Mourou-Vikström (Monaco), Antonella Mularoni (San Marino), Kristina Pardalos (San Marino), Nona Tsotsoria (Georgia), Ganna Yudkivska (Ukraine), Ineta Ziemele (Latvia).

[75] Ledi Bianku, judge in respect of Albania, was 37 years old when he was elected in 2008.

[76] Jean-François Flauss, 'Les élections de juges à la Cour européenne des droits de l'homme (2005–08)' (2008) 75 Revue trimestrielle des droits de l'homme 713, 738.

was established were all from small countries or countries historically more open to gender equality.[77]

3.4. The Professional Backgrounds of Judges

The data also allowed an examination of the professional background of male and female judges at the time of their election. Given that most of the judges pursued several occupations before their elections, only the occupations they held immediately prior to their elections were taken into consideration.

The following two graphs (Figures 10.5 and 10.6) divide judges of both genders into four categories: former judges, academics, lawyers (barristers), and public officials (excluding judges).

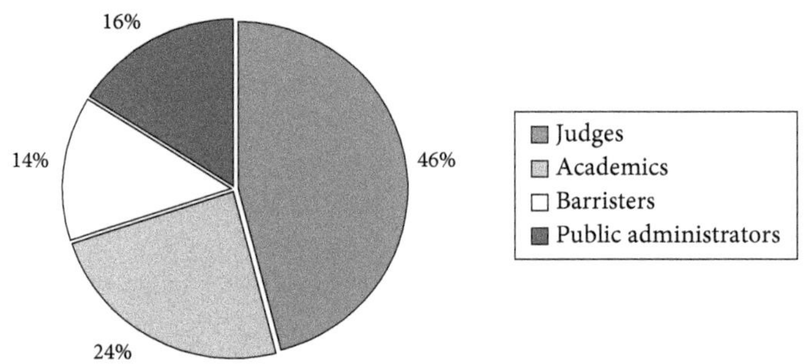

Figure 10.5 Professional background of female judges before being appointed

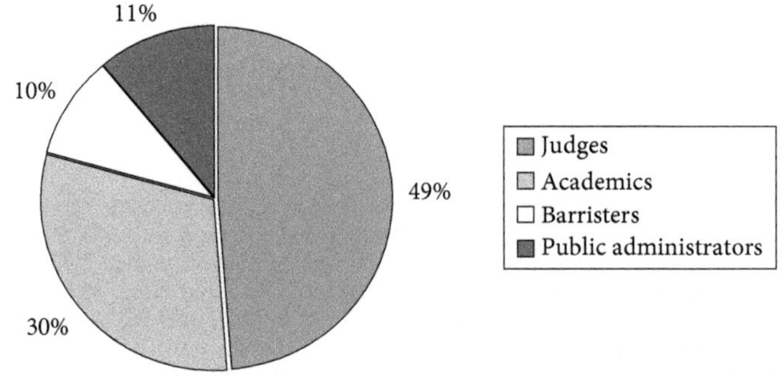

Figure 10.6 Professional background of male judges before being appointed

[77] Helga Pedersen (Denmark), Elisabeth Palm (Sweden). See also the election of Denise Bindschedler in respect of Switzerland, as discussed below, who however—although she did come from a small country—did not come from a country that was necessarily historically open to gender equality.

Thus, 46% of female judges were judges before their election,[78] 24% were academics,[79] 14% were lawyers,[80] and 16% were public officials or politicians.[81]

Of the male judges, 49% were judges before their election,[82] 30% were academics,[83] 10% were lawyers,[84] and 11% were public officials or politicians.[85]

This shows that nearly half of judges from both genders worked as judges immediately preceding their election. The main differences are that more men than women came from academia (24% of female judges and 30% of male judges).

[78] Alvina Gyulumyan (Armenia), Pauliine Koskelo (Finland), Renate Jaeger (Germany), Päivi Hirvelä (Finland), Siofra O'Leary (referendar, Ireland), Isabelle Berro (Monaco), Stéphanie Morou-Vikström (Monaco), Jolien Schukking (Netherlands), Wilhelmina Thomassen (Netherlands), Hanne Sophie Greve (Norway), Iulia Motoc (Romania), Alena Polackova (Slovak Republic), Helena Jäderblom (Sweden), Elisabeth Palm* (Sweden), Mirjana Lazarova Trajkovska (North Macedonia), Margarita Tsatsa-Nikolovska (North Macedonia), and Ganna Yudkisvksa ((deputy) legal secretary, Ukraine). The asterisk (*) indicates that a given judge served as a member of the 'old' Court or of the now defunct European Commission of Human Rights.

[79] Gabriele Kucsko-Stadlmayer (Austria), Françoise Tulkens (Belgium), Ksenija Turkovic (Croatia), Nina Vajic (Croatia), Julia Laffranque (Estonia), Angelika Nussberger (Germany), Ineta Ziemele (Latvia), Helen Keller (Switzerland), and Isil Karakas (Turkey).

[80] Elisabeth Steiner (Austria), Zdravka Kalaydjieva (Bulgaria), Ann Power-Forde (Ireland), Kristina Pardalos (San Marino), and Elisabet Fura (Sweden).

[81] Ljiljana Mijovic (prosecutor, Bosnia and Herzegovina), Snejana Botoucharova (politician and ambassador, Bulgaria), Danute Jociene (agent of the government, Lithuania), Nona Tsotsoria (prosecutor, Georgia), Antonella Mularoni (politician, San Marino), and Viera Straznicka (ambassador, Slovak Republic).

[82] Josep Casadevall* (Andorra), Pere Pastor Vilanova (Andorra), Khanlar Hajiyev (Azerbaijan), Faris Vehabovic (Bosnia and Herzegovina), Loukis Loucaides* (Cyprus), George Nicolaou (Cyprus), Georgios Serghides (Cyprus), Karel Jungwiert* (Czech Republic), Jon Fridrik Kjolbro (Denmark), Peer Lorenzen (Denmark), Rait Maruste (Estonia), Matti Pellonpää* (Finland), André Potocki (France), Mindia Ugrekhelidze (Georgia), Georg Ress* (Germany), Andras Baka* (Hungary), Peter Paczolay (Hungary), Gaukur Jörundsson* (Iceland), Benedetto Conforti* (Italy), Vladimiro Zagrebelsky (Italy), Egils Levits* (Latvia), Carlo Ranzoni (Liechtenstein), Pranas Kuris* (Lithuania), Georges Ravarani (Luxembourg), Vincent de Gaetano (Malta), Tudor Pantiru* (Republic of Moldova), Mihai Poalelungi (Republic of Moldova), Johannes Silvis (Netherlands), Erik Mose (Norway), Sverre Erik Jebens (Norway), Lech Garlicki (Poland), Jerzy Makarczyk* (Poland), Ireneu Cabral Barreto* (Portugal), Corneliu Birsan* (Romania), Dmitry Dedov (Russian Federation), Luzius Wildhaber* (Switzerland), Volodymyr Butkevych* (Ukraine), Paul Mahoney (United Kingdom). The asterisk (*) indicates that a given judge served as a member of the 'old' Court or of the now defunct European Commission of Human Rights.

[83] Ledi Bianku (Albania), Kristaq Traja (Albania), Letif Hüseynov (Azerbaijan), Paul Lemmens (Belgium), Linos-Alexandre Sicilianos (Greece), Andras Sajo (Hungary), David Thor Björgvinsson (Iceland), Robert Spano (Iceland), Martins Mits (Latvia), Lucius Caflisch (Liechtenstein), Mark Villiger (Liechtenstein), Nebojsa Vucinic (Montenegro), Egbert Myjer (Netherlands), Krzysztof Wojtyczek (Poland), Paulo Pinto de Albuquerque (Portugal), Anatoly Kovler (Russian Federation), Luigi Ferrari Bravo (San Marino), Branko Lubarda (Serbia), Dragoljub Popovic (Serbia), Marko Bosnjak (Slovenia), Bostjan Zupancic (Slovenia), Luis Lopez Guerra (Spain), Antonio Pastor Ridruejo (Spain), Giorgio Malinverni (Switzerland), and Jovan Ilievski (North Macedonia).

[84] Yonko Grozev (Bulgaria), Ales Pejchal (Czech Republic), John Hedigan (Ireland), Dean Spielmann (Luxembourg), Giorgio Bonello (Malta), Valeriu Gritco (Republic of Moldova), Javier Borrego Borrego (Spain), and Tim Eicke (United Kingdom).

[85] Armen Harutyunyan (ombudsman, Armenia), Willi Fuhrmann (politician, Austria), Jean-Paul Costa (politician, France), Lado Chanturia (ambassador and minister, Georgia), Guido Raimondi (legal adviser of the International Labour Organization, Italy), Marc Fischbach (politician, Luxembourg), Stanislav Pavlovschi (prosecutor, Republic of Moldova), Jan Sikuta (United Nations, Slovak Republic), and Riza Türmen (ambassador, Turkey).

This might be a result of the low number of women in high academic posts. More women than men were former practicing lawyers and public officials.

3.5. Motherhood at the Court

As will be further detailed below, the permanent Court originally had no policy in place to allow judges to take parental leave. This type of deficit affects potential new mothers in particular, and suggests that the idea of a Strasbourg judge was not considered compatible with maternity, either because it was associated with a stereotyped understanding of judges as men who were not heavily involved in childcare or because of the perception that judgeship was reserved for older candidates. In light of this and the younger average age of female judges, and also given anecdotes about the difficulty of combining (new) motherhood and judicial office shared with us by some judges, we decided to gather data about motherhood at the Court. The idea is not to reinforce the stereotype that mothers should be primary caregivers to their children, or to argue that men do not give care, but to respond to the persistence of societal attitudes that penalize working mothers.[86]

Our inquiry showed that the female judges elected in 1998 had no minor children when they were elected. Today, most female judges have children, and many of these children were minors at the time of their mothers' election. This seems to indicate that the Court has become a more motherhood-friendly workplace for judges, or that more women feel confident in combining motherhood and judgeship.

In order to further explore the compatibility of motherhood and election to the Strasbourg bench, we considered it relevant to take into account the family situation of female ECtHR judges. In this regard, we contacted all 36 living women who have, since 1998, been judges at the Court. Of these, six did not respond to our inquiry. The remaining 30 judges had, on average, 1.9 children. Overall, including two female judges who did not have children, this amounts to an average of 1.8 children per female judge. While female ECtHR judges do not constitute a representative sample of women in Council of Europe member States, this number is above the EU average fertility rate, which in 2015 was 1.58 live births per woman.[87]

The average ages of these children at the time of their mothers' election was 16.6 years. However, the children's average ages vary strongly by region. Thus, the children of female Scandinavian judges were 22.5 years old on average when their mothers were elected onto the Court. The children of female Western European judges were, on average, 16.0 years of age. As concerns female South Eastern European

[86] See for example European Commission, 'Report on Equality between Women and Men in the EU' (2018) <https://publications.europa.eu/en/publication-detail/-/publication/950dce57-6222-11e8-ab9c-01aa75ed71a1> accessed 31 July 2019.

[87] Eurostat, 'Fertility Statistics' <http://ec.europa.eu/eurostat/statistics-explained/index.php/Fertility_statistics> accessed 19 December 2017. Similar data for the Council of Europe was not available.

judges, their children were 19.8 years old on average. For female Eastern and Central European judges, this average was much lower, at 8.1 years. This last finding is in line with the above results relating to the age of the elected judges. On average, female Eastern and Central European judges were by far the youngest group at the time of their election, with an average age of 41.6. This also explains the finding that three female judges had at least one child during their mandate, and that two of these three women were elected in respect of 'new democracies'. Female Scandinavian judges, by contrast, were the oldest regional group of female judges, which also explains the average ages of these women's offspring when their mothers took office.

4. Drawing Conclusions from the Data

4.1 Regional Variations and Nomination Processes

The data shows that small countries, countries historically open to gender equality and 'new democracies' have had the most female judges elected to the Strasbourg Court. It could be argued that the pool of qualified men in these countries is smaller, and so States turn more readily to female candidates. Supporters of this argument could rely on the fact that, while it is not a formal requirement to do so, all Contracting States (except Liechtenstein) clearly prefer to nominate nationals. Small countries therefore have smaller male samples from which to draw their candidates, which could arguably, although certainly not in all cases,[88] encourage their governments to turn to female candidates. Conversely, this argument would go, large countries, such as France, Italy, the United Kingdom, or the Russian Federation, have many more qualified men at their disposal.

However, the fact that these four States Parties have never had a female judge elected to the Strasbourg Court cannot be explained purely by referring to the widespread availability of qualified men. Regarding France, it is interesting to recall the abundance of women in the French judiciary, even in its highest echelons,[89] and the fact that about half of male and female ECtHR judges worked as judges directly before their election. This situation is indicative of the so-called 'leaky pipeline' problem, wherein qualified women disappear from the career ladder.[90]

[88] Malta being one very significant exception in this regard, as outlined above.

[89] European Parliament, Policy Department for Citizens' Rights and Constitutional Affairs, 'Mapping the Representation of Women and Men in Legal Professions Across the EU', Study for the JURI Committee (August 2017), 25. We noted the representation of women in the *Conseil constitutionnel* (four women and five men), the *Cour de cassation* (120 women and 127 men if all of the *conseillers* and all of the *avocats généraux* are considered; if these are not included, women have a clear majority, and three of the six chambers are presided over by women). The *section du contentieux du Conseil d'Etat* (the highest domestic administrative instance) is presided over by a man, who has four male deputies. Of the *section's* 10 Chambers, seven are presided over by men and three by women, and of the *section* presidents' deputies, 14 are male and six are female.

[90] On this, see Farah Dubois-Shaik and Bernard Fusulier, 'Academic Careers and Gender Inequality: Leaky Pipeline and Interrelated Phenomena in Seven European Countries', *Garcia Working*

In the French context, support for the existence of such a problem comes from the fact that, as Nienke Grossman has argued, there had been no female judges in respect of France elected to the European Court of Justice, the International Court of Justice (ICJ), the ECtHR, the International Criminal Court (ICC), the International Criminal Tribunal for Rwanda, the International Criminal Tribunal for the former Yugoslavia, or the International Tribunal for the Law of the Sea as of 2016. Thus, France has failed to produce a single female international judge, despite the fact that (1) an estimated 50% of French lawyers are women and (2) there is a predominance of women in the judiciary.[91] All 25 of its international judges have been male.[92] Despite the abundance of qualified women available in the French judicial branch and in legal practice, candidates for international judicial election tend to be drawn from areas in which women may be less well represented, perhaps the top judicial positions or public office: only one of the French judges elected to the ECtHR worked as a judge prior to his election.[93] Furthermore, France rarely selects academics for international judicial positions, preferring instead to nominate candidates who have held public office.[94]

It is also relevant, in this regard, to consider the case of Italy. In the context of gender and the domestic courts, a Council of Europe study found that, while more than half of all of Italy's professional judges in 2014 were women, only 25% of Supreme Court judges were female.[95] This gender imbalance still persists, although it has perhaps become less extreme. Thus, the *corte costituzionale* had only three female judges in its ranks in 2017 out of a total of 13 judges.[96] Things were quite a bit better, however, at the *corte di cassazione*, where 25 out of the 55 new nominees in 2017 were female.[97] In this regard, it can—given the findings below about young women's chances of election—be noted that Italy's first (unsuccessful) female

Paper 611737 <http://eige.europa.eu/sites/default/files/garcia_working_paper_5_academic_careers_gender_inequality.pdf> accessed 6 December 2017.

91 European Parliament (n 90).

92 Nienke Grossman, 'Achieving Sex-Representative International Court Benches' (2016) 110 The American Journal of International Law 82, at 85.

93 This being André Potocki, who has served as the judge in respect of France since 2011.

94 See, on this process, Laurence Burgorgue-Larsen, 'Des idéaux à la réalité: Réflexions comparées sur les processus de sélection et de nomination des membres des Cours européenne et interaméricaine des droits de l'homme' (2014) 6 La Revue des droits de l'homme <https://journals.openedition.org/revdh/949> accessed 31 July 2019, para 19.

95 European Commission on the Efficiency of Justice, 'European Judicial Systems: Efficiency and Quality of Justice', Edition 2016 (2014 data), CEPEJ STUDIES 23 <https://rm.coe.int/european-judicial-systems-efficiency-and-quality-of-justice-cepej-stud/1680788228> accessed 13 August 2020, 101.

96 Italian Corte Costituzionale, 'I Giudici costituzionali' <www.cortecostituzionale.it/actionGiudiciCostituzionali.do> accessed 20 December 2017.

97 Zero Zero News, 'Nomine Csm: 55 nuovi Consiglieri di Cassazione e il sorpasso di Davigo' (15 June 2017) <www.zerozeronews.it/nomine-csm-55-nuovi-consiglieri-di-cassazione-e-il-sorpasso-di-davigo/> accessed 20 December 2017.

candidate to the full-time Court to date, Andreana Esposito, was listed with two men who were both more than a decade her seniors.[98]

With regard to the United Kingdom, the lack of female judges on the national and international levels seems instead to be down to domestic judicial selection practices, which were traditionally based around the idea of the 'tap on the shoulder', described by one recent EU report as 'a form of self-reproduction of older male members of the profession'.[99] This tradition seems to have left its mark, as—despite the existence of statutory responsibility of the Lord Chancellor and the Lord Chief Justice to ensure gender parity through judicial recruitment—less than a third of the UK's professional judges are women, putting the nation in 46th place in the Council of Europe, ahead only of Azerbaijan's 11%.[100]

Regarding the formerly communist member States, the situation is quite surprising, as one might expect a higher percentage of female judges coming from these parts of Europe. Indeed, the increase of women in the judiciary started earlier here, likely due to the more pronounced gender equality dogma present in these countries and the low reputation and income opportunities linked with judicial positions.[101] Despite this, top judicial posts seem to be largely reserved to men: thus, for example, the Russian Constitutional Court is composed of three women and 16 men,[102] and the Constitutional Court of the Republic of Moldova has only one woman on its bench.[103] Hence, it seems that a glass ceiling exists even in these parts of Europe.

This indicates the existence of a gender problem in many member States, whether it is termed a glass ceiling or a leaky pipeline. For the ECtHR, a comparison can be made to the pool of legal counsel representing State governments before the Court: in this regard, there is approximate overall gender parity between the number of women and men who have recently represented States before the Court.[104] In considering the merits of the pool argument, ie the argument that qualified female candidates are simply less plentiful, attention should also be paid to the list of potential ad hoc ECtHR judges. Both large and small States that have

[98] PACE, 'List and Curricula Vitae of Candidates Submitted by the Government of Italy' (16 September 2009) doc 12020.

[99] European Parliament (n 90) 25.

[100] See European Commission on the Efficiency of Justice, 'European Judicial Systems: Efficiency and Quality of Justice', Edition 2016 (2014 data), CEPEJ STUDIES 23 <www.coe.int/t/dghl/cooperation/cepej/evaluation/2016/publication/REV1/2016_1%20-%20CEPEJ%20Study%2023%20-%20General%20report%20-%20EN.pdf> accessed 7 December 2017, 84–85, and 101. In England and Wales, 30% of professional judges were women; in Northern Ireland and Scotland it was 23%.

[101] European Parliament (n 90) 25, 48–49.

[102] Constitutional Court of the Russian Federation, 'Judges' <www.ksrf.ru/en/Info/Judges/Pages/default.aspx> accessed 6 December 2017.

[103] Government of Moldova, 'Panel of Judges: Constitutional Judges' <www.constcourt.md/tabview.php?l=en&idc=18&t=/Composition-and-organization/Constitutional-judges> accessed 6 December 2017.

[104] The agents who represented the Governments of each State in the five most recent judgments on the merits delivered in its regard were determined on 30 October 2017.

not sent any female judges to Strasbourg—notably France, Russia, and Malta—have, nevertheless, listed female ad hoc judicial candidates, indicating that qualified female candidates are available.[105]

In this regard, it is relevant to note that the number of female judges at the ECtHR is currently 31.9%, and compare this with figures recently released by the Council of Europe finding that, on average in the member States, 26% of Constitutional Court judges are female, along with 33% of High or Supreme Court justices, and 28% of members of High Councils of the Judiciary.[106] Thus, the Court is actually closer to adequate gender representation than many of the national courts from which its candidates may be drawn.

In summary, the PACE policy regarding gender, as an attempt to increase fair gender representation at the Court by requiring that the list of three State candidates must contain at least one member of the underrepresented gender, seems to have been effective to some degree in the sense that the number of female judges has increased overall since 1998. Of course, this could be a matter of sheer correlation, with no causality attributable to the PACE policy itself, and the argument could for example be made that improved gender equality in the Member States has led to these developments. However, again, the situation at the ECtHR is overall more equal than that in the domestic jurisdictions, which indicates some influence of the PACE policy.

In addition, it is striking that this number is dropping again, and it is clear that Strasbourg is far from a post-gender situation, despite the CDDH's recent argument to the contrary.[107] This issue begins at the State level, and is not (just) a problem for the Council of Europe. In this regard, Françoise Tulkens has noted that an examination of gender at the Court has to begin with the national level: in some States, she has argued, 'behind [the] argument of competence and qualifications, an apparently neutral and worn out argument, lies merely the expression of an entrenched discrimination'.[108]

4.2 Election by PACE

The voting method which PACE uses to select judicial candidates once it has received the lists of three is also relevant to the court's lack of gender parity. In

[105] ECtHR, 'List of Ad hoc Judges for the Year 2017' <www.echr.coe.int/Documents/List_adhoc_judges_BIL.pdf> accessed 17 January 2018.

[106] Council of Europe, 'Balanced Participation of Women and Men in Decision-Making', analytical report based on the 2016 data by the Gender Equality Commission <https://rm.coe.int/analytical-report-data-2016-/1680751a3e> accessed 6 December 2017, 10.

[107] CDDH (n 2) 5, para 10; see also at 10, para 75. See on this also Hennette Vauchez (n 10), especially 221.

[108] Françoise Tulkens, 'More Women – But Which Women? A Reply to Stéphanie Hennette Vauchez' (2015) 26 European Journal of International Law 223, 226.

reviewing the CVs of both successful and unsuccessful female candidates (and successful male candidates) for the Strasbourg bench since 1 January 2013, in continuation of the work begun by Stephanie Hennette Vauchez, it is almost always possible to justify the selection on the basis of the successful applicants' qualifications. In a few cases, however, it was difficult to determine why particular male candidates succeeded over their female counterparts, particularly when it is PACE's policy to elect a member from the underrepresented gender where the available candidates are equally qualified.[109] That is not to say that the chosen men were not qualified, but simply that they were not head and shoulders above their female competitors. In all other cases, the election of the successful candidate seemed evident based on the qualifications of all three candidates on the relevant list.

The fact that a State includes a female candidate on its list of three candidates does not provide clear evidence of a commitment to gender equality on the Strasbourg bench or elsewhere. States could deliberately include a less-experienced or 'weaker' female candidate who is unlikely to succeed in the PACE elections.[110] It is then up to PACE to reject the list in question, as it will likely do if the discrepancies are glaring. In other words, there are ways for States to comply with the Council of Europe's gender policy without actually having a female judge in Strasbourg. And indeed, nominating female candidates to the Court has never necessarily meant that a State had a deep or long-standing commitment to gender equality. Thus, for example, Switzerland nominated Denise Bindschedler-Robert to the Court in 1972, just one year after female suffrage was passed on the federal level in Switzerland and 19 years before suffrage on the local level was universalized in the country.[111]

4.3 Traits of Successful Female Judicial Candidates

Previous work on the topic of gender (in)equality among ECtHR judges has looked not only at quantitative elements concerning female judges, but also at the specific qualities and traits of the individuals who are elected to judicial office at the Court. For example, Fionnuala Ní Aoláin argues that, in documenting and evaluating the Court's judicial selection process for female candidates, simply counting the number of women appointed only provides part of the picture. In addition, she argues, it is also necessary to determine whether these women display 'any

[109] PACE, Resolution 1366 (2004) (n 1) para 6.

[110] Hennette Vauchez (n 10) 216.

[111] In 1972, she was nominated as an alternative candidate to sitting judge Antoine Favre (Consultative Assembly of the Council of Europe (28 September 1972) doc 3171), who was re-elected. In 1975, after Judge Favre's death, she succeeded him in office (PACE, 'Communication on the Election of a Member of the European Court of Human Rights in Respect of Switzerland' (9 April 1975) doc 3599).

discernible commitment ... to feminist method, practice and outcomes'.[112] Thus, judicial appointment processes are part of an institutional culture that contains performance requirements that create 'pathways for certain kinds of women who perform in particular ways' to access the bench.[113]

So far, the pathway to the Court for female judges seems to favour active feminists. As Stéphanie Hennette Vauchez highlights, all 120 or so female candidates to the Court between 1959 and 2012 displayed feminist engagement. By this, she describes a wide range of activities described as 'distinctively feminist', including membership in female professional networks, engagement with international organizations working on women's equality, teaching feminist legal theory, or activist work in a similar vein.[114] However, all but one of the women who have taken up office on 1 January 2013 or later[115] have not mentioned any similar feminist activity in their CVs.[116] This is a significant change. In her article, Hennette Vauchez wrote that the presence of these engagements on candidates' CVs either signals that women consider these engagements to be advantageous for the judicial selection process, and therefore include them, or that States seek out self-identified feminist women as candidates.[117] The fact that the presence of feminist engagements on the CVs of female judges has decreased indicates a possible change in one or both of these regards.

Another factor that characterizes the female judges at the Court is that they tend to be younger than their male counterparts—on average by 6.2 years, but with greater discrepancies in certain areas, with female judges from Eastern and Central European countries being, on average, 41.6 years old at the time of their election and the youngest woman ever elected being aged 33 at the time of her election. This is interesting, given that youth is usually accompanied by fewer years of experience (although not necessarily having anything to do with the qualifications of the person concerned, of course, and being, in post-totalitarian States, a potential asset). States nominating younger women may put PACE in a position of having to decide whether to elect a relatively young and comparatively inexperienced person whose participation on the Court may lead the highest national courts, which are generally populated with much older and male judges, to question Strasbourg's findings. In this regard, a recent proposal to introduce a minimum age limit for judges—in addition to the maximum age limit of 70 years[118]—led to

112 Fionnuala Ní Aoláin, 'More Women – But Which Women? A Reply to Stéphanie Vauchez' (2015) 26 The European Journal of International Law 229, 230.

113 ibid 231.

114 Hennette Vauchez (n 10) 214.

115 Ksenija Turkovic (Croatia) was a member of the ad hoc Committee on Preventing and Combatting Violence against Women and Domestic Violence. Furthermore she was a member of the Croatian Expert Committee Drafting Law on Gender Equality back in 2008.

116 Gabriele Kucsko-Stadlmayer (Austria), Pauliine Koskelo (Finland), Siofra O'Leary (Ireland), Stéphanie Morou-Vikström (Monaco), Jolien Schukking (Netherlands), Iulia Motoc (Romania), Alena Polackova (Slovak Republic), Helena Jäderblom (Sweden).

117 Hennette Vauchez (n 10) 215.

118 As enshrined in Article 23(2) ECHR.

hefty discussions at the Court and an ultimate decision not to do so. Proponents argued that the Court's legitimacy vis-à-vis the highest national instances suffers if it is perceived as too young and female by the largely older, male domestic judges. The CDDH has made plain that it is against the introduction of a minimum age limit for judges, but it has not framed this as an issue that is relevant to gender, even though—given the fact that younger judges tend to be female—it is an important element to consider.[119]

The compatibility of judgeship and motherhood has increased over time. The average age of children of female judges at the time of their mothers' election between 1998 and 2017 is 16.6 years. In contrast, there were no female judges with minor children when the full-time court was established. This seems to indicate that the road to the Strasbourg bench has become more compatible with motherhood over time. Anecdotal evidence provided by judges shows a transformation over time when the Court has been faced with concrete needs. Thus, for example, the permanent Court originally had no policy in place to allow judges to take maternity leave, and had to quickly introduce such a policy when first faced with the reality of a pregnant judge in 2005.[120] Beyond this, however, and independently of gender, schooling is a problem for judges who are parents of minor children and who relocate their families to Strasbourg. For years, judges have faced difficulties in enrolling their children in the international schools in Strasbourg, and access to the Council of Europe's on-site day-care for younger children can also be an issue.[121]

The odds of a female candidate's success in seeking judicial office seems to vary depending on her region of origin. Thus, female candidates from countries where women have been well-represented in society and on the bench for decades tend to be older women with adult children. In small countries or countries that have recently undergone political transition, successful female candidates tend to be younger. Their success, in recently-transitioned States, may be due to language abilities or uncorrupted records; in small States, it may be linked to a smaller pool of eligible male candidates.

In conclusion, a woman has the best chances of becoming a judge at the ECtHR today, according to the above findings, if she does not emphasize her feminist activities and comes from a small country; in addition, in most regions, she is more likely to succeed if she faces opponents more or less (give or take five years) her own age. Having minor children does not seem to be a drawback (anymore). Regarding this potential candidate's ideal professional background, the information analysed does not allow for any specific or generalizable conclusions, except that she is

[119] CDDH (n 2) 17–18, paras 70–74.

[120] This change took place in light of the principled refusal of the judge in question to accept prolonged sick leave as an alternative, arguing that she was 'not sick, but pregnant'.

[121] CDDH (n 2) 38, para 153.

unlikely to win if she has less experience than a male counterpart (contrary to the concerns in this regard that prompted the introduction of the gender parity policy to begin with), and that she may not necessarily win if she has the same or even slightly better qualifications than her male opponents.

Despite the efforts by PACE, the number of female judges has been decreasing in recent years, as indicated above. This mirrors the current global gender gap, which seems to be widening.[122] It may be that the diminishing number of women on the Court can be ascribed to a loss of interest in gender parity on the bench on the part of PACE, or to a backlash against PACE's gender balance policy on the part of the States nominating the judges, or perhaps simply to the fact that the terms of a number of female judges have expired, and they have been replaced by men.[123] Whatever the reason for this development, it is worrying, and one that will need to be closely monitored and addressed by PACE.

5. Effectiveness, Compliance, Legitimacy

These trends provoke several questions. Does gender on the Strasbourg bench matter for the normative or social legitimacy of the ECtHR? Do we need more women on the Strasbourg bench? What effect do female judges have on the Court's jurisprudence? There are numerous arguments for increased gender representation in the judiciary and elsewhere, and it is impossible to address them all here. Françoise Tulkens very reasonably argues that: '... [w]omen are not on the bench to "legitimate" or "justify" anything. Women are present at the European Court of Human Rights simply because there is no reason for them not to be there.'[124]

However, it can also be argued that the Court benefits, in the sense of its legitimacy as an institution, from having an equitable representation of both genders among its judges. Without going too deeply into the issue of the institutional legitimacy of international courts or of the ECtHR specifically, it is possible to argue that it would be difficult to justify an institution dedicated to protecting human rights and democratic principles, including the prohibition of discrimination on the basis of gender, without adequate respect and consideration for the representation of women.

It is impossible to answer the delicate question of whether female judges decide differently than male judges (thus, the question of a particular female 'adjudicatory style') here. In any event, this question certainly should not be seen as implying that women per se think differently from men, which is a problematic idea that lends

[122] World Economic Forum, 'The Global Gender Gap Report 2017' <http://www3.weforum.org/docs/WEF_GGGR_2017.pdf> accessed 19 December 2017, viii and *passim*.

[123] In this regard, compare the 'token woman' argument made by Françoise Tulkens (n 110).

[124] Tulkens (n 110) 224.

itself to stereotyping. To avoid doing so would require very solid empirical analysis. It would be required to have access to the Court's decision-making process to do this: the first author, who does have such access, cannot share the relevant information without breaking her duty of confidentiality concerning proceedings before the Court. The alternative, to base such arguments on the dissenting opinions of judges, would be highly questionable in a methodological sense.

However, it can be noted that female judges have experienced being female and, as such, being part of a specific underrepresented and historically oppressed group. This may allow them to take a different perspective than their male counterparts when it comes to specific issues. That is not to argue that men may not belong to (other) underrepresented groups, or that women necessarily have a natural affinity for human rights,[125] but simply to say, based on the experience of the first author, that members of minorities—including women in this particular context—may sometimes have a basic understanding for certain experiences of vulnerability.[126] Thus, for example, in the context of rape, former ICC Judge and former UN High Commissioner for Human Rights Navanethem Pillay suggested that although women do not 'decide in a different way', they have a 'particular sensitivity and understanding about what happens to people who are raped'.[127]

This argument holds despite the fact that judges must be impartial. Human decision-makers are necessarily influenced by their backgrounds and experiences, which is one reason why adequate representation of diversity is so important. Thus, it could be that having members of an affected group present when discussing certain issues (such as, for example, gender equality, reproductive rights, or domestic violence) improves the dialogue and balances the discussion within the Court, leading to well-reasoned holdings that render Convention rights practical and effective. However, whether the presence of women has an impact on the outcome of cases is hard to determine empirically.

In addition, although this is rather obvious, it should be emphasized that female judges do not always agree with each other. For example, when the Grand Chamber decided the reproductive rights issues at stake in *SH and Others v Austria*, of the eight female judges in the composition, all four judges in the minority (and thus also four members of the majority) were women.[128] There are, naturally, opposite examples: in the Chamber judgment in *Couderc and Hachette Filipacchi Associés v France*,[129] which was eventually confirmed by the Grand Chamber[130] and which

[125] Hennette Vauchez (n 10) 212–13.

[126] Grossmann, 'Glass Ceiling' (n 31) 75 et seq.

[127] Cited in Daniel Terris, Cesare PR Romano, and Leigh Swigart, *The International Judge: An Introduction to the Men and Women Who Decide the World's Cases* (Oxford University Press 2007) 48, as noted and discussed in Grossmann, 'Glass Ceiling' (n 31) 76.

[128] *SH and Others v Austria*, App no 57813/00 (ECtHR 3 November 2011), Joint Dissenting Opinion of Judges Tulkens, Hirvelä, Lazarova, Trajkoska, and Tsotoria.

[129] *Couderc and Hachette Filipacchi Associés v France* App no 40454/07 (ECtHR, 12 June 2014).

[130] *Couderc and Hachette Filipacchi Associés v France*, Reports 2015 (extracts).

concerned the attempts by Prince Albert of Monaco to prevent the publication of statements about his paternity made by the mother of his son, a majority made up of four women and one man faced off against a minority made up of three men. However, this does not mean that there is any reason to expect female judges to be particularly progressive or to decide in a certain way, but there is a potential that moving away from an overwhelmingly male Court can improve the case-law in some way. In addition, former judge Elisabet Fura has written about the signalling function of gender representation on the Court: thus, the presence of women on a judicial body sends a message about that body's inclusivity regardless of any differences in their judicial style.[131]

6. Improving the Representation of Women on the Strasbourg Bench

What can be learned from this analysis, and how can the Court's gender balance be improved? There seem to be three main categories of female candidates. The first are 'strong' candidates ('*des hommes comme des autres*'), ie those who are as or more qualified and experienced than the other candidates on a given list, and who have often gone on to win their elections and become judges at the Court. The second category consists of 'weaker' female candidates (in terms of qualifications and experience), who are perhaps listed by States simply to pay lip service to the requirement to have a female candidate, in the knowledge that they are unlikely to win and thus as a form of low-cost compliance.[132] The third category consists of women who are successful because of their political capital, which they can use to lobby for their judicial nomination or election. Men can do this too, of course; however, States cannot use the success of 'weaker' but well-connected male candidates as evidence of 'progressiveness' or 'inclusivity'.

States can also be put into similar categories. One group of States, often the Scandinavian countries, puts forth strong, qualified, and experienced female candidates. A second category, into which young democracies often fall, proposes younger, and therefore, less experienced female candidates. A third group of States has an unabashedly shabby record with regards to its three-candidate lists (for example, Malta has twice submitted an all-male list, in March 2004 and September 2007).

If the Strasbourg Court is far from being able to claim a post-gender position, ie one in which it is no longer necessary to maintain the current policy on judicial lists or to take other measures to advance gender parity among judges, and given

[131] Elisabet Fura, 'The "Feminization" of the Court' in Jonathan Sharpe (ed), *The Conscience of Europe: 50 Years of the European Court of Human Rights* (Third Millennium 2011) at 188.

[132] Hennette Vauchez (n 10) 220.

the desirability of adequate gender representation, it is necessary to ask how to best achieve that goal. Ensuring the transparency of judicial selection undeniably helps to improve and equalize this process, thus benefitting qualified female candidates (of whom there are many). In this regard, PACE has formulated a number of recommendations to States, which include issuing open calls for judicial candidates, being transparent about the selection criteria applied domestically, and ordering candidates' names alphabetically when transmitting them to PACE.[133]

However, transparency alone cannot solve the problem of gender inequality in the judicial selection process. Thus, the PACE Judicial Selection Committee should examine the lists of three candidates submitted by States in order to determine whether States have proposed an obviously weaker female candidate unlikely to win merely in order to pay lip service to their obligations in this regard. It would also be relevant to gain a better understanding of how candidates and their supporters lobby PACE preceding elections, and how the gender composition of PACE itself has changed over the years. Of the 22 full members of the PACE Committee on the Election of Judges to the ECtHR—which, since early 2015, notably also includes the Chairperson of the Committee on Equality and Non-Discrimination and the Chairperson of the Committee on Legal Affairs and Human Rights as *ex officio* members[134]—only five are female.[135] The membership of the Advisory Panel of Experts on Candidates for Election as Judge to the ECtHR, however, is quite a bit more gender-equitable. This panel, established in 2010 by the Committee of Ministers and originally made up of one woman and six men,[136] is currently made up of five men and three women, although this means that women constitute 37.5% of its composition, and that—according to the 40% rule applied to lists of judges—women are still underrepresented here as well.[137]

Of course, the Council of Europe can only do so much in this regard. Thus, factors such as the absence of women in the highest echelons of a country's government will also influence the availability and selection of female candidates. In addition, even though all judges have equal standing at the ECtHR, States that play a less important geopolitical role may perceive the impact of judicial elections before the Court, and thus also of electing a female candidate, to be less crucial politically. This perception that the role brings less power with it may mean that women

[133] PACE, Resolution 1646 (2009) (n 3) para 5.

[134] Compare PACE, 'Rules of Procedure of the Assembly' (4 November 1999) Resolution 1202 (1999), with subsequent modifications, status as of October 2017, Rule 44.1 on the appointment of committees. See, on this, Drzemczewski (n 15).

[135] PACE, 'Committee on the Election of Judges to the European Court of Human Rights' http://www.assembly.coe.int/nw/xml/AssemblyList/AL-XML2HTML-EN.asp?lang=en&XmlID=Committee-Cdh accessed 20 December 2017.

[136] Committee of Ministers, 'Establishment of an Advisory Panel of Experts on Candidates for Election as Judge to the European Court of Human Rights' (10 November 2010) Resolution CM/Res(2010)26; Grossmann, 'Glass Ceiling' (n 31) 43.

[137] Council of Europe, 'Secretariat of the Advisory Panel' <www.coe.int/en/web/dlapil/advisory-panel> accessed 20 December 2017.

have a greater chance of success. In this same vein, it is important to study the differences between the nomination practices of States vis-à-vis different courts to determine whether they are perhaps more willing to nominate female judges to a human rights court than to, for example, the ICJ; unfortunately, the present chapter cannot speak to this argument.

The Council of Europe has tried—but not always succeeded—to convince intractable States to comply with its gender policy. Thus, when Belgium submitted its all-male list, the (then) Sub-Committee on the Election of Judges made repeated efforts to obtain an explanation from the Belgian government, and conducted two special meetings in this regard along with a long telephone conversation with the then (female) Belgian Minister of Justice.[138] At the time, Eva Brems, a highly qualified female Belgian academic—who was once listed as a potential ad hoc judge in respect of Belgium[139]—had submitted her candidacy. The Government's refusal to list this excellent candidate (whom the domestic authorities nevertheless described as 'underqualified')[140] can be understood as a political trade-off.[141] Ultimately, the all-male list was accepted by the Committee on the Election of Judges, which was at the time notably chaired by a woman.[142] Judicial appointments to regional and international courts are, of course, highly political decisions, and PACE may be hard-pressed to influence such a decision by a recalcitrant State.

7. Conclusion

The data shows that female judges on the Strasbourg bench are generally younger and fewer in number than their male colleagues. It also shows strong discrepancies between States on a regional basis. All-male lists are not entirely a thing of the past, and strikingly, 23 member States had never sent a female judge to Strasbourg at the time of writing (in early 2018).[143]

[138] Open Society Justice Initiative and International Commission of Jurists, *Strengthening from Within: Law and Practice in the Selection of Human Rights Judges and Commissioners* (Open Society Foundations 2017) 92, n 95, referring to an e-mail communication with Andrew Drzemczewski dated 21 July 2017 and to David Kosar, 'Selecting Strasbourg Judges: A Critique' in Michael Bobek (ed), *Selecting Europe's Judges: A Critical Review of the Appointment Procedures to the European Courts* (Oxford University Press 2015) 130–33. On the telephone call with Annemie Turtelboom, see PACE, 'Synopsis AS/Jur No 2012/ 01' (1 February 2012), 4. On one of the two meetings, held in Paris with representatives of the Belgian Ministry of Justice, see PACE, 'Synopsis AS/Jur No 2011/09' (15 December 2011), 2.

[139] PACE Committee on Legal Affairs and Human Rights, 'Ad hoc Judges at the European Court of Human Rights: An Overview' (19 October 2011) AS/Jur (2011), 36.

[140] Tulkens (n 110) 226.

[141] ibid, calling these events 'clearly insulting' to the candidate in question.

[142] This was Renate Wohlwend (PACE, 'Synopsis AS/Jur No 2012/ 01' (1 February 2012), 4).

[143] This number sank to 21 States later in 2018, when female judges were elected in respect of two States that had never previously sent a female judge to Strasbourg (namely Montenegro (n 57) and Spain (n 63)).

While it is true that, today, the Court is closer to adequate gender representation than it was at the time of the establishment of the permanent Court two decades ago, or even in 2004, when PACE introduced the requirement that three-person lists of judicial candidates must contain a member of the underrepresented gender, there is still work to be done. Enthusiasm for ensuring gender parity on the Strasbourg bench seems to be flagging, as reflected in the diminishing number of female ECtHR judges and the idea that additional measures are not necessary in this regard.

It is safe to say, then, that the Court has not entered a post-gender age. Increased transparency and scrutiny of judicial selection procedures both by States and by PACE would be helpful to ensure that qualified female candidates are listed and given a fair chance to be elected. Of course, however, the Council of Europe is significantly dependent on the collaboration of States when it comes to the creation of the three-candidate lists. However, over the past decades, it has made key changes that have improved judicial selection, from publicity requirements concerning the search for candidates to the matter discussed here, namely the gender requirement for candidate lists. To ensure continuing perceptions of fairness and legitimacy, as well as the diversity of its composition, the Court should continue to improve the selection process as well as take efforts to reinvigorate support for the gender parity rule.

PART II
ON THE INTERNATIONAL BENCH

11
The Identity Conundrum
Legitimacy and Doubt on the International Bench

Catharine Titi

1. Introduction

The identity of an international judge or arbitrator can affect international judicial or arbitral decision-making. Adjudicators cannot be expected to arrive at a court or tribunal as *tabulae rasae*,[1] nor by donning judicial robes do they '[cease] to be human', '[strip themselves] of all predilections' and become 'passionless thinking machine[s]'.[2] Nationality, ethnicity, country of legal education, country of residence, a public or private international law background, coming from an industrialized or a developing country, and an adjudicator's socio-economic background are some of the elements of identity that can come into play in decision-making. Research has shown, for example, that judges tend to favour States with a level of wealth similar to that of the State of their nationality;[3] judges from democratic States tend to vote in favour of democracies, and judges from nondemocratic States in favour of nondemocratic States; and there is evidence of bias when the judge's home State and the respondent have a common religion or common language.[4] While extensive empirical studies are necessary to reveal the exact impact that different aspects of a judge's identity can have on how he or she decides, this chapter focuses on nationality and offers some preliminary thoughts on the varying degrees to which it matters for selection and appointment to the international bench.[5]

[1] Tom Dannenbaum, 'Nationality and the International Judge: The Nationalist Presumption Governing the International Judiciary and Why it Must Be Reversed' (2012) 45 Cornell International Law Journal 77, 120, citing Rosalyn Higgins.

[2] Manfred Lachs, 'Some Reflections on the Nationality of Judges of the International Court of Justice' (1992) 4 Pace Yearbook of International Law 49, 58, n. 17, citing Jerome Frank, *Law and the Modern Mind* (1949).

[3] Eric A Posner and Miguel de Figueiredo, 'Is the International Court of Justice Biased?' (2004) John M Olin Program in Law and Economics Working Paper No. 234.

[4] Posner and Figueiredo (n 3) 22, 26.

[5] It is outside the scope of the present chapter to consider other elements, such as gender diversity on the international bench. On that related topic, see Nienke Grossman, 'Shattering the Glass Ceiling in International Adjudication' (2016) 56 Virginia Journal of International Law 339; Nienke Grossman, 'Sex on the Bench: Do Women Judges Matter to the Legitimacy of International Courts?' (2012) 12 Chicago Journal of International Law 647; Susan Franck and others, 'The Diversity Challenge: Exploring the "Invisible College" of International Arbitration' (2015) 53 Columbia Journal of Transnational Law 429, *passim*; Kimi Lynn King and Megan Greening, 'Gender Justice or Just Gender? The Role of Gender in

Catharine Titi, *The Identity Conundrum* In: *Identity and Diversity on the International Bench.* Edited by: Freya Baetens, Oxford University Press (2020). © The several contributors. DOI: 10.1093/oso/9780198870753.003.0011.

A caveat is however in order: the impact of the adjudicator's identity can only be analysed in a holistic manner within the broader context of the design of an international court or tribunal.

The chapter commences by reviewing nationality in the statutes of international courts, before turning to the nationality of arbitrators in investment arbitration. Next, it draws on lessons from the experience of investment arbitration with respect to identity and decision-making. This allows the chapter to give an overview of the rules but also to move to practice statistics concerning identity and voting. Ultimately, this chapter considers the peculiar case of judges ad hoc. The final section concludes.

2. Nationality in the Statutes of International Courts

Nationality is an important element in the identity of an international adjudicator, capable of both decreasing and increasing the legitimacy of the adjudicative process. It can lessen legitimacy when national judges[6] are seen as partial to their home States; it can bolster legitimacy, when States consider the presence of a national judge a *sine qua non* in order to submit to the jurisdiction of a court or tribunal. Legal scholarship has often been wary of judges deciding cases involving the State of their nationality and voting in its favour, such as in the case of a judge sitting at the ECtHR on behalf of Italy, who 'dissented on a set of 133 judgments on alleged Italian Article 6 violations using the same dissenting opinion'.[7] Judges have often 'spent their careers in national service as diplomats, legal advisors, administrators, and politicians', therefore they are more likely to identify with the interests of their home State.[8] ICJ judges tend to vote in favour of their national State, although it has been observed that this experience is not borne out by the WTO Appellate Body.[9]

The statutes of most international courts and tribunals ordinarily regulate nationality. In doing so, they seek to reconcile the challenges attached to the

Sexual Assault Decisions at the International Criminal Tribunal for the Former Yugoslavia' (2007) 88 Social Science Quarterly 1049.

[6] In this context, the term 'national judge' is used to refer to a judge hearing a case involving the State of his or her nationality.

[7] For the criticism, see Erik Voeten, 'The Politics of International Judicial Appointments: Evidence from the European Court of Human Rights' (2007) 61 International Organization 669, 684. The judge was Luigi Ferrari Bravo. The 133 cases concerned similar petitions (violation of the right to a hearing 'within a reasonable time') and were all decided on 28 February 2002. The dissenting opinion, inserted in each judgment, was drafted in broad language to encompass all 133 judgments but was not modulated to take into account the particular case. For instance, the awarded amounts mentioned do not apply to all cases, but a *mutatis mutandis* statement is included ('*La même chose arrive, mutatis mutandis, pour la grande majorité des autres arrêts*'). Eg Dissenting Opinion of Judge Ferrari Bravo, *Lucia Riccardi v Italy*, App No 51095/99 (ECtHR, 28 February 2002). See also n 34.

[8] Posner and Figueiredo (n 3) 11.

[9] Dannenbaum (n 1) 166.

presence of national judges on the bench and the difficulties that their absence would entail, such as by debarring individuals of the same nationality from sitting together or by allowing the appointment of judges ad hoc when a disputing party does not have one of its nationals on the bench. The statutes of a minority of international courts and tribunals do *not* make reference to nationality. In this section, I will examine the two types of statutes in turn.

2.1 Court Statutes that Make Provision for Nationality

The statutes of 'classic' international courts tend to make explicit reference to nationality. The Statute of the International Court of Justice (ICJ), the archetypal international judicial forum, first aims to ensure that nationality does not function as a limitation: it provides that judges shall be elected 'regardless of their nationality'.[10] However, the significance of this statement is immediately circumscribed by the ensuing article, according to which no two members of the Court may be nationals of the same State.[11] The ICJ Statute makes further provision for persons who for the purposes of the membership of the Court could be considered to be nationals of more than one State and establishes that the latter shall be regarded as nationals of the State in which they typically exercise their civil and political rights.[12] But the Statute further enjoins the electors of the judges to bear in mind elements beyond nationality *stricto sensu*, and notably 'that in the body as a whole the representation of the main forms of civilization and of the principal legal systems of the world should be assured'.[13] To some extent, but only to some extent, this provision appears to contradict the need for the election of judges to be 'regardless of their nationality'.[14]

However, benefits as well as limitations arise from a judge's nationality. The Statute affirms that judges of the nationality of each disputing party retain their right to sit in the case.[15] If there is no judge of the nationality of a disputing party, the Statute allows the appointment of judges ad hoc. First, if the Court includes on the bench a judge of the nationality of one of the disputing parties, 'any other party may choose a person to sit as judge'.[16] Second, if the Court does not include on the

[10] Art 2 of the Statute of the ICJ, 33 UNTS 993. Although judges are elected without reference to their nationality, there appears to be an informal understanding according to which the permanent members of the UN Security Council are guaranteed to have a judge of their nationality on the bench. Exceptionally, in 2017, the UK 'lost' its judge. See Owen Bowcott, 'No British judge on world court for first time in its 71-year history' *The Guardian* (20 November 2017) <www.theguardian.com/law/2017/nov/20/no-british-judge-on-world-court-for-first-time-in-its-71-year-history> accessed 29 August 2019.

[11] Art 3(1) of the Statute of the ICJ, 33 UNTS 993.

[12] Art 3(2) of the Statute of the ICJ, 33 UNTS 993.

[13] Art 9 of the Statute of the ICJ, 33 UNTS 993.

[14] Shabtai Rosenne, *The Law and Practice of the International Court* (Martinus Nijhoff 1965) 168.

[15] Art 31(1) of the Statute of the ICJ, 33 UNTS 993.

[16] Art 31(2) of the Statute of the ICJ, 33 UNTS 993.

bench a judge of the nationality of the parties, each party may choose a person to sit as judge.[17] However, there is no need for the judge ad hoc to have the nationality of the appointing party. The institution of judges ad hoc is discussed in section 5.

A further provision in the Statute of the ICJ reveals the assumption that the judge's nationality has an impact on his or her decision-making. Article 32 of the Statute states that in the event that the President of the Court shall be a national of one of the disputing parties he shall relinquish his presidential functions in respect of the given case.[18] Similar provision is made for the Vice-President or senior judge when called to act as President.[19]

The provisions of the Statute of the ICJ are mirrored in the Statute of the International Tribunal for the Law of the Sea (ITLOS) almost to the letter. According to the ITLOS Statute no two members of the tribunal may be nationals of the same State.[20] Provision is made for persons who for the purposes of the membership of ITLOS could be regarded as nationals of more than one State.[21] Judges of the nationality of each party retain their right to sit in the case,[22] and provision is made for judges ad hoc.[23] The ITLOS Statute further stipulates that the Tribunal will include 'no fewer than three members from each geographical group as established by the General Assembly of the United Nations'.[24]

Analogous provisions exist in the American Convention on Human Rights (ACHR) and the Statute of the Inter-American Court of Human Rights (IACtHR),[25] and in the Rome Statute of the International Criminal Court (ICC).[26] The Rome Statute is worth a particular mention, because it also aims to guarantee diversity. It states that when selecting judges, State parties should take into account the 'need' in respect of the membership of the Court for '(i) The representation of the principal legal systems of the world; (ii) Equitable geographical representation; and (iii) A fair representation of female and male judges'.[27] While representation

17 Art 31(3) of the Statute of the ICJ, 33 UNTS 993.

18 Art 32 of the Statute of the ICJ, 33 UNTS 993.

19 ibid.

20 Art 3(1) of the ITLOS Statute, 1833 UNTS 561.

21 ibid.

22 Art 17(1) of the ITLOS Statute, 1833 UNTS 561.

23 Art 17(2)–(3) of the ITLOS Statute, 1833 UNTS 561.

24 Art 3(2) of the ITLOS Statute, 1833 UNTS 561. The geographical groups are the African Group, the Asia-Pacific Group, the Eastern European Group, the Latin American and Caribbean Group, and the Western European and Others Group.

25 Eg Art 52 of the ACHR, 1144 UNTS 123, and Art 4 of the IACtHR Statute, OAS Off. Rec. OEA/Ser.P/IX.0.2/80, Vol 1 at 88, provide that no two judges may be nationals of the same State.

26 Art 36(7) of the Rome Statute of the International Criminal Court, 2187 UNTS 3, states that no two judges of the same nationality can sit on the Court and makes provision for persons who for the purposes of membership of the Court have dual nationality.

27 Art 36(8)(a) of the Rome Statute of the International Criminal Court, 2187 UNTS 3. Interestingly, Art 12(2) of the Protocol to the African Charter on Human and Peoples' Rights on the Establishment of an African Court on Human and Peoples' Rights (OAU Doc OAU/LEG/EXP/AFCHPR/PROT (III)) also requires that '[d]ue consideration shall be given to adequate gender representation in nomination process'. It is expected that the statutes of new international courts established in the future are likely to include provisions on representativeness, including gender parity.

of the principal legal systems of the world and equitable geographical representation are not unique to the Rome Statute, the latter goes to some lengths to stress the need for representativeness.

2.2 Courts whose Statutes Are Silent on Nationality

In contrast with the above-mentioned statutes that take nationality into account, some courts' statutes follow what has been termed the 'cosmopolitan approach' and are silent on nationality.[28] The Caribbean Court of Justice, a regional integration court, is an example of this approach. A number of judges sitting on the Caribbean Court of Justice are or have been nationals of States that are neither CARICOM members nor signatories to the Court.[29] Another example is the Appellate Body of the World Trade Organization (WTO). The latter, while broadly agnostic about nationality, states that membership of the Appellate Body 'shall be broadly representative' of WTO membership.[30] Even so, typically, the Appellate Body does not include adjudicators of the same nationality. A further example is the Court of Justice of the European Free Trade Association (EFTA Court), another court of regional integration, comprising Norway, Iceland, and Liechtenstein. According to the Statute of this Court, '[a] party may not apply for a change in the composition of the Court on the grounds of either nationality of a Judge or the absence from the Court of a Judge of the nationality of that party'.[31]

The European Court of Human Rights (ECtHR) used to include a provision on nationality, requiring that no two judges may be nationals of the same State, but this was removed with Protocol 11's entry into force in 1998. Article 20 of the European Convention on Human Rights (ECHR) replaced old Article 38 and now states that the ECtHR 'shall consist of a number of judges equal to that of the High Contracting Parties'. This and the fact that judges are elected 'with respect to' each party from a list of three candidates nominated by the party[32] seemed to remove the need to specify that no two judges may be nationals of the same State. However, a party may nominate nationals of other parties or of non-parties. According to the Explanatory Report to Protocol 11:

> In principle, there should be no more than two judges of the same nationality on the Court. A State Party will have the possibility to put forward the name of a

28 Dannenbaum (n 1) 101.
29 ibid 102.
30 Art 17(3) of the Understanding on Rules and Procedures Governing the Settlement of Disputes, 1869 UNTS 401.
31 Art 15 of Protocol 5 to the ESA/Court Agreement on the Statute of the EFTA Court.
32 Art 22 of the ECHR, 213 UNTS 221.

> judge who is a national of another State Party rather than propose a judge from a State which has not ratified the Convention.[33]

This statement shows that while in principle the drafters of the Protocol considered preferable to avoid the situation where two judges with the nationality of the same State would sit on the Court, the possibility was envisaged. Consequently, a small number of co-nationals have served as judges simultaneously. At least San Marino and Liechtenstein (the latter repeatedly) have had Italian and Swiss nationals respectively elected as judges at the ECtHR.[34] At least one non-European judge has also served on the ECtHR. Ronald St. John Macdonald, a Canadian national, served on the ECtHR between 1980 and 1998. He was elected in respect of Liechtenstein.[35] Such appointments are not unique to the ECtHR. Liechtenstein has also selected at least one Swiss national to serve on the EFTA Court.[36] But this approach has also been used in courts whose statutes do not allow adjudicators of the same nationality to serve in parallel. Panama, for instance, has appointed a Costa Rican national to serve on the ICC. It bears noting that some of the judges appointed in respect of a State other than the State of their nationality may have held important positions in their home State, and could therefore be presumed to have strong government links with it.[37] It is notable that the examples discussed here tend to concern micro-States, or at least relatively small States, which leads to a reasonable assumption that the pool of qualified individuals available to serve on international courts may be limited.

The ECHR further provides that the judge elected in respect of the High Contracting Party concerned shall sit as an *ex officio* member of the Chamber and the Grand Chamber of the Court, and '[i]f there is none or if that judge is unable to sit, a person chosen by the President of the Court from a list submitted in advance by that Party shall sit in the capacity of judge'.[38]

[33] Council of Europe, Explanatory Report to Protocol No. 11 to the Convention for the Protection of Human Rights and Fundamental Freedoms, restructuring the control machinery established thereby, 1994, para. 59.

[34] See <www.echr.coe.int/Pages/home.aspx?p=court/judges&c> accessed 29 August 2019. See also William A Schabas, *The European Convention on Human Rights: A Commentary* (Oxford University Press 2015) 646.

[35] See list of judges of the ECtHR <www.echr.coe.int/Documents/List_judges_since_1959_BIL.pdf> accessed 29 August 2019.

[36] Daniel Terris and others, *The International Judge: An Introduction to the Men and Women who Decide the World's Cases* (Brandeis University Press 2007) 28.

[37] For instance, Luigi Ferrari Bravo, an Italian national elected in respect of San Marino, was legal adviser to the Italian government and sat as judge at the ICJ for Italy between 1995 and 1997; Elizabeth Odio Benito, a Costa Rican national, was nominated for election to the International Criminal Court by Panama, was previously minister in her home State.

[38] Art 26(4) of the ECHR, 213 UNTS 221.

3. Nationality of Arbitrators in Investment Arbitration

Nationality plays a different role in dispute settlement mechanisms where adjudicators are appointed directly by the disputing parties. In contrast with international courts, investment tribunals, like commercial tribunals, are constituted ad hoc to hear a dispute and the parties usually appoint their own arbitrators. While the term 'ad hoc' is sometimes employed to draw a distinction with 'institutional arbitration', ie arbitration administered by an institution, it is used in this chapter to indicate that the tribunal is constituted to hear a specific case once the dispute has been filed. In this light, all arbitration is ad hoc. In this respect, arbitral institutions resemble courts which allow judges ad hoc and considerations concerning the appointment of permanent judges—preselected to sit in a standing body where disputes are randomly allocated—do not apply in principle.

Under the Convention on the Settlement of Investment Disputes between States and Nationals of Other States (ICSID Convention), the default method for constituting a three-member arbitral tribunal is for each disputing party to appoint one arbitrator and for the third arbitrator, who is the president of the tribunal, to be appointed by agreement of the parties.[39] If the tribunal cannot be constituted by agreement, the Chairman of ICSID's Administrative Council appoints the remaining arbitrators at the request of a party and 'after consulting both parties as far as possible'.[40] Where the Chairman appoints arbitrators pursuant to this procedure, these arbitrators cannot be nationals of the State party to the dispute or have the nationality of the investor's home State.[41] In other words, the Chairman cannot select an arbitrator who is a national of, or who has the same nationality as, one of the disputing parties. This rule is not without significance. According to the ICSID database, in about 200 out of 656 original proceedings brought under the ICSID Convention at least one member of the tribunal was appointed by the Chairman of the ICSID Administrative Council.[42] The ICSID Convention further provides that the majority of the arbitrators cannot have the nationality of the disputing parties, unless the parties agree.[43] According to Aron Broches, this provision was inserted to 'avoid a situation in which the third arbitrator, as the only one appointed by a neutral party, might find himself in the position of a sole arbitrator in having to maintain a balance between two other arbitrators who were more inclined to act as advocates for the parties appointing them'.[44] By the same token, arbitrators with the nationality of the disputing parties

39 Art 37(2)(b) of the ICSID Convention, 575 UNTS 159.

40 Art 38 of the ICSID Convention, 575 UNTS 159.

41 Art 38 of the ICSID Convention, 575 UNTS 159.

42 See <https://icsid.worldbank.org/en/Pages/cases/AdvancedSearch.aspx> accessed 29 August 2019 (information correct as of 29 August 2019).

43 Art 39 of the ICSID Convention, 575 UNTS 159. See also Rule 1(3) of the ICSID Arbitration Rules.

44 ICSID, *History of the ICSID Convention* (ICSID Vol II, Part 2 1968) 983.

are allowed if they constitute the minority, notably if the tribunal is composed of five or more arbitrators.[45]

When it comes to annulment, all three members of an ICSID annulment committee are appointed by the Chairman. In that case, certain additional limitations apply, for example the Chairman cannot appoint an individual who sat on the original tribunal that issued the award under review or who acted as conciliator in the dispute.[46] In addition, the Chairman cannot appoint an individual who is a national of the State party to the dispute or of the home State of the investor, an individual who has the same nationality as any member of the original tribunal that issued the award, nor an individual who has been designated to the Panel of ICSID Arbitrators by either of those States.[47]

Although the parties select their adjudicators in investment arbitration, some limitations are imposed with respect to nationality. In the case of judges ad hoc before international courts, one issue of legitimacy, discussed below, is whether it is appropriate to actually choose one's adjudicator, while in investment arbitration, the default rule is that disputing parties can choose who to appoint (therefore the bench is 'tailor-made'), but are ordinarily prevented from choosing among their own nationals.[48]

That said, the ICSID Convention is also in some ways similar to the Statute of the ICJ, if only because it was at least in part modelled on it.[49] Interestingly, like the statutes of some international courts, it requires that when the Chairman of ICSID's Administrative Council designates persons to serve on the Panels of ICSID Arbitrators,[50] he shall 'pay due regard to the importance of assuring representation on the Panels of the principal legal systems of the world and of the main forms of economic activity'.[51] The Chairman may designate ten

[45] ICSID, 'Report of the Executive Directors on the Convention on the Settlement of Investment Disputes between States and Nationals of Other States' (World Bank 1965), para 36; Christoph H Schreuer and others, *The ICSID Convention: A Commentary* (OUP 2nd edn, 2009) 499.

[46] Art 52(3) of the ICSID Convention, 575 UNTS 159.

[47] Art 52(3) of the ICSID Convention, 575 UNTS 159.

[48] The method of selection and appointment of investment arbitrators has been criticized in the literature and it forms part of the debate in the multilateral reform negotiations at UNCITRAL Working Group III. Eg see the *Report of the Working Group on Selection and Appointment of International Adjudicators: Structural Options for ISDS Reform*, prepared by Andrea K. Bjorklund, Marc Bungenberg, Manjiao Chi, and Catharine Titi for the Academic Forum on ISDS and the UNCITRAL Working Group III Meeting of October 2019.

[49] Summary Record of Proceedings, Consultative Meetings of Legal Experts, 19 February 1964, in ICSID, *History of the ICSID Convention: Documents Concerning the Origin and the Formulation of the Convention on the Settlement of Investment Disputes between States and Nationals of Other States* Vol II-1 (1968) 423 (According to Aron Broches, the parallel between the ICSID Convention and 'commercial arbitration should not be drawn too closely because the Convention sought to establish a new jurisdiction. The parallel if any lay with the International Court of Justice rather than with commercial arbitration', ibid).

[50] ICSID maintains a Panel of Arbitrators (Art 3 of the ICSID Convention, 575 UNTS 159).

[51] Art 14(2) of the ICSID Convention, 575 UNTS 159.

persons to the Panel of Arbitrators.[52] These arbitrators must each have a different nationality.[53]

However, individuals on the Panel of Arbitrators are especially nominated by States. Each contracting State may, but is not obliged to, designate four persons to the Panel of Arbitrators.[54] These individuals may or not have the nationality of the State that designates them.[55] In reality, arbitrators appointed to hear ICSID cases do not have to be appointed from the Panel of Arbitrators, except when the appointment is made by the Chairman.[56]

Other arbitration rules also deal with the issue of the appointment of arbitrators of the same nationality as one of the disputing parties. The Arbitration Rules of the United Nations Commission on International Trade Law (UNCITRAL) remain somewhat agnostic about the desirability of doing so. These Rules provide that the appointing authority 'shall take into account the advisability of appointing an arbitrator of a nationality *other than* the nationality of the parties'.[57] In effect, this seems to favour the appointment of arbitrators of the nationality of one of the disputing parties.[58] The Arbitration Rules of the Stockholm Chamber of Commerce (SCC) provide that 'the sole arbitrator or the Chairperson of the Arbitral Tribunal shall be of a different nationality than the parties, unless the parties have agreed otherwise or the Board otherwise deems it appropriate'.[59] In appointing arbitrators, the Board must consider several aspects, such as the circumstances of the dispute and the applicable law, but also the nationality of the disputing parties.[60] Similar provisions exist in the Arbitration Rules of the London Court of International Arbitration (LCIA).[61] A different clause is included in the Arbitration Rules of the International Chamber of Commerce. While in confirming or appointing arbitrators their nationality shall be taken into account, and the sole arbitrator or the president of the tribunal cannot be of the nationality of one of the parties, these Rules also provide that 'in suitable circumstances and provided that none of the parties objects within the time limit fixed by the Court, the sole arbitrator or the president of the arbitral tribunal may be chosen from a country of which any of the parties is a national'.[62]

52 Art 13(2) of the ICSID Convention, 575 UNTS 159.
53 ibid.
54 Art 13(1) of the ICSID Convention, 575 UNTS 159.
55 ibid.
56 Art 40 of the ICSID Convention, 575 UNTS 159.
57 Art 6(7) of the UNCITRAL Arbitration Rules (2010), emphasis added.
58 Catharine Titi, 'Nationality and Representation in the Composition of the International Bench: Lessons from the Practice of International Courts and Tribunals and Policy Options for the Multilateral Investment Court' (15 January 2020) CERSA Working Papers on Law and Political Science 1/2020 <https://cersa.cnrs.fr/wp-content/uploads/2020/01/CTiti-Nationality-1.pdf 47> accessed 14 August 2020, with examples from NAFTA appointments.
59 Art 17(6) of the SCC Arbitration Rules (2017).
60 Art 17(7) of the SCC Arbitration Rules (2017).
61 Art 6 of the LCIA Arbitration Rules (2014).
62 Art 13 of the Arbitration Rules of the International Chamber of Commerce (2017).

4. Identity, Appointments, and Decision-Making: Some Observations from the Experience of Investment Arbitration

The fact that arbitrators are appointed by the disputing parties although they tend not to have their nationality leads to a complex matrix of considerations when it comes to appointments. The majority of investment arbitrators come from industrialized countries. A study published in 2014 found that while 87 nationalities were represented among the appointees in ICSID arbitration, most arbitrators come from a handful of industrialized countries.[63] Contrariwise, while 83% of ICSID cases have been filed against developing countries, fewer than 30% of appointments were of developing country nationals.[64] According to 2019 data from ICSID, Western European arbitrators account for about half of all appointments, although only 8% of disputes involve a Western European State as respondent.[65] Arbitrators from North America (Canadian, Mexican, and US) correspond to 20% of appointments, although a mere 4% of disputes involve a North American State as a respondent.[66] Already in 2014, nationals of seven States (Australia, Canada, France, New Zealand, Switzerland, the UK, and the US) accounted for almost 50% of appointments.[67] In ICSID arbitration, French, UK, and US nationals represent close to one-third of all appointments.[68] In 2018, French, UK, and US arbitrators corresponded to one quarter of all ICSID appointments,[69] while collectively arbitrator appointments from North America (Canada and US only) and Western Europe amounted to 57% of all 2018 appointments.[70] By contrast, arbitrators from South and Central America and the Caribbean represent only 13% of appointments, although the States in this region are respondents in almost 30% of disputes.[71] In 2018, Latin America and the Caribbean corresponded to 19% of appointments.[72]

[63] Sergio Puig, 'Social Capital in the Arbitration Market' (2014) 25 European Journal of International Law 387, 405.

[64] Joost Pauwelyn, 'The Rule of Law without the Rule of Lawyers? Why Investment Arbitrators Are from Mars, Trade Adjudicators from Venus' (2015) 109 American Journal of International Law 761, 771.

[65] World Bank, The ICSID Caseload Statistics, Issue 2019-1 <https://icsid.worldbank.org/en/Documents/resources/ICSID%20Web%20Stats%202019-1(English).pdf> accessed 29 August 2019, 11 and 19.

[66] ibid.

[67] ibid; Puig (n 63) 405.

[68] Pauwelyn (n 64) 769–70. Outside the ICSID Convention, it appears that appointments of Mexican arbitrators are also high, see the earlier study Susan D Franck, 'Empirically Evaluating Claims about Investment Treaty Arbitration' (2007) 86 (1) North Carolina Law Review 78.

[69] The corresponding numbers are 26 appointments of French nationals, 20 appointments of UK nationals, and 20 appointments of US nationals. ICSID, '2018 Annual Report' (2018) 33 in combination with <https://icsid.worldbank.org/en/Pages/cases/AdvancedSearch.aspx> accessed 29 August 2019. Note that ICSID, ibid, mentions 27, instead of 26 appointments of French nationals but one appointment concerns a conciliation case.

[70] ibid.

[71] World Bank (n 65) 11 and 19.

[72] ICSID (n 69) 32–33 and <https://icsid.worldbank.org/en/Pages/cases/AdvancedSearch.aspx> accessed 29 August 2019.

Similarly, arbitrators from Eastern Europe and Central Asia obtain a meagre 3% of appointments, while these regions have attracted 26% of claims.[73]

Another interesting finding is that nationals of developing countries who are appointed as arbitrators tend to have a law degree from an industrialized country. For instance, it appears that, with a single exception, all Latin American arbitrators known to have been appointed to an ICSID tribunal or committee until 2014 have had a graduate degree from France, the UK, or the US.[74] The question remains of whether the discrepancy between the percentages of disputes attracted by a State and the percentages of arbitrator appointments with the nationality of that State can be explained by the fact that the ICSID Convention in principle debars nationals of the respondent State from being appointed as arbitrators. However, in principle the ICSID Convention also prevents appointments of arbitrators with the same nationality as the claimant, and yet most claimants come from Western Europe and North America, the regions with the highest percentages of arbitrator appointments.[75]

While the possibility of appointing one's own national or co-national is generally precluded by the ICSID system, and appointment of nationals with the same developed-developing country background does not seem to gain currency, selection necessarily follows other criteria. Some arbitrators are thought to be pro-State (and tend to be appointed by respondent States), while others are thought to be pro-investor (and tend to be appointed by claimant investors).[76] A minority of arbitrators have repeat appointments as presidents of the tribunal or annulment committee, demonstrating that they are trusted by ICSID or by their peers, in cases where the president is appointed with the agreement of his or her co-arbitrators.[77] The arbitrators obtaining most appointments in the original proceeding are not necessarily repeatedly appointed to annulment committees.[78] This could be due to the different method of appointment of arbitrators who sit in the original proceeding and of those who are appointed as members of an annulment committee. That said, the fact that repeat arbitrators in original proceedings are not necessarily repeat members of annulment committees may also be explained by taking into account that members of an annulment committee cannot be chosen among those who sat in the original proceeding deciding the same case. The more frequently a person has sat in original proceedings, the less one is likely to be appointed—at least repeatedly—in follow-up proceedings.

73 World Bank (n 65) 11. However, in 2018, the percentage appointments from this region was slightly higher (6%). See ICSID (n 69) 32.

74 Puig (n 63). The exception is Rodrigo Oreamuno, Costa Rica's former First Vice-President, ibid.

75 Pauwelyn (n 64) 789–90.

76 Puig (n 63) 404.

77 ibid.

78 UNCTAD, ISDS Navigator <https://investmentpolicyhub.unctad.org/ISDS> accessed 29 August 2019.

How the identity of the arbitrator, including the fact that he or she comes from a State with a similar level of economic development or from the same region, impacts the outcome of the arbitration remains however unclear. Consider the following example: in some regions, neighbouring countries have been engaged in warfare over long periods of time or in non-violent inter-State disputes. Is the fact that an appointed arbitrator—or a judge for that matter—comes from the same region as one of the disputing parties likely to make him or her favour the party in question, or the contrary? In addition, the presumed preference of arbitrators from developing countries for countries or nationals of countries with a similar level of development has been questioned,[79] and it is not unusual for arbitrators from developed countries to be selected to sit in South-South disputes.[80]

A recent empirical study of arbitrator appointments and decision-making in investment law provides some astonishing results. The study found that overall arbitrators from developing countries are likely to reject jurisdiction and liability of the respondent State.[81] However, amongst them those more likely to uphold jurisdiction are claimant-appointed arbitrators.[82] Respondent-appointed arbitrators with work experience as investor counsel—ordinarily seen as pro-investor—are less likely to uphold jurisdiction and liability.[83] In general, arbitrators with experience in private practice are more likely to affirm jurisdiction, and when they are appointed by the respondent State, they are more likely to hold their appointing party liable.[84] Finally, while there is some evidence that work experience in the private sector is linked to pro-investor decisions, government experience and public international law background do not appear to be significantly correlated with pro-State decisions.[85] Further empirical research is necessary in this field in order to fully explore how the arbitrator's identity influences decision-making.

5. The Peculiar Case of Judges Ad Hoc

The presence of national judges sitting in cases involving the State of their nationality has been extensively canvassed, at least since the drafting of the Statute of the Permanent Court of International Justice.[86] Almost nowhere is scepticism towards

[79] Eg Jan Paulsson, 'Third World Participation in International Investment Arbitration' (1987) 2 ICSID Review – Foreign Investment Law Journal 19, 22–23 and *passim*.

[80] ibid 32–33.

[81] Michael Waibel and Yanhui Wu, 'Are Arbitrators Political? Evidence from International Investment Arbitration' 18 (January 2017) <www.yanhuiwu.com/documents/arbitrator.pdf> accessed 15 August 2020.

[82] ibid.

[83] ibid.

[84] ibid.

[85] ibid 19. However, the authors appear to be making a slightly different argument on 18.

[86] Stephen M Schwebel, 'National Judges and Judges Ad Hoc of the International Court of Justice' (1999) 48 International and Comparative Law Quarterly 889, 889 et seq; Iain Scobbie, '"Une heresie

appointments of national judges so evident, as in the discussion of the institution of judges ad hoc, in light of the supposition that willingness to be reappointed may make judges conform to the wishes of the State that appointed them.[87]

Accordingly, in his dissenting opinion in *Land, Island and Maritime Frontier Dispute*, Judge Shahabuddeen remarked that '[i]t is not easy to think of any concept of judicial independence which is consonant with particular judges being named to sit in a particular case practically at the behest of the parties'.[88]

> On the face of it, the very idea that a litigant may appoint a judge of its own choice to the bench would appear to be in flagrant breach of the *nemo iudex in sua causa* principle and the general idea of judicial independence. In a domestic legal system, any judge with an interest in a case would be expected to stand down.[89]

Some have gone so far as to describe the judge ad hoc as a 'judge-advocate'[90] and it has been observed that the '*dependence* of the judge *ad hoc* is in stark contrast to the judicial ideal presented with respect to the permanent judge'.[91]

The institution of judges ad hoc has been included in the statutes of international courts for a number of reasons. A rationale for the presence of a national judge ad hoc on the bench is that he or she can help the Court understand issues of national jurisprudence or law that require specialized knowledge.[92] The judges' ad hoc knowledge of the 'legal traditions' and 'problems' of their home State are seen as useful to better inform the Court in relation to some aspects of a case.[93] Judges ad hoc could 'influence the drafting of the judgment so that it would not unduly ruffle the susceptibilities of the losing State'.[94] In addition, it has been argued that a judge ad hoc 'must always ensure that the appointing State's arguments are fully

en matière judiciaire" – The Role of the Judge ad hoc in the International Court' (2005) 4 The Law and Practice of International Courts and Tribunals 421, 430 et seq; Dannenbaum (n 1) 167–69.

87 Jeffrey Dunoff and Mark Pollack, 'The Judicial Trilemma' (2017) 111 American Journal of International Law 225; Posner and Figueiredo (n 3) 11.

88 *Land, Island and Maritime Frontier Dispute (El Salvador/Honduras), Application to Intervene* (Order of 28 February 1990) [1990] ICJ Rep 3, Dissenting opinion of Judge Shahabuddeen, 45.

89 Scobbie (n 86) 428.

90 Michael Reisman, 'Nullity and Revision: The Review and Enforcement of International Judgments and Awards' (1971) 479, as cited in Dannenbaum (n 1) 146.

91 Dannenbaum (n 1) 146, emphasis added.

92 Scobbie (n 86) 434. In reality, this argument holds only partly true: in international adjudication, domestic law tends to be considered as a fact and international courts rarely engage in extensive analysis of domestic law, see ibid, 459; Dannenbaum (n 1) 169; Titi (n 58) 36–37. Exceptionally, in investment dispute settlement domestic law has to be applied and it is not considered a fact. For an exception to the exception, see investment agreements negotiated by the European Union, where EU law is to be considered as a fact, eg Comprehensive Economic and Trade Agreement (CETA) between Canada and the European Union.

93 Gilbert Guillaume, 'Some Thoughts on the Independence of International Judges vis-à-vis States' (2003) 2 The Law and Practice of International Courts and Tribunals 163, 164.

94 Scobbie (n 86) 434.

addressed by the Court, whether or not they convince the majority of the judges'.[95] Judges ad hoc are the first to address the Court,[96] thus having the opportunity to set the tone of the debate.

Some of these arguments had already been raised by Judge ad hoc Elihu Lauterpacht in his separate opinion in *Application of the Convention on the Prevention and Punishment of the Crime of Genocide*.[97] He explained that the institution of ad hoc judges was created to give a party, which would not otherwise have a judge of its nationality on the bench, the opportunity to have such a judge. But that a judge ad hoc should be 'regarded as a representative of the State that appoints him' is 'contrary to principle and cannot be accepted'.[98] Lauterpacht added that the judge ad hoc has the obligation 'to ensure that, so far as is reasonable, every relevant argument in favour of the party that has appointed him has been fully appreciated in the course of collegial consideration and, ultimately, is reflected—though not necessarily accepted—in any separate or dissenting opinion that he may write'.[99] Judges ad hoc do not always vote in favour of their appointing State,[100] and it has been famously argued that 'if judges *ad hoc* sometimes do little good, they usually do little harm'.[101] Sometimes even judges of the same nationality can arrive at different results between them.[102] Disputing parties have sometimes foregone the opportunity to appoint judges ad hoc, and this independently of whether the other disputing party had a judge of its nationality on the bench.[103] On occasion, a disputing party may appoint a judge ad hoc of the nationality of the *other* disputing party.[104]

In reality, the votes of national or ad hoc judges in favour of the State of their nationality or their appointing State can have the effect of cancelling each other out.[105] It is possible that the same holds true for arbitrators selected by the parties in a three-member panel, where the final decision may be left to the presiding

[95] *Sovereignty over Pulau Ligitan and Pulau Sipadan (Indonesia/Malaysia)* (Judgment) [2002] ICJ Rep 625, Dissenting opinion of Judge ad hoc Franck, para 10.

[96] Freya Baetens and Pierre Bodeau-Livinec, 'Face-à-face: Interview with President Yusuf – President of the International Court of Justice' (2019) 18 The Law and Practice of International Courts and Tribunals 267.

[97] *Application of the Convention on the Prevention and Punishment of the Crime of Genocide* (Provisional Measures, Order of 13 September 1993) ICJ [1993] Rep 325, Separate opinion of Judge ad hoc Lauterpacht.

[98] ibid 409.

[99] ibid. See also Stephen M Schwebel, 'National Judges and Judges Ad Hoc of the International Court of Justice' (1999) 48 International and Comparative Law Quarterly 889, 893 et seq.

[100] Eg Judge ad hoc Suzanne Bastid in *Application for Revision and Interpretation of the Judgment of 24 February 1982 in the Case concerning the* Continental Shelf (Tunisia/Libyan Arab Jamahiriya) *(Tunisia v Libyan Arab Jamahiriya)* (Judgment) [1985] ICJ Rep 192, 231.

[101] Schwebel (n 86) 898–99.

[102] Lachs (n 2) 63.

[103] Schwebel (n 86) 897.

[104] *Certain Criminal Proceedings in France (Republic of the Congo v France)* (Provisional Measure – Order of 17 June 2003) [2003] ICJ Rep 102. For a discussion of the nationality of judges ad hoc, see Titi (n 58) 39–43.

[105] Scobbie (n 86) 448.

arbitrator.[106] For this and other reasons, the judge ad hoc has also been described as 'functionally useless'.[107] Either way, judges ad hoc, more than permanent judges, do indeed tend to vote for their appointing State,[108] although it is also probable that sometimes they do so because they genuinely agree with the legal arguments presented.[109]

The institution of judges ad hoc also serves to underline that while nationality weighs in decision-making, it is not the only element that matters. Indeed, judges ad hoc are not required to have the nationality of the disputing party that appoints them and as of the time of writing about 60% of all appointments of judges ad hoc at the ICJ do not concern a judge of the nationality of the appointing State.[110] This narrows the relevance of the conclusions that can be drawn as to how much nationality matters. A recent review of ITLOS cases has revealed that national judges ad hoc tend to vote in favour of their appointing State more often than non-national judges ad hoc do.[111]

So should national judges and judges ad hoc be banned from the bench? In some international courts, both national judges and judges ad hoc have been prevented from sitting in cases involving the State of their nationality or their appointing State; for instance, there was a decisive shift in that direction after long contrary practice in the context of individual (as opposed to interstate) cases in the IACtHR.[112]

International courts depend on States' consent to submit disputes to their jurisdiction. The fact that a State may choose a judge to sit in a case concerning it, may convince it to submit to the jurisdiction of the court.[113] Indeed, some States are more comfortable with arbitration than international courts, because in arbitration in principle all adjudicators are ad hoc.[114] The question is after all political,

[106] Waibel and Wu (n 81) 18.
[107] Scobbie (n 86) 462.
[108] Eg see *Sovereignty over Pulau Ligitan and Pulau Sipadan (Indonesia/Malaysia)* (Judgment) [2002] ICJ Rep 625, Dissenting opinion of Judge ad hoc Franck, para. 10, observing that '[b]etween March 1948 *(Corfu Channel (United Kingdom v Albania))* and July 2002 *(Ahmadou Sadio Diallo (Republic of Guinea v Democratic Republic of the Congo))* there have been ad hoc judges in 45 cases and 53 phases of cases before this Court. Of these, 29 have written dissenting opinions, corresponding quite closely to the number of ad hoc judges appointed by losing parties'.
[109] Scobbie (n 86) 441 ('A mere head-counting approach to the voting record of judges ad hoc is simplistic: there are other factors in play apart from the fact of being appointed by a litigant State.').
[110] Titi (n 58) 40 and Appendices C and D. While some judges ad hoc have been repeatedly appointed by the State of their nationality (eg this is the case of Judge ad hoc Milenko Kreća), several have received repeat appointments by States other than their home State. For instance, Gilbert Guillaume, a French national, has been appointed nine times as judge ad hoc by a State other than France (and twice by France); Yves Daudet, also a French national, has been appointed eight times by States other than France—he has not been appointed as judge ad hoc by France; Christopher J. R. Dugard (South Africa) and Jean-Pierrre Cot (France) have both been appointed seven times by a State other than the State of their nationality—neither has been appointed by his State of nationality. These examples appear to show a certain popularity of French nationals as judges *ad hoc*. In reality, French judges ad hoc correspond to about 15% of appointments.
[111] Titi (n 58) 39–43 and Appendix E.
[112] ibid 29–33.
[113] Scobbie (n 86) 463; Dannenbaum (n 1) 172; Guillaume (n 93) 164.
[114] For instance, this has become obvious in the arguments used by a number of States in the negotiations in UNCITRAL Working Group III that express scepticism vis-à-vis the

not legal.[115] Decisions in international courts are taken collectively and collegially which allows for 'collective independence'.[116] However, in mixed disputes, especially when the right to appoint a judge ad hoc is conferred only on the disputing State party, the institution of judges ad hoc may be inappropriate.

6. Conclusion

This chapter has presented some preliminary thoughts on how certain elements of the identity of the international judge and arbitrator matter in international adjudication. The stark differences between nationality requirements or restrictions in different international court statutes and arbitration rules offer in this respect food for thought, as do the differences more broadly contemplated between international courts and arbitration. The chapter has drawn particular attention to the institution of judges ad hoc, although more often than not judges ad hoc are not nationals of their appointing State. In any case, the full impact of the adjudicator's identity, of which nationality is only one aspect, cannot be interpreted in a detached manner but needs to be seen in a holistic approach in the context of the design of an international court or tribunal. But this would need to be the topic of a dedicated study.

establishment of international investment court. Catharine Titi, 'Who's Afraid of Reform? Beware the Risk of Fragmentation' (2018) 112 AJIL Unbound 232.

[115] Scobbie (n 86) 463. See also Baetens and Bodeau-Livinec (n 95).
[116] Guillaume (n 93).

12
Judicial Education and International Courts
A Proposal Whose Time has Come?

SI Strong

1. Introduction

For an international court to be considered legitimate, it must feature an impartial, independent, and above all competent international judiciary. Traditionally, States and scholars have believed the best way to ensure competence on the international bench is through appropriate selection processes.[1] However, no selection method can ensure the long-term fitness of the judiciary. Indeed, experts in judicial studies have argued that 'most judges are ill-prepared for the challenges, personal and professional, of a judicial career, and many of them turn out to be ill-suited for the job', despite having survived rigorous selection procedures.[2]

In other professions, the solution would be easy: mandatory post-selection continuing education requirements. However, this prospect is seldom discussed in policy circles, even though experts in judicial education have long recognized that 'good judges can be made'.[3] Academics have also overlooked the importance of judicial education,[4] preferring to conceptualize judicial competence largely if not exclusively in terms of substantive and procedural expertise that can (ostensibly) be measured at the time of appointment, even though research shows that judges

[1] Burgh House Principles on the Independence of the International Judiciary, Principle 2.1 (International Law Commission 2004) (Burgh House Principles); see also Basic Principles on the Independence of the Judiciary, Adopted by the Seventh United Nations Congress on the Prevention of Crime and the Treatment of Offenders held at Milan from 26 August to 6 September 1985 and endorsed by General Assembly resolutions 40/32 of 29 November 1985 and 40/146 of 13 December 1985, Principle 10 (Basic Principles) <www.ohchr.org/EN/ProfessionalInterest/Pages/IndependenceJudiciary.aspx> accessed 29 February 2020.

[2] Keith R Fisher, 'Education for Judicial Aspirants' (2010) 54 Akron Law Review 163, 164.

[3] Livingston Armytage, *Educating Judges: Towards Improving Justice – A Survey of Global Practices* (Brill Nijhoff 2015) 162 (discussing the classic nature versus nurture debate).

[4] Cheryl Thomas, *Review of Judicial Training and Education in Other Jurisdictions*, report prepared for the Judicial Studies Board (May 2006) 113.

SI Strong, *Judicial Education and International Courts* In: *Identity and Diversity on the International Bench.* Edited by: Freya Baetens, Oxford University Press (2020). © The several contributors. DOI: 10.1093/oso/9780198870753.003.0012.

must master a wide range of hard and soft skills if they are to carry out their duties properly.[5]

The situation is exacerbated by the fact that many judges have been hesitant about discussing the need for judicial education.[6] This restraint may stem from a desire to safeguard the 'mystique' of the judge[7] or from the realization that 'even the most learned judges ... do not understand how judges make decisions'.[8] Unfortunately, the lack of information about the hardships experienced by both new and experienced judges hinders both academic and policy work on this subject.

This is not to say that there is no data on judicial education. To the contrary, recent innovations in judicial studies have led to an increasing respect for the role that judicial education plays in a well-functioning legal system,[9] and contemporary forms of judicial education are seen as promoting rather than detracting from judicial independence,[10] perhaps because education providers adopt an interdisciplinary and multidisciplinary perspective, with only minimal focus on 'law' per se.[11]

As encouraging as these developments may be, they are currently limited to national judiciaries. Not only does the leading document on international judicial ethics (the Burgh House Principles on the Independence of the International Judiciary (Burgh House Principles)) fail to even mention judicial education, but international judges are not required to undertake any form of

[5] National Judicial Institute (NJI), *Judicial Education Overview and Education Resources* <www.nji-inm.ca/> accessed 29 February 2020. (clicking on NJI Course Calendar).

[6] Some exceptions exist. David Baragwanath, 'The Interpretive Challenges of International Adjudication Across the Common Law/Civil Law Divide' (2014) 3 Cambridge Journal of International and Comparative Law 450 (New Zealand and international perspective); Judge Jeremy Fogel and SI Strong, 'Judicial Education, Dispute Resolution and the Life of a Judge: A Conversation with Judge Jeremy Fogel, Director of the Federal Judicial Center' (2016) Journal of Dispute Resolution 259 (US perspective); Peter Mason, 'The Good Judge' (1991) 57 Arbitration 181 (English perspective); Richard A Posner, *How Judges Think* (Harvard University Press 2010) (US perspective); Richard A Posner, 'The Role of the Judge in the Twenty-First Century' (2006) 86 Boston University Law Review 1049 (US perspective); Patricia M Wald, 'Reflections on Judging: At Home and Abroad' (2004) 7 University of Pennsylvania Journal of Constitutional Law 219 (US and international perspective); Leon R Yankwich, 'The Art of Being a Judge' (1957) 105 University of Pennsylvania Law Review 374 (US perspective).

[7] Emily Kadens, 'The Puzzle of Judicial Education: The Case of Chief Justice William de Grey' (2009) 75 Brooklyn Law Review 143, 143–44.

[8] Chris Guthrie, Jeffrey J Rachlinski, and Andrew J Wistrich, 'Inside the Judicial Mind' (2001) 86 Cornell Law Review 777, 782.

[9] Armytage (n 3) xv, 23.

[10] Basic Principles (n 1) Principle 9; European Judicial Training Network (EJTN), Judicial Training Principles (EJTN 2016), Principles 1–4 (EJTN Judicial Training Principles); Office of the High Commissioner on Human Rights in cooperation with the International Bar Association, *Human Rights in the Administration of Justice: A Manual on Human Rights for Judges, Prosecutors and Lawyers: Professional Training Series No. 9* (United Nations 2003) 115, 133 (OHCHR/IBA) <www.ibanet.org> accessed 29 February 2020; José Zeitune, *International Principles on the Independence and Accountability of Judges, Lawyers and Prosecutors, Practitioners Guide No. 1* (International Commission of Jurists 2007) 205 (discussing judicial education under the Principles and Guidelines on the Right to a Fair Trial and Legal Assistance in Africa); ibid 222 (discussing judicial education under the Latimer House Guidelines for the Commonwealth on Parliamentary Supremacy and Judicial Independence).

[11] European Judicial Training Network (EJTN), *EJTN Handbook on Judicial Training Methodology in Europe* (European Union 2016) 2, 17–19.

judicial education whatsoever, despite the fact that approximately 67% of international judges have never served in a judicial capacity or received any specialized judicial training prior to their elevation to the international bench.[12] While some judges do serve as arbitrators prior to their elevation to the bench and thus could be said to have a certain amount of hands-on experience,[13] arbitrators are typically not required to undertake significant amounts of specialized education before or after becoming arbitrators.[14] The situation is further exacerbated by the fact that efforts to encourage international judges to engage voluntarily in judicial education programs often meet with considerable resistance from the judges themselves.[15]

The inextricable link between legitimacy and competence demands further investigation of the role that judicial education can and should play in international adjudication. This Chapter therefore outlines the various practical and theoretical problems associated with judicial education of international judges and offers a number of suggestions regarding further academic inquiries and reform initiatives.

The discussion proceeds as follows. First, section 2 discusses the conventional wisdom that judicial selection procedures can and do constitute a proxy for judicial competence. Next, section 3 outlines a number of lessons that proponents of international judicial education can learn from common law countries, while section 4 identifies a number of shortcomings in the current common law model. section 5 considers issues regarding self-regulation of judicial education, while section 6 provides several recommendations on how the international legal regime can move forward.

[12] The concept of mandatory judicial education is fraught even at the national level, even though many authorities believe that judicial education should be considered part of a judge's continuing ethical duty. National Judicial Education Program, *Testimony to the ABA Joint Commission to Evaluate the Model Code of Judicial Conduct* (April 2004) 15 <www.ncsc.org/__data/assets/pdf_file/0021/15438/2007abamodelcode.pdf> accessed 14 August 2020; see also Basic Principles (n 1) Principle 9; EJTN Judicial Training Principles) (n 10) Principles 1–4; OHCHR/IBA (n 10) 115, 133; Zeitune (n 10) 205, 222.

[13] While it is unclear how many international judges acted as arbitrators prior to elevation to the international bench, an empirical study published in 2020 suggests that such movement does in fact occur. SI Strong, *Legal Reasoning Across Commercial Disputes: Comparing Judicial and Arbitral Analyses* (OUP 2020) Fig. 3.2 (Strong, *Legal Reasoning*) (noting that of the 465 domestic and international judges and arbitrators who participated in an international survey on legal reasoning in commercial disputes, 14 had served as arbitrators prior to becoming judges, as compared to 35 judges who had moved to arbitration). Although some people believe that there are significant differences between acting as a judge and acting as an arbitrator, recent empirical research suggests that the process of legal reasoning is essentially the same across the two groups, at least in commercial matters. ibid ch 6 (analysing data from a multi-pronged empirical study that included a large-scale international survey, a series of semi-structured interviews and textual analysis of judicial decisions and arbitral awards).

[14] ibid ch 2, ch 6; SI Strong, 'Reasoned Awards in International Commercial Arbitration: Embracing and Exceeding the Common Law-Civil Law Dichotomy', (2015) 37 Michigan Journal of International Law 1, 5–9.

[15] Daniel Terris, Caesare PR Romano, and Leigh Swigart, *The International Judge: An Introduction to the Men and Women Who Decide the World's Cases* (OUP 2007) 209.

Before beginning, it is necessary to note that the term 'international judicial education' is used in this chapter to refer to judicial education programs aimed at judges sitting on international courts or tribunals. The term is not used to refer to cross-border judicial education programs that are aimed at domestic judges and that seek to (1) increase competence in international or regional law; (2) facilitate the development of the rule of law at the domestic level; or (3) promote cross-border judicial cooperation.[16]

2. Rebutting Conventional Wisdom: Judicial Selection as a Proxy for Judicial Competence

Judicial education is only important if traditional means of ensuring judicial competence (ie, superior judicial selection procedures) cannot adequately perform that function. As it turns out, judicial selection cannot serve as a proxy for ongoing judicial competence due to problems relating to the conventional definition of judicial competence and the disconnect between judicial selection procedures and the qualities of a good international judge.

2.1 Qualities of a Good International Judge

If the best way to ensure judicial competence is to select good judicial candidates, then it is critical to know the qualities of a good international judge. Unfortunately, this is a more difficult task than it seems, for despite the extensive consideration of judicial qualities in domestic,[17] comparative,[18] and philosophical analyses,[19] very little research exists involving the qualities of a good international judge.[20] Even those principles that do exist (such as the admonition that international judges

[16] Toby S Goldbach, 'From the Court to the Classroom: Judges' Work in International Judicial Education' (2016) 49 Cornell International Law Journal 617, 671; Hon Justice Michael Kirby AC CMB, 'Transnational Judicial Dialogue, Internationalisation of Law and Australian Judges' (2008) 9 Melbourne Journal of International Law 171, 176 (discussing the Judicial Reference Group convened by the United Nations High Commissioner for Human Rights).

[17] Robert G Bone, 'Judging as Judgment: Tying Judicial Education to Adjudication Theory' (2015) Journal of Dispute Resolution 129; Chris Guthrie, 'Blinking on the Bench: How Judges Decide Cases' (2007) 93 Cornell Law Review 1 (2007); Chris Guthrie, 'Misjudging' (2007) 7 Nevada Law Journal 420; Guthrie, Rachlinski, and Wistrich (n 8) 782; Chad M Oldfather, 'Of Judges, Law, and the River: Tacit Knowledge and the Judicial Role' (2015) Journal of Dispute Resolution 155.

[18] Thomas (n 4) 131–36 (discussing judicial 'best practices' in a variety of common law and civil law jurisdictions).

[19] Ronald Dworkin, *Law's Empire* (Harvard University Press 1985) 240 (discussing Hercules, an ideal judge).

[20] A few exceptions exist. Baragwanath (n 6) 478; Caroline Foster, 'The Role of the International Judge and Arbitrator', forthcoming; Ruth Mackenzie and others, *Selecting International Judges: Principle, Process, and Politics* (OUP 2010) 61–62.

must learn to transcend their national experiences and training) are either contested or ignored in practice.[21]

The absence of any significant research on this issue means that those charged with selecting international judges have had to rely on very general criteria such as 'competence' and 'high moral character'.[22] Traditionally, the concept of competence has been narrowly defined in terms of subject matter expertise and considered to be a relatively static quality that can be ascertained at the time of appointment.[23] However, recent research in judicial studies shows that judges must master a wide range of personal and professional skills if they are to do their jobs properly, although judicial selection committees often do often recognize or prioritize these qualities as central to the process of judging.[24]

2.2 Judicial Selection Methods

Traditionally, the selection of international judges has focused on the candidates' substantive knowledge of international law, based on the belief that judicial competence can and should be measured solely in terms of subject matter expertise.[25] As a result, it should not come as a surprise that existing selection procedures produce judicial candidates who meet that particular criterion.[26] However, existing processes have not been as successful in producing candidates with pre-existing judicial experience.[27] Indeed, according to a study conducted in the mid-2000s, only about 33% of all international judges had any experience on the bench prior to joining an international court or tribunal, with the remaining judges coming from the civil service, academia and, to a lesser extent, the international bar.[28] This is clearly problematic, since the 67% of individuals who do not have prior experience as a judge will not have had any formal training in judicial matters.[29]

[21] Terris, Romano, and Swigart (n 15) xii, 208–09 (noting some international judges believe that they do not need to learn about other legal systems or the underlying social conditions of the jurisdictions the serve after they are elevated to the bench).

[22] ibid 26–29 (noting nationality and fluency in the working language of the court also play a role); see also Burgh House Principles (n 1) ¶2.1.

[23] David Salter, 'Some Observations on a Report by Justice – The Judiciary in England and Wales (London 1992)' (1993) 12 Civil Justice Quarterly 329, 332 (suggesting post-appointment education could be comprised primarily of top-up 'refresher' courses).

[24] Armytage (n 3) 7–8; Thomas (n 4) 13–17 (constituting a worldwide report prepared for the British Judicial Studies Board); J Clifford Wallace, 'Globalization of Judicial Education' (2003) 28 Yale Journal of International Law 355, 357, 358–59 (noting needs of civil law and common law judges).

[25] Mackenzie and others (n 20) 152–53; Terris, Romano, and Swigart (n 15) 16, 23–25.

[26] Terris, Romano, and Swigart (n 15) 16, 23–25.

[27] ibid.

[28] ibid 20 (claiming approximately 40% of 215 international judges came from academia and 28% from the civil service). Each group reflects different strengths and weaknesses. Mackenzie and others (n 20) 51–60; Terris, Romano, and Swigart (n 15) 64–65.

[29] Some individuals with international judicial experience have criticized the practice of naming those without any practical experience as counsel to adjudicative positions (ie, positions as judges or

The lack of judicial experience, combined with the lack of judicial education after elevation to the bench, is extremely concerning, since there significant differences between acting as a judge and acting as an advocate, academic, or civil servant.[30] Traditionally, international judges were believed to learn their craft through 'socialization' rather than through formal education,[31] which was for many years also a hallmark of the judicial education method used in common law countries.[32] However, many common law jurisdictions have reconsidered their reliance on socialization (also known as acculturation) as their primary means of educating judges due to concerns about the risk of perpetuating questionable behavioural norms based on unconscious bias (implicit bias) and depressing the benefits of diversity on the bench through unspoken adherence to standards developed exclusively by those who have traditionally held power.[33] This shift in thinking at the domestic level suggests a similar move by the international judicial community would be beneficial.

This recommendation makes sense given the number of similarities between the common law and international bench. Both systems appoint judges mid-career, after the candidate has distinguished himself or herself as an advocate, academic, or civil servant, which is very different than the civil law approach, which appoints judges at a much more junior level.[34] However, civil law judges typically take specialized coursework in judicial studies from the earliest stages of their legal schooling, while common law judges do not take any classes in judging prior to their elevation to the bench.[35] Instead, international and common law judges simply '[take] the oath, step[] onto the bench, and proceed[] to fill the judicial role as if born in the robe'.[36] This tradition is rooted in medieval English practice and

arbitrators). Strong, *Legal Reasoning* (n 15) ch. 4.II.H (comments from Interviewee 16, an international judge-arbitrator).

[30] Fisher (n 2) 168–69; Kadens (n 7) 143.

[31] Lyndel V Prott, 'The Role of the Judge of the International Court of Justice' (1974) 10 Revue belge de droit international 473, 502–06. International judges may therefore join various judicial organizations in the belief that professional networking and informal congresses will help them learn how to carry out their judicial functions. A variety of general organizations exist as well as those that are subject-specific, although no known group focuses on international judges per se. Eg Global Institute for the Environment <www.iucn.org/news/world-commission-environmental-law/201607/judges-establish-global-judicial-institute-environment> accessed 29 February 2020; International Association of Women Judges<www.iawj.org/> accessed 29 February 2020.

[32] Kadens (n 7) 143–46.

[33] Kathleen E Mahoney, 'The Myth of Judicial Neutrality: The Role of Judicial Education in the Fair Administration of Justice' (1996) 32 Willamette Law Review, 785, 786 n. 2, 814–19 (discussing the use of judicial education mechanisms to overcome unconscious bias); Nancy Scherer, 'Diversifying the Federal Bench: Is Universal Legitimacy for the US Judicial System Possible?' (2011) 105 Northwestern University Law Review 587, 615.

[34] Kadens (n 7) 143–45.

[35] ibid; Charles H Koch, Jr, 'The Advantages of the Civil Law Judicial Design as the Model for Emerging Legal Systems' (2004) 11 Indiana Journal of Global Legal Studies 139, 143.

[36] Kadens (n 7) 143.

is based on the assumption that anyone who has become a senior litigator is sufficiently well-prepared to act as a judge.[37]

While the common law approach may have been appropriate in medieval times, contemporary judges face demands never experienced by medieval judges.[38] As a result, common law countries have reformed their approach to judicial education by expanding curricular offerings and professionalizing the delivery of content. The international legal community can and should look to these developments and initiatives when considering how to approach international judicial education.[39]

Judicial education can assist with the selection of international judges in other ways.[40] For example, some commentators have suggested that the process of selecting international judges reflects a number of 'significant vulnerabilities' that threaten the legitimacy and effectiveness of international courts and tribunals.[41] Several of these concerns can be resolved through post-appointment education of international judges. For example, questions have been raised about the representativeness of international courts and the possibility that selection procedures discriminate on the basis of race, gender, or socio-economic status.[42] Indeed, in 2006, one report showed only 21% of all international judges were women.[43] In 2018, an analysis of seven different international courts and tribunals (the International Criminal Court (ICC), the European Court of Human Rights, the Inter-American Court of Human Rights, the African Court on Human and Peoples' Rights, the International Court of Justice (ICJ), the International Tribunal on the Law of the Sea, and the Iran-United States Claims Tribunal) showed only 27% of the judges were women.[44] While efforts can and should continue to be made to increase the

[37] ibid 144.

[38] Fisher (n 2) 8, at 182–85. For example, judicial caseloads have increased dramatically, particularly in the last few decades. SI Strong, 'Writing Reasoned Decisions and Opinions: A Guide For Novice, Experienced and Foreign Judges' (2015) Journal of Dispute Resolution 93, 95 (Strong, Writing). Judges are also having to take on additional duties, ranging from case management (leading to the rise of the 'managerial' judge rather than the professional adjudicator) to alternative dispute resolution (as a result of the increased emphasis on settlement). See Fisher (n 2) 164, 182; Judith Resnik, 'Managerial Judges' (1982) 96 Harvard Law Review 374, 378.

[39] Some improvements have yet to be made. SI Strong, 'Judicial Education and Regulatory Capture: Does the Current System of Educating Judges Promote a Well-Functioning Judiciary and Adequately Serve the Public Interest?' (2015) Journal of Dispute Resolution 1, 16–22 (Strong, Regulatory Capture).

[40] Although it is difficult and in some cases dangerous to generalize about international judicial selection, since the means by which judges are appointed to the international bench varies significantly, depending on the appointing country and/or the tribunal in question. Terris, Romano, and Swigart (n 15) 15–16; see also Mackenzie and others (n 20) 63–136. Many international judges are appointed by their national governments, although it is also possible for an international judge to be appointed or elected by a regional or intergovernmental organization like the European Union or the United Nations. Terris, Romano, and Swigart (n 15) xi.

[41] Terris, Romano, and Swigart (n 15) 16.

[42] Mackenzie and others (n 20) 161–71.

[43] Terris, Romano, and Swigart (n 15) 18.

[44] Priya Pillai, 'Women in International Law: A Vanishing Act?' (*Opinio Juris*, 3 December 2018) <http://opiniojuris.org/2018/12/03/women-in-international-law-a-vanishing-act/> accessed 29 February 2020.

representativeness of the international bench, some of the more invidious effects of a non-diverse bench could be mitigated through judicial education regarding the social realities of underrepresented groups.[45]

Concerns also exist as to whether and to what extent the qualities that lead to recognition by a selection committee can be tied to long-term judicial competence.[46] For example, selection committees may be attracted to advocates who have 'made a name for themselves' in their previous professions, even though being a good advocate, a good academic, or a good civil servant is not the same as being a good judge.[47] Domestic judges have also remarked that appointment procedures often favour those who are good at social networking, although there is no correlation between networking skills and judicial competence.[48]

Other appointment mechanisms (for example, judicial elections, which are relatively rare in domestic settings but not uncommon in international settings) reflect an even more tenuous link between the qualities necessary to gain the bench and the qualities associated with being on the bench.[49] Not only can the appointment process be marred by 'undignified electioneering', but those voting on international judgeships may not even have sufficient information about the candidates' qualifications to make a considered decision.[50] The situation is exacerbated by the fact that there is little if anything that can be done at the international level to combat improper appointment procedures at the national level or to address improper behaviour or incompetence once an individual has been elevated to the international bench.[51] Of course, judicial education could eliminate or minimize some of the problems that arise post-appointment.

3. Judicial Education in Common Law Countries: Lessons for International Judicial Education?

The last ten to fifteen years have seen judicial education become 'big business' around the world, with numerous public, quasi-public, and private organizations entering the field.[52] The movement began in common law countries in the 1960s

[45] Livingston Armytage, 'Judicial Education on Equality' (1995) 58 Modern Law Review 160; T Brettel Dawson, 'Judicial Education on Social Context and Gender in Canada: Principles, Process and Lessons Learned' (2014) 21 International Journal of the Legal Profession 259; T Brettel Dawson, Ulrike Schultz, and Gisela Shaw, 'Gender and Judicial Education' (2014) 21 International Journal of the Legal Profession 255; Kathleen Mahoney, 'Judicial Bias: The Ongoing Challenge' (2015) Journal of Dispute Resolution 43 (Mahoney, Judicial Bias).

[46] Wayne Doane, Note, 'The Membership of Judges in Gender Discriminatory Clubs' (1987) 12 Vermont Law Review 459, 461; Fisher (n 2) 164.

[47] Strong, Regulatory Capture (n 39) 2–3.

[48] Scherer (n 33) 595.

[49] Terris, Romano, and Swigart (n 15) 16, 31–36.

[50] ibid xx, 36.

[51] OHCHR/IBA (n 10) 129–32; Terris, Romano, and Swigart (n 15) 23–24.

[52] Armytage (n 3) 15 (citation omitted).

with the creation of the National Judicial College and the Federal Judicial Center (FJC) in the United States, with other jurisdictions eventually following suit.[53] Most developed countries have established their own national institutes for educating their judges, with regional bodies serving smaller jurisdictions that cannot afford to support their own independent centres.[54] Privately funded judicial education programs also exist, although questions exist about the potential for bias in course offerings.[55] Cross-border educational initiatives are quite common, although those programs typically focus on educating domestic rather than international judges.[56]

At one time, these organizations focused primarily if not exclusively on substantive issues of law.[57] However, leading programs like the National Judicial Institute/Institut National de la Magistrature (NJI) of Canada now offer a sophisticated and comprehensive curriculum that ranges from social science-based offerings on social context and the judicial role to practical courses on 'judge craft' (communication skills and crafting judgments), 'court craft' (managing the trial process and assisting with settlement efforts), and 'profession craft' (engaging with technology).[58] The European Judicial Training Network (EJTN) offers a similarly broad range of coursework, supplementing programming on European and comparative law with classes in judicial skills, linguistics, professional practice, and societal issues.[59]

The range of subject matters and the emphasis on 'soft skills' may come as a surprise to those who do not work frequently in judicial education, but those courses are often extremely popular and have been developed through formal and informal needs assessments.[60] Indeed, many of the qualities that sitting judges believe are most important to the task of judging and that are the most difficult to master have little if anything to do with the substantive law.[61]

[53] 28 USC §620(b) (creating the Federal Judicial Center). Formal programs of judicial education also exist in civil law countries, beginning in 1959 with the creation of what is now known as *L'Ecole Nationale de la Magistrature* in France. Armytage (n 3) xvi.

[54] Armytage (n 3) xvi–xix.

[55] Strong, Regulatory Capture (n 39) 3.

[56] Goldbach (n 16) 671.

[57] Fogel and Strong (n 6) 262–63, 265; T Brettel Dawson, 'Judicial Education: Pedagogy for Change' (2015) Journal of Dispute Resolution 175, 182 (Dawson, Pedagogy).

[58] NJI (n 5) (clicking on NJI Course Calendar) (including a course calendar that discusses the 'craft of judging', including judge craft, court craft, and professional craft).

[59] EJTN, Catalogue General <www.ejtn.eu/About-us/Projects--Programmes/Catalogue-General/> accessed 29 February 2020.

[60] Armytage (n 3) 69–83 (discussing pros and cons of needs assessments as well as various methodologies).

[61] One leading judicial education expert has described the 'eight pillars' of judging as including qualities such as remaining aware of one's judicial responsibilities, regardless of the setting; remaining aware in the courtroom by being conscious of what is said by all parties, including the judge, and remembering to notice one's own reactions, emotions and thoughts with respect to proceedings; respecting the rule of law; avoiding assumptions by challenging preconceptions and prejudices; keeping a professional distance by not taking things personally or acting as an advocate; ensuring honesty and integrity in terms of both process and outcome; exhibiting integrity and courage by knowing what is proper under the law and acting accordingly; and being accountable for one's actions on the bench. David M Rothman, *California Judicial Conduct Handbook*, Appendix 3, 1–4 (2013 Supplement), as reproduced in Diane E Cowdrey, 'Teaching New Judges: What It Means to "Be" a Judge' (2015) 4 Journal of the

4. Problems with Adopting the Common Law Model for International Judicial Education

The similarities between international and common law judges, along with the increasing maturity and sophistication of the common law approach to judicial education, suggest that the international community could look to common law jurisdictions for inspiration in developing international judicial education norms. While the common law model could indeed provide some useful insights, reformers need to keep several issues in mind.

4.1 Issues Relating to the Perceived Need for International Judicial Education

4.1.1 Public perception of judicial performance

Judge Theodor Meron has spoken about the 'crucial' importance of 'public respect for the courts and the judge's conduct',[62] which suggests a need to consider the connection between judicial education and public perception of the judiciary. On the one hand, requiring international judges to take continuing education courses could be interpreted as diminishing the esteem surrounding international courts, since it would suggest that judges are fallible or less than perfect. However, it is also possible that a formal program of international judicial education would be seen as addressing some of the key shortfalls of the international court system and thereby improving the quality of international justice.

In some ways, this analysis is quite difficult, since relatively little is known about the public perception of international courts.[63] However, empirical research suggest that 'opinions of international courts are strongly correlated with attitudes towards the international organizations most closely associated with a particular court and with legal values more generally'.[64] Thus, concerns about the legitimacy of the United Nations may affect the legitimacy of the ICJ, just as concerns about the legitimacy of the European Union may affect concerns about the legitimacy of the Court of Justice of the European Union (CJEU).[65] An as-of-yet untested hypothesis could also see correlations in the opposite direction, such that concerns about the CJEU could affect perceptions of the EU.[66]

International Organization for Judicial Training 82, 84–88; see also Fogel and Strong (n 6) 278; Mason (n 6) 181 (providing an English perspective).

62 Terris, Romano, and Swigart (n 15) 191.

63 Erik Voeten, 'Public Opinion and the Legitimacy of International Courts' (2013) 14 Theoretical Inquiries in Law 411, 412.

64 ibid 413.

65 ibid.

66 ibid 412. This may have been a factor in the United Kingdom's decision to withdraw from the EU.

Empirical research also suggests that 'international courts quickly lose support when they get embroiled in public controversy'.[67] While no distinction is made between controversies generated by disparate views of the law and controversies associated with improper judging techniques (such as those involving bias or a lack of appreciation for social context, as has been alleged of the ICC),[68] some of these issues might have been avoided through judicial education, either by helping judges be aware of issues such as social context and unconscious bias or by helping judges write decisions that were more persuasive to the losing party.[69]

4.1.2 Judicial perception of judicial performance

As important as public perception of judicial performance is, judicial perception is perhaps even more critical to the issue of judicial education, since judges will resist mandatory judicial education if they believe they are already competent at their jobs. Interestingly, empirical research has suggested not only that judges can and do become overconfident in their own abilities (a phenomenon known as 'judicial hubris') but that judges are often unaware of their own shortcomings (a phenomenon known as the 'bias blind spot').[70] Although judges are not the only ones prone to overconfidence, 'one can make a persuasive argument that the natural human foibles such as ... overconfidence ... become exacerbated, rather than reduced, because of the isolation in which judges work and the pedestal upon which they are placed'.[71] Indeed, some judges appear to 'wrap themselves in a mantle of infallibility' and find it very difficult to admit that they do not know something.[72] As a result, judges—including international judges—may avoid educational programming for fear of seeming less than competent.[73]

Concerns about overconfidence and its corollaries are particularly relevant to the current discussion because international judges are entirely in control of their own educational agendas, even though only approximately 33% of international judges have any prior experience on the bench.[74] Furthermore, international judges do not appear to be required to undertake any form of judicial education before or after their elevation to the bench, despite the acknowledged importance of judicial education to the proper functioning of the judiciary.[75]

[67] ibid 435.
[68] ibid 412.
[69] Writing judicial decisions is much more difficult than it seems, yet judges often lack detailed instruction in such matters. Strong, Writing (n 38) 95–97.
[70] Jeffrey M Stempel, 'In Praise of Procedurally Centered Judicial Disqualification – And a Stronger Conception of the Appearance Standard: Better Acknowledging and Adjusting to Cognitive Bias, Spoliation, and Perceptual Realities' (2011) 30 Review of Litigation 733, 741, 743–44 (Stempel, Praise). International judges are not immune to these concerns. Terris, Romano, and Swigart (n 15) 191, 208–09.
[71] Stempel, Praise (n 70) 744.
[72] Terris, Romano, and Swigart (n 15) 214.
[73] ibid 209.
[74] ibid 16, 23–25.
[75] OHCHR/IBA (n 10) 115, 133.

A system that allows individuals to choose for themselves the content and timing of their professional education is somewhat questionable in light of research indicating that persons 'who are overconfident ... make poor [educational] choices compared to learners who are uncertain about their knowledge'.[76] Empirical evidence also shows that those persons (such as judges) who are more socially dominant are more confident in their judgments, regardless of actual ability,[77] and may be more likely to act unethically.[78] The situation is further exacerbated by the fact that some supremely overconfident people—particularly those who are given a great deal of deference in their jobs—are highly unlikely to learn from experience.[79]

Overconfidence can affect other aspects of international judicial education. For example, judges may be inclined to over-prioritize intellectual prowess in comparison to interpersonal and other types of skills necessary to the judicial process.[80] Studies also show that people tend to avoid material they perceive as difficult to learn, particularly if they are (as judges often are) under time pressure, or may avoid coursework in subjects they erroneously believe they have already mastered.[81]

This latter concern is particularly relevant to educational programming that concerns social context and implicit bias because 'these cognitive processes can operate implicitly, or at a level below conscious awareness, ... [and thus] can bias judgment and behavior in ways that go unnoticed by the individual'.[82] As a result, judges may not believe that they themselves could be prone to unconscious biases and may therefore choose not to receive training in this particular subject matter area,[83] even though social scientists research has shown that '[e]veryone, judges ... included, harbors attitudes and stereotypes that influence how he or she

[76] Jennifer M Cooper, 'Smarter Law Learning: Using Cognitive Science to Maximize Law Learning' (2016) 44 Capital University Law Review 551, 574–75.

[77] Stephen V Burks and others, 'Overconfidence and Social Signalling' (2013) Review of Economic Studies 1, 4.

[78] Gary Warth, 'Connection Found in Elitism, Unethical Behavior, Study Says,' *San Diego Union-Tribune* (2 January 2018) <www.sandiegouniontribune.com/pb-monthly/news/education/sd-me-sdsu-ethics-20171227-story.html> accessed 29 February 2020.

[79] Troy A Paredes, 'Too Much Pay, Too Much Deference: Behavioral Corporate Finance, CEOs, and Corporate Governance' (2005) 32 Florida State University Law Review 673, 693.

[80] Debra Cassens Weiss, 'Lawyers in Failed Firms Overestimated the Importance of Being Smart, Law Dean Says,' ABA Journal (9 March 2015) <www.abajournal.com/news/article/lawyers_in_failed_firms_overestimate_the_importance_of_being_smart_law_dean> accessed 29 February 2020 (quoting Dean Frank Wu of Hastings Law School as saying '[s]mart people overestimate the importance of being a smart person').

[81] Cooper (n 76) 574–75; Terris, Romano, and Swigart (n 15) 208–09.

[82] National Center for State Courts, Helping Courts Address Implicit Bias: Resources for Education <www.ncsc.org/ibeducation> accessed 29 February 2020; see also Jerry Kang and others, 'Implicit Bias in the Courtroom' (2012) 59 UCLA Law Review 1124, 1146–48, 1172–79. Similar problems occur with respect to domestic violence cases. Lynn Hecht Schafran, 'There's No Accounting for Judges' (1995) 58 Albany Law Review 1063, 1075.

[83] Gregory S Parks and Matthew W Hughey, 'Opposing Affirmative Action: The Social Psychology of Political Ideology and Racial Attitudes' (2014) 57 Howard Law Journal 513, 537.

perceives and interacts with the social world'.[84] Interestingly, experts in judicial studies have suggested that conservative judges may be more opposed to judicial education programs attempting to demonstrate the existence and effect of implicit bias because conservatives 'may be more inclined than liberals to justify and use their implicit biases for explicit judgment'.[85]

4.2 Issues Relating to the Shape of International Judicial Education

Problems also exist with respect to the shape of international judicial education. International judges are not currently required to undertake any type of pre-appointment or continuing judicial education, even though approximately 67% of international judges have no prior experience on the bench. Indeed, there are reports that

> there is little formalized training or mentoring about the practical aspects of being an international judge ... Novice judges are mostly left alone to figure out how things work.... Only one court seems to have made a more formal attempt to help incoming judges learn the ropes of their institution ... But this scheme was, in the end, more an idea than a reality.[86]

It is also unclear how well-prepared the 33% of international judges who come from national courts are, given that some jurisdictions—particularly those following the common law tradition—do not require their national judges to undertake any form of initial or continuing judicial education.[87] Indeed, some insiders suggest that former national judges can experience significant difficulties on the international bench, since they find it hard to switch from a purely domestic mind set to an international perspective.[88]

Experience suggests that voluntary systems of judicial education can be extremely problematic.[89] Part of the difficulty arises because judges are often pressed for time and prioritize other tasks over educational opportunities. No matter how good the educational programs are, they cannot improve judicial performance unless the

[84] National Center for State Courts (n 82); see also Mahoney, Judicial Bias (n 45) 77, at 815; Paul M Secunda, 'Cultural Cognition at Work' (2010) 38 Florida State University Law Review 107, 109; Paul M Secunda, 'Cognitive Illiberalism and Institutional Debiasing Strategies' (2012) 49 South Dakota Law Review 373, 375 (Secunda, Debiasing).

[85] Parks and Hughey (n 83) 537.

[86] Terris, Romano, and Swigart (n 15) 65–66.

[87] Strong, Regulatory Capture (n 39) 3–4.

[88] Terris, Romano, and Swigart (n 15) 64–65, 88.

[89] ibid 208–09.

individual in question attends class.[90] However, voluntary systems of judicial education also experience problems in terms of course selection, since those persons who are most in need of instruction on particular issues (such as unconscious bias or social context) are perhaps least likely to attend programs on those topics.[91]

Some of these difficulties could be overcome by requiring international judges to take a certain number or type of courses after their appointment to the bench. However, efforts to impose mandatory judicial education requirements in common lave countries have triggered strenuous opposition, with a number of judges claiming that such initiatives are 'insulting'.[92] Some international judges are so opposed to the notion of judicial education that providers have had to rename the process 'strengthening judicial capacity' or 'judicial capacity-building' to avoid giving offense.[93]

A related issue involves the degree of control exerted by the judiciary over the scope, content, and methods of judicial education. National and international authorities have traditionally suggested that judges should take primary responsibility over the content and delivery of judicial education because of concerns about (1) expertise (namely the notion that only judges can appreciate the particular pressures and demands of acting as a judge and are therefore the only people qualified to act as instructors) and (2) judicial independence.[94] As a result, judicial education has long been an insider initiative. Indeed, the vast majority of faculty members on judicial education courses are judges,[95] even if they have no special expertise in education or in the subject matter under discussion.[96]

Judicial influence over the educational curriculum can also be seen at the institutional level, as illustrated by the number of judges serving on the advisory boards of organizations specializing in judicial education.[97] Although judicial input into

[90] Jane Goodman-Delahunty and others, 'Insightful or Wishful: Lawyers' Ability to Predict Case Outcomes' (2010) 16 Psychology, Public Policy, and Law 133, 153; Mahoney, Judicial Bias (n 45) 815; Secunda, Debiasing (n 84) 375.

[91] Cooper (n 76) 568, 574–75.

[92] National Judicial Education Program (n 12) 15; see also Armytage (n 3) 29–41.

[93] Armytage (n 3) 170 n16; Terris, Romano, and Swigart (n 15) 209 (noting 'considerable resistance' to educational initiatives by international judges); see eg United Nations Office on Drugs and Crime, *Resource Guide on Strengthening Judicial Integrity and Capacity* (United Nations 2011). Some judges have also criticized the term 'judicial training' (preferring the more elevated 'judicial education'), although the former is broadly used.

[94] ABA Commission on the 21st Century Judiciary, *Preserving the Judiciary's Institutional Legitimacy*, 37 Brief 54, 56 (2008) <http://apps.americanbar.org/tips/faic/16_PreservingJudiciary.pdf> accessed 29 February 2020); see also Thomas (n 4) 32–33 (constituting a report prepared for the British Judicial Studies Board); J Clifford Wallace, 'Judicial Education and Training in Asia and the Pacific' (2000) 21 Michigan Journal of International Law 849, 858–59 (Wallace, Asia).

[95] Basic Principles (n 1) Principle 9; see also EJTN Judicial Training Principles (n 10) Principle 6; OHCHR/IBA (n 10) 119, 133.

[96] Wallace, Asia (n 94) 17, at 856 (reflecting the judicial perspective).

[97] 28 USC §621 (listing members of the supervisory board of the FJC); The National Judicial College, Faculty Council www.judges.org/about/faculty-council.html; accessed 29 February 2020; see also 2014 FJC Annual Report 14 <www.fjc.gov/content/299416/annual-report-2014> (accessed 29 February 2020) (listing members of various FJC Committees, some of which are entirely made of judges).

programming is of course necessary, 'the conservative nature of the judicial branch, its many stakeholders, and its resulting reluctance to change' can thwart efforts to improve or modify existing approaches to judicial education.[98]

Another way that judges can affect both content and format of educational programming is through their choice of courses and educational providers. Because judges can choose which courses to attend, any program that is considered too difficult or too controversial will gain few attendees, thereby decreasing the likelihood that the program will be offered again in the future.[99] Indeed, commentators have noted a significant lag in institutional adoption of programs that are seen as particularly challenging for judicial audiences.[100]

Finally, even if a program of international judicial education is adopted, it is unclear how such coursework will be funded. Although the Burgh House Principles indicate in Principle 6 that 'States parties and international organisations shall provide adequate resources ... to enable courts and the judges to perform their functions effectively',[101] many international courts are in financial straits, and judges may be unwilling to elevate international judicial education over other priorities.[102] Given the apparent lack of public funding mechanisms, international judges will have to either pay for educational programming themselves (which will likely suppress attendance) or will be forced to attend privately funded educational programs, which carry with them the risk of political influence and bias.[103]

5. Regulation of International Judicial Education: Who and How?

At this point, no legal or political body has the authority to require or regulate international judicial education. Instead, self-regulation is the norm, not only because of the desire to protect the independence of the judiciary[104]

[98] Elizabeth Dennis, 'Leading Into the Future: Securing the Public Trust in Texas Courts' (2010) 51 South Texas Law Review 839, 840.

[99] Jeffrey W Stempel, 'Refocusing Away From Rules Reform and Devoting More Attention to the Deciders' (2010) 87 Denver University Law Review 355, 363 n116 (Stempel, Refocusing) (noting that judicial education is highly susceptible subject to market pressures); see also (nn 75) (noting that learners tend to avoid difficult material, if given the chance).

[100] Stempel, Refocusing (n 99) 363 n116.

[101] Burgh House Principles (n 1); see also OHCHR/IBA (n 10) 121.

[102] Terris, Romano, and Swigart (n 15) 226.

[103] Center for Public Integrity, *Corporations, Pro-Business Nonprofits Foot Bill for Judicial Seminars* (27 May 2014) 13 <www.publicintegrity.org/2013/03/28/12368/corporations-pro-business-nonprofits-foot-billjudicial-seminars> accessed 29 February 2020; Bruce A Green, 'May Judges Attend Privately Funded Educational Programs? Should Judicial Education Be Privatized?: Questions of Judicial Ethics and Policy' (2002) 29 Fordham Urban Law Journal 941, 941–44. Reliance on public expenditures can also create problems to the extent the political branches can wield control over attendance at various programs. Goldbach (n 16) 671.

[104] Burgh House Principles (n 1) preamble.

but also because of the preferential status enjoyed by the legal profession in general.[105]

The concept of the judiciary as a profession is an interesting one, since it raises questions about the nature and limits of self-regulation. For example,

> [p]rofessionalism has been defined as a 'peculiar type of occupational control' where the members themselves retain control over their work and as a result enjoy state sanctioned autonomy.... [A] core feature of the notional profession-state bargain sees professions promising to ensure expertise and appropriate behaviour from their members in return for certain, typically monopolistic, privileges. The state doesn't seek to ensure the competence and trustworthiness of each individual member of a profession, but instead motivates the profession collectively to seek to ensure this.[10] ... The bargain model implicitly assumes that if the profession fails to meet its obligations the terms may need to be renegotiated or, at the extreme, the profession's privileges withdrawn. Indeed, it has been argued that the only effective discipline against a whole profession is to remove the power to self-regulate.[106]

While the international bench has thus far been immune to cases of patent dishonesty or corruption, there have unfortunately been various 'lapses of character or judgment' that 'contribute to a public perception of international judges as callous, incompetent, arrogant, or all of those combined'.[107] For example, '[t]he International Criminal Court (ICC) has been charged with bias against Africa and insufficient sensitivity to the politics of conflict resolution',[108] while the International Criminal Tribunal for the former Yugoslavia has been criticized for a variety of inefficiencies and improprieties.[109]

Although judges tend to view these as 'aberrations' stemming from too much stress, experts link these phenomena to difficulties in establishing and communicating appropriate ethical standards and the absence of any institutional system of accountability.[110] Notably, these types of issues can be and often are routinely addressed in domestic forms of judicial education and could easily be incorporated into a well-designed program of international judicial education.

Self-regulation of international judicial education has a number of benefits, including flexibility, speed, expertise by those creating the regulations, acceptance by those subject to regulations, cost-efficiency, and cross-border application.[111]

[105] Mark Davies, 'The Demise of Professional Self-Regulation? Evidence From the "Ideal Type" Professions of Medicine and Law' (2010) 26 Professional Negligence 3, 4–5.

[106] ibid.

[107] Terris, Romano, and Swigart (n 15) 191.

[108] Voeten (n 63) 412.

[109] Wald (n 6) 226–27

[110] Terris, Romano, and Swigart (n 15) 192.

[111] Eva Hupkes, 'Regulation, Self-Regulation, or Co-Regulation?' (2009) 4 Journal of Business Law 427, 429.

However, even those who support self-regulation recognize that '[t]he overall social, political and statutory framework for self-regulation should nurture the positive aspects of self-regulation without ceding so much discretion to market participants that they corrupt the system by favouring their own interests over the public good'.[112] Improper self-regulation can lead to a number of problems, including rules that are inadequate to the task of protecting third parties and the public interest, inadequate enforcement, and conflict of interests between those doing the regulating and those that are regulated.[113]

States tend to defer to self-regulated industries so long as no problems appear to arise.[114] However, waiting until significant problems occur is not an option in the case of international courts and tribunals. Furthermore, international judicial education appears to reflect a number of concerns already, particularly with respect to (1) the high degree of control currently wielded by international judges on matters relating to their own educational requirements; (2) resistance by judges to any independent external oversight on matters relating to judicial education; and (3) the potentially significant number of negative externalities generated by the current system. Increased attention therefore needs to be paid to this issue by scholars, non-governmental organizations, and other relevant stakeholders, so as to create a shared regulatory regime.[115]

6. Recommendations

There are a number of ways to overcome problems with excessive self-regulation in the area of international judicial education. Three suggestions relate to the general concept of international judicial education and four relate to academic involvement in international judicial education.

6.1 General Recommendations Regarding International Judicial Education

6.1.1 Increasing accountability in international judicial education

The first way to improve the international judicial education regime is to include an element of personal accountability by requiring international judges to meet certain minimal standards regarding judicial education post-appointment.

[112] ibid.
[113] ibid 429–30.
[114] ibid 430.
[115] While most commentary on self-regulation contemplates public-private sector regulatory regimes, one must be careful about state involvement so as to not interfere with judicial independence. ibid 446.

A strong version of this recommendation would indicate not only the minimum number of hours but also the type of coursework that a new or experienced judge would need to undertake to comply with his or her obligations. A weak version of this requirement would only identify the number of hours that need to be completed.

The educational requirement could be made even more meaningful if it were tied to judicial assessment procedures, including either judicial evaluations or needs assessments, similar to the type used in various domestic settings.[116] Although judicial evaluations can trigger concerns about judicial independence, particularly in the international realm, where judges must often be re-appointed or re-elected after a term of years,[117] such mechanisms can nevertheless identify areas where individual or institutional improvement is needed.[118] Judicial assessment mechanisms can also promote the legitimacy of international courts and tribunals by rebutting negative allegations from critics.[119]

Evaluating judicial performance can be extremely difficult, given the number of elements that are outside the judge's control.[120] However, experts in judicial education have developed a number of instruments that can effectively identify the type of judicial programming that would be most useful to judges.[121] In conducting these evaluations, experts should be careful not to rely solely on judicial self-assessment, since that data can be misleading.[122]

6.1.2 Increasing external participation in international judicial education

The second way to improve the international judicial education regime is to increase external input regarding international judicial education. While non-judges have traditionally been excluded from discussions about judicial education because of concerns about judicial independence,[123] experts in judicial studies believe that judicial education actually enhances judicial independence.[124]

[116] Thomas (n 4) 115.

[117] Mackenzie (n 20) 120–21; Joanne M Shepard, 'Are Appointed Judges Strategic Too?' (2009) 58 Duke Law Journal 1589, 1592; Thomas (n 4) at 115. However, judicial evaluations can be used for entirely benign purposes. James B Eaglin and Matthew Alex Ward, 'Enhancing the Administration of Justice and Strengthening Judicial Independence Through Independent, Judicial-Based Research Centers' (2014) 7 Journal of Legal Technology and Risk Management 77, 78–88 (discussing judicial research centres).

[118] Report: Regarding a Judicial Evaluation Form (December 1999) 3 Hawai'i Bar Journal 9; Eaglin and Ward (n 117) 78–88; Shepard (n 117) 1592.

[119] Penny J White, 'Using Judicial Performance Evaluations to Supplement Inappropriate Voter Cues and Enhance Judicial Legitimacy' (2009) 74 Missouri Law Review 635, 652–54.

[120] Strong, Regulatory Capture (n 39) 17–18.

[121] Armytage (n 3) 69–83 (discussing pros and cons of needs assessments as well as various methodologies); see also EJTN, Good Judicial Training Practices <www.ejtn.eu/Resources/Good-judicial-training-practices/> accessed 29 February 2020 (containing various types of needs assessments).

[122] Strong, Regulatory Capture (n 39) 19.

[123] OHCHR/IBA (n 10) 120–35 (discussing both institutional and individual independence).

[124] Eaglin and Ward (n 117) 108; see also Russell Wheeler, *Judicial Administration: Its Relation to Judicial Independence* (National Center for State Courts 1988) 42.

Input should be sought regarding the content of judicial education as well as the question of whether and to what extent mandatory programming is necessary and appropriate.

This approach complies with best practices in judicial education, as illustrated by organizations like Canada's NJI, which has adopted a 'three pillar' approach to judicial education that considers input from judges, academics (including those from multiple fields, such as law, management, adult education, and the social sciences), and the community,[125] and the EJTN, which has also created a broad curriculum built on multidisciplinary and interdisciplinary expertise.[126] Individual judges, most notably US federal appellate Judge Richard Posner, have also supported increased academic participation in judicial education.[127]

6.1.3 Increasing the transparency of international judicial education

The third way to improve international judicial education would be to increase transparency regarding both the content and the process of educating international judges. Although the primary burden for this particular process will likely fall to the academic community, other members of civil society can and should become involved in analysing and developing international judicial education.

At this point, virtually no information exists about how individuals learn to act as international judges, and the 'corporate solidarity' of the international bench makes it difficult to identify what is working and what is not.[128] However, much can be learned from internationally renowned judicial education organizations, such as the FJC, the NJI, and the EJTN, and from the International Organization for Judicial Training (IOJT), which helps facilitate information-sharing about best practices in judicial education.[129]

6.2 Academics' Role in International Judicial Education

After decades of relative neglect, judicial education has begun to garner a certain amount of scholarly interest. However, much has yet to be done, particularly in the international context. Going forward, scholars must work with international judges and specialist research institutes on four related issues.[130] Although this

125 Thomas (n 4) 50. In this context, the 'community' includes lay individuals from the relevant geographic area. Dawson, Pedagogy (n 57) 176, 180.

126 EJTN (n 11) 2, 17–19 (noting that 'keeping abreast of legal matters is essentially a personal task for judges').

127 Richard A Posner, *Divergent Paths: The Academy and the Judiciary* (Harvard University Press 2016) (Posner, *Divergent Paths*).

128 Terris, Romano, and Swigart (n 15) 204–07.

129 International Organization of Judicial Training <www.iojt.org/About-Us.aspx> accessed 29 February 2020.

130 Additional suggestions are available elsewhere. Posner, *Divergent Paths* (n 127); SI Strong, 'Richard A Posner, Divergent Paths: The Academy and the Judiciary – How Legal Academics Can Participate in

work can and likely should build off work done in the domestic setting, it must also take the special needs of the international judiciary into account.

First, academics must consider the often-overlooked question of what it means to be a judge. This issue is critical to questions relating to judicial education, since it is impossible to develop an appropriate curriculum without knowing what it is that judges do. This strand of research can also assist the process of selecting international judgeships, since it will identify the qualities that are needed to succeed as an international judge.

Second, academics need to become much more involved in identifying the goals and purposes of international judicial education. Numerous issues need further investigation, including the ways in which judicial independence is promoted by judicial education and the connection between judicial competence (broadly defined) and the real and perceived legitimacy of international courts.

Third, academics should become involved not only in developing the content of international judicial education but also in the delivery of that content. Judicial education experts in the domestic sphere have relied heavily on research into adult learning practices and the distinctive attributes of judges as learners,[131] and those involved in creating international judicial education programs can use these materials as templates to help create effective and successful programming that meets the needs of new and experienced international judges.

Last but not least, academics need to collaborate with international judges to create a centralized research-based judicial institute similar to those established in domestic settings.[132] Although a number of useful initiatives have been established, including the iCourts program sponsored by the Danish National Research Foundation,[133] the PluriCourts project at the University of Oslo,[134] and the Brandeis Institute for International Judges,[135] these efforts do not address international judicial education per se. Furthermore, they do not reflect the kind of close and permanent collaborative relationship between judges, researchers, and judicial education experts that is the hallmark of leading judicial education institutes. However, these organizations may be well-placed to develop joint competence in judicial research and education in the future.

Judicial Education: A How-To Guide by Richard Posner' (2017) 66 Journal of Legal Education 421, 425–37; Strong, Regulatory Capture (n 39) 16–22.

131 Armytage (n 3) 105–11, 127–30, 137–38.

132 Eaglin and Ward (n 117) 108; Yigal Mersel and Keren Weinshall-Margel, 'Establishing a Judiciary-Based Research Centre: The Israeli Experience' (2014) 2 Journal of the International Organization of Judicial Training 35.

133 iCourts <http://jura.ku.dk/icourts/about/> accessed 29 February 2020.

134 PluriCourts <www.jus.uio.no/pluricourts/english/> accessed 29 February 2020.

135 Brandeis Institute for International Judges <www.brandeis.edu/ethics/internationaljustice/index.html> accessed 29 February 2020.

7. Conclusion

Questions of competence are central to the real and perceived legitimacy of international courts and tribunals. However, the traditional emphasis on judicial selection as a means of ensuring judicial competence has proven insufficient in guaranteeing excellence on the international bench. Fortunately, a solution is at hand: international judicial education.

Developing a program of international judicial education would require collaboration between the international bench, the academic community, and experts in judicial education. However, the benefits of such an initiative would be immeasurable and would have real and immediate effects on the quality and efficiency of international judicial decisions and procedures. Although this Chapter has provided only a brief analysis of some of the more salient issues, hopefully the analysis reflected herein has been sufficient to trigger interest in this vitally important issue.

13

Additional Opinions and Judicial Diversity at the International Court of Justice

A Research Methodology

*Hemi Mistry**

1. Introduction

In the context of international law, there has always been a formal acknowledgement that the identity of judges matters.[1] Traditionally, the degree to which diversity has been embraced has been dictated by the extent to which such diversity has aligned with the interests of the States subject to the jurisdiction of the court or tribunal in question. Thus, the diversity we see on the international bench has been largely along nationality-based lines. This has resulted in judicial diversity on related grounds such as legal culture and political and philosophical orientations. This focus on the State, rather than upon the individual judges per se, has meant that characteristics such as gender, race, ethnicity, and religion have not traditionally featured within the diversity discourse in the international sphere. As this Collection demonstrates, greater attention is now being paid to these latter forms of judicial diversity in the context of international law. While judicial diversity on the basis of race, ethnicity, and religion may have only just entered the mainstream spotlight, the mainstreaming of gender issues within socio-political and legal discourse over the last two to three decades has resulted in (or coincided with) efforts to promote greater gender diversity within the international judiciary. While some courts have made greater strides in this regard than others,[2] there has been little

* All statistics in this paper are accurate as of 1 July 2019. The author wishes to thank Professor Freya Baetens and PluriCourts, organizers of the workshop 'Identity on the International Bench: Workshop 1 – Gender on the Bench' (11–12 January 2018, The Hague)' for which an earlier draft of this chapter was prepared. The author also wishes to thank in particular Judge James Crawford and Professor Andreas Føllesdal for their invaluable comments on that draft, and to the anonymous reviewers for their comments on subsequent drafts.

[1] Evidenced in the 'diversity clauses'; provisions within the statutes of international courts and tribunals setting out the criteria for the composition of the Court. For discussion, see Vera Shikhelman, 'Diversity and Decision-Making in International Judicial Institutions: The United Nations Human Rights Committee as a Case Study' (2018) 36 Berkeley Journal of International Law 60.

[2] A notable example would be the International Criminal Court, where one of the many successes claimed by the feminist advocacy groups during the negotiation and drafting of its Statute was the

Hemi Mistry, *Additional Opinions and Judicial Diversity at the International Court of Justice* In: *Identity and Diversity on the International Bench.* Edited by: Freya Baetens, Oxford University Press (2020). © The several contributors.
DOI: 10.1093/oso/9780198870753.003.0013.

scrutiny of what effect this relatively new form of diversity has had upon international adjudication.

This chapter focuses on (gender) diversity at the International Court of Justice (ICJ). As the principal judicial organ of the United Nations (UN),[3] and in light of its unparalleled general jurisdiction and its unique status as the *only* permanent judicial institution until 2002,[4] the ICJ has historically been the principal prism through which understandings of the functions and nature of international judicial institutions and the role of the international judge have developed.[5] Owing to this historical dominance, and notwithstanding the structural, procedural, and cultural differences between international judicial institutions, ICJ judges have had particular influence upon shaping the 'juridical field', that is, the 'area of structured, socially patterned activity or "practice"' of international judges'.[6] Put differently, in theory, the ICJ (and its institutional predecessor, the Permanent Court of International Justice (PCIJ)) has been at the centre of the development of the 'sets of values, norms, and practices that influence' how international judges, not just those of the ICJ, behave.[7]

Yet, whereas it may have led the way on geographic and nationality-based diversity, on the matter of gender diversity the ICJ has been—at best—a follower rather than a leader. At worst, it might be said that precisely owing to its systemic position the failure of the ICJ to embrace gender diversity until so recently in its long history has served to *reinforce* gender inequalities in the field of international law.[8] Either way, in light of its systemic role and despite (or even, perhaps, owing to) its lack of gender diversity, there is good argument to start any systemic enquiry into the gender diversity in international adjudication with the ICJ.

Section Two elaborates upon the notion of judicial diversity, the rationales for diversity and will explain the extent to which diversity—and, specifically, gender diversity—has been embraced at the ICJ. When developing an understanding

imposition of an obligation upon States Parties to 'take into account the need [for] ... [a] fair representation of female and male judges' when selecting judges (Article 36(8)(a)(iii)). Seven of the first 18 judges appointed to the Court in 2003 were female, while Stefan Barriga, a representative of Liechtenstein, has observed that during the 2011 judicial elections 'male judges were at risk of being underrepresented, which ... led to affirmative action for male candidates (!)'. See, Stefan Barriga, 'Election Rules for ICC Judges: A Balanced Bench Through Quasi-Quotas' (*EJIL:Talk!*, 4 December 2017) <www.ejiltalk.org/election-rules-for-icc-judges-a-balanced-bench-through-quasi-quotas/>accessed 01 July 2019. On current count in July 2019 the ICC has 12 male and 6 female judges.

[3] Charter of the United Nations (adopted 26 June 1945, entered into force 24 October 1945) 1 UNTS XVI (UN Charter) Article 92; Statute of the International Court of Justice (ICJ Statute), Article 1.

[4] Excluding dispute settlement bodies such as the Appellate Body of the World Trade Organisation.

[5] Lyndel V Prott, *The Latent Power of Culture and the International Judge* (Professional Books 1979).

[6] Richard Terdiman, 'The Force of Law: Towards a Sociology of the Juridical Field by Pierre Bourdieu. Translator's Introduction' (1986–1987) 38 Hastings Law Journal 805, 805.

[7] Erik Voeten, 'International Judicial Behaviour' in R C Romano, K Alter, and Y Shany (eds), *The Oxford Handbook of International Adjudication* (OUP 2014) 564.

[8] Hilary Charlesworth, Christine Chinkin, and Shelley Wright, 'Feminist Methods in International Law' (1999) 8 American Journal of International Law 379, 381.

of how female judicial participation has influenced ICJ adjudication one might make recourse to any number of possible of research methods and methodologies. Additional opinions (that is, dissenting opinions, separate opinions, and declarations), as manifestations of the individual judge, are by definition, the public expression of the *individuality* of judges. Therefore, when looking for evidence of the impact of individual judges, and specifically the impact of various diversity characteristics that they possess, we might be inclined to look to additional opinions, particularly those authored individually but also those co-authored by two or more judges.

Section Three examines the relationship between additional opinions and the normative rationales for the diversification of the ICJ bench. When doing so, it shows how additional opinions play an important institutional role in operationalizing diversity in practice. Consequently, additional opinions are undoubtedly a significant and highly relevant subject for study, Yet, when turning to consider how their analysis may assist efforts to evaluate the impact of any individual variable—identity-factor or otherwise—upon additional opinions and, in turn, the processes and outcome of adjudication at the ICJ, the picture becomes more complex. Additional opinions—as expressions of the individual judge—are the site upon which an innumerable number of variables intersect to influence how a judge uses the platform that additional opinions offer. Therefore, while certainly a rich source of data and information about what diversity means in practice, attempts to identify and isolate the causal relationship between any single characteristic of an author of an additional opinion—whether that be, for example, gender, race, ethnicity, disability, or sexual orientation—and the nature, content, and effects of that additional opinion runs the risk of essentialism and an overly reductionist evaluation of the significance of identity-based diversification to international adjudication.[9] This does not mean that additional opinions are not a useful subject of study. Rather, as this chapter concludes, the study of additional opinions through the lens of judicial diversity can help us to build a more nuanced understanding the impact of judicial identity upon the processes and outcomes of international adjudication.

2. Diversity and the ICJ

These days, diversity in the composition of the international judiciary—whether that be in terms of gender, ethnicity, nationality, race, or religion—can often be an assumed 'good'. There are various normative rationales for such diversity.[10] A judiciary whose composition reflects and represents the diversity of those subject to its

[9] Kate Malleson, Justifying Gender Equality on the Bench: Why Difference Won't Do' (2003) 11 Feminist Legal Studies 1, 12–13.

[10] ibid 1–2; and specifically in the context of international adjudication, see Shikhelman (n 1) 67–71.

jurisdiction is a more (democratically) legitimate judiciary.[11] From the perspective of equity and notions of fairness, if individuals with different characteristics are equally capable of performing a function, it can then be asked why should they be excluded from being able to perform those functions?[12] A third rationale—more radical in orientation—focuses upon the substantive contribution that difference can make to improving the quality of the process and outputs of adjudication.[13] Typically, such arguments are premised upon observations of the inequities in society and the manner in which the law generates and perpetuates those inequities, in part by the exclusion of certain categories of actors from legal processes.[14] By increasing participation of individuals representative of those groups historically silenced, oppressed, or subjugated through the law, they are in a position to disrupt the status quo and effect change in the law so as to make it and the society within which is has effect fairer and more just for members of those groups. For example, within domestic legal systems, greater gender diversity can be viewed by some as a mechanism by which structural gender inequalities ingrained within the law and perpetuated by a traditionally male-dominated judiciary and profession, could be remedied.

Alternatively, diversity can have a catalysing effect beyond the bench; rather than the individual judge being the direct agent of change (ie through influencing the decision-making and reasoning of the Court), the presence of difference on the bench and its manifestation as a diverse judiciary can influence the thinking and actions of others by 'render[ing] contingent particular but dominant forms of judicial reasoning' and 'uncovering alternative ways of seeing, understanding and judging'.[15] On this understanding, Erika Rackley explained, 'difference – found in the distinctiveness of perspective and experience – is not an end in itself but rather a route to engendering diverse perspective on adjudication, justice, and law'.[16] There are merits to all these rationales, and while there may be some normative contradictions between them, it is not necessary for the purposes of this paper to resolve any such inconsistencies. Whatever the rationale for the push for greater diversity within the international judiciary, at various times and with varying degrees of alacrity, international courts and tribunals have widened their diversity in ways that align with these different rationales.

In the context of the ICJ its representative diversity is often posited as one of its greatest legitimizing attributes.[17] The ICJ takes a selective representation approach

[11] ibid.

[12] ibid.

[13] ibid.

[14] Marie-Claire Belleau and Rebecca Johnson, 'Judging Gender: Difference and Dissent at the Supreme Court of Canada' (2008) 15 International Journal of the Legal Profession 57, 68.

[15] Erika Rackley, 'What Difference Makes' (2008) 15 International Journal of the Legal Profession 37, 38–39.

[16] ibid 41.

[17] Yuval Shany and Rotem Giladi, 'The International Court of Justice' in Yuval Shany, *Assessing the Effectiveness of International Courts* (OUP 2014) 185; Kenneth Keith, 'The International Court of

to judicial membership, one based upon geographical groupings or legal systems/cultures.[18] Echoing that of the PCIJ, the ICJ Statute stipulates that the composition of the Court as a whole should represent 'the main forms of civilization and of the principal legal systems of the world'.[19] As more nations (and more diverse nations) were embraced within the 'international community' of States and as participants in the international legal system, so too did the diversity of the individual judges that make up the international judiciary. More substantively, this requirement is understood as ensuring that 'the divergent ways of political thought and social action as well as the diverse juridical ideas in the world today' are represented and which feed into and enhance the process of deliberation and decision-making.[20] On this view, diversity strengthens representational legitimacy not simply by mere virtue of presence around the table, a form of 'numerical aestheticism',[21] but because diversity brings to that table a range of experiences and perspectives that are necessary for the Court to understand and operate effectively in the society within which it exists and the context and consequences of its judgments.[22] Looking to the writings (both judicial and extra-judicial) of individual judges, there is support for both the 'equality' and the 'difference' based rationales for diversity. For some, like Taslim Olawale Elias (Nigerian jurist and former ICJ Judge (1976–91) and President of the Court (1982–85)), the participation of judges, whether as scholars or as judges, from newly-independent African States in international legal discourse was driven by the imperative to demonstrate sameness or equality between African States and the European States.[23] The practice of others, such as Alejandro

Justice: Reflections on the Electoral Process' (2010) 9 Chinese Journal of International Law 49, 73–74. However, at the same time it must be acknowledged that the degree to which the diversity requirements translate to substantive plurality and diversity of viewpoints in practice can be questioned, particularly given that most ICJ judges – despite their national origin – will have received at least part of their legal education in Western Europe or the United States of America, thereby affecting their legal philosophy. See Gleider-Hernández,-*The International Court of Justice and the Judicial Function*-(OUP-2014) 133; Georges Abi-Saab, 'The Newly Independent States and the Rules of International Law: An Outline' (1962) 8 Howard Law Journal 95, 100; Michelle Burgis, *Boundaries of Discourse in the International Court of Justice: Mapping Arguments in Arab Territorial Disputes* (Brill 2009) 23.

[18] Ruth Mackenzie and others (eds), *Selecting International Judges: Principle, Process, and Politics* (OUP 2010) 7–8.

[19] ICJ Statute, Article 9.

[20] Taslim Olawale Elias, 'Report on "Does the International Court of Justice, as it is Presently Shaped, Correspond to the Requirements which Follow from its Function as the Central Body of the International Community?"' in Max Planck Institute for International and Comparative Law, *Judicial Settlement of International Disputes: International Court of Justice, other Courts and Tribunals, Arbitration and Conciliation: An International Symposium* (Springer 1974) 23.

[21] Rackley (n 15) 40.

[22] The degree to which representational legitimacy is valued within the ICJ context is embodied by the retention of the system of *ad hoc* judges. See *Application of the Convention on the Prevention and Punishment of Genocide* (*Bosnia and Herzegovina v Serbia and Montenegro*) (Further Requests for the Provision of Additional Measures) [1993] ICJ Rep 325, Separate Opinion of Judge *ad hoc* Lauterpacht, 409.

[23] C L Lim, 'Neither Sheep Nor Peacocks: T. O. Elias and Post-Colonial International Law' (2008) 21 Leiden Journal of International Law 295.

Álvarez (ICJ Judge 1946–1955), was more influenced by the 'difference'-based conception of diversity.[24] On this view, by participating in international adjudication, judges from semi-peripheral and peripheral States could influence changes in international law to reflect not only the interests of central (ie primarily European) but also those of States at the (semi)-periphery.[25]

2.1 The ICJ and Gender Diversity

While there has long been a recognition of the value of diversity at the ICJ, the discussion has been relatively silent on gender diversity specifically. The matter of gender diversity in the international legal profession—whether that be among judges or other participants in the international legal system—only emerged on the international law agenda in the 1990s and 2000s.[26] Writing in 1999, Hilary Charlesworth, Christine Chinkin, and Shelley Wright noted how, historically, gender perspectives on international law and international adjudication were overlooked (with the notable exception of international human rights law) since the traditional focuses of intentional law—sovereignty, territorial integrity, use of force and State responsibility—were issues that were assumed not to have a gender dimension.[27] The first female judge to participate as a judge in ICJ proceedings was Suzanne Bastid who—in 1985—sat as an ad hoc judge.[28] The first *permanent* ICJ judge (Dame Rosalyn Higgins) was not appointed until a decade later, in 1995, who also went on to become the Court's first (and, so far, only) female President in 2006. Since Judge Higgins' appointment to the Court, the ICJ has seen six further female judges at the ICJ: four as ad hoc Judges (Judges Christine van den Wyngaert,[29] Hilary Charlesworth,[30] Louise Arbour,[31] and Navanethem

[24] ibid. See also Liliana Obregón, 'Noted for Dissent: The International Life of Alejandro Álvarez' (2006) 19 Leiden Journal of International Law 983.

[25] For this notion of the 'periphery' and 'semi-periphery' see Arnulf Becker Lorca, *Mestizo International Law* (CUP 2014). Mohammed Bedjaoui, 'From an Oligarchic Law to a Law of Community' in Mohammed Bedjaoui (ed), *International Law: Achievements and Prospects* (Martinus Nijhoff 1991) 5–11; Goerges Abi-Saab, 'The International Court as a World Court' in Vaughan Lowe and Malgozia Fitzmaurice (eds), *Fifty Years of the International Court of Justice* (CUP 1996); Edward McWhinney *The World Court and the Contemporary Law-Making Process* (Sijthoff and Noordhoff 1979); Nagendra-Singh,-*The Role and Record of the International Court of Justice*-(Martinus Nijhoff-1989) 257; Anthony Anghie, *Imperialism, Sovereignty and the Marking of International Law* (CUP 2007) 198.

[26] Generally, and for references, see Mackenzie and others (n 18) 161.

[27] Charlesworth, Chinkin, and Wright (n 8) 614.

[28] *Application for Revision and Interpretation of the Judgment of 24 February 1982 in the Case Concerning the Continental Shelf (Tunisia/Libyan Arab Jamahiriya)* (*Tunisia v Libyan Arab Jamahiriya*) (Judgment) [1985] ICJ Rep 192 (appointed by Tunisia).

[29] *Arrest Warrant of 11 April 2000* (*Democratic Republic of Congo v Belgium*) (Judgment) [2002] ICJ Rep 3 (appointed by Belgium).

[30] *Whaling in the Antarctic* (*Australia v Japan, New Zealand intervening*) (Judgment) [2014] ICJ Rep 226 (appointed by Australia) and *Arbitral Award of 3 October 1899* (*Guyana v Venezuela*) (Application Instituting Proceedings of 29 March 2018) (appointed by Guyana).

[31] *Obligation to Negotiate Access to the Pacific Ocean* (*Bolivia v Chile*) (Judgment) (appointed by Chile).

Pillay[32]) and a further three as permanent judges. Judges Xue Hanqin and Joan Donoghue joined the Court in 2010 and Judge Julia Sebutinde in 2012. All three are incumbents on the Court, and Judge Xue has been Vice-President of the Court since February 2018.[33]

Little has been written upon the rationale for gender diversity at the ICJ. Among academics, Hilary Charlesworth and Christine Chinkin have written about the symbolic and representational legitimacy brought about by female participation in the ICJ proceedings.[34] Speaking extra-judicially, President Higgins has tended towards the equality-based rationale for gender diversity, downplaying the significance of her gender to her membership and activities on the Court and instead emphasizing her expertise and experience that qualified her for judicial office at the ICJ.[35] In contrast, Judge Sebutinde has more recently adopted a participatory approach to justifying gender diversity on the ICJ.[36] Taking a purposive view of the Court's systemic function, Judge Sebutinde drew upon UN Security Council Resolution 1325, which mandates that Member States of the UN must ensure women participate on an equal basis to men in the advancement of international peace and security,[37] in order to argue for female participation in the ICJ. By invoking Resolution 1325, she drew upon the Resolution's recognition of the significance of women's experience and perspectives of conflicts, conflict resolution, and peacebuilding and the importance of ensuring their equal participation in conflict resolution and peacebuilding.[38] Through her invocation of Resolution 1325, Judge Sebutinde signalled the international community's acceptance that the female experience and perspective *should* contribute to the maintenance and restoration of international peace and security—including through judicial means. On this understanding not only is female participation in the judicial process 'right' from the perspective of the equality of the individual judge, but it also contributes towards enhancing the effectiveness of dispute resolution by the ICJ.

Against the backdrop of the relative dearth of literature on the contribution of gender diversity at the ICJ, this chapter asks how the study of the individual

[32] *Application of the Convention on the Prevention and Punishment of the Crime of Genocide (The Gambia v Myanmar)* (Application instituting proceedings and Request for the indication of provisional measures) 11 November 2019 (appointed by The Gambia).

[33] Note, both Judge Xue Hanqin and Judge Julia Sebutinde's current terms of office are due to expire on 5 February 2021. Both have been nominated for re-election. See, UNGA, 'Election of members of the International Court of Justice: list of nominations by national groups' (29 June 2020) UN Doc A/75/129-S/2020/615. There is one further female nominee, Maja Seršić (Croatia).

[34] Hilary Charlesworth and Christine Chinkin, *The Boundaries of International Law: A Feminist Analysis* (Manchester University Press 2000) 81.

[35] Amrin Amin and Cheah Wuiling, 'In Conversation: An Interview with Her Excellency Judge Rosalyn Higgins' (2002) 22 Singapore Law Review 2.

[36] American Society of International Law, 'Plenary Discussion: A Conversation with International Court of Justice Judges Joan Donoghue, Julia Sebutinde, and Xue Hanqin' (2014) 108 American Society of International Law Proceedings 383, 387.

[37] UNSC Res 1325 (31 October 2000) UN Doc S/RES/1325.

[38] ibid, preambular para 5, and paras 1 and 2.

practice of individual female judges when issuing additional opinions might contribute to enhancing understanding of the nature of that contribution.

3. Additional Opinions and Judicial Diversity

When seeking to understand the 'impact' of female judicial participation at the ICJ we could be speaking of both their contribution to (1) the processes and outcomes of ICJ adjudication specifically; and (2) more broadly to the development of international law. From both perspectives, a lawyer's principal subject of analysis would be the jurisprudence of the Court, the publicly available written account of the Court's decision-making activities.[39] One might subject this jurisprudence to a range of analytical methods—whether that be qualitative textual analysis,[40] quantitative analysis,[41] or a mixture of both.[42] When focusing specifically on the jurisprudential *output* of the Court, the analysis of the Court's judgments, advisory opinions, or interlocutory orders ('decisions' unless otherwise stated) is unlikely to prove fruitful for the purpose of tracing the manner in which individual judges have contributed to it.[43] Decisions pronounced in the name of the Court are—by design—designed to obscure the individuals behind it: they are written by the drafting Committee in a 'disembodied, collective voice' and finalized by the plenary bench.[44] However, one of the defining characteristics of the Court's jurisprudence is the plurality of individual and joint opinions that are invariably issued alongside the univocal decision of the Court. It is these opinions—rather than the Court's decisions—that offer a window both into the contribution of individual judges to adjudication and to the wider development of international law.

[39] As Judge Crawford observes in this collection (Chapter 20), non-text based methods might include the ethnographic study of oral hearings to observe how female judges conduct themselves in the course of hearings and how other judges and counsel interact with the Court in general and female judges in particular. Insights into the impact of female judges to judicial deliberations is somewhat more limited, owing to secrecy of deliberations. However, interviews with judges – both male and female – to ascertain their experience of deliberations where there has (and has not) been female judicial participation would be a gainful method. Similarly, interviews with those who appear before the ICJ may provide insight into the extent to which the experience of appearing before the Court has been influenced by the gender composition of the bench, and how that influences their argumentative practices.

[40] For an example of a discourse analysis of argumentative practices of parties to disputes before the ICJ and, in turn, the judgments, advisory opinions and additional opinions issued by the Court and its members in those disputes, see Burgis (n 17).

[41] For recent quantitative work and the use of 'network analysis' to track citation patterns in, *inter alia*, the jurisprudence of the ICJ, see N Ridi, 'The Shape and Structure of the 'Useable Past': An Empirical Analysis of the Use of Precedent in International Adjudication' (2019) 10 Journal of International Dispute Settlement 200.

[42] An example from the context of international criminal tribunals is N Stappart, 'A New Influence of Legal Scholars? The Use of Academic Writings at International Criminal Courts and Tribunals (2018) 31 Leiden Journal of International Law 963.

[43] On the limits of the Court's judgment as a window into the impact of gender diversity, see Charlesworth and Chinkin (n 32) 82.

[44] Hernández (n 17) 95.

The discussion that follows aims to achieve two different things. First, it sets out how additional opinions support or advance the normative rationales for (gender) diversity. Second, it explores the utility of their analysis to empirically verify (or refute) the impact of diversity upon international adjudication and international law.

3.1 A Spectrum of Differences

Additional opinions are written texts attached to court decisions under a plethora of guises: 'dissenting opinions', 'separate opinions', 'minority opinions', 'individual opinions', 'declarations', and permutations thereof are all familiar terms by which additional opinions are referred to within the wider context of international adjudication. They can be authored by individual judges or jointly, by two or more judges. At the ICJ, judges confined the labels that they use to describe their opinions to those terms found in the Court's Statute and Rules: dissenting opinion, separate opinion, and declaration.[45] Irrespective of the label assigned to them, all additional opinions share the purpose of being a platform upon which judges can express their personal views on aspects of a case as distinct from that of 'the Court', as expressed in the judgment.[46]

Additional opinions, as spaces both created and occupied by difference, are beyond the courtroom—both geographically and temporally—the primary public manifestation of 'the individual' international judge. From the perspective of the individual judge, the level of discretion afforded to judges to determine how (and indeed, whether) they utilize their right to issue additional opinions means that they offer judges—as individuals—an unparalleled and platform upon which to communicate with the authority of an ICJ judge to the wider international law-making and -interpreting community. That communication may by its very fact have an expressive or symbolic function;[47] quite apart from their substantive content the additional opinion is a public performance of that judge's membership of the Court and participation in its activities, in turn lending credence to the Court's claims to participatory and representative legitimacy.[48] From the perspective of gender diversity, although gender diversity is not a *formal requirement* under the Court's Statute,[49] gender diversity may be normative (if not yet an empirically verified) criterion for institutional legitimacy.

[45] ICJ Statute, Article 57 and ICJ Rules of Court (adopted 14 April 1978, entered into force 1 July 1978), Articles 95(2) and 107(3).

[46] For a more detailed discussion of the institutional significance of additional opinions in the context of the ICJ, see H Mistry, '"The Different Sets of Ideas at the Back of Our Heads": Dissent and Authority at the International Court of Justice' (2019) 32 Leiden Journal of International Law 293.

[47] Charlesworth and Chinkin (n 32).

[48] For a detailed account of how additional opinions interact with institutional legitimacy and authority, see Mistry (n 44) and for a ritual theory of judicial dissent in international law, see H. Mistry, *Rebellious Jurisprudence: Judicial Dissent and International Law* (under contract, Hart).

[49] ICJ Statute, Article 9.

Representational and participatory legitimacy aside, from the perspective of diversity as an agent of change—either directly through participation in and influencing internal deliberation and decision-making or indirectly by catalysing change-agents beyond the bench—additional opinions are a means of judicial empowerment. Internally, the prospect of the publication of a critical dissenting opinion could incentivize a majority to, if not accommodate or adopt compromise to satisfy the putative dissenter, then at least to pre-empt the dissent and include stronger analysis to refute the dissentient critique.[50]

From an indirect perspective, the platform offered by additional opinions empowers individuals to contribute to wider international legal discourses with the authority of an ICJ judge. Individual ICJ judges possess semantic authority, that is, the capacity to 'shape meanings as well as the ability to establish its communications as authoritative reference points in legal discourse'.[51] The semantic authority of any actor is a function of three variables: the first is the nature and substantive content of the expression of power; second are the interests and standards of legitimacy held by the 'accepting' actor, and third are the particular attributes of the power-wielding actor.[52] The consequence of this semantic authority, as Venzke has explained, is to 'increase an actor's capacity to create and its faculty to control – to make law and to constrain by way of law'.[53] While the ICJ, through its judgments and opinions, has a high degree of semantic authority, the semantic authority of an individual judge can only be determined on a case-by-case basis, in light of the substantive content of their opinion and the degree of authority that the law-interpreting actor accords to individual judges. Nevertheless, at a minimum that individual ICJ judges possess a certain degree of authority simply because they hold the title, or the hold the office of, 'judge'.[54]

As ICJ judges from semi-peripheral and newly-independent States demonstrated during the 1950s, 1960s, and 1970s demonstrated, the platform offered by additional opinions can be used by judges to highlight the contingencies of mainstream international law; to highlight its euro-centricity and to invite participants in the international legal community to think about international law from different perspectives.[55] Where the circumstances of the case deem it appropriate,

[50] Hugh Thirlway, 'The Drafting of ICJ Decisions: Some Personal Recollections and Observations' (2006) 5 Chinese Journal of International Law 15, at 19.

[51] Ingo Venzke, *How Interpretation Makes International Law: On Semantic Change and Normative Twists* (OUP 2012) 63.

[52] ibid.

[53] ibid.

[54] Max Weber, *Economy and Society: An Outline of Interpretive Sociology*, vol 1 (UCP 1978) 219; Belleau and Johnson (n 14) 59.

[55] In addition to Judges Alvarez and Elias previously mentioned (see text accompanying n.24–26), see the Separate Opinions by Judge Ammoun in, *inter alia*, the advisory proceedings in *Legal Consequences for States of the Continued Presence of South Africa in Namibia (South West Africa) Notwithstanding Security Council 276 (1970)* (Advisory Opinion) [1971] ICJ Rep 16 and *Western Sahara* (Advisory Opinion) [1975] ICJ Rep 12.

additional opinions offer similar opportunities for judges to highlight aspects of international law and its operation that their personal experiences by reason of aspects of their identity—such as, say, race or gender—that may not be appreciated by those who have not shared those experiences. By doing this, not only do judges deepen understanding of the nature and effect of international law, but their opinions can empower out-of-court participants in international legal discourse by providing them with authoritative support for their legal argumentation and advocacy within other fora—whether academic, policy, or adjudicatory—in their efforts to promote change in the law.[56]

While the individual judge may have failed in the course of deliberations to persuade their colleagues of their view, a powerful additional opinion will shape the appraisal by other participants in the international law-making process of the Court's semantic authority for the purposes of the correct articulation of the law.[57] To this end, Sir Franklin Berman stated 'with confidence that an ICJ bench that tried to be too adventurous would find its judgment encircled by an array of trenchant separate or dissenting opinions that would weigh in as a useful corrective in the process of absorbing the judgment into the international bloodstream'.[58] Similarly, former ICJ judge, Mohamed Shahabuddeen, identified a 'precedential value' of additional opinions in their potential to reveal a 'false consensus' as the basis of the Court's judgment.[59] Using the *Lotus* case as an example, he demonstrated how separate opinions can reveal how the Court's judgment can contain a statement of the law which is in fact rejected by half of the members of the Bench.[60]

It is clear, therefore, that irrespective of which conception of diversity one has in mind, additional opinions are a valuable institutional mechanism through which the objectives behind diversification can be advanced. At the same time, it is necessary to consider how we might analyse and interpret additional opinions for the purposes of evaluating both the impact of diversification in general and the impact of the participation of individuals bearing particular identity characteristics upon the ICJ. Here, matters start to become more complex. Certainly, a content analysis of additional opinions would help us identify how judges work within the space of difference.[61] A doctrinal legal analysis of which issues of law and procedure individual judges have written on, and the substantive views on those

[56] On the 'out of court leverage' offered by judicial pronouncements, see Karen Alter, *The New Terrain of International Law* (Princeton University Press 2014) 19.

[57] Mita Manouvel, *Les Opinions Séparées à la Cour Internationale: Un Instrument de Contrôle du Droit International Prétorien par les Etats* (L'Harmattan 2005).

[58] Franklin Berman, 'The International Court of Justice as an "Agent" of Legal Development' in Christian Tams and James Sloan (eds), *The Development of International Law by the International Court of Justice* (OUP 2013) 13; Rainer Hofmann and Tilmann Laubner, 'Article 57' in Andreas Zimmermann and others (eds), *The Statute of the International Court of Justice: A Commentary* (2nd edn, OUP 2012) 1397.

[59] Mohamed Shahabuddeen, *Precedent in the World Court* (CUP 1996) 180.

[60] ibid.

[61] Belleau and Johnson (n 14) 66.

matters would reveal which areas of international law those judges are most engaged with—whether that be from the perspective of their activities on the Court or their contributions to wider international legal discourse—and which areas they are less so. Reading additional opinions through the prism of different theoretical approaches—such as feminist theory, critical theory, or perhaps drawing upon insights from law and literature—can help uncover different qualities of judicial practice, which may be unseen through 'traditional' doctrinal analysis alone.[62] Methods drawn from other disciplines, such as linguistic discourse analysis, will reveal *how* individual judges communicate using additional opinions and will allow the comparison between their styles of communication with that of their colleagues.[63]

Beyond qualitative analysis, there may also be utility in recourse to quantitative methods when looking at the practice of issuing (or perhaps, not issuing) additional opinions. For example, taken together the simple metrics of the (1) issue rate of additional opinions; and (2) page length of individual opinions, can together offer an insight into the 'vocality' of individual judges. Such analysis can be of interest from the perspective of diversity discourse in a number of ways. From the perspective of representational and participatory diversity—if the visibility of the female judge is something that strengthens the legitimacy of the ICJ and its decisions—we might hypothesize that when it comes to additional opinions, more is better. If the practice of female judges is disproportionately lower than that of their male counterparts, this may warrant further investigation via other, qualitative methods order to understand *why* female judges have or are making less recourse to additional opinions. From the perspective of international law and its development through the jurisprudence of the Court, a quantitative analysis of how prolific individual judges are—both in terms of frequency and page length—can supplement our content analysis of the substantive of opinions, to understand the nature of the contributions to international legal discourse. Are particular individual judges using additional opinions in order to write lengthy and comprehensive treatises on a range of matters raised by the case at hand? Alternatively, are they more laconic: writing less frequently and/or shorter and more focused opinions?

While labels assigned to additional opinions might be descriptively arbitrary,[64] they can nevertheless be normatively significant. A quantitative analysis of the labelling practices of individual judges—how they style their opinions, and

[62] Andrea Bianchi, *'International Law Theories: An Inquiry into Different Ways of Thinking* (OUP 2016).

[63] On the rhetoric of dissent, see Erin Rand, 'Fear the Frill: Ruth Bader Ginsburg and the Uncertain Futurity of Feminist Judicial Dissent' (2015) 101 Quarterly Journal of Speech 72; Robert Ferguson, 'The Judicial Opinion as a Literary Genre' (2013) 2 Yale Journal of Law and the Humanities 204; Gerald Wetlaufer, 'Rhetoric and its Denial in Legal Discourse' (1990) 76 Virginia Law Review 1555; Katie Gibson, 'In Defense of Women's Rights: A Rhetorical Analysis of Judicial Dissent' (2012) 35 Women's Studies in Communication 123.

[64] For discussion, see Mistry (n 44).

themselves—might be one method of exploring individual judicial identity: how judges wish themselves to be perceived in relation to the institution of which they are a member.[65] A judge who frequently labels their opinion (and, by extension, themselves) as 'dissenting' or 'separate' may, for example, be perceived as an 'outsider' on the Court,[66] with the labels of their opinions highlighting the difference or disagreement between its author and the Court. By contrast, a judge who rarely uses the labels 'dissenting' and 'separate' and instead prefers to use the neutral label of 'declaration' (or indeed does not issue additional opinions at all) could be perceived to be downplaying their difference or individuality in relation to the Court. To the extent that any patterns or trends can be detected, recourse to supplementary methods—such as content analysis of opinions and interviews with judges to ascertain the subjective motives informing labelling practice—could help explain those trends.[67]

However, while it may be the case that additional opinions may be subjected to a variety of methods of analysis that can help us to describe what judges bearing particularly identity characteristics do, while they may prompt us to make certain hypotheses and can help us to identify further research questions, the answers to which can help us test those hypotheses, these methods cannot tell us (1) the effectiveness with which those judges have utilized additional opinions; or (2) the causal link between any identity-characteristic and the nature, content, or effect of an additional opinion.

In terms of effectiveness, quite often the evidence of their effect—if there is any evidence to be found—is found elsewhere. When considering the use of additional opinions to influence the deliberations and decision-making of the Court, evidence of the successful leveraging of an additional opinion is—in principle—more likely to be found in the Court's decision, rather than in the additional opinion. Yet for reasons discussed earlier in this section, it is unlikely that this could be easily discerned from an ICJ judgment.[68] From this perspective, one might ultimately interpret an additional opinion—in particular a dissenting opinion—as evidence of the failure of an individual judge to exercise their power in the course of deliberations: that they are a 'space of failed possibilities'.[69] Of course, this too could be informative. If dissenting opinions are 'spaces of failed possibilities',[70] a pattern of routine dissent or of being repeatedly in the minority may suggest that the judge

[65] Belleau and Johnson (n 14) 66.

[66] On the connotations associated with the term 'dissent', see Mistry (n 46).

[67] An excellent example of a mixed methods analysis of individual judicial practice, combining the triangulation of quantitative and qualitative analysis of voting practices, additional opinions and Court judgments, and interviews with current and former members of a Court is A Paterson, *Final Judgment: The Last Law Lords and The Supreme Court* (Hart 2013).

[68] Although, for reasons mentioned (text accompanying n.43) there would be little evidence in the Court's judgment to attribute its contents to a particular judge.

[69] Belleau and Johnson (n 14) 67.

[70] ibid.

is an 'outsider' to the decision-making process.[71] Looking beyond the internal dynamics within the Court, given the ostensibly representative composition of the Court's bench, this perception of 'exclusion' may extend beyond the individual judge in relation to the Court to the conception of international law that their additional opinions represent, in relation to the 'mainstream' of international law.[72] By contrast, a judge who infrequently writes individually may create the perception that they are an effective 'power-broker' within the Court's deliberations: they do not *need* to write individually because they have successfully exerted their power within deliberations in order to secure the reflection of their views in the Court's judgment. Turning to additional opinions as catalysts of change beyond the courtroom, to find evidence of the effectiveness with which they are deployed for this purpose it is necessary to look elsewhere for reference to and use of those opinions by other actors (litigants, courts and judges, academics, students) in their legal argumentation.[73]

More to the point, however, is the matter of isolating the causal relationship between 'what judges do' and any individual identity-characteristic, such as gender. While—for example—content analysis and quantitative analysis may tell us what judges who bear particular attributes have been doing while members of the Court, and while it may help identify patterns in that practice, such methods of analysis do not tell us the extent to which those attributes explain that practice. Moreover, the relational nature of additional opinions—in that they have meaning only in the context of the judgments against which they stand in opposition to—requires the consideration of whether patterns in judicial practice reflect a change in the author's thinking, or a change in that of the majority from which they depart.[74] While it is one thing to state that additional opinions are an expression of difference, it would be wrong to assume a relationship between the difference represented in and by the opinion and the differences embodied in the opinion's author. Specific personal characteristics such as gender can conceivably influence the manner in which individual judges utilize the right to issue additional opinions, but the practice of judges is likely to be the result of a number of intersecting characteristics or attributes. These may include 'political outlooks, philosophical tendencies and ideological and cultural affinities'.[75] ICJ judges are drawn from a particularly

[71] ibid, referring to the work of P McCormick, *Supreme At Last: The Evolution of the Supreme Court of Canada* (James Lorimer & Co 2000) 138.

[72] One might argue that this is the case with the jurisprudence of Judge Cançado Trindade at the ICJ and the conception of international law that he espouses in his separate opinions. His voluminous additional opinions simply serve to highlight just how peripheral his particular human-centric conception of international law is. See M Milanovic, 'Judging Judges: A Statistical Exercise' (*EJIL:Talk!*, 12 March 2012) <http://www.ejiltalk.org/judging-judges-a-statistical-exercise/> accessed 1 July 2019.

[73] See the growing body of empirical scholarship looking at citation practices and footnote-analysis, eg Stappart (n 40), Ridi (n 38) and L Boer, '"The Greater Part of Jurisconsults": On Consensus Claims and Their Footnotes in Legal Scholarship' (2016) 29 Leiden Journal of International Law 1021.

[74] Belleau and Johnson (n 14) 64.

[75] Charlesworth and Chinkin (n 32) 82.

narrow social field, in terms of educational background, wealth, class, and age.[76] Candidates for judicial office at the ICJ must not only bear the requisite level of experience and expertise,[77] but must also must possess sufficient professional social and political capital to secure their success in the nomination and election process,[78] and sufficient mastery of 'English as the lingua franca of international law' to participate effectively in ICJ proceedings.[79] Consequently—irrespective of their gender, race, religion, sexual orientation, or disability, or any other typical identity characteristic—ICJ judges embody a highly socialized and professionally homogenous elite.[80]

Other factors include professional background, legal-cultural background, and the capacity in which a judge is participating in the case (ie whether they are a permanent judge or an ad hoc judge and, if they are a permanent judge, whether they are a national of a party to the case). Judges who hail from a civil law background, where additional opinions are commonly understood to be inconsistent with institutional authority and undermining of it,[81] may be less inclined to issue additional opinions than those judges hailing from the common law tradition where additional opinions as expressions of individual judicial authority are not only considered consistent with institutional authority, but to a certain degree constitutive of it.[82] Similarly, the professional background of judges may also influence their practices when writing individually. Whereas those judges whose professional identity was cultivated in the civil service may be less inclined towards expressing their personal views when discharging their professional role, those judges with an academic background will be more accustomed to expressing their own view independent of the institution to which they affiliated.[83] Within international law

[76] Malleson (n 9) at 12.

[77] ICJ Statute, Article 2.

[78] Keith (n 17); D. Akande, 'ICJ Elections 2017: UN General Assembly and Security Council Elect Four Judges to the ICJ But Fail to Agree on a Fifth, Yet Again! + Trivia Question' (*EJIL:Talk!* 11 November 2017)<www.ejiltalk.org/icj-elections-2017-un-general-assembly-and-security-council-elect-four-judges-to-the-icj-but-fail-to-agree-on-a-fifth-yet-again-trivia-question/>accessed 1 July 2019.

[79] Jean d'Aspremont, 'The Professionalisation of International Law' in Jean d'Aspremont and others (eds), *International Law as a Profession* (CUP 2017) at 35.

[80] ibid.

[81] Mirjan Damaška, *The Faces of Justice and State Authority: A Comparative Approach to the Legal Process* (Yale University Press 1986) 18–23; John Merryman, *The Civil Law Tradition: An Introduction to the Legal Systems of Europe and Latin America* (Stanford University Press 1985); transposed to the ICJ context, see Gilbert Guillaume, 'Some Thoughts on the Independence of International Judges Vis-à-Vis States' (2003) 2 Law and Practice of International Courts and Tribunals 163, 166.

[82] Damaška (n 79) 24; William Brennan, 'In Defense of Dissents' (1985) 37 Hastings Law Journal 427; Lord Browne, cited by Brian Kerr, 'Dissenting Judgments – Self Indulgence or Self Sacrifice?' (*The Birkenhead Lecture*, 8 October 2012) <www.supremecourt.uk/docs/speech-121008.pdf>accessed 1 July 2019; Brenda Hale, 'Judgment Writing in the Supreme Court' (First Anniversary Seminar, 30 September 2010)<www.supremecourt.uk/docs/speech_100930.pdf>accessed 1 July 2019, 2; Claire L'Heureux-Dubé, 'The Dissenting Opinion: Voice of the Future?' (2000) 38 Osgoode Hall Law Journal 495, 513; Michael Kirby, 'Judicial Dissent' (*James Cook University*, 26 February 2005) <www.hcourt.gov.au/assets/publications/speeches/former-justices/kirbyj/kirbyj_feb05.html>accessed 1 July 2019.

[83] Alternatively, judges from a civil service legal background are – perhaps – more likely to be generalist international lawyers, rather than academics who may have over the course of their academic

academia too, the privilege enjoyed by particular academic cultural traditions in academic publishing may be reproduced in the context of which academics attain the professional prominence and 'capital' required to secure their nomination and election to the Court.[84] Nevertheless, even if characteristics other than gender are more directly influential upon their practice with regard to additional opinions, this does not preclude the indirect relevance of gender to that practice. If, for example, particular judicial systems bearing particular legal-cultural attributes or particular professions have been historically more facilitative of female career progression,[85] then one might hypothesize that female ICJ judges are more likely to come from those backgrounds that might lead to greater reticence when it comes to additional opinions. If this is the case, then the potential that additional opinions offer for the projection of the female judicial voice—both institutionally and systemically—may not be realized.

Finally, given the comparatively small population size of female judges at the ICJ in comparison to that of male judges, any study aimed at ascertaining the impact of gender upon judicial practice would be purely descriptive in nature: its aim can only be to describe and explain the behaviour of the particular judges that have sat on the Court. While it may—depending upon the data—be possible to identify patterns in the practice within that population, it would be inappropriate to extrapolate or generalize further, beyond that population.

4. Conclusion

The purpose of this chapter has been to reintroduce additional opinions both as a vehicle for the expression of judicial diversity and their analysis as a methodology for the appraisal of the impact of different forms of diversity upon the processes and outcomes of ICJ adjudication. On the first point, whether speaking in terms of equality, participatory and representative legitimacy, or whether we are

career carved out an area of highly specialised expertise. Thus, academics are more likely to author lengthier and more detailed additional opinions on specific issues raised by a case that fall within their area of expertise, in comparison to the governmental lawyer-judge. On the differences in the approach to judging based upon professional background, see American Society of International Law (n 34) 388–99 (Judges Donoghue and Sebutinde).

[84] Alonso Gurmendi and Paula Baldini Miranda da Cruz, 'Writing in International Law and Cultural Barriers (Part I)' (*Opinio Juris*, 7 August 2020) <www.opiniojuris.org/2020/08/07/writing-in-international-law-and-cultural-barriers-part-i/>accessed 17 August 2020. As discussed by Gurmendi and Baldini Miranda da Cruz, even if judges conforming to more 'peripheral' legal academic writing styles do make it onto the Court, the dominance of particular conventions may reduce the likelihood that their additional opinions will be engaged with by the 'mainstream' of international law, accustomed as it is to a particular style of legal writing.

[85] Ulrike Schultz and Giselle Shaw, 'Editorial: Gender and Judging' (2008) 15 International Journal of the Legal Profession 1, 2–3; see also Chapter 10, Helen Keller, Corina Heri and Myriam Christ, Fifty years of women at the European Court of Human Rights: successes and failure of the Council of Europe's gender agenda.

speaking with a more radical orientation towards change, the expressive and functional operation of additional opinions make them an important site upon which the normative objectives underpinning the diversification of the international judiciary—whether that be on the grounds of gender or other identities, such as race, ethnicity, or religion—are advanced. With this in mind, additional opinions *must* be a subject of analysis for those seeking to understand the implications of identity and diversity on the international bench. However, this takes us to the second point: what their analysis can—and cannot—tell us.

In this regard, this chapter has demonstrated that the interpretation of additional opinions for the purposes of evaluating the impact of any individual identity borne by their authors should be undertaken with caution. Additional opinions are the product of the intersection of innumerable factors and a complex institutional process, and the accurate interpretation of additional opinions for the purpose of ascertaining the influence of one variable—such as gender identity—cannot be undertaken by isolating that variable from those other intersecting factors. This does not mean that the additional opinions are not a fruitful subject for analysis. To the contrary, precisely because of this complexity, the study of additional opinions, which includes not just their substantive content but also the processes of which they are an output and the processes into which they feed, offers the opportunity to build a richer and more nuanced understanding of how identity intersects and interacts with other variables (such as professional background, nationality, legal-philosophical culture) and to what ends. While we must exercise caution when drawing inferences from judicial practice, additional opinions force us to confront the multidimensional nature of identity and its impact upon professional life of the individuals who comprise the international bench and upon the regimes and systems of international adjudication and international law.

14

Citing Religious Texts in Individual Opinions to Judgments of the International Court of Justice

Do Judges Incorporate Their Religious Identity in Judicial Decision-Making?

*Mubarak Waseem**

1. Introduction

In its judgments, the International Court of Justice ('the Court' or 'the ICJ') rarely cites from documents outside the primary and subsidiary sources of law enumerated in its Statute. However, this citational conservatism is not as prevalent in the Separate and Dissenting Opinions of the Court's judges. In those individual opinions, ICJ judges have been known to cite from a wider range of texts, both legal and otherwise.[1] This chapter explores one particular narrow sub-set of that wider range of texts—religious texts—and proceeds in three steps. First, it sets out the methodology used to obtain the data set for this study. Secondly, it discusses whether any patterns or correlations can be divined from the (infrequent) use of religious texts in the Court's judgments and individual opinions, and importantly whether there is any link between the citation of religious texts and the identity of those judges citing them. Thirdly, it explores the normative argument that the citation of religious sources can bring important benefits to the judgments of the Court. As a preliminary note: for the purpose of this chapter, the term 'religious texts' refers not only to sacred texts (eg the Torah, the Bible, and the Qur'an), but also to texts on religion, whether these are academic texts which expand upon the

* This chapter is dedicated to the memory of Professor David D. Caron, a mentor and a friend, who always encouraged us to look at the virtue behind the law. His lessons, qualities and virtues were an inspiration to all those who knew him. Thanks also to Andrew Brown and Caleb Kirton for their research assistance. I owe you both a Nando's. Finally, thank you to Professor Michael Peil for the invaluable use of his database, as explained below. All errors and misstatements remain, of course, my own.

[1] Michael Peil, 'Scholarly Writings as a Source of Law: A Survey of the Use of Doctrine by the International Court of Justice' (2012) 1(3) Cambridge Journal of International and Comparative Law 136.

Mubarak Waseem, *Citing Religious Texts in Individual Opinions to Judgments of the International Court of Justice* In: *Identity and Diversity on the International Bench.* Edited by: Freya Baetens, Oxford University Press (2020). © The several contributors. DOI: 10.1093/oso/9780198870753.003.0014.

history and context of religious teachings, or quasi-legal texts such as religious jurisprudential codes.

2. A Survey of the Citations of Religious Texts in ICJ Judgments

2.1 The use of Individual Opinions

First, a word on methodology. The reason that this piece focusses on individual opinions[2] (as opposed to judgments and advisory opinions of the Court itself), is because the Court has rarely cited from "highly qualified publicists" (see below, section 4.2).[3] Materials that are frequently cited include first and foremost the primary sources of international law (treaties, customary law and general principles of law) as well as (from the subsidiary sources) its own jurisprudence, or, less frequently, judicial decisions of other courts and tribunals. In fact, it was intended that this chapter would also cover ICJ judgments and advisory opinions. However, during the initial survey, only one, fleeting allusion to religious texts could be found in a judgment, namely in *Tehran Hostages*,[4] where the ICJ made a brief reference to Islam's contribution to the law of diplomatic immunity:

> But the principle of the inviolability of the persons of diplomatic agents and the premises of diplomatic missions is one of the very foundations of this long-established régime, to the evolution of which the traditions of Islam made a substantial contribution.[5]

We can, of course, hazard a guess as to why the Court tipped its hat to Islam's contribution to international law in the *Tehran Hostages* case. In light of the case's historical-political context, Iran's unwillingness to participate in the proceedings, and the importance given to 'the deep-rootedness and the essential character of the Islamic revolution'[6] in Iran's communications, the citation is perhaps unsurprising.

[2] By the phrase 'individual opinions', I include joint declarations, joint separate opinions and joint dissents. Perhaps unsurprisingly, however, I found in my survey that no joint opinions contained citations of religious texts. Those opinions are marked by agreement and its necessary corollary, compromise.

[3] Statute of the International Court of Justice [hereafter ICJ statute] 33 UNTS 993; Alain Pellet, 'Article 38' in Andreas Zimmermann and others (eds), *The Statute of the International Court of Justice: A Commentary* (2nd edn, OUP 2012) 336, where it is said that those citations are 'very proximate to nil'; Peil (n 1) 151.

[4] *United States Diplomatic and Consular Staff in Tehran (United States of America v Islamic Republic of Iran)* (Judgment) [1980] ICJ Rep 3 .

[5] ibid 40, para 86.

[6] Letter of 9 December 1979 (transcribed in Order of 15 December 1979) [1979] ICJ Rep 7, para 8); Letter of 16 March 1980 (contained in the Judgment of 24 May 1980) [1980] ICJ Rep 3, para 10.

However, even there, the Court limited itself to making an allusion without explicit citation. Other than this one reference to a religious tradition, however, there appear to be no other citations of religious texts in the Court's main judgments. Given the way that the Court's judgments are drafted, this is not at all surprising. The position is, however, different in individual opinions.

2.2 The Scope of the Search

The method adopted for the survey conducted in 2018 was as follows:

- First, a sample of the individual opinions on the Court's website (including those that are not PDF-searchable) were read, and references to religious texts were identified;
- Secondly, from the results of that initial survey, an extrapolated list of 57 keywords was created.[7] Those keywords were then used to search through all PDF-searchable individual opinions available on the Court's website; and
- Thirdly, the accuracy of those searches and keywords were then cross-referenced against a database of individual opinions of ICJ judges compiled by Professor Michael Peil.[8] Given that the database was last updated on 1 May 2012, the cross-referencing does not encompass judgments issued after that date. However, judgments cross-referenced to that date suggest that the sample list of keywords suffices to capture most, or even all, religious references.

2.3 Exclusion of Results

The next step was to decide which of the results were relevant for the purposes of this chapter. At the start, the survey was over-inclusive, and included all references to religious texts that were found. Within the scope of religious texts, the survey included sacred texts, and texts expanding upon religious beliefs[9] or

[7] Those keywords were: Bible; Biblical; Quran; Qur'an; Koran; Quranic; Qur'anic; Koranic; Torah; Old Testament; New Testament; Sharia; Shariah; Shari'a; Islam; Christianity; Judaism; Hinduism; Buddhism; Zoroastrianism; Muslim; Jewish; Hindu; Christian; Islamic; Buddhistic; Abraham; Jesus; Muhammad; Mohamed; Mohammad; Genesis; Exodus; Leviticus; Numbers; Deuteronomy; Joshua; Matthew; Mark; Luke; John; Roman; Peter; Psalm; God; Allah; Ramayana; Mahabharatha; Tribe; Tribal; Saint; Prophet; Zoroaster; Buddha; Sura; Surah; Christ.

[8] Professor Peil created this database in 2012 in the process of compiling an insightful article in the Cambridge Journal of International and Comparative Law on the citation of scholarly authorities in ICJ judgments, which is cited above, n 1.

[9] See eg *Legality of the Threat or Use of Nuclear Weapons* (Advisory Opinion) [1996] ICJ Rep 226 (Dissenting Opinion of Judge Weeramantry) 481, which refers to Walpola Rahula's *What the Buddha Taught* (Oneworld Publications 1959).

jurisprudence.[10] Excluded from the results were: (1) references to the divine beings of classical mythology (though there are modern adherents to those faiths,[11] those texts were not cited as religious texts per se, but allegorically as myths);[12] (2) religious references which were not part of the judicial reasoning in any way, for example where religious texts were quoted in a witness statement which was reproduced within an individual opinion;[13] (3) references to religious texts contained within quotations of other judgments;[14] (4) historical references to religion for the purposes of, for example, the delimitation of territory;[15] and (5) fleeting references which form no part of judicial reasoning whatsoever.[16] This left a small body of results, which form the basis of the analysis conducted in the next section.

3. Analysis

3.1 The Citation of Religious Authorities is Exceptionally Rare

Amongst over 1,200 Declarations, Separate and Dissenting Opinions appended to ICJ Judgments, there are only 43 references to religious texts,[17] contained

[10] See eg *North Sea Continental Shelf Cases (Federal Republic of Germany v Denmark; Federal Republic of Germany v Netherlands)* [1969] ICJ Rep 3 (Separate Opinion of Judge Fouad Ammoun) 139–40, in which he cites, amongst other texts, Islamic *Shari'ah* jurisprudence, and Hindu jurisprudence.

[11] Polytheistic Hellenism has modern adherents (some 2,000 according to a US State Department survey of Greece in 2006): US Bureau of Democracy, Human Rights, and Labour: 'International Religious Freedom Report 2006: Greece' <www.state.gov/j/drl/rls/irf/2006/71383.htm> accessed 19 Sept 2018a.

[12] See eg the fleeing reference to the Goddess Themis (Lady Justice) in *Certain Expenses of the United Nations (Article 17, paragraph 2 of the Charter)* (Advisory Opinion) [1962] ICJ Rep 151 (Dissenting Opinion of Judge Koretsky), p 268.

[13] See eg *Application of the Convention on the Prevention and Punishment of the Crime of Genocide (Croatia v Serbia)* [2015] ICJ Rep 3 (Separate Opinion of Judge Ad Hoc Kreća), pp 449–50, citing a statement of Marjan Durić, a Deputy in the Croatian Parliament who said, of the idea of killing Serbs, that: 'This is something that my Christian, Catholic faith would not allow me, because Father Stanko Bogeljic has taught me that there is one commandment in those ten commandments: "thou shall not kill", and it does not allow me to say that this is right, but it would be right for me if ten Serb intellectuals would get the sack in Zagreb, Rijeka, Split or Osijek for every policeman killed.'

[14] See eg *Maritime Delimitation and Territorial Questions Between Qatar and Bahrain (Qatar v Bahrain)* (Judgment) [2001] ICJ Rep 40 (Separate Opinion Judge Kooijmans), para 9, in which Judge Kooijmans cites from the *Eritrea v Yemen* Arbitral Award (*Territorial Sovereignty and Scope of the Dispute (Eritrea v Yemen)* (1998) XXII UNRIAA 211 (Award Phase I), para 525) which refers to 'Islamic Tradition'.

[15] See eg the numerous references in *Western Sahara* (Advisory Opinion) [1975] ICJ Rep 12 (Separate Opinion Vice-President Ammoun) to the historians Vernet, Domenech, Lafuente, Seco de Lucena, Huici, and Romeu, who describe the legal and Islamic ties between Morocco and the territory of the Western Sahara (at 94–95).

[16] See eg *Maritime Delimitation in the Caribbean Sea and the Pacific Ocean (Costa Rica v Nicaragua)* (Judgment) (2018 unreported), (Dissenting Opinion Judge ad hoc Al-Khasawneh), at 5 footnote 9, who comments that 'Shams-ud-din Mohammed, better known as Hafez of Shiraz (born circa 1320 CE) is one the greatest poets not only of Iran and Islam but of humanity at large.'

[17] We should pause here to note that the Dissenting Opinions of Judge Cançado Trindade in the *Nuclear Arms Race* cases each contained four relevant but identical references to religious texts (in all

within 13 individual opinions in 13 different cases.[18] The first references to religious texts are in Judge Fouad Ammoun's Separate Opinion in the *North Sea Continental Shelf* cases.[19] That Opinion contains seven references to religious texts, most of which are used to support an argument for a general principle of equity.[20] After dismissing the idea that Article 6 of the Convention on the Continental Shelf could have attained a status in either general or regional customary international law,[21] Judge Ammoun analysed the existence of a general principle of equity, which was absent in the reasoning underlying the judgment. Arguing in favour of the existence of this general principle, Judge Ammoun cited both Islamic and Hindu law.[22] These citations, which referred to African custom, Chinese law, Western European law, and Soviet law amongst others, led Judge Ammoun to conclude that it was a general principle of law that legal relations between States are governed by equity.[23] There are so few references to religious texts that the exploration of trends and causal relationships is a statistically

material ways the opinions are identical). Technically, this produced 12 references, but they have been included as only four.

[18] Those are: *North Sea Continental Shelf* (n 10) (Separate Opinion of Judge Ammoun); *Legal Consequences for States of the Continued Presence of South Africa in Namibia (South West Africa) notwithstanding Security Council Resolution 276* (Advisory Opinion) [1971] ICJ Rep 16 (Separate Opinion of Vice-President Ammoun); *Aegean Sea Continental Shelf (Greece v Turkey)* (Judgment) [1978] ICJ Rep 3 (Separate Opinion of Judge Tarazi); *Tehran Hostages* (note 4) (Dissenting Opinion of Judge Tarazi); *Arbitral Award of 31 July 1989 (Guinea-Bissau v Senegal)* (Judgment) [1989] ICJ Rep 53 (Dissenting Opinion of Judge Weeramantry); *Questions of Interpretation and Application of the 1971 Montreal Convention arising from the Aerial Incident at Lockerbie (Libyan Arab Jamahiriya v United Kingdom)* (Provisional Measures) [1992] ICJ Rep 3 (Dissenting Opinion of Judge El-Khosheri); *Maritime Delimitation in the Area between Greenland and Jan Mayen (Denmark v Norway)* (Judgment) [1993] ICJ Rep 38 (Separate Opinion of Judge Weeramantry); *Nuclear Weapons Advisory Opinion* (n 9) Dissenting Opinion of Judge Weeramantry); *Gabčíkovo-Nagymaros Project (Hungary/Slovakia)* (Judgment) [1997] ICJ Rep 7 (Separate Opinion of Vice-President Weeramantry); *Legality of the Use of Force (Serbia and Montenegro v Belgium)* (Provisional Measures) [1999] ICJ Rep 124 (Dissenting Opinion of Vice-President Weeramantry); *Request for Interpretation of the Judgment of 15 June 1962 in the Case Concerning the Temple of Preah Vihear (Cambodia v Thailand) (Cambodia v Thailand)* (Provisional Measures) [2011] ICJ Rep 537 (Separate Opinion Judge Cançado Trindade); *Croatian Genocide* (n 13) (Dissenting Opinion of Judge Cançado Trindade); *Obligations Concerning Negotiations Relating to Cessation of the Nuclear Arms Race and to Nuclear Disarmament (Marshall Islands v India)* [2016] ICJ Rep 225 (Dissenting Opinion Judge Cançado Trindade) (and see n 17).

[19] *North Sea Continental Shelf* (n 10) (Separate Opinion of Judge Ammoun).

[20] *North Sea Continental Shelf* (n 10) (Separate Opinion of Judge Ammoun), para 12 (note 3): a citation of *Al Majallat al Akham* (or *Mecelle*, the Ottoman civil code) for a general principle of *quieta non movere* ('do not move settled things'); ibid para 22: a citation of the *Majallat al Akham* for a general principle of estoppel; ibid para 35 (note 1) and para 38 (notes 2, 3, and 4) for citations of the *Majallat al Akham*, the *Qur'an* and an academic text on Hinduism for a general principle of equity; and ibid para 41 (note 4): a citation of *Majallat al Akham* for a general principle of *preater legem* as part of equity.

[21] *North Sea Continental Shelf* (n 10) (Separate Opinion of Judge Ammoun), para 32.

[22] As to Islamic law, Judge Ammoun cited both the Qur'an and the *Majallat al-Akham al-Adliyyah*, the Ottoman Court manual, for the proposition that the *Shari'a* requires, among other sources of law, *Istihsan*, the use of fairness and equity to avoid an overly harsh result. As to Hindu Law, Judge Ammoun cited René David, *Les Grand Systèmes de Droit Contemporain* (Dalloz 1966) 152 for the proposition that Hindu law recommends justice according to equity in the absence of a formal rule of law.

[23] *North Sea Continental Shelf* (n 10) (Separate Opinion of Judge Ammoun), para 38.

difficult task. Nevertheless, there are a few observations that can be made from the 43 citations identified.

3.2 Islamic Texts are Cited More than Texts of any Other Religion

Within the 43 identified citations of religious sources, 18 are citations to Islamic texts.[24] One reason for this high number is that six of those 18 references were to two jurisprudential documents pertaining to the Ottoman empire: *Al Majallat al Akham* (the Ottoman civil code)[25] and the book *Corps de Droit Ottoman*.[26] The frequency of their citation is explained by the fact that these texts also set out principles of domestic law since the Ottoman empire had a domestic legal system based upon the *Shari'ah*. Therefore, when they were cited, these texts were described as examples of both Islamic and domestic law.[27] In contrast, the citations of texts of other religions did not fulfil this dual function. For example, although there are references to Christian and Hindu jurisprudential documents,[28] these documents were not cited as examples of domestic law.

3.3 Citations of Religious Texts Seem to Have Waned in Popularity

It appears as though the citation of religious texts enjoyed relative prominence between the late 1960s and the late 1990s, in which 37 of the 43 identified citations were made. By contrast, between 2002 and 2010, there were no citations of religious texts. This conclusion requires some obvious moderation. As mentioned below, very few judges account for the majority of citations[29] (and those citations are rare). The paucity of these references renders statistical analysis difficult. Considering that 40 of the 43 references come from three judges,[30] an increased number of

[24] The next are is Christianity with 11; Buddhism with nine; Hinduism with six; Judaism with three and Zoroastrianism with one. The reason that the total number of mentions amounts to 48 although there are only 43 citations is that in *Interpretation of Preah Vihear*, Judge Cançado Trindade, in his Separate Opinion, cites all six of these religious in one academic citation (*Interpretation of Preah Vihear* (n 18) (Separate Opinion Judge Cançado Trindade), 605–06).

[25] *Al Majallat al Akham* <www.iium.edu.my/deed/lawbase/al_majalle/index.html> accessed 19 September 2018.

[26] George A Young, *Corps de Droit Ottoman* (Clarendon Press 1906).

[27] *Aegean Sea Continental Shelf* (n 18) (Separate Opinion of Judge Tarazi), p 56; *North Sea Continental Shelf* (n 10) (Separate Opinion of Judge Ammoun), paras 12, 22, 35, 38, and 41.

[28] *Nuclear Weapons Advisory Opinion* (n 9) (Dissenting Opinion of Judge Weeramantry), pp 478–79 (Laws of Manu) and p 480 (Second Lateran Council of 1139).

[29] See section 3.5.

[30] ibid.

citations in one decade as opposed to another is likely more reflective of the composition of the Court and individual judges' career paths and personal beliefs, than any particular judicial trend.

3.4 Those Citations are most often used to establish a general principle of law

In 20 of the 43 references, judges explicitly disclosed that their citation of religious texts was in pursuit of the establishment of general principles of law. In 13 references, judges used religious texts to explain the contribution of a religion to a particular sphere of law or that religion's perspective on a particular idea or rule, without explicitly clarifying whether a particular binding norm was being referred to.[31] Otherwise, religious texts are cited fleetingly, or as judicial flourishes (to make a moralistic point, for example).[32]

3.5 The Citation of Religious Texts and the Identity of the Judges

Although this study began as an attempt to draw patterns and establish correlations, it identified only 13 relevant individual opinions that contain citations of religious texts. Only five judges are responsible for those 13 opinions. Strikingly, Judge Weeramantry and Judge Cançado Trindade are the authors of eight of these 13 opinions. When individual citations are considered, the picture is even more striking; Judge Weeramantry is responsible for over half of the individual citations (26 of the 43). Judge Ammoun has eight, and Judge Cançado Trindade has six. Bearing that in mind, can we see any correlations between the citation of religious texts and the identity of the judges? It does not appear that there is any correlation between the religious identity of the judge and the religious texts that they cite. Judge Weeramantry, for example, was Christian, but only four of his 26 citations are to Christian sources. The majority of his citations are to sources of Islamic law, in which he was a published expert.[33] Judge

[31] *Legality of the Use of Force* (n 18) (Dissenting Opinion of Vice-President Weeramantry), p 199; and *Nuclear Weapons Advisory Opinion* (n 9) Dissenting Opinion of Judge Weeramantry), pp 478–81.

[32] See eg the reflective comment in *Marshall Islands v India* (n 18), (Dissenting Opinion of Judge Cançado Trindade), para 189: '*Is there anything quintessentially more cruel? To use nuclear weapons appears like condemning innocent persons to hell on earth, even before they are born.* That seems to go even further than the Book of Genesis's story of the original sin. *In reaction to such extreme cruelty, the consciousness of the rights inherent to the human person has always marked a central presence in endeavours towards complete nuclear disarmament*' (emphasis added. Note that the same paragraph can be found in the cases against the United Kingdom (at para 185) and Pakistan (at para 179).

[33] See eg C G Weeramantry, *Islamic Jurisprudence: An International Perspective* (1988 Palgrave)

Cançado Trindade has stated that whilst he considers himself very religious, he does not follow any particular religion,[34] though the majority of his citations are to Christian sources.

However, it does appear that there is a correlation between the religious tradition in the Judges' home States and their citation of religious texts. Judge Cançado Trindade is Brazilian, Judge Ammoun (of whose eight citations, six were to Islam, one to Christianity and one to Hinduism) was Lebanese, and Judge Weeramantry was Sri Lankan. The latter Judge has written in his memoirs that his desire to bring religious texts into the jurisprudence of the Court was in part a product of the multi-cultural background to which he was accustomed in Sri Lanka.[35] The relationship does not seem to go both ways, though. There have been many judges who did not cite any religious texts in their judgments, even though they came from a background which would have exposed them to this. For example, although Sir Muhammad Zafarullah Khan served two terms at the Court, including as President and Vice-President, was involved in the partition of India, and published numerous books of Islamic principles, his individual opinions contain no citations to religious texts.

4. Is There a Place for Religious Texts in Judgments of the ICJ?

Considering the above, it is fair to conclude that while religious texts are cited rarely in ICJ judgments, it is not wholly unknown for individual opinions to feature such citations. The normative question that follows is: *should* those texts be cited? Our starting point must of course be Article 38(1) of the Statute of the Court, which lists the sources of law on which the Court must base its decisions:

1. The Court, whose function is to decide in accordance with international law such disputes as are submitted to it, shall apply:
   (a) international conventions, whether general or particular, establishing rules expressly recognized by the contesting states;
   (b) international custom, as evidence of a general practice accepted as law;
   (c) the general principles of law recognized by civilized nations;
   (d) subject to the provisions of Article 59, judicial decisions and the teachings of the most highly qualified publicists of the various nations, as subsidiary means for the determination of rules of law.[36]

[34] Lauri R Tanner and Antônio A Cançado Trindade, 'Interview with Judge Antônio A Cançado Trindade, Inter-American Court of Human Rights' (2009) 31(4) Human Rights Quarterly 985, at 1004.

[35] C G Weeramantry, *Towards One World: Volume III (The International Court and Thereafter)* (Stamford Lake 2014).

[36] Art 38(1), Statute of the International Court of Justice (1945) 15 UNCIO 355.

Religious texts do not explicitly feature in Article 38(1). There are three possible justifications for their citation within individual judgments. The first is that their citation falls within Article 38(1)(c) of the Statute, ie the establishment of a general principle of law. The second possibility is that the particular religious text is a 'teaching of the most highly qualified publicists'. There is also a third possibility. Article 38(1) lists the sources of law to be applied when the Court is discharging its primary function, ie 'to decide in accordance with international law such disputes as are submitted to it'. As we have noted, some judges cite texts as a simple flourish, to make a particular normative point that is not directly connected with the resolution of the dispute (in the same way that many judges use allegories and examples from literature). Those citations would fall outside of Article 38(1) on its face.

4.1 Religious Texts as General Principles of Law?

The first possibility is that religious texts, laws, and traditions are able to form or inform 'general principles of law'. This third source of primary law in the ICJ Statute has received comparatively less academic attention than the other two primary sources, or the subsidiary sources of law. Often, general principles of law are considered a 'gap-filling' source, to be used to avoid a situation of *non liquet*.[37] Nevertheless, they have been an important storehouse of norms applied by international courts and tribunals.[38] Bin Cheng described them as 'general propositions underlying the various rules of law which express the essential qualities of juridical truth itself'.[39] Waldock argued that the application of general principles is the result of law and lawyers being 'imbued through and through with the principles and notions of one or more systems of national law'.[40]

The *travaux préparatoires* of the Statute of the Permanent Court of International Justice (PCIJ) are helpful as to the identification, interpretation, and application of general principles. Lord Phillimore described general principles at the *procés-verbaux* as 'maxims',[41] suggesting a softer and more open-textured approach than rules contained within treaties and customary international law. One might therefore argue that general principles of law can temper the voluntarist nature of treaty and customary law with certain base principles resembling natural law.[42]

[37] Sir Robert Jennings QC and Sir Arthur Watts KCMG QC, *Oppenheim's International Law: Volume I (Peace)* (1992 Longman) 40; Bin Cheng, *General Principles of Law as Applied by International Courts and Tribunals* (1953 Steven & Sons).

[38] *Oppenheim* (n 37) 37–38; *see*, generally, Bin Cheng (n 37).

[39] Bin Cheng (n 37) 24.

[40] Sir Humphrey Waldock, *General Course on Public International Law* (1962) 106 *Recueil des Cours* 1, p 54.

[41] *Procés-Verbaux of the Proceedings of the Committee of Jurists* (Van Langenhuysen Brothers 1920) 335.

[42] *See* Bin Cheng (note 37) p xi (foreword by George Schwarzenberger): Art 38(1)(c) is a 'channel though which concepts of natural law could be received into international law'.

Those general principles that are regular players on the World Court's stage, such as 'good faith', 'abuse of rights', and 'equity', all have a ring of morality about them. This was the view of Judge Ammoun in his Separate Opinion in the *North Sea Continental Shelf Cases*, where he opined that:

> the general principles of law, when they effect a synthesis and digest in foro domestico of the nations—of all the nations—seem closer than other sources of law to international morality. By being incorporated in the law of nations, they strip off any tincture of nationalism, so as to represent, like the principle of equity, the purest moral values.[43]

Still, it is one thing to say that these principles have a naturalistic or moral *core*, and quite another to say that their content can be *defined by* religious texts. The distinction is (perhaps) a thin one, but it is nevertheless important. Bin Cheng suggested the necessity for a clear demarcation between principles of *law* and principles of religion or morality.[44] The *travaux* tell us that only those principles recognized in domestic systems qualify as principles of law, rather than those of natural justice or of a sense of what is right and lawful.[45]

Nevertheless, in this context, references to religious law might be considered to fall appropriately within the realm of Article 38(1)(c) where what is being explored is either: (1) the law of a State where religious principles are part of the constitution or are in some way embedded within the national law; or (2) the historical context or historical examples of a particular general principle. Indeed, the former occurs particularly with Islamic texts which can form part of domestic *Shari'ah* law.[46] The latter of these possibilities is a fairly regular reason for the citation of religious texts in judgments of the ICJ.[47]

4.2 The Teachings of Highly Qualified Publicists?

As other writers have pointed out, Article 38(1)(d) of the Court's Statute is intentionally ambiguous, as a result of disagreements between the drafters of the original

43 *North Sea Continental Shelf Cases* (n 10) (Separate Opinion of Judge Fouad Ammoun), pp 134–35. See also p 136: 'The general principles of law are indisputably factors which bring morality into the law of nations, inasmuch as they borrow from the law of nations principles of the moral order'.

44 Bin Cheng (note 37) 24.

45 *Procés-Verbaux* (n 41) 335.

46 Mashood A Baderin, 'Religion and International Law: Friends or Foes?' (2009) 5 European Human Rights Law Review 637, at 652.

47 See eg *Nuclear Weapons Advisory Opinion* (n 9) (Dissenting Opinion of Judge Weeramantry), pp 479–81 (citations of religious texts relating to Hinduism, Judaism, Christianity, Islam, and Buddhism).

text from the PCIJ Statute, upon which the ICJ Statute is based.[48] The Court's use of the teachings of publicists is couched within a number of requirements, all of which point to the exclusion of religious texts from Article 38(1)(d), for at least two reasons. First, although Article 38(1)(d) does not qualify the term 'publicists', it seems clear from the *travaux* of the PCIJ Statute that the Committee of Jurists intended only to include legal jurists within the meaning of 'qualified publicists'.[49] This would exclude sacred texts and authors of religious commentaries from the Statute. Secondly, the teachings referred to in Article 38(1)(d) may only be used as a 'subsidiary means for the determination of rules of law'. In other words, the use of publicists must be evidentiary in nature,[50] used as a method of clarification, determination or confirmation of 'rules of law'. Citing a text which expands upon a particular religious belief or a sacred text is not a citation for the purpose of determining a rule of law. It would seem, therefore, that religious texts cannot fall within Article 38(1)(d) of the Court's Statute.

There are, of course, theoretical exceptions to this general exclusion. States may specify that their relations in a particular sphere are to be governed by a religious law or principle, in which case examination of the dispute would naturally require recourse to religious texts as a subsidiary source. An example of this approach can be found in Article 20(3) of the UN Convention on the Rights of the Child, which provides that State protection of children deprived of their family environment can include the concept of *kafalah* in Islamic Law.[51] Article 20(3) of that treaty therefore presents the opportunity for States to govern their obligations on the basis of *Shari'ah* law, which in turn requires an examination of Islamic religious texts in order to determine the extent of the obligation. This, however, is a rare exception. Consequently, at least insofar as the general position is concerned, religious texts do not fall within Article 38(1)(d) of the Court's Statute.

4.3 Do Citations of Religious Texts Undermine the Legitimacy of the Court?

But for the limited exceptions considered above, it is doubtful that religious texts can ever be truly considered primary or subsidiary sources of law proper under

48 Michael Peil, 'Scholarly Writings as a Source of Law: A Survey of the Use of Doctrine by the International Court of Justice' (2012) 1(3) Cambridge Journal of International and Comparative Law 136, 13–40.

49 *Procés-Verbaux* (n 41) 322 et seq. See, in particular, the comment of Baron Descamps, at p 323 that there is a presumption in favour of a rule where 'the greater part of jurisconsults agree upon a certain rule', citing Chancellor Kent; and p 332, where Baron Descamps accepts that judges must use 'the coinciding doctrines of jurists as auxiliary and supplementary means, only'; p 333 where Mr. Ricci-Busatti asked Lord Phillimore whether 'England would accept a sentence based not on a rule of law [. . .] but upon the doctrine of legal writers'.

50 Sir Humphrey Waldock (n 40) 88.

51 United Nations Convention on the Rights of the Child (1990) 1157 UNTS 3.

Article 38(1) of the Court's Statute. Perhaps, then, we could argue that religious sources should never be cited within individual opinions. After all, if judges base their decisions on sources extraneous to the Court's Statute, the very core of consent-based international dispute resolution begins to come apart at the seams. In none of its cases has the Court been asked by the parties to a dispute to decide the case on the basis of *ex aequo et bono*,[52] and we may agree that this evidences a 'deep suspicion' with which States view decisions made outside the realms of positive law.[53] However, the citation of religious sources is not a case of the usurpation of law by morality, for two reasons.

First, the survey conducted demonstrates that as a matter of fact religious texts are not used *instead* of positive rules of law but as *supplements to* those rules. For example, in the 20 references identified above[54] in which religious texts were used to establish a general principle of law, those references were combined with national laws, judicial decisions and other positivist sources to strengthen them, rather than to dilute them.

Secondly, even once we accept (as we should do) that the citation of religious sources brings some moral content to the law or augments it with a moral dimension, that is not an antithesis to judicial dispute resolution on the basis of positive law. The judicial function necessarily contains a moral, virtue-based dimension.[55] This has been acknowledged by judges in their individual opinions[56] and, at times, indirectly by the Court itself.[57] These 'moral suasions', to adopt the nomenclature of Hernández,[58] can supplement rather than supplant judicial decision-making on the basis of Article 38(1) of the ICJ Statute. They need not affect the decisional authority of the court, which is still grounded firmly in the sources of Article 38(1) and Article 59, far less replace law with morality. That being the case, if those 'moral

[52] Art 38(2), ICJ Statute (n 36).

[53] Gleider I Hernández, *The International Court of Justice and the Judicial Function* (OUP 2014) 68.

[54] See section 2.6.

[55] Samantha Besson, 'Legal Philosophical Issues of International Adjudication: Getting over the *amour impossible* between International Law and Adjudication' in Cesare P R Romano, Karen Alter, and Yuval Shany (eds), *The Oxford Handbook on International Adjudication* (OUP 2013) 428.

[56] *Nuclear Weapons Advisory Opinion* (n 9) (Dissenting Opinion of Judge Higgins), para 41: 'It may well be asked of a judge whether, in engaging in legal analysis of such concepts as "unnecessary suffering", "collateral damage" and "entitlement to self-defence", one has not lost sight of the real human circumstances involved. The judicial lodestar, whether in difficult questions of interpretation of humanitarian law, or in resolving claimed tensions between competing norms, must be those values that international law seeks to promote and protect. In the present case, it is the physical survival of peoples that we must constantly have in view.'

[57] Hernández, (n 53) 207–08; See *The Corfu Channel Case (United Kingdom of Great Britain and Northern Ireland v People's Republic of Albania)* [1949] ICJ Rep 4, at 22: 'Such obligations [of Albania] are based […] on general and well-recognized principles, namely: elementary considerations of humanity' (a self-evidently naturalist inclination in the finding of Albanian responsibility); See also a rejection of this dictum in *South West Africa (Ethiopia v South Africa; Liberia v South Africa)* (Second Phase) [1966] ICJ Rep 6, paras 49–51, in which the court made clear that it would not take account of moral principles until they were 'clothed in legal form', and the acerbic academic criticism of that rejection cited in Hernández (n 53) 211 note 98.

[58] Hernández (n 53) 207–08.

suasions' are drawn from a variety of traditions and histories (including religious ones), and are used only to supplement decision-making on the basis of positive law, rather than to replace it, it is unclear how the legitimacy of the Court is undermined. That forms the basis for the argument in the final section of this piece.

5. An Argument for the Citation of Religious Texts in ICJ Judgments

5.1 The 'World Court'

Many scholars have written about the Eurocentric origins of international law,[59] which has tended to overlook the developments of (even older) civilizations in other continents, including those developed through religions,[60] to which the Court alluded in the *Tehran Hostages* case. There is, however, ample evidence that these cultures and religions have contributed to the development of modern international law.[61] The ICJ's place in the international legal order is unique: in addition to being the principal judicial organ of the UN,[62] it is the only court than can claim universality both in the scope of its subject matter and its geographical mandate.[63] That the ICJ truly is the *world* court is alluded to in its Statute, which demands that, within the Court as a whole, 'the representation of the main forms of civilization and of the principal legal systems of the world should be assured',[64] an obligation which arguably touches not only upon the election of the bench, but also its operation.[65] If there is any judicial body in modern international

[59] Particularly striking examples can be found in: Manlohar L Sarin, 'The Asian-African States and the Development of International Law' in René-Jean Dupuy (ed), *The Future of International Law in a Multicultural World* (Colloques, Académie de droit international de La Haye/Brill 1984) 117; R P Anand, 'The Role of Asian States in the Development of International Law', at p 105 of the same volume.

[60] Manfred Lachs, *The Teacher in International Law* (Martinus Nijhoff 1982) 31; Alexander Orakhelashvili. 'The Idea of European International Law' (2006) 17 European Journal of International Law 315, at 320–28, especially at 328: 'The thesis put forward by the proponents of European international law that non-Europeans were incapable of understanding international law was based on pure prejudice. Their writings ignored the fact that the cultural and intellectual heritage of non-European nations had long embraced and developed fundamental ideas of international law. Kautilya's Arthasastra and the Code of Manu, to mention only a couple of examples, provide evidence of non-European concepts of the sanctity of treaties, inviolability of ambassadors, principles of humanity in conducting wars and fundamental principles of the law of the sea, which, it may be noted, anticipated to a certain extent the modern law of the sea. Ancient Greeks praised the generosity of the Indian conception of the laws of war, which was based on a fundamental distinction between combatants and non-combatants.'

[61] Manlohar L Sarin (n 59) 123;. R P Anand, (n 59) 109–10; *Orakhelashvili* (n 60) 330–31.

[62] Art 92, Charter of the United Nations (1945) 1 UNTS 16.

[63] Yuval Shany and Rotem Giladi, 'The International Court of Justice' in Yuval Shany, *Assessing the Effectiveness of International Courts* (OUP 2014) 163

[64] Art 9, ICJ Statute (n 36).

[65] See eg Bardo Fassbender, 'Article 9' in Zimmermann (n 3), para 46; See also *Jan Mayen* (n 18) (Separate Opinion Judge Weeramantry), para 234: 'The International Court of Justice, specifically

law that is able and, perhaps, mandated to act to ensure that international law is truly *international*, it is the ICJ.[66]

5.2 The Function and Legitimacy of the Court in Light of Increased Citations of Religious Texts

Considering the above, it is submitted that when judges choose to cite religious texts in their individual opinions, they are not simply displaying individual judicial style and identity, but they are also conducting a normative activity that affects the function and legitimacy of the Court. The citation of religious texts is a route by which judges can acknowledge the long-term contributions of other societies to international law.

While it cannot be ignored that the *chapeau* to Article 38(1) of the ICJ Statute discloses the critical function of the Court (to apply the sources listed therein to decide international disputes),[67] that statement is not an *exhaustive* list of the functions of the Court. Indeed, the Court answers questions submitted to it in its advisory capacity; develops and cements international law by creating precedent in all but name; and, in the view of some authors, the ICJ has, in recent years, developed a trusteeship function.[68]

As Besson notes, one way in which domestic and international tribunals can differ is in the identification of law. In pursuit of its overall function of dispute resolution, the ICJ must first identify the relevant applicable law. In the sphere of international judicial dispute resolution, this is necessarily an exercise bordering on law-making. To say that a treaty entails one obligation rather than another, or that *x* and *y* are examples of relevant State practice is necessarily to engage both in interpretation *and* a form of law-making, even if at a superficial level. Such an exercise involves the validation and supplementation of the various texts, methods, and reasoning styles that are involved in dispute resolution.[69]

structured to embody a "representation of the main forms of civilization and of the principal legal systems of the world" (see Article 9 of the Statute of the Court), is under a particular obligation to search in all these traditions and legal systems for principles and approaches that enrich the law it administers, and in the context of the present case, this applies to the contributions that equity can make to the law of the sea.'

[66] See eg Bardo Fassbender, 'Article 9' in Zimmermann (n 3), para 44.

[67] Art 38(1), ICJ Statute (n 36).

[68] Karen Alter, 'Agents or Trustees? International Courts in Their Political Context' (2008) 14 European Journal of International Relations 33; Armin von Bogdandy and Ingo Venzke, 'On the Functions of International courts: An Appraisal in Light of Their Burgeoning Public Authority' (2013) 26(1) Leiden Journal of International Law 49.

[69] Samantha Besson, 'Legal Philosophical Issues of International Adjudication: Getting over the *amour impossible* between International Law and Adjudication' in Cesare P R Romano, Karen Alter, and Yuval Shany (eds), *The Oxford Handbook on International Adjudication* (OUP 2013) 426.

Therefore, the choice to include religious, cultural, or other sources[70] within the identification of a legal obligations validates their existence within the sphere of dispute resolution. The benefit of citing religious texts is thrown into sharp relief in the case of general principles of law. As observed above,[71] general principles of law have an almost moralistic character. By citing religious texts, which have for centuries been part of the warp and weft of our collective moral compasses, judges bring these texts into the sphere of international law-making and validate their place within the international order. It is suggested that this can strengthen international law. This was the view of Judge Weeramantry in his Separate Opinion in the *Gabčíkovo-Nagymaros* case and his Dissenting Opinion in the *Nuclear Weapons* Advisory Opinion. In *Gabčíkovo-Nagymaros*, he argued that the case was 'an opportunity to tap the wisdom of the past and draw from it some principles which can strengthen the concept of sustainable development'.[72] He continued:

> This is a legitimate source for the enrichment of international law, which [. . .] is perhaps not used to the extent which its importance warrants. In drawing into international law the benefits of the insights available from other cultures, and in looking to the past for inspiration, international environmental law would not be departing from the traditional methods of international law, but would, in fact, be following in the path charted out by Grotius [. . .] Environmental law is now in a formative stage, not unlike international law in its early stages. A wealth of past experience from a variety of cultures is available to it. It would be pity [sic] indeed if it were left untapped merely because of attitudes of formalism which see such approaches as not being entirely de rigueur [. . .] Moreover, especially at the frontiers of the discipline of international law, it needs to be multi-disciplinary, drawing from other disciplines such as history, sociology, anthropology, and psychology such wisdom as may be relevant for its purpose.[73]

In the *Nuclear Weapons Advisory Opinion*, Judge Weeramantry commented on the use of religious and cultural texts to eschew Eurocentrism and to bring validity to those texts within the sphere of international law:

> In rendering an advisory opinion on a matter of humanitarian law concerning the permissibility of the use of force to a degree capable of destroying all of humanity, it would be a grave omission indeed to neglect the humanitarian perspectives available from this major segment of the world's cultural traditions [. . .] It is against such a varied cultural background that these questions must be

70 This piece has only focussed on religious texts, but this argument applies equally to other categories of text, for example cultural.

71 See section 3.1.

72 *Gabčíkovo-Nagymaros Project* (n 18) (Separate Opinion of Vice-President Weeramantry) , p 96

73 ibid 96–97.

considered and not merely as though they are a new sentiment invented in the nineteenth century and so slenderly rooted in universal tradition that they may be lightly overridden.[74]

The citation of religious texts allows the Court to extend both the geographic and temporal support it can call upon to reinforce basic norms of international law. As to the geographic scope, an examination of international law gains legitimacy when that examination is itself international. As to the temporal scope, an understanding that some modern-day rules are rooted in traditions older than those of the 19th century can inform our modern-day approaches to these norms. When the development of international law reflects the diverse range of histories and cultures subject to its reign, it can only gain legitimacy and strength.[75]

Therefore, when the Court (and its judges) take the opportunity to cite from religious texts and cultural texts, this provides three benefits. First, it fulfils the obligation in Article 9 of the Court's Statute. Secondly, it gives the Court true claim to the mantle and legitimacy of its position as the *World Court*. Finally, it allows the Court to draw on 'that plenitude of universal authority which is available to give it added strength'.[76]

6. Conclusion

This chapter's aim has been to explore, through a survey of individual Separate and Dissenting Opinions, the treatment of religious texts within the Court, and to provide an argument for their continued usage. This argument is straightforward: in order to maintain its legitimacy, ICJ judges are under an obligation to serve the international community and its principles, in all their variety. International law is already, at least in part, based on natural law. Ultimately, the answer to the central question, whether ICJ judges should be more willing or more hesitant to express their own identity through citing religious texts, depends on one's view of the role of the Court. If we view the ICJ as a quasi-arbitral forum for the clinical resolution

[74] *Nuclear Weapons Advisory Opinion* (n 9) (Dissenting Opinion Judge Weeramantry) pp 481–82.

[75] Others have gone further than the normative argument about legitimacy. Manlohar L. Sarin (n 59) suggests (at p 127) that taking into account a diverse range of cultures will encourage more States to submit to the jurisdiction of the Court: 'As novel international norms are drawn up which are not only juridical in the sense of reflecting a general practice, but are also norms that reflect justice and take into account the needs and opinions of these countries, then the latter would be more inclined to submit themselves voluntarily to their application. The principles of international law have got to be adjusted to the novel structure and conditions of post-war international society. The naked positivism that had reigned supreme over the formulation of prevailing norms had to be replaced by an idealism and spirit of innovation based on the new requirements and values, incorporated in the purposes and principles of the United Nations as enunciated in its Charter, of the modem world. The peaceful co-existence of all States has to be maintained. The sovereign equality of all States has to be respected.'

[76] *Nuclear Weapons Advisory Opinion* (n 9) (Dissenting Opinion of Judge Weeramantry), p 478.

of disputes,[77] then the answer to the question is probably negative, and judges like the late Judge Christopher Weeramantry would be labelled as idealists, or even 'activists'. Naturally, the political realities of international dispute resolution make this view a compelling one. But if we view the Court as something more, an apex forum for a truly international legal order, one that is geographically, religiously, and culturally diverse, and whose legal concepts are the result of long and storied histories, then perhaps we can agree with that very same judge when he said:

> The ingrained values of any civilization are the source from which its legal concepts derive, and the ultimate yardstick and touchstone of their validity. This is so in international and domestic legal systems alike [...] The formalism of modern legal systems may cause us to lose sight of such principles, but the time has come when they must once more be integrated into the corpus of the living law.[78]

This chapter ends with a call for further research as it would be interesting to expand the present survey either horizontally, to look at the religious identity of judges serving on other international courts and tribunals—and their concomitant use of religious texts; or vertically, to take into account the religious identity and submissions of parties before the ICJ. Moreover, the cultural identity of judges, and their use of cultural texts, would also make for interesting study material.

[77] Yuval Shany and Rotem Giladi, 'The International Court of Justice' in Yuval Shany, *Assessing the Effectiveness of International Courts* (OUP 2014) 180–81.
[78] *Gabčíkovo-Nagymaros Project* (n 18) (Separate Opinion of Vice-President Weeramantry), pp 108–09.

15

A Question of Impartiality

Who are the Dissenting Arbitrators in Investment Treaty Arbitration?

*Szilárd Gáspár-Szilágyi and Laura Létourneau-Tremblay**

1. Introduction

Investment treaty arbitration (ITA), the central feature of the international investment regime, has come under increased criticism in recent years. An ITA tribunal is typically constituted of three arbitrators: two arbitrators appointed by each of the disputing parties (the wing arbitrators) and one presiding arbitrator appointed either by agreement of the disputing parties or by an arbitral institution.[1] This selection process differs from other international adjudicatory bodies, such as the International Tribunal for the Law of the Sea (ITLOS)[2] or the European Court of Human Rights (ECtHR),[3] where a body/committee appoints the members of the judiciary for a fixed term.

The effects of the selection procedures of international adjudicators on potential adjudicator bias is a topic that affects multiple international courts.[4] For example, Posner and de Figueiredo find strong evidence that members of the International Court of Justice (ICJ) favour the appointing State and States at similar levels of development with a related political system.[5] While concluding that judges in the

* The authors would like to thank Daniel Behn, Øyvind Stiansen, Anton Strezhnev, and the participants of the two conferences—*The 2018 ASIL IEcLIG Biennal- Managing International Economic (Dis)Integration: Challenges and Opportunities* and *Geography and Legal Culture on the International Bench*—for their valuable comments, as well as Maxim Usynin for providing data from the PITAD database.

[1] See eg Convention for the Settlement of Investment Disputes between States and Nationals of Other States (opened for signature 18 Mar. 1965, entered into force 14 Oct. 1966) 575 UNTS 159 (ICSID Convention) Art 37.

[2] Statute of the International Tribunal for the Law of the Sea (opened for signature 10 Dec. 1982, entered into force 16 Nov. 1994), Art 4.

[3] Convention for the Protection of Human Rights and Fundamental Freedoms (European Convention on Human Rights, as amended) (ECHR) Arts 22 and 23.

[4] Ruth Mackenzie and Philippe Sands, 'International Courts and Tribunals and the Independence of the International Judge' (2003) 44(1) Harvard International Law Journal 271. For dissents issued by the Supreme Courts of EU member states, see European Parliament, 'Dissenting Opinions in the Supreme Courts of the Member States' (2012) Study, Directorate General for Internal Policies, PE 462.470.

[5] Eric A Posner and Miguel FP de Figueiredo, 'Is the International Court of Justice Biased?' (2005) 34(2) The Journal of Legal Studies 599.

Szilárd Gáspár-Szilágyi and Laura Létourneau-Tremblay, *A Question of Impartiality* In: *Identity and Diversity on the International Bench*. Edited by: Freya Baetens, Oxford University Press (2020). © The several contributors.
DOI: 10.1093/oso/9780198870753.003.0015.

context of the ECtHR do not employ cultural or geopolitical biases in their rulings, Voeten finds some evidence that judges might favour their national governments when party to the dispute.[6]

ITA is no stranger to such criticisms either. Some of the critics challenging the legitimacy of the international investment regime specifically question the selection process of arbitrators, arguing that party-appointed arbitrators might have innate biases in favour of the party appointing them.[7] They claim that investment arbitrators favour their appointing party 'in a self-interested effort to increase the likelihood of future appointments'.[8] This discussion found its way into academic commentaries tackling the relevance of dissents by party-appointed arbitrators, resulting in a heated academic debate between prominent arbitrators, such Jan Van den Berg and Jan Paulsson, on the one side, and Charles Brower, on the other.[9] Van den Berg's original claim that 'nearly 100% of dissenting opinions are drafted by arbitrators appointed by the losing party'[10] was met with scepticism and abundant discussions on the role of dissents in ITA.[11]

In light of these controversies surrounding dissenting opinions in ITA, this chapter aims to contribute to the ongoing discussion by identifying some of the

[6] Erik Voeten, 'The Impartiality of International Judges: Evidence from the European Court of Human Rights' (2008) 102(4) American Political Science Review 425–27; on international human rights courts see also Daniel Naurin and Øyvind Stiansen, 'The Dilemma of Dissent: Split Judicial Decisions and Compliance with Judgments from the International Human Rights Judiciary' (2019) Comparative Political Studies 33.

[7] See Jan Paulsson, 'Moral Hazard in International Dispute Resolutions' (2010) 25(2) ICSID Review – Foreign Investment Law Journal 339; Chiara Giorgetti, 'Who Decides Who Decides in International Investment Arbitration?' (2014) 35(2) University of Pennsylvania Journal of International Law 431; Sergio Puig, 'Affiliation Bias in Arbitration: An Experimental Approach' (2017) 46(2) The Journal of Legal Studies 398; in the context of the ISDS reform process see also UNCITRAL, 'Possible reform of investor-State dispute settlement (ISDS) Arbitrators and decision makers: appointment mechanisms and related issues' (30 August 2018) A/CN.9/WG.III/WP.152.

[8] Catherine A Rogers, 'The Politics of International Investment Arbitration' (2013) 12 Santa Clara International Law Review 223, 226.

[9] Albert Jan van den Berg, 'Dissenting Opinions by Party-Appointed Arbitrators' in Mahnoush Arsanjanu and others (eds), *Looking at the Future: Essays on International Law in Honor of W. Michael Reisman* (Brill Academic 2011) 842; Albert Jan van den Berg, 'Charles Brower's Problem With 100 Per Cent – Dissenting Opinions by Party-appointed Arbitrators in Investment Arbitration' (2015) 31 Arbitration International 381; Paulsson (n 7); Charles N Brower, Michael Pulos, and Charles B Rosenberg, 'So Is There Anything Really Wrong with International Arbitration as we Know It?' in Arthur W Rovine (ed), *Contemporary Issues in International Arbitration and Mediation: The Fordham Papers 2012* (Martinus Nijhoff 2013); Charles N Brower and Charles B Rosenberg, 'The Death of the Two-Headed Nightingale: Why the Paulsson-Van der Berg Presumption that Party-Appointed Arbitrators are Untrustworthy is Wrongheaded' (2013) 29(1) Arbitration International 39.

[10] Van den Berg, 'Dissenting Opinions by Party-Appointed Arbitrators' (n 9) 831.

[11] See n 9; see also Pedro J Martinez-Fraga and Harout Jack Samra, 'A Defense of Dissents in Investment Arbitration' (2012) 42(3) Inter-American Law Review 446; VV Veeder, 'The Historical Keystone to International Arbitration: The Party-Appointed Arbitration—From Miami to Geneva' in David D Caron and others (eds), *Practicing Virtue: Inside International Arbitration* (Oxford University Press 2016); Anton Strezhnev, 'You only Dissent Once: Re-appointment and Legal Practices in Investment Arbitration', Research Note (2015) <http://scholar.harvard.edu/files/astrezhnev/files/dissent_draft_1.pdf> accessed 18 August 2020; Catharine Titi, 'Investment Arbitration and the Controverted Right of the Arbitrator to Issue a Separate or Dissenting Opinion (2018) 17 The Law and Practice of International Courts and Tribunals 197.

common characteristics of the dissenting arbitrators and discussing those in light of the independence and impartiality required on the bench. Taking into account all existing dissents issued in ITA proceedings until the end of 2016, we look at a series of arbitrator-level (nationality, gender, education, professional background) and case-level (party appointment, appointment by States or investors) variables to test six hypotheses that are meant to provide a more accurate profile of dissenting arbitrators. Such a socio-legal study of dissenting arbitrators can provide unique insights into the workings of ITA.[12]

Following the Introduction, in section 2 of the chapter, we lay out the theoretical framework of our analysis, focusing on four key points: (a) dissents as a feature of common law; (b) the underrepresentation of women in ITA; (c) dissenting arbitrators acting as advocates of the appointing party; and (d) the perception that ITA and arbitrators favour investors. While discussing these points, the hypotheses are tested in sections 4 and 5 following the description of the methodology in section 3. We then examine the broader implications of our findings in section 6, focusing on the effects of dissents on arbitral tribunals' perceived independence and impartiality, as the cornerstones of the credibility and legitimacy of international courts. We finally consider possible ways of remedying the perceived lack of impartiality of dissenting arbitrators.

2. The Theoretical Underpinnings

This section provides the theoretical framework supporting our argument. Arbitrators are selected for a particular dispute on an ad hoc basis. Parties (and institutions) select arbitrators with certain characteristics for specific disputes. On this basis, we aim to explore the various characteristics dissenting arbitrators might have.

2.1 Dissents—A Feature of Common Law

Dissenting opinions are common to many international adjudicatory bodies, such as the ICJ,[13] the ECtHR,[14] ITLOS,[15] or ITA,[16] with some notable exceptions, such

[12] Generally on socio-legal studies of adjudicators, see Yves Dezalay and Bryant G Garth, *Dealing in Virtue: International Commercial Arbitration and the Construction of a Transnational Legal Order* (University of Chicago Press 1996); Thomas Schultz and Robert Kovacs, 'The Rise of a Third Generation of Arbitrators: Fifteen Years after Dezalay and Garth' (2012) 28 Arbitration International (updating the scholarship of Dezalay and Garth); Mikael R Madsen, 'Sociological Approached to International Courts' in Cesare P R Romano and others (eds), *The Oxford Handbook of International Adjudication* (OUP 2013).

[13] Statute of the International Court of Justice, Art 57.

[14] Rules of the Court, European Court of Human Rights (2018), rule 75(2).

[15] Statute of the International Tribunal for the Law of the Sea, Art 30(3).

[16] ICSID Convention, Art 48(4); ICSID Convention Arbitration Rules (came into effect on 10 April 2006), Art 47(3); Other international arbitration rules are however silent on dissenting opinions (but

as the Court of Justice of the European Union (CJEU).[17] Their origins, however, are not to be found in international law, but in national legal systems.

Scholars, with some exceptions,[18] argue that the idea of a judge expressing an opinion that is different from the majority's decision finds its roots in common law systems, reflecting their understanding of the role of adjudicators as law-creators.[19] A major challenge for international courts is to blend the main legal traditions of the world.[20] For some it appears that divergences between legal cultures are persisting primarily due to the fundamentally different legal *mentalités* internalized by practitioners from different legal cultures.[21] As dissenting opinions are more widely used in common law systems, we expect arbitrators with such a legal *mentalité* to write more dissenting opinions than those without such a background. We therefore look at whether dissenting arbitrators have a common law or a civil law background.

How exactly one should categorize an arbitrator with a 'common law' background, however, is not an easy question. A simplistic way of looking at it would be to verify whether an arbitrator holds the nationality of a common or a civil law country. Studying whether the nationality of arbitrators matters for outcomes in ITA, Langford and others find that most arbitrators come from Western countries even though the majority of cases concern respondent States from non-Western countries.[22] They highlight that non-Western arbitrators are mainly from Latin

not prohibiting either): United Nations Commission on International Trade Law (UNCITRAL), Permanent Court of Arbitration (PCA); the International Chamber of Commerce (ICC), and the London Court of International Arbitration (LCIA).

[17] The notable outlier being the Court of Justice of the EU; Consolidated Version of Protocol No 3, annexed to the EU Treaties, on the Statute of the Court of Justice of the European Union, Art 35—provides for secret deliberations, which due to the continental tradition has been interpreted as prohibiting separate opinions. See European Parliament, 'Dissenting Opinions in the Supreme Courts of Member States' (2012) PE.462.470, 34 <www.europarl.europa.eu/RegData/etudes/etudes/join/2012/462470/IPOL-JURI_ET(2012)462470_EN.pdf> accessed 18 August 2020.

[18] Martinez-Fraga and Samra (n 11) 450.

[19] Ruth Breeze, 'Dissenting and Concurring Opinions in International Investment Arbitration: How the Arbitrators Frame Their Need to Differ' (2012) 25 International Journal for the Semiotics of Law 393: 'In theory, the option of publicly declaring and explaining a divergent opinion is related to the Common Law understanding of the role of the judge as creating law [...]'; Michael Kirby, 'Judicial Dissent – Common Law and Civil Law Traditions' (2007) Law Quarterly Review 123; Martinez-Fraga and Samra (n 11) 450; Alan Redfern, 'The 2003 Freshfields Lecture - Dissenting Opinions in International Commercial Arbitration: The Good, the Bad and the Ugly' (2004) 20(3) Arbitration International 223, 225.

[20] Daniel Terris, Cesare PR Romano, and Leigh Swigart, *The International Judge: An Introduction to the Men and Women Who Decide the World's Cases* (OUP 2007).

[21] Pierre Legrand, 'European Legal Systems are not Converging' (1996) 45(1) The International and Comparative Law Quarterly 52, 79–81; see also Voeten (n 6) 430 who finds that there is no evidence that the heterogeneity in legal cultures is a source of concern.

[22] Malcolm Langford, Daniel Behn, and Maxim Usynin, 'The West and the Rest: Geographic Diversity and the Role of Arbitrator Nationality in Investment Arbitration' in Daniel Behn, Ole Kristian Fauchald, and Malcolm Langford (eds), *The Legitimacy of Investment Arbitration: Empirical Perspectives* (CUP 2020) (forthcoming); (dataset: examining the nationality of 695 individual arbitrators appointed

America and mostly appointed as respondent wing arbitrator.[23] Puig's research conducted on ICSID appointments from 1972 to 2014 has shown that seven countries represent almost half of the total arbitrator appointments, five of which (the US, Canada,[24] the UK, Australia, and New Zealand) adhere to common law traditions (the other two being France and Switzerland).[25] Therefore, in addition to dissenting opinions being a more usual practice in common law systems, the predominance of common law source countries also supports the expectation that most dissenting opinions are written by arbitrators with a common law nationality.

Nevertheless, as Franck notes, '[d]efining a person's nationality can be difficult because arbitrators can be dual nationals, born one place, live in another, practice in another, and have law degrees from different countries'.[26] Thus, education may also play a significant role in determining whether someone adheres more to the common law or the civil law traditions.[27]

A recent survey by Franck and others on both commercial and investment arbitrators shows that common law was the dominant legal training, 38.5% of the arbitrators surveyed had been trained exclusively in common law jurisdiction, while 27.7% had a hybrid training in both common law and civil law jurisdictions.[28] More generally, in his study on the educational background of international judges (the 'transnational power elite'), Madsen illustrates the role of elite universities

until 1 August 2018); see also Michael Waibel and Yanhui Wu, 'Are Arbitrators Political? Evidence from International Investment Arbitration' (2017) Research Paper (dataset: 341 ICSID arbitrators appointed between 1978 and 2011, finding that most ICSID arbitrators were from OECD countries); Susan Franck, 'Empirically Evaluating Claims about Investment Treaty Arbitration' (2007) 86 North Carolina Law Review 1, 75–82 (finding that for the awards prior to 2007, most arbitrators involved were from OECD states); Susan Franck, 'Development and Outcomes in Investment Treaty Arbitration' (2009) 50 Harvard International Law Review 435 (also concluding that most arbitrators were from OECD states); Noah Rubins and Anthony Sinclair, 'ICSID Arbitrators: Is there a club and who gets invited?' (November 2006) Global Arbitration Review <http://globalarbitrationreview.com/ journal/article/16468/icsid-arbitrators-club-gets-invited/> accessed 18 August 2020) (examining the nationality of 279 ICSID arbitrators from 57 countries with pre-2007 data and finding that nationals from the United States have the largest number of appointments, followed by French, British, Swiss, and Canadian nationals, but observing that several Mexican arbitrators were appointed).

23 Langford and others (n 22) 11; on the issue of diversity in ITA, see also Andrea K Bjorklund and others, 'The Diversity Deficit in International Investment Arbitration' (2020) 21 Journal of World Investment and Trade 410.

24 With the exception of Quebec.

25 Sergio Puig, 'Social Capital in the Arbitration Market' (2014) 25 European Journal of International Law 387; see also UNCTAD, World Investment Report (2018) 95 (finding that in the small group of most appointed arbitrators, all, with the exception of one, are Western European or North American).

26 Franck, 'Empirically Evaluating Claims about Investment Treaty Arbitration' (n 22) footnote 355.

27 ibid 80; see also more generally Mikael R Madsen, 'Who Rules the World? The Educational Capital of the International Judiciary' (2018) 3 UC Irvine Journal of International, Transnational, and Comparative Law 97.

28 Franck and others, 'International Arbitration: Demographics, Precision and Justice' (2015) ICCA Congress Series No18, Legitimacy: Myths, Realities, Challenges (survey on 552 participants of which 262 served as arbitrators: 200 international commercial arbitrators and 62 international investment arbitrators); see also Waibel and Wu (n 22) 15 (finding that most ICSID presiding arbitrators have had their education in OECD countries).

in the formation of international judges, as well as the frequency of international judges having a doctoral degree (54% of the international judges analysed, after 1990).[29] The study reveals that the five most attended universities are University of Cambridge, University of London, Harvard University, University of Paris, and University of Oxford.

In light of the above, we hypothesize that the elite common law background that is dominant among international adjudicators will be reflected amongst dissenting arbitrators as well. In other words, being educated in legal systems that favour dissents could potentially be more important for an arbitrator's inclination to dissent, than the arbitrator's country of nationality. Therefore, we expect that:

> (Hypothesis 1) Arbitrators possessing the nationality of a common law country dissent more than those possessing the nationality of a civil law country;
>
> (Hypothesis 2) Arbitrators with a law degree from a common law country dissent more than those with a civil law degree.

2.2 The Underrepresentation of Women in ITA

One of the often-voiced legitimacy concerns of ITA is the domination of 'pale, male and stale' arbitrators.[30] The last decade has seen a considerable amount of research dedicated to studying the representation of women in ITA appointments. In 2007, Franck concluded—based on a pool of 145 investment treaty arbitrators selected from all publicly available ITA awards before 1 June 2006—that only 3.5% of them were women, who appeared in only nine cases.[31] In 2014, Puig's research has shown that women made up only 7% of ICSID arbitrator appointments.[32]

[29] Madsen 2018 (n 27). Madsen's study covers nine international and regional courts: the European Court of Human Rights, the Inter-American Court of Human Rights, the African Court of Human and Peoples Rights, the Court of Justice of the European Union, the East African Court of Justice, the Caribbean Court of Justice, the International Court of Justice, the World Trade Organization's Appellate Body, and the International Criminal Court. The statistics for each individual court can be found on pages 114–16.

[30] See eg Lucy Greenwood and C Mark Baker, 'Getting a Better Balance on International Arbitration Tribunals' (2012) 28 Arbitration International 653; see also Susan Franck and others, 'The Diversity Challenge: Exploring the "Invisible College" of International Arbitration' (2015) 53 Columbia Journal of Transnational Law 429; Gus Van Harten, 'The (Lack of) Women Arbitrators in Investment Treaty Arbitration' (6 February 2012) Columbia FDI Perspectives No 59.

[31] Franck, 'Empirically Evaluating Claims about Investment Treaty Arbitration' (n 22) 82.

[32] Puig 2014 (n 25) 406; see also Daniel Behn and others, 'Empirical Perspectives on Investment Arbitration: What Do we Know? Does it Matter?' (2020) 21 Journal of World Investment and Trade 233–36; Lucy Greenwood and C Mark Baker, 'Is the Balance Getting Better? An Update on the Issue of Gender Diversity' (2015) 31(3) Arbitration International 413 (finding that 5.61% of women were appointed in 2014), and Waibel and Wu 2017 (n 22) (finding less than 10% of women were appointed in 2017).

More recently, St. John and others analysed all publicly known ITA appointments up until 1 January 2017. Out of a total of 2810 appointments, 253 (9%) were women. Interestingly though, of the 253 female appointments, 57% was shared by only two 'formidable women' of investment arbitration, Gabrielle Kaufmann-Kohler and Brigitte Stern.[33] Even though roughly a third of individuals active in investment arbitration (as arbitrators, counsel, experts, and tribunal secretaries) are women, 'women are more likely to appear in roles with formalized appointment procedures and less prestige, like tribunal secretaries'.[34] Furthermore, informal norms within the appointment process, such as 'previous experience' might reinforce this phenomenon .[35]

In addition, previous academic findings are mixed when looking at empirical research on the role of gender in dissenting opinions. On the one hand, an experimental study on decision-making processes indicates that women tend to prefer universalistic outcomes and group cooperation, whereas men favour individualistic and competitive solutions.[36] Such a finding could indicate a tendency for female adjudicators to dissent less. On the other hand, while some studies on US Courts show that female justices bring a different worldview than their male counterparts to the deliberative process[37], others find little or no effect of gender on dissent.[38] In the context of Canadian courts, studies show that female judges are more liberal than men and that they dissent more often.[39] Noting the limitations of domestic analogies, such studies still provide valuable insights to our analysis.

Given the existing evidence on the underrepresentation of women in the appointment of investment arbitrators and the potential for arbitrators to be influenced by their gender attribute, we expect that:

(Hypothesis 3) Female arbitrators dissent less than male arbitrators reflecting the overall underrepresentation of female appointments.

[33] Taylor St John and others, 'Glass Ceilings and Arbitral Dealings: Explaining the Gender Gap in Investment Arbitration' (2018) PluriCourts Working Paper; see also Lucy Greenwood, 'Tipping the Balance: Diversity and Inclusion in International Arbitration' (2017) 33(1) Arbitration International 99 (arguing that the situation might be slowly improving with regards to gender diversity).

[34] ibid.

[35] ibid.

[36] Carole Kennedy, 'Gender Differences in Committee Decision-Making: Process and Outputs in an Experimental Setting' (2003) 25(3) Women and Politics 40–41.

[37] See for example Christina L Boyd, Lee Epstein, and Andrew D Martin, 'Untangling the Causal Effects of Sex on Judging' (2010) 54(2) American Journal of Political Science 406–407.

[38] See for example Virginia A Hettinger, Stefanie Lindquist, and Wendy L Martinek, 'Comparing Attitudinal and Strategic Accounts of Dissenting Behavior on the U.S. Courts of Appeals' (2004) 48(1) American Journal of Political Science 133.

[39] Marie-Claire Belleau and Rebecca Johnson, 'Judging Gender: Difference and Dissent at the Supreme Court of Canada' (2008) 15(1–2) International Journal of the Legal Profession 57; see also Donald R Songer and Susan W Johnson, 'Judicial Decision Making in the Supreme Court of Canada: Updating the Personal Attribute Model' (2007) 40(4) Canadian Journal of Political Science 931.

If the assumption is correct, then this would indicate that the low proportion of female dissenting arbitrators is reflective of the overall state of investment arbitrator appointments, and not an indication that women are less prone to dissent than men, or vice versa.

2.3 Dissenting Arbitrators Acting as Advocates of the Appointing Party?

The right of each party to appoint an arbitrator is a significant characteristic of ITA. As suggested by Veeder, this right is arguably 'one manifest reason' for users to prefer arbitration over litigation as it gives 'the sense of ownership by a party over the arbitral process because it has participated in the formation of the tribunal as to which all parties have consented'.[40]

However, it is this very sense of ownership flowing from party appointments that might cause concern. Critics suggest that party-appointed arbitrators tend to be biased in favour of 'their' party,[41] which in turn can affect the impartiality and independence of the arbitral tribunal.[42] For example, Puig and Strezhnev's 2017 survey of 257 arbitrators focused on the affiliation bias of arbitrators and found that arbitrators appointed by one of the two litigants 'tended to make decisions more favourable to that party compared with arbitrators appointed by the opposite party', even when the selection effects were removed.[43] Puig's 2016 study has also shown that tribunals *without* party-appointed arbitrators tend to handle cases faster, they settle more often and their decisions tend to be unanimous.[44] Nevertheless, the rate of challenges of arbitrators is higher for such tribunals than for party-appointed ones.[45]

Scholarship has also explored the link between arbitrator impartiality and dissents. Van den Berg's original study on dissenting arbitrators questioned the neutrality of party-appointed arbitrators as he found that 'dissenting opinions are almost universally issued in favour of the party that appointed the dissenter',[46]

[40] Veeder (n 11).
[41] Chiara Giorgetti, 'Who Decides Who Decides in International Investment Arbitration?' (2013) 35(2) University of Pennsylvania Journal of International Law 431.
[42] Sergio Puig and Anton Strezhnev, 'Affiliation Bias in Arbitration: An Experimental Approach' (2017) 46 Journal of Legal Study 371; Susan D Franck and others, 'Inside the Arbitrator's Mind' (2017) 66 Emory Law Journal 1115.
[43] Puig and Strezhnev (n 42) 373; see also Behn and others (n 32) 240-249. In statistics when a sample from a population is not selected randomly, then one runs the risk of having a biased sample, even if that bias is unintentional or difficult to discern. This is often called *selection bias* or *selection effect*. See David M Diez, Christopher D Barr, and Mine Cetinkaya-Rundel, *OpenIntro Statistics. Third Edition* (OpenIntro 2015) 16.
[44] Sergio Puig, 'Blinding International Justice' (2016) 56 Virginia Journal of International Law 647, 693–4.
[45] ibid.
[46] Van den Berg 2011 (n 9); see also Paulsson (n 7) and Titi (n 11).

a conclusion later confirmed by Kapelniuk as well.[47] He therefore questioned the legitimacy of dissents in ITA and suggested that ITA should 'observe the principle *nemine dissentiente*'. As a response to Van den Berg's conclusions, Brower and Rosenberg emphasized the importance of dissents, highlighting that dissenting opinions may contribute to the development of the law.[48] They further explained that 'dissenting opinions play a critical role in fostering the legitimacy of international arbitration'.[49]

Furthermore, career motivations—as an important determinant of judicial behaviour—is widely recognized in US legal literature.[50] In the context of the ECtHR, Voeten finds modest evidence of the effect of career motivations on the behaviour of judges.[51] He also shows that career insecurities might incentivize judges to favour their national government when it is party to a dispute.[52] Evidence indicates that ECtHR judges reaching the mandatory retirement age show less national bias than judges who face reappointment pressures.[53] Voeten also argues that judges appointed on a case-by-case basis have much stronger national bias than regular judges.[54] Similar career insecurities could also motivate arbitrators to favour the party appointing them.

In the context of ICSID arbitrations, Strezhnev finds that dissents may reduce the re-appointment of presiding arbitrators. This effect, however, is not applicable to appointments by individual parties. Thus, it indicates that dissents may have less impact on the perception that arbitrators act as advocates for either claimants or respondents.[55] However, according to Tucker, the dissent of party-appointed arbitrators—especially wing arbitrators—might benefit their career if they wish to be consistently appointed by either claimants or respondents.[56] Some arbitrators claim that 'reputation is "all you have" as an arbitrator in a system without tenure' and 'for arbitration to become your "bread and butter" and to make a "nice living" on it, you need the support of others in the arbitration community'.[57] Thus, even

[47] Daphna Kapelniuk, 'Collegial Games: analyzing the Effect of Panel composition on Outcome in Investment Arbitration' (2012) 31 The Review of Litigation 267, 309-310. However, Kapelniuk finds that there is a lack of tendency of party-appointed arbitrators to display bias in favour of the appointing party through dissents.

[48] Brower, Pulos, and Rosenberg (n 9); Brower and Rosenberg (n 9).

[49] See (n 11); Martinez-Fraga and Samra (n 11) 462, criticizing Van den Berg's conclusions, arguing that the latter's 'purely descriptive account is certainly hapless as to any revelation directly or indirectly related to the nature or character of dissenting opinions'.

[50] Richard A Posner, 'What Do Judges and Justices Maximize? (The Same Thing Everybody Else Does)' (1993) 3 Supreme Court Economic Review 41.

[51] Voeten (n 6) 427–28; see also Erik Voeten, 'International Judicial Behavior' in Cesare Romano, Karen Alter, and Yuval Shany (eds) *The Oxford Handbook of International Adjudication* (OUP 2013) 553.

[52] Voeten (n 6).

[53] Voeten (n 6) 417–33.

[54] Erik Voeten, 'International Judicial Behavior' (n 51) 554.

[55] Strezhnev (n 11) 5.

[56] Todd Tucker, 'Inside the Black Box: Collegial Patterns on Investment Tribunals' (2016) 19 Journal of International Dispute Settlement 190.

[57] ibid; see also Waibel and Wu (n 22).

though dissenting opinions might benefit the development of the law and generate better awards, as Tucker further explains:

> [by] creating a long paper trail of dissents, [arbitrators] document what [they] in particular (rather than the tribunals as a whole) believe. On the one hand, this advertises [that they] have not been bought off in a given case. On the other, dissents do advertise to law firms and potential appointers. They say, *Here is what I believe. Appoint me if this belief's useful to you.*[58]

When looking at factors influencing the outcomes of arbitral decisions, Waibel and Wu indicate, *inter alia*, that work experience in corporations positively correlates with holding host States liable while experience as private practitioners or as an academic has a strong negative effect on the decision on liability.[59] In the context of the ECtHR, Voeten finds that judges who were diplomats in their previous careers were more likely to favour their national governments than judges with a different career background.[60] As arbitrators are dependent on their reputation to survive in the arbitration community, the incentive to maintain a good reputation might be higher for those primarily working in a private law firm.[61]

In light of the above, we expect that:

> (Hypothesis 4) Arbitrators appointed by the losing party write more dissents;

> (Hypothesis 5) Arbitrators with a private practice background write more dissents than arbitrators without such a professional background.

2.4 The Perception that ITA and Arbitrators Favour Investors

ITA has also been criticized over the years for 'favouring' investors to the detriment of States.[62] This criticism was initially fuelled by the large number of ITA awards rendered as a result of the measures adopted by Argentina during its 2001–2002

[58] Tucker (n 56) 194; see also Pia Eberhardt and Cecilia Olivet, 'Profiting from Injustice: How Law Firms, Arbitrators, and Financiers are Fueling an Investment Arbitration Boom', Corporate Europe Observatory (November 2012); Puig and Strezhnev (n 42).

[59] Waibel and Wu (n 22) 17; see also Franck and others 2017 (n 42).

[60] Voeten (n 6) 430.

[61] Ana Fernandez Perez, 'Conflicts of interests of arbitrators in international law firms' (2018) 34 Arbitration International 105.

[62] On the issue of bias towards investors, see for example Mavluda Sattorova, *The Impact of Investment Treaty Law on Host States: Enabling Good Governance?* (Hart 2018); Gus Van Harten, 'Leaders in the Expansive and Restrictive Interpretation of Investment Treaties: A Descriptive Study of ISDS Awards to 2010' (2018) 29(2) European Journal of International Law 507.

economic crisis.[63] Many saw these awards as restricting a State's regulatory autonomy in times of national emergency in favour of protecting the interests of private companies.[64] Furthermore, ITA has also been criticized for its asymmetrical nature, since only investors are able to bring claims and investment treaties prescribe obligations for States but not for investors.[65] Finally, one could argue that evidence indicating that arbitrators appointed by investors dissent more often, would further fuel the perception that ITA favours investors.

However, the results of several empirical studies on some of the aforementioned criticisms paint a more nuanced picture. Langford and Behn's 2017 study find that in the period 1990–2001 investors rarely lost at the jurisdiction stage (94% success rate in 32 decisions) and they won approximately three quarters of finally resolved cases (72%) and liability/merits awards (78%).[66] Nevertheless, from 2002 to 2017, they identify a downwards trend for investors,[67] which is arguably driven by arbitrators' concern to maintain the perceived legitimacy of the system.

Likewise, Franck and Wylie's study demonstrates that ITA reflects 'a [S]tate-favourable or rough balance in outcomes'.[68] Similarly, the World Investment Report of 2017 (WIR) released by the United Nations Conference on Trade and Development (UNCTAD), has concluded that for the period 1987–2016, out of 495 investor-state dispute settlement (ISDS) proceedings, 36% were decided in favour of the State, 27% in favour of the investor, 25% were settled, 10% discontinued, and 2% found a breach without awarding damages.[69] Conversely, Tucker's study on the collegial dynamics within investment tribunals shows that collegial interactions lead to making awards more investor-friendly or fact specific.[70]

63 Malcolm Langford and Daniel Behn, 'Managing Backlash: The Evolving Investment Treaty Arbitrator?' (2018) 29(2) European Journal of International Law 551, 556 (dataset: 453 jurisdiction decisions and 291 liability/merits decisions).

64 ibid.

65 Jonathan Bonnitcha, Lauge N S Poulsen, and Michael Waibel, *The Political Economy of the Investment Treaty Regime* (OUP 2016) 14.

66 Langford and Behn (n 63) 566–67.

67 ibid, 567 (between 2002–17, the success rates of investors dropped to 44% in finally resolved cases and 59% in finally resolved cases and in liability/merits awards, while the number of investor wins in the jurisdictional phase also decreased to 69% from 2011 onwards).

68 Susan Franck and Lindsey Wylie, 'Predicting Outcomes in Investment Treaty Arbitration' (2015) 65 Duke Law Journal 520 (using publicly available awards prior to 2012); see also Franck (2007) (n 22) 54 (finding that investors were more successful at the jurisdictional stages whereas governments had higher success rates on the merits); see also Alec Stone Sweet and Florian Grisel, *The Evolution of International Arbitration: Judicialization, Governance, Legitimacy* (OUP 2017).

69 UNCTAD, 'World Investment Report 2017 – Investment and the Digital Economy' (2017) UNCTAD/WIR/2017, 117. However, Bonnitcha and others (n 65) 26–27 argue that this win-loss ratio in and of itself says little to us, 'because investors are likely to take their probability of success into account when deciding whether to bring particular disputes to investment treaty arbitration'.

70 Tucker (n 56) 204 (dataset: 44 interviews with 44 individuals that served in over 90% of the over 260 concluded cases from 1990 through mid-2015, finding eight types of arbitrators); see also Van Harten (n 62) (finding that a small group of elite arbitrators favour investors and particularly those from major Western capital-exporting countries).

One explanation to the findings is that investors have asymmetric control over the caseload and thereby indirectly on the reappointments.[71]

Given the existing perceptions that ITA might favour investors, while noting the mixed findings from empirical studies, we expect that:

> (Hypothesis 6) Arbitrators appointed by investors write more dissents than those appointed by States.

3. Delimitation and Data Gathering

When conducting empirical legal research, several questions have to be considered.[72] First, how does one delimit the central concept of the research? Second, what data should be gathered and what is the source of the data? Third, to what end should the data be used? Fourth, what type of conclusions can be drawn from the data? One cannot prove causation, but correlation at most, and due to the politicization of investment law and ITA one has to be careful to present the data as objectively as possible. Therefore, proposals for reform in section 6 are made cautiously.[73]

3.1 Delimitation

What exactly is a dissent? A dissenting opinion may be defined as 'the reasons for which a judge could not agree with the majority'.[74] If one looks at ITA awards, arbitrators often issue 'dissenting' opinions,[75] 'separate' opinions, 'concurring' opinions, or 'dissenting and concurring' opinions to express divergent views. *Lato sensu*, a dissent means any additional comments or opinions that are different from the majority's decision, which leads to the same or a different outcome. In other words, dissents *lato sensu* cover so called dissenting, concurring, and separate opinions. On the other hand, a *stricto sensu* dissent would entail that the arbitrator does not agree with the overall outcome of the case or the outcome of one/several claims raised in the case. In a separate or concurring opinion, the arbitrator would agree with the outcome of the case but not fully or in part with the reasoning through which the tribunal reached the outcome. For the purposes of this chapter, both *lato*

[71] Tucker (n 56).

[72] See Lee Epstein and Andrew D Martin, *An Introduction to Empirical Legal Research* (OUP 2014).

[73] Rogers (n 8) 233.

[74] R P Anand, 'The Role of Individual and Dissenting Opinions in International Adjudication' (1965) 14(3) The International and Comparative Law Quarterly 788, 806.

[75] Some arbitrators name them 'declarations'.

sensu and *stricto sensu* dissents are discussed. Furthermore, this chapter does not aim to take a stance on whether ITA and dissents are desirable or not.

3.2 Data Gathering

We used the PITAD database[76] in order to identify all dissenting, concurring, and separate opinions issued in ITA proceedings until 31 December 2016, the last time the database was fully updated when the data was gathered for this study. In total, we found 117 dissenting opinions *lato sensu*, a considerably higher number than the 34 dissents used in Van den Berg's original 2011 study. Of the 117 dissents in the broad sense, 70 (59.8%) were dissenting opinions in the narrow sense, 37 (31.6%) were separate/concurring opinions, and 10 (8.6%) were both dissenting and concurring/separate opinions.[77] The coded dissents (see Annex 2) include dissenting opinions on final awards, partial awards, or decisions on jurisdiction. Dissenting opinions on procedural/interim orders were excluded.[78] We coded for appointments by the winning party,[79] the losing party, and the president of the tribunal, as well as the arbitrators appointed by the investor, the State, and the presiding arbitrator. We tested for both dissents in the broad and the narrow sense in order to minimize selection bias.

We also looked at publicly available information[80] on the dissenting arbitrators to gather further data on their nationality, gender, educational, as well as professional backgrounds. In total, for the 117 dissenting opinions *lato sensu* we identified 87 arbitrators. We found limited information on two arbitrators: Jürgen Voss and Yawovi Agboyibo. In the case of nationality, we looked at both first and second nationality and gender. The educational background included the *almae matres* for undergraduate, postgraduate, and doctoral studies. Finally, the professional background included four categories: 'academia', 'government', 'private practice', and 'other international' (excluding ITA, but including international organizations or other international courts). Many arbitrators had experience in at least three professional fields (see Annex 1).

76 PluriCourts database (PITAD) <https://pitad.org/index#welcome> accessed 18 August 2020.

77 Because the classification of dissents creates the potential for selection bias, when testing assumptions for which the number of dissents was crucial, we tested for both dissents in the broad (*lato sensu*) and the narrow (*stricto sensu*) sense; see also Rogers (n 8) 245.

78 We only included dissents on matters relating to legal issues (jurisdiction, admissibility and merits) rather than purely procedural matters. This approach is also taken by other authors examining dissents in ITA (see eg Breeze (n 19); van den Berg 2011 (n 9).

79 A 'winning party' includes all decisions in favour of the party whether it is a partial win or a full win.

80 The relevant information was collected using: the arbitrators' professional profile in the ICSID database (if available), the arbitral awards detailing their nationality, information found on ITALAW, as well as professional CVs available on the websites of governments, universities, and private law firms.

It is also important to highlight that dissents in ITA are not the norm. As mentioned, we looked at 117 dissents *lato sensu*, until the end of 2016. If we corroborate this data with the number of concluded (388 with a final award, 124 settled, and 67 discontinued) cases by the end of 2016 in the PITAD database,[81] then 20.2% of the concluded cases had a dissent *lato sensu*. If we count the 70 dissents *stricto sensu* and only the cases that had a final award, then 18% of them had a dissent. Whilst, these numbers are not high, they are also not negligible.

The use of dissenting and concurring opinions is relatively infrequent in ITA compared to other international courts.[82] This might be a result of the different set-up of a standing court, such as the ICJ, compared to an ad hoc arbitral tribunal. The ICJ normally sits as a full bench of 15 judges compared to the three arbitrators usually appointed in ITA. Thus, the higher number of judges might also result in a higher number of dissents, as the possibility of divergent opinions rises. Despite this seemingly low percentage of ITA dissents,[83] one should not overlook the importance and the potential problems relating to this feature in ITA.

4. Meeting the Dissenting Arbitrators: Arbitrator-Level Variables

Parties to investment disputes (and their lawyers) spend a considerable amount of time and effort scrutinizing the social, legal, and professional background of arbitrators in order to appoint an arbitrator who might have some favourable predisposition towards their case, without rising to the level of conflict of interest and partiality.[84] Therefore, in this part of the study, we focus on four arbitrator level variables that could influence dissents: nationality, gender, education, and professional experience.

4.1 Legal Culture: Common Law *v* Civil Law

In order to test the first hypothesis (H1) this section first takes a more simplistic look at the nationality of arbitrators and whether their nationality belongs to a civil law or common law country. Then, we focus on the educational background

[81] Daniel Behn, 'The Performance of Investment Treaty Arbitration' in Theresa Squatrito and others (eds), *The Performance of International Courts and Tribunals* (CUP 2018) 77–113, 97.

[82] Strezhnev (n 11); see also Breeze (n 19) 396 (arguing that the low number of dissents might be because of the high desirability of unanimity in ITA); Jeffrey L Dunoff and Mark A Pollack, 'International Judicial Dissent: Causes and Consequences' (2015) Conference Proceedings: European Union Studies Association, Biennial Conference, 4–7 March 2015.

[83] As Rogers rightly asks, low or high compared to what? Rogers (n 8) 242.

[84] See Waibel and Wu (n 22).

of the arbitrators in order to offer a more nuanced analysis and test the second hypothesis (H2).

4.1.1 The nationality test

4.1.1.1 Nationality

When looking at the *nationality* of the dissenting arbitrators (see Figure 15.1), the following can be said: 18 arbitrators came from the United States (20.7%), 7 came from Canada (8%), 6 from Spain (6.9%), 6 from the United Kingdom (6.9%), 6 from France (6.9%), 4 from Argentina (5%), 3 from Italy (3.4%), 3 from the Netherlands (3.4%), 3 from Mexico (3.4%), 3 from Germany (3.4%), 2 from Australia (2.3%), 2 from Russia (2.3%), 2 from Poland (2.3%), 2 from Colombia (2.3%), 2 from Venezuela (2.3%), and 2 from Chile (2.3%). The rest of the 16 arbitrators (18.2%) came from: Uruguay, Guyana, Egypt, Senegal, Ghana, Jordan, Togo, Pakistan, Sweden, Czech Republic, Bulgaria, Serbia, Switzerland, Cyprus, Costa Rica, and South Africa. Out of the 87 arbitrators, 6 had a double nationality.[85]

Based on this data, one should not hastily conclude that US arbitrators—coming from a system where dissents have a long-rooted tradition—dissent more often than non-US arbitrators. This number needs to be corroborated with the overall high percentage of US arbitrators appointed as arbitrators. Puig's research conducted on ICSID appointments between 1972 and 2014 places the US appointments on top of the list, with 11.54%.[86] Franck and others' 2015 study of 260 international commercial and investment treaty arbitrators also found that the

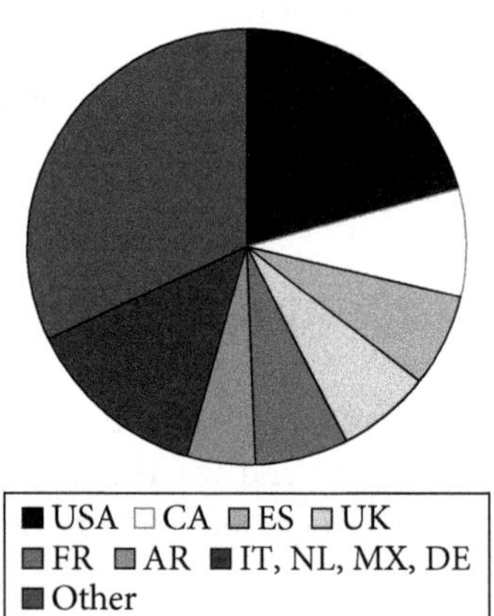

Figure 15.1 Dissenting arbitrators by nationality (87 arbitrators)

[85] Philippe Sands (France and UK); Laurence Boisson de Chazournes (France and Switzerland); Raúl Emilio Vinuesa (Argentina and Spain); Jan Paulsson (Sweden and France); Donald McRae (Canada and New Zealand); Ibrahim Fadlallah (France and Lebanon).

[86] Puig 2014 (n 25) 406.

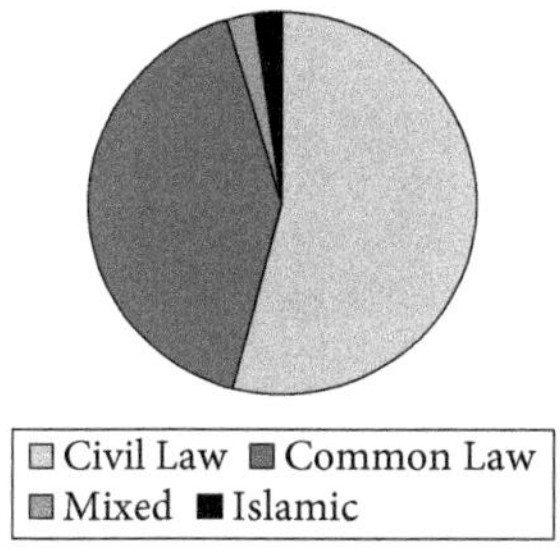

Figure 15.2 'Common law' v 'Civil law' by nationality (87 arbitrators)

United States leads the list with 23.2%.[87] Therefore, the high percentage of US dissenters might simply reflect the overall high representation of appointed US arbitrators, as indicated by Puig's and Franck's studies.

4.1.1.2 Common v civil law nationality

In order to test H1, we grouped the nationality of the dissenting arbitrators according to whether they belong to a common law country, a civil law country, or a country with a different legal system (see Figure 15.2).

According to this 'crude' classification based on nationality, 47 (54%) out of the 87 dissenting arbitrators have the nationality of a civil law country, 36 (41.3%) came from common law jurisdictions, 2 (2.3%) from a partial Islamic legal system,[88] and 2 (2.3%) from 'mixed' jurisdictions.[89]

Given that some arbitrators dissented more than once, we decided to look at the civil/common law nationality divide also with regard to the overall number of 117 dissents *lato sensu* (see Figure 15.3). Arbitrators possessing a civil law nationality issued 58 (49.6%) dissents, those with a common law nationality issued 51 (43.6%), 4 (3.4%) came from a partial Islamic legal system, 2 (1.7%) from mixed jurisdictions, and for 2 (1.7%) dissents the authors were unknown.[90]

Contrary to our expectations (H1), over half (54%) of dissenting arbitrators, if one looks at nationality, come from civil law and *not* common law countries! Furthermore, the number remained roughly unchanged when we looked at the overall number of dissents *lato sensu*. When looking at the larger pool of arbitrators, Puig and Strezhnev found that, among the number of ICSID arbitrators they

[87] Franck and others (n 30) 52.

[88] Georges Abi-Saab (Egypt) and Omar Nabulsi (Jordan). It is debatable to what extent can Georges Abi-Saab be considered as someone coming from a partial Islamic System and not a Civil Law system.

[89] Andreas Jacovides (Cyprus) and P M Nienaber (South Africa). We counted the entirety of Canada (including Quebec) as a common law system.

[90] *Ahmonseto, Inc. and others v Arab Republic of Egypt* Ahmonseto, ICSID Case No ARB/02/15, Award 18 June 2007; and *Banro American Resources, Inc. and Société Aurifère du Kivu et du Maniema S.A.R.L. v Democratic Republic of the Congo*, ICSID Case No ARB/98/7, Award, 1 September 2000.

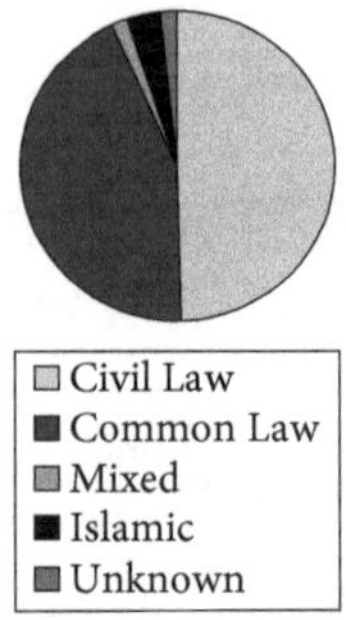

Figure 15.3 'Common law' v 'Civil law' by nationality (117 dissents *lato sensu*)

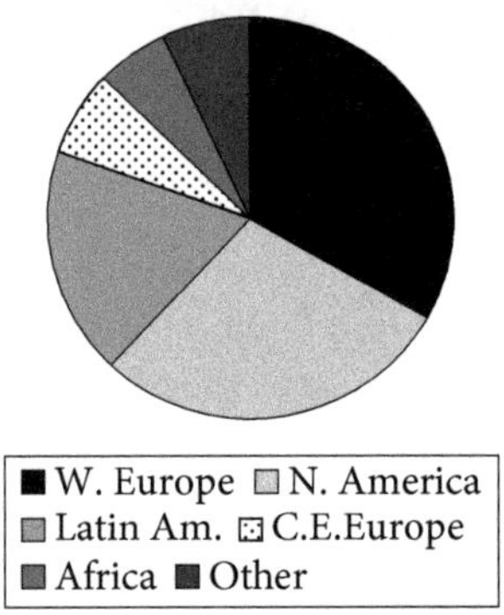

Figure 15.4 Dissenting arbitrators by geographical area (87 arbitrators)

surveyed, more than half come from 'exclusively civil-law backgrounds' whereas 41% are from a country with a common law background.[91] In light of these numbers, we can assume that the nationality of the dissenters reflects the overall higher percentage of arbitrators possessing a civil law nationality.

4.1.1.3 Geographical regions

For the sake of curiosity, we also decided to group the dissenting arbitrators by major geographical regions (see Figure 15.4). A third of dissenting arbitrators (29, 33.3%) come from Western Europe (including Italy and Spain), while 25 dissenters come from North America (28.7%), excluding the Latin American States. The third geographical area, with 16 arbitrators (18.4%) is Latin America (including

[91] See Puig and Strezhnev (n 42) 391; see also Franck and others (n 30) 52. They found that 40% of arbitrators have the nationality of a common law country using a survey on 552 participants of which 262 served as arbitrators: 200 as international commercial arbitrators and 62 as international investment arbitrators.

Guyana). In other words, Western Europe, North America, and Latin America dominate dissents with 80.4%. Central Eastern Europe (excluding Russia) gave 6 dissenting arbitrators (6.9%), while Africa gave 5 (5.7%). Asia, the most populous continent, is only represented by 2 (2.3%) dissenters, while the rest of the dissenting arbitrators came from Australia and Russia (4, 4.7%).

The large number of North American, Western European, and Latin American dissenters should *not* be viewed as proof that the arbitrators from these regions are more prone to dissenting, compared to arbitrators coming from other regions. It is in fact a further reflection of the existing disparities between the geographical areas from which most appointed arbitrators come from. One of the criticisms of ITA is that the number of appointed arbitrators does not adequately reflect the various geographical regions of the world, North America, Western Europe, and Latin America providing a large chunk of the appointed arbitrators. According to Puig's research conducted on appointed ICSID arbitrators until 2014, arbitrators from seven Western nations (the UK, the US, Canada, France, Switzerland, Australia, New Zealand) represent almost half of the total appointments, while arbitrators from five Latin American countries make up close to 15% of the appointed arbitrators.[92]

In conclusion, contrary to our expectation (H1)—that most dissents are issued by arbitrators holding the nationality of a common law country—we find that most dissenting arbitrators do not have the nationality of a common law country. In fact, dissents were fairly evenly split between the two groups, with those possessing a civil law nationality representing slightly over half of dissenting arbitrators. This reflects the similar split between the common and civil law nationalities of the broader pool of arbitrators and further displays one of the inherent problems in ITA: the limited geographic representation of appointed arbitrators.

4.1.2 The educational background

According to our second hypothesis (H2) arbitrators possessing a degree from a (top) common law institution wrote more dissents than arbitrators with civil law degrees. In order to test this hypothesis, we took into account the arbitrators' undergraduate, postgraduate and doctoral degrees and the percentage of these degrees that came from top US or UK law schools.[93]

4.1.2.1 Undergraduate degrees

We managed to find information on the *undergraduate degrees* of 75 arbitrators out of 87 (86.2%). For 13 arbitrators, the name of the undergraduate *alma mater* was not available. Of the 74 arbitrators, the great majority of them (61, or 82.4%)

[92] Puig 2014 (n 25) 405; see also discussion above in section 2.1.

[93] Florian Grisel, 'Competition and Cooperation in International Commercial Arbitration: The Birth of a Transnational Legal Profession' (2017) 51 (4) Law and Society Review 790.

pursued their undergraduate studies in the countries of their first nationality, while the remaining 13 pursued it in a different country, or their country of first nationality and another country. Thus, the nationality of the arbitrators and the institutions where they pursued their undergraduate degrees roughly coincide. In other words, there might be no significant correlation between dissents and whether the undergraduate degrees were obtained at a top UK or US law school.

4.1.2.2 Postgraduate degrees

The outcome differs once we consider the postgraduate degrees. We counted master's degrees in law (LLM), diplôme d'études supérieures spécialisées (DESS) in France and the JD degree in the United States as postgraduate degrees. For 12 arbitrators, we did not find any information on their postgraduate degrees. This does not completely overlap with the previous 12 arbitrators lacking undergraduate degrees. Thus, we had information on 75 arbitrators. Of the 75 dissenting arbitrators, 16 did not possess a postgraduate degree (21%).

What we see is that during their postgraduate degrees a number of dissenting arbitrators pursued their education at institutions located outside their original country of nationality. If we look at top law-schools from the US, UK, or France (see Figure 15.5), then 12 (16%) out of the 75 arbitrators obtained their postgraduate degree (or one of them) from Harvard, 5 (6.7%) from Cambridge, 4 (5.3%) from Oxford, 4 (5.3%) from Yale, 2 (2.7%) from Michigan, 11 (14.7%) from other leading US law schools (New York University, Miami Law School, Columbia, Fordham, Chicago, etc.), 4 (5.3%) from other leading UK universities (eg LSE), and 3 from leading French universities.

In other words, 38.7% of dissenting arbitrators for whom we found information concerning their postgraduate education have obtained their degree at top US universities, while 17.3% have obtained it at a top UK university. This amounts to over half (42, 56%) of the 75 arbitrators for whom information is available on their postgraduate studies. If we deduct the 16 arbitrators who do not possess a postgraduate

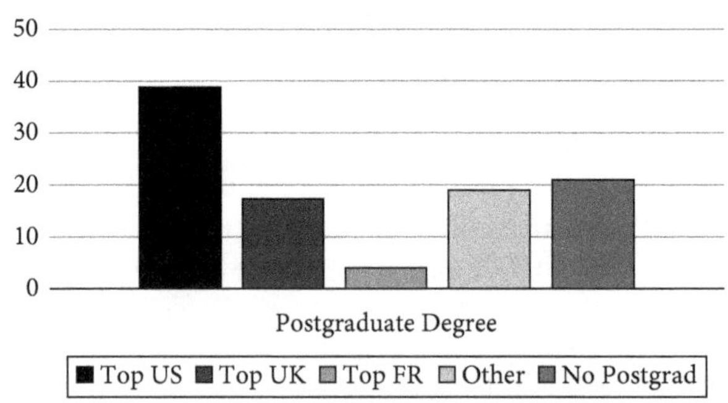

Figure 15.5 Postgraduate education at top law schools (75 arbitrators)

degree, then 71.2% of the remaining 59 arbitrators—who possess a postgraduate degree—have received their degrees at leading US or UK universities.

For the 42 arbitrators possessing a UK or US postgraduate degree we also looked at whether they possessed the nationality of a common or a civil law country. Of the 42 dissenting arbitrators who received their postgraduate degrees at top UK or US institutions, 25 possessed a common law nationality, 14 possessed a civil law nationality, 1 came from a country with a mixed system, and 2 arbitrators came from a country with partial Islamic law.

iii. *Doctorate:* When looking at the existence of a doctorate degree or equivalent, we found the following. For 6 out of the 87 dissenting arbitrators we did not find any information on whether they possess a doctorate. Another 43 indicated that they do not possess such a degree. We know for sure that 38 arbitrators do possess a doctorate (43.6% of the 87), 14 (16.1% of the 87) of whom obtained it at a top US or UK university. If we only count the arbitrators who possess a doctorate, then a large number of them (36.8%) received their doctoral degrees at top UK or US universities (common law universities).

In conclusion, our second hypothesis (H2)—that arbitrators with a common law degree wrote more dissents than those with a civil law degree—is partially true. One needs to differentiate between the levels of education. The vast majority of dissenters obtained their undergraduate degrees in their countries of nationality. However, during their postgraduate studies a significant part of the dissenting arbitrators moved abroad and 71.2% of those who pursued a postgraduate degree had done so at top US or UK law schools. But is that really a notable characteristic of dissenting arbitrators? Probably not. Recent studies show that the international judges predominantly receive their legal training in elite universities mainly situated in common law jurisdictions.[94]

4.2 Gender

According to our third hypothesis (H3) the proportion of female arbitrators and dissents rendered by female arbitrators will reflect the overall low representation of women in ITA. In order to minimize selection bias resulting from some arbitrators dissenting more often than others, we decided to look at (a) the number of female dissenters compared to the overall number of dissenting arbitrators, and (b) the number of dissents rendered by female arbitrators compared to the overall number of dissents.

Of the 87 dissenters, only four (4.6%) were women, namely: Brigitte Stern, Susana Czar De Zalduendo, Laurence Boisson de Chazournes, and Carolyn

[94] See Franck and others (n 30); see also more generally on international adjudicators, Madsen (n 27).

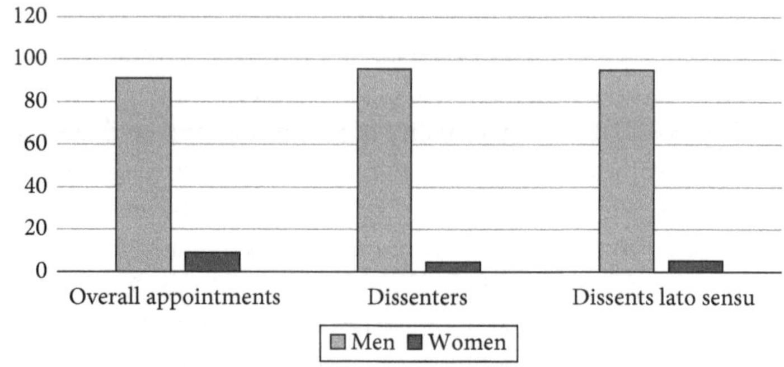

Figure 15.6 The gender of the dissenters

Lamm. With the exception of Brigitte Stern, the other women arbitrators only dissented once. Of the total number of 117 dissents *lato sensu* only six (5.1%) came from female arbitrators. Based on these findings one could arrive at the erroneous conclusion that men dissent more often than women. However, when the data is corroborated with the afore-mentioned studies (see section 2.2) that place the percentage of overall female appointed arbitrators between 3.5–9%, then our hypothesis might be confirmed: the very low proportion of female dissenters and dissents rendered by women arbitrators reflects the overall underrepresentation of women appointed as investment arbitrators (see Figure 15.6).

4.3 Professional Backgrounds

According to our fifth hypothesis (H5), we would expect arbitrators with a professional background from private law firms to write more dissents than arbitrators without such a professional background. To test this hypothesis, we grouped the professional backgrounds of dissenting arbitrators into four categories: private practice, academia, government, and other international experience (experience in international organizations or international courts, other than ITA).[95] For two arbitrators (Jürgen Voss and Yawovi Agboyibo) we did not find information on their professional backgrounds. Of the remaining 85 arbitrators for whom we found ample information on their professional backgrounds: 65 (76.5%) had experience in private practice, 56 had academic experience, (65.7%), 50 had government experience (58.8%), and 39 had other international experience (45.9%). The

[95] International experience refers mainly to experience with international courts and tribunals and/or UN agencies.

total number is higher than 100% because most dissenting arbitrators had more than one type of professional experience.[96]

The data seems to confirm the fifth hypothesis, as more arbitrators with a professional background in private practice wrote dissents than arbitrators with other professional backgrounds. Nevertheless, our conclusions are nuanced. Firstly, it cannot be clearly concluded that there is a significant correlation between writing dissents and having experience in private practice, since the number of dissenters who had experience in private practice is not considerably higher than those who had academic experience. Furthermore, over half (58.8%) of the dissenting arbitrators also had government experience.

Secondly, we do not have data on the professional background of *all* appointed arbitrators. Thus, we do not know whether these numbers reflect or not the characteristics of the overall pool of arbitrators. The 2015 study of Franck and others—on both commercial and investment treaty arbitrators—concluded that 87.3% of the arbitrators surveyed acted as arbitration counsel.[97] This data, however, refers to international experience, not other experience in private practice.

5. Case-Level Variables: Party Appointment

If in section 4 we focused on arbitrator-level variables, in this section we look at two case-level variables: appointment by the losing party and appointment by investors/host States.

5.1 Appointment by the Losing Party

We hypothesized, based on Van den Berg's earlier study, that arbitrators appointed by the losing party will dissent more than the other arbitrators (H4). The relevant dataset for this question included 98 dissenting opinions in the broad sense. From the original dataset of 117 dissents, we eliminated 19 dissenting opinions. As we needed to find information on the appointing parties' success in the case, we excluded dissents rendered in ICSID Annulment proceedings (in such cases there is no party appointment); in cases that were settled/discontinued (no clear winner/loser); in cases in which the information on the parties' success was not available; and even one case in which the claimant appointed the two wing arbitrators.[98]

[96] 11 out of the 85 arbitrators have experience in all 4 fields (13%), 35 have experience in 3 fields (41.1%), 22 have experience in two fields (25.9%), and 17 have experience in only one field (20%).

[97] Franck and others (n 30) 43.

[98] *Patrick Mitchell v Democratic Republic of the Congo*, ICSID Case No ARB/99/7, Award, 9 February 2004.

We found that in our dataset of 98 dissenting opinions *lato sensu* (see Figure 15.7), 72.4% of the opinions were written by arbitrators appointed by the losing party (71 opinions); 24.5% were by arbitrators appointed by the winning party (24 opinions); and 3.1% by the president of the tribunal (3 opinions). We then looked at dissenting opinions in the narrow sense. Out of the 58 dissents *stricto sensu*, 43 (74.1%) were rendered by arbitrators appointed by the losing party, 13 (22.4%) by the arbitrator appointed by the winning party, and 2 (3.5%) by the presiding arbitrator. These percentages (see Figure 15.8) are remarkably similar to the ones for dissents in the broad sense minimizing selection bias.

Several conclusions follow from these results. Firstly, our analysis confirms our hypothesis (H4) that dissents are written much more often by arbitrators appointed by the losing party than those appointed by the winning party. Therefore, there is a strong correlation between dissenting opinions and arbitrators appointed by the losing party. Arbitrators appointed by the losing party are almost three times more likely to dissent than the other two arbitrators combined.

Secondly, while this data supports Van den Berg's original findings with a considerably larger dataset, it also moderates his claim according to which arbitrators appointed by the losing party issue almost 100% of dissenting opinions. Actually,

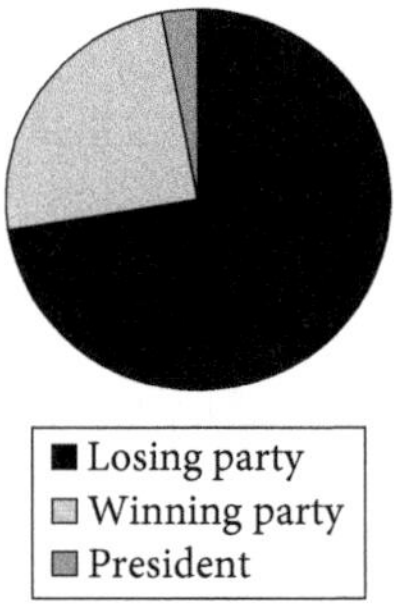

Figure 15.7 Dissenters *lato sensu* appointed by losing party (98 dissents).

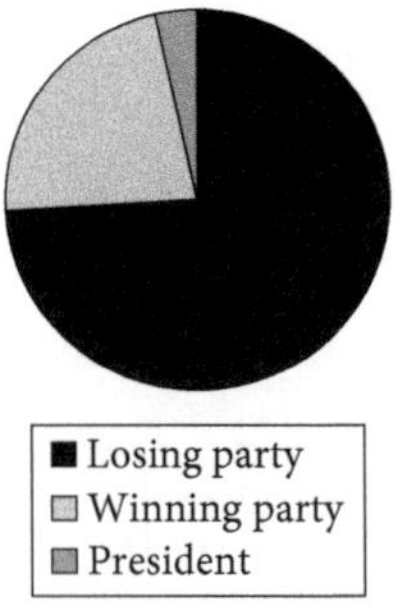

Figure 15.8 Dissenters *stricto sensu* appointed by losing party (58 dissents).

approximately a quarter of dissents *lato* and *stricto sensu* come from the arbitrator appointed by the winning party.

5.2 Appointment by the State or the Investor

According to our last hypothesis (H6), arbitrators appointed by the investors write more dissents. The dataset for this question included 104 dissents in the broad sense. Since the assumption concerns the appointing parties' quality as investor or host State, we excluded 13 dissents from the original dataset of 117 dissents: those rendered in ICSID annulments and those without information available on the appointing party.

In the dataset of 104 dissents in the broad sense (see Figure 15.9), appointments of the dissenting arbitrator by the investor accounted for 51.9% (54), by the respondent State for 45.2%, and by the president of the tribunal for 2.9%. In order to minimize selection bias, we also tested for dissents *stricto sensu*. Of the 61 dissents in the narrow sense (see Figure 15.10), 31 were issued by the investor-appointed arbitrator (50.8%), 28 by the State-appointed arbitrator (45.9%), and two by the president of the tribunal (3.3%). Once again, the numbers are very similar.

Corroborating this data with the overall pool of appointments is once again simple, as the appointment of wing arbitrators by the State or the investor is evenly

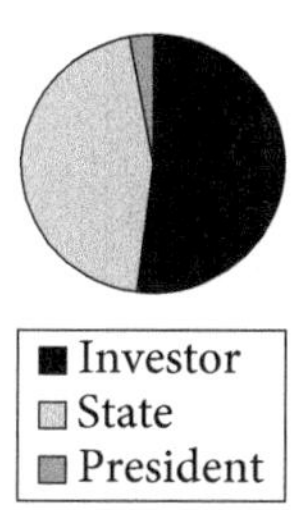

Figure 15.9 Dissenters *lato sensu* appointed by disputing parties (104 dissents).

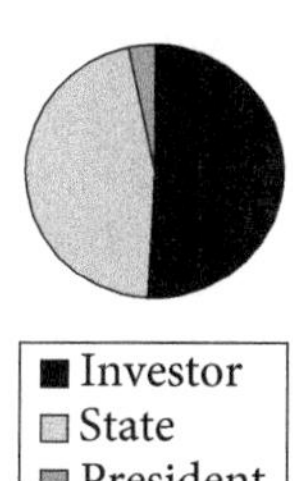

Figure 15.10 Dissenters *stricto sensu* appointed by disputing parties (61 dissents).

split. Since the dissents rendered by the investors and States are roughly evenly split, there might be no significant correlation between dissents and being appointed by the investor. This data *disproves* our hypothesis (H6) that arbitrators appointed by the investor dissent more often.

6. The Broader Implications

Back in 1965, Anand noted that dissents by ICJ judges were a common phenomenon,[99] even though ICJ judges are not appointed by the disputing parties, such as in investor-State arbitration. The opponents of ICJ dissents argued that they diminish the prestige of the Court and lower the persuasive authority of the judgments and opinions.[100] Those in favour of them argued that dissents are an assurance that the judges fully considered the case, and that a well-argued dissent can help the development of the law.[101] Furthermore, the 'losing party may get considerable satisfaction if the arguments in support of its case are cogently set out in a reasoned statement'.[102]

Similar discussions have unfolded in the investment arbitration literature as well, with arguments raised both in favour and against dissenting opinions. In the following sections, using the data presented in sections 4 and 5, we discuss whether dissents encourage partiality and thereby impair the legitimacy of the decision-making process in the context of ITA. This is followed by a discussion on possible remedies to the perceived partiality of dissenting arbitrators.[103]

6.1 Dissents and the Perceived Lack of Impartiality of Party-Appointed Arbitrators

One of the focal points of the *Paulsson and Van Den Berg v Brower and Rosenberg* controversy centred on the effect that dissenting opinions and dissenting arbitrators might have on the legitimacy, independence, and impartiality of arbitral tribunals. Independence relates to the absence of relevant legal relationships between the adjudicators and the parties to a dispute, whereas impartiality requires the absence of bias or prejudices of the adjudicator in relation to the case or the parties.[104]

[99] Anand (n 74) 788–89.
[100] ibid 789.
[101] ibid 788–808.
[102] ibid 794.
[103] For a summary of the discussion in ITA see Titi (n 11); on dissents in international commercial arbitration, see Redfern (n 19).
[104] See for example ECtHR, *Mutu and Pechstein v Switzerland*, App Nos 40575/10 and 67474/10, Judgment (2 October 2018) paras 138–68 (referring to the notion of independence and impartiality in the context of sports arbitration from the perspective of the European Convention on Human Rights).

A lack of independence and impartiality could result in biased decision-making and the unfair treatment of one of the disputants.

According to Paulsson and Van den Berg, dissenting arbitrators act as 'quasi-advocates' among the members of the tribunal.[105] In other words, some dissenting arbitrators could perceive their role not that much as an adjudicator, but as an advocate of the appointing party who will reassure the appointers that even if the majority decided against them, their views and arguments have been taken into consideration in the dissent. In a similar fashion, Smit argues that in US domestic arbitration a party-appointed arbitrator is an 'advocate on the panel'.[106] An international party-appointed arbitrator is however 'expected to be objective and impartial'.[107] Smit, citing also his personal experience, explains that 'the incentive of the party and its counsel is to appoint an arbitrator who will win the case for them'.[108] Such a party-appointment process can exert pressure on the arbitrator to decide in favour of the appointing party.

Brower and Rosenberg, on the other hand, differentiate between the 'advocate-arbitrator' and an arbitrator appointed by a party who perceives that the arbitrator might share their views.[109] They condemn the former practice, but consider the second practice to be commonplace and benign. They further argue that the perceived legitimacy of international arbitration has two important elements: 'the significant and timeless' right of the parties to choose their arbitrators and the ability of a disagreeing member of the tribunal to express different views.[110] Furthermore, they argue that there might be 'a close nexus between the perceived legitimacy of international arbitration and the parties' appointment of the arbitrators'.[111]

The data gathered allows us to add some nuance to the afore-mentioned debate. The common law/civil law nationality of the dissenters seems to reflect the common law/civil law nationality divide of the overall pool of arbitrators. The same holds true for gender and for appointment by the investor or the host State. In other words, there seems to be no significant correlation between the nationality of the dissenters, their gender, as well as appointment by the investor or the State, and the number of dissents written.

In the absence of clearer data on the educational and professional background of *all* appointed arbitrators, our findings concerning education and the professional background are much more tentative. Arbitrators with a postgraduate degree from a top US or UK law school wrote more dissents than arbitrators with other postgraduate degrees. Nonetheless, we cannot conclude whether this reflects

[105] Van Den Berg 2011 (n 9) 830; Paulsson (n 7) 347.

[106] Hans Smit, 'The Pernicious Institution of Party-appointed Arbitrator' (2010) Columbia FDI Perspective No. 33.

[107] ibid; Redfern (n 19) 224.

[108] ibid.

[109] Brower and Rosenberg 2013 (n 9) 17.

[110] ibid 8.

[111] ibid 19.

the tendencies in the overall arbitral pool or whether arbitrators with such degrees are more likely to dissent, as we do not possess information on the educational background of all appointed arbitrators and considering that international judges are mainly trained in elite universities in common law countries. Furthermore, more dissents were written by arbitrators who had experience in private practice. However, an almost equally high number of dissents were written by arbitrators who had academic experience. Thus, we cannot conclude that experience in private practice makes arbitrators more likely to dissent. However, where we do see significant correlation, is between dissents and appointment by the losing party. Arbitrators appointed by the losing party dissented three times more often than the other two arbitrators combined.

Even if a dissenting arbitrator is not biased in favour of the appointing party, the fact that the losing party appoints most dissenting arbitrators creates the appearance that dissenting arbitrators act more as advocates of their appointing party as opposed to impartial adjudicators. It might indicate—as some argue—that 'many dissents seem merely to advise the appointing party of the arbitrator's fidelity to that party, as if to advertise his suitability for another appointment of that arbitrator'.[112]

The role of an adjudicator should always be to decide a case in an independent and impartial manner,[113] without letting the decision-making process be influenced by his/her prior convictions. The risk exists that party-appointed arbitrators may represent the interests of their appointing party, thereby assuming the role of advocates. This in turn casts doubts on the legitimacy and perceived neutrality of arbitrators and of ITA, a core issue addressed in the ISDS reform process initiated by UNCITRAL.[114]

Some clarifications are warranted. Whenever one speaks of legitimacy, one needs to define from whose perspective legitimacy is perceived. Whilst Brower and Rosenberg do not mention it specifically, one can infer that they refer to the perception of the disputing parties. However, is this the only perception one needs to take into account? As Venzke argues, international investment tribunals exercise international public authority, 'in the sense that they have the capacity of affecting the freedom of others in pursuance of the common interest'.[115] Given the public law implications of international investment law and arbitration,[116]

[112] James D Wangelin, 'Buttressing the Pillars of Arbitration' (2004) 19 Mealey's International Arbitration Report 1, 8; see also Breeze (n 19).

[113] See UNCITRAL Arbitration Rules Art 6, UNGA Res. 31/98 (15 December 1976), UN Doc A/RES/31/98 <www.uncitral.org/pdf/english/texts/arbitration/arb-rules/arb-rules.pdf> accessed 18 August 2020 (UNCITRAL Rules); ICSID Convention Arts 14 and 40.

[114] UNCITRAL, 'Possible reform of investor-State dispute settlement (ISDS): Arbitrators and decision makers: appointment mechanisms and related issues' (30 August 2018) A/CN.9/WG.III/WP.152.

[115] Ingo Venzke, 'Investor-State Dispute Settlement in TTIP from the Perspective of A Public Law Theory of International Adjudication' (2016) 17 The Journal of World Investment and Trade 374, 376.

[116] See Stephan W Schill, *International Investment Law and Comparative Public Law* (OUP 2010).

it would be short sighted not to consider the perception of the system by the public. Lord Chief Justice Hewart famously said that it is of 'fundamental importance that justice should not only be done, but should manifestly and undoubtedly *be seen to be done*'.[117]

The perception of justice being done is thus of paramount importance for an adjudicative body. It is not only important that investment arbitrators are independent and impartial, but they also have to be perceived as independent and impartial, not only by the disputing parties, but by the public as well. As Redfern asks 'when a dissenting arbitrator disagrees with the majority, and does so in terms which are likely to find favour with the party which appointed him or her, does not that cause some concern?'[118]

6.2 Reform Options Addressing Impartiality

As a response to the current legitimacy crisis of the international investment system, four reform scenarios are being discussed under the UNCITRAL multilateral initiative to reform ISDS: no ISDS, improved ISDS, an appellate mechanism, and a standing Multilateral Investment Court (MIC).[119] For the purposes of this chapter the most relevant issue is: which reform option can remedy the perceived lack of independence and impartiality of dissenting arbitrators resulting from the party-appointed system? This section explores this question in light of the possible reform options with respect to the selection and appointment of ISDS arbitrators.[120]

As suggested in the UNCITRAL ISDS reform process, one remedy could be to eliminate the party-appointment system. For example, the EU began including provisions on the Investment Court System (ICS) in its bilateral international economic agreements. Recently, the Court of Justice of the EU held that the ICS under the EU-Canada agreement (CETA) is compatible with EU Law.[121] These standing bilateral 'courts' would consist of a Tribunal of First Instance and an Appellate Tribunal. Furthermore, the disputing parties would not have a (direct) say in the appointment of the judge-arbitrators, which would be left to the contracting parties via a Joint Committee.[122] The nationalities of the judges would be split evenly

[117] *R v Sussex Justices, Ex parte McCarthy* [1924] 1 KB 256 (emphasis added).

[118] Redfern (n 19) 234.

[119] See UNCITRAL, 'Possible reform of investor-State dispute settlement (ISDS)' (30 July 2019) A/CN.9/WG.III/WP.166.

[120] UNCITRAL, 'Possible Reform of investor-State dispute settlement (ISDS): Selection and appointment of ISDS tribunal members' (31 July 2019) A/CN.9/WG.III/WP.169 para 13.

[121] CJEU, Opinion 1/17 (*CETA Investment Court System*) ECLI:EU:C:2019:341.

[122] The arbitrator-judges would be appointed by a bilateral committee, made up of officials from both contracting parties. This of course means that states will have a say in the appointment of the tribunal members, while investors will not.

between the two contracting parties and third States. Furthermore, the standards of independence and impartiality are relatively high.[123] The EU is also seeking the creation of a Multilateral Investment Court (MIC). Interestingly, neither the provision on the ICS, nor the negotiating directives for a MIC issued by the Council of the EU include any provisions on dissents.[124]

The 2018 Dutch Model Bilateral Investment Treaty (BIT) can also provide guidance as it also abolishes the party-appointment system. Instead, it provides that '[a]ll members of the Tribunal [...] shall be appointed by an appointing authority'.[125] The appointing authority, depending on the arbitration rules under which the claim is initiated, will be the Secretary-General of ICSID or the Secretary-General of the Permanent Court of Arbitration.[126]

However, such systems make one of the key features— party-appointment—of arbitration obsolete. An extensive 2012 survey of arbitrators and private practitioners shows a general disapproval of abolishing unilateral party-appointments.[127] Other possible remedies to the perceived lack of independence and impartiality of party-appointed arbitrators are discussed. For example, Giorgetti considered it unwise to move away from the party-appointment system. Instead, she recommends a code of conduct improving the current system with stricter rules for challenging arbitrators and enlarging the pool of arbitrators.[128] Dimitropoulos looked at various ways of ensuring arbitrator independence and impartiality, among others by creating various accountability mechanisms, either via an appellate mechanism, the abolishment of party-appointed arbitrators, the creation of a

[123] See EU-Canada Comprehensive and Economic Trade Agreement, provisionally entered into force on 21 September 2017 (CETA), Code of Conduct for Arbitrators (Annex 29-B).

[124] Council of the EU, 'Negotiating Directives for a Convention Establishing a Multilateral Court for the Settlement of Investment Disputes' (20 March 2018) 12981/17 ADD 1.

[125] Netherlands Draft Model BIT, Art 20(1) <https://globalarbitrationreview.com/digital_assets/820bcdd9-08b5-4bb5-a81e-d69e6c6735ce/Draft-Model-BIT-NL-2018.pdf> accessed 18 August 2020.

[126] ibid.

[127] Paul Friedland and Stavros Brekoulakis, 'International Arbitration Survey: Current and Preferred Practices in the Arbitral Process' (2012) Study prepared by the School of International Arbitration at Queen Mary University of London, sponsored by White and Case, at 5 <www.arbitration.qmul.ac.uk/media/arbitration/docs/2012_International_Arbitration_Survey.pdf> accessed 18 August 2020; see also UNCITRAL, 'Possible reform of investor-State dispute settlement (ISDS): comments by the Kingdom of Bahrain' (29 August 2019) A/CN.9/WG.III/WP.180 paras 26–50 (on the concerns regarding a permanent investment court system).

[128] See Giorgetti 2014 (n 7); see also ICSID and UNCITRAL, 'Draft Code of Conduct for Adjudicators in Investor-State Dispute Settlement' (1 May 2020) <https://uncitral.un.org/en/codeofconduct> accessed 18 August 2020; Chiara Giorgetti and others, 'Independence and Impartiality of Adjudicators in Investment Dispute Settlement: Assessing Challenges and Reform Options' (2020) 21 The Journal of World Investment and Trade 441; Chiara Giorgetti, 'A Common Code of Conduct for Investment Arbitrators?' 113 (2019) Proceedings of the ASIL Annual Meeting 217–19 (highlighting the need for a code of conduct for arbitrators as a mean to reform ISDS); International Bar Association, '2014 IBA Guidelines on Conflict of Interest in International Arbitration' 23 October 2014 <www.ibanet.org/ENews_Archive/IBA_July_2008_ENews_ArbitrationMultipleLang.aspx> accessed 18 August 2020.

standing Investment Court, the inclusion of codes of conduct, etc.[129] Another option suggested to address criticism against biased appointed arbitrators is 'blind appointments' which is a means to increase impartiality without abolishing unilateral appointments.[130]

Research on cognitive biases in judicial decision-making suggests 'that arbitrators often make intuitive and impressionistic decisions rather than fully deliberative ones'.[131] Thus, a successful reform might need not focus too much on the identity of the arbitrators, but rather on providing enough safeguards to guarantee their impartiality and independence.[132] Such a shift in approach can be seen in recently signed investment treaties, which increasingly tackle the issue of independence and impartiality of arbitrators. For example, some explicitly include the possibility to challenge arbitrators lacking impartiality or independence[133] while other treaties explicitly stipulate that arbitrators shall be independent and impartial[134] and impose compliance with a code of conduct.[135]

There is of course the problem that no matter which remedy is preferred to enhance the impartiality of arbitrators, it may be that adjudicators subject to reappointment might face a 'Judicial Trilemma' where only two of the three core judicial values—judicial independence, judicial accountability, or judicial transparency—can be maximized.[136]

While preserving all the three core values is difficult, if not impossible, we argue that the creation of a standing, two-tier investment court, in which a joint committee of the contracting parties or an appointing authority appoints the arbitrators on a non-renewable term, can not only ensure the survival of dissents, but it can also increase the perception that arbitrators decide in an impartial and

[129] Georgios Dimitropoulos, 'Constructing the Independence of International Investment Arbitrators: Past, Present, and Future' (2016) 36(2) Northwestern Journal of International Law and Business 371, 421 and following; see also UNCITRAL (n 120).

[130] See Puig and Strezhnev (n 42); Puig 2016 (n 44); Brower and Rosenberg 2013 (n 9).

[131] See Franck and others (2017) (n 42) 1115.

[132] ibid; on the issue of biases see also Stavros Brekoulakis, 'Systemic Bias and the Institution of International Arbitration: A New Approach to Arbitral Decision-Making' (2013) 4 Journal of International Dispute Settlement 553; Gus Van Harten, 'Leaders in the Expansive and Restrictive Interpretation of Investment Treaties: A Descriptive Study of ISDS Awards to 2010' (2018) 29(2) European Journal of International Law 507; Sergio Puig and Anton Strezhnev, 'The David Effect and ISDS' (2017) 28(3) European Journal of International Law 731.

[133] See for example Agreement between the Argentine Republic and Japan for the Promotion and Protection of Investment (Argentina–Japan BIT) (signed on 1 December 2018, not in force) Art 26(6); Agreement for the Reciprocal Promotion and Protection of Investment between the Argentine Republic and the United Arab Emirates (Argentina - UAE BIT) (signed on 16 April 2018, not in force) Art 41.

[134] See for example Treaty between the Republic of Belarus and the Republic of India on Investments (Belarus–India BIT) (signed on 24 September 2018, not in force) Art 18.2; Agreement between the Government of Canada and the Government of the Republic of Moldova for the Promotion and Protection of Investments (Canada–Moldova BIT) (signed on 12 June 2018, not in force) Art 25(2).

[135] See for example Argentina–UAE (n 133) Art 25(2), Arts 34–41.

[136] Jeffrey L Dunoff and Mark A Pollack, 'The Judicial Trilemma' (2017) 111(2) American Journal of International Law 225.

independent way.[137] Firstly, this would mean that arbitrator-judges of the first level Tribunal would know that their actions can be scrutinized in the appellate phase, which would create an incentive to act in an impartial way. Furthermore, since the judges are not appointed by the disputing parties (or not directly by one of them), there is no incentive for the arbitrators to dissent for the purpose of acting as an 'advocate' of the appointing party. Thus, the incentive to dissent would be based on disagreements with the rest of the panel on points of law, which then could contribute to the development of the law. However, if the two-tier mechanism is kept *without* abolishing party-appointment, this could affect dissents in two ways. On the one hand, even if dissents could not be appealed as they do not form part of the award, the presence of a second tier of adjudication could make some arbitrators less inclined to dissent, if the purpose of the dissent is to favour the appointing party. On the other hand, the possibility to appeal the first level Tribunal's award could also prompt some arbitrators to dissent in order to favour their appointing party, as the Appellate Tribunal might be inspired by the arguments contained in the dissent.

Secondly, ad hoc arbitrators, whose income mostly depends on their reappointment, might purposely write dissents in order to illustrate their stance on a specific issue, which might help them during a future reappointment and consequently deter public confidence in the legitimacy of their decision-making.[138] On the other hand, judges with a non-renewable, long-term appointment (eg nine years) and a fixed, high salary would not have such reappointment and financial pressures. Thus, the dissents that they publish could genuinely help the development of the law. The current system envisaged by CETA does not seem to adequately relieve the future 'arbitrator-judges' of reappointment and financial pressures, even if the Court of Justice of the EU held that the system—as it stands now—does not affect the independence and impartiality of the future members of the ICS (!).[139] Instead of long, non-renewable terms, CETA provides that members of the First Instance Tribunal shall have five-year terms, renewable once (Article 8.27(4) CETA). Furthermore, instead of a fixed salary, they shall be paid a monthly retainer fee with other fees and expenses that are incurred when hearing a claim

[137] UNCITRAL, 'Possible reform of investor-State dispute settlement (ISDS): Submission from the European Union and its Member States' (24 January 2019) A/CN.9/WG.III/WP.159/Add.1 para 47; see also a similar suggestion made by Voeten in the context of the ECtHR in Voeten 2013 (n 51) 554 '(. . .) longer, non-renewable terms, as the ECtHR recently implemented, should help reduce national bias if career motivations are to blame, but would be of little use if culture is primarily responsible'.

[138] See David Gaukrodger, 'Adjudicator Compensation Systems and Investor-State Dispute Settlement', OECD Working Papers on International Investment 2017/05, OECD Publishing (2017) 20 'As a matter of institutional design, permanent appointments and salaries are generally seen as important elements in achieving public confidence on these issues. Beyond institutional matters, domestic legal systems also apply rules to the individual pecuniary interests of particular judges. Like the provision of salaries, these rules are generally seen as contributing to judicial independence and public confidence in the justice system'.

[139] Opinion 1/17 (n 121) paras 223–44.

(Article 8.27(12)–(14) CETA), to be determined by the CETA Joint Committee. The Joint Committee can later decide to convert the retainer fee and other fees into a regular salary (Article 8.27(15) CETA). Moreover, the administrative and organizational specifics of the CETA Appellate Tribunal are not included in the text of the Agreement and shall be set out in a subsequent decision of the Joint Committee (Article 8.28(7) CETA).

Thirdly, because the disputing parties would not appoint the adjudicators for each case, the perception that the adjudicators have to act in the interests of one of the disputing parties would be greatly lowered.

Of course, this does not mean that bias will be fully eliminated. This is impossible and as the studies mentioned in the Introduction show, potential for bias still exists in the ECtHR and the ICJ, despite the fact that their members are appointment by specific bodies/institutions of international organizations and not directly by the disputing parties. Furthermore, contracting parties would be the ones appointing the arbitrator-judges, which at least from the investors' perspective could create the perception of bias. However, the aforementioned structural changes, such as a two-tier mechanism, long-term, non-renewable appointments, and fixed salaries, would ensure that potential bias could be better controlled, and that the perceived impartiality of a standing investment court could be a lot higher.

7. Conclusion

Arbitrators, dissenting or not, carry the responsibility to uphold the integrity of ITA as a just and effective institution for the settlement of investor-State disputes. In the last decades, ITA processes and outcomes have nevertheless raised doubts whether arbitrators are truly impartial and independent.[140] As part of the larger debate on the legitimacy of the international investment regime, our study of 117 dissents *lato sensu* and 87 dissenting arbitrators looked at a series of arbitrator-level (nationality, gender, education, professional background) and case-level (party appointment, appointment by States or investors) variables to test six hypotheses that are meant to provide a more accurate profile of dissenting arbitrators.

We found that the common law/civil law nationality of the dissenters largely reflects the common law/civil law nationality divide of the overall pool of arbitrators. The same holds true for gender and for appointment by the investor or the host State. In other words, we found no significant correlation between the nationality of the dissenters, their gender, and the appointment by the investor or the State, and the number of dissents written.

[140] See UNCITRAL, 'Possible reform of investor-State dispute settlement (ISDS)' (2017) A/CN.9/WG.III/WP.142.

In the absence of data on the educational and professional background of *all* arbitrators, our findings concerning education and the professional background of dissenting arbitrators are more tentative. Arbitrators with a postgraduate degree from a top US or UK law school wrote more dissents than arbitrators with other postgraduate degrees. In addition, more dissents were written by arbitrators who had experience as private parties. Nonetheless, more research is needed to find out whether these reflect the tendencies in the overall arbitral pool. Where there might be significant correlation, is between dissents and appointment by the losing party. Arbitrators appointed by the losing party dissented roughly three times more often than the other two arbitrators combined did.

The findings of this study are meant to describe the dissenting arbitrators and to challenge the formalistic view that dissenting arbitrators apply the law irrespective of their appointing party. The fact that most dissents are written by arbitrators appointed by the losing party creates the perception that some arbitrators act more like the advocates of their appointers instead of impartial adjudicators. If, as suggested by Pauwelyn, the legitimacy of ITA depends on the neutrality and impartiality of its arbitrators, the predispositions of dissenting arbitrators (and arbitrators more generally)[141] pose a serious challenge to ITA.[142]

Critics of dissenting opinions in ITA propose various solutions to remedy what is perceived as creating bias.[143] We do not argue that the abolition of dissenting opinions is a viable alternative.[144] Instead, having looked at several reform options, we propose that a standing, two-tier investment court that provides for non-renewable, long-term appointments and fixed salaries could ensure both the survival of dissents and remedy the perceived partiality of party-appointed arbitrators. The impartiality of adjudicators remains crucial for the continued functioning and legitimacy of investor-State arbitration.

[141] See Waibel and Wu (n 22).

[142] Joost Pauwelyn, 'The Rule of Law without the Rule of Lawyers? Why Investment Arbitrators are from Mars, Trade Adjudicators from Venus' (2015) 109 (4) The American Journal of International Law 761.

[143] Van den Berg 2011 (n 9) 832–34.

[144] ibid; see also Patricia Jimenez Kwast, 'Prohibitions on Dissenting Opinions in International Arbitration' in C Ryngaert and other (eds), *What's Wrong with International Law?* (Brill 2015).

Annex 1 The Dissenting Arbitrators

	NAME	NATIONALITY		GENDER		EDUCATION			PROFESSION			
		Nat 1	Nat 2	F	M	Undergrad	Postgrad	Doctorate	Priv	Acad	Gov.	Other
1	Stuart E Eizenstat	USA	x	x	1	Univ North Carolina	Harvard Law	Honorary	1	x	1	1
2	José Luis Shaw	URY	x	x	1	N/A	N/A	Uruguay State Univ	1	1	x	x
3	Brigitte Stern	FRA	x	1	x	Institut d'Et Politiques	NYU Univ Strasbourg	Univ Paris	x	1	x	x
4	Charles N Brower	USA	x	x	1	Harvard Coll Hochschule für Politik	Harvard Law	x	1	x	1	1
5	Alberto Feliciani	ITA	x	x	1	N/A	Perugia Univ	N/A	1	x	x	x
6	Stephen Schwebel	USA	x	x	1	Harvard Coll Cambridge, Yale Law	x	x	1	1	1	1
7	Joaquín M Godoy	CHL	x	x	1	Univ Chile	American Univ, LSE	x	1	1	1	1
8	Joseph Matthews	USA	x	x	1	N/A	Univ Miami	x	1	x	x	x
9	José M C Medina	ESP	x	x	1	Barcelona Univ	x	Paris 1 Sorbonne	1	1	1	1
10	Jürgen Voss	DEU	x	x	1	N/A	N/A	N/A	N/A	N/A	N/A	N/A
11	Eduardo Zuleta	COL	x	x	1	Univ del Rosario	Univ del Rosario Queen Mary	x	1	x	x	x

(continued)

	NAME	NATIONALITY		GENDER		EDUCATION			PROFESSION			
		Nat 1	Nat 2	F	M	Undergrad	Postgrad	Doctorate	Priv	Acad	Gov.	Other
12	Horacio A G Naón	ARG	x	x	1	Univ Buenos Aires	Harvard Law	Harvard Law Univ Buenos Aires	1	x	1	1
13	Francisco O Vicuña	CHL	x	x	1	Univ Chile	x	LSE	1	1	x	1
14	Arthur W Rovine	USA	x	x	1	Harvard Univ	x	Columbia Univ	1	1	1	x
15	M Shahabuddeen	GUY	x	x	1	Univ London	Univ London	Univ London	1	x	1	1
16	W Michael Reisman	USA	x	x	1	Hebrew Univer.	Yale Law	Yale Law	x	1	x	x
17	Gary Born	USA	x	x	1	Haverford Coll	Univ Pennsylvania	x	1	x	x	x
18	O de Witt Wijnen	NLD	x	x	1	Univ Leiden	x	x	1	x	1	1
19	Grant D Aldonas	USA	x	x	1	Univ Minnesota	Univ Minnesota	x	1	x	1	x
20	Georges Abi-Saab	EGY	x	x	1	Univ Cairo	Univ Cairo, Paris, Michigan, Harvard	Cambridge, Geneva, Harvard	1	1	1	1
21	Susana C Zalduendo	ARG	x	1	x	Univ Buenos Aires	Univ Buenos Aires	x	x	1	1	1
22	A F Lowenfeld	USA	x	x	1	Harvard Law	Harvard Law	x	1	1	1	1
23	Guido S Tawil	ARG	x	x	1	Univ Buenos Aires	Univ Buenos Aires	Univ Buenos Aires	1	1	1	x
24	Pedro Nikken	VEN	x	x	1	Univ Cat Andrés Bello	Univ de Paris II; Univ de Carabobo	x	1	1	x	1
25	B M Cremades	ESP	x	x	1	Univ de Sevilla	x	Univ de Sevilla Universität Köln	1	x	x	x

26	Dominique Schmidt	FRA	x	x	1	Univ Strasbourg	x	Univ Strasbourg	1	1	x	1
27	Franklin Berman	GBR	x	x	1	Univ Cape Town Oxford	Oxford	x	1	1	1	1
28	Aron Broches	NLD	x	x	1	Univ Amsterdam	Univ Amsterdam Fordham Univ	x	x	x	1	1
29	Kéba Mbaye	SEN	x	x	1	Ecole National de la FRA d'Outre-mer	x	x	x	x	1	1
30	Prosper Weil	FRA	x	x	1	N/A	N/A	Univ Paris	x	1	1	1
31	Daniel M Price	USA	x	x	1	Cambridge	Harvard Law	x	1	x	1	x
32	Ian Sinclair	GBR	x	x	1	Cambridge	Cambridge	x	1	1	1	1
33	Samuel K B Asante	GHA	x	x	1	Nottingham Univ	London Univ	Yale Univ	1	1	1	1
34	Heribert Golsong	DEU	x	x	1	Univ Cologne	Univ Wuerzberg	Univ Bonn	x	1	1	1
35	David Suratgar	GBR	x	x	1	N/A	Oxford, Columbia, Harvard Business	x	1	x	1	1
36	Jan H Dalhuisen	NLD	x	1	1	Univ Amsterdam	Univ Berkley	Univ Amsterdam	1	1	x	1
37	Domingo B Janeiro	ESP	x	x	1	Santiago de Compostela	x	Santiago de Compostela	x	1	x	x
38	Keith Highet	GBR	x	x	1	Harvard Univ	Harvard Law	x	1	1	1	1
39	Omar Nabulsi	JOR	x	x	1	Univ Cairo	Univ Cairo	x	1	x	1	x
40	Antonio Crivellaro	ITA	x	x	1	Univ Padua	N/A	x	1	1	x	1
41	Jorge C Bravo	MEX	x	x	1	Univ Argentina	x	x	1	1	x	x
42	Yawovi Agboyibo	TGO	x	x	1	N/A	N/A	N/A	N/A	N/A	N/A	N/A
43	José L Alberro-Semerena	MEX	x	x	1	Instituto Tecnológico Autónomo de México	Univ Chicago	Univ Chicago	1	1	1	x

(continued)

	NAME	NATIONALITY		GENDER		EDUCATION			PROFESSION			
		Nat 1	Nat 2	F	M	Undergrad	Postgrad	Doctorate	Priv	Acad	Gov.	Other
44	Marc Lalonde	CAN	x	x	1	Univ de Montréal	Oxford, Univ Ottawa	x	1	1	1	x
45	Philippe Sands	FRA	GBR	x	1	Univ Cambridge	Univ Cambridge	x	1	1	x	x
46	Santiago T Bernárdez	ESP	x	x	1	Univ Valladolid	Saar Univ	Univ Al de Henares Univ Carlos III	1	1	x	1
47	William W Park	USA	x	x	1	Yale; Columbia	Cambridge	x	1	1	x	x
48	M Sornarajah	AUS	x	x	1	Univ Ceylon	Yale Law, LSE	King's College	1	1	1	1
49	Steven A Hammond	USA	x	x	1	Maine Law	Free Univ Brussels	x	1	x	x	x
50	Enrique G Pinzón	COL	x	x	1	Univ de Los Andes	Harvard Law	x	1	x	1	x
51	Tadeusz Szurski	POL	x	x	1	Jagiellonian Univ	Jagiellonian Univ	Jagiellonian Univ	x	1	1	1
52	Ricardo R Hernández	MEX	x	x	1	Univ A Metropolitana	Univ Washington	x	1	1	1	1
53	M R-Sammartano	ITA	x	x	1	Univ of Milan	x	x	1	1	x	1
54	Gavan Griffith	AUS	x	x	1	N/A	Melbourne Univ	Univ Oxford	1	x	1	1
55	Edward Nottingham	USA	x	x	1	Cornell Univ	Univ Colorado Law	x	1	x	1	x
56	Michael E Jaffe	USA	x	x	1	Rice Univ Columbia Univ	x	x	1	1	x	x

57	L B de Chazournes	FRA	CHE	1	x	Univ Lyon II	Univ Lyon III	Graduate Institute	x	1	x	1
58	Raúl Emilio Vinuesa	ARG	ESP	x	1	Univ Argentina	Harvard Univ; Tufts Univ; Cambridge	x	x	1	1	1
59	Makhdoom Ali Khan	PAK	x	x	1	Univ of Karachi; Cambridge	LSE	x	1	x	1	x
60	J C Thomas	CAN	x	x	1	Univ British Columbia	Columbia Univ; Sussex Univ	x	1	1	1	x
61	Jan Paulsson	SWE	FRA	x	1	Harvard Coll	Yale Law; Univ of Paris	x	1	1	x	1
62	Antonio R Brotóns	ESP	x	x	1	N/A	N/A	Univ Bologna	X	1	X	X
63	Henri Alvarez	CAN	x	x	1	Univ British Columbia; Univ Ottawa	x	Graduate Institute of International Studies	1	x	x	x
64	Luis H Marcano	VEN	x	x	1	N/A	N/A	Univ C Venezuela	x	1	1	x
65	Jaroslav Hándl	CZE	x	x	1	N/A	N/A	N/A	1	x	x	x
66	Ian Brownlie	GBR		x	1	Hertford Coll Oxford	N/A	Oxford	1	1	x	x
67	Stanimir Alexandrov	BGR	x	x	1	Moscow Institute of International Relations	George Washington Univ	George Washington Univ	1	1	1	x
68	Jerzy Rejski	POL	x	x	1	Univ Warsaw	Univ Warsaw	Univ Warsaw	1	1	x	x
69	Manuel Conthe	ESP	x	x	1	Univ Comp de Madrid (UCM)	Univ Aut de Madrid (UAM)	x	1	x	1	1
70	Dobrosav Mitrović	SRB	x	x	1	Univ Belgrade	Univ Belgrade	Univ Belgrade	x	1	1	x
71	Donald McRae	CAN	NZL	x	1	Univ Otago	Univ Otago; Cambridge; Columbia	x	x	1	1	x

(continued)

	NAME	NATIONALITY		GENDER		EDUCATION			PROFESSION			
		Nat 1	Nat 2	F	M	Undergrad	Postgrad	Doctorate	Priv	Acad	Gov.	Other
72	Ivan S Zykin	RUS	x	x	1	N/A	N/A	N/A	1	1	1	x
73	Todd Weiler	CAN	x	x	1	Univ W Ontario	Univ Ottawa Univ Michigan	Univ Michigan Univ W Ontario	1	1	x	x
74	Robert Volterra	CAN	x	x	1	Univ W Ontario; Osgoode Hall Law	Cambridge	x	1	1	1	x
75	Michael Chertoff	USA	x	x	1	Harvard Univ	Harvard Law	x	1	x	1	x
76	Dominic Pellew	GBR	x	x	1	Merton Coll Oxford	Oxford Polytechnic	x	1	x	x	x
77	Bryan Schwartz	USA	x	x	1	Queen's Univ	Yale Univ	Yale Univ	1	x	x	x
78	David Haigh	CAN	x	x	1	Univ Alberta Univ Toronto	x	x	1	x	x	x
79	Sergei Lebedev	RUS	x	x	1	Michigan Univ	N/A	N/A	x	1	1	1
80	Ronald A Cass	USA	x	x	1	Univ Virginia	Univ Chicago	x	1	1	1	x
81	Andreas Bucher	CHE	x	x	1	Univ Zurich	N/A	Univ Basel	x	1	x	x
82	Andreas Jacovides	CYP	x	x	1	Middle Temple	Middle Temple	x	x	1	1	1
83	Carolyn B Lamm	USA	x	1	x	State University of New Yord (SUNY)	Univ Miami Law	Honorary Drexel Univ; honorary SUNY	1	1	1	x
84	Thomas Waelde	DEU	x	x	1	Univ Heidelberg	Harvard Law	Frankfurt	x	1	x	1
85	Rodrigo Oreamuno	CRI	x	x	1	Univ de Costa Rica	x	x	1	x	1	1
86	P M Nienaber	ZAF	x	x	1	Rand Afrikaans Univ	x	Cambridge	1	1	1	x
87	Ibrahim Fadlallah	FRA	LBN	x	1	NA	Saint Joseph Univ; Univ Paris II	Univ Paris II	x	1	x	x

Annex 2 The Dissents

	CASE NAME (shortened)	LEGAL REF	DISSENTING ARBITRATOR	TYPE*	APPOINTER**		DETAILS
					W/L	I/S	
1	*Railroad Dev Corp v Guatemala (Rectification req)*	ARB/07/23	Stuart Eizenstat	1	1	1	Attached to the Decision on claimant's request. Dissent on whether amount of damages to be changed due to new evidence.
2	*Iberdrola Energía SA v Guatemala (ICSID Annul)*	ARB/09/5	José Luis Shaw	1	N/A	N/A	Did not agree with the other two members of the annulment committee on the grounds of annulment.
3	*Impregilo SpA v Argentina*	ARB/07/17	Brigitte Stern	3	2	2	Concurring and dissenting on the Award (tribunal's jurisdiction and the scope of MFN clause).
4	*Impregilo SpA v Argentina*	ARB/07/17	Charles Brower	3	1	1	Concurring and dissenting on the Award (on the issue of expropriation and the standard of compensation).
5	*Toto Costruzioni Generali SpA v Lebanon (Jurisdiction)*	ARB/07/12	A Feliciani (changed to Schwebel)	1	2	1	Voted in favour of Chapters I, II, III, and IV. He dissents in several respects on the other parts of the decision.
6	*Toto Costruzioni Generali SpA v Lebanon (Final Award)*	ARB/07/12	S Schwebel	2	2	1	Concurring opinion. He agrees with the overall conclusion but not with certain interpretations.
7	*Renée Rose Levy v Peru*	ARB/10/17	Joaquín Godoy	1	2	1	Did not find a common position on how the other two arbitrators construed the facts and the law to dismiss the Claimant's complaint.
8	*Piero Foresti, Laura de Carli v South Africa*	ARB(AF)/07/1	J Matthews	2	1	2	Concurring statement evidencing that the costs were reduced due to claimants' policy towards historically disadvantaged South Africans.

(continued)

	CASE NAME (shortened)	LEGAL REF	DISSENTING ARBITRATOR	TYPE*	APPOINTER**		DETAILS
					W/L	I/S	
9	*Nations Energy Inc v Panama*	ARB/06/19	José Medina	1	2	1	Attached to the Award. Does not disagree with the whole award, but with some of the formal and structural elements (in Spanish).
10	*Joseph C Lemire v Ukraine*	ARB/06/18	Jürgen Voss	1	2	2	Dissent concerns the majority's disregard of the Settlement Agreement (on the Award).
11	*Murphy Exploration v Ecuador*	ARB/08/4	Horacio Naón	1	2	1	Partial dissenting opinion. He departs from the reasoning of the tribunal and the conclusions of the award.
12	*Siag and Vecchi v Egypt (Jurisdiction)*	ARB/05/15	F O Vicuña	1	2	2	Finds the nationality connection based on which the tribunal had jurisdiction to be artificial.
13	*Siag and Vecchi v Egypt (Aw)*	ARB/05/15	F O Vicuña	1	2	2	Different conclusions on the merits.
14	*EDF Ltd v Romania (Aw)*	ARB/05/13	Arthur Rovine	1	2	1	Dissent regarding costs.
15	*Malaysian Historical Salvors, v Malaysia (ICSID Annul)*	ARB/05/10	Mohamed Shahabuddeen	1	N/A	N/A	Different opinion on the outcome.
16	*Roussalis v Romania*	ARB/06/1	W M Reisman	1	1	2	Declaration. He does not join the part of the award that rejects jurisdiction over counterclaims.
17	*Biwater Gauff Ltd v Tanzania*	ARB/05/22	Gary Born	3	2	1	Concurring and dissenting. Agrees with many of the conclusions of the award, but writes separately on several aspects of the analysis.
18	*African Holding Co v DR Congo*	ARB/05/21	De Witt Wijnen	1	2	1	Opinion on issues of *rationae temporis* and the Tribunal's jurisdiction (in French).

19	*Archer Daniels v Mexico (Consolidation Tribunal)*	ARB(AF)/04/5	Arthur Rovine	2	N/A	N/A	Concurring opinion. Provides his own opinion on the role of countermeasures.
20	*TSA Spectrum v Argentina*	ARB/05/5	G Aldonas	1	2	1	Dissent on jurisdiction.
21	*TSA Spectrum v Argentina*	ARB/05/5	G Abi-Saab	2	1	2	Concurring opinion. Agrees with overall outcome of the award, but adds some of his own conclusions.
22	*Sociedad Anónima Eduardo Vieira v Chile*	ARB/04/7	Susana Czar de Zalduendo	1	2	1	Dissent on jurisdiction (in Spanish).
23	*Corn Products Int v Mexico*	ARB(AF)/04/1	AF Lowenfeld	2	N/A	1	Concurs with parts of the decision but has a different opinion on the 'countermeasures defence' discussion of the majority (not public).
24	*Duke Energy Int v Peru*	ARB/03/28	Guido S Tawil	3	1	1	Partial dissent.
25	*Duke Energy Int v Peru*	ARB/03/28	Pedro Nikken	3	2	2	Partial dissent. Agrees on the breach of the guarantee of legal stability, dissents on the estoppel issue.
26	*Fraport Frankfurt Airport v Philippines (Aw)*	ARB/03/25	Bernardo M Cremades	1	2	1	Attached to the Award. He does not agree that the secret shareholder agreement violates the Anti-Dummy Law.
27	*Klöckner Industrie v Cameroon*	ARB/81/2	Dominique Schmidt	1	1	1	Case analysed by Jan Paulsson and Friedrich Niggemann (not public)
28	*Industria Nacional v Peru (ICSID Annul)*	ARB/03/4	F Berman	1	N/A	N/A	Dissents because of 'manifold shortcomings' of the majority decision.

(continued)

	CASE NAME (shortened)	LEGAL REF	DISSENTING ARBITRATOR	TYPE*	APPOINTER**		DETAILS
					W/L	I/S	
29	*SOABI v Senegal (Jurisdiction)*	ARB/82/1	Aron Broches	2	3	3	Regarding a Declaration of the President of the Tribunal on the Tribunal's Decision of August 1, 1984 (in French).
30	*SOABI v Senegal (Award)*	ARB/82/1	Kéba Mbaye	1	2	2	Disagrees with the majority on fundamental issues (in French).
31	*Tokios Tokelės v Ukraine (Jurisdiction)*	ARB/02/18	Prosper Weil	1	3	3	Dissents as chair. Argues that the approach taken by the tribunal is at odds with the object and purposed of the ICSID Convention.
32	*Tokios Tokelės v Ukraine (Aw)*	ARB/02/18	Daniel M Price	1	2	1	Agrees with most conclusions but dissents from Section L of the Award
33	*Ahmonseto Inc v Egypt*	ARB/02/15	N/A	1	N/A	N/A	Dissenter is unknown.
34	*Salini Costruttori v Jordan*	ARB/02/13	Ian Sinclair	2	1	2	Separate Declaration relating to the costs of proceedings.
35	*Asian Agricultural v Sri Lanka*	ARB/87/3	Samuel Asante	1	2	2	Dissent on the issue of liability.
36	*American Manufacturing v DR Congo*	ARB/93/1	Kéba Mbaye	2	2	2	Concurs with opinion but disagrees with the amount of compensation.
37	*American Manufacturing v DR Congo*	ARB/93/1	H Golsong	2	1	1	Statement of individual opinion. Agrees with outcome but not with legal reasoning.
38	*Mihaly Int Corp v Sri Lanka*	ARB/00/2	David Suratgar	2	2	1	Individual opinion (attached to the award).

39	*Comp de Aguas del Aconquija v Argentina (ICSID Annul)*	ARB/97/3	Jan Hendrik Dalhuisen	2	N/A	N/A	Dissent in annulment (attached to the decision).
40	*Siemens AG v Argentina*	ARB/02/8	D B Janeiro	2	2	2	Agrees with conclusions but disagrees on the amount of damages.
41	*Banro American v DR Congo*	ARB/98/7	N/A	1	N/A	N/A	Dissenter and award not public.
42	*Waste Management v Mexico*	ARB(AF)/98/2	Keith Highet	1	2	1	Proceedings initiated in Mexico differed in substance from the ICSID arbitration. Pursuing these remedies in Mexico did not render the claimant's waiver moot.
43	*Hussein Soufraki v UAE (ICSID Annul)*	ARB/02/7	Omar Nabulsi	1	N/A	N/A	Partially agrees but differs on the claimant's argument that the tribunal failed to apply Italian law.
44	*SGS v Philippines (Jurisd)*	ARB/02/6	A Crivellaro	3	2	1	Dissent limited to Section VII(d) of the Decision.
45	*Marvin Roy Feldman Karpa v Mexico*	ARB(AF)/99/1	Jorge C Bravo	1	2	2	Agrees with description of the facts, on procedural and jurisdictional issues, and on the Claimant's actions with regard to expropriation and due process. Disagrees on national treatment and discrimination.
46	*Patrick Mitchell v Dr Congo*	ARB/99/7	Yawovi Agboyibo	1	N/A	N/A	Excerpts. Full Dissenting Opinion not available.
47	*Aguas del Tunari v Bolivia*	ARB/02/3	José Semerena	1	N/A	N/A	Dissenting declaration on the decision on jurisdiction
48	*Daimler AG v Argentina*	ARB/05/1	Charles Brower	1	2	1	Disagrees with majority view on the effect of the BIT's MFN clause.

(continued)

	CASE NAME (shortened)	LEGAL REF	DISSENTING ARBITRATOR	TYPE*	APPOINTER**		DETAILS
					W/L	I/S	
49	*Daimler AG v Argentina*	ARB/05/1	Domingo Bello Janeiro	2	1	2	Fully subscribes to the decision. Disagrees only on aspects with greater actual relevance, repercussion, and substantive content.
50	*Sempra Energy v Argentina*	ARB/02/16	Marc Lalonde	1	1	1	Partial dissent on final date of payment of interest.
51	*Mobil Investments v Canada*	ARB(AF)/07/4	Philippe Sands	1	2	2	Concludes that the question of damages did not arise and cannot support the other arbitrators in their conclusions.
52	*Ambiente Ufficio v Argentina*	ARB/08/9	S T Bernárdez	1	2	2	Dissenting opinion on the decision on jurisdiction and admissibility.
53	*Kılıç İnşaat İthalat v Turkmenistan*	ARB/10/1	W Park	2	2	1	Separate opinion to a unanimous decision (award) of the tribunal. Does not agree with some of the tribunal's interpretations.
54	*UAB 'ARVI' v Serbia*	ARB/09/21	Charles Brower	2	N/A	1	Not public (dissent on the award).
55	*Rafat Ali Rizvi v Indonesia*	ARB/11/13	M Sornarajah	2	1	2	Separate opinion. Agrees with the conclusions of the tribunal but arrives to it through a different reasoning.
56	*Mamidoil Jetoil v Albania*	ARB/11/24	Steven A Hammond	1	2	1	Dissenting opinion. Disagrees with the tribunal's analysis of the alleged violation of claimant's right to FET and non-discrimination
57	*Venoklim Holding v Venezuela*	ARB/12/22	E G Pinzón	3	2	1	Concurrent and dissenting opinion on the award (in Spanish).
58	*Sociedad General de Aguas de Barcelona v Argentina*	ARB/03/19	Pedro Nikken	2	2	2	Separate opinion. Agrees that state violated FET, but disagrees that this was due to the frustration of legitimate expectations.

59	*Saar Papier v Poland*	UNCITRAL	Tadeusz Szurski	1	2	2	*Votum separatum*. Dissents to the treatment of the measures as equivalent to expropriation.
60	*Cervin Investissements v Costa Rica*	ARB/13/2	R R Hernández	1	2	1	First dissent: on the existence of a plausible violation of the BIT. Second, partial dissent on costs.
61	*Marco and Stefano Gavazzi v Romania*	ARB/12/25	M Rubino-Sammartano	1	2	2	Three dissenting opinions on: decision on jurisdiction, admissibility, and liability; final award; the calculation of costs.
62	*RSM Production Corp v Saint Lucia (discontinuation)*	ARB/12/10	Gavan Griffith	2	1	2	Assenting reasons. Arrives to same conclusion but takes different path.
63	*RSM Production Corp v Saint Lucia (security for costs)*	ARB/12/10	Edward Nottingham	1	2	1	Questions the state's right to costs reimbursement (not public).
64	*Tulip Real Estate v Turkey*	ARB/11/28	Michael E Jaffe	2	2	1	Separate opinion on the Decision on bifurcated jurisdictional issue.
65	*Garanti Koza LLP v Turkmenistan*	ARB/11/20	L B de Chazournes	1	2	2	Dissenting opinion on the Decision on the Objection to Jurisdiction for Lack of Consent.
66	*Vincent J Ryan v Poland*	ARB(AF)/11/3	F O Vicuña	1	2	1	Partial dissenting opinion on the award.
67	*Flughafen Zürich v Venezuela*	ARB/10/19	Raúl Vinuesa	1	2	2	Partially Dissenting (in Spanish).
68	*Deutsche Bank AG v Sri Lanka*	ARB/09/2	Makhdoom Ali Khan	1	2	2	Dissenting on: a) whether the agreement constitutes an investment; b) expropriation; c) FET.
69	*HOCHTIEF v Argentina (jurisdiction)*	ARB/07/31	J Christopher Thomas	3	2	2	Separate and dissenting opinion.

(continued)

	CASE NAME (shortened)	LEGAL REF	DISSENTING ARBITRATOR	TYPE*	APPOINTER**		DETAILS
					W/L	I/S	
70	*Giovanni Alemanni v Argentina*	ARB/07/8	J Christopher Thomas	2	N/A	2	Concurring opinion regarding the multi-party investment treaty dispute component.
71	*Abaclat v Argentina*	ARB/07/5	G Abi-Saab	1	N/A	2	Dissenting opinion to decision on jurisdiction and admissibility pertaining to substance and method (e.g. issue of mass claims).
72	*Abaclat v Argentina*	ARB/07/5	ST Bernárdez	1	N/A	2	Declaration appended to the award.
73	*Occidental v Ecuador (Award)*	ARB/06/11	Brigitte Stern	1	2	2	Dissenting opinion on quantum.
74	*Quiborax SA v Bolivia*	ARB/06/2	Brigitte Stern	1	2	2	Partially dissenting opinion on legal findings (agrees with outcome).
75	*Hrvatska Elektroprivreda v Slovenia*	ARB/05/24	Jan Paulsson	2	2	2	Individual opinion on the decision on the treaty interpretation issue: impossible to subscribe to the decision.
76	*Micula v Romania (I)*	ARB/05/20	G Abi-Saab	2	2	2	Separate opinion on interpretation of the law (legitimate expectations; remedies).
77	*Mobil Exploration v Argentina (Award)*	ARB/04/16	A R Brotóns	1	N/A	2	Dissenting opinion on the award (not public).
78	*Sociedad General de Aguas de Barcelona v Argentina*	ARB/03/17	Pedro Nikken	2	2	2	Separate opinion on the grounds for finding a violation of FET (Decision on liability).
79	*AWG Group Ltd v Argentina*	UNICTRAL	Pedro Nikken	2	2	2	Separate opinion on the reasoning for finding a violation of FET.
80	*Total SA v Argentina*	ARB/04/1	Henri Alvarez	1	1	1	Dissenting opinion (Decision on liability).
81	*Mesa Power v Canada*	PCA 2012–17	Charles Brower	3	2	1	Concurring and Dissenting (on issues relating to Art 1105, 1108(7)(a) and 8(b) NAFTA).

82	*Total SA v Argentina*	ARB/04/1	Luis H Marcano	2	2	2	Concurring opinion (Decision on liability) relating to the interpretation of FET.
83	*Austrian Airlines v Slovakia*	UNCITRAL	Charles Brower	2	2	1	Separate opinion on the final award (tribunal lacks jurisdiction). Different interpretation of the applicability of MFN clause.
84	*Chevron Texaco v Ecuador*	UNCITRAL PCA 2009–23	Horacio Naón	1	1	1	Note of dissent on Decision on Track 1B (dissenting on substantive determinations of issues, regarding the Lago Agrio complaint).
85	*CME v Czech Republic*	UNCITRAL	Jaroslav Hándl	1	2	2	Dissenting opinion on the partial award (legal conclusions).
86	*CME v Czech Republic*	UNCITRAL	Ian Brownlie	2	2	2	Separate opinion on calculation of quantum.
87	*Erhas v Turkmenistan*	UNICTRAL	S Alexandrov	2	1	1	Separate declaration on the award (arguing that the case should be dismissed on lack of commonality of claims).
88	*Eureko BV v Poland (partial award)*	UNCITRAL	Jerzy Rejski	1	2	2	Dissenting opinion relating to inconsistency of the decision with the BIT and principles of international law
89	*Guaracachi America v Bolivia*	PCA 2011–17	Manuel Conthe	1	1	1	Dissent on tribunal's finding of compliance with due process and lack of jurisdiction.
90	*HICEE BV Slovakia*	PCA 2009–11	Charles Brower	1	2	1	Dissenting opinion on jurisdiction.
91	*Mytilineos Holdings v Serbia and Montenegro (I)*	UNCITRAL	Dobrosav Mitrović	1	2	2	Dissenting opinion on jurisdiction.
92	*Mobil Investments v Canada*	ARB(AF)/07/4	Philippe Sands	1	2	2	Partial dissenting opinion on the issue of subordinate measure.
93	*InterTrade Holding v Czech R*	2009–12	Henri Alvarez	2	2	1	Separate opinion on the reasoning and conclusions relating to attribution.

(continued)

	CASE NAME (shortened)	LEGAL REF	DISSENTING ARBITRATOR	TYPE*	APPOINTER**		DETAILS
					W/L	I/S	
94	*Oxus Gold v Uzbekistan*	UNCITRAL	Marc Lalonde	1	1	1	Partially dissenting opinion on the degree of liability.
95	*Bilcon v Canada (jurisdiction)*	PCA 2009–04	Donald McRae	1	2	2	Dissenting opinion relating to application of the minimum standard of treatment, national treatment and MFN.
96	*EnCana Corp v Ecuador (jurisdiction)*	LCIA UN 3481	Horacio Naón	1	2	1	Partial dissenting, determination of direct expropriation.
97	*Franz Sedelmayer v. RUSSIA*	SCC	Ivan S. Zykin	1	2	2	Dissenting opinion on the qualifications an investor and as the proper respondent (not public).
98	*Berschader v Russia*	SCC 080/2004	Todd Weiler	2	2	1	Separate opinion on indirect invest and availability of disp. settl.
99	*Renta 4 SVSA v Russia*	SCC 24/2007	Charles Brower	2	1	1	Separate opinion relating to the MFN clause and on the qualification of one of the claimants (award on preliminary objections),.
100	*Eastern Sugar BV v Czech R*	SCC 088/2004	Robert Volterra	1	1	1	Partial dissent on some conducts not amounting to a violation.
101	*Detroit Intern v Canada*	PCA 2012–25	M Chertoff	2	2	1	Separate dissenting opinion on jurisdictional statement.
102	*Energoalians Sarl v Moldova*	UNCITRAL	Dominic Pellew	1	3	3	Dissenting opinion on jurisdiction (in Russian).
103	*SD Myers v Canada (partial Award)*	UNCITRAL	Bryan Schwartz	2	1	1	Separate opinion concurring except with respect to performance requirements.
104	*SD Myers v Canada (final Award)*	UNCITRAL	Bryan Schwartz	1	1	1	Dissent on apportionment of costs.

105	*Ascom v Kazakhstan*	SCC 116/2010	David Haigh	1	1	1	Dissent on quantum.
106	*Ascom v Kazakhstan (jurisdiction)*	SCC 116/2010	Sergei Lebedev	1	2	2	Dissenting opinion.
107	*UPS v Canada (Award)*	UNCITRAL	Ronald A Cass	2	N/A	N/A	Separate statement on the award on the merits (on issues pertaining to like circumstances, national treatment).
108	*Zhinvali v Georgia*	ARB/00/1	A Jacovides	2	2	1	Separate opinion (not public).
109	*İçkale İnşaat v Turkmenistan*	ARB/10/24	C B Lamm	1	2	1	Partially dissenting on jurisdiction and allocation of costs.
110	*İçkale İnşaat v Turkmenistan*	ARB/10/24	Philippe Sands	1	1	2	Partial dissent on treaty interpretation, admissibility of the claims.
111	*Int Thunderbird v Mexico*	UNCITRAL	Thomas Wälde	2	2	1	Separate opinion on national treatment, legitimate expectations.
112	*Philip Morris v Uruguay*	ARB/10/7	Gary Born	3	2	1	Concurring and dissenting opinion on the interpretation of the Agreement.
113	*Swissbourgh v Lesotho*	PCA 2013–29	P M Nienaber	1	2	2	Dissent on the partial award on jurisdiction and merits (not public).
114	*RSM Production v Saint Lucia*	ARB/12/10	Gavan Griffith	2	N/A	N/A	Assenting reasons on a decision on a request for provisional measures (not public).
115	*RSM Production v Saint Lucia*	ARB/12/10	Edward Nottingham	1	N/A	N/A	Dissenting opinion on a decision on a request for provisional measures (not public).
116	*Getma International v Guinea*	ARB/11/29	B M Cremades	1	1	1	Dissenting opinion addressing the denial of justice claim.
117	*Lieven J van Riet v Croatia*	ARB/13/12	I Fadlallah	1	2	1	Attached to the award (not public see IAReporter).

Explanations:

* (1) Dissent *stricto sensu*; (2) Separate/concurring opinion; (3) Dissenting and concurring opinion

** Column 1 (W/L) 1: (1) Winning Party; (2) Losing Party; (3) President; Column 2 (I/S): (1) Investor; (2) State; (3) President

16

Adjudicating International Trade Cases in the World Trade Organization

Does Gender Make a Difference?

Valerie Hughes

1. Introduction

Does gender make a difference in the adjudication of international trade cases in the World Trade Organization (WTO)? Like many cautious lawyers, I would answer this question with 'it depends'. It depends on what one means by 'a difference': does it refer to the notion that including women on the WTO bench ensures or enhances its institutional legitimacy, or does it allude to a possible effect on the substantive response to the legal question at hand? Perhaps it is both.

The question posed in the title of this chapter has been asked many times before in the context of different courts, be they domestic or international. The WTO, however, has not been the subject of detailed study in this regard.[1] The WTO presents a special context for this inquiry because its adjudicatory system is unique in the international law field in a number of ways, including that decisions are signed by all three adjudicators even where there is a separate or dissenting opinion. This may explain the lack of detailed study on this subject thus far.

In this chapter, I will first describe how the WTO adjudicatory system works, including how adjudicators are selected. I will then turn to examine how many women have served as WTO adjudicators and what their backgrounds are. Finally, I will explain why providing an evidence-based answer to the question posed in the title of this chapter is not yet possible, but that WTO dispute settlement procedures as well as current approaches to trade policy development suggest that the answer is 'yes'.

[1] See Nienke Grossman, 'Sex on the Bench: Do Women Judges Matter to the Legitimacy of International Courts?' (2012) 12 (2) Chicago Journal of International Law 647, 653–54, which refers briefly to the WTO.

Valerie Hughes, *Adjudicating International Trade Cases in the World Trade Organization* In: *Identity and Diversity on the International Bench.* Edited by: Freya Baetens, Oxford University Press (2020). © The several contributors.
DOI: 10.1093/oso/9780198870753.003.0016.

2. The WTO Dispute Settlement System

2.1 General Overview

The WTO dispute settlement system was established in 1995 when the World Trade Organization itself was established. The system was not entirely new; many of its features have their origin in the practices and procedures developed during the latter years of the General Agreement on Tariffs and Trade (GATT), the predecessor to the WTO. But the new WTO system was intended to improve the GATT system by eliminating some aspects that tended to undermine its effectiveness and favour stronger economies that could block dispute settlement actions taken against them. Thus, on 15 April 1994, trade ministers representing 124 governments and the European Communities adopted a Declaration in which they welcomed 'the stronger and clearer legal framework they ha[d] adopted for the conduct of international trade, including a *more effective and reliable* dispute settlement mechanism'.[2]

WTO dispute settlement is governed by the *Understanding on the Rules and Procedures Governing the Settlement of Disputes*,[3] referred to as the Dispute Settlement Understanding, or the DSU. The aim of WTO dispute settlement is to 'secure a positive solution to a dispute' and a mutually agreed solution is to be preferred to an adjudicated outcome.[4] The first objective of WTO dispute settlement is to secure withdrawal of the offending measures. For this reason, the first phase of a dispute includes a period of compulsory consultations, where disputing parties meet without the involvement of an adjudicator with a view to resolving the issues in dispute. If consultations fail to settle the dispute, the complaining party may move to the adjudicative phase.[5]

The adjudicative phase includes two levels—a first instance level (decided by what is referred to as 'a panel') and an appellate level (decided by what is called 'the Appellate Body').[6] Jurisdiction of panels is compulsory in that, according to the DSU, WTO Members 'shall have recourse to, and abide by the rules and procedures of' the DSU when seeking the 'redress of a violation' of WTO obligations.[7] Appeal from a panel report by the complainant or respondent is as of right; there is no need to obtain leave to appeal.[8] A very high percentage (67%) of panel reports are appealed.[9]

[2] Marrakesh Declaration <www.wto.org/english/docs_e/legal_e/marrakesh_decl_e.htm>accessed 29 February 2020 (emphasis added).

[3] 1869 UNTS 401.

[4] DSU, Art 3.2.

[5] DSU, Art 4.

[6] There was no appellate level under the GATT system.

[7] DSU, Art 23.1.

[8] DSU, Art 17.4.

[9] During the period 1996 through 2018, 67% of all panel reports were appealed. Annual rates of appeal range from as low as 40% of panel reports (2013) to as high as 100% (2008). (There were no appeals

First instance panels are composed of three persons who are required to examine whether or not certain measures imposed by a WTO Member are consistent with cited provisions of the WTO agreements. There is no standing panel body; as discussed in the next section of this chapter, panels are composed on an ad hoc basis as and when disputes arise. Panels are to 'make an objective assessment of the matter before [them], including an objective assessment of the facts of the case and the applicability of and conformity with the relevant [WTO] agreements . . .'[10] In other words, panels make findings of fact and law. In making their legal findings, panels are required to apply 'the customary rules of interpretation of public international law', understood in the WTO as Articles 31 and 32 of the Vienna Convention on the Law of Treaties.[11]

The Appellate Body is a standing body of seven members, but each appeal is determined by a division of three Appellate Body members (see next section of this chapter for additional explanation about the Appellate Body). The Appellate Body's jurisdiction is limited to issues of law covered in a panel report and legal interpretations developed by a panel.[12] It has no authority to make factual findings so must rely on the factual findings of the panel. Like the panels, the Appellate Body also must also apply Articles 31 and 32 of the Vienna Convention.

The DSU also provides for arbitration proceedings in other circumstances, including to determine the reasonable period of time to comply with a ruling, the level of retaliation for failure to comply with a ruling, and whether measures taken to comply with a ruling are consistent with the complying Member's WTO obligations.[13] The latter two procedures are to be carried out by the original panel members, if available. The procedures for determining the reasonable period of time for compliance do not specify who is to serve as the arbitrator, but as explained in the next section, usually a serving or former Appellate Body member conducts these arbitrations sitting alone and serving in a personal capacity.[14]

in 1995, the first year the system was in operation. Although several disputes were filed in 1995, no panel reports were circulated until the following year.) See World Trade Organization, *Appellate Body Annual Report for 2018*, WT/AB/29, 28 May 2019, 142. One reason for the high appeal rate could be the fact that there is no retroactive remedy in the WTO, which means that a party that loses at the panel stage may choose to appeal simply to keep its impugned measure in place throughout the appeal period. For additional information about how the WTO dispute settlement system functions in practice, see World Trade Organization, *A Handbook on the WTO Dispute Settlement System* (2nd edn, Cambridge University Press 2017).

[10] DSU, Art 11.
[11] 1155 UNTS 331.
[12] DSU, Art 17.6.
[13] These procedures are governed by DSU, Arts 21.3(c), 22.6, and 21.5, respectively.
[14] *Appellate Body Annual Report for 2018* (n 9) 112.

2.2 Use of the System and Types of Disputes

Before turning to the mechanics of adjudicator selection, which informs the question whether gender makes a difference in international trade adjudication, it is useful to highlight that the WTO dispute settlement system has been used often, by a large number of WTO Members, to resolve all manner of trade disputes. This is relevant to the inquiry we make in this chapter because, if the system were not used regularly by a large number of WTO Members to resolve significant trade disputes, it would have little impact, with the result that gender on the WTO bench could have little relevance for international trade law.

The WTO dispute settlement is one of the busiest State-to-State international adjudicative systems in the world. Some numbers illustrate this point: during the period 1995 through 31 December 2019, 593 disputes were filed with the WTO.[15] During approximately the same period, 29 cases were received by the International Tribunal for the Law of the Sea,[16] while three State-to-State disputes were heard under the North Atlantic Free Trade Agreement (NAFTA).[17] Looking over a longer perspective, there were 316 trade disputes under the 47 years of the GATT (from 1947 to 1994).[18] The International Court of Justice, the principal judicial organ of the United Nations, has received 179 cases in its 72-year history.[19]

Of the WTO's 164 Members, 109 (66%) have participated in WTO disputes in some capacity, be it as a complainant bringing a challenge, a respondent defending a case, or by contributing views as a 'third party' in a dispute because the Member has a systemic or other interest in the matter being adjudicated.[20] Fifty-one WTO Members have brought at least one case to the WTO, while 60 different Members have been named as respondent in at least one dispute. More than 50% of the membership (88 different members) have participated as a 'third party' in a dispute.[21]

15 <www.wto.org/english/tratop_e/dispu_e/dispu_status_e.htm> accessed 29 February 2020.

16 <www.itlos.org/en/cases/> accessed 29 February 2020.

17 <https://can-mex-usa-sec.org/secretariat/report-rapport-reporte.aspx?lang=eng> accessed 6 July 2020. State-to-State disputes are governed by Chapter Twenty of the NAFTA. This mechanism is separate from the investor-State dispute settlement regime provided for in Chapter Eleven of the NAFTA: 32 ILM 289.

18 Arti Gobind Daswani, Roy Santana, and János Volkai, *GATT disputes: 1948-1995, Volume 1: Overview and one-page case summaries* (World Trade Organization 2018) 9.

19 <www.icj-cij.org/en/cases> accessed 29 February 2020.

20 The DSU provides in Article 10.1 that any WTO Member with 'a substantial interest in a matter before a panel and having notified its interest to the [Dispute Settlement Body] ... shall have an opportunity to be heard by the panel and to make written submissions to the panel'. Such participants are referred to as third parties. Although third parties do not have a right to appeal a panel report, they are permitted to file written submissions to and be heard by the Appellate Body in accordance with DSU, Art 17.4.

21 Dispute settlement statistics referred to in this paragraph are current as of 31 December 2019. WTO dispute settlement statistics by WTO Member are available on the WTO website at <www.wto.org/english/tratop_e/dispu_e/dispu_by_country_e.htm> acccessed 29 February 2020.

The United States and the European Union[22] are far and away the most frequent users of the system, which is not surprising given their significant trade volumes. Other frequent participants include Argentina, Australia, Brazil, Canada, China, India, Japan, Korea, and Mexico.[23] It is noteworthy that reliance on the system to resolve international trade irritants has not generally divided down development status lines in the WTO; in other words, WTO dispute settlement is not exclusively a case of the developed world versus the developing one, or vice versa. In 1995, the first year the WTO dispute settlement mechanism system was in operation, developed country Members filed 50% of the cases, while the other half were filed by developing/emerging country Members.[24] The split has fluctuated to some degree over the years, but the overall usage of the system to challenge alleged WTO violations is roughly even between developed and developing/emerging country members.[25] As for defending WTO challenges, developed country Members have more often been on the receiving end of disputes brought by developed and developing/emerging country Members alike.[26]

Members have not hesitated to bring to WTO panels and the Appellate Body complex and highly important issues for resolution. WTO disputes have often been highly significant either in terms of subject-matter, economic impact, or both.[27] Some examples include: hormone-treated beef, genetically modified products, dolphin-safe labelling, country of origin labelling for meat products, protection of sea turtles, public morals and the seal hunt, taxation of foreign sales corporations, activities of State trading enterprises, cross-border supply of gambling and betting services, measures related to financial services and tax transparency, copyright and music in bars, a preferential arrangement tied to combatting drug trafficking, packaging requirements for tobacco products and their impact on intellectual property rights, export restrictions on rare earths, transmission of natural gas and electricity and access to natural gas and electricity network capacity by transmission service operators, billions of dollars in alleged subsidies granted to aircraft companies, electronic payment services in China, fairness of softwood lumber pricing, protection of halal as a public moral,

[22] Unlike in the United Nations, the European Union is a WTO Member in its own right, as are each of the EU member states.

[23] See (n 21).

[24] <www.wto.org/english/tratop_e/dispu_e/dispu_status_e.htm>accessed 29 February 2020.

[25] However, no 'least developed country' has ever pursued a trade dispute to the panel phase. Although Bangladesh filed a dispute against India in 2004 (*India—Anti-Dumping Measures on Batteries from Bangladesh*, WT/DS306), the matter was resolved before the case reached the panel stage <www.wto.org/english/tratop_e/dispu_e/cases_e/ds306_e.htm>accessed 29 February 2020.

[26] Arie Reich, 'The effectiveness of the WTO dispute settlement system: A statistical analysis', European University Institute, Department of Law Working Paper, LAW 2017/11, 8.

[27] William J. Davey, 'The WTO and Rules-Based Dispute Settlement: Historical Evolution, Operational Success, and Future Challenges' (2014) 17 (3) Journal of International Economic Law 679, 679–700.

application of WTO rules to illicit trade, and subsidies granted in the renewable energy sector.[28]

Although the WTO dispute settlement mechanism continues to be used actively by WTO Members,[29] the system has been undergoing challenges in recent years due in large measure to the increased breadth and complexity of individual disputes, which have put a strain on the system.[30] More significant, however, is what many have called a crisis at the appellate level due to the inability, since early 2017, of WTO Members to appoint replacements to the Appellate Body following completion of sitting members' terms.[31] Such appointments are by consensus and one WTO Member, the United States, has refused to permit the launch of selection processes for replacements due to its profound dissatisfaction with the functioning of the Appellate Body.[32] As mentioned above, the rules require that three Appellate

[28] Panel and Appellate Body reports are available on the WTO website and may be located by the DS number <www.wto.org/english/tratop_e/dispu_e/dispu_status_e.htm> accessed 29 February 2020. Citations for reports in the cases referred to above, in the order mentioned, are as follows: *European Communities—Measures Concerning Meat and Meat Products (Hormones)* (16 January 1998) WT/DS24/AB/R, WT/DS48/AB/R; *European Communities—Measures Affecting the Approval and Marketing of Biotech Products* (29 September 2006) WT/DS291/R, WT/DS292/R, WT/DS293/R; *United States—Measures Concerning the Importation, Marketing and Sale of Tuna and Tuna Products* (16 May 2012) WT/DS381/AB/R; *United States—Certain Country of Origin Labelling Requirements* (29 June 2012) WT/DS384/AB/R, WT/DS386/AB/R; *United States—Import Prohibition of Certain Shrimp and Shrimp Products* (12 October 1998) WT/DS58/AB/R; *European Communities—Certain Measures Prohibiting the Importation and Marketing of Seal Products* (22 May 2014) WT/DS400/AB/R, WT/DS401/AB/R; *United States—Tax Treatment for Foreign Sales Corporations* (24 February 2000) WT/DS108/AB/R; *United States—Definitive Anti-Dumping and Countervailing Duties on Certain Products from China* (11 March 2011) WT/DS397/AB/R; *United States—Measures Affecting the Cross-Border Supply of Gambling and Betting Services* (7 April 2005) WT/DS285/AB/R; *Argentina—Measures Relating to Trade in Goods and Services* (14 April 2016) WT/DS453/AB/R; *United States—Section 110(5) of US Copyright Act* (15 June 2000) WT/DS160/R; *European Communities—Conditions for the Granting of Tariff Preferences to Developing Countries* (7 April 2004) WT/DS246/AB/R; *Australia—Certain Measures Concerning Trademarks, Geographical Indications and Other Plain Packaging Requirements Applicable to Tobacco Products and Packaging* (28 June 2018) WT/DS435/R, WT/DS441/R, WT/DS458/R, WT/DS467/R; *China—Measures Related to the Exportation of Rare Earths, Tungsten and Molybdenum* (7 August 2014) WT/DS431/AB/R, WT/DS432/AB/R, WT/DS433/AB/R; *European Union—Certain Measures Relating to the Energy Sector* (10 August 2018) WT/DS476/R; *United States—Measures Affecting Trade in Large Civil Aircraft* (12 March 2012) WT/DS353/AB/R; *European Communities—Measures Affecting Trade in Large Civil Aircraft* (18 May 2011) WT/DS316/AB/R; *China—Certain Measures Affecting Electronic Payment Services* (16 July 2012) WT/DS413/R; *United States—Final Countervailing Duty Determination with Respect to Certain Softwood Lumber from Canada* (19 January 2004) WT/DS257/AB/R; *Indonesia—Importation of Horticultural Products, Animals and Animal Products* (19 November 2017) WT/DS477/AB/R, WT/DS478/AB/R; *Colombia—Measures Relating to the Importation of Textiles, Apparel and Footwear* (7 June 2016) WT/DS461/AB/R; *Canada—Certain Measures Affecting the Renewable Energy Sector* (6 May 2013) WT/DS412/AB/R, WT/DS426/AB/R.

[29] Thirty-eight and 20 new disputes were filed in 2018 and 2019, respectively. See (n 15).

[30] Speech by WTO Director-General Roberto Azevedo to the WTO Dispute Settlement Body on 28 October 2015 and annexed document 'Current Dispute Settlement Activity' <www.wto.org/english/news_e/spra_e/spra94_e.htm>accessed 29 February 2020.

[31] Robert McDougall, *Crisis in the WTO: Restoring the WTO Dispute Settlement Function*, CIGI Papers No. 194 (Center for International Governance Innovation, October 2018); Tetyana Payosova, Gary Clyde Hufbauer, and Jeffrey J. Schott, *The Dispute Settlement Crisis in the World Trade Organization: Causes and Cures*, Policy Brief 18-5 (Peterson Institute for International Economics, March 2018).

[32] The United States is of the view that the Appellate Body regularly exceeds its authority and strays beyond the role agreed for it by WTO Members when the WTO dispute settlement system was put in

Body members sit on an individual appeal. In December 2019, all but one Appellate Body member had completed their terms, with the result that the Appellate Body can no longer hear new appeals.[33]

2.3 The Adjudicators

WTO adjudicators are not referred to as judges; they are either panellists or Appellate Body Members. This harks back to the early days of trade dispute settlement under the GATT, when trade disputes were resolved by the GATT members (then called Contracting Parties) initially in plenary and then later in smaller groups called working parties. The effort was more diplomatic than legal, and lawyers were not involved in the process. The result was negotiated with the disputing parties and the solution was often the result of a compromise.[34] Over time, the GATT system became increasingly legalistic. Today, WTO dispute settlement is highly legalistic, with very few remaining vestiges of the early GATT approach.[35]

2.3.1 Panellists

2.3.1.1 Panel selection process

WTO panels are established on an ad hoc basis as disputes arise because there is no standing panel body. The DSU specifies the qualifications of panellists as follows:

> Well-qualified governmental and/or non-governmental individuals, including persons who have served on or presented a case to a panel, served as a representative of a [WTO] Member or of a contracting party to GATT 1947 or as a representative to the Council or Committee of any [WTO] agreement or its predecessor

place in 1995. For example, the United States believes that, contrary to the dispute settlement rules, the Appellate Body issues advisory opinions by making findings that are not necessary to resolve the dispute at hand, wrongly considers that its previous rulings serve as precedent, engages in review of fact-finding carried out by panels when its mandate is confined to making legal findings, and repeatedly issues reports beyond the 90-day deadline stipulated in the rules. See statement delivered by United States Ambassador Dennis Shea at the meeting of the WTO General Council held on 9 December 2019 available at <https://geneva.usmission.gov/2019/12/09/ambassador-shea-statement-at-the-wto-general-council-meeting/>accessed 29 February 2020.

[33] Appeals already in the system at that time could continue, however, because the Appellate Body working procedures permit a person who ceases to be a member of the Appellate Body to complete the disposition of any appeal to which that person was assigned while a member of the Appellate Body: World Trade Organization, *Working Procedures for Appellate Review*, Rule 15, WT/AB/WP/6 (16 August 2010) (*Working Procedures*).

[34] Paul Luyten, 'We were young together: at the GATT, 1956-58' and Peter Williams, 'Law and Lawyers in the Multilateral Trading System: Back to the Future' in Gabrielle Marceau (ed), *The History of Law and Lawyers in the GATT/WTO: The Development of the Rule of Law in the Multilateral Trading System* (CUP 2015) 79, 82–84 and 85, 97–103.

[35] This evolution is best described in Robert E. Hudec, *Enforcing International Trade Law – The Evolution of the Modern GATT Legal System* (Butterworth Legal Publishers 1993.)

agreement, or in the Secretariat, taught or published on international trade law or policy, or served as a senior trade policy official of a Member.[36]

The DSU notes further that:

> Panel members should be selected with a view to ensuring the independence of the members, a sufficiently diverse background and a wide spectrum of experience.[37]

Panellists serve in their personal capacity and do not represent their country of nationality or, if the panellist is a government employee, their government.[38] It is not necessary to be a lawyer to serve as a panellist; although most panels contain at least one or two lawyers, many have also included economists, trade policy specialists, or sector specific experts (such as in agriculture, financial services, intellectual property, animal health, or food safety).[39] Nationals of the disputing parties can sit on panels provided that the disputing parties agree,[40] although this has rarely occurred.[41]

Panels are composed of three persons and panellists are selected on an ad hoc basis by the parties to the dispute. There is no roster from which panellists must be chosen, but the Secretariat maintains an indicative list of individuals nominated by WTO Members from which panellists *may* (but not must) be selected.[42] The Indicative List of Panellists currently contains the names of 446 individuals nominated by 71 different WTO Members (including the European Union and each of its Member States counted individually).[43] Only 91 individuals (20%) on the list are women. Of the 71 WTO Members who have one or more names of individuals on the list, 36 (51%) do not include women on their lists. Only 12 Members (17%) include 50% or more women among their nominated individuals.[44] Even raising the criterion to women making up one third of the names on the list, only

[36] DSU, Art 8.1.

[37] DSU, Art 8.2.

[38] DSU, Art 8.9.

[39] Reto Malacrida, 'WTO panel composition: searching far and wide for administrators of world trade justice' in Gabrielle Marceau (ed.) (n 34) 311, 322–23.

[40] DSU, Art 8.3.

[41] Malacrida (n 39) 321.

[42] DSU, Art 8.4. The Dispute Settlement Body, an organ of the WTO composed of the entire WTO membership that meets on a monthly basis to administer the dispute settlement system, approves the nominations. No nomination has ever been rejected.

[43] The Indicative List is updated on a regular basis as WTO Members propose names to be added. The list referred to in this paragraph is dated 13 January 2020, the most recent available at the time of writing: WT/DSB/44/Rev 48.

[44] These are: Cote D'Ivoire, Cuba, Denmark, Dominican Republic, France, Ghana, Hungary, Indonesia, Moldova, Romania, Sweden, and the Separate Customs Territory of Taiwan, Penghu, Kinmen, and Matsu.

18 Members (25%) meet it.[45] Although concerning, this is less significant than it appears because many 'off roster' panellists have been chosen to serve on panels and the Indicative List is not considered by WTO Members as a primary source for panel selection.

Disputing parties can select panellists through mutual agreement and then inform the WTO Secretariat of their choices. However, panel selection is almost always carried out with the assistance of the Secretariat because agreement on three individuals can be difficult to reach.[46] The process is conducted on a confidential basis and usually takes several weeks and sometimes even months, as parties try to buy time to prepare their cases, find a settlement, or simply avoid the litigation phase.

The process when selecting panellists with the assistance of the Secretariat is as follows: representatives of the disputing parties meet with the WTO Secretariat[47] shortly after a dispute settlement panel is established by the Dispute Settlement Body (DSB) at the request of a complainant.[48] During the meeting, the disputing parties provide their respective lists of preferred panellist qualifications and request the Secretariat to provide names of proposed panellists that meet these criteria.[49] Disputing parties invariably request that panellists have prior WTO panel experience; this of course limits the pool from which to select people to serve. Parties might also ask for sector specific experience (such as intellectual property or financial services or industrial policy), depending upon the nature of the case to be decided. Parties almost always request that one or more of the panellists be qualified lawyers. Experience in economics or animal health, or some other profession is often requested, depending on the subject-matter of the dispute. Parties almost always exclude nationals of disputing parties and often exclude nationals of third parties to the dispute, as well as nationals of WTO Members with similar measures or policies to those being challenged. Some disputing parties will make clear that they prefer not to have individuals with certain backgrounds, such as academics. Sometimes ability to conduct a panel in Spanish without requiring interpretation is requested, although this is rare because the vast majority of panels are conducted in English.[50] Finally, developing country disputing parties are entitled to have a developing country national on the panel if they so request, which they invariably

[45] The additional Members under this criterion are Australia, Brazil, Colombia, Italy, Malaysia, and Norway.

[46] Malacrida (n 39) 313–16.

[47] The Secretariat is represented by the Director of the Legal Affairs Division or the Director of the Rules Division, depending upon the subject of the dispute. If the dispute concerns trade remedies (namely, subsidies, dumping, or safeguards), the Director of the Rules Division will assist with panel selection. If the dispute concerns any other WTO matter, the Director of the Legal Affairs Division will assist with panel selection.

[48] The authority of the DSB to establish panels is found in DSU, Art 2.1.

[49] DSU, Art 8.6.

[50] The three official languages of the WTO are English, French, and Spanish.

do.[51] Not surprisingly, the qualifications enumerated by the complainant on the one hand and the respondent on the other usually have little in common and are often contradictory; for example, one side will consider that the expertise of an economist will greatly inform the panel's analysis while the other side will consider such expertise will be a distraction from the essential questions at issue. Naturally, the more qualifications that are enumerated and the more nationalities that are excluded, the more challenging the selection process becomes.[52]

The Secretariat usually provides a list of six or more names within a few days and another meeting is held to discuss the proposals. The DSU stipulates that disputing parties shall not oppose nominations 'except for compelling reasons',[53] but in practice this does not really constrain rejections. It is rare to reach agreement on any of the names at this initial meeting. Most often, some names will be rejected while one or two might be identified as a possible candidate and kept on a 'possibles' list. The Secretariat will then seek to come up with another list of names and another meeting will be held to discuss the new proposals. This usually goes on for a few weeks; eventually, one or even two panellist names might be agreed upon.[54] But agreement on all three names occurs infrequently.[55] The more usual scenario is that one of the disputing parties will lose patience with the lack of progress and will request the WTO Director-General (DG) to choose the three panellists. In fact, either disputing party is entitled to request the DG to compose the panel if there is no agreement within 20 days after establishment of the panel.[56]

The DG selection process is very efficient: the DG is required to select the panel within 10 days of receiving a request to do so.[57] The DG must consult with the disputing parties to hear their selection criteria, after which she/he must select the three panellists whom she/he 'considers most appropriate'.[58] In other words, the DG has considerable discretion in selecting panellists. However, experience shows that DGs generally try to accommodate both sides' selection criteria as much as possible. Once the DG selects the three panellists, the disputing parties are informed of the names in writing. At that point, the disputing parties cannot object

[51] DSU, Art 8.10. The WTO does not publish a list WTO Members that have developing country status; each Member determines its own status.

[52] Information in this paragraph and the next is based to a large degree on the author's experience in numerous panel selection procedures while serving as Director of the WTO Legal Affairs Division during the period 1 September 2010 through 31 August 2016. See also Malacrida (n 39) 314–16, 320–27.

[53] DSU, Art 8.6.

[54] Malacrida (n 39) 314–16.

[55] Of the 38 panels established in 2018 and 2019, only 6 (16%) were composed by agreement of the disputing parties. See also Malacrida (n 39) 317–18.

[56] DSU, Art 8.7.

[57] DSU, Art 8.7. The DG selects the panellists in consultation with the chairperson of the DSB and the Chairperson of one of the WTO Councils or Committees: which of those chairpersons is consulted depends upon the subject matter of the dispute in question. For example, if the dispute concerns a provision under the General Agreement on Trade in Services, the DG will consult the Chairperson of the Services Council. WTO ambassadors serve as chairpersons of the Councils and Committees.

[58] DSU, Art 8.7. There have been five Directors-General of the WTO, all male.

to the composition of the panel, unless of course there is a conflict of interest with one of the panellists. This, however, is unlikely. Selected panellists' backgrounds are researched thoroughly. Moreover, panellists are required to affirm in writing that no such conflict exists when accepting the appointment.[59]

2.3.1.2 The role of gender in the panel selection process

Until very recently, gender was never a stated consideration in panel selection processes; the gender of the panellist would simply never arise when discussing preferences (such as area of expertise, experience serving as a panellist) with the disputing parties.[60] However, this appears to have changed during the past two years. A few WTO members (including Canada and New Zealand) regularly request the Secretariat to include women in the list of proposed candidates for panels and, even without such prodding, the Secretariat seeks to include women when proposing candidates.[61]

2.3.1.3 Women panellists

Of the 819 panellist appointments made from 1995 through 2019 (some of which are repeat appointments of the same person), 145 went to women (18%). Of the 301 different individuals appointed as panellists from 1995 through 2019, 51 are women (17%).[62] Overall representation of women on three-person panels presents a better picture: of the 280 three-person panels composed from 1995 through 2019, 128 panels—or 46%—have included at least one woman. However, 100% of panels have included at least one man. Although there have been a number of panels composed of two women and one man (19, or seven percent), there has never been a panel composed of three women. This compares with 152 panels composed of three men (54%).[63]

[59] See *Rules of Conduct for the understanding on rules and procedures governing the settlement of disputes*, Rules II, III and IV, and Annexes 2 and 3: WT/DSB/RC/1 (96-5267), 11 December 1996.

[60] Not once during the six years (2010–16) of the author's involvement in panel selection processes as Director of the WTO Legal Affairs Division did a party request that the Secretariat's list of proposed panellists include women.

[61] This information is based on interviews with delegates and WTO Secretariat staff conducted on a non-attribution basis. Panel selection processes are conducted on a confidential basis and specific information on individual selection processes has not been made public.

[62] From 1995 through 2019, the percentage of women panellists appointed ranged from 0 (in 2006 and 2009) to a high of 71 (in 2013); the next highest was 35%, in 2003. During 12 of those years, appointments of women were below 20% of total appointments; in seven of them, they were below 10%: Dispute Settlement Statistics and Tables, Count of WTO Panellist Positions, by Gender <www.worldtradelaw.net>accessed 29 February 2020.

[63] The statistics in this section are based on data found on the WTO website <www.wto.org/english/tratop_e/dispu_e/dispu_status_e.htm>as well as statistics presented in <www.worldtradelaw.net>accessed 29 February 2020. The number of panel appointments refer to appointments to original panels as well as to compliance panels established under DSU, Art 21.5. There can be slight variations in the relevant statistics because sources may count disputes with multiple complainants differently. If more than one WTO Member challenges the same measure imposed by a single WTO Member, the WTO may establish a single panel to deal with all of the challenges, or it may establish a separate panel for each challenge (DSU, Art 9). Often, in the latter situation, the same panellists will serve on all of the

The women who have been chosen to serve as panellists have served at diplomatic missions in Geneva or in trade positions in their governments. Some have enjoyed very senior government positions including minister and vice-minister; one was a former deputy Prime Minister.[64] A few are private legal practitioners, while others are former WTO Secretariat staff members.

Of the 51 different women who have served as panellists, 16 have served several times.[65] Claudia Orozco, a former Colombian diplomat, has served on 15 panels—more than any other woman. Canada and Colombia have had the most women panellists, each at five.[66] Four women have served from each of Australia and Chile, while three have served from each of Argentina, Brazil, Jamaica, Mexico, Singapore, South Africa, and Switzerland. Despite some women's considerable experience serving on panels, however, relatively few have chaired them. Statistics reveal that of the 280 panels composed thus far, only 23 (eight percent) were chaired by women. Five women have served as panel chair more than once.[67]

It is difficult to know for certain why some women have been chosen to serve several times. Nationality is likely a factor. Those countries that have provided the most panellists overall have also provided many of the repeat women panellists: Canada has provided the highest number of total panellists (men and women combined) at 21, followed closely by Australia (16), Switzerland (16), Chile (14), Brazil (13), South Africa (13), and Mexico (10). In addition, a high repetition rate appears to be a characteristic more generally in WTO panel selection.[68] As noted above, experience serving as a panellist is a common criterion set forth by disputing parties in the panel selection process.

Despite the increased demand for women panellists mentioned above, appointments of men still far outnumber appointments of women. In 2018, appointments

panels and the proceedings will be conducted simultaneously. Some sources count these as separate panels, while others count them as one single panel. In this section, panels composed to deal with multiple complaints are counted as single panels.

[64] Dame Billie Miller (Barbados).

[65] The 16 women who have served more than twice are: Stephanie Sin Far Lee (Australia), Delilah Cabb (Belize), Marta Lemme (Brazil), Elaine Feldman (Canada), Claudia Orozco (Colombia), Deborah Milstein (Israel), Andrea Marie Dawes (Brown) (Jamaica), Usha Dwarka-Canabady (Mauritius), Gloria Peña (Mexico), Luz Elena Reyes de la Torre (Mexico), Penelope Ridings (New Zealand), Elizabeth Chelliah (Singapore), Margaret Liang (Singapore), Leora Blumberg (South Africa), Maria-Gabrielle Ineichen-Fleisch (Switzerland), and Eni Neri De Ross (Venezuela).

[66] The Canadians are Elain Feldman, Heather Forton, Kirsten Hillman (all of whom served at one time at the Permanent Mission of Canada to the WTO), Debra Steger (former WTO staff member) and the author (former WTO staff member). The five Colombians are Claudia Orozco (private legal practitioner), Angela María Orozco Gómez (Minister of Transport), Marta Lucia Ramírez De Ricón (Vice-President), Olga Lucía Lozano (Vice-Minister of Trade) and Mónica Rolong (diplomat).

[67] Elaine Feldman (Canada, former diplomat), Carmen Luz Guarda (former Ambassador of Chile to the WTO), Claudia Orozco (Colombia, private practitioner), Luz Elena Reyes de la Torre (Mexico, private practitioner), and Margaret Liang (former Deputy Permanent Representative of Singapore to the WTO).

[68] Joost Pauwelyn, 'The Rule of Law without the Rule of Lawyers? Why Investment Arbitrators are from Mars, Trade Panelists are from Venus', CTEI Working Papers CTEI-2015-05, Center for Trade and Economic Integration, Graduate Institute Geneva (2015) 14–15.

of women amounted to only 29%; the percentage was higher in 2003 (35%), 2005, 2007, and 2008 (all at 30%), 2012 (38%), and 2013 (71%). Of the 74 people serving as panellists at the end of 2019, 34% are women. One positive development seems to be that most panels composed recently include at least one woman: at the end of 2019, of the 32 active panels, women were serving on 21 of them (66%).

Why have members traditionally chosen comparatively fewer women than men to serve on panels? A partial explanation lies in the fact that women continue to comprise a much smaller pool of candidates for appointment. A high percentage of panellists are Geneva-based trade diplomats[69] and men are dominant in that pool. This may also influence the choice in that the diplomats responsible for panel selection might be inclined to appoint their peers because they know and have confidence in them; this would limit efforts to look beyond their immediate circles that are dominated by men. Another reason that relatively few women have been chosen could be related to the selection procedure itself: it is conducted on a confidential basis behind closed doors in the presence only of the two disputing parties and the Secretariat. There is no peer pressure to seek diversity as there would be in a more public process.

WTO Members have been discussing for many years possible amendments to several of the WTO dispute settlement procedures with a view to making improvements, achieving efficiencies, and addressing lacunae in the rules.[70] Although numerous proposals for change have been made over the years covering a wide variety of subjects, none has addressed a means of increasing representation of women on the WTO bench. Perhaps this is just as well, because it has not been possible to arrive at a consensus on any proposal for change, with the result that no amendments have been adopted. Nevertheless, I offer a suggestion for consideration: the DSU provides in Article 8.10 that when a dispute is between a developing country Member and a developed country Member the panel shall, if the developing country so requests, include at least one panellist from a developing country. This provision could be used as a model for a new gender-based provision that would provide as follows: if a disputing Member so requests, the panel shall include at least one women panellist.

2.3.2 Appellate Body members

2.3.2.1 Appellate Body members selection process

The WTO Appellate Body is composed of seven persons, each of whom serves a four-year term.[71] Appellate Body members may be reappointed once.[72] Three members of the Appellate Body (referred to as a Division) sit and decide on an

[69] ibid 26.

[70] Information about these negotiations may be found on the WTO website <www.wto.org/english/tratop_e/dispu_e/dispu_negs_e.htm>accessed 29 February 2020.

[71] DSU, Art 17.1.

[72] DSU, Art 17.2.

appeal, although all seven Appellate Body members discuss each Appellate Body report prior to its issuance.[73] This practice is referred to as 'collegiality' and is designed to 'ensure consistency and coherence in decision-making, and to draw on the individual and collective expertise' of the Appellate Body members.[74]

When the Appellate Body was established in 1995, WTO Members anticipated that appeals would be rare and hence the 'job' was considered a part time one. In fact, it turned out to be quite different from expectations. As noted above, most panel reports are appealed and the challenges in almost every appeal are numerous and complex.

The DSU stipulates the following qualifications for Appellate Body members:

> Persons of recognized authority, with demonstrated expertise in law, international trade and the subject matter of the covered agreements generally. They shall be unaffiliated with any government. The Appellate Body membership shall be broadly representative of membership in the WTO.[75]

Appellate Body Members must have legal expertise and must not be affiliated with any government. They serve in their personal capacity and do not represent their country of nationality. Unlike with panellists, Appellate Body members may (and regularly do) sit on appeals involving their country of nationality and they do not require the agreement of the disputing parties to do so.

The Appellate Body selection process is not prescribed in the DSU; it is set forth in a June 1995 decision of the Dispute Settlement Body.[76] The process begins with the adoption by consensus of a DSB decision to launch a selection process for an upcoming vacancy.[77] This is followed several weeks later by the submission to the DG of written nominations by any Member wishing to nominate a

[73] DSU, Art 17.1 and Rules 4 and 6, *Working Procedures* (n 33).

[74] Rule 4(1), *Working Procedures* (n 33).

[75] DSU, Art 17.

[76] World Trade Organization, WT/DSB/1, 19 June 1995, para 13 (WT/DSB/1). Some steps in the selection procedure are not specified in the document but they have been developed over time.

[77] There is an ongoing debate as to whether or not voting is permitted for purposes of launching an Appellate Body selection process or appointing an Appellate Body Member, or whether such processes require consensus. See, for example, Jennifer Hillman, 'Three Approaches to Fixing the World Trade Organization's Appellate Body: The Good, the Bad and the Ugly', Issue Brief Series, Institute of International Economic Law, Georgetown University Law Center (December 2018) 11-14; Pieter Jan Kuijper, 'US Attack on the Appellate Body' (*International Economic Law and Policy Blog*, 15 November 2017) <https://worldtradelaw.typepad.com/ielpblog/2017/11/guest-post-from-pieter-jan-kuiper-professor-of-the-law-of-international-economic-organizations-at-the-faculty-of-law-of-th.html>accessed 29 February 2020; Mary E. Footer, 'Effecting Global Economic Governance Through the WTO: One Step at a Time?' in Denise Prévost, Iveta Alexovicová, and Jens Hillebrand Pohl (eds), *Restoring Trust in Trade, Liber Amicorum in Honour of Peter Van den Bossche* (Hart Publishing 2019) 17, 22. Thus far, there has never been a vote to launch an Appellate Body selection process, with the result that, as mentioned above, the United States has blocked the launch of selection processes since early 2017.

candidate. Nomination documents are circulated by the DG to all WTO Members. Nominating Members usually propose one person although some have proposed two candidates,[78] and Members almost always propose their own nationals.[79]

Candidates attend an interview conducted by a selection committee, which is composed of the DG as well as the chairpersons of several WTO bodies: the Dispute Settlement Body, the General Council, the Goods Council, the Services Council, and the TRIPS Council,[80] all of whom are ambassadors from different WTO Members. The interviews are confidential. Once the committee has completed the interviews, it receives the views (written or oral) of those WTO Members wishing to submit indications as to which candidate(s) they can or cannot support for selection. WTO Members (especially those that are very active in dispute settlement) often form their views based on private meetings they hold with candidates on an individual basis.

After considering the results of the interviews as well as the views submitted by those WTO Members that choose to provide views, the selection committee draws up a proposal setting forth the candidate whom they believe will receive consensus support of the WTO membership. The proposal is circulated to WTO Members and is considered for approval at a subsequent meeting of the DSB. Usually, the selection committee has determined informally, in advance of that meeting, that the proposal will be approved on a consensus basis. On one occasion, the committee determined that none of the proposed candidates would be acceptable to the entire membership, such that consensus approval would not be possible. The DSB reopened the selection process and called for new nominees, which engendered some controversy at the time.[81]

The Appellate Body selection process is currently undergoing its biggest challenge to date. As mentioned above, it has not been possible to reach consensus among the WTO membership to launch a selection process since early 2017. Several Appellate Body members' terms have expired since then, with the result that on 11 December 2019, the Appellate Body had only one member left (Hong Zhao of China). As it is necessary to have three Appellate Body members to hear each appeal, the Appellate Body can no longer hear new appeals. Although WTO

[78] The United States and the European Union have nominated two candidates in the same process on a number of occasions.

[79] Canada put forward a Uruguayan (Ambassador Julio Lacarte Muró) in the first selection process in 1995 because of his stellar qualifications and long-time GATT experience. He had served as Deputy Executive Secretary of the GATT at its inception in 1947.

[80] WT/DSB/1, para 13.

[81] This occurred in 2013–14 when none of the four nominees (Joan Fitzhenry from Australia, Yenkong Ngangjoh from Cameroon, Hamid Mamdouh from Egypt, and James Gathii from Kenya) was able to secure consensus support. Eventually, Shree Baboo Chekitan Servansing (Mauritius) was appointed to the post. See minutes of the meeting of the DSB held on 22 January 2014, WT/DSB/M/341, 20-24. See also Gregory Shaffer, Manfred Elsig, and Sergio Puig, 'The Extensive (But Fragile) Authority of the WTO Appellate Body' (2016) 79 Law and Contemporary Problems 237, 271.

Members continue to make efforts to respond to the United States' concerns so that a selection process can be launched, the issue remains unresolved.[82]

2.3.2.2 The role of gender in the Appellate Body member selection process

Since 1995, several women have been put forward for a seat on the Appellate Body, although male candidates have consistently outnumbered women candidates in selection processes.[83] Thus far, gender has not been a stated consideration in selecting Appellate Body members. Members emphasize the criteria listed in Article 17.3 of the DSU ('persons of recognized authority, with demonstrated expertise in law, international trade and the subject matter of the covered agreements generally ... unaffiliated with any government ... broadly representative of membership in the WTO')[84] and support candidates they believe will support their positions on substantive legal issues.[85]

The three Appellate Body members who sit on an individual appeal (called a Division) are selected internally 'on the basis of rotation, while taking into account the principles of random selection, unpredictability, and opportunity for all Members to serve regardless of their national origin'.[86] The precise selection process is secret and is intended to work so that disputing parties cannot seek to time their appeals in order to draw a particular composition of Appellate Body members on a Division. Given that selection is on a random basis, it is clear that gender considerations do not enter into the composition of Appellate Body Divisions.

[82] New Zealand Ambassador David Walker was appointed in January 2019 to assist Ambassador Junichi Ihara, Chair of the WTO General Council (the highest decision-making body composed of representatives of all WTO Members), in finding a solution to the impasse. Ambassador Walker convened several meetings with WTO Members throughout 2019 and presented a proposed solution in the form of a General Council decision on 9 December 2019, which set forth guidance and suggestions to improve the functioning of the Appellate Body. However, the proposal did not receive consensus approval: 'Informal Process on Matters Related to the Functioning of the Appellate Body – Report by the Facilitator H E Dr David Walker (New Zealand) and Draft Decision on the Functioning of the Appellate Body', 9 December 2019, WTO document JOB/GC/225 <www.wto.org/english//news_e/news19_e/gc_09dec19_e.htm>accessed 29 February 2020.

[83] Although nominations are not always made public by nominating Members and a comprehensive list of Appellate Body nominees has not been published by the WTO, the author served in the Appellate Body Secretariat and the Legal Affairs Division of the WTO for more than 10 years and relies on personal recollections as well as interviews of WTO Secretariat staff conducted on a non-attribution basis. The author is aware of nine nominations of women out of over 70 nominees in total from 1995 to the present (three from the United States, two from China, and one each from Australia, Brazil, the Philippines, and Zimbabwe).

[84] See, for example, interventions by Australia and Canada during meetings of the Dispute Settlement Body in July and September 2014, respectively, when the Appellate Body selection process launched in 2013 failed to identify a candidate who had consensus support of the membership: WT/DSB/M/345, 19 and WT/DSB/M/350, 15-16.

[85] Manfred Elsig and Mark A. Pollack, 'Agents, Trustees, and International Courts: The Politics of Judicial Appointment at the World Trade Organization' (2014) 20 (2) European Journal of International Relations 391, 408, 410.

[86] Rule 6.2, *Working Procedures* (n 33).

2.3.2.3 Women Appellate Body members

Of the 27 Appellate Body members who have served so far since 1995, five (19%) have been women. Two have come from China (Yeujiao Zhang and Hong Zhao), two from the United States (Merit Janow and Jennifer Hillman), and one from the Philippines (Lilia Bautista). The first woman who served on the Appellate Body (Merit Janow) is from the United States; she was the only woman on the Body for her entire four-year term from 2003 to 2007. Two women (Jennifer Hillman and Lilia Bautista) served concurrently in 2007, and they were joined by a third woman (Yeujiao Zhang) in 2008. The three served together until 2011. Currently, the sole member of the Appellate Body is a woman (Hong Zhao). She was appointed in December 2016 and her term expires on 30 November 2020.[87]

The women who have served on the Appellate Body had all previously served in their national governments as advisers and negotiators. Two served in judicial and quasi-judicial positions,[88] another in private legal practice,[89] another in the securities field,[90] and another in international organizations.[91]

2.3.3 Selection process for other WTO arbitrators and the role of gender

As mentioned above, in addition to panellists and Appellate Body members, the WTO dispute settlement system also provides for arbitration to determine the reasonable period of time to comply with a ruling, the level of retaliation for failure to comply with a ruling, and whether measures taken to comply with a ruling are consistent with the complying Member's WTO obligations.[92]

Selection of arbitrators for 'reasonable period of time' arbitrations is carried out on a confidential basis and involves the disputing parties, the director of the Appellate Body Secretariat, and the DG. Such arbitrations have usually, but not exclusively, been carried out by serving or former Appellate Body members serving alone. On two of the three occasions when a non-Appellate Body member served in that capacity, the arbitrator had served as a member of the underlying panel in the dispute.[93] Only one woman has served as an arbitrator in 37 such arbitrations since 1995, and she had been a panellist in the underlying dispute.[94] Therefore, it

[87] <www.wto.org/english/tratop_e/dispu_e/ab_members_descrp_e.htm>accessed 29 February 2020.

[88] Jennifer Hillman (United States), International Trade Commission, and Hong Zhao (China), Economic Tribunal of the Second Intermediate Court of Beijing.

[89] Merit Janow (United States).

[90] Lilia Bautista (Philippines), Securities Exchange Commission.

[91] Yeujiao Zhang (China), Asian Development Bank, and World Bank.

[92] These procedures are governed by DSU, Arts 21.3(c), 22.6, and 21.5, respectively.

[93] The arbitrator has served in the underlying panel in *United States—Anti-Dumping Measures on Certain Shrimp from Viet Nam* (15 December 2015) WT/DS429/12 and *United States—Anti-Dumping and Countervailing Measures on Large Residential Washers from Korea* (13 April 2017) WT/DS464/RPT, but not in *United States—Certain Methodologies and their Application to Anti-Dumping Proceedings Involving China* (19 January 2018) WT/DS471/RPT.

[94] Claudia Orozco (Colombia) in *United States—Anti-Dumping and Countervailing Measures on Large Residential Washers from Korea* (13 April 2017) WT/DS464/RPT.

is safe to assume that gender had nothing to do with arbitrator selection in these proceedings.

Retaliation and compliance arbitrations are carried out by members of the original panel who are available to serve again. If one or more members of an original panel is not available, however, the selection process follows that used in selecting original panellists. In other words, the Secretariat seeks to assist parties to select one or more replacement panellists, and either party can go to the DG for selection if agreement proves elusive. As with panel selection, gender has not generally been a stated consideration until quite recently for a few WTO members.

3. Does Gender Make a Difference in WTO Adjudication?

Having explained the procedures for panel and Appellate Body selection and reviewed the experience with woman adjudicators in the WTO, we turn now to consider whether gender makes a difference in WTO adjudication.

3.1 The Paucity of Data

Unfortunately, it is far from easy to answer the question whether gender matters in WTO adjudication. One reason has to do with the difficulty of making assessments when there are very limited data. As explained above, women have not been absent from the WTO bench, and their presence seems to be more extensive than it is in some other fields—international investment arbitration being one example. Nevertheless, based on the events thus far, one cannot say that women have played a significant role as adjudicators in WTO dispute settlement. For one thing, as described above, women have been far outnumbered by men as WTO adjudicators. In addition, there has never been a WTO panel composed exclusively of women, or an Appellate Body Division composed of all women. There has been only one occasion since 1995 when a woman has made a decision as a sole arbitrator, and this regarding the relatively less weighty issue of the time period permitted for compliance with a ruling.[95] Her arbitral award reveals nothing to suggest she approached the issue before her differently than any male arbitrator had: the award follows the structure and style of previous awards; like all the male arbitrators, she followed the guideline set forth in the DSU not to award a compliance time period of more than 15 months; her determination was the same as or similar to nine determinations made by male arbitrators in terms of the time allotted for compliance but was markedly different (much less exigent) from eight others; and the reasons

[95] ibid.

supporting her decision include reliance on a number of previous arbitration awards issued by men.[96] In sum, this one example provides no insight into whether or not gender makes a difference in WTO adjudication.

3.2 Individual Opinions Must Be Anonymous

Even using the data we have presents challenges because of the way panels and the Appellate Body work. As mentioned above, a panel is composed of three individuals. All three panellists sign the panel report as a whole. Even if one of the panellists authors a separate or dissenting opinion, it remains anonymous: all three names appear at the end of the report. The author of the individual or dissenting opinion cannot be revealed.[97] Of the panels where women have been present, there has always been at least one man and usually two serving on the panel. Hence when a woman and two men serve on a panel that does not issue a unanimous decision, we cannot determine whether the woman authored the separate or dissenting opinion or whether she and one of the male panellists formed the majority. Nor can we know, when two women and one man serve as panellists on a panel that issues a split decision, whether or not the two women formed the majority or whether the women split on the result.

It may be that some intelligence could be gleaned by studying the panel reports authored by two women and one man, but that represents only seven percent of all panel reports. The same difficulty arises with panel reports where a woman chaired the panel; one might speculate that as chair, she might have more influence or be able to exercise persuasion over other panellists. But only eight percent of panel reports fall into this category, so there is not enough experience on which to base solid conclusions.

As mentioned above, 16 individual women have served on several panels so one might consider studying their respective decisions to seek to draw conclusions about whether a common approach might be discerned that sets them apart from decisions of all male panels. However, limited data undermine such research: only two women have served on more than 10 panels, while only eight have served more than five times.[98] Most women have only served on one or two panels. Moreover,

[96] There were 37 such proceedings but there were no determinations in four of them because the disputing parties came to an agreement between themselves.

[97] DSU, Art 14.3.

[98] The two who have served more than 10 times are Claudia Orozco (Colombia, 15 times) and Enie Neri de Ross (Venezuela, 13 times). Those who have served more than five times are, in addition to the two just mentioned, Leora Blumberg (South Africa, 8), Luz Elena Reyes (Mexico, 8), Deborah Milstein (Israel, 7), Mary Elizabeth Chelliah (Singapore, 6), Andrea Marie Brown Dawes (Jamaica, 6), and Marta Lemme (Brazil, 6): 'List of WTO panelists with Number of Panels Served On' www.worldtradelaw.net accessed 29 February 2020.

given the wide variety of subjects covered in panel reports, it would be very difficult to find any trend at all.

A similar issue arises in the context of examining Appellate Body Reports. All three members of the Division hearing the appeal sign the Appellate Body Report and separate and dissenting opinions are anonymous.[99] However, given that Appellate Body Members sit for at least four years rather than on an ad hoc basis as panellists do, there will be more relevant data to examine (ie Appellate Body Reports where one or two women have been on the Division as compared to reports where no women have been on the Division) with a view to determining whether the reports involving women Appellate Body Members show any differences in the decisions. Again, however, the current study sample is too small to be helpful: so far, only five women have served as Appellate Body members.

3.3 What Do We Mean By 'Difference'?

Data and other issues aside, we return to the issue raised at the outset of this chapter: whether 'difference' should be understood in terms of the institutional legitimacy of the adjudicative body and its decisions, or whether it should focus on the substantive response to the legal question or issue before the adjudicative body?

If the question is about institutional legitimacy, the answer is clear, or at least it should be. When Canadian Prime Minister Justin Trudeau was asked shortly after he was elected in 2015 why he insisted on gender parity in his Cabinet, he answered 'because it's 2015'.[100] Similarly, the answer to whether including women on trade adjudicating bodies enhances the body's institutional legitimacy is rather simple: 'of course it does, because it's 2020'. In other words, it is not legitimate or acceptable in 2020 to have adjudicative bodies composed only of men because this does not reflect the general population or the population of law graduates, 50% of which is female for both groups.[101] Moreover, adjudicative bodies composed only of men suggest the selection process is not fair, based on merit and non-discriminatory. Finally, the presence of women on the bench not only provides encouragement for junior female lawyers and female law students to aspire to such appointments, but also affords opportunities for women judges to mentor those seeking to obtain judicial appointments.[102]

[99] DSU, Art 17.11.

[100] CBC News <www.cbc.ca/news/politics/canada-trudeau-liberal-government-cabinet-1.3304590> accessed 29 February 2020.

[101] World Bank data <https://data.worldbank.org/indicator/SP.POP.TOTL.FE.ZS?view=map> accessed 29 February 2020.

[102] Rosemary Hunter, 'More than Just a Different Face? Judicial Diversity and Decision-making' (2015) 68 (1) Current Legal Problems 119, 123.

The more difficult question to answer is whether gender affects outcomes in international trade adjudication. In a paper written 30 years ago, Bertha Wilson, the first woman to be appointed to the Supreme Court of Canada, addressed a similar issue.[103] Justice Wilson referred to being daunted by the expectations expressed by so many that her presence on the bench of Canada's highest court would usher in a new era for women. She wondered whether, despite wanting to live up to expectations, she would be able to do so given, among other things, the 'nature of judicial office itself'.[104] Justice Wilson wrote of the requirement of judges to be both impartial and independent, and the requirement 'not to approach his or her task with preconceived notions about law or policy . . . .'[105] She quoted Lord MacMillan's admission that:

> . . . impartiality is not easy of attainment. For a judge does not shed the attributes of common humanity when he assumes the ermine. The ordinary human mind is a mass of prepossessions inherited and acquired . . . Few minds are as neutral as a sheet of plate glass . . . every legal mind is apt to have an innate susceptibility to particular classes of arguments.[106]

She also quoted Justice Rosalie Abella, appointed to the Supreme Court of Canada in 2004, who said that '[e]very decisionmaker who walks into a courtroom to hear a case is armed not only with the relevant legal texts, but with a set of values, experiences and assumptions that are thoroughly embedded'.[107]

Justice Wilson opined that whether or not one considers that women on the bench will make a difference depends on one's perception of 'the degree to which the existing law reflects [] judicial neutrality or impartiality . . . .'[108] She reasoned that '[i]f the existing law can be viewed as the product of judicial neutrality or impartiality, even although the judiciary has been very substantially male, then you may conclude that the advent of increased numbers of women judges should make no difference, assuming, that is, that these women judges will bring to bear the same neutrality and impartiality'.[109]

Justice Wilson continues to explain that scholarship at the time suggested that gender was a factor in judicial decision-making, particularly in certain areas of

103 Bertha Wilson, 'Will Women Judges Really Make a Difference?' (1990) 28 (3) Osgoode Hall Law Journal 507. Justice Wilson was appointed in 1982.

104 ibid 507.

105 ibid 508.

106 ibid 508–09.

107 ibid 510. Justice Abella made this statement in a speech entitled 'The Dynamic Nature of Equality' delivered at a conference held in Banff, Alberta in 1986. Conference papers are published in Sheilah L Martin and Kathleen E Mahoney (eds), *Equality and Judicial Neutrality*, Conference Proceedings edition (Carswell 1987).

108 Wilson (n 103) 510

109 Wilson (n 103) 511.

law. She opined that, based on her experience as a judge, there were certain areas of the law on which there was 'no uniquely feminine perspective'.[110] She mentioned the law of contract, the law of real property, and the law applicable to corporations where 'the principles and the underlying premises are so firmly entrenched and so fundamentally sound [that] no good would be achieved by attempting to re-invent the wheel, even if the revised version did have a few more spokes in it'.[111] For Justice Wilson, however, there were areas of the law—she mentioned aspects of criminal law—that bore a 'distinctly male perspective', such that the 'legal principles [were] not fundamentally sound and that should be revisited . . .'.[112]

Is international trade law an area of law where there is or could be a uniquely feminine perspective? The fact that gender has not played much of a role in selecting panellists or appointing Appellate Body Members (except very recently for a few members) suggests that WTO Members generally do not believe that there is a uniquely feminine perspective in international trade law. But is it equally the case that the membership considers that the WTO adjudicator brings absolute neutrality to her or his task—a mind as neutral as a sheet of plate glass, in the words of Lord MacMillan? As explained below, it seems it does not.

The WTO membership took pains to ensure that developing country Members would have at least one developing country panellist for certain disputes between developing and developed country Members.[113] One might assume that this rule is aimed at ensuring the legitimacy or perceived fairness of the process in such cases. But there seems to be more to it than that because the rule does not apply in all situations. Specifically, it is not applied in disputes involving one developing country against another developing country. Nor does it apply in situations when the disputing developing country Member does not specifically request the presence of a developing country panellist. If the aim of including developing country panellists were solely to ensure legitimacy or perceived fairness of the process when developing countries are involved in disputes, one would expect that the rule would apply whenever a developing country is involved in disputes with developed Members, and not only when the developing country Member specifically makes a request for such inclusion in a developed versus developing Member dispute. In this light, it is legitimate to suggest that, in creating the dispute settlement system, WTO Members believed that developing country panellists would bring a unique perspective when deciding disputes between developed and developing countries, and thereby make a 'difference' to the result.

110 Wilson (n 103) 515.
111 ibid.
112 ibid.
113 DSU, Art 8.10.

3.4 Trade and Gender: What Might be?

Having demonstrated that the WTO membership appears to be open at least in some circumstances to engaging adjudicators specifically because of a perceived special perspective that they might bring to the task of resolving disputes (such as a developing country perspective), we turn to consider whether being a woman might conceivably give one a unique perspective in the context of adjudicating international trade disputes. In other words, harking back to Justice Bertha Wilson's approach, is international trade an area of law that might have a 'uniquely feminine perspective'?

Justice Wilson thought that the law of contract, the law of real property, and the law of corporations had no uniquely feminine perspective. In this same vein, it is hard to imagine that the law related to the calculation of a dumping margin[114] or a legal analysis of whether a product fits within one or other tariff heading[115] could have a gender perspective. But it is less difficult to contemplate a possible feminine perspective in other areas of trade law, such as the consideration of whether an otherwise WTO-inconsistent measure might be justified under the general exceptions clause of the GATT 1994 because it is necessary to protect public morals, or necessary to protect human or animal health, or related to the conservation of exhaustible natural resources.[116] It is possible to conceive that some women (though perhaps not each and every one) could bring a unique perspective to such analyses in the light of their particular life or work experiences as a woman.

This notion is more easily received if one accepts that trade affects women and men differently. In recent years, trade policy analysts have come to realize that it is important to approach trade policy with a gender lens. Consider the following examples. In Cambodia, 86% of employees in the silk industry are women,[117] which means that trade policies affecting the textile industry will have a significant and perhaps disproportionate impact on women. In many countries, men tend to be employed in traditional export sectors such as natural resources and manufacturing. Thus, trade policies affecting these sectors generally will impact

[114] Dumping occurs when goods are exported at a price less than their normal value, generally meaning they are exported for less than they are sold in the domestic market or in third-country markets, or at less than production cost. The margin of dumping is the difference between the comparable price of the like product when exported to a third country and the cost of production in the country of origin, plus a reasonable amount for administrative, selling and general costs, and for profits.

[115] The Harmonized Commodity Description and Coding System (known as the HS Code) is an internationally standardized system of names and numbers used to classify traded products. The classification determines the level of duty imposed on the product when imported.

[116] Article XX of the GATT 1994 sets forth a number of exceptions for justifying a measure that is otherwise WTO-inconsistent, including the necessity to protect public morals, the environment, and human and animal and plant life and health <www.wto.org/english/docs_e/legal_e/gatt47_01_e.htm> accessed 29 February 2020.

[117] WTO Director-General Roberto Azevêdo, 'Promoting Inclusive Trade Through Gender Empowerment', speech, 11 July 2017 <www.wto.org/english/news_e/spra_e/spra185_e.htm> accessed 29 February 2020.

men more than women. Women comprise 43% of the agricultural labour force in developing countries.[118] This explains why agricultural trade policy in some countries can have a more profound effect on women than on men. Women-owned companies tend to be smaller and produce less volume so they suffer disproportionately from trade-related fixed costs (such as non-tariff measures like lengthy customs procedures).[119] Finally, analysts point out that when governments reduce tariffs there is less revenue for social safety nets, education, child care, and elder care—areas that disproportionately involve women.

Having understood the potential for differential impact of trade on men and women, some trade policy makers seek to formulate trade policy using a gender-based analysis, with the goal of devising trade rules that address the inequalities that hold back the ability of women to participate fully in, and benefit from, the multilateral trading system.[120] Is there an analogy to be made, if not to the adjudicator herself, then to the adoption of a gender-based analysis in trade adjudication?

The 20-plus WTO agreements address a wide range of subjects, from agriculture to human and animal and plant life and health, to standards, customs, import licensing, subsidies, trade in a variety of services, intellectual property rights, anti-dumping, and import licensing, to name only a few. It seems likely that a gender-based analysis would be relevant in disputes between WTO Members regarding obligations undertaken in at least some areas of these agreements. The close to 600[121] disputes filed thus far have raised a vast range of legal issues. For example, challenges have addressed measures relating to: hormone-treated beef, genetically modified products, dolphin-safe labelling, protection of sea turtles, marketing products obtained through the seal hunt, cross-border supply of gambling services, preferential trade arrangements tied to combating drug trafficking, packaging requirements for tobacco products, export restrictions on rare earths, prohibition of cultural content that could have a negative impact on public morals, subsidies granted to aircraft companies, protection of halal requirements as a public moral, and subsidies in the renewable energy sector. Perhaps not all trade disputes will require or benefit from a feminist perspective, but given the considerable range of

[118] State of Food and Agriculture Team and Cheryl Doss, Agricultural Development Economics Division, Food and Agriculture Organization, 'The Role of Women in Agriculture', EAS Working Paper No. 11-02, March 2011, 1, 3.

[119] Arancha Gonzalez, Executive Director, International Trade Centre, 'How Does Gender Affect the Participation of SMEs in International Trade?', speech, Queen's University Institute on Trade Policy Annual Policy Forum, Kingston, Canada, 16 October 2016 <www.intracen.org/news/How-does-gender-affect-the-participation-of-SMEs-in-international-trade/>accessed 29 February 2020.

[120] See, for example, Global Affairs Canada, 'Summary of Initial GBA+ for Canada-Mercosur FTA Negotiations'<www.international.gc.ca/trade-commerce/gender_equality-egalite_genres/gba_plus_summary-acs_plus_resume.aspx?lang=eng>accessed 29 February 2020.

[121] 593 disputes had been filed as of 30 January 2020 <www.wto.org/english/tratop_e/dispu_e/dispu_e.htm>accessed 29 February 2020.

trade obligations and the frequency with which Members litigate trade issues, it is reasonable to suspect that some could.

It must be acknowledged that not everyone accepts the merits or validity of the gender-based approach to trade policy development mentioned above. The sceptics decry gender-sensitive trade policies as a 'pink herring'.[122] In addition, we cannot be sure without more data and research whether gender has made or is making a difference in the adjudication of international trade law disputes. But it is certainly worth asking the question and giving the issue serious study and thought.

4. Conclusion

This chapter explains how the WTO dispute settlement mechanism works and explains how adjudicators are selected to serve on WTO panels and the Appellate Body. It reveals that women have served on many panels and that several women have been appointed to the Appellate Body. But it also shows that most WTO Members generally have not thought about—or at least referred explicitly—to gender in identifying criteria for panellist selection, and that Members have not required gender parity or even significant representation of women on panels or the Appellate Body.

This chapter suggests that the presence of women on WTO panels and the Appellate Body makes a difference from the perspective of the overall institutional legitimacy of those adjudicative bodies and their decisions. But it has also made clear that, given the paucity of data and the limited experience with women adjudicators on the WTO bench, and the fact that the WTO system requires adjudicator anonymity in decision-making, it is not possible to point to any empirical evidence of whether or not women have in fact made a difference by bringing a unique perspective to WTO adjudication. Nevertheless, it is suggested that this may indeed be the case for at least two reasons. The first is that, as demonstrated above, WTO Members believe that the individual perspective or life experience of an adjudicator can inform her or his decision-making, at least in the case of developing country adjudicators. Second, some trade policy makers have come to realize that trade policies and approaches can affect women and men differently, and hence that a gender-based analysis is essential in the development of trade policy. With this in mind, it may not be too far a leap to suggest that there is a gender-based approach to WTO adjudication and that women on the WTO bench do indeed make a difference beyond just providing institutional legitimacy to the adjudicative body itself.

[122] Balakrishnan Rajagopal, 'Women and Trade at the WTO: Pink Herring, Trojan Horse or Historic Advance?' in Centre for International Governance Innovation, *Reshaping Trade through Women's Economic Empowerment*, CIGI Special Report 2018, 39.

17

The Contribution of Women Judges and Prosecutors to the Development of International Criminal Law

Teresa Doherty

A photo of the first modern international criminal tribunal, the Nuremberg Tribunal, shows a court composed of male judges, prosecutors, and defence lawyers (as well as male defendants) with women relegated to the back rooms, standing in a sea of papers.[1] More recently, the photo of the Principals of the International Criminal Tribunal for the Former Yugoslavia (ICTY), taken at the ICTY's closure, was reminiscent of the Nuremberg image: again, only male judges and one female administrator (despite the ICTY having had two female judges in its early years).[2] Overall, the situation is similar in all international courts. Of the international courts with no representativeness requirements built into their selection procedures, surveyed by Nienke Grossman in 2016, only 15% of judges were women.[3] She also found that '[o]n courts with either aspirational representativeness language or mandatory targets, however, 33% were women'.[4] This underrepresentation is not limited to the judicial profession: the BBC, for example, reported in 2018 that only 11% of engineers in the UK are women.[5] There is also a lack of female representation in some national judiciaries. My own region, Northern Ireland, only appointed women High Court judges for the first time in 2015,[6] although the Republic of Ireland has had women judges, including a woman Chief Justice, for

[1] For records and photographs of the Nuremburg Trials, see <trumanlibrary.gov/library/online-collection/war-crimes-at-Nuremburg> accessed 29 February 2020.

[2] For the transition into the International Residual Mechanism for Criminal Tribunals, in December 2017, see: icty.org/en/press (accessed 29 February 2020).

[3] Nienke Grossman, 'Shattering the Glass Ceiling in International Adjudication' (2016) 56 (2) Virginia Journal of International Law 339–406, 342.

[4] ibid.

[5] BBC Radio 4: Women's Hour (January 2018) discussing women in STEM professions, in particular engineering, see <www.bbc.co.uk/programmes/m0006149>accessed 29 February 2020.

[6] Justices Keegan and McBride were the first women to be appointed to the High Court of Northern Ireland on 23 October 2015. There had been female District Court judges and female magistrates in Northern Ireland prior to this date.

Teresa Doherty, *The Contribution of Women Judges and Prosecutors to the Development of International Criminal Law*
In: *Identity and Diversity on the International Bench.* Edited by: Freya Baetens, Oxford University Press (2020).
 DOI: 10.1093/oso/9780198870753.003.0017.

decades before that.[7] For over 10 years I was the only woman among 17 judges in Papua New Guinea.[8]

Negative attitudes to the appointment of women judges may be shown in subtle ways. When I was appointed to the High Court and Court of Appeal of Sierra Leone in 2003, all judges and lawyers were addressed as if they were men. Sierra Leone is a former British colony and followed English common law, its procedures, and traditions. These included addressing a judge (who was always male in the colonial period) as 'My Lord'. Whilst other common law jurisdictions slowly changed to addressing female judges as 'My Lady',[9] Sierra Leone persisted in addressing all judges of the higher courts as 'My Lord'. When I objected to this, the Senior Counsel and leader of the Bar answered by saying 'there are no women at the Bench or Bar of Sierra Leone'. Initially this statement puzzled me because there were female judges and counsel in the Sierra Leone courts but I then realized that all judges were addressed as 'My Lord' and all lawyers as 'Mr'. Hence all female judges and lawyers wishing to practice in that jurisdiction had to pretend to be token males. I insisted that I would not be addressed as if I were a man and slowly succeeded in changing the mode of address of female judges to 'My Lady' and female lawyers to Ms or Mrs. However, this change occurred in the face of considerable resistance. In my experience, therefore, the paucity of female representation in courts is not limited to international tribunals.

In addition to a negative attitude to women judges, the common law jurisprudence and attitudes concerning crimes of sexual violence were also incorporated into the British colonial legal systems and were maintained in most of them after independence. I observed myself how this influenced the judges of many former colonies in Africa and Australasia. I recall discussions with my male colleagues in Papua New Guinea who persisted in applying the 'maxim' 'rape is easy to allege and hard to rebut' and demanded corroboration of a complainant's evidence in sexual violence trials. This 'maxim' was a statement formulated in the writings (not in an actual court hearing) of Lord Hale in the English courts some centuries earlier.[10]

[7] The first woman judge, Justice Mella Carroll was appointed to the High Court of Ireland on 6 October 1980. Justice Susan Denham was first woman Chief Justice of Ireland (2011–17).

[8] At the time of my tenure (1987–1997) there were 16 national and Supreme Court judges and some acting judges of the National Court. There were several women magistrates in the District and Local Courts but no women in the Village Courts. The Village Courts touched the majority of the population who sought legal redress and were responsible for administration of traditional and customary rules. Some of their decisions were discriminatory towards women and girls.

[9] Justice Mella Carroll ensured that this change of address was implemented in Ireland's courts, Justice Butler-Sloss, the first woman to be appointed a High Court judge in England and Wales, implemented this change and some African jurisdictions, eg. Uganda and Kenya adopted the style of address 'My Lady'.

[10] This maxim persisted in some jurisdictions into the 21st century. For a history of this maxim and its application, see: A Thomas Morris, 'The Empirical, Historical and Legal Case Against the Cautionary Instruction: A Call for Legislative Reform' (1988) Duke Law Journal 154–173.

The view persisted in the common law courts of the former British colonies for years and was repeated by judges during rape trials.[11]

In my view, we are looking at a much wider phenomenon than merely the poor proportion of female representation on the benches of international tribunals. Appointment procedures for international judicial positions involve international as well as domestic political input. For example, depending on the court, candidates may have to be nominated by a country's government and have to campaign for their position. This may involve considerable self-promotion, which some people find distasteful or difficult. International judicial positions frequently require leaving one's home country for several years which, again, is not acceptable to everyone.

Recent history has proven that women judges are capable of dealing well with international legal issues, including in international criminal law—initially an exclusively male field. The first (few) female judges in the international criminal law tribunals were appointed to the ICTY and International Criminal Tribunal for Rwanda (ICTR). Justice Gabrielle Kirk MacDonald was appointed to the ICTY bench in 1993 and served as its President from 1997 to 1999, which included presiding over the first trial, that of Duško Tadić.[12] She was a major initiator and contributor to the Court's Rules of Procedure and Evidence.[13] At the 20th anniversary commemorations of the ICTY in 2013, she described the discussions between the common law and civil law judges concerning different evidentiary concepts, recalling going several 'rounds' with Justice Cassese on some issues.[14] The ad hoc and hybrid tribunals developed a more adversarial mode of procedure in the succeeding years. Another woman, Justice Elizabeth Odio-Benito, served as the ICTY's Vice-President from 1993 to 1995, and then went on to become a judge at the International Criminal Court (ICC).

Following their appointments, women judges made important contributions to the development of the jurisprudence of the criminal tribunals. The jurisprudence on sexual offences is an example of this. When discussing these contributions to the jurisprudence of the international tribunals, it is essential to stress that the Rules of Procedure and Evidence of the ad hoc and international tribunals do not permit judges to make their deliberations public.[15] Therefore, unless a judge issued a separate dissenting or concurring opinion, it is not possible to indicate precisely which judge formulated a particular decision. Initially, there were not many

[11] I have also heard male judges (not, I stress, my Papua New Guinea or Special Court for Sierra Leone (SCSL) colleagues) describe rape as 'assault with a friendly weapon', or stating 'everyone knows when a woman says NO, she really means YES', and making other remarks that showed a lack of sensitivity and/or preconceived views about sexual violence.

[12] *Prosecutor v Tadic* IT-94-1-T (7 May 1997) 112 ILR 1.

[13] Rules of Procedure and Evidence of the International Criminal Tribunal for the former Yugoslavia (IT/32/Rev.50, 8 July 2015)

[14] Discussions during the *ICTY Conference - Marking the 20th anniversary of the Tribunal*, see <www.icty.org/en/features/legacy-conferences/icty-conference-marking-the-20th-anniversary-of-the-tribunal>accessed 29 February 2020.

[15] For example, Rule 87(a) of the Rules of Procedure and Evidence of the SCSL provided '[a]fter [...] the hearing closed, the Trial Chamber shall deliberate in private'.

prosecutions for sexual offences at either the ICTY or the ICTR, a fact conceded by Justice Richard Goldstone, an early prosecutor.[16] One proffered explanation was that victims, both male and female, did not want to give evidence or re-live the trauma or embarrassment of the violence perpetrated upon them.[17] As pointed out by Chen Reis,[18] various factors might influence under-reporting and not-prosecuting sexual violence, including sexual violence in armed conflicts. Such factors include 'facing social stigma, abandonment by an intimate partner, fear that she (the victim) may be blamed, fear that the victim may be considered unfit for marriage, feelings of shame, fears for personal safety or fear of reprisals and fear of the risk of "being put on trial with charges of adultery"'.

In the Preliminary Report of the Special Rapporteur on the Situation of Systematic Rape, Sexual Slavery and Slavery-like Practices during Periods of Armed Conflict, Linda Chavez explains that reluctance to report wartime rape is due to shame and social stigma, fear of awakening bad memories, fear of reprisals and a lack of trust in the judicial system and national legislature.[19] One example is the human rights campaigner Jan Ruff O'Herne who was held as a 'comfort woman' by Japanese soldiers who invaded Indonesia during World War II and subjected to sexual violence. When telling of her own ordeal, many years after it occurred, she stated '[f]or fifty years, the "Comfort Women" maintained silence; they lived with a terrible shame, of feeling soiled and dirty. It has taken 50 years for these women's ruined lives to become a human rights issue'.[20]

A further explanation may be a historical attitude to sexual violence in wartime. In her work on the history of attitudes to sexual violence in conflict, Kelly Askin argues that '[t]raditionally women were regarded as legitimate spoils of war or rape as an inevitable by-product of war'[21]—thereby confirming the finding made by Peter Karsten in 1978, explaining why prosecutions for sexual violence were not pursued.[22]

16 Oral remarks by Richard Goldstone at a conference held at the Peace Palace (The Hague) in 2009.

17 Chen Reis, 'Ethical, Safety and Methodological Issues Related to Collection and Use of Data on Sexual Violence in Conflict' in Anne-Marie De Brouwer and others (eds), *Sexual Violence as an International Crime: Interdisciplinary Approaches* (Intersentia 2013) 194–5. See also Guidelines for medico-legal care for victims of sexual violence (Geneva, World Health Organisation 2003); 'Preliminary report of the Special Rapporteur on the situation of systematic rape, sexual slavery and slavery-like practices during periods of armed conflict, Ms. Linda Chavez', Sub-Commission on Prevention of Discrimination and Protection of Minorities, UN DOC E/CN.4/Subpr.2/1996/26 (16 July 1996). In a dissent, SCSL Justice Boutet stated: '[v]ictims of sexual violence have the right to have crimes that are committed against them prosecuted with all due respect to the Rule of Law', Dissenting Opinion of Justice Pierre Boutet on Decision on Prosecution Application for Leave to file an Interlocutory Appeal against the Decision on the Prosecution's Request for Leave to Amend the Indictment against Norman, Fofana, and Kondewa, 5 August 2004, SCSL-2004-14-T, para 18.

18 Reis (n 17) 194.

19 UN DOC E/CN.4/Sub.2/1996/26 (16 July 1996), para 87.

20 Statement by Jan Ruff O'Herne at the Hearing on Protecting the Human Rights of 'Comfort Women', US House of Representatives (Committee on Foreign Affairs) (15 Feb. 2007) see <https://foreignaffairs.house.gov/2007/2/protecting-human-rights-comfort-women>accessed 29 February 2020.

21 Kelly Askin, 'Treatment of Sexual Violence in Armed Conflicts: A Historical Perspective and the Way Forward' in Anne-Marie De Brouwer and others (eds), *Sexual Violence as an International Crime: Interdisciplinary Approaches* (Intersentia 2013) 15–56.

22 Peter Karsten, *Law, Soldiers and Combat* (Greenwood Press 1978).

Regardless of the reason or attitudes, crimes of sexual violence were not prosecuted at the ICTR or ICTY until the trial of a town mayor, Jean-Paul Akeyesu, before the ICTR.[23] Initially, Akeyesu's indictment did not contain any sexual crime counts but when a witness described the gang rape of her very young daughter, Justice Navenethem Pillay intervened and asked the Prosecutor why the rape was not being prosecuted. The Prosecutor amended the indictment to include counts of rape, sexual violence as genocide, and outrages against personal dignity. Akayesu was convicted on all of these counts on the grounds of individual criminal responsibility pursuant of Article 6(1) of the Statute of the ICTR.[24] The Trial Judgment noted that there was 'no commonly accepted definition [of rape] in international law',[25] giving it a broad conceptual definition ('physical invasion of a sexual nature, committed on a person under circumstances which are coercive')[26] and ultimately declaring it 'an act of genocide'. The decision was a landmark both for its definition of rape and establishing that rape is a crime in war as it is in peacetime.

With the appointment of women investigators and prosecutors, more prosecutions for crimes of sexual violence followed. Justice Louise Arbour (who had commented on the 'remarkable vision and sensitivity of the [*Akayesu*] judgement')[27] was appointed Chief Prosecutor of both the ICTY and the ICTR. Patricia Sellers was the Legal Adviser for Gender for the Office of the Prosecutor, including in the case of *Prosecutor v Furundzija*,[28] in which rape and sexual torture were recognized as war crimes. Brenda Hollis held various legal positions in the Office of the Prosecutor including as a co-counsel in the *Furundzija* case and also in *Prosecutor v Tadić*,[29] in which rape was charged as torture. She subsequently was appointed as Prosecutor in the Special Court for Sierra Leone (SCSL). Maxine Marcus was a prosecuting attorney at the ICTY and later at the SCSL. She particularly worked in the investigation and prosecution of crimes of sexual violence under international law.

When considering the role of judges and prosecutors in developing international criminal law, it is essential to recognize that the statutes of the international criminal tribunals give virtually sole responsibility to the Prosecutor to decide on the charges to be brought.[30] Hence the role of prosecutors and

[23] *Prosecutor v Jean-Paul Akayesu*, ICTR-96-4.

[24] *Prosecutor v Jean-Paul Akayesu*, ICTR-96-4-T (Trial Judgment), 2 September 1998; ICTR-96-4-A (Appeal Judgment), 1 June 2001.

[25] *Prosecutor v Akayesu* (Trial Judgment), para 596.

[26] ibid para 598.

[27] Arbour praised its 'remarkable vision and sensitivity'. Press Release CC/PIU/342-E (September 1998).

[28] *Prosecutor v Furundzija* IT-95-17/1-T (10 December 1998) 121 ILR 213.

[29] *Prosecutor v Tadic* IT-94-1-T (n 12) and IT-94-1-A (15 July 1999) 124 ILR 61.

[30] Agreement between the United Nations and the Government of Sierra Leone on the establishment of a Special Court for Sierra Leone (with Statute) (concluded 16 January 2002, entered into force in 12 April 2002), 2178 UNTS 137. Art 15(1) provides '[t]he Prosecutor shall be responsible for the investigation and prosecution of persons who bear the greatest responsibility for serious violations of international humanitarian law and crimes under Sierra Leonean law committed in the territory of

investigators (particularly of women prosecutors) was pivotal in bringing charges and presenting evidence that developed international criminal jurisprudence in this field.

In my opinion, the inclusion of women on the bench and in the Office of the Prosecutor led to the development of the field of international criminal law in areas that had not previously been adjudicated upon by international courts. In the trial of *Prosecutor v Mucić et al* (*Čelibići* trial)[31] at the ICTY, which included Justice Odio Benito on the bench, the judgment emphasized the extraordinary harm caused by sexual violence in wartime and interpreted facts of widespread rape and sexual violence as constituting elements of other crimes such as genocide, torture, enslavement, extermination, and persecution.[32] Justice Florence Mumba was a member of the *Furundzija* bench which, after reviewing the international instruments and the laws and definitions of sexual assault and rape in various national jurisdictions in the world, defined the elements of rape as the sexual penetration, however slight of the vagina or anus of the victim by the penis of the perpetrator or any other object used by the perpetrator; or of the mouth of the victim by the penis of the perpetrator; by coercion or force or threat of force against the victim or a third person. Arguably, according to Catharine MacKinnon, it broadened rape to include oral penetration.[33]

Further contributions to the development of law relating to crimes against humanity were made at the ICTR. Justice Khalida Khan was Presiding Judge in the case of *Prosecutor v Muhimana*, in which the court noted the Furundjiza Appeal Chamber ruling that 'any form of captivity vitiates consent', before finding that

> coercion is an element that may obviate the relevance of consent as an evidentiary factor in the crime of rape. Further, this Chamber concurs with the opinion that circumstances prevailing in most cases charged under international criminal law, as either genocide, crimes against humanity, or war crimes, will be almost universally coercive, thus vitiating true consent.[34]

Sierra Leone since 30 November 1996. The Prosecutor shall act independently as a separate organ of the Special Court. He or she shall not seek or receive instructions from any Government or from any other source'; Art 42 Rome Statute of the International Criminal Court (ICC Statute) 2187 UNTS 3.

[31] *Prosecutor v Delalic et al*, IT-96-21-T (16 Nov. 1998). Until the trial judgment in which Judge Odio Benito sat, this case is known as *Prosecutor v Delalic, Mucic, Delic, Landzo*. Delalic was acquitted in the trial judgment, and his acquittal was affirmed on appeal. Therefore, the case proceeded in subsequent phases (especially sentencing) as *Prosecutor v Mucic, Delic, Landzo*.

[32] See also Niamh Hayes, 'Creating a Definition of Rape in International Law: The Contribution of the International Criminal Tribunals' in Shane Darcy and Joseph Powderly (eds), *Judicial Creativity at the International Criminal Tribunals* (OUP 2010) 137.

[33] *Prosecutor v Furundzija* Trial judgment (n 28), paras 183–84; and C MacKinnon, 'Defining Rape Internationally: A Comment on *Akayesu*' (2006) 44 Col JTL 940.

[34] *Prosecutor v Muhimana*, ICTR -95-1B-T (28 April 2005), paras 545–46.

Justice Andresia Vaz was Presiding Judge in the case of *Prosecutor v Gacumbitsi,* which recognized that the 'fact that rape victims were attacked by those they were fleeing from, adequately establish[ed] the victims' lack of consent to the rapes'.[35] The judgment also found that penetration of the victims' vaginas by either the perpetrator's genitals or by 'insert[ing] sticks into them' fell within the definition of the crime of rape.

The work of the SCSL on sexual violence was hailed by the United Nations Entity for Gender Equality and the Empowerment of Women (commonly referred to as UN Women) as 'a critical landmark for international justice in prosecuting sexual and gender based crimes committed during conflict'.[36] It further stated that 'jurisprudence of the Special Court for Sierra Leone [has] played an essential role in advancing the recognition in law for such crimes'.[37] The preliminary Report of the UN Secretary-General on the SCSL noted that: 'the subject matter jurisdiction shall include *inter alia* ... the most egregious practice of ... sexual violence against girls and woman, and sexual slavery and abduction of thousands of children and adults'.[38] Perhaps as a result of this observation, the SCSL's Statute provided that 'due consideration should be given in the appointment of staff to the employment of prosecutors and investigators experienced in gender-related crimes and juvenile justice'.[39] In *Prosecutor v Hinga Norman,* Justice Renate Winter was the sole female member of the SCSL Appeal Chamber which dealt with (and rejected) a challenge against the indictment for the crime of conscripting, recruiting, and use of children under the age of 15 years in armed conflict (commonly referred to as 'child soldiers') on the grounds that it was not part of international law when the alleged events took place.[40]

The trial of *Prosecutor v Brima et al* (commonly referred to as AFRC trial) indicted the three accused with conscripting, recruitment, and use of child soldiers in hostilities, as breaches of international humanitarian law, and sexual slavery and forced marriages as crimes against humanity. No international criminal tribunal had previously ruled on these crimes. The Trial Chamber had two women judges, Justice Sebutinde and the writer (Justice Doherty). The judgment defined 'use of children in hostilities' as

[35] *Prosecutor v Gacumbitsi,* ICTR-2001-64-T, at paras 321 and 325.

[36] 'UN Women hails historic work done by Special Court for Sierra Leone strengthening women's access to justice' (press release of 9 Oct. 2012), see <www.unwomen.org/en/news/stories/2012/10/un-women-hails-historic-work-done-by-special-court-for-sierra-leone-strengthening-women-s-access-to>accessed 29 February 2020.

[37] ibid.

[38] Report of the Secretary-General of the United Nations to the Security Council on the Establishment of a Special Court for Sierra Leone, 4 October 2000 (UN Doc S/2000/915), Part III (on the Competence of the Special Court and subject-matter jurisdiction), para 12.

[39] Art 15(4) SCSL Statute.

[40] *Prosecutor v Hinga Norman*, Decision on Preliminary Motion Based on Lack of Jurisdiction (Child Recruitment) SCSL-2004-14-AR(E) (31 May 2004).

> not limited to participation in combat. An armed force requires logistical support to maintain its operations. Any labour or support that gives effect to, or helps maintain, operations in a conflict constitutes active participation. Hence carrying loads for the fighting faction, finding and/or acquiring food, ammunition or equipment, acting as decoys, carrying messages, making trails or finding routes, manning checkpoints or acting as human shields are some examples of active participation as much as actual fighting and combat.[41]

Evidence was presented on the impact and trauma of women and girls who had been abducted and forcefully 'married' to rebel soldiers and commanders, as well as on the trauma and injury inflicted on other women and girls who were abducted but had not been coerced in an exclusive relationship (forced marriage). The latter group was held in captivity and raped and made available to any rebel for sexual purposes.

Defence counsel argued that indicting the accused for sexual slavery and any other form of sexual violence in the same count was bad for duplicity. This followed an earlier separate concurring opinion of Justice Sebutinde that Count 7 of the indictment (which charged 'sexual slavery and any other form of sexual violence') was 'defective or bad for duplicity'.[42] In the judgement, the majority opinion upheld this submission and struck out the count entirely but this was overruled on appeal (by an Appeal Chamber bench that included two women judges, Justices Fisher and Winter).[43] Both Justice Sebutinde and I wrote separate opinions on forced marriage and we both distinguished forced marriage from traditional arranged marriages. Justice Sebutinde compared it with traditional and arranged marriages, stating that:

> a clear distinction should be drawn between traditional or religious marital unions involving minors (early or arranged marriages), during times of peace; and the forceful abduction and holding in captivity of women and girls ('bush wives') against their will, for purposes of sexual gratification of their 'bush husbands' and for gender-specific forms of labour including cooking, cleaning, washing clothes (conjugal duties). In my view, while the former is proscribed as a violation of human rights under international human rights instruments or treaties like CEDAW, it is not recognised as a crime in International Humanitarian law. The latter conduct on the other hand, is clearly criminal in nature and is liable to attract prosecution.[44]

[41] *Prosecutor v Brima et al*, SCSL-2004-16-T-613 (20 June 2007), para 737.

[42] ibid, Separate Opinion, para 4.

[43] *Prosecutor v Brima et al*, SCSL-2004-16A (22 February 2008) (Judgment) SCSL Appeals Chamber.

[44] *Prosecutor v Brima et al*, SCSL-2004-16-T-613 (20 June 2007), Separate Concurring Opinion of Justice Julia Sebutinde appended to Judgement pursuant to Rule 88 (C) para 12.

In my dissenting opinion (relying on international instruments, legislation of civil and common law jurisdictions and laws of Islamic and other jurisdictions, and general principles of international law), I set out that forced marriage is a crime against humanity: '[t]he crucial element of 'forced marriage' is the imposition, by threat or physical force arising from the perpetrator's words or other conduct, of a forced conjugal association by the perpetrator over the victim'.[45] This resulted in mental and physical suffering. Moreover, I explained that the submission that Count 7 was bad for duplicity was an abuse of process and that sexual slavery should have been severed in Count 7. More precisely, I stated that:

> [w]hilst I do have no doubt of the fundamental nature of the accused's right to be informed of the nature and cause of the charge against him, the defence is under a corresponding duty to raise the issue prior to the commencement of trial or at the earliest opportunity thereafter. I do not consider it to be in the interests of justice to allow the accused to invoke this right to quash an indictment after the case has closed, without showing that he was materially prejudiced. This is particularly so in cases such as the present, when the Accused were not only silent on the issue throughout the trial, but proceeded to adduce evidence and defended themselves on the charge.[46]

In the later trial of *Prosecutor v Sesay et al* (commonly referred to as the RUF trial) convictions for the crime of forced marriage and sexual slavery were returned.[47] As Oosterveld pointed out, 'the RUF trial judgment brought the first-ever convictions in an international or internationalized tribunal for the crimes against humanity of sexual slavery and forced marriage (as an inhumane act)'.[48] This opinion was later upheld by an Appeal Chamber (including two women judges, Justices Fisher and Winter), in line with the arguments I had set out earlier in my dissenting opinion in *Prosecutor v Brima et al.*[49] As a final example of the contribution of women judges to the development of international criminal law at the SCSL, I refer to the *Prosecutor v Charles Taylor* case, in which it was held that the public humiliation of women and girls being raped in front of family and community amounted to an act of terror.[50] The SCSL hereby became the first tribunal since the Nuremburg trials to convict a sitting head of State.[51] The bench was composed of the same judges as

[45] *Prosecutor v Brima et al*, SCSL-2004-16-T-613 (20 June 2007), Partly Dissenting Opinion of Justice Doherty on Count 7 (Sexual Slavery) and Count 8 ('Forced Marriages') para 53.
[46] *Prosecutor v Brima et al*, SCSL-2004-16-T-613 (20 June 2007), Partly Dissenting Opinion of Justice Doherty on Count 7 (Sexual Slavery) and Count 8 ('Forced Marriages') para 10.
[47] *Prosecutor v Sesay et al*, SCSL-2004-15-T-1234 (2 March 2009).
[48] Valerie Oosterveld, 'The Gender Jurisprudence of the Special Court for Sierra Leone: Progress in the Revolutionary United Front Judgments' (2011) 44 (1) Cornell International Law Journal 49–74.
[49] *Prosecutor v Sesay et al*, Appeal Judgment, SCSL-2004-15-A-1321 (26 Oct. 2009).
[50] *Prosecutor v Charles Taylor*, SCSL-03-01-T-1283 (26 Sept. 2013).
[51] Mr Taylor was President of Liberia at the time the indictment was preferred against him.

in *Prosecutor v Brima* (two female judges, Justices Doherty and Sebutinde, and one male judge, Justice Lussick).

Judges can only develop the law on the basis of the evidence in the trials before them. For this reason, it is important to acknowledge the contributions of the witnesses who overcame their feelings of shame or stigma and the trauma of re-living violent experiences. I observed in the trials at the SCSL how some women and men became upset as they gave their evidence. Some witnesses F feared reprisals. The tribunal issued protective measures such as using pseudonyms or allowing them to speak behind a screen. However, witnesses also made clear that they wanted 'the world' to know how they suffered, that they wanted 'justice'. These witnesses belied the earlier conceptions that women would not speak about the sexual violence inflicted upon them. Clearly witnesses appreciated the opportunity to speak out.[52] As Sandesh Sivakumaran has written, '[s]exual violence has been inflicted upon men and boys for centuries' but it 'remains ... hidden'.[53] The RUF judgment, for example, was innovative in this respect as it addressed male sexual violence committed during the armed conflict in Sierra Leone.

Whilst I have emphasized the contribution of women judges in this chapter, I also recognize the contribution of male judges and prosecutors to the development of international criminal law relating to sexual violence in conflict. I highlight in particular the work of David Crane, the first SCSL prosecutor, who indicted the accused in the RUF and AFRC cases with the crimes of rape, outrages upon personal dignity, forced marriage, and sexual slavery. As noted above, the latter two crimes were the first such indictments in the ad hoc or hybrid tribunals. Noteworthy too is Justice Pierre Boutet (SCSL), whose dissenting opinions, cited above, reviewed the findings of such reports as the ICRC study on the impact of armed conflict on women (Charlotte Lindsay)[54] and the Preliminary Report of the Special Rapporteur on the Situation of Systematic Rape, Sexual Slavery and Slavery-like Practices during Periods of Armed Conflict (Linda Chavez),[55] to emphasize that victims of sexual violence have the right to have crimes that are committed against them prosecuted.

Naimh Hayes has highlighted the 'substantial contributions' to the development of the law relating to sexual violence that have emanated from a Trial Chamber

[52] A witness in *Prosecutor v Brima et al* spoke with feeling and dignity when thanking the SCSL for the opportunity she had been given to tell 'the world' of the gang rape of herself and her daughter. That statement was made after and despite a lengthy cross examination.

[53] Sandesh Sivakumaran, 'Prosecuting Sexual Violence against Men and Boys' in Anne-Marie De Brouwer and others (eds), *Sexual Violence as an International Crime: Interdisciplinary Approaches* (Intersentia 2013) 79–98.

[54] Charlotte Lindsey, 'Women facing war: ICRC study on the impact of armed conflict on women' (International Committee of the Red Cross, 2001).

[55] 'Preliminary report of the Special Rapporteur on the situation of systematic rape, sexual slavery and slavery-like practices during periods of armed conflict, Ms. Linda Chavez', Sub-Commission on Prevention of Discrimination and Protection of Minorities, UN DOC E/CN.4/Subpr.2/1996/26 (16 July 1996).

with a female judge. She stated that '[o]ne of the most significant elements of the judicial interpretation of the crime of rape by the ad hoc Tribunals has undoubtedly been the role played by female judges',[56] citing Justice Pillay who 'noted that although all three judges on the bench in the *Akayesu* trial introduced questions regarding sexual violence, only her alleged impartiality was raised as an issue on appeal'.[57] Those objections were dismissed. Justice Mumba was also accused of bias and of advancing 'a legal and political agenda' by Counsel for the Defence in the *Furundžija* case because of her membership of the UN Commission on the Status of Women.[58] Defence Counsel applied to have Justice Winter recuse herself from hearing the challenge to the child soldier indictments on the grounds of her membership on the UN Committee on the Rights of the Child.[59] The objections to Justices Mumba and Winter were dismissed by their respective Chambers as being unfounded.

The Convention for the Elimination of Discrimination Against Women (CEDAW) calls for equality of opportunity for men and women but the percentage of male to female judges in the international tribunals indicates that far from all countries are complying with what appears to be a mandatory obligation.[60] Organizations which promote and support women judges, such as the International Association of Women Judges and gqualcampaign.org (GQUAL) make their members aware of vacancies in the international tribunals and encourage women to apply. Whilst important, this work alone is insufficient; more must be done at the domestic political level to inform qualified women of positions, encourage and then support their candidacies if we are to have more female judges at the international level. One example of such positive action might be a mandatory quota, or a system similar to the European Court of Human Rights nomination system whereby States have to nominate three candidates, only two of whom can be of the same gender. Only then, real change in the composition of the international bench will be possible.

[56] Hayes, 154–55.

[57] N. Pillay, 'Equal Justice for Women' (2008) Arizona Law Revue 657, 687.

[58] *Prosector v Furundzija*, IT -95-17/1-A, paras 211–12.

[59] *Prosecutor v Hinga Norman*, Decision on Preliminary Motion Based on Lack of Jurisdiction (Child Recruitment) SCSL-2004-14-AR(E) (31 May 2004).

[60] Convention on the Elimination of All Forms of Discrimination against Women (concluded 18 December 1979, entered into force 3 September 1981) 1249 UNTS 1, Article 8: 'States Parties shall take all appropriate measures to ensure to women, on equal terms with men and without any discrimination, the opportunity to represent their Governments at the international level and to participate in the work of international organizations'.

18

The Contribution of Female Judges to the Victim Jurisprudence of the International Criminal Court

Juan-Pablo Pérez-León-Acevedo

1. Introduction

The special attention given to victims of mass atrocities constitutes an important feature of the law and practice of the International Criminal Court (ICC). ICC chambers have included female judges, with diverse professional backgrounds, and benefited from their expertise in these matters. This chapter seeks to determine whether and to what extent female judges have contributed to the ICC jurisprudence on victims, focusing on the procedural aspects of victim-witness protection, victim participation, and victim reparations. Under the ICC Rules of Procedure and Evidence (ICC-RPE), the term 'victims' is defined as 'natural persons who [have] suffered harm as a result of the commission of any crime within the jurisdiction of the Court'.[1] Victim participation at the ICC extends beyond that of domestic criminal courts. Under the ICC-Statute (ICCS): 'where the personal interests of the victims are affected, the Court shall permit their views and concerns to be presented and considered at stages of the proceedings determined to be appropriate by the Court and in a manner which is not prejudicial to or inconsistent with the rights of the accused and a fair and impartial trial'.[2] Victim participants and witnesses may also benefit from protective measures and victims can claim reparations against the convicted.[3]

This chapter argues that female ICC judges have made important contributions to the ICC case-law on victims. Their contributions have included interpreting and/or applying ICC legal framework provisions on victims for the first time, fleshing out the contours and scope of these provisions, and facing substantive and procedural challenges in victim matters. This chapter uses standards

[1] Rule 85(a), ICC Rules of Procedure and Evidence (ICC-RPE) UN Doc PCNICC/2000/1/Add.1 (2000).

[2] Art 68(3) ICC-Statute (ICCS) 2187 UNTS 3.

[3] Arts 68, 75 ICCS.

Juan-Pablo Pérez-León-Acevedo, *The Contribution of Female Judges to the Victim Jurisprudence of the International Criminal Court* In: *Identity and Diversity on the International Bench.* Edited by: Freya Baetens, Oxford University Press (2020). DOI: 10.1093/oso/9780198870753.003.0018.

from international human rights law (IHRL) to assess the legitimacy of the jurisprudence. Identification of 'female' ICC victim jurisprudence presents difficulties: most ICC-Chambers have female and male judges and separate/dissenting opinions are exceptional. This chapter seeks to find and analyse specific instances of victim jurisprudence to which female ICC-judges have contributed, primarily examining three kinds of decisions. The first is decisions of ICC Appeals, Trial, and Pre-Trial Chambers (AC, TC, PTC respectively) exclusively ('all-female') or mainly ('majority-female') constituted by female judges, ie when at least two out of the three TC or PTC judges were women or at least three out of the five AC judges were women. The second is decisions rendered by single female judges on behalf of their PTCs and the third is single/concurrent dissenting votes of female judges. This chapter starts off by examining professional profiles of female ICC judges. It then analyses their contributions to ICC victim jurisprudence under three sections: victim-witness protective measures; victim participation; and victim reparations.

2. Female ICC Judges

Since its establishment, the ICC has had the most gender-balanced representation among international courts.[4] This helps to enhance the ICC's normative legitimacy, that is, whether the court objectively meets normative criteria or 'has the right to rule' based on objective criteria, and sociological legitimacy, ie whether the court is perceived to be legitimate or is believed to hold the right to rule.[5] Albeit conceptually distinct, these types of legitimacy are interrelated.[6] Nevertheless, as then International Criminal Tribunal for the former Yugoslavia (ICTY) Judge Patricia Wald highlighted, the numbers are still insufficient: 'women judges (men too of course) have to be recognized as smart, fair, and hardworking if they are to wield influence, not only inside the courtroom and among their judicial peers, but also outside the court, in the concerned world of commentators and media'.[7] As Judge Wald cautioned, to avoid disappointing results similar to those experienced by previous international and hybrid criminal tribunals (ICTs) in their early years, women (and men) judges must possess relevant experience and knowledge, and supporters of women at the ICC 'must

[4] Nienke Grossman, 'Sex on the Bench: Do Women Judges Matter to the Legitimacy of International Courts?' (2012) 12(2) Chicago Journal of International Law 647, 649.

[5] Nienke Grossman, 'Sex Representation on the Bench and the Legitimacy of International Criminal Courts' (2011) 11 International Criminal Law Review 643, 645; Silje Langvatn and Theresa Squatrito, 'Conceptualizing and Measuring the Legitimacy of International Criminal Tribunals' in Nobuo Hayashi and Cecilia Bailliet (eds), *The Legitimacy of International Criminal Tribunals* (CUP 2017)? 43.

[6] ibid 44.

[7] Patricia Wald, 'Women on International Courts-Some Lessons Learned' (2011) 11 International Criminal Law Review 401, 402.

continue to be critical and cautious regarding whom they support for crucial judicial [. . .] positions'.[8]

The purpose of improving gender representation and ensuring candidates fulfil the requisite qualifications is preserving (the perception of) the ICC's authority and quality of its decisions.[9] Indeed, some critical voices emphasize the need for more ICC judges with suitable national or international judicial experience to enhance the ICC's legitimacy and effectiveness.[10] Selection criteria like geographical distribution or gender representation may occasionally be in tension with the quality of judges elected.[11] Thus, analysis of professional profiles of female ICC judges[12] who have contributed to ICC victim jurisprudence is arguably important to see how well-prepared they were to handle complex victim matters and make meaningful jurisprudential contributions in substantive and procedural matters. Experiences at ICTs, where highly qualified female judges such as Judges Wald (ICTY), Odio-Benito (ICTY, ICC), and Pillay (International Criminal Tribunal for Rwanda (ICTR, ICC)) contributed to develop *inter alia* jurisprudence on sexual violence, powerfully illustrate this point.[13] As Judge Odio-Benito explains, contributions of female judges to ICT jurisprudence relate to both substantive law (eg rape as a war crime) and procedural/evidential issues.[14] Some of these developments have been qualified as judicial activism.[15] However, as Judge Odio-Benito suggests, the ICC has to enforce its mandate to protect victims and guarantee their rights, which demands female perspectives.[16]

Including the six judges who assumed their functions in March 2018 (5 female judges), 20 out of the 47 ICC-judges who ever served at the ICC have been women (42.55%).[17] Under ICCS Article 36 ('Qualifications, nomination and election of judges'), this universe of 20 female judges can be broken down in different ways. Whereas five judges (25%) were elected from List B (competence in international law), the other 15 judges were elected from List A (competence in criminal law and procedure).[18] Concerning 'representation of the principal legal systems of the world' and 'equitable geographical distribution',[19] there have been seven female judges from African States (35%), five from Latin-American and Caribbean States

[8] ibid.

[9] Grossman (n 4) 674–75.

[10] Ruth MacKenzie and others, *Selecting International Judges* (OUP 2010) 175.

[11] ibid.

[12] See <www.icc-cpi.int/about/judicial-divisions/biographies> accessed 29 February 2020; <www.icc-cpi.int/iccdocs/PIDS/publications/ContinuingJudgesENG.pdf> accessed 29 February 2020. <www.iccnow.org/documents/CVDigest200212Eng.pdf> accessed 12 August 2020.

[13] Grossman (n 5) 647–49.

[14] Louise Chappell and Andrea Durbach-Interview with Judge Odio-Benito, 'A View of Gender Justice from the Bench' (2014) 16(4) International Feminist Journal of Politics 648, 649–50.

[15] ibid 650.

[16] ibid 650–51.

[17] See also ICCS, Art 36(8)(a)(iii).

[18] ICCS, Arts 36(3)(b)(i)–(ii), 36(5).

[19] ICCS, Art 36(8)(a).

(25%), three from Asian-Pacific States (15%), two from Eastern European States (10%), and three from 'Western European and other' States (15%).

As of February 2018, of the 15 female ICC judges who ever served at the ICC until February 2018 and whose jurisprudential contributions are examined in this chapter, most have held judicial and/or quasi-judicial positions at the national and/or international levels *prior to* their ICC appointments, which the following examples show. Judges Odio-Benito, Christine Van den Wyngaert, Maureen Harding Clark, and Fatoumata Diarra had served as ICTY Judges, and Judge Pillay had served as an ICTR Judge where she critically contributed towards ground-breaking case-law on categorising mass rape as part of genocide.[20] Judge Van den Wyngaert also served as an International Court of Justice (ICJ) ad-hoc Judge in the *Arrest Warrant Case*.[21] Judges Sylvia Steiner, Joyce Aluoch, Sanji Monageng, Olga Herrera-Carbuccia, Anita Ušacka, and Pillay had been high-level court national judges. Judge Ekaterina Trendafilova had been a deputy district attorney. Judges Aluoch, Fumiko Saiga, Monageng, and Akua Kuenyehia had been members of regional and/or international human rights bodies. Judge Maureen Harding Clark had been a Senior Counsel. Additionally, Judges Silvia Fernández-de-Gurmendi and Steiner participated in the negotiation and/or drafting of ICC instruments.

In fulfilment of 'the need to include judges with legal expertise on specific issues, including, but not limited to, violence against women or children',[22] several female ICC Judges had had professional experience on issues related to women and/or children.[23] ICC-judges need to have qualifications for appointment to the highest judicial offices in their respective States.[24] Almost all the female judges also had academic experience: professorships, research experience, and/or publications. In sum, female ICC judges have professional expertise in international and domestic criminal law and procedure, international humanitarian law (IHL), IHRL, general international law, and/or vulnerable victims such as women and children, which largely meets the ICCS qualification requirements.[25] The Advisory Committee on Nominations, established by the Assembly of States Parties in 2012,[26] and legal literature[27] have specially remarked the importance of competence in criminal or international law.

[20] See <www.icc-cpi.int/about/judicial-divisions/biographies/Pages/former-judges.aspx>accessed 12 August 2020.<http://iccnow.org/documents/CVDigest20021 2Eng.pdf> accessed 12 August 2020.

[21] See <www.icc-cpi.int/about/judicial-divisions/biographies/Pages/former-judges.aspx> accessed 29 February 2020.

[22] ICCS, Art 36(8)(b).

[23] See <www.icc-cpi.int/about/judicial-divisions/biographies/Pages/former-judges.aspx> accessed 29 February 2020.

[24] ICCS, Art 36(3)(a).

[25] ICCS, Arts 36(3) and 36(8)(b)

[26] ICCS, Art 36(4)(c); Report of the Bureau Working Group on the Advisory Committee on Nominations (ICC-ASP/11/47), paras 7–8.

[27] Michael Bohlander, 'Article 36' in Otto Triffterer and Kai Ambos (eds), *Commentary on the Rome Statute of the International Criminal Court* (3rd edn, C.H. Beck/Nomos/Hart 2016) 1220–21.

3. Protective Measures for Witness-Victims

This section focuses on findings of the only all-female trial chamber, TC-III (Judges Steiner (Presiding), Aluoch, and Ozaki) in *Bemba*, and the majority-female TC-II (2/3 were female judges: Judges Diarra and Van den Wyngaert) in *Katanga* and *Ngudjolo-Chui* before and after their division in two cases.

3.1 Protective Measures

As the all-female TC-III (*Bemba*) noted, when Chambers rule on protective measures, they must comply with Article 68 obligations 'to protect the safety, physical and psychological well-being, dignity and privacy of victims and witnesses' in a manner that is not 'prejudicial to or inconsistent with the rights of the accused and a fair and impartial trial'.[28] Articles 64(7) and 67(1), and ICC Regulation 20 oblige TCs to observe the principle of public proceedings.[29] This principle is not absolute but it must be considered when protective measures will limit public proceedings.[30] The majority-female TC-II (*Katanga*, *Ngudjolo-Chui*) and the all-female TC-III (*Bemba*) considered that protective measures should be granted exceptionally, under a case-by-case assessment of the necessity to protect witness safety, where it was proportional to and balanced against the accused's rights to a fair and impartial trial, and the principle of public proceedings.[31] Protective measures were ordered to protect the identity of many witnesses because of concerns for their personal or family safety; this is why they are referred to with numbers and certain identifying details are omitted in the *Bemba*, *Katanga* and *Ngudjolo-Chui* judgments.[32]

However, whenever the majority-female TC-II (*Katanga*, *Ngudjolo-Chui*) and the all-female TC-III (*Bemba*) ordered protective measures, the parties, participants, and their lawyers knew relevant identifying information.[33] During trial, protective measures granted aimed to protect the witnesses' identity vis-à-vis general public/media but not to 'curtail the defence's knowledge of the witness' identity'.[34] This was consistent with the ICC practice of inadmissibility of anonymous

[28] *Bemba* (Decision on protective measures for Witness 44) ICC-01/05-01/08-2107-Red (29 June 2016), para 7 (invoking ICCS, Art 68(1)–(2); Rule 87).
[29] ibid.
[30] ibid.
[31] *Katanga/Ngudjolo-Chui* (Order on protective measures for certain witnesses called by the Prosecutor and the Chamber) ICC-01/04-01/07-1667-Red (9 December 2009), para 9; *Bemba* (n 28) para 10.
[32] *Bemba* (Judgment) ICC-01/05-01/08-3343 (21 March 2016), para 247; *Katanga* (Judgment) ICC-01/04-01/07-3436-tENG (7 March 2014), para 97; *Ngudjolo-Chui* (Judgment) ICC-01/04-02/12-3-tENG (26 December 2012), para 63.
[33] *Ngudjolo-Chui* (n 32) para 63; *Bemba* (n 32) para 247; *Katanga* (n 32) para 97.
[34] *Bemba* (n 28) para 11.

witnesses during trials. Witness identities were timely disclosed to the defence which could listen to, see, and question witnesses in court.[35] According to Judge Sylvia Steiner (on behalf of PTC-I), non-disclosure of victim identities to public and media during the pre-trial phase minimized the risks they faced.[36]

3.2 Set of Protective Measures

This section discusses judicial protective measures, including closed sessions and redactions of documents. The first is the exception to the general rule that ICC trials are public.[37] As the majority-female TC-II (*Katanga, Ngudjolo-Chui*) noted, 'to protect the safety, physical and psychological well-being, dignity and privacy of victims and witnesses', ICC instruments provide for exceptions to the principle of public hearings: the Chamber may order that (parts of) the proceedings be conducted in closed session.[38] To ensure effective protective measures, the majority-female TC-II (*Katanga, Ngudjolo-Chui*) and the all-female TC-III (*Bemba*) frequently heard testimony in closed sessions.[39] Nevertheless, the majority-female TC-II aimed to develop best practices such as keeping closed sessions to a minimum and ordering that portions of testimony transcripts from closed sessions which posed no security risk be reclassified as public.[40] The need for closed sessions was assessed on a case-by-case basis.[41] The principle of public hearings is important, protective measures must be necessary, and these measures must involve minimal restrictions not substantially affecting defence rights.[42] The majority-female TC-II (*Katanga, Ngudjolo-Chui*) ordered closed sessions when certain witnesses would enter and exit the courtroom and when they would be asked potentially identifying questions.[43] As a result, testimony has been frequently heard in closed or 'private session,[44] negatively affecting the general rule of public hearings.

The second protective measure, acknowledged by the majority-female TC-II (*Katanga, Ngudjolo-Chui*), is allowing witnesses to testify by 'electronic or other special means',[45] including by altering images and voices, and through closed circuit

[35] ibid.

[36] *Katanga/Ngudjolo-Chui* (Decision on the Set of Procedural Rules Attached to Procedural Status of Victim at the Pre-Trial Stage of the Case) ICC-01/047-01/07-474 (13 May 2008), paras 20–22.

[37] ICCS, Art 67(1).

[38] *Katanga/Ngudjolo-Chui* (n. 31) para 8; ICCS, Art 68(1).

[39] *Katanga* (n 32) para 98; *Bemba* (n. 32) para 248; *Ngudjolo-Chui* (n 32) para 64.

[40] *Ngudjolo-Chui* (n 32) para 64; *Bemba* (n 32) para 248; *Katanga* (n 32) para 98; ICCS, Arts 64(7) and 67(1).

[41] *Katanga/Ngudjolo-Chui* (Decision Granting Protective Measures for Witness 323 during In-Court Testimony) ICC-01/04-01/07-1795-Red-tENG (27 January 2010), para 11.

[42] ibid para 13.

[43] *Katanga/Ngudjolo-Chui* (Decision on the application for the institution of protective measures) ICC-01/04-01/07-2663-Red (22 February 2011), para 15.

[44] *Ngudjolo-Chui* (n 32) para 64; William Schabas, *The International Criminal Court-A Commentary on the Rome Statute* (2nd edn, OUP 2016) 1058.

[45] ICCS, Art 68(2); Rule 87(3)(c).

television testimony.[46] TC-II used voice and image distortion and pseudonyms to preserve witness anonymity vis-à-vis the public and media to guarantee witness safety.[47] Trial fairness was not affected as the defence knew witness identities and the accused could see witnesses and hear witness undistorted voices.[48] The Prosecutor disclosed witness identities to the defence 45 days prior to witness testimonies.[49] Apart from closed sessions, the public was able to follow the proceedings and know their contents.[50] Arrangements were made to prevent anyone outside the courtroom from identifying witnesses.[51] Also the all-female TC-III (*Bemba*) qualified voice and image distortion and pseudonyms as limited protective measures because they are not generally intrusive.[52] The majority-female TC-II granted distortion of witness images and voices before being publicly broadcasted due to harassment suffered by other witnesses upon their return to the Democratic Republic of Congo (DRC) and fear that new witnesses would undergo the same.[53] Judge Van den Wyngaert (dissent) considered that the non-refoulement principle binds the ICC (TC-II's position), and added that in-custody witnesses must be released under IHRL.[54] According to TC-III, a witness' personal circumstances, including his or her well-being, determines the admissibility of viva voice (oral) testimony through video technology.[55]

Under the third measure, redactions of certain documents can be authorized to protect sensitive information.[56] TCs can review redactions and lift them during trial or after closing submissions.[57] In fleshing out ICC-RPE Rule 87(3)(a), majority-female TC-II (*Katanga, Ngudjolo-Chui*) and all-female TC-III (*Bemba*) indicated that redactions may include this witness identifying information: name, aliases, gender, previous/current location, specific dates and times, information concerning family members, nationality, ethnic origin, religious affiliations, current/previous profession or functions, identifying characteristics, and Protection Programme-related information.[58] Judges order redactions when revealing information would lead to identify witnesses, ordered case-by-case, and granted if disclosure would put witnesses at risk in light of the context.[59]

46 *Katanga/Ngudjolo-Chui* (n. 31) paras 8, 14.
47 *Katanga/Ngudjolo-Chui* (n. 41) para 10.
48 ibid para 12.
49 *Katanga/Ngudjolo-Chui* (n 31) para 13.
50 *Katanga/Ngudjolo-Chui* (n 41) para 12.
51 *Katanga/Ngudjolo-Chui* (n 31) para 12.
52 *Bemba* (n 28) para 8.
53 *Katanga/Ngudjolo-Chui* (n 43) para 15.
54 *Katanga* (Dissenting opinion) ICC-01/04-01/07-3405-Anx (1 October 2013).
55 *Bemba* (Public Redacted Decision on the 'Prosecution Request to Hear Witness CAR-OTP-PPPP-0036's Testimony Via Video-link') ICC-01/05-01/08-2101 (3 February 2012), para 7.
56 *Katanga* (n 32) para 99; *Ngudjolo-Chui* (n 32) para 65; *Bemba* (n 32) para 248.
57 ibid para 249.
58 *Katanga/Ngudjolo-Chui* (n. 31) para 20; *Bemba* (Decision on Directions for the Conduct of the Proceedings) ICC-01/05-01/08-1023 (19 November 2010) para 27.
59 ibid para 28.

The fourth measure, as set out by majority-female TC-II in the *Katanga* judgment, maintains confidential information as much as possible to avoid putting witnesses at risk.[60] The all-female TC-III in the *Bemba* judgment publicly referred to former confidential information if its classification as confidential was no longer necessary.[61] This Chamber found that documents pertaining to the Prosecution may be classified as confidential to protect the psychological well-being, dignity, and privacy of witnesses.[62] However, it sought to strike a balance between witness protection and the Chamber's duty to ensure public proceedings.[63] Finally, non-disclosure of witness identities to the defence (anonymous witnesses) has only been allowed during pre-trial,[64] not during trial. This is consistent with ICCS Article 68(5) and Rule 81(4), which require such disclosure before trial and, thus, protect the defendant from anonymous accusations.

3.3 Special Measures

Under Rule 88(1), the ICC can order 'special measures' including, 'measures to facilitate the testimony of a traumatized victim or witness, a child, an elderly person or a victim of sexual violence, pursuant to article 68, paragraphs 1 and 2'. As the majority-female TC-II (*Katanga, Ngudjolo-Chui*) noted, special measures adopted to facilitate testimony of vulnerable witnesses such as sexual violence witnesses and victims may include testimony via closed circuit television, reference to witnesses by protection numbers, prevention of eye contact with the accused, image distortion, and pseudonyms.[65] However, as the majority-female TC-II (*Katanga, Ngudjolo-Chui*) appropriately added, the defence should know witness identities, the public should generally be able to follow the hearings, and special measures must be minimal and proportionate to defence rights.[66] As TC-II remarked, the ICC-Victim and Witness Unity should be able to meet vulnerable witnesses to assess their needs so that the Chambers can decide on protective measures.[67] The all-female TC-III (*Bemba*) also reminded parties of their obligation to control their manners of questioning vulnerable witnesses.[68]

The majority-female TC-II (*Ngudjolo-Chui*) granted in-court protective measures to 19 prosecution witnesses and two victim participants, including women.[69]

[60] *Katanga* (n 32) para 100.
[61] *Bemba* (n 32) para 250.
[62] *Bemba* (n 55) para 12; ICCS, Art 68(1).
[63] *Bemba* (n 55) para 12; ICCS, Arts 64(7), 67(1).
[64] Eg *Katanga/Ngudjolo-Chui* (n 31).
[65] *Katanga/Ngudjolo-Chui* (n. 31) paras. 14–15, 17.
[66] ibid para 19.
[67] ibid paras 14–15.
[68] *Bemba* (n 58) para 15; Rule 88(5).
[69] *Ngudjolo-Chui* (n 32) footnotes 43–44; Rules 87–88.

TC-II remarked on its vigilance to preserve the psychological well-being and privacy of an under-age victim.[70] The all-female TC-III (*Bemba*) rejected the proposed questioning of a witness concerning her resistance during rape because this was considered unacceptable and would set a dangerous precedent, and it reminded all parties and participants of Rule 70 for guidance on evidence principles in sexual violence cases.[71] Corroboration to prove ICC-jurisdiction crimes, particularly sexual violence crimes, is prohibited.[72] TC-II and TC-III found that the extent to which a piece of evidence alone suffices to prove a fact beyond reasonable doubt depends on the respective issue and evidentiary strength (case-by-case approach).[73]

4. Victim Participation

4.1 Application

The victim participation application procedure has demanded a significant amount of time and resources at the ICC. For example, in *Bemba* and *Ongwen* there were over 5,000 and 4,000 victim participants, respectively. As Judge Van den Wyngaert warned, the ICC 'may soon reach the point where an individual case-by-case approach becomes unsustainable'.[74] Judge Silvia Fernandez (on behalf of PTC-I) in *Gbabgo*, followed by Judge Hans-Peter Kaul (on behalf of PTC-II), introduced collective application forms: victims applied collectively, but victim participation was individual.[75] In *Ntaganda*, after considering *inter alia Gbagbo* problems to physically bring together victim groups due to victim discomfort and security concerns, Judge Ekaterina Trendafilova (on behalf of PTC-II) ordered the Victim Participation and Reparations Section to implement a simplified victim application process.[76]

Majority-female TC-V (female Judges Kuniko Ozaki (Presiding), Van den Wyngaert) introduced in *Ruto/Sang* and *Muthaura/Kenyatta* (Kenyan cases) a new victim application procedure to simplify proceedings.[77] However, this departed from

[70] *Katanga/Ngudjolo-Chui* (n. 43) para 15.

[71] *Bemba* (Transcripts) ICC-01/05-01/08-T-47-Red-ENG-CT2-WT (14 January 2011), p 47.

[72] Rule 63(4).

[73] *Bemba* (n 32) paras 245–46; *Katanga* (n. 32) para 110; *Ngudjolo-Chui* (n 32) para 72.

[74] Christine Van den Wyngaert, 'Victims before International Criminal Courts-Some Views and Concerns of an ICC Trial Judge' (2011) 44 Case Western Reserve Journal of International Law 475, 483.

[75] *Gbagbo* (Second Decision on Issues Related to the Victims' Application Process) ICC-02/11-01/11-86 (5 April 2012); *Situation in Uganda*, (Decision on Victims' Participation in Proceedings Related to the Situation in Uganda) ICC-02/04-191 (9 March 2012).

[76] *Ntaganda* (Decision Establishing Principles on the Victims' Application Process) ICC-01/04-02/06-67 (28 May 2013).

[77] *Ruto/Sang* (Decision on Victims' Representation and Participation) ICC-01/09-01/11-460 (3 October 2012), paras 8–62; *Muthaura/Kenyatta* (Decision on Victims' Representation and Participations) ICC-01/09-02/11-498 (3 October 2012), paras 7–61.

previous ICC practice. Victims were divided into two categories. Those who wished to appear personally/via video-link to present their views and concerns followed standard Rule 89 proceedings: applications individually assessed by the Chamber and subject to party observations. Conversely, victims who wished to participate only under common legal representation system could register with the Registry not subject to Chamber assessment or party observations. Under Rule 89, as consistently applied by the ICC, victim participant status is granted on judicially assessed applications, not on mere 'registration'. Furthermore, ICCS Article 68(3) refers to ICC-RPE proceedings (applications). Therefore, the ICC instruments do not foresee the majority-female TC-V's system. TC-V considered victim interests due to security concerns, the large numbers of victims, efficient proceedings, and defence rights. Nevertheless, other TCs did not go beyond ICC instruments.

4.2 Investigation

In *Lubanga*, the majority-female PTC-I (female Judges Akua Kuenyehia and Steiner) extended victim participation to investigations.[78] First, 'proceedings', as referred to in Article 68(3), does not necessarily exclude investigations. Second, Article 68(3) is in the ICCS 'Trial' Section; however, no procedural stage for victim participation is mentioned. Third, Article 68(3) application to investigations is consistent with the ICCS object and purpose of victim participation, especially under IHRL and IHL (case-law of the Inter-American Court of Human Rights (IACtHR) and the European Court of Human Rights (ECtHR) was invoked). Since victim participation must not be 'prejudicial or inconsistent with the rights of the accused', PTC-I concluded that victim participation during investigation per se neither affects investigations nor compromises efficiency and security. PTC-I added that victim personal interests are generally affected during investigation because such participation can help to clarify facts, sanction offenders, and claim reparations.

This participation is consistent with restorative goals,[79] and was well-received by victim advocates. It may also guarantee viable further proceedings because victims' accounts are important for investigation and prosecution. However, the above-mentioned decision may be partially criticized. Unrealistic expectations about the role of victims may arise and be counter-productive with restorative-oriented goals. There may be also tension with the ICC's responsibility to guarantee efficient and fair proceedings. Finally, early victim participation could jeopardize the Prosecutor's independence and duty to establish the truth. The then all-male

[78] *Situation in DRC* (Decision on the Applications for Participation in the Proceedings of VPRS1 *et al.*) ICC-01/04-101-tEN-Corr (17 January 2006), paras 28–63.

[79] War Crimes Research Office, *Victim Participation Before the ICC* (2007) 42.

AC partially reversed the PTCs' decisions that allowed broad victim participation during investigation. Compared to the majority-female PTC-I, the all-male AC adopted more restrictive considerations. The AC found that participation can take place only within judicial proceedings (investigations are not judicial proceedings), and general victim participation during investigation would contravene the ICCS.[80] However, by partially upholding the *Lubanga* decision of majority-female PTC-I, it concluded that victims are not precluded from participation in judicial proceedings, including those during investigations.[81] Thus, PTC-I (and other PTCs) established an amended framework: victims could participate during investigation but only within judicial proceedings.[82] Consideration of the whole investigation stage made the requirement of affected 'personal interests' for participation redundant. The previous approach was also contradictory. Victims granted general participation during investigation could later be deprived of participation, which frustrated victims and raised doubts about participation benefits.

4.3 Pre-trial

In *Katanga/Ngudjolo-Chui,* Judge Sylvia Steiner (on behalf of PTC-I) adopted a seminal systematic approach of making a clear determination of victim participant procedural rights to make victim participation meaningful.[83] Under the principle of proportionality, she divided these procedural rights into six groups,[84] which other judges have largely adopted. The first is a right to access all filings/decisions (public or not) in the case-record, including evidence filed by the parties, and public and closed hearings; however, *ex-parte* materials were excluded. Judge Steiner (on behalf of PTC-I) allowed non-anonymous victim participants' lawyers to access confidential materials and attend closed session hearings but not to transmit related materials/information to their clients.[85] Nevertheless, Judge Hans-Peter Kaul (on behalf of PTC-III) found that all victim participants could access all public materials (excepted *ex-parte*/confidential materials).[86] However, Judge Ekaterina Trendafilova (on behalf of PTC-II) allowed case-by-case victim participant access

[80] *Situation in the DRC* (Judgment on Victim Participation in the Investigation Stage of the Proceedings in the Appeal of the OPCD against the Decision of Pre-Trial Chamber I of 7 December 2007 and in the Appeals of the OPCD and the Prosecutor against the Decision of Pre-Trial Chamber I of 24 December 2007) ICC-01/04-556 (19 December 2008), paras 45–52.

[81] ibid para 56.

[82] *Situation in the DRC* (Decision on Victims' Participation in Proceedings Relating to the Situation in the Democratic Republic of Congo) ICC-01/04-593 (11 April 2011).

[83] *Katanga/Ngudjolo-Chui* (n 36) paras 49–51.

[84] ibid paras 124–45.

[85] *Katanga/Ngudjolo-Chui* (Decision on Limitations of Set of Procedural Rights for Non-Anonymous Victims) ICC-01/04-01/07-537 (30 May 2008), p 12.

[86] *Bemba* (Fourth Decision on Victims' Participation) ICC-01/05-01/08-320 (12 December 2008), paras 103–05.

to confidential materials.[87] Regardless of anonymous/non-anonymous distinctions, anonymous victims cannot access confidential filings and closed hearings.

The second victims' right is to file submissions on admissibility and probative value of party evidence related to the confirmation of charges hearing and examine such evidence at this hearing. Unlike Judge Steiner (on behalf of PTC-I), Judge Kaul (on behalf of PTC-III) found that this right also benefited anonymous victim participants.[88] Judge Trendafilova (on behalf of PTC-II) considered that anonymous victim participants could case-by-case be allowed.[89] The third is to examine witnesses called by the parties during confirmation of charges hearing. Under the principle of non-anonymous accusations, anonymous victim participants were not granted this right.[90] The majority-female PTC-I (Judges Steiner (Presiding) and Monageng) in *Abu-Garda* followed this approach.[91] Judge Trendafilova (PTC-II) followed a case-by-case approach.[92] The fourth is to attend public and closed hearings leading up to and during the confirmation of charges hearing; however, *ex-parte* hearings were excluded. Judge Kaul (PTC-III) limited attendance to public hearings;[93] and, Judge Silvia Fernandez (on behalf of PTC-I) followed a case-by-case approach.[94]

Fifth, victim participants can participate via oral motions, responses, and submissions in all hearings to which they were allowed to attend. Victims cannot extend the Prosecution Charging Document factual basis; however, they may try to extend the legal characterization of facts and the PTC may ask the Prosecution to make amendments. The majority-female PTC-I (*Banda/Jerbo*) established that victims could make oral and written submissions during hearings.[95] Sixth, victim participants can file written motions, responses, and replies on all matters not excluded by the ICC instruments, including submissions on evidentiary and legal issues to be discussed at the confirmation of charges hearing, and objections/observations on proper conduct of the proceedings prior to this hearing. Judge Steiner (on behalf of PTC-I) determined that the Prosecution is in charge of investigations and cases, and grant of investigative powers to victim participants would be inconsistent with ICC instruments, and victim participants may request the

[87] *Ruto et al.* (Second Decision on the 'Request by the Victims' Representative to Access to Confidential Materials') ICC-01/09-01/11-340 (23 September 2011), paras 9–17.

[88] *Bemba* (n 86) paras 99, 110.

[89] *Ruto et al.* (Decision on Victims' Participation at the Confirmation of Charges Hearing and in the Related Proceedings) ICC-01/09-01/11-249 (8 August 2011), para 126.

[90] ibid paras 136–37.

[91] *Abu-Garda* (Decision on Victims' Modalities of Participation at the Pre-trial Stage of the Case) ICC-02/05-02/09-136 (6 October 2009), paras 23–24.

[92] *Ruto et al.* (n 89) para 126.

[93] *Bemba* (n 86) para 101.

[94] *Gbagbo* (Decision on Victims' Participation and Victims' Common Legal Representation at the Confirmation of Charges Hearing and in the Related Proceedings) ICC-02/11-01/11-138 (4 June 2012), para 50.

[95] *Banda/Jerbo* (Decision on Issues Related to the Hearing on the Confirmation of Charges) ICC-01/05-03/09-13 (17 November 2010).

Prosecution to investigate.[96] Furthermore, she rejected introduction of evidence by victim participants because this would infringe defence rights.[97] As she added, these findings are justified because the confirmation of charges hearing is not a 'mini-trial'.[98] Additionally, victims are participants, not parties.

4.4 Trial

Five important victim participant procedural rights are examined here. First, concerning access to documents, all-female TC-III (*Bemba*) and majority-female TC-II (*Katanga, Ngudjolo-Chui*) stated that the access of victims' lawyers is limited to public and confidential filings (*ex-parte* filings are excluded).[99] TC-II limited this access to legal representatives, and victims themselves were not given access.[100] Nevertheless, TC-III and the majority-female TC-V in the Kenyan cases allowed victims to access confidential materials upon approval.[101] Second, according to the majority-female TC-II (*Katanga, Ngudjolo-Chui*) and all-female TC-III (*Bemba*), victims' right to attend and participate in public hearings (Rule 91(2) included all closed sessions (*ex-parte* hearing attendance determined case-by-case).[102] Majority-female TC-V (Kenyan cases) case-by-case decided participation in *ex-parte* hearing.[103]

Third, TC-I in *Lubanga* (including Judge Elizabeth Odio-Benito),[104] upheld by the AC (Judge Pillay presiding),[105] and followed by other TCs,[106] found that the right to file evidence and file submissions on evidence admissibility is not reserved to the parties and, thus, TCs may allow victims' lawyers to produce and challenge evidence pertaining to the accused's guilt/innocence. As the AC determined, although this right lies primarily with the parties, victims may be allowed to exercise it if this assists the TC to determine the truth.[107] The AC emphasized that this is

[96] *Katanga/Ngudjolo-Chui* (n 36) paras. 82–83.

[97] ibid para 112–13.

[98] ibid para 100.

[99] *Bemba* (Decision on the Participation of Victims in the Trial and on 86 Applications by Victims to Participate in the Proceedings) ICC-01/05-01/08-807 (30 June 2010), para 47; *Katanga/Ngudjolo-Chui* (Decision on the Modalities of Victim Participation at Trial) ICC-01/04-01/07-1788-tENG (22 January 2010), para 121.

[100] ibid paras 121–23.

[101] *Bemba* (n 99) para 47; *Ruto/Sang* (n 77) para 68; *Muthaura/Kenyatta* (n 77) para 67.

[102] *Katanga/Ngudjolo-Chui* (n 99) para 71. Concerning *Bemba*, see Brianne McGonigle-Leyh, *Procedural Justice?-Victim Participation in International Criminal Proceedings* (Intersentia 2011) 292.

[103] Eg *Muthaura/Kenyatta* (n 77) para 70.

[104] *Lubanga* (Decision on Victims' Participation) ICC-01/04-01/06-1119 (18 January 2008), paras 108–09.

[105] *Lubanga* (Judgment on the Appeals of the Prosecutor and The Defense against Trial Chamber I's Decision, on Victims' Participation of 18 January 2008) ICC-01/04-01/06-1432 (11 July 2008), paras 86–105, 109.

[106] Eg *Bemba* (n 99) paras 30–32; *Ruto/Sang* (n 77) para 77.

[107] *Lubanga* (n 105), paras 93–96; ICCS, Art 66(2).

not 'an unfettered right for victims' because victims must 'demonstrate why their interests are affected by the evidence or issue'.[108] Two AC male Judges (Kirsch and Pikis) in their partially dissenting opinions considered that only parties can file evidence. Thus, Judge Pillay's vote was decisive to constitute majority (alongside male Judges Song, and Kourula) to recognize this key right. In applying the above-detailed AC principles, all-female TC-III (*Bemba*) correctly found that: victims are not parties and, hence, not vested with a self-standing right to present evidence; and victims may be authorized to present evidence to assist the Chamber to determine the truth (Article 69(3)) and to make victim participation meaningful.[109] The majority-female TC-V (Kenyan cases) reached similar findings.[110] However, whereas the all-female TC-III (*Bemba*) frequently allowed victim participants to lead evidence on the accused's guilt, overlapping with prosecutorial mandate, the majority-female TC-II (*Katanga, Ngudjolo-Chui*) proceeded in a manner in which even victim participants were aware of their limited role.[111]

Fourth, concerning witness questioning by victim participants' lawyers, TCs differently approached the relationship between victim evidence and the ICC's goal of determination of the truth.[112] The all-female TC-III (*Bemba*) frequently permitted victims' lawyers to question witnesses about the accused's guilt and adopted a broad approach to this relationship.[113] Not only did they question Prosecution witnesses on the context of crimes, victim suffering, or reparations, but they also often tried to determine the accused's guilt.[114] Conversely, the majority-female TC-II (*Katanga, Ngudjolo-Chui*) adopted a more limited approach to victim participation. It exceptionally let victims question witnesses on the accused's guilt,[115] reminded lawyers to stay within their clients' interestes,[116] established that questioning must mainly aim at the truth, reminded that victims 'are not parties', and remarked that victims do not support the Prosecutor.[117] This approach overlooks victim participation bias. However, it better ensures defence rights: the accused does not face two accusers. In any event, as the majority-female TC-V (Kenyan cases) correctly determined, victim participants' lawyers when questioning witnesses/accused 'may not formulate any new allegations against the accused'.[118]

[108] *Lubanga* (n 105) para 4.
[109] *Bemba* (Decision on the Supplemented Applications by the Legal Representatives of Victims to Present Evidence and the Views and Concerns of Victims) ICC-01/05-01/08-2138 (22 February 2012), paras 13–18.
[110] Eg *Ruto/Sang* (n 77) para 77.
[111] McGonigle-Leyh (n 101), 320.
[112] ibid 298; Rule 91(3).
[113] *Bemba* (n 99) para. 33–40.
[114] McGonigle-Leyh (n 101) 299.
[115] *Katanga/Ngudjolo-Chui* (n 85) para 60.
[116] *Katanga/Ngudjolo-Chui* (Transcripts) ICC-01/04-01/07 (22 March 2010), p 4; (12 July 2010), p 15.
[117] *Katanga/Ngudjolo-Chui* (Directions for the Conduct of the Proceedings and Testimony in Accordance with Rule 140) ICC-01/04-01/07-1665 (20 November 2009), para 82.
[118] Eg *Muthaura/Kenyatta* (n 77) para 74.

Fifth, the ICC instruments are silent on whether victim participants may be also witnesses; however, *inter alia* the majority-female TC-II (*Katanga*, *Ngudjolo-Chui*) and the all-female TC-III (*Bemba*) allowed them to testify under these conditions: attention to Article 67(1) accused's rights, victims are not auxiliary prosecutors, testimony genuinely contributes to truth determination, and anonymous testimonies are forbidden.[119] These TCs also developed criteria to determine which victims are best placed to personally provide evidence at the ICC, including whether testimonies are repetitive, representative, pertinent, and substantially new.[120]

Additional victim participation matters will now be examined. First, the majority-female TC-V (Kenyan cases) designed, for victim participants who did not appear in person, participation proceedings under a common legal representative and the Office of Public Counsel for Victims (OPCV) acting on his/her behalf.[121] Whereas the former became the contact point for victims and appeared on their behalf at critical junctures, the OPCV was the interface between the common legal representative and TC-V in the court-room. This aimed to benefit victims and ensure safe/secure handling of confidential information. However, this extra victims-Chamber intermediation makes victim participation more symbolic. Moreover, victims' lawyers should exercise victims' basic rights like attendance at hearings.

Second, on the question of victim participants who also testified as witnesses (dual status victims) in *Lubanga*, the majority-male TC-I due to inconsistencies regarding their ages and true identities found their evidence unreliable and inaccurate, and as a result, withdrew these victims' right to participation.[122] Non-consideration of such testimonies is sound because these were unreliable evidence. However, in agreement with Judge Odio-Benito's dissent, depriving dual status victims of their participant status was excessive. She considered that the problems with the testimonies of dual status victims should not affect their participant status because they were after all victims of crimes for which Lubanga was charged.[123] She added that imposing a higher evidentiary threshold on dual status victims than that imposed on victims who were only participants and who were not thoroughly examined is 'unfair and discriminatory'.[124] According to her, inadmissibility of evidence provided by those dual status victims would have been enough because when evaluating reparation claims TCs can determine whether

[119] *Katanga/Ngudjolo-Chui* (n 117) paras 19–22; *Bemba* (n 109) paras 22–23.

[120] ibid para 24; *Katanga/Ngudjolo-Chui* (n 117) para 30.

[121] *Ruto/Sang* (n 77) paras 41–43; *Muthaura/Kenyatta* (n 77) paras 40–42.

[122] *Lubanga* (Judgment Pursuant to Art 74 of the Statute) ICC-01/04-01/06-2842 (14 March 2012), para 484.

[123] *Lubanga* (Separate and Dissenting Opinion of Judge Odio Benito) ICC-01/04-01/06-2842 (14 March 2012), paras 25–34.

[124] ibid para 35.

those victims meet the criteria.[125] Furthermore, this loss of participant status may cause re-victimization.

Finally, only parties can appeal TCs/PTCs interlocutory decisions.[126] Nonetheless, victim participation is allowed during interlocutory appeals proceedings. In separate opinions to AC decisions that stemmed from appeals against TCs decisions, Judge Song concluded that victims who participated in trial/pre-trial should automatically be allowed to participate in related interlocutory appeals.[127] Judge Christine Van den Wyngaert agreed with him in a separate opinion.[128] The AC (female Judges Ozaki and Monageng plus three male judges) finally followed the approach adopted by Judges Song and Van den Wyngaert.[129]

5. Victim Reparations

5.1 Victimhood Scope

The majority-female AC (female Judges Monageng, Ušacka, and Trendafilova) clarified in *Lubanga* that only victims who suffered harm as a result of crimes that led to conviction are eligible to claim reparations against the convicted.[130] The majority-male TC-I's *Lubanga* reparation order found that the ICC 'should formulate and implement reparations awards that are appropriate for the victims of sexual and gender-based violence' and 'shall implement gender-sensitive measures'.[131] However, the AC did not consider sexual or gender-based violence as harm resulting from the crimes for which Lubanga was convicted: war crimes of recruitment and use of child soldiers.[132] This majority-female AC's finding may be partially criticized. Under Rule 85(a), there is no direct causal link requirement between crime and harm concerning natural persons for ICC reparations. For reparations, Judge Odio-Benito's dissent to the *Lubanga* judgment is important. She concluded that 'sexual violence committed against children in the armed groups causes irreparable

[125] ibid.

[126] ICCS, Art 82.

[127] *Katanga/Ngudjolo-Chui* (Separate Opinion of Judge Song) ICC-01/04-01/07-2124 (24 May 2010), p 8.

[128] *Lubanga* (Separate Opinion of Judge Song and Judge Van Der Wyngaert with respect to the 'Decision on the participation of victims in the appeals') ICC-01/04-01/06-2205 (8 December 2009).

[129] *Gbagbo/Blé-Goudé* (Reasons for the "Decision on the 'Request for the Recognition of the Right of Victims Authorized to Participate in the Case to Automatically Participate in any Interlocutory Appeal Arising from the Case and, in the alternative, Application to Participate in the interlocutory appeal against the ninth decision on Mr Gbagbo's Detention (ICC-02/11-01/15-134-Red3)'") ICC-02/11-01/15-172 (31 July 2015).

[130] *Lubanga* (Judgment on the appeals against the "Decision establishing the principles and procedures to be applied to reparations" of 7 August 2012) ICC-01/04-01/06-3129 (3 March 2015), para 8.

[131] *Lubanga* (Decision Establishing the Principles and Procedures to be Applied to Reparations) ICC-01/04-01/06-2904 (7 August 2012), paras 207–08.

[132] *Lubanga* (n 130) paras 196–98.

harm and is a direct and inherent consequence to their involvement with the armed group', ie 'sexual violence is an intrinsic element of the criminal conduct of "use to participate actively in the hostilities"'.[133] She appropriately clarified that 'crimes of sexual violence are distinct and separate crimes that could have been evaluated separately by this Chamber if the Prosecutor would have presented charges against these criminal conducts'.[134] She added that sexual violence/enslavement may inflict harm directly caused by the war crime of enlisting, conscripting, and using children in support of combatants.[135]

The majority-female Appeals Chamber should have upheld the majority-male TC-I's reparation order finding of reparable harm resulting from sexual/gender violence to redress this dimension of harm related to crimes for which Lubanga was convicted. In any event, victims of sexual crimes committed by Lubanga's forces would not have been included because the Prosecutor filed no sexual crimes charges. Additionally, quite a flexible application of the causal link would cause an exponential increase in victims, worsening the lack of available resources. In confirming and refining TC-I's *Lubanga* reparation order, the majority-female AC upheld that indirect victims are those who suffer harm as a result of the harm inflicted on direct victims and can benefit from reparations, including family members.[136] This consideration of the socio-cultural context of victims is welcome. Many victims at the ICC come from societies where extended family relationships are prevalent. The majority-female AC appropriately identified material, physical, and psychological harm for reparations.[137] Furthermore, after differentiating between identification and assessment of harm, the AC defined sub-categories of harm specific to direct and indirect victims.[138] The majority-male TC-II (female Judge Olga Herrera-Carbuccia) in *Katanga* and *Lubanga*, applied these principles/standards,[139] promoting consistency.

5.2 Reparation Principles and Reparation Orders

Under ICCS Article 75(1), the Chambers have a quasi-legislative competence to determine reparation principles.[140] By largely confirming TC-I's findings, the majority-female AC presided by Judge Pillay in *Lubanga* identified

[133] *Lubanga* (n 123) para 20.
[134] ibid.
[135] ibid para 21.
[136] *Lubanga* (Order for Reparations) ICC-01/04-01/06-3129-AnxA (3 March 2015), para 6.
[137] ibid para 10.
[138] *Lubanga* (n 130) para 191.
[139] *Katanga* (Order for Reparations pursuant to Art 75 of the Statute) ICC-01/04-01/07-3728-rEng (24 March 2017); *Lubanga* (Décision fixant le montant des réparations auxquelles Thomas Lubanga Dyilo est tenu) ICC-01/04-01/06-3379-Red (15 December 2017).
[140] Conor McCarthy, *Reparations and Victim Support in the International Criminal Court* (CUP 2012) 131.

thirteen categories of reparation principles: beneficiaries, harm, causation, non-discrimination, a convicted person's liability, proof, child victims, accessibility/consultation with victims, reparation modalities, proportional and adequate reparations, defence rights, States/other stakeholders, and publicity.[141] Some principles identified by the Chambers were arguably defined by the ICCS but others went beyond Article 75.[142] It may also be that the Chambers identified more principles than there are in reality.[143] However, the *Lubanga* reparation principles are largely not mere re-statements of ICC instruments. Some flesh out and clarify normative language to guide complex ICC reparation proceedings whereas others fill in normative lacunas.[144] In upholding TC-I's findings, the majority-female AC also invoked IHRL, including regional case-law. This promotes coherence of ICC reparation case-law vis-à-vis other international sources on reparations, and convergence amidst institutional diversification/fragmentation. The majority-male TC-II (female Judge Olga Herrera-Carbuccia) in *Katanga* invoked those principles.[145] This promotes internal judicial consistency. ICC Chambers should continue to look to IHRL sources for guidance in reparations but they should remain aware that ICC reparations are ordered against individuals not States.

By filling in important normative gaps, the majority-female AC in the *Lubanga* reparation judgment identified essential elements of Article 75 reparation orders: be issued against the convicted; establish and inform the convicted of his/her liability; provide reasons for reparation types (collective and/or individual); define the harm caused to direct and indirect victims as a result of the crimes for which the accused was convicted and identify reparation modalities (compensation, etc.); and identify eligible reparation beneficiaries or set out eligibility criteria under the link between harm and crimes that led to conviction.[146] The majority-male TC-II, including female Judge Herrera-Carbuccia, applied these elements,[147] promoting consistent and predictable case-law.

5.3 A Convicted Person's Accountability

According to the ICCS *travaux préparatoires,* literature, and Article 82(4) (the convicted (not the Trust Fund for Victims (TFV)) may appeal reparation orders), the majority-female AC (*Lubanga*) properly determined that ICC reparations orders must be made against the convicted based on his/her criminal liability.[148] It was

[141] *Lubanga* (n 136).
[142] David Donat-Cattin, 'Article 75' in Triffterer and Ambos (n 27) 1861.
[143] ibid.
[144] ibid.
[145] *Katanga* (n 139).
[146] *Lubanga* (n 130) paras 1, 32.
[147] *Katanga* (n 139) para 31.
[148] *Lubanga* (n 130) paras 65–68.

not persuaded by TC-I's interpretation of 'through the Trust Fund' as replacing 'against the convicted' when this is indigent.[149] The AC concluded through their own textual interpretations that even if reparations are ordered 'through' the TFV, TCs must direct reparation orders 'against' the convicted.[150] It noted that collective reparations made through the TFV are 'against a convicted'.[151] By invoking Article 128 and the Vienna Convention on the Law of the Treaties, the AC also relied on the equally authoritative French version of Article 75(2), and ICC practice.[152] Therefore, according to the AC, TC-I erred in not issuing the reparation order against Lubanga.[153]

In *Lubanga*, the majority-female AC upheld the majority-male TC-I's application of the principle of the obligation of the convicted to remedy harm caused by the crimes for which (s)he was found guilty; however, the AC determined that TC-I did not actually hold Lubanga liable for reparations.[154] Under textual interpretation of ICC instruments and drafting history thereof, the AC correctly found that TC-I erred by: considering Lubanga's indigence to be relevant to his/her reparation liability; and assuming, when the convicted is indigent, that TCs may control TFV resources collected through voluntary contributions without establishing the offender's liability for these awards.[155] The TFV may advance resources when needed; however, the convicted remains liable (he/she must refund the TFV), and the TFV (not the Chambers) decides whether and how much of its 'other resources' may be used to fund ICC awards.[156] Therefore, the AC's findings were consistent with the principle of the offenders' liability for reparations to victims.

5.4 Reparation Types and Modalities

Concerning reparation types (individual/collective), the majority-female AC (*Lubanga*) found that some aspects of the majority-male TC-I's community-based approach to collective reparations were inconsistent with ICC reparation provisions.[157] By considering the plain meaning of 'community' and 'victims' within ICC instruments, the AC found that when an award is granted to a community, only community members who meet the relevant criteria are eligible: they must have suffered harm resulting from crimes that led to conviction.[158] Not all community

[149] ibid para 70.
[150] ibid; ICCS, Art 75(2).
[151] *Lubanga* (n 130) para 72; Rule 98(3).
[152] *Lubanga* (n 130) paras 74–75.
[153] ibid para 76.
[154] ibid paras 99–101.
[155] ibid paras 101–17.
[156] ibid paras 114–15.
[157] ibid.
[158] ibid paras 210–14.

members are necessarily reparations beneficiaries. Conversely, the IACtHR has ordered reparations for whole communities.[159] However, the majority-female AC's approach is sound since the ICC is a criminal court: unlike human rights courts, it determines criminal liability rather than State responsibility. The majority-female AC (*Lubanga*) rejected victims' request for both collective and individual reparations based upon textual interpretation of ICC instruments and its drafting history.[160]

According to the AC, victims could not demonstrate a right to consideration of individual reparation applications when the applicable law provides for both individual and collective reparations and a collective award was already made.[161] This may be criticized under teleological/purposive and dynamic/evolutive interpretations. Additionally, under Article 21(3), the AC should have closely considered a victim's general right to claim and receive reparations. However, this finding may be justified as reparation funding is scarce at the ICC and only a limited number of victims filed reparation claims in *Lubanga*. By considering IACtHR case-law, the AC remarked that individual and collective reparations are not mutually exclusive, and individual reparations should not divide communities.[162] Although TC-I in *Lubanga* only ordered individual awards, the majority-male TC-II (female Judge Olga Herrera-Carbuccia) in *Katanga* ordered collective and individual awards. TC-II's approach is more consistent with international standards.

Regarding reparation modalities, Article 75 only states that reparations include 'restitution, compensation and rehabilitation'. In upholding and refining the majority-male TC-I's findings, the majority-female AC (*Lubanga*) also invoked IHRL, in particular the UN-General Assembly Basic Principles and Guidelines on the Right to a Remedy and Reparation for Victims of Gross Violations of International Human Rights Law and Serious Violations of International Humanitarian Law (UNGA Reparation Principles),[163] IACtHR, and ECtHR case-law to flesh out these modalities.[164] The purpose of restitution is to restore the victim to his/her circumstances before the crime(s). Compensation includes physical, moral, and material damage, lost opportunities, and expenses. Rehabilitation includes medical, psychological, and socio-legal services. Conviction/sentence and measures raising awareness about crimes and harm are also reparations as they possess symbolic, preventative, or transformative value. By following similar principles/standards, the majority-male TC-II (female Judge Olga Herrera-Carbuccia) in *Lubanga* and *Katanga* identified and quantified material, physical,

[159] *Plan de Sánchez Massacre Case* (Reparations and Costs) IACtHR Series C no 116 (19 November 2004).
[160] *Lubanga* (n 130) paras 147–53, 157.
[161] ibid para 154.
[162] *Lubanga* (n 136) para 33.
[163] Resolution 60/147, 16 December 2005.
[164] *Lubanga* (n 136) paras. 34–43.

and psychological harm partially under IHRL.[165] Like other reparation matters, the all-male TC-VII (*Al-Mahdi*) followed these principles/standards.[166] This promotes coherent jurisprudence.

6. Conclusion: Human Rights-based Legitimacy Assessment

There are a number of legitimacy standards in literature and practice:[167] these concern both normative legitimacy (right to rule based on objective criteria) and sociological legitimacy (perceptions/beliefs).[168] This chapter uses human rights (specifically IHRL) to assess the examined jurisprudence for the following reasons. First, human rights constitute a (legitimacy) standard to assess the law and practice of international courts,[169] and are related to other (legitimacy) criteria such as rule of law, democracy, effectiveness, and efficiency.[170] Second, empirical studies show how important is for victims to participate and receive reparations at the ICC (sociological legitimacy).[171] Justice for victims is an important goal of the ICC: restorative justice, transitional justice, and IHRL victim standards have had an increasing influence,[172] which is related to normative legitimacy. Third, human rights may increase interpretative consistency or integration of the international judiciary amidst substantive/institutional fragmentation.[173] The ICC at which victims of mass atrocities exercise their rights belongs to a network of national/international (judicial) bodies. Fourth, under ICCS Article 21(3), 'application and interpretation of [ICC] law […] must be consistent with internationally recognized human rights'. Also, under Articles 21(1)(b) and 21(3), human rights are applicable at the ICC. ICC instruments contain defence and victim rights provisions. Therefore, human rights are useful to assess the legitimacy of ICC victim jurisprudence in which development female judges have played an important role as seen.

Overall, female ICC judges have clearly contributed to the development of the jurisprudence concerning victim rights to protection, participation, and reparations in criminal proceedings. Traditionally, international and regional human

165 ibid para 10; *Lubanga* (n 139) para. 245–81; *Katanga* (n 139) paras 181–264.

166 *Al-Mahdi* (Reparations Order) ICC-01/12-01/15-236 (17 August 2017).

167 Eg Carsten Stahn, 'Between 'Faith' and 'Facts'-By What Standards Should we Assess International Criminal Justice?' (2012) 25 Leiden Journal of International Law 251–282; UN-Secretary-General, *The Rule of Law and Transitional Justice in Conflict and Post-Conflict Societies* (2004), S/2004/616.

168 Langvatn and Squatrito (n 5) 43.

169 Eg Anne-Marie Brouwer and Mikaela Heikkilä, 'Victim Issues-Participation, Protection, Reparation, and Assistance' in Göran Sluiter and others (eds), *International Criminal Procedure* (OUP 2013) 1299–1374.

170 Jan Klabbers and others, *The Constitutionalization of International Law* (OUP 2011).

171 Eg Human Rights Center, *The Victims' Court? A Study of 622 Victim Participants at the International Criminal Court* (Berkeley, 2015).

172 Luke Moffett, *Justice for Victims before the International Criminal Court* (Routledge 2014) 39–50.

173 See Annika Jones, 'Insights Into an Emerging Relationship-Use of Human Rights Jurisprudence at the International Criminal Court' (2016) 16(4) Human Rights Law Review 701.

rights treaties did not explicitly recognize victim rights to protection and participation in criminal proceedings. In turn, regional human rights treaties recognized victim right to reparations, but without specifying criminal procedure-related reparations against the convicted. However, these gaps have been filled in by various international instruments: ECtHR/IACtHR case-law in examining alleged State violations of human rights treaties;[174] soft-law instruments, particularly, the UNGA Declaration of the Basic Principles of Justice for Victims of Crime and Abuse of Power, and the UNGA Reparation Principles; binding instruments, particularly, Directive 2012/29/EU on Victims; some (human rights) treaties like the UN Conventions against Torture and other Ill-Treatments, Enforced Dissapearance, and Transnational Organized Crime; and general principles as State practice evidences[175] despite common/civil-law and national systems differences.[176]

The jurisprudence on defence rights, to which female judges have contributed substantially, has largely sought to strike a balance between defence and victim rights. It has been largely consistent with the ICCS which requires protective measures and victim participation to not be 'prejudicial to or inconsistent with the rights of the accused and a fair and impartial trial'.[177] Inadmissible anonymous witnesses during trials and limited anonymous victim participation illustrate this. In turn, as the majority-female AC (*Lubanga*) determined, reparations are not to 'prejudice or be inconsistent with the rights of the convicted'.[178] Apart from some instances of pro-victim decisions, contributions of female ICC-judges to ICC victim jurisprudence have been generally consistent with ICC instruments and respect for defence rights. In any event, some jurisprudence on victims (partially) construed by female judges prompts questions on whether respect for defence rights or other ICC goals may have been compromised. Authors, including Salvatore Zappalà, Guido Acquaviva, Mikaela Heikkila, and Anne-Marie de Brouwer, have raised concerns about the negative effects of a judicially expanded victim status (particularly participation) on defence rights, including rights to: expeditious proceedings, an independent and impartial tribunal, fair trial and equality of arms, presumption of innocence, public trials, witness examination, and evidence-related matters.[179] Additionally, certain ICC victim jurisprudence has been partially questioned

[174] Eg *Kelly and Others v. UK* App no 30054/96 (ECtHR, 4 August 2001); *Blake Case* (Judgment) IACtHR Series C No. 36 (24 January 1998).

[175] Liesbeth Zegveld, 'Victims' Reparations Claims and International Criminal Courts' (2010) 8(1) Journal of International Criminal Justice 79, 85–86; Brouwer and Heikkilä (n. 167) 1367; Jean-Marie Henckaerts and Louise Doswald-Beck, *Customary International Humanitarian Law*, vol I (ICRC/CUP 2005) 554–555.

[176] Guido Acquaviva and Mikaela Heikkilä, 'Protective and Special Measures for Witnesses' in Sluiter and others (n 169) 854; Brouwer and Heikkilä (n 167) 1341–42.

[177] ICCS, Arts 68(1), 68(3).

[178] *Lubanga* (n 136) para 49.

[179] Salvatore Zappalà, 'The Rights of Victims v. the Rights of the Accused' (2010) 8(1) Journal of International Criminal Justice 137–164; Acquaviva and Heikkila (n 174) 1140; Brouwer and Heikkila (n 167) 1340–41; Van den Wyngaert (n 73) 475–96.

because of disruption of efficient and effective proceedings;[180] inconsistent judicial practices and interpretation;[181] and counter-productive effects by not meeting victims' expectations and victim-oriented goals,[182] amidst the need for State cooperation and involvement.[183] To address the said problems, female ICC judges may meaningfully contribute and/or continue their contributions due to their expertise and professional backgrounds. It is important for all ICC judges, including female judges, to take distance from excessive pro-victim judicial activism to fully respect defence rights, and avoid victim frustration.

[180] ibid 493.
[181] Sergey Vasiliev, 'Victim Participation Revisited?' in Carsten Stahn (ed), *The Law and Practice of the International Criminal Court* (OUP 2015) 1200–1202.
[182] Brouwer and Heikkilä, (n 167) 1346–47.
[183] See Moffett (n 172) 143–95.

19

Judicial Legal Culture and Victim Procedural Status at the Special Tribunal for Lebanon and Extraordinary Chambers in the Courts of Cambodia

Juan-Pablo Pérez-León-Acevedo

1. Introduction

This chapter examines the relationship between judicial legal culture and victim procedural practices at the Special Tribunal for Lebanon (STL) and the Extraordinary Chambers in the Courts of Cambodia (ECCC). Starting with judicial composition, judges are categorized by their professional and educational backgrounds *before* assuming their STL/ECCC judicial positions: whether they originate from the common law/adversarial system, the civil law/inquisitorial system, or the 'international' system. The mandatory quotas of Lebanese and Cambodian judges, in place due to the courts' hybrid nature, constitute an important factor: 3 out of 9 STL judges and 11 out of 17 ECCC judges must originate from the host countries—which have civil law legal systems. The chapter then investigates connections between STL/ECCC practices concerning victim procedural status and the typical features of the common law/adversarial, the civil law/inquisitorial, and the international system. In doing so, it identifies areas in which the legal culture of STL/ECCC judges may have impacted their approach towards victim procedural status.

When construing victim status, ECCC judges have largely adopted the inquisitorial system. Thus, victims participate as civil parties in the criminal proceedings and claim reparations. STL judges have combined civil law/inquisitorial and common law/adversarial elements. Victims can participate in criminal proceedings (civil law/inquisitorial system) but they cannot claim reparations (common law/adversarial system). Overall, STL and ECCC judges have adapted several civil law/inquisitorial and common law/adversarial features to make victim procedural status fit the mandate and characteristics of the STL and ECCC, namely, the presence of *sui generis* international features.

Juan-Pablo Pérez-León-Acevedo, *Judicial Legal Culture and Victim Procedural Status at the Special Tribunal for Lebanon and Extraordinary Chambers in the Courts of Cambodia* In: *Identity and Diversity on the International Bench.* Edited by: Freya Baetens, Oxford University Press (2020). © The several contributors. DOI: 10.1093/oso/9780198870753.003.0019.

2. Legal Culture of Judges

2.1. Legal Traditions and Legal Culture

This chapter considers the leading common law and civil law legal traditions. The civil law or continental European tradition is the most common legal tradition.[1] The common law tradition, originating from England, is currently applied in the United States, Canada, Australia, etc. Adversarial systems are associated with common law traditions and inquisitorial systems with civil law ones.[2] An adversarial proceeding takes 'its shape from a contest or dispute: it unfolds as an engagement of two adversaries before a relatively passive decision maker whose principal duty is to reach a verdict'.[3] A non-adversarial system is 'an official inquiry'.[4] The common law/adversarial system has passive judges, confrontational/dominant parties, and strict evidence rules, whereas the civil law/inquisitorial system contains active judges, more restrained parties, and more relaxed evidence rules. These features impact victim status: in common law systems, the role of victims is largely limited to that of witnesses.

However, the classification of national systems as inquisitorial or adversarial is difficult as 'criteria remain uncertain for the inclusion of specific features into the adversarial and the inquisitorial types'.[5] Moreover, inquisitorial systems have adopted adversarial features and vice-versa.[6] As for the purposes of this chapter, the main factor in terms of STL/ECCC judges' legal culture is their professional and educational background. For the majority of STL/ECCC judges, there is arguably a direct relationship between their legal education (concerning mainly their undergraduate law degrees) and their professional profiles/careers. A third category, besides common law and civil law, is 'international': this comprises of judges who had previously been judges at international(ized) criminal tribunals (ICTs) and/or international courts, or who had professional experience at international courts or international organizations *before* their judicial appointments at the STL/ECCC.

These disclaimers/caveats are made. This chapter summarizes/includes only career/bio information of each judge's highly accomplished career considered most relevant to this study and within length constraints. Career/bio information

[1] John Merryman, *The Civil Law Tradition* (2nd edn, Stanford University Press 1985) 1–3.

[2] George Cole and others, *Major Criminal Justice Systems* (2nd edn, Sage 1987) 23–26.

[3] Mirjan Damaška, *The Faces of Justice and State Authority-A Comparative Approach to the Legal Process* (Yale University Press 1986) 3.

[4] ibid.

[5] ibid 4.

[6] Alphons Orie, 'Accusatorial v. Inquisitorial Approach in International Criminal Proceedings Prior to the Establishment of the ICC and in the Proceedings Before the ICC' in Antonio Cassese and others (eds), *The Rome Statute of the International Criminal Court-A Commentary*, vol II (OUP 2002) 1441.

was obtained mainly from STL/ECCC websites—as of 1 July 2019. The categories employed and which judges correspond to each category are based on judges' profiles *before* their STL/ECCC appointments and are only for illustrative purposes of this study. Under other/additional considerations, the judicial composition of each category can change or there may be different categories. Judges may fall or fall in more than one category.

2.2 Special Tribunal for Lebanon (STL)

Based on an Agreement between the UN and the Lebanon (enforced by the Security Council), the STL was given jurisdiction over terrorist attacks who killed Lebanese Prime Minister Rafiq Hairiri and others. Article 8 of the STL Statute (Composition of the Chambers) establishes that the chambers consist of the following: one international Pre-Trial judge, three Trial Chamber judges (one Lebanese and two international judges), five Appeals Chamber (AC) judges (two Lebanese and three international judges), and two alternate judges (one Lebanese judge and one international judge). Article 9 of the STL Statute (Qualification and appointment of judges) establishes that:

1. The judges shall be persons of high moral character, impartiality and integrity, with extensive judicial experience […].
2. In the overall composition of the Chambers, due account shall be taken of the established competence of the judges in criminal law and procedure and international law.

As of 1 July 2019, there have been 14 STL judges, including current, former, and alternate judges.[7] Based on the information on their profiles obtained mainly from the STL's web-page,[8] this chapter divides them in three main groups. First, while there are ten STL judges who have civil law/inquisitorial background in terms of their (first) law degrees, six of them are considered under the 'international' category due to their experience as judges, etc. at international(ized) (criminal) courts and/or their positions/experience at international organizations/international institutions *before* their STL appointments. This would leave four judges (or 28.57%) in the civil law category. Pre-Trial Judge Daniel Fransen (Belgium) worked as a defence lawyer and an investigating judge in Brussels. He specialized in international

[7] <www.stl-tsl.org/en/about-the-stl/biographies/judges-of-the-special-tribunal-for-lebanon> accessed 1 July 2019.

[8] ibid. Concerning some judges, these websites were also consulted: <www.geneva-academy.ch/masters/study-with-us/faculty/detail/34-robert-roth> <www.waikato.ac.nz/law/about-us/staff/honorary/david-baragwanath> <www.linkedin.com/in/kjell-bj%C3%B6rnberg-ab6660119/?originalSubdomain=se&fbclid=IwAR38Tl_yZAlXMDOtThbDwSvrb49PYj2VbvS6K9AjGyl2lk4k463U3CX-5xc> <www.worldlitigationforum.org/speaker/ivana-hrdlickova/> accessed 1 July 2019.

humanitarian law (IHL)/terrorism cases. AC Judge Afif Chamseddine (Lebanon) worked in the Lebanese judiciary, namely, he was president of the Third Criminal Chamber of the Court of Cassation, a member of both the Court of Justice and the Supreme Council of the Judiciary, etc. Trial Chamber Judge Micheline Braidy (Lebanon) also developed a career in the Lebanese judiciary, more precisely she was a judge at the Service des Législations et des Consultations, the Criminal Chamber of the Court of Appeal of Mount Lebanon, and the Court of Cassation. Trial Chamber-Alternate Judge Walid Akoum (Lebanon) also came from the Lebanese judiciary, including that he was a Court of Cassation member and presided the Indictment Chamber of South Lebanon.

Second, while there are four STL judges who have a common law/adversarial background, they are considered under the 'international' category as they had been international judges and/or had experience at international(ized) (criminal) courts/international organizations before their STL appointments.

Third, ten out of the 14 STL judges (or 71.42%) had experience as international judges and/or acquired experience at international organizations/international institutions before their STL appointments. Judge Ralph Riachi (Lebanon) served as *ad-litem* judge at the International Criminal Tribunal for the former Yugoslavia (ICTY). He developed his career in the Lebanese judicial system, including president of both the Court of Appeal of Mount Lebanon and the Court of Cassation Criminal Chamber. AC Judge Daniel Nsereko (Uganda) was a judge at the Appeals Chamber of the International Criminal Court (ICC). Additionally, he worked as an advocate in the High Court of Uganda and studied law in Tanzania and the United States. In addition to his law practice in Australia, Trial Chamber-President Judge David Re (Australia) was an ICTY senior prosecuting trial attorney and an international judge at the War Crimes Chamber of the Court of Bosnia and Herzegovina. Trial Chamber Judge Janet Nosworthy (Jamaica) served as an ICTY *ad-litem* judge in trial, pre-trial, and sentencing cases. She was also, *inter alia*, an international criminal law consultant at the Caribbean Community. Trial Chamber-Alternate Judge Nicola Lettieri (Italy) was a European Court of Human Rights (ECtHR) ad-hoc judge, and a co-agent before the ECtHR. He also worked, *inter alia*, at the Supreme Court of Cassation (Italy) and was a judge at the Constitutional Court (San Marino).

Late STL-President Antonio Cassese was previously president of the ICTY, Chairman of the Council of Europe Steering Committee on Human Rights, President of the Council of Europe Committee against Torture, Chairman of the UN International Commission of Inquiry into Genocide in Darfur (Sudan), and Independent Expert appointed by the UN Secretary-General to review the efficiency of the Special Court for Sierra Leone (SCSL). Appeals Chamber (AC) Judge and STL-President Ivana Hrdličková (Czech Republic) served as a domestic judge. She wrote a PhD on international and Islamic law. She was a Council of Europe Expert on human rights, money laundering, and terrorism financing, and participated in international legal projects on transitional justice, judicial independence, and the rule of law. AC Judge David Baragwanath (New Zealand), *inter alia*, was a Permanent Court of Arbitration member, a judge of the High Court and Court of Appeal of New Zealand, and president of the Samoan Court of Appeal. Former STL-Trial Chamber Judge Robert Roth (Switzerland) has been an international criminal law professor and was law faculty dean at the University of Geneva, contributing to create the Geneva Academy of IHL/Human Rights. He has been a steering committee member of the European Criminal Law Academic Network. Former AC Judge Kjell Bjornberg (Sweden), *inter alia*, was Chamber President of the Court of Appeal for Western Sweden, was a European Commission Expert, and headed the UN Judicial System Assessment Programme in Bosnia-Herzegovina.

Out of the ten STL judges considered here as having an 'international' profile, six originally had a civil law background while four had a common law background. Concerning first law degrees (and, where applicable, post-graduate law degrees), four STL judges hold common law degrees (28.57%), and ten STL judges hold civil law degrees (71.43%). Out of the ten non-Lebanese STL judges: nine had international experience as judges, etc. at international(ized) (criminal) courts and/or experience at international organizations/institutions before their appointment at the STL. Four hold common law degrees and six hold civil law degrees. As for the four Lebanese STL judges: one had international judicial experience before his STL appointment; all of them hold civil law degrees but seemingly none holds a (first) common law degree.

2.3 Extraordinary Chambers in the Courts of Cambodia (ECCC)

Under Article 3(2) ('Judges') of the Agreement between the UN and Cambodia concerning the prosecution of crimes committed during Democratic Kampuchea (ECCC-Agreement)[9] and Article 9 of the Law on the Establishment of the Extraordinary Chambers (ECCC-Law),[10] the ECCC-Chambers consist of three Cambodian and two international judges (Trial Chamber), and four Cambodian and three international judges (Supreme Court Chamber). Under Article 20new, the ECCC-Pre-Trial Chamber has three Cambodian and two international judges. Like Article 10new of the ECCC-Law, ECCC Agreement Article 3 provides for:

> 3. The judges shall be persons of high moral character, impartiality and integrity who possess the qualifications required in their respective countries for appointment to judicial offices […]

[9] UNGA Res 57/228B (22 May 2003) (Annex).
[10] Including amendments promulgated on 27 October 2004 (NS/RKM/1004/006).

4. In the overall composition of the Chambers due account should be taken of the experience of the judges in criminal law, international law, including international humanitarian law and human rights law.

As of 1 July 2019, there have been identified 29 ECCC Pre-Trial, Trial, and Supreme Court Chambers Judges, including current, former, and reserve judges. Since these chambers adopted the case-law decisions examined herein and for better comparisons with the STL, ECCC-Co-Investigating Judges are excluded here. Under the three categories (civil law/inquisitorial, common law/adversarial, international) used, this chapter relies largely on the information found on the online profiles of the judges (ECCC website).[11]

First, 16 ECCC judges (or 55.17%) would fall in the civil law category. Current Pre-Trial Chamber-President, Judge Prak Kimsan (Cambodia), has been a Supreme Court Judge and was a Prosecutor before the Supreme Court. Pre-Trial Chamber Judge Huot Vuthy (Cambodia), *inter alia*, has been a prosecutor and was an Advisor of the Documentation Center for Cambodia (Cambodian genocide research). Pre-Trial Chamber Judge Ney Thol (Cambodia) has presided over the Cambodian Military Court. Pre-Trial Chamber Judge (Reserve) Pen Pichsaly (Cambodia) has been a national judge. Pre-Trial Chamber Judge Kang Jin Baik (South Korea) was a Seoul High Court judge, etc. and obtained a US LL.M. degree and completed a SJD programme (Seoul). Former Pre-Trial Chamber Judge Katinka Lahuis (Netherlands) has been an appeal criminal justice, and was a Public Prosecutor, and a lawyer. She was also an investigating judge, and presiding judge in the criminal law, pre-trial, and extradition divisions.

Trial Chamber-President Judge Nil Nonn (Cambodia) has been Siem Reap Court President after presiding over the Battambang Court. Trial Chamber Judge Thou Mony (Reserve) (Cambodia) has been a Cambodian Court of Appeals Judge, and served at the Ministry of Justice. Former Trial Chamber Judge Jean-Marc Lavergne (France) was Presiding Judge of the Criminal Appeals Court of Loire-Atlantique and Morbihan, and was a Parole Judge at the High Civil Court of Angers. Trial Chamber Judge Ya Sokhan (Cambodia) has been nominated Supreme Court Judge (2009), was a Banteay Meanchey Court Judge, a Phnom Penh Municipal Court Judge, etc. Trial Chamber Judge You Ottara (Cambodia) has been a Supreme Court Judge. He worked in the Justice Ministry (international affairs, etc.). Judge Kong Srim (Cambodia), who is the Supreme Court Chamber-President, *inter alia*, has been (recently) Deputy Chief at the Supreme Court and a Supreme Council of Magistracy member and he was Deputy General Prosecutor. Supreme Court Chamber Judge Som Sereyvuth (Cambodia) has been a Judge of the Cambodian Supreme Court

[11] <www.eccc.gov.kh/en/organs/judicial-chambers> <www.eccc.gov.kh/en/judicial-chamber/supreme-court-chamber> Concerning some judges, these web-pages were also consulted: <www.icc-cpi.int/CourtStructure/Pages/judge.aspx?name=Judge%20Chang-ho%20Chung>web-pages accessed 1 July 2019.

and Head of Examination Department. Supreme Court Chamber Judge Sin Rith (Reserve) (Cambodia) was, *inter alia*, appointed as the Lead Prosecutor before the Cambodian Supreme Court, a Ministry of Justice Legal Officer, and a Deputy Prosecutor. Supreme Court Chamber Judge Ya Narin (Cambodia) is Mundulkiri Court President, and served as a Rattanakiri Court President. Supreme Court Chamber judge Mong Monichariya (Cambodia) has been Preah Sihanouk Provincial Court Chief Judge from 2009. He was appointed as a Supreme Court Judge, was a Phnom Penh Judge, etc.

Second, there have been eight ECCC judges who hold first common law degrees. Among them, there would be two ECCC judges (or 6.89%) whose legal careers had seemingly developed predominantly in common law/adversarial systems before their ECCC appointments. Pre-Trial Chamber-Reserve Judge Steven Bwana (Tanzania) was a judge and administrator of the High Court of Tanzania, Court of Appeal of Tanzania and Court of Appeal of Seychelles. Supreme Court Chamber judge Chandra Nihal Jayasinghe (Sri Lanka) was, *inter alia*, Presiding Judge of the Supreme Court of Sri Lanka, President of the Court of Appeal of Sri Lanka, and Sri Lanka High Commissioner to the United Kingdom.

Third, eleven identified ECCC judges (37.93%) had experience as international judges and/or experience at international criminal justice institutions or international bodies/international organisations before their ECCC appointments. Trial Chamber Judge Claudia Fenz (Austria) was an international judge with the UN Interim Administration Mission in Kosovo (UNMIK), including war crimes, and Head of the Rule of Law Section within the EUPOLCOPPS Mission in Palestine. Additionally, she served as a national judge. Trial Chamber Judge Martin Karopkin (Reserve) (USA) was a UNMIK international judge. He was also, *inter alia*, a New York City Criminal Court Judge and an Acting Justice of the New York Supreme Court. Supreme Court Chamber Judge Florence Ndepele Mwachande Mumba (Zambia) was a Judge at the ICTY and International Criminal Tribunal for Rwanda (ICTR) AC. She also served on the UN Commission on the Status of Women, participating in resolutions that characterized rape as a war crime. She is also a Zambian Supreme Court Judge. Former Supreme Court Chamber Judge Agnieszka Klonowiecka-Milart (Poland) was a UNMIK international judge, worked (seconded) at the Polish Justice Ministry, etc. Former Trial Chamber Judge Silvia Cartwright (New Zealand) had been a High Court Judge and a member of the UN Committee on the UN Convention to Eliminate All Forms of Discrimination against Women. Former Pre-Trial Chamber Judge Rowan Downing (Australia) was a Judge of the Court of Appeal and Supreme Court of Vanuatu, worked with multilateral organizations, etc. Former Pre-Trial Chamber Judge Chang-ho Chung (South Korea) was a Legal Advisor and Korean Delegate to the UN Commission on International Trade Law at the Republic of Korea's Embassy/Permanent Mission in Vienna, a high court judge, a district court judge, a court martial judge, etc. He holds a LLM in international law. Pre-Trial Chamber judge Olivier Beauvallet (France), *inter alia*, was a prosecutor within the Special Investigative Task Force and within the Special Prosecution Office of the EULEX Mission in Kosovo, involving war crimes, was an investigative judge (France), etc.

Reserve Supreme Court Chamber Judge Phillip Rapoza (USA) was an international judge at the Special Panels for Serious Crimes in Timor-Leste, dealing with crimes against humanity and other serious offenses. In the USA, he is court of appeals' chief justice, and was a prosecutor, a defence lawyer, and a trial judge. Former Pre-Trial Chamber judge Catherine Marchi-Uhel (France) was, *inter alia*, a UNMIK international judge, an ICTY/ICTR Appeals Chamber Senior Legal Officer, and ICTY Head of Chambers. Former Supreme Court Chamber Judge Motoo Noguchi (Japan) had been a national prosecutor, a visiting professional at the ICC, a legal counsel (seconded) at the Asian Development Bank, etc. He also professionally/academically worked on international (criminal) law.

Out of the eleven ECCC judges of 'international' profiles, six had original civil law backgrounds and five had original common law backgrounds. Concerning first law degrees, seven ECCC judges hold common law degrees (24.14%) while 22 ECCC Judges have civil law degrees (75.86%). Out of the 16 international judges (non-Cambodian nationals) 11 had international judicial experience at international(ized) courts and/or experience in international bodies/ international(ized) courts before their ECCC appointments, 3 have civil law profiles, and 2 have common law profiles. Seven hold first common law degrees while 9 hold first civil law degrees. Concerning the 13 Cambodian ECCC judges, their ECCC appointments constituted their first international level judicial positions and all of them hold civil law degrees.

3. Judicial Practices on Victim Procedural Status

3.1 Context

In civil law/inquisitorial and common law/adversarial systems and at ICTs, victims may be witnesses,[12] and thus provide evidence (testimony) of their personal knowledge of relevant facts. Additionally, in civil law/inquisitorial systems such as France,[13] Lebanon,[14] and Cambodia,[15] victims can be civil parties to criminal

[12] Marion Brienen and Ernestine Hoegen, *Victims of Crime in 22 European Criminal justice Systems* (Wolf Legal Publishers 2000) 27; Jonathan Doak, *Victims' Rights, Human Rights and Criminal Justice* (Hart 2008) 245; Orie (n 6) 1446, 1458, 1466, 1478.

[13] Code of Criminal Procedure (CPP-France), Arts 2, 85, 87.

[14] 2001 CPP-Lebanon, Arts 7, 68.

[15] 2007 CPP-Cambodia, Arts 13–14, 138, 142.

Table 19.1 Judges' profiles

Hybrid criminal courts	STL	ECCC
Some analytical categories		
I. Judicial legal culture/legal profile *before* appointment at STL or ECCC		
Common law/adversarial	0 (0%)	2 (6.9%)
Civil law/inquisitorial	4 (28.6%)	16 (55.2%)
International profile	10 (71.4.%)	11 (37.9%)
Number of current and former judges	14 (100%)	29 (100%)
II. National vs. international judges		
National judges, ie, Lebanese (STL) or Cambodians (ECCC)	4 (28.6%)	13 (44.8%)
International judges	10 (71.4%)	16 (55.2%)
Number of current and former judges	14 (100%)	29 (100%)

proceedings to obtain the accused's guilt and compensation.[16] Civil claims adhere to criminal proceedings ('adhesion model').[17] Not all civil parties seek reparations; however, victims who seek reparations in criminal proceedings must be civil parties.[18] In common law adversarial/adversarial systems, victims are not civil parties, they are witnesses.[19] However, in common law/adversarial systems, there can be victim participation via victim impact statements[20] during sentencing in, for example, the USA[21] and England.[22] Occasionally, victims can participate during certain appeals.[23] Moreover, victims may benefit from compensation orders (penalties against the convicted)[24] in, *inter alia*, England[25] and USA.[26] At ICTs, victims were traditionally only witnesses, reflecting the common law/adversarial tradition.[27] The practice of the ICTY, ICTR, and SCSL illustrates this. However, victims at the ICC can also apply to be victim participants to express their own views and

16 Valérie Dervieux, 'The French System' in Mireille Delmas-Marty and John Spencer (eds), *European Criminal Procedures* (CUP 2002) 227.
17 Brienen and Hoegen (n 12) 27.
18 Nathalie Pignoux, *La Réparation des Victimes d'infractions Pénales* (L'Harmattan 2008) 253, 262.
19 John Spencer, 'The English System' in Mireille Delmas-Marty and John Spencer (eds), *European Criminal Procedures* (CUP 2002) 156.
20 Brienen and Hoegen (n 12) 481.
21 Crime Victims' Rights Act (CVRA), 18 U.S.C § 3771(a)(4).
22 Practice Direction (Victim Personal Statements) [2002] 1 Cr App R (S) 482.
23 Eg CVRA, § 3771(d)(3).
24 Brienen and Hoegen (n 12) 28.
25 Powers of Criminal Conducts (Sentencing) Act 2000, Section 130(4).
26 CVRA, § 3 771(a)(6).
27 Orie (n 6) 1446, 1458, 1466, 1478.

concerns.[28] Additionally, victims can apply for reparations against defendants in ICC post-conviction proceedings.[29]

The judicially-drafted STL-Rules of Procedure and Evidence (STL-Rules) incorporated adversarial and inquisitorial features,[30] but the STL-Procedure is inquisitorial-oriented in several aspects.[31] Under Article 28(2) of the STL Statute, Judges were guided in drafting the STL Rules by 'the Lebanese Code of Criminal Procedure [and] […] materials reflecting the highest standards of international criminal procedure'. According to Rule 3, interpretation of STL Rules requires consideration of the Vienna Convention on the Law of Treaties, international human rights standards, general principles of international criminal law and procedure, and the Lebanese Code of Criminal Procedure. The judicially-adopted STL Rules Explanatory Memorandum (Rules Memorandum) acknowledge the inquisitorial system, particularly the Lebanese one, while the STL Procedure is 'substantially based on the adversarial system'.[32] By invoking the ECCC Agreement and ECCC Law, the ECCC Trial Chamber determined that it operates under applicable Cambodian procedural law as consolidated via ECCC Internal Rules (ECCC Rules) tailored to ECCC proceedings and, in cases of uncertainty, 'guidance is also sought from procedural rules established at the international level, where appropriate'.[33] International criminal procedure has been generally more adversarial-oriented. For example, ECCC Rule 21(1)(a) states that 'ECCC proceedings shall be fair and adversarial'.

3.2 STL

3.2.1 Victim status

As before other ICTs, victims are witnesses at the STL. Witnesses (and also victim participants) are entitled to protective measures,[34] which mainly follow the common law/adversarial tradition.[35] Under the STL-Statute, victim participation involves that:

> Where the personal interests of the victims are affected, the Special Tribunal shall permit their views and concerns to be presented and considered at stages of the

[28] ICC-Statute, Art 68(3).
[29] ICC-Statute, Art 75.
[30] STL-President, Rules of Procedure and Evidence-Explanatory Memorandum, 2009, paras 2–4.
[31] Salvatore Zappalà, 'Comparative Models and the Enduring Relevance of the Accusatorial-Inquisitorial Dichotomy' in Göran Sluiter and others (eds), *International Criminal Procedure* (OUP 2013) 44, 52–53.
[32] STL-President (n 30) para 4.
[33] *Case 001* (Judgment) 001/18-07-2007/ECCC/TC (26 July 2010), para 35.
[34] STL-Statute, Art 28; STL-Rule 133.
[35] Juan-Pablo Perez-Leon-Acevedo, *Victims' Status at International and Hybrid Criminal Courts* (Abo Akademi 2014) 228–35, 278–80.

> proceedings determined to be appropriate by the Pre-Trial Judge or the Chamber and in a manner that is not prejudicial to or inconsistent with the rights of the accused and a fair and impartial trial.[36]

As the Rules-Memorandum details, victim participation may take place at various procedural stages.[37] Article 25 does not provide for 'civil parties' since victim participants cannot claim reparations for crime-related harm.[38] The Rules-Memorandum invoked the UN Secretary General's Report on the STL to clarify that the presentation of victims' views and concerns does not make them civil parties so the concept of 'civil parties' as a distinctive civil law feature is absent.[39] As the Rules-Memorandum states: 'the main *raison d'être* of "*parties civiles*", namely, their participation in criminal proceedings for the purpose of seeking compensation, is removed'.[40] Unlike in common law systems and at previous ICTs, victims at the STL cannot receive judicial compensation orders as penalties against the convicted. However, Article 25 of the STL Statute and Rule 86(G) foresaw victims' compensation claims at national courts for which STL judgments are binding. As the Rules-Memorandum stipulates victim participation at the STL 'may prove of enormous value' for identifying purposes related to national compensation.[41] According to the STL-Appeals Chamber, victim participation is not a condition to seek national judicial compensation.[42]

According to the Rules-Memorandum, the STL-Rules drafters (STL judges), 'deemed it fair and appropriate to grant extensive participation in proceedings to victims' although STL proceedings do not seek to determine compensation but rather to establish the accused's criminal responsibility.[43] By invoking the French system, the Rules-Memorandum emphasizes that victim action does not depend on damages claims nor does civil action admissibility imply that damages will be awarded to victims.[44] STL Rules drafters (STL judges) remarked that active victim participation may be important because victims can present views and concerns that the prosecution and defence may have neglected.[45] As for victim participant definition, STL judges drafted the Rules to limit the number of victim participants and to avoid 'flooding' the Tribunal.[46] A 'victim participant' is someone 'granted leave by the Pre-Trial Judge to present his views and concerns' at one or more procedural stages, whereas a 'victim' is 'a natural person who has

36 STL-Statute, Art 25.
37 STL-President (n 30) para 14.
38 ibid.
39 ibid.
40 ibid.
41 ibid para 15.
42 *Ayyash et al.* (Decision on Appeal by Legal Representative of Victims Against Pre-Trial Judge's Decision on Protective Measures) STL-11-01/PT/AC/AR126.3 (10 April 2013), para 34.
43 STL-President (n 30) para 15.
44 ibid.
45 ibid.
46 ibid para 17.

suffered physical, material, or mental harm as a direct result of an attack within the Tribunal's jurisdiction'.[47]

Unlike the ICC or the Lebanese Code of Criminal Procedure, Rule 86(A) of the STL Statute does not authorize victim participation before the confirmation of indictment.[48] As the Rules Memorandum explains, this is to avoid hampering prosecution and to prevent delays.[49] This exclusion may be justified by prosecutorial consideration of factors other than victim interests, 'fabricated requests' to infiltrate investigation, and lack of civil law investigating judges who gather evidence and lead investigations.[50] Subsequent revocation of the victim participant status and problems with defence rights may also be relevant.[51] However, prosecutorial actions during investigation may affect victims. Such an exclusion is a step backwards from the ICC and civil law/inquisitorial proceedings. As the ICC did,[52] STL judges could have considered balanced solutions, including victim participation limited to judicial proceedings within investigation. Compared to the ICC and the ECCC, victim participants are (much) less numerous at the STL. Thus, concerns about delays are not fully justified. Actually, victim status is already limited: victims cannot claim reparations at the STL.

Under Rule 86, alleged victims of crimes under STL jurisdiction have to apply for victim participant status before the Pre-Trial Judge who shall consider whether 'the applicant provided *prima facie* evidence that he/she is a Rule 2 victim'; an 'applicant's personal interests are affected'; an applicant intends to express his/her views and concerns; and an applicant's participation would be prejudicial to or inconsistent with the accused's rights and a fair and impartial trial.[53] The Pre-Trial Judge noted that these criteria are cumulative for granting the victim participant status and that applicants do not need to prove other factors.[54] Nevertheless, the victim participant status does not grant automatic participation. The Pre-Trial Judge or competent Chamber decides whether and how victim participants may present their views and concerns if this 'is not prejudicial or inconsistent with the rights of the accused and a fair and impartial trial'.[55] Like at the ICC, this need for judicial authorization to participate corresponds to the victim status at the STL: participants and not civil parties, unlike at the ECCC or in civil law

47 STL-Rule 2(A).

48 STL-President (n 30) para 19.

49 ibid.

50 Jérôme de-Hemptinne, 'Challenges Raised by Victims' Participation in the Proceedings of the Special Tribunal for Lebanon' (2010) 8 Journal of International Criminal Justice 165 173.

51 ibid 174.

52 *Situation in the DRC* (Decision on Victims' Participation in Proceedings Relating to the Situation in the Democratic Republic of Congo) ICC-01/04-593 (11 April 2011).

53 STL-Rule 86(B)(i)(iv).

54 *Ayyash et al.* (Decision on Victims' Participation in the Proceedings) STL-11-01/PT/PTJ (8 May 2012), paras 24–25. See also Anne-Marie de-Brouwer and Mikaela Heikkilä, 'Victim Issues' in Sluiter and others (n 31) 1306.

55 STL-Statute, Art 17.

jurisdictions. Victim participants have to show that, *inter alia*, their personal interests are affected to be judicially allowed to participate.

Rule 150(D) (Testimony of Witnesses) originally precluded that victim participants could also be witnesses (dual status): victim participants 'shall not be permitted to give evidence unless a Chamber decides that the interests of justice so require'. Victims had to decide whether to be participants or witnesses. The Rules-Memorandum reckoned that parties may later realize the importance of certain victims as witnesses and respectively apply to the Chamber.[56] However, the Plenary of STL judges in February 2012 amended Rule 150(D): victim participants 'may be permitted to give evidence if a Chamber decides that the interests of justice so require'. As the Plenary stated, the original Rule 150 (D) was unduly restrictive.[57] This amendment reverses the presumption of inadmissible dual status victim participants/witnesses via the admissibility of dual status victim participants/witnesses. As the Rules-Memorandum points out, this amendment also harmonizes Rule 150(D) with Article 17 of the STL Statute, which recognizes that victim participants shall be permitted or even required to express their views and concerns through their legal representatives when the Pre-Trial Judge or Chamber considers it appropriate.[58] Since Rule 150(A) requires that witnesses make a solemn declaration before testifying, it is implied that victim participants should give evidence 'under oath'. Finally, as the STL judges plenary pointed out,[59] the Trial Chamber determines the manners in which witnesses who are also victim participants must give evidence. In *Ayyash et al.*, it was determined that tailored protective measures may be required for dual status victim participants/witnesses and that these 'must be managed carefully in order to safeguard the rights of the accused to a fair and expeditious trial, as well as the interests of the Prosecution and [victim participants] themselves'.[60]

3.2.2 Procedural rights

On the question of victim participant procedural rights, the ICC practice and law have arguably influenced the STL judges. Several victim procedural rights applied by STL judges *mutatis mutandis* resemble procedural rights held by civil parties in civil law/inquisitorial systems. Victim participant procedural rights during the pre-trial phase resemble those at the ICC,[61] as well as those held by civil parties in civil law/inquisitorial systems. However, since victims can only participate after confirmation of the indictment, procedural rights during the pre-trial phase are

56 STL-President (n 30) para 20.
57 Fourth Plenary of Judges, February 2012, p 19.
58 STL-President, Rules of Procedure and Evidence-Explanatory Memorandum, 2012, para 21.
59 ibid para 19.
60 *Ayyash et al.* (Decision on the VPU's Access to Materials and the Modalities of Victims' Participation in Proceedings before the Pre-Trial Judge) STL-11-01/PT/PTJ (18 May 2012), para 61.
61 Eg *Katanga/Ngudjolo-Chui* (Decision on the Set of Procedural Rules Attached to Procedural Status of Victim at the Pre-Trial Stage of the Case) ICC-01/047-01/07-474 (13 May 2008).

more limited than those at the ICC and in civil law/inquisitorial jurisdictions. At the STL, victim participants hold the following procedural rights: access by their common legal representatives to case files (except for confidential/*ex parte* documents), *inter parte* 'disclosed' materials under restrictions, and confidential information under conditions; attendance at hearings, except for those excluded by the Pre-Trial Judge; participation in hearings not excluded by the Pre-Trial Judge; and written submissions not excluded by STL instruments.[62]

There are similarities between victim participant procedural rights at the STL vis-à-vis civil party rights in civil law jurisdictions/ECCC and, especially, victim participant rights at the ICC,[63] during both trials and appeals. Overall, STL Rules follow the law and practice of the ICC, including procedural rights not listed in the ICC Rules but developed in the ICC jurisprudence. Procedural rights during trial include the right to notification of decisions; access to documents though confidential and *ex parte* materials are excluded from this; attend and participate in public and closed hearings; participate orally, including opening and closing statements; file written motions and briefs; tender evidence; question witnesses and the accused; testify under oath; and propose/call witnesses to testify.[64] As well as establishing that victim participants are not parties, the STL Trial Chamber has invoked the ICC's practice on victim participation.[65]

Unlike civil parties, victim participants at the STL lack the right to support the prosecution. Nevertheless, they may be allowed to lead and challenge evidence on the accused's guilt, which could be considered as support of the prosecution. This right may be controversial: the defendant would face two accusers and victim participants are not civil parties. However, determination of the judicial truth as part of the mandate of ICTs, including the STL, may exceptionally justify this. Nevertheless, judges must respect defence rights. To exercise this and other procedural rights such as calling, examining, or cross-examining witnesses, and filing motions and briefs, Rule 87(B) soundly requires that the Trial Chamber authorizes these rights after hearing both parties. STL judges have banned anonymous victim participation during trial to protect defence rights.[66] This may be criticized. STL-Rules exceptionally authorizes anonymous witnesses. Moreover, witness anonymity is allowed in several common law[67] and civil law national jurisdictions.[68] Unlike witness testimonies, victim participant statements are not evidence. Therefore, anonymous victim participation should have been allowed. STL judges should have adopted half-way approaches to balance victim and defence rights.

[62] *Ayyash et al.* (n 54).
[63] Eg *Lubanga* (Decision on Victims' Participation) ICC-01/04-01/06-1119 (18 January 2008).
[64] STL-Rules 87(B), 143, 144(B), 146(A), 146(B)(ii), 147(A), 168(A).
[65] *Ayyash et al.* (Directions on the Conduct of the Proceedings) STL-11-01/T/TC (16 January 2014), para 2.
[66] *Ayyash et al.* (n 42) paras 27–39.
[67] Eg England, New Zealand, USA.
[68] Eg The Netherlands, Poland, Germany.

For example, the ICC allows anonymous victim participation during trial but with limited procedural rights.

Concerning appeals, STL-Rules recognize potential victim participation, including participation in appeals of the judgment (verdict), sentence, and interlocutory appeals triggered by the parties. However, victim participants cannot appeal the Trial Chamber judgment/sentence. Rule 177(B) only mentions 'party' as holders of this right. The Rules-Memorandum explicitly stresses it.[69] Besides victim participation in interlocutory appeals, the STL-Appeals Chamber determined that victim participants hold a narrow non-automatic right to appeal interlocutory decisions in confined circumstances when their personal interests are fundamentally affected, namely, decisions on victim participant status applications,[70] victim participation modalities, protective measures, and variations thereof,[71] and certain disclosure matters.[72] The STL-Appeal Chamber considered not to be bound by ICC jurisprudence under which victim participants cannot appeal interlocutory decisions.[73] That victim participants can appeal certain interlocutory decisions at the STL partially resembles the civil party right to appeal several interlocutory decisions in national civil law jurisdictions[74] and the ECCC.[75] Regarding sentencing, Rule 87(C) establishes that, subject to Trial Chamber's authorization, victim participants 'may be heard […] or file written submissions relating to the personal impact of the crimes on them'. This resembles ICC practice. Rule 87(C) is *mutatis mutandis* similar to victim impact statements for sentencing in common law/adversarial jurisdictions.

Under Article 17 of the STL Statute, victim participation shall be conducted in 'a manner that is not prejudicial to or inconsistent with the rights of the accused and a fair and impartial trial'. Thus, STL judges included specific STL Rules. First, the Trial Chamber can under Rule 87(B) discretionally authorize the exercise of certain victim procedural rights such as calling witness, authorization to tender other evidence, witness examination and cross-examination and filing of motions and briefs. Second, under Rule 86(C)(ii), victim participants may only participate 'through a legal representative unless the Pre-Trial Judge authorizes otherwise' as applied in *Ayyash et al.* This resembles the ECCC but differs from the ICC Rules under which legal representation is mainly a right rather than a requirement. However, the STL Rules are consistent with the fact that victims generally participate via lawyers at ICTs. Under Rule 86(C), victim participants are in principle

69 STL-President (n 30) para 16.
70 Rule 86(C).
71 *Ayyash et al.* (n 42) paras 9, 15.
72 Rules 116(D)-(E).
73 *Ayyash et al.* (n 42) para 17.
74 Eg CPP (France), Arts 81, 82–81, 87, 156, 167, 175(1), 186(1).
75 Rule 74(4).

treated as a single group unless valid reasons under Rule 86(D)(i) justify otherwise. In *Ayyash et al.*, victim participants have participated as a single group via common legal representatives.[76] STL judges envisioned legal representation on behalf of multiple victims to avoid 'flooding' the STL.[77] Grouping of victim participants by the Pre-Trial Judge and exceptional direct victim participation may save time and other resources as *Ayyash et al.* demonstrates.[78] Third, Rule 86(C) originally contemplated that the Pre-Trial Judge could limit the number of victim participants. Although STL judges have deleted this, the Trial Chamber may still adopt similar practices.

These measures reflect an active judicial role: a feature of civil law/inquisitorial systems.[79] They are necessary to allow victim participation whilst not affecting defence rights and/or procedural efficiency. However, victim participation at the STL is almost always exercised throughout common legal representatives, which differs from the direct victim participation in national civil law jurisdictions where there is no need for common lawyers, letting alone mandatory legal representation. Nevertheless, this is justified because the numbers of victim participants are higher at the STL than in national civil law/inquisitorial systems.

3.3 The ECCC

3.3.1 Victim status

Judges have modified ECCC Rules several times, including the civil party regime. However, as the Supreme Court Chamber noted, the civil party definition had 'remained essentially unchanged'.[80] Due to the influence of the French civil law/inquisitorial system via Cambodian law as reflected in the ECCC-Rules, the ECCC introduced civil parties at ICTs and, once victims are admitted as civil parties, they hold several procedural rights as highlighted by the Supreme Court Chamber.[81] Under Rule 23(1), the dual purpose of civil party action is to 'participate in criminal proceedings against those responsible within the jurisdiction of the ECCC by supporting the prosecution' and 'seek collective and moral reparations'. This reflects civil law jurisdictions.[82] Under Rule 23 *quinquies*, 'if an Accused is convicted, the Chambers may award only collective and moral reparations to Civil Parties'. As

[76] *Ayyash et al.* (n 54) paras 112, 119–20, 127.
[77] STL-President (n 30) paras 17–18.
[78] *Ayyash et al.* (n 54) paras 108–28.
[79] Orie (n 6) 1443–44.
[80] *Case 001* (Appeal Judgment) 001/18-07-2007-ECCC/SC (3 February 2012), para 412.
[81] ibid para 488.
[82] Brienen and Hoegen (n 12) 129, 320.

the Supreme Court Chamber stated, 'civil party participation before the ECCC includes both the right for victims to participate as parties in the criminal trial of an accused in support of the Prosecution and to pursue a related civil action for collective and moral reparations against an accused'.[83]

By applying Article 33 of the new ECCC Law, the Supreme Court Chamber determined that the civil party notion must be interpreted under Cambodian procedure and, if this provides no answer, international procedural rules may provide guidance.[84] The Supreme Court Chamber added that although reparations for civil parties draw from Cambodian criminal procedure and international human rights law, these sources have limited importance because the ECCC Rules are tailored to the ECCC's mandate and mechanisms.[85] However, ECCC jurisprudence actually has (as adapted) relied on international human rights law. As the Supreme Court Chamber stated in *Case 001*, victims are parties at the ECCC unlike at the ICC and STL: once admitted in the proceedings, they acquire procedural rights.[86] In turn, civil party admissibility, especially in cases where there are many civil parties, may impact the equality of arms due to the civil party role related to civil claims and prosecutorial support, including leading evidence, audience right in trial, and appeals.[87] However, the Pre-Trial Chamber in *Case 002* correctly remarked that parties in criminal proceedings hold different positions which may vary across procedural stages and civil parties do not need to have the same procedural rights of other parties.[88]

Although civil parties are not required to seek reparations, victims need to become civil parties to claim reparations at the ECCC. This reflects the practice in civil law/inquisitorial jurisdictions. At the ICC, there are no civil parties so victims can claim reparations without trial participation. As the Supreme Court Chamber clarified, civil party reparation claims are also recognized under Cambodian Law; however, the scope of civil action is wider at the national level.[89] Whereas civil parties at the ECCC may claim reparations only against the accused and their reparations cannot include individual awards or compensation, civil parties at the national level may also claim reparations against other liable persons and awards include individual compensations.[90] To respect defence rights, which include facing only one prosecutor, the ECCC Trial Chamber has stated that civil party support of the prosecution does not make civil parties additional prosecutors

83 *Case 001* (n 80) para 639.
84 ibid para 414.
85 ibid para 641.
86 ibid paras 488–89.
87 ibid.
88 *Case 002* (Decision on Preliminary Matters Raised by the Lawyers for the Civil Parties in Ieng Sary's Appeal Against Provisional Detention Order) 002/19-09-2007-ECCC/OCIJ (1 July 2008), para 4.
89 *Case 001* (n 80) para 643.
90 ibid.

and parties have different roles in accordance with their particular interests and responsibilities during trial.[91] Although civil parties are entitled to assist/support the Co-Prosecutors, they lack 'a general right of equal participation with the Co-Prosecutor'.[92] However, the ECCC rejected defence argumentation, allegedly French law-based, whereby civil party questioning of witnesses should be limited to reparation/harm-related aspects.[93]

As the ECCC has determined, once victims become civil parties, they do not need to demonstrate how their personal interests are affected to participate.[94] This follows civil law systems and differs from victim participant status (STL, ICC). Similar to civil law systems,[95] civil party admissibility at the ECCC is subject to clear identification and demonstration of material or psychological injury as a consequence of a crime against the defendant upon which collective and moral reparations may be invoked.[96] Under Rule 23*bis*(2), Co-Investigating judges decide civil party admissibility, subject to appeal at the Pre-Trial Chamber. Judge Lavergne said that 'during the substantive proceedings we [the Trial Chamber] shall examine each of the applications to be perfectly certain that the alleged harm did in fact occur'.[97] The Supreme Court Chamber noted that *prima facie* assessment of civil party applications is distinct from merits assessments of these applications because 'a more rigorous standard of proof would be applied to finally determine civil party admissibility' which relates to 'the ultimate finding on eligibility of the civil party applicant for reparation'.[98]

ECCC jurisprudence has differentiated between victims as witnesses and civil parties. Upon becoming civil parties, victims can no longer be questioned as witnesses.[99] The ECCC has distinguished between witness testimony subject to adversarial argument, and 'general statements of suffering, which the Civil Party can freely make at the conclusion of their testimony'.[100] Civil party lead co-lawyers have been directed to structure the questioning of civil parties to distinguish between testimony on facts and statements pertaining to suffering,[101] and to assist civil parties

[91] *Case 001* (Decision on Civil Party Co-Lawyers' Joint Request for a Ruling on the Standing of Civil Party Lawyers to Make Submissions on Sentencing and Directions Concerning the Questioning of the Accused, Experts and Witnesses Testifying on Character) 001/18-07-2007/ECCC/TC (9 October 2009), paras 26–27.

[92] ibid para 25.

[93] *Case 001* (Transcripts) (22 June 2009), p 98, lines 11–12.

[94] *Case 002* (Decision on Civil Party Participation in Provisional Detention Appeals) 002/19-09-2007-ECCC/OCIJ-(PTC01) (20 March 2008), para 49.

[95] Eg CPP (France), Arts 2, 85–87, 418.

[96] Rule 23*bis*(1).

[97] *Case 001* (Transcripts) (17 February 2009), p 42, lines 5–10.

[98] *Case 001* (n 80) paras 511, 519.

[99] *Case 001* (n 33) para 53.

[100] *Case 002/01* (Decision on Request to Recall Civil Party TCCP-187, for Review of Procedure Concerning Civil Parties' Statements on Suffering and Related Motions and Responses) 002/19-09-2007/ECCC/TC (2 May 2013), para 14.

[101] ibid p 10.

in preparing their statements of suffering to discourage new allegations against the accused and limit these statements to the purpose for which they are intended.[102] Should these statements introduce new factual allegations, especially inculpatory, the defence can challenge and re-examine them on adversarial basis.[103]

Victims at ECCC trials have to choose between being witnesses or civil parties since the deadline for civil party application is before trial.[104] Accordingly, unlike civil law jurisdictions like France,[105] victims cannot first be witnesses and then civil parties during trial. This puts victims at a crossroads with almost irreversible effects. Victims could withdraw their civil party status[106] and, later, be witnesses. Although victims cannot simultaneously be civil parties and witnesses, civil parties can provide unsworn testimony and the ECCC has seemingly given this as much weight as sworn testimony.[107] Nevertheless, the former is generally less persuasive than the latter.[108] Civil parties have been examined and cross-examined like witnesses at the ECCC. Thus, the testimony of victims may in practice hold a 'dual status' (civil party witness).[109] Judges must be attentive when examining evidence contents. Witnesses (and civil parties) are entitled to protective measures,[110] which reflect international standards mainly based on the common law/adversarial tradition.[111] Similar to civil law and common law jurisdictions,[112] victims may be complainants to ensure ECCC Co-Prosecutors are aware of specific crimes. However, victim-complainants do not have as many rights as civil parties do.[113] Moreover, the introductory submission of the ECCC Co-Prosecutors, which identifies suspects, distinguishes between victims and civil parties.[114] Whereas Khmer Rouge victims can complain within the framework of the Co-Prosecutors' investigation,[115] only victims of crimes under introductory submissions may become civil parties.[116]

3.3.2 Procedural rights

According to the ECCC, victims hold 'active rights' to participate in investigations.[117] Unlike the STL but similar to civil law jurisdictions, civil

[102] ibid paras 17–18.
[103] ibid para 19.
[104] ECCC-Rule 23*bis*(2).
[105] Brienen and Hoegen (n 12) 322.
[106] ECCC-Rule 23*bis*(5).
[107] *Case 001* (n 33) paras 52–54; *Case 002/01* (n 100) para 21.
[108] Brianne McGonigle-Leyh, *Procedural Justice?Victim Participation in International Criminal Proceedings* (Intersentia 2011) 206.
[109] ibid.
[110] Rule 29.
[111] Perez-Leon-Acevedo (n 35) 228–35, 278–80.
[112] Brienen and Hoegen (n 12) 26, 481.
[113] McGonigle-Leyh (n 108) 174.
[114] Rule 53(1).
[115] Rule 49.
[116] *Case 002* (n 88) para 36.
[117] ibid paras 36, 43.

parties can participate during ECCC judicial investigation (pre-trial), and hold several procedural rights. These largely resemble civil party rights found in civil law jurisdictions.[118] For example, civil parties at the ECCC may undertake dossier examination.[119] Co-investigating judges are able to call civil parties to confront a charged person who then can be questioned by civil party lawyers.[120] Civil parties can, unlike victim participants (ICC/STL), request co-investigating judges to conduct investigations on civil party's behalf though these investigations must be related to judicial investigations.[121] They may also request co-investigating judges to interview them, question witnesses, visit sites, order expert reports or collect evidence on their behalf.[122] They can request and propose witnesses, attend, and participate in proceedings via written/oral interventions though they are excluded from certain proceedings, and support the prosecution.[123]

At the trial stage, ECCC practice has sometimes restricted some civil party procedural rights in contrast to the STL where victim participation has been judicially expanded. This has determined that procedural rights of victim participants and civil parties at the STL and ECCC respectively present important similarities. Those restrictions/controls may indicate the ECCC's unwillingness to fully acknowledge civil parties as parties.[124] Nevertheless, as the ECCC has determined, restrictions to the scope of civil party rights may be necessary because 'features of more traditional Civil Party models, devised for less complex proceedings with fewer victims, required adaptation'.[125] The number of civil parties skyrocketed from 93 in *Case 001* to 3869 in *Case 002*. Indeed, the ECCC divided *Case 002* into *Case 002/01* and *Case 002/02* for trial and subsequent stages, involving 794 and 3075 civil parties respectively. However, civil party procedural rights crafted by ECCC judges in the ECCC Rules and applied in ECCC jurisprudence largely resemble civil party procedural rights in civil law/inquisitorial systems,[126] as adapted to the ECCC.

In ECCC trials, ten civil party rights, generally exercised by common legal counsels, can be identified.[127] First is the right to be heard (or the right to audience). Second is the right to provide unsworn testimony: unlike the STL/ICC, civil parties do not need to take an oath, but they can be cross-examined. Besides testimony, civil parties can provide statements of suffering. Third is the right to support the prosecution and, thus, tender evidence on the accused's

[118] Dervieux (n 16) 238–39; Brienen and Hoegen (n 12) 320.
[119] Rules 55(11), 86.
[120] Rule 55(5)(a).
[121] Rule 55(10).
[122] Rules 31(10); 59(5).
[123] Rules 23(1)(a), 80(2); *Case 001* (n 80) paras 488–89.
[124] Eric Stover and others, 'Confronting Duch-Civil Party Participation' (2011) 93 International Review of the Red Cross 503, 523–524.
[125] *Case 001* (n 91) para. 12.
[126] Dervieux (n 16) 247, 263; Brienen and Hoegen (n 12) 328–29.
[127] Rules 23(4), 80(1), 80(2), 80*bis*(2), 86, 87(4), 89(1), 89(2), 90(2), 91(1)–(2), 94(2)–(3); *Case 001* (n 80) paras 488–89.

guilt. Nevertheless, civil parties lack a general right to equal participation with the Co-Prosecutors: they cannot advance their own case theory because they are not additional/auxiliary prosecutors: the accused must only face one prosecutor. Nonetheless, the right to support the prosecution is determined by civil parties' interest in reparations and establishment of the truth. Fourth is the right to question the witnesses and the accused via the Chamber's President provided that questions correspond to matters discussed in the proceedings. Fifth is the right to propose witnesses to be called by the Trial Chamber and ask to summon new witnesses. Sixth is the right to respond preliminary objections. Seventh, is the right to make written submissions. Eighth is the right to access the dossier. Ninth is the right to make closing statements. Tenth is the right to file written evidence.

Regarding sentencing, civil party participation is quite restricted: civil parties cannot file submissions on sentencing, relevant to sentencing and on evaluation of sentencing factors.[128] Similar limitations exist in France; however, civil parties can testify on the accused's character in France.[129] This is judicially banned for sentencing at the ECCC. Nevertheless, ECCC-Rules prohibit no civil party participation for sentencing. Such prohibition disempowers and frustrates civil parties. As stated in a dissent by Judge Lavergne, civil party participation for sentencing relates to the determination of the accused's guilt, not in the abstract, but in consideration of particular circumstances, and focuses not only on the crimes committed but also the underlying reasons for those crimes.[130] Such exclusions place civil parties in a weaker status than victim participants (STL, ICC), and even victims in common law jurisdictions. For example, victims in the US can participate in sentencing via victim impact statements[131] albeit the lack of civil party or victim participant status. However, civil parties at the ECCC can only present statements of suffering during the trial.

Concerning appeals, civil parties at the ECCC have judicially been modelled after civil law/inquisitorial jurisdictions like France.[132] Although civil parties can appeal the trial judgment when the Co-Prosecutors have appealed it, they cannot appeal the sentence.[133] However, civil parties can via their lawyers appeal reparation orders at the ECCC.[134] Additionally, they can appeal certain interlocutory decisions, including refusal of requests for investigation, expert reports, or protective measures and inadmissibility of civil party applications.[135]

[128] *Case 001* (Transcripts) (27 August 2009), pp 41–42.
[129] CPP (France), Art 444.
[130] *Case 001* (n 91) (Dissenting Opinion judge Lavergne), paras 27–28.
[131] CVRA, 18 U.S.C § 3771(a)(4); Kenna v. United States D. Ct. For C. Dist. Ca. 435 F.3d 1011, 1015–16 (9th Cir. 2006).
[132] ECCC-Rules 81, 82–81, 87, 156, 167, 175(1), 186, 380, 386, 567–68, 573. See Dervieux (n 16) 273–75.
[133] ECCC-Rule 105(1).
[134] ibid.
[135] ECCC-Rule 74(4).

Additionally, the ECCC has allowed appeals against revoked civil party statuses.[136] Thus, civil parties have the right to appeal as well as to participate during interlocutory appeals. Conversely, victim participants' right to appeal is limited at the STL. Civil party procedural rights during appeals have included written and oral participation at the ECCC. Interestingly, the US system has endowed victims with the right to appeal certain interlocutory decisions that affect their rights.[137]

Concerning legal representation, ECCC judges amended the ECCC Rules in March 2009 to consolidate early decisions on the role of civil parties and their lawyers.[138] Thus, ECCC Rule 23*ter*(1) states that civil parties 'shall at all times be represented by a Civil Party Lawyer' from the closing order onwards—this includes the judicial investigation, trial, and appeals stages. Moreover, ECCC judges modified the ECCC Rules to handle the much higher number of civil parties in *Case 002* efficiently. Under ECCC Rule 23(3), civil parties from the trial stage onwards 'shall comprise a single, consolidated group, whose interests are represented by the Civil Party Lead Co-Lawyers […]supported by the Civil Party Lawyers'. As the Trial Chamber stated, 'civil Parties no longer participate individually on the basis of their particular harm suffered, but instead comprise a consolidated group whose collective interests are represented by the Civil Party Lead Co-Lawyers'.[139]

The ECCC Rules introduced continuous intermediation between victims and the ECCC: it is lawyers rather than civil parties who participate. Legal representation also becomes an obligation rather than a right. For example, the French system requires no mandatory common legal representation for civil parties: legal representation is a right.[140] However, ECCC cases involve many more civil parties than those in domestic civil law jurisdictions. As the Pre-Trial Chamber determined, the 'balance between the procedural rights of the parties was an important and ongoing process'.[141] As ECCC judges in one of its Plenary Sessions considered, civil party rights are not limited but only the manners to exercise these rights are modified.[142] In US class actions, which involve civil litigation for international crimes,[143] common lawyers have represented large numbers of victims.[144]

136 *Case 001* (n 80) paras 537–622.
137 CVRA, 18 U.S.C. § 3771(d)(3).
138 ECCC, Fifth Plenary Session of Judicial Officers, Closing Press Statement, 6 March 2009.
139 *Case 002* (Severance order pursuant to internal rule 89ter) 002/19-09-2007-ECCCITC (22 September 2011), para 8.
140 CPP (France), Art 424.
141 *Case 002* (Decision on Application for Reconsideration of Civil Party's Right to Address the Pre-Trial Chamber in Person) 002/19-09-2007-ECCC/OCIJ (PTC03) (28 August 2008), para 5.
142 ECCC, Fifth Plenary Session of Judicial Officers, Closing Press Statement, 6 March 2009.
143 Alien Tort Claims Act 28 USC § 1350; Torture Victim Protection Act (T 28 USC § 1350 note).
144 Federal Rules of Civil Procedure, Rule 23.

4. Conclusion

There is arguably a link between the legal culture of STL and ECCC judges and their judicial practices concerning victim procedural status, including procedural rights. The civil law/inquisitorial background of judges matches the oriented civil law/inquisitorial procedural framework of the STL and the predominantly civil law/inquisitorial procedural framework of the ECCC. The existence of the civil party status at the ECCC demonstrates a higher level of influence of the civil law/inquisitorial legal tradition as compared to the STL where civil law/inquisitorial and common law/adversarial elements are more evenly balanced. However, international criminal procedure, which has traditionally been influenced by common law/adversarial features and which features in the professional and education background of many judges, has also impacted the interpretation and application of victim procedural status at both the STL and ECCC. This reflects the presence of an 'international' component, as complemented by common law/adversarial elements, in the legal culture prevalent in the practice of the ECCC and, especially, the STL.

20

Appearing Before and Sitting With Female Adjudicators

Reflections from Practice

*James Crawford**

1. Introduction

To this day, only one bust of a woman has been found worthy to decorate the halls of the Peace Palace: Baroness Bertha Felicie Sophie von Suttner (9 June 1843–21 June 1914). The posthumous daughter of a field marshal and the granddaughter, on her mother's side, of a cavalry captain, she was an Austrian-Bohemian pacifist and a novelist.[1] In 1889, Suttner became a leading figure in the Austrian peace movement with the publication of her pacifist novel, *Die Waffen nieder!* (*Lay Down Your Arms!*),[2] which went through 37 editions and was translated into 12 languages.

In 1897, Suttner presented Emperor Franz Joseph I of Austria with a list of signatures urging the establishment of an international court of justice. She attended both Hague Peace Conferences.[3] In 1905, she was the first woman to be awarded the Nobel Peace Prize and only the second female Nobel laureate after Marie Curie's shared 1903 award for physics;[4] she was also the first Austrian laureate.[5] In some respects she paved the way for the 1915 International Congress of Women by organizing annual peace congresses in Vienna[6] and by participating in the Peace Conferences in The Hague and other international peace congresses such as the Rome Congress on Disarmament in 1891.[7] Some of the causes that Suttner had

* Thanks to Freya Baetens, Rose Cameron, Yulia Ioffe, and Nikiforos Panagis for their help with this chapter. Needless to say, the views expressed are purely personal.

1 'Bertha von Suttner – Biographical' (The Nobel Prize) <www.nobelprize.org/prizes/peace/1905/suttner/biographical/> accessed 13 August 2020.

2 ibid.

3 'Suttner, Bertha von (1843–1914)' (Women in World History: A Biographical Encyclopedia) <www.encyclopedia.com> accessed 13 August 2020.

4 'Nobel Prize awarded women' (The Nobel Prize) <www.nobelprize.org/prizes/lists/nobel-prize-awarded-women/> accessed 13 August 2020.

5 Arthur Herman, 'What Life Was Like: At Empire's End: Austro-Hungarian Empire Ad 1848-1918' (*Time Life Education* 2000).

6 Hella Pick, 'Bertha Von Suttner, Living for Peace' (Austrian Federal Ministry for Foreign Affairs 2005) 30.

7 ibid 32.

James Crawford, *Appearing Before and Sitting With Female Adjudicators* In: *Identity and Diversity on the International Bench.* Edited by: Freya Baetens, Oxford University Press (2020). © The several contributors.
DOI: 10.1093/oso/9780198870753.003.0020.

campaigned for, such as the creation of international judicial mechanisms for the peaceful resolution of disputes, were taken up at the International Congress of Women in 1915.[8] Suttner died the year before the Congress was held, but she contributed to its preparation.[9]

This third, unofficial, Hague Peace conference is now largely forgotten but it represents an innovative attempt to re-think the international legal system. As Baetens explains, '[w]here the previous Conferences primarily aimed at protecting States against a war which was deemed unavoidable, a much greater belief in the "creatability" of a well-functioning international legal system prevailed at the 1915 Conference'.[10] The Resolutions of the Congress set out 'principles of justice' which were innovative for their time. These included '[t]hat no territory should be transferred without the consent of the men and women in it, and that the right of conquest should not be recognized' and '[t]hat foreign politics should be subject to democratic control'.[11] Baetens sums up the 'visionary' character of the Congress by noting that, despite the fact that none of the Congress' Resolutions was adopted by States or international organizations, '[i]t remains remarkable that this Congress had the enlightenment of mind to predict the development of the international legal system over the subsequent century'.[12]

The 1915 Congress produced what it termed the 'Five Principles for a Permanent Peace'. The fifth principle was the 'Enfranchisement of Women',[13] with which the Congress 'drew a link between the attainment of peace and women's acquisition of equal political rights with men'.[14] In fact all participants in the Congress were to adhere to the principle that 'the parliamentary franchise should be extended to women'.[15] For the participants at the Congress, political rights for women included 'not only the right to vote but also to be elected and equally represented on all levels of government, as well as in the judiciary and academia'.[16] As Baetens remarks, '[s]een in its historic context, this is a spectacular demand in light of the fact that in 1915 only five countries in the world gave fully equal voting rights for all women'.[17] Since the Congress, the principle of enfranchisement of women has been widely adopted. Examples include the provisions of the Covenant of the League

[8] ibid 30; Freya Baetens, 'The 1915 International Congress of Women' in *Max Planck Encyclopedia of Public International Law* (OUP 2011—online edition), para 10.
[9] 'Bertha von Suttner - Biographical' (n 1).
[10] Freya Baetens (n 8), para 17.
[11] Report of the International Congress of Women (Women's Peace Party 1915).
[12] Freya Baetens (n 8), para 17.
[13] Report of the International Congress of Women (Women's Peace Party 1915).
[14] Hilary Charlesworth and Christine Chinkin, *The Boundaries of International Law, A Feminist Analysis* (Melland Schill Studies in Law 2000) 14–15.
[15] Jane Addams, Emily Balch, and Alice Hamilton, 'Women in the Hague, The International Congress of Women and Its Results', Introduction by Harriet Alonso (University of Illinois Press 2003) xvi.
[16] Freya Baetens (n 8), para 17.
[17] Freya Baetens (n 8), para 17.

of Nations[18] and the Charter of the United Nations[19] allowing for the participation of men and women equally in the organizations, and the Convention on the Elimination of All Forms of Discrimination against Women.[20]

In this chapter, I highlight the two sides of my experience with female adjudicators: first, my experience as counsel appearing before women judges, and second, my experience as arbitrator and judge, sitting on the bench with female colleagues. Third, I would like to draw some cautious conclusions as to how these experiences reflect on the legitimacy of the international adjudicatory process in this context.

2. Appearing as Counsel Before Female Adjudicators

The first case I ever argued was *Phosphate Lands in Nauru, Nauru v Australia*,[21] initiated in 1989 before the International Court (ICJ) where I appeared as junior counsel on behalf of Nauru (not my own country, Australia). There were no women on the ICJ bench in those days, neither were there any female agents or counsel on Nauru's team. Australia's counsel, however, included Ms Susan Kenny of the Australian Bar, who later became the first woman to be appointed to the Victorian Court of Appeal and, since 1998, has been a judge of the Federal Court of Australia.[22]

The first woman to be elected as a judge to the ICJ was Dame Rosalyn Higgins in 1995 (re-elected in 2000; she retired in 2009).[23] Higgins became the first woman president in 2006.[24] I had the honour of appearing before her in several cases; first of these was *Oil Platforms (Iran v USA)* initiated in 1992, decided in 2003, to which she made a major contribution.[25] Later I appeared in a number of cases before women judges who later became my colleagues—Hanqin Xue of China and Joan Donoghue of the United States of America (both elected in 2010),[26] and Julia Sebutinde of Uganda (who was elected in 2012).[27]

[18] Covenant of the League of Nations, 28 June 1919, Art 7. Hilary Charlesworth and Christine Chinkin attribute this Article to the 'women's deputations to the Paris Peace Conference in 1919': Hilary Charlesworth and Christine Chinkin (n 14) 14–15.

[19] Charter of the United Nations, San Francisco, 26 June 1945, Art 8.

[20] Convention on the Elimination of All Forms of Discrimination against Women, New York, 18 December 1979.

[21] *Certain Phosphate Lands in Nauru (Nauru v Australia)* (Preliminary Objections) (Judgment) [1992] ICJ Rep 240.

[22] 'The Hon Susan Coralie Kenny' (Federal Court of Australia) <www.fedcourt.gov.au/about/judges/current-judges-appointment/current-judges/kenny-j> accessed 13 August 2020.

[23] International Court of Justice, 'All Members' <www.icj-cij.org/en/all-members> accessed 13 August 2020.

[24] UN News, 'International Court of Justice names its first female president', 6 February 2006 <https://news.un.org/en/story/2006/02/168322-international-court-justice-names-its-first-female-president> accessed 13 August 2020.

[25] *Oil Platforms (Islamic Republic of Iran v United States of America)* (Judgment) [2003] ICJ Rep161. Judge Higgins wrote individual opinions in both stages of the proceedings.

[26] International Court of Justice, 'Current Members' <www.icj-cij.org/en/current-members> accessed 13 August 2020.

[27] ibid.

I cannot say that appearing before women judges ever consciously affected my litigation strategy or pleading style. No doubt my subjective perception could differ from someone else's observations and I cannot speak for my co-counsel throughout the years. But one reason why a change of litigation strategy or pleading style would, in my view, be unlikely, is that even if one or two women are sitting, this still leaves 13 or more male judges—and the purpose of a pleading always remains to persuade the Court as a whole. I doubt my 'success rate' (if that is a meaningful term) in arguing before women judges at the Court is any different than that before their male colleagues. Focusing on two cases that I pleaded shortly before joining the Court, in *Croatia v Serbia*, in which I appeared as counsel for the Applicant, the three female judges sided with the majority, rejecting Croatia's claim.[28] Conversely, in *Whaling in the Antarctic*, in which I appeared as counsel for the Applicant (Australia), all four female sitting judges (including judge ad hoc Charlesworth) voted in favour of Australia's argument that Japan had not acted in conformity with some of its obligations under the International Convention for the Regulation of Whaling.[29]

Since 2010, pleadings before the ICJ have been web-streamed live and remain available online,[30] so perhaps it would be interesting for sociologists, anthropologists, or linguists to watch the pleadings in a more systematic manner. In particular, it might be interesting to analyse whether parties advocate differently depending on the number of female judges on the bench; whether parties spend equal time addressing questions from female and male judges; whether counsel refer to previous separate decisions of female judges to the same extent as they do to separate decisions of male judges, for example. Since the election of Judge Higgins, there has always been at least one woman on the ICJ bench, so it could be too late to try to examine any differences in this regard; no web streaming is available of cases in which there is no woman judge on the bench. Moreover, the procedure during oral hearings at the ICJ includes only very limited unplanned interaction between counsel and the bench, making meaningful analysis of varying dynamics according to the judicial officer's gender difficult.

Turning to arbitration, women remain a small minority: most of the arbitral tribunals before which I have appeared have not included a female arbitrator, nor has any tribunal before which I appeared ever included more than one woman (out of three or five arbitrators). It is difficult to formulate discrete reasons for this, but research suggests one reason has to do with the limited willingness of parties to

[28] *Application of the Convention on the Prevention and Punishment of the Crime of Genocide (Croatia v Serbia)* (Judgment) [2015] ICJ Rep 3.

[29] *Whaling in the Antarctic (Australia v Japan: New Zealand intervening)* (Judgment) [2014] ICJ Rep 226.

[30] International Court of Justice, 'Multimedia galleries' <www.icj-cij.org/en/multimedia-cases> accessed 13 August 2020.

appoint women.[31] On the whole, in approximately 30 arbitration cases in which I appeared as counsel, only a handful had a female arbitrator. In two cases, she was also the president of the tribunal—this was Gabrielle Kaufmann-Kohler, who has built up a remarkable career as an arbitrator. Mention may also be made at this point of Brigitte Stern who has similarly developed an impressive career in arbitration. Together, Kaufmann-Kohler and Stern make up 75% of appointments of women in the field.[32]

If any change in litigation strategy or pleading style based on the gender of one's adjudicators would make a difference, it would rather be in the context of arbitration, where one faces more often a panel of three or perhaps five judges—and where persuading one or two female arbitrators could more readily tip the balance. Moreover, representing clients in an arbitration is also a more engaging exercise than it is before a court. Counsel in arbitral cases normally interact intensively with the bench; if there is any scope for female adjudicators to 'stand out', it is more likely to become apparent in arbitration. For myself, I have never detected any differences in this regard.

3. Sitting with Female Adjudicators

In total, I have served as an arbitrator in about 40 cases but in only about 10% did I serve with a female co-arbitrator (including again Gabrielle Kaufmann-Kohler; also Loretta Malintoppi). I am unable to detect any clear gender-based differences from my female colleagues on arbitral tribunals, perhaps due to their fluctuating and ad hoc composition. The same was true with my experience as counsel appearing in arbitral proceedings. There are studies, however, which have attempted to test whether women have a unique impact on arbitral decision-making. For example, a 2011 study by Michael Waibel and Yanhui Wu found that female decision-makers are more likely than men to rule in favour of jurisdiction in ICSID cases.[33]

Since 2015, in all the cases in which I have been able to participate, I have had the good fortune of sitting with the three female judges: the Chinese judge (Hanqin Xue), the US judge (Joan Donoghue), and the Ugandan judge (Julia Sebutinde). As was my experience as arbitrator, I cannot identify differences between my male and female colleagues on the bench, although I would think that the women judges on the Court seem more flexible and open to differing

[31] Victoria Pernt, 'Women in Arbitration Are on the Rise' (*Kluwer Arbitration Blog*, 4 June 2017) <http://arbitrationblog.kluwerarbitration.com/2017/06/04/women-arbitration-rise/> accessed 13 August 2020.

[32] Gus Van Harten, 'The (Lack of) Women Arbitrators in Investment Treaty Arbitration', *FDI Perspectives*, Vale Columbia Center on Sustainable International Investment, February 2012.

[33] Nienke Grossman, 'Sex on the Bench: Do Women Judges Matter to the Legitimacy of International Court' (2012) 12 Chicago Journal of International Law Journal 647, at 656, referring to Michael Waibel and Yanhui Wu, 'Are Arbitrators Political?', ASIL Research Forum, UCLA, November 2011.

arguments than the average male colleague. This conclusion finds some support in research which suggests that women judges may assist in changing the working environment.[34] But since the sample size of female judges at the ICJ has been so small, any such observations may be without significance. More importantly, since so much depends on the individual, it can be illusory and misleading to generalize the behaviour of all female judges.

I tend to agree with the literature which sees 'the very question of whether women would judge differently as both "dangerous and unanswerable"'.[35] Judging involves the procedural running of a case, the deliberations held amongst members of the court or tribunal and the ultimate decision-making.[36] My own experience has led me to conclude that female adjudicators do not approach these stages any differently than their male colleagues.

4. Representation of Women and the Legitimacy of International Adjudication

4.1 Personal Impressions

In preparing for this Chapter, I have (for the first time) reflected upon the performance of female adjudicators that I personally dealt with as counsel or as co-adjudicators and, as I have said, I could not come up with any defining features which characterizes their style, that could be linked to the fact that they are women. Part of the reason for this could be that, again, my experience involves simply too small a sample on which to build any defensible theories regarding the 'different' contribution of female adjudicators.

More specifically, I cannot think of any questions they asked that one could not envisage coming from male arbitrators or judges. There also seemed no difference between the handling of factual matters or legal questions (whether of substance or procedure) they were particularly concerned about.[37] They did not treat counsel in any noticeably different manner and they do not behave differently in deliberations. In arbitration cases, women presidents do not seem to conduct proceedings any differently either. Of course, there were differences between individuals (for example, in how active they are during oral hearings and how they deal with

[34] Dermot Feenan, 'Women Judges: Gendering Judging, Justifying Diversity' (2008) 35 Journal of Law and Society 490, at 509.

[35] ibid, quoting Sandra Day O'Connor, 'Portia's Progress' (1991) 66 New York University Law Review 1546, at 1557.

[36] ibid 493, in which Feenan complains that some studies on gender differences in decision-making have ignored aspects of judging other than the 'decisional outcome'.

[37] In a similar vein, Bertha von Suttner herself is reported to have seen 'no difference between men's and women's viewpoints on peace': Ruth Roach Pierson (ed), 'Women and Peace: Theoretical, Historical and Practical Perspectives' (Routledge 2019).

certain procedural matters) but these do not seem to me to have been specifically gendered. I have never had a moment where I thought 'only a woman would have come up with this question' or 'only a woman would have decided this issue in this manner'.

This could imply that the thinking and reasoning processes of women who do 'make it' in this overwhelmingly male environment are conditioned to such an extent that any 'difference' in approach is ironed out or minimized. Prominent female judges, as well as researchers, have suggested that an 'occupational socialization' may occur accompanied by 'assimilation to the [historical] gender norms of the legal profession'.[38] On the other hand, it could also be that there is little or no difference between the approach of female and male adjudicators—or at least, no differences that can be linked, either in a correlative or causal manner, to their gender. The law is after all a powerful socializing factor. Feenan referred to this as the 'legal professional socialization' of women—and it would impact upon men too—in her argument against the rationalization of gender equality because women judges judge differently.[39]

Nor have I noticed that being the first female or only female judge affected their adjudicatory 'style', any more than it would have affected the behaviour of male colleagues. Research on the US Supreme Court suggests that female judges tend to be interrupted in oral argument or deliberations more often than male judges,[40] but I cannot recall any arbitration or court proceeding in which I was involved where this was the case. As noted above, in terms of the ICJ, this might be because of the limited interactions between counsel and the bench, or it might be because of the formal, ceremonial—rather than adversarial—procedure with which the ICJ's oral proceedings are conducted.

Equally, I do not believe that gender observably affects the interpretation of legal principles, facts, precedent, or rules of procedure or evidence. Some women judges tend to exhibit a higher or lower level of judicial restraint in participation in oral hearings, written decisions, separate or concurring opinions, and dissenting opinions—but this seems rather linked to their national origin, place of legal education, and the legal system they functioned in before becoming a judge, rather than their gender, as I see the same pattern of participation in male judges from particular regions and legal systems. For some judges, the time on the bench since appointment does indeed have an impact upon their restraint, but this is mostly true for judges who were highly restrained at the outset, and become somewhat

[38] Dermot Feenan (n 34) 515, with reference to Justice Mary Gaudron of the Australian High Court and US Judge Patricia Wald.

[39] Dermot Feenan (n 34) 492.

[40] Tonja Jacobi and Dylan Schweers, 'Justice, Interrupted: The Effect of Gender, Ideology and Seniority at Supreme Court Oral Arguments' (2017) 103 Virginia Law Review 1379 conclude that 'judicial interactions at oral argument are highly gendered, with women being interrupted at disproportionate rates by their male colleagues, as well as by male advocates'.

'bolder', when confronted with the conduct of their colleagues—again, this seems to have little or nothing to do with gender, at least in civil litigation.

My legal practice focused on questions of general international law and investment law—far less on disputes involving trade law, human rights, or criminal law. It is therefore hard for me to say whether some areas of international law call for legal and professional socialization in judicial decision-making while others call for more personal discretionary modes of decision-making. Lady Hale has suggested that, as a female judge, in some cases her 'experience and perceptions of life made a difference to "[her]" view on the law'.[41] She cites examples of cases involving issues such as 'the damage done to a woman by an unwanted pregnancy' and 'the definition of violence'.

Similarly, Nienke Grossman argues for gender equality on the benches of international criminal tribunals because, in her view, it is 'necessary for normative legitimacy because men and women bring different perspectives to bear in judging, at least in cases involving experiences unique to each sex'.[42] Grossman gives examples pertaining to criminal law, such as a study of International Criminal Tribunal for the former Yugoslavia (ICTY) sentencing in which 'ICTY panels with female judges imposed more severe sanctions on defendants who assaulted women'.[43] Recent research suggests that men and women are affected differently by the type of crimes prosecuted in international criminal tribunals,[44] and female victims might feel more comfortable describing their trauma to a female judge.[45] Judge Patricia Wald, formerly of the ICTY, writing extra-curially, suggests that '[w]omen judges may well have a special sensitivity to the degradation suffered by victims of ... crimes [such as rape, perpetrated most often against women]'.[46] There might be an argument for rationalizing gender equality on criminal courts benches in terms of the particular role women judges might play, for example in 'shaping international law relating to gender-based violence'.[47] But I would not make any such distinction in terms of gender for my own areas of specialization, where adjudicators search for the best solution to resolve a dispute, rather than thinking of theoretical models within which to frame their ruling.

[41] Lady Hale, 'Women in the Judiciary: the Fiona Woolf Lecture for the Women Lawyers' Division of the Law Society', 27 June 2014, p 21.

[42] Nienke Grossman, 'Sex Representation on the Bench and the Legitimacy of International Criminal Courts' (2011) 11 International Criminal Law Review 643, at 645.

[43] ibid.

[44] Leila Sadat, 'Avoiding the Creation of a Gender Ghetto in International Criminal Law' (2011) 11 International Criminal Law Review 655, at 658, with reference to the ICC Trust Fund for Victims, 'Learning from the TVF's Second Mandate: From Implementing Rehabilitation Assistance to Reparations', Fall 2010 Programme Progress Report.

[45] ibid 660.

[46] Patricia Wald, 'Women on International Courts: Some Lessons Learned' (2011) 11 International Criminal Law Review 401, at 403.

[47] Sandra Day O'Connor and Kim Azzarelli, 'Sustainable Development, Rule of Law, and the Impact of Women Judges' (2011) 44 Cornell International Law Journal 3, at 7.

Finally, and insofar as I can say, I do not think that women are more likely to be selected to adjudicate any specific type of case. It may be true that parties in arbitration are more hesitant to appoint women, but one reason may well be that the first question every client asks when presented with a potential list of arbitrators is 'how many cases (or how many of the relevant type) has this person adjudicated before?'. With women, the number is usually lower—so to those who have, still more is given.

I have been discussing arbitration, but I do not think any different conclusion can be reached for the International Court. Once women get to the bench, they are not allocated any specific roles due to their gender, as most roles (eg procedural rules committee, hiring committee) are distributed among the judges with a view to achieving the equal distribution of tasks among judges. In deliberations, each judge speaks in turn, in reverse order of seniority. Gender has nothing to do with this, formally and, as far as I can detect, informally as well. All women judges elected to the Court are likely to be well able to present their views—so far, this has certainly been the case.

4.2 The Goal of Equal Representation

These reflections, even if warranted, do not detract from the conclusion that the current imbalance as between male and female adjudicators is deeply regrettable. As Lady Hale, former President of the United Kingdom's Supreme Court, has stated extra-curially, there is both a 'moral' and a 'business case' for diversity, in terms of gender and otherwise.[48] The moral argument includes the need to ensure that suitably qualified women and men have equal opportunity to become a judge.[49] The business case is perhaps best stated as the simple notion that the best candidates—of whatever gender and from whatever background—must be able to access important judicial positions, thereby enriching the courts. Lady Hale also described well how, in terms of domestic courts, '[t]he public should be able to feel that the courts are their courts' and that '[i]n a democracy governed by the people ... the judiciary should reflect the whole community, not just a small section of it'.[50] It should be likewise with the international judiciary sitting on international courts. However, current estimates vary as to when the 1915 Congress of Women's goal of equal representation of women in the international judiciary could realistically be achieved at the current rate of progress. But, despite an overall increase in the

[48] Lady Hale (n 41) 2, citing Fiona Woolf's 'The Power of Diversity' series of events.

[49] Dermot Feenan (n 34), 493.

[50] Lady Hale (n 41) 4; see also Report commissioned by the UK Shadow Secretary of State for Justice authored by Sir Geoffrey Bindman QC and Karon Monaghan QC, 'Judicial Diversity, Accelerating Change', 6 November 2014, p 5: lack of gender and ethnic diversity amongst judges 'undermines the democratic legitimacy of our legal system'.

number of female judges in international courts,[51] there is no doubt it will be a long time.

The International Court has had only four women judges in its 74-year history, of which three are currently serving, whereas there have been 100 male judges. In addition, there have been 5 female ad hoc judges sitting in four cases (compared with more than 110 male ad hoc judges, several of whom have sat in multiple cases). The five are Louise Arbour (Canadian), Suzanne Bastid (French), Hilary Charlesworth (Australian), Navanethem Pillay (South African), and Christine van den Wyngaert (Belgian). On a different note, the Statute of the Court uses only the masculine when referring to members of the Court (and the Registrar of the Court).[52] This simply reflects the historical reality that in 1945 all the members of the Court were men (and there has never been a female Registrar).[53] But it also marks the Statute as anachronistic in relation to the fostering of gender parity and perpetuates the image of the male judge.[54] What also perpetuates the image of the judge as male is the plethora of photographs and paintings of the male judges of the ICJ, and its predecessor the Permanent Court of International Justice, which line the halls of the Court. Given that three of the four female judges are still sitting, only one portrait of a woman judge, that of former President Rosalyn Higgins, sits amongst them.

It should be stressed that the 'feedstock' for careers in international law and adjudication has been more or less gender-balanced, at least for the past 20 years.[55] But this situation has not, or not yet, flowed through to the most senior levels of the profession. For example, at the last election for the 34 members of the International Law Commission (ILC) only four women were elected—but there were only four women candidates, all from the Western European and Others Group (WEOG) (so all female candidates were elected).[56] Not a single nominee from any other group was a woman! The Institut de Droit International has 170 titular, associate, honorary, and emeriti members, of which only 21 are women.[57]

[51] Stéphanie Vauchez, 'More Women – But Which Women? The Rules and the Politics of Gender Blance at the European Court of Human Rights' (2015) 26 European Journal of International Law 195, at 198.

[52] Statute of the International Court of Justice, 26 June 1945. See for example Arts 20, 40, and 55. Only very recently, and quite fragmentarily, did the Court introduce gender neutrality in some provisions of its Rules: see Arts 22, 23, 29, as amended on 21 October 2019: <www.icj-cij.org/files/press-releases/0/000-20191021-PRE-01-00-EN.pdf> accessed 13 August 2020.

[53] International Court of Justice, 'The Registrar', <www.icj-cij.org/en/registrar> accessed 13 August 2020.

[54] See Dermot Feenan (n 34), 495, in relation to the perpetuation of the male judge through media, film, and portraiture,

[55] See for example: Elizabeth Olson, 'Women Make Up Majority of U.S. Law Students for First Time' (*New York Times* – Online) 16 December 2016; Justin Levinson and Danielle Young, 'Implicit Gender Bias in the Legal Profession: An Empirical Study' (2010) 18 Duke Journal of Gender Law & Policy 1.

[56] International Law Commission, 'Membership: 2016 Election of the International Law Commission', <http://legal.un.org/ilc/elections/2016election_outcome.shtml> accessed 13 August 2020.

[57] Institut de droit international, 'Members', <http://www.idi-iil.org/en/membres/> accessed 13 August 2020.

All this suggests that we could be looking at a very long period before there is equal representation on the ICJ bench, perhaps more than two centuries after the International Congress of Women's call. As long as women are not reaching the higher echelons of the legal profession, it will be difficult for them to become 'visible'[58] enough for consideration for appointment for international judicial office. Lady Hale used the concept of visibility to describe how '[l]ess conventional candidates' in the United Kingdom (eg to paraphrase Lady Hale's view, not men who had attended a boarding school and then an Oxbridge college) would struggle to gain a judicial appointment.[59]

The low number of female advocates appearing before the ICJ may also render an increase in female candidates for positions on the Court more unlikely. In a study conducted of oral proceedings before the Court from 1999 to 2012, Shashank Kumar and Cecily Rose highlighted the male dominance of these proceedings.[60] Their study revealed that just twenty-three of the 205 lawyers who appeared before the Court in that period were women, accounting for just 7.4% of the total speaking time for oral argument.[61] The study also notes that, of 63 counsel who appeared two or more times before the Court during the period in question, there were only four women.[62]

The statistics for female arbitrators are similar to those at the ICJ, although progress seems to materialize at a somewhat faster pace. It has been reported that the number of women arbitrators (in public as well as private arbitration) appointed in 2016 was 209 compared to 136 in 2015: a rise of 4.4% to 14.8% of total appointments.[63] Focusing on dispute resolution in the International Chamber of Commerce in 2019, 312 female arbitrators were appointed or confirmed, representing 21% of all appointments and confirmations.[64] If one looks at the appointments of sole arbitrators in the context of the International Chamber of Commerce, 33% were women in 2019. Interestingly, the case management system of the International Chamber of Commerce's International Court of Arbitration does not permit the collection of gender data so that the manual collection of this data, and its analysis, exemplifies a relatively recent commitment to working towards gender parity in arbitral appointments.[65]

58 Lady Hale (n 41) 11.
59 Lady Hale (n 41) 10–11.
60 Shashank Kumar and Cecily Rose, 'A Study of Lawyers Appearing before the International Court of Justice, 1999-2012' (2014) 25 European Journal of International Law 893.
61 ibid 904.
62 ibid 909.
63 'Recent Gender Statistics Show More Women Arbitrators Appointed' (*Lexology*, 20 July 2017) <www.lexology.com/library/detail.aspx?g=377f3352-7e23-4b46-b86c-48660d552a93> accessed 13 August 2020.
64 International Chamber of Commerec Dispute Resolution 2019 Statistics, p 13 <https://iccwbo.org/publication/icc-dispute-resolution-statistics/> accessed 13 August 2020.
65 Mirèze Philippe, 'How Has Female Participation at ICC Evolved?', International Chamber of Commerce Dispute Resolution Bulletin, Issue 3, 2017, p 38.

According to Lucy Greenwood, driving the trend of greater gender parity in arbitral appointment is the Equal Representation in Arbitration Pledge launched in May 2016.[66] As Greenwood explains, the Pledge was 'a global initiative addressing the gender imbalance in arbitration [which] has led to a considerable rise in female arbitrator appointments in a single year.'[67] However, 'the success of the Pledge has so far rested on the shoulders of the arbitral institutions.'[68] As Greenwood concludes, parties have the power to appoint arbitrators in the majority of cases (the International Chamber of Commerce making direct appointments in only 25% of its cases). Unfortunately, parties 'lag far behind the [arbitral] institutions in appointing women.'[69]

It is difficult to determine why parties hesitate to appoint female arbitrators, or why States do not propose female candidates more often for positions at the ILC or on the ICJ. Statistics reveal that many States, at least in Europe, in fact have gender parity on their domestic benches. The Council of Europe's 2012 data reveals a mixed picture: seventeen States or entities (up from fourteen in 2010) present 'male-female parity within a range from 40% to 60%'.[70] While three States (Slovenia, Latvia, and Romania) had more than 70% female judges, six States had more than 70% male judges.[71]

In this context, the European Commission's current proposal for an Investment Court System or a Multilateral Investment Court, which does not impose any specific requirements regarding gender representation, might damage the prospects of gender equality in the field of international investment law. Perhaps more alarmingly, the Council of the European Union included only one woman in its five nominations for the List of Arbitrators under Article 29.8 of the Comprehensive Economic and Trade Agreement (CETA) between Canada and the European Union and its Member States, while not a single one of the suggested chairpersons was female.[72] Other international legal institutions do have institutional mechanisms which aim to ensure a certain level of gender equality. For example, the procedure for the nomination and election of judges at the International Criminal Court (ICC) contains 'minimum voting requirements' aimed at achieving a gender-balanced result,[73] reinforcing the Rome Statute's exhortation that 'States Parties

[66] Victoria Pernt (n 31),.
[67] ibid.
[68] ibid.
[69] ibid.
[70] European Commission for the Efficiency of Justice, 'European judicial systems, Edition 2014 (2012 data): Efficiency and quality of justice, An overview', p 35.
[71] ibid.
[72] Council Decision (EU) 2019/2246 of 19 December 2019 on the position to be taken on behalf of the European Union in CETA Joint Committee as regards the adoption of the List of Arbitrators pursuant to Art 29.8 of the Agreement, OJ L 336/288, 30.12.2019.
[73] Procedure for the nomination and election of judges, the Prosecutor and Deputy Prosecutors of the International Criminal Court, Doc No. ICC-ASP/3/Res.6, 10 September 2004. See also Assembly of States Parties, 'Informal guide and commentary to the procedure for the nomination and election of judges of the International Criminal Court', Doc No. ICC-ASP/16/INF.2, 5 May 2017.

shall, in the selection of judges, take into account the need, within the membership of the Court, for ... [a] fair representation of female and male judges'.[74] Regardless, as at August 2020, just six of the eighteen judges on the International Criminal Court are women.[75] In 2010 women made up more than half of the ICC bench.[76] Further examples of institutional mechanisms promoting gender equality include that States proposing judicial candidates for the European Court of Human Rights (ECtHR) must include at least one woman (and at least one man) on their list of candidates, unless exceptional circumstances apply.[77] The Protocol on the establishment of the African Court on Human and Peoples' Rights mandates that when States Parties nominate judicial candidates, '[d]ue consideration shall be given to adequate gender representation'.[78] As of August 2020, sixteen of the forty-seven judges of the ECtHR are women[79] and, representing a majority of members, six of the eleven judges of the African Court on Human and Peoples' Rights are women.[80]

5. Conclusion

To conclude, gender parity on the bench (whether domestic or international) is highly desirable for many reasons and is currently not being achieved in many international legal institutions. I have not observed any notable differences between male and female adjudicators from my experience as counsel and now as judge, although it appears that some research—especially in international criminal law—suggests that women judges can make unique contributions on the bench. It is to be hoped that the rate at which female adjudicators are being appointed increases, or it will be many years before gender parity exists in many international legal institutions. The role of these institutions in speeding up the process towards equality should be carefully considered. In some respects, institutional mechanisms can ensure a certain level of gender parity. In other institutions, such as arbitral tribunals, it will be primarily for parties nominating decision-makers to consider gender parity in appointing individuals.

[74] Rome Statute of the International Criminal Court, 17 July 1998, Art 36(8).

[75] International Criminal Court, 'Current Judges'<www.icc-cpi.int/bios-2> accessed 13 August 2020. There are also two further judges (one male, one female) continuing in office to complete proceedings.

[76] Nienke Grossman (n 42), 643.

[77] Council of Europe Parliamentary Assembly, 'Candidates for the European Court of Human Rights', Resolution 1366 (2004); see also Council of Europe Parliamentary Assembly, 'Procedure for the election of judges to the European Court of Human Rights as of 15 April 2019', 8 July 2019.

[78] Protocol to the African Charter on Human and Peoples' Rights on the Establishment of the African Court on Human and Peoples' Rights, 10 June 1998, Art 12.

[79] ECHR, 'Composition of the Court' <www.echr.coe.int/Pages/home.aspx?p=court/judges&c=> accessed 13 August 2020.

[80] African Court on Human and Peoples' Rights, 'Current Judges' <http://en.african-court.org/index.php/judges/42-former-judges> accessed 13 August 2020.

PART III

BEYOND THE INTERNATIONAL BENCH

21

Diversity and Legitimacy of the World Trade Organization's Bench

Cosette D Creamer and Zuzanna Godzimirska

1. Introduction

The past few years have been a gloomy period for the crown jewel of the World Trade Organization (WTO), with the slow dismemberment of its Appellate Body (AB), previously lauded as the most successful international court of universal membership.[1] Since mid-2017, the US has been blocking a selection process for new AB members—effectively its judges—which has slowly forced the 'supreme court of trade' into a coma, facing limited personnel and a growing number of appeals.[2] While the identity of those on the bench is not the root cause of the current impasse, it may very well be at the core of present concerns with the WTO's dispute settlement mechanism and its future.

Indeed, WTO members expend considerable resources to acquire information about future adjudicators' views on issues of interest to them.[3] This in itself suggests that governments are invested in who ends up on the bench. In light of the extensive authority in the hands of the WTO Dispute Settlement Mechanism (DSM)—comprising dispute panels and the AB—scholars have tried to understand the effects that certain adjudicator characteristics have on the functioning and legitimacy of the DSM. For instance, Busch and Pelc find that experienced panel chairs—presumably jurists with the ability to render 'better and more consistent rulings'—are less likely to have their judgments reversed by the Appellate Body than their less experienced counterparts.[4] We might expect, then, that panellists' experience and professional background may similarly matter for how their rulings are received by member governments. Yet Pauwelyn argues that the DSM's

[1] Cosette D Creamer, 'From the WTO's Crown Jewel to Its Crown of Thorns' [2019] AJIL Unbound.

[2] The Appellate Body is normally composed of seven members; at the time of writing, it is down to one and can no longer deal with appeals (for which a minimum of three is required).

[3] Manfred Elsig and Mark A Pollack, 'Agents, Trustees, and International Courts: The Politics of Judicial Appointment at the World Trade Organization' (2014) 20 European Journal of International Relations 391.

[4] Marc L Busch and Krzysztof J Pelc, 'Does the WTO Need a Permanent Body of Panelists?' (2009) 12 Journal of International Economic Law 579.

Cosette D Creamer and Zuzanna Godzimirska, *Diversity and Legitimacy of the World Trade Organization's Bench* In: *Identity and Diversity on the International Bench*. Edited by: Freya Baetens, Oxford University Press (2020). © The several contributors. DOI: 10.1093/oso/9780198870753.003.0021.

'sociological legitimacy as evidenced by patterns of adjudicator appointments',[5] rests less on the expertise and experience of adjudicators and more on 'the quality of the broader system (its representativeness and diversity)' including the WTO Secretariat.[6]

In this chapter, we look beyond how identity factors into appointment patterns, given that WTO panellists are largely appointed by the Director General and powerful countries disproportionately influence the AB appointment process. Instead we focus on the importance of the WTO bench's composition for the legitimacy of the DSM in the eyes of the broader membership. We use aggregate levels of governments' expressed support for and criticism of dispute rulings as a proxy for the DSM's legitimacy. Once on the bench, do certain characteristics of the WTO's judges matter for the WTO bench's sociological legitimacy? Does judicial identity shape how governments evaluate and respond to dispute reports (or 'rulings')?

To answer these questions, the next section briefly clarifies the concept of legitimacy and the potential role that the composition of the bench may have for the DSM's sociological legitimacy. We then describe the data analysed, before turning to a descriptive analysis of dispute panellist and AB member diversity over the past twenty years, focusing on gender, nationality, legal tradition, and professional experience. The final section explores the relationship between adjudicators' characteristics and the DSM's sociological legitimacy.

2. Legitimacy and Bench Composition

Existing research on the sociological legitimacy of international courts largely focuses on assessing the degree to which various court constituents believe that the exercise of judicial authority is legitimate.[7] In contrast to scholarship on normative legitimacy, which relies on theoretical assessments of an institution's *worthiness* of support, this research seeks to empirically measure various actors' *beliefs* about a court's exercise of authority.[8] A plethora of factors might influence these beliefs. For example, we have found that expansive interpretations by the WTO's judicial bodies tend to undermine its legitimacy in the eyes of its members, whereas

[5] Joost Pauwelyn, 'Who Decides Matters: The Legitimacy Capital of WTO Adjudicators Versus ICSID Arbitrators' in Nienke Grossman and others (eds), *Legitimacy and International Courts* (Cambridge University Press 2018) 224.

[6] Pauwelyn (n 5) 225.

[7] Daniel Bodansky, 'The Legitimacy of International Governance: A Coming Challenge for International Environmental Law?' (1999) 93 The American Journal of International Law 596. See also Nienke Grossman, 'Legitimacy and International Adjudicative Bodies' (2009) 41 George Washington International Law Review 107.

[8] Daniel Bodansky, 'The Concept of Legitimacy in International Law' in Rüdiger Wolfrum and Volker Roben (eds), *Legitimacy in International Law* (Springer 2008) 309.

'majoritarian activism'[9] increased its legitimacy among the same constituents.[10] Yet the outcome of a dispute is arguably not the only factor to shape assessments of a court's legitimacy; there are good reasons to believe that the composition of the bench—or judges' characteristics—also matter for how a court is perceived by various constituents. We divide such characteristics into two categories: those related to the identity of the adjudicators and those related to their professional experience.

2.1 Identity: Gender, Geographical Representation, and Legal tradition

Most States—at least publicly—want to ensure that the international bench is gender diverse and representative of the world's regions.[11] A recent study of UN General Assembly debates on the International Court of Justice's (ICJ's) annual report found that the bench's composition is one of the key topics mentioned in negative evaluations of the Court.[12] States have called for increased representation of women and 'the main forms of civilization', arguing that assuring representativeness would strengthen the Court as 'a universal organ imparting justice and promoting respect for the rules of international law'.[13]

Most constitutive treaties contain provisions that set forth more or less specific requirements for who can be elected as a judge, and the composition of a bench in specific cases. In the context of the WTO, Dispute Settlement Understanding (DSU) Articles 8 and 17 provide guidance on the characteristics required—or desired—in panellists and Appellate Body members (ABMs). To ensure representativeness, Article 8(10) stipulates that when a dispute involves a developing country, the panel 'shall ... include at least one panellist from a developing country', if requested by said country. As with panels, the AB 'shall be broadly representative of the membership in the WTO'. Notably, there are no formal rules in the DSU to ensure gender balance, although the absence of such a requirement does not necessarily mean that gender does not play a role in the DSM's sociological legitimacy.

A judge's gender and their nationality are likely not the only factors to shape assessments of a court's legitimacy. As Mitchell and Powell argue, States 'look to similarity between [a court's] legal principles and rules' when they design treaties

[9] Alec Stone Sweet and Thomas L Brunell, 'Trustee Courts and the Judicialization of International Regimes. The Politics of Majoritarian Activism in the European Convention on Human Rights, the European Union, and the World Trade Organization' (2013) 1 Journal of Law and Courts 61.

[10] Cosette Creamer and Zuzanna Godzimirska, '(De)Legitimation at the WTO Dispute Settlement Mechanism' (2016) 49 Vanderbilt Journal of Transnational Law 275.

[11] Zuzanna Godzimirska, 'Delegitimation of Global Courts: Lessons from the Past' in Avidan Kent, Jamie Trinidad, and Nikos Skoutaris (eds), *The Future of International Courts* (Routledge 2019).

[12] ibid.

[13] ibid.

and are more likely to accept the jurisdiction of an international court that rests on a similar legal tradition.[14] For example, a State with a common law tradition—as compared with its civil law counterpart—may be more familiar with the doctrine of precedent applied by the WTO's judicial organs,[15] resulting in more favourable assessments of the DSM's exercise of authority.

Why might it matter that the international bench is representative of diverse genders, world regions or legal traditions? Under a deontological argument for diversity, as outlined in the introductory chapter, States believe that diversity is 'a good in and of itself' and that representativeness across various dimensions is an important democratic value that itself justifies a court's exercise of authority.[16] But does it have any effect beyond that? In the language of this volume, are there consequentialist arguments for ensuring diversity and representativeness? This chapter turns to these questions by examining whether *once on the bench*, identity matters for how governments evaluate the WTO's exercise of judicial authority. Does the presence of a female panellist or ABM positively influence members' evaluations of trade rulings? Does an AB division with mostly civil law members affect how governments respond to its legal analysis or findings?

2.2 Professional Experience: Sensitivity to Political Considerations

Recent research suggests that professional experiences—particularly sensitivity to political considerations—affect a court's sociological legitimacy.[17] In the context of the ICJ, we found that professional experience signalling a probability of independence or insensitivity to political considerations reduced a candidate's probability of being elected to the bench. Importantly, the WTO's DSU establishes guidelines regarding adjudicator experiences. Article 8 specifies that panellists should represent 'well-qualified governmental and/or non-governmental individuals' with prior experience within the WTO, and each panel 'should be selected with a view to ensuring the independence of the members, a sufficiently diverse background and a wide spectrum of experience'.[18] For ABMs, the requirements are slightly different. Article 17 requires that they have 'demonstrated expertise in law, international trade and the subject matter of the covered agreements generally'. In

[14] Sara McLaughlin Mitchell and Emilia Justyna Powell, *Domestic Law Goes Global. Legal Traditions and International Courts* (Cambridge University Press 2011).

[15] Krzysztof Pelc, 'The Politics of Precedent in International Law: A Social Network Application' (2014) 108 American Political Science Review 547.

[16] Freya Baetens, Chapter 1, 'Identity and Diversity on the International Bench: Implications for the Legitimacy of International Adjudication' in this volume.

[17] Cosette D Creamer and Zuzanna Godzimirska, 'The Job Market for Justice: Screening and Selecting Candidates for the International Court of Justice' (2017) 30 Leiden Journal of International Law 1.

[18] DSU, Art 8(2). With respect to independence, see further Arts 8(3) and 8(9).

contrast to panels that may consist of government officials, ABMs 'shall be unaffiliated with any government', though they are permitted to have held government positions prior to their appointment.[19]

Madsen has argued that a key component of legitimation rests with how elected judges develop the court and its jurisprudence, finding that the Cold War composition of the European Court of Human Rights (ECtHR) helped increase its legitimacy and establish itself as a 'supreme court of human rights' during a critical existential phase.[20] The court was initially composed of a 'legal-political elite of law professors who were keenly aware of how the structural challenges faced by key member States had to be considered in the development of the court's practices'.[21] In the 1990s, however, the bench transformed to one primarily consisting of human rights law experts with less sensitivity to the political considerations of European member States, which has arguably contributed to a decline in the court's legitimacy in more recent decades.[22] Similar arguments have been made in the WTO context, with trade officials and scholars suggesting that the absence of lawyers in settling disputes during the GATT's first decade contributed to the success of and support for the system, because panellists 'felt they knew exactly what was meant by all of the provisions in the agreement they had drafted'.[23] In light of current critiques of interpretive 'overreaching' by the WTO's AB, there are thus good reasons to believe that professional experiences play a role in assessments of the DSM's legitimacy.

3. Data

To explore the relationship between WTO bench composition and the DSM's sociological legitimacy, this chapter draws on two original datasets. We limit the analysis to the period between 1995 and 2016, the year in which deadlock over new Appellate Body appointments began. The first dataset consists of background information on all individuals appointed to sit on WTO dispute panels and all individuals elected as ABMs. To compile this data, we first collected all individuals' curriculum vitae (CVs) and biographical narratives available online[24] and created

[19] Working procedures for appellate review Art 2(3) specify this further: 'A Member shall exercise his/her office without accepting or seeking instructions from any international, governmental, or non-governmental organization or any private source.'

[20] Mikael Rask Madsen, 'The Legitimization Strategies of International Judges: The Case of the European Court of Human Rights' in Michal Bobek (ed), *Selecting Europe's Judges: A Critical Review of the Appointment Procedures to the European Courts* (Oxford University Press 2015) 262.

[21] Madsen (n 20).

[22] ibid.

[23] Robert E Hudec, 'The Role of the GATT Secretariat in the Evolution of the WTO Dispute Settlement Procedure' in Jagdish Bhagwati and Mathias Hirsch (eds), *The Uruguay Round and Beyond: Essays in Honour of Arthur Dunkel* (Springer-Verlag 1998) 104.

[24] Both on the WTO website as well as other institutional sources.

a timeline of each judge's professional experiences and background. We then coded various characteristics of professional background, pre- and post-appointment, as well as a number of identity traits.

For both panellists and ABMs, an individual's country of nationality was used to code whether they came from a common law, civil law, or mixed legal tradition.[25] It was also used to code region, employing the World Bank's regional classifications. The gender of all panellists and ABMs was coded using titles prefixing a person's name within WTO dispute documents. These metadata were collected to examine the relevance of gender, geographical representation, and legal tradition.

Studies stress the importance of judges' professional profiles for the sociological legitimacy of an international court,[26] so we coded adjudicators' CVs for a number of professional experiences. For panellists, we identified whether they had any prior experience in the GATT or WTO. If so, information was collected on whether this was as a government representative or delegate to the GATT/WTO, within the GATT or WTO Secretariat, as a previous Appellate Body Member, and/or whether the panellist had experience working within their home ministry dealing with international trade. We also coded a panellist's occupation at the time of appointment, namely whether they worked (predominantly) within government, academia, private practice, an international organization, or retired. Finally, data was gathered on whether the panellist had previously served on a WTO dispute panel (hereinafter a 'repeat panellist').

For Appellate Body members, occupation at the time of appointment was coded, in addition to whether the ABM had any prior academic experience, any experience working within their home government in the area of trade (including as a GATT/WTO delegate), any international arbitral experience, and whether the ABM had previously served as a dispute panellist. For ABMs, we coded two educational characteristics, namely whether they had earned some type of law degree and whether they had any educational training in the United States.

The second dataset consists of government statements on panel and Appellate Body dispute reports over the past twenty years. Member statements made prior to the adoption of a dispute report typically comment on legal interpretations or procedural decisions, and are likely to reflect governments' views on how panellists and ABMs exercise their judicial authority, providing a valid proxy for the sociological legitimacy of panels and the AB. Between 1995 and 2016, the period we analyse, the DSB considered, discussed and adopted 195 dispute or compliance reports, with an average of 8.86 reports adopted per year. While the WTO Agreement permits all governments to express views prior to report adoption, only a select group of countries make use of this opportunity in practice, with only thirty-nine

[25] Classification of legal tradition draws from the University of Ottawa's JuriGlobe—World Legal Systems project. Available at <www.juriglobe.ca/eng/>accessed October 20, 2019.

[26] Madsen (n 20); Hudec (n 23).

percent of the WTO membership (fifty-one Members in total) having expressed at least one view on an Appellate Body or panel report. Thus, while we are examining aggregate expressed views, this is still only a subset of the membership and largely those who participate as disputing or third parties.

In order to classify the sentiment expressed within each statement, a coding scheme was developed consisting of six categories: (1) strongly critical; (2) predominantly critical; (3) neutral; (4) predominantly supportive; (5) strongly supportive; and (6) other.[27] Statements that fall within the *strongly supportive* category express strong support for the dispute settlement system as a whole and panel and/or Appellate Body proceedings or reports. To fall within this category, the language employed in relation to the DSM must convey strong support, despite the inclusion of one or two indirectly critical comments. This category also includes statements that express exclusive support for the DSM, even if the statement does not employ strongly supportive language. For example, Members often stress that the report under adoption was 'generally well-reasoned' or that the Member 'support[s] the Appellate Body's interpretation' on a specific question, and uses the rest of the statement to recap the findings, without expressing any further view on the issue.[28] Similarly, statements that fall within the *strongly critical* category include those that express strong criticism of the DSM despite the presence of indirectly supportive comments. As with the *strongly supportive* category, this category also includes statements that are exclusively critical, even if the language is not strongly critical.

Statements that fall within the *predominantly supportive* category express both criticism and support for the DSM, but overall—both qualitatively and quantitatively—convey greater support. Similarly, statements that fall within the *predominantly critical* category express both criticism and support for the DSM, but overall convey greater criticism.[29] Statements classified as *neutral* in some way reference the DSM by mentioning the dispute or the report at hand, without expressing criticism or support for it or the DSM.[30] Finally, the *other* category ensures that statements not about the operation of the DSM are excluded from the

[27] Coding rules are on file with the authors.

[28] See eg Dispute Settlement Body, *Minutes of Meeting Held in the Centre William Rappard on 18 August 2003*, para 40, WTO Doc WT/DSB/M/154 (22 October 2003) ('The representative of the United States said that her country welcomed the opportunity to comment on what it considered a generally well-reasoned report.'); Dispute Settlement Body, *Minutes of Meeting Held in the Centre William Rappard on 25 November 1998*, para 19, WTO Doc WT/DSB/M/51 (22 January 1999). ('The representative of Japan said that his country supported the Appellate Body's interpretation ... ').

[29] See eg Dispute Settlement Body, *Minutes of Meeting Held in the Centre William Rappard on 27 July 2000*, para 71, WTO Doc WT/DSB/M/86 (July 27, 2000) (describing the representative of Hong Kong, China's overall acceptance of the report but high concern regarding third party filings).

[30] See eg Dispute Settlement Body, Minutes of Meeting *Held in the Centre William Rappard on 22 September 1998*, para 19, WTO Doc WT/DSB/M/48 (Sept 22, 1998) ('The representative of the United States said that references had been made to the reports of the panel and the Appellate Body adopted on 16 January 1998 in the case of the US—India dispute on the same matter. The United States still awaited India's action to comply with the DSB's recommendations concerning this issue. He therefore wished to ask India whether it could provide any information on steps to be taken towards compliance.').

analysis. Two coders manually classified all 1161 statements made between 1995 and 2016.[31] For ease of presentation, the six categories described are collapsed into four in the subsequent analysis, i.e. Critical, Supportive, Neutral, and Other.

4. How Diverse are WTO Panellists and Appellate Body Members?

Before turning to the sociological legitimacy of the WTO's DSM, we first describe the composition of—and diversity within—panels and the AB up until 2016. We focus on gender, nationality, and legal tradition, and the professional profiles of panels and the ABM, and relate to current critiques of the DSM where relevant.

Between 1995 and 2015, the DSB composed 161 panels to hear and help settle trade disputes.[32] Of these, the Director General selected roughly two thirds of the panellists (for 102 panels), in lieu of agreement on composition between disputing parties.[33] This represents over five hundred appointments and 246 distinct individuals. In contrast, only twenty-seven individuals have sat on the Appellate Body, all selected by the entire WTO membership under a consensus decision-making norm.[34] So how diverse are these panellists and ABMs? Is the settlement of trade disputes dominated by a group of individuals with specific identities?

In terms of geographical representation, 22.5% of appointed panellists came from Europe and Central Asia; 24.6% from Latin America and the Caribbean; and 31% from East Asia and the Pacific. The Middle East and North Africa (MENA) is less well-represented (only 4% of appointed panellists), as is Sub-Saharan Africa (4.7% of panellists) and South Asia (5.2% of panellists). In fact, these figures overrepresent these regions, as all but four appointed panellists hailed from South Africa, and those four panellists consist of two individuals (Usha Dwarka-Canabady from Mauritius and Darlington Mwape from Zambia). Similarly, MENA panellists all came from Egypt or Israel, with the exception of one individual from Morocco. A little less than half (40.7%) of ABMs came from the East Asia and Pacific region, with two of these individuals hailing from the Philippines. Sub-Saharan Africa has been represented on the AB by one South African and one Mauritian, while two Indians have represented the South Asian region and two Egyptians the MENA region. Only three Latin Americans and three Europeans have sat on the Appellate Body, which contrasts with these regions' strong representation on dispute panels.

[31] Following an initial round of coding, the inter-coder reliability measure calculated using Krippendorff's alpha coefficient was 0.859.

[32] Analysis ends at 2015 due to length of time it takes to issue a report (especially if appealed), and thus allow for possibility of DSB statement on report. This data do not include panels established under DSU, Art 21.5 to evaluate compliance with previous reports, so-called 'compliance panels'.

[33] Pauwelyn (n 5) 221.

[34] Though note disproportionate influence of economically powerful countries. See Elsig and Pollack (n 3).

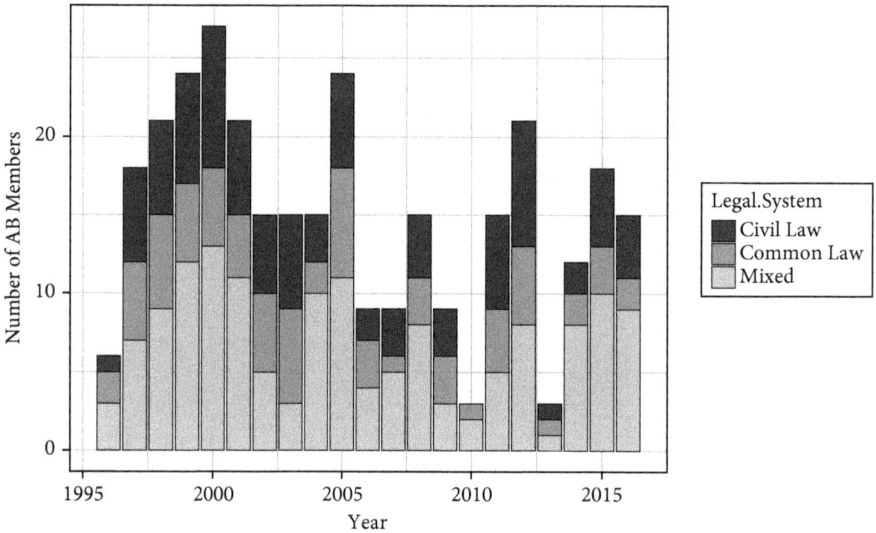

Figure 21.1 Number of ABMs from three primary legal cultures on each division composed, 1995–2016

The Director General and disputing parties seem to prefer panellists from a civil law tradition; panellists from a country with a strong civil law background were a majority for 46% of panels composed. This differs from the 22% of panels composed with a majority of common law panellists, with an average of about one common law panellist per panel. While slightly lower than the average number of civil law panellists (1.4) per panel, it is higher than the average for panellists coming from mixed legal traditions (0.63). This contrasts starkly with the AB, where only six members come from a country with a civil law tradition, seven from a common law country, and 14 from a country with a mixed legal tradition (see Figure 21.1). Indeed, there have been six disputes heard by an appellate division composed entirely of members from mixed legal traditions and none by a bench of all common law or all civil law ABMs. This need not necessarily translate into a stronger influence on rulings, however, given the practice of all members exchanging views on each dispute prior to drafting the report.[35]

US nationals are rarely selected to sit on panels, indirectly supporting the Trump Administration's claim that the US does not 'have the judges'.[36] In terms of

[35] 'This exchange of views is intended to give effect to the principle of collegiality in the Appellate Body and serves to ensure consistency and coherence in the jurisprudence of the Appellate Body (Rule 4(1) of the Working Procedures).' See <www.wto.org/english/tratop_e/dispu_e/disp_settlement_cbt_e/c6s5p3_e.htm> (accessed Oct. 30, 2019).

[36] Tom Miles, 'Trump's Bonfire of the Treaties Sweeps towards the WTO' *Reuters* (18 May 2018) <www.reuters.com/article/us-usa-trade-wto-analysis/trumps-bonfire-of-the-treaties-sweeps-towards-the-wto-idUSKCN1IJ1K9> accessed 1 November 2018.

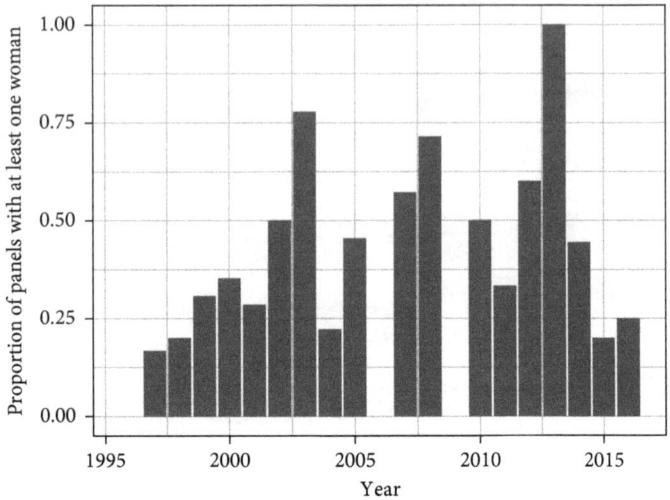

Figure 21.2 Gender diversity on WTO panels, 1995–2016

geographical representation, fourteen panels have had a US panellist, though this represents only nine separate individuals, as a few have sat on multiple panels. In fact, out of the 597 panellists appointed (including for compliance panels), only 48 (12.4%) have come from the US or Canada. This likely derives from the fact that DSU Article 8.2 prohibits nationals from the disputing or third parties to sit on panels, unless otherwise agreed to by the disputing parties, and the fact that the US participates as a direct or third party in nearly every dispute, with Canada not far behind. At the appellate level, nationality prohibitions do not exist and the Appellate Body has always had a sitting US member, in contrast to Trump's claims. In addition, well over half of appointed members received some form of education in the United States. Yet despite the fact that Canada has been a direct party in 18% of disputes that have reached the AB up until 2016,[37] to date there has not been a single Canadian ABM.

As for gender, women have comprised only 14.9% of all panellists, representing a mere 31 individuals. After two full decades of WTO dispute settlement, not a single female South Asian had been appointed to sit on a panel. Figure 21.2 displays the proportion of panels that have been composed with at least one female panellist. Notably, only 11 panels were composed with a majority of women and as of 2016 there has never been an all-female panel. Gender diversity is only slightly better for the Appellate Body, with women constituting 18.5% of the 27 ABMs appointed. Two of these five women were American

[37] 19 out of 105 disputes reaching the AB up until 2016. This excludes compliance reports.

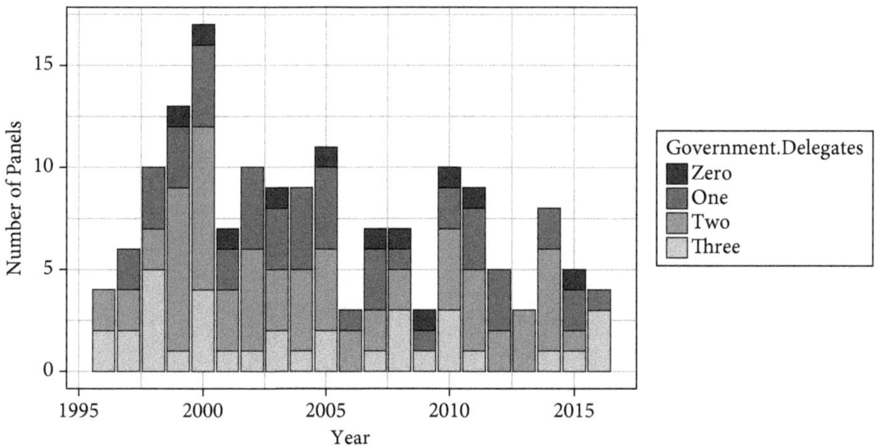

Figure 21.3 Number of panellists with government delegate experience on each WTO panel, 1996–2016

nationals and two Chinese. The first female ABM—Merit Janow—did not start her term until 2003.

Turning to professional background, 153 of the 161 panels composed from 1995–2015 were comprised of at least two panellists that had some form of experience with or in the WTO, in line with what is encouraged in DSU Article 8.[38] Two-thirds of all panels have been composed of a majority of panellists with experience as a government delegate to the GATT/WTO (see Figure 21.3). Some degree of familiarity with the organization is evidently seen as an essential professional experience to rule on a trade dispute. Indeed, this seems to be a holdover from early GATT dispute panels, comprised largely of diplomats who had negotiated the treaty.[39] The same holds true with respect to the Appellate Body, with roughly 60% of members having some experience in or with the WTO, and 17 of the 27 members appointed to date having some government trade experience.

As for experience with WTO dispute settlement, roughly half of all panels have been composed of at least two (if not three) repeat panellists (see Figure 21.4). This excludes compliance panels, which tend to re-appoint the original panellists. However, only seven AB members have previously served on a dispute panel.

Few panels have been composed without at least one panellist holding a government position at the time of appointment (only 10 panels in total). In fact,

[38] As mentioned previously, this includes one or more of the following: GATT/WTO Secretariat, former AB member, government delegate to the GATT/WTO, or official within the home trade ministry.

[39] Gabrielle Marceau, 'A History of Law and Lawyers in the GATT/WTO: The Development of the Rule of Law in the Multilateral Trading System' (Cambridge University Press 2015) 11–12.

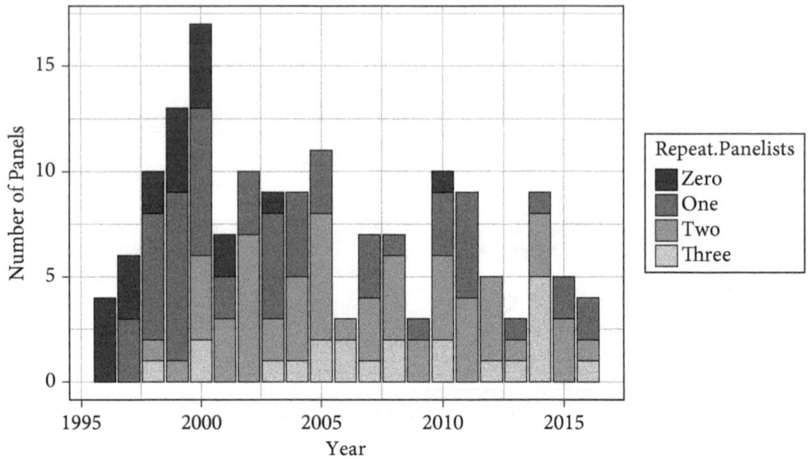

Figure 21.4 Number of repeat panellists on each WTO panel composed, 1995–2016

the vast majority of panellists over the years have held some sort of political or government position while sitting on a panel. In contrast to the Appellate Body, few 'pure' or primary academics have been selected as panellists. Still, many selected panellists with primary occupations in the private sector or government have adjunct academic affiliations or some sort of academic teaching experience.

ABMs typically possess a distinct profile from that of panellists, in that fewer held government positions at the time of appointment and many more have extensive legal experience (in government or academia). Indeed, 85% of ABMs hold a law degree, and only three AB reports have been issued by a division composed without a majority of lawyers sitting on it. Yet this difference in professional profiles should not be overstated. Over half of appointed AB members have had experience working within their home governments in the area of trade, although a little over half of AB Divisions to date have been composed with a majority of academics at the time of their appointment.

5. Bench Composition and Legitimacy

Does the background of individuals tasked to interpret WTO rules matter for how member governments react to their rulings? Do certain identity traits increase the likelihood that a government will be more critical of a report's content? Drawing on manual sentiment classification of report statements discussed above, this

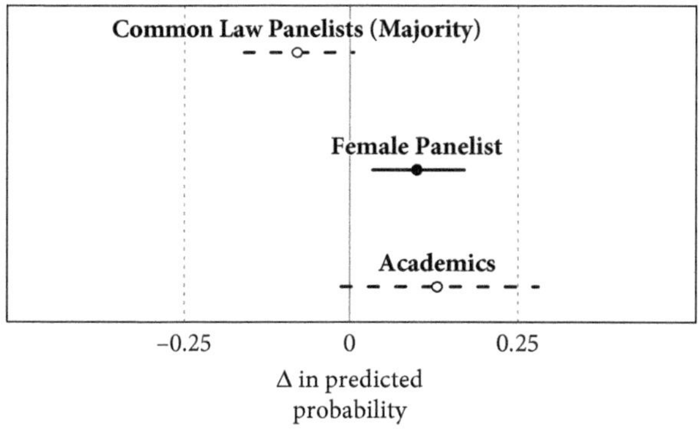

Figure 21.5 Likelihood of critical report statement*

* Simulated estimates of probability that a given report statement will garner criticism. Circles represent the expected effect on the probability of criticism as the number of common law panellists moves from non- majority (0–1 members) to majority (2–3), the number of academics on a panel moves from 0 to 2 panellists, and all other variables are held constant at their means. For female panellists, the circle represents the expected effect on the probability of criticism as a panel moves from no women to one or more women. The lines are 95% confidence intervals. When the circles and lines are solid, there is at least a 95% confidence of a positive or negative effect on the probability of criticism. Otherwise lines are dotted. The common law and academic covariates retain significance at $p < 0.1$. See Table 21.1 for full results of the pooled logistic odds regression.

section employs bivariate associations and multivariate analysis to identify factors associated with voicing criticism of or expressing support for a panel or Appellate Body report.

5.1 WTO Dispute Panels

In the early years of the WTO, the DSB decided that it would not adopt panel and AB reports separately and instead discuss both reports together. If a panel ruling is appealed by one or both parties, the DSB simultaneously discusses the panel and AB reports. If a panel ruling is not appealed, the DSB will discuss the panel report alone. In practice, statements on appealed reports tend to comment on both the panel's and AB's legal analysis and findings. This does, however, make it difficult to fully disentangle the relationship between report reception and panellist background from that of AB background. One place to start would be by examining the sentiment of statements made only on panel reports not appealed. Unfortunately, very few panel reports during the period we analyse have not been appealed, fifty-six total, making any inferences drawn from this subset of reports questionable. Instead, we examine all panel reports, with the understanding that criticism for appealed reports can be aimed at the AB, panels, or both.

We report bivariate correlations between criticism and each element of panel composition, and findings from a multivariate analysis that controls for other factors likely to influence the probability of criticism (see Figure 21.5 for significant multivariate findings and Table 21.1 for all multivariate

Table 21.1 Panel composition and critical statements

	Estimated Probability of Critical Statement
Majority Common Law Panellists	–0.408[a] (0.239)
Any Panellist from Underrepresented Region	0.099 (0.168)
Any Female Panellist	0.493[c] (0.173)
Majority GATT/WTO Delegates	–0.056 (0.182)
One Academic Panellist	0.261 (0.193)
Two Academic Panellists	0.542[a] (0.328)
Majority Repeat Panellists	–0.114 (0.179)
GDP per capita (logged)	–0.141[b] (0.063)
Total Population (logged)	0.124[a] (0.064)
Anti-Dumping Dispute	–0.618[c] (0.238)
Zeroing Dispute	–0.573 (0.414)
EU Statement	–0.762[c] (0.295)
US Statement	0.322 (0.263)
Constant	1.022 (1.269)
Observations	920
Log Likelihood	–555.532
Akaike Inf. Crit.	1,139.064

Note: [a] p<0.1; [b] p<0.05; [c] p<0.01

results).[40] Notably, our analysis finds no significant bivariate correlation between the number of panellists with a mixed law tradition or from an underrepresented region and criticism, and only a very weak (negative) association with number of civil and common law panellists. In multivariate specifications, panel reports with a majority of common law panellists are weakly correlated with a slightly lower likelihood of criticism.

The presence of a panellist from an underrepresented region (MENA, South Asia, and Sub-Saharan Africa) is unrelated to the probability of criticism in all model specifications. A significant bivariate relationship does exist, however, between gender and criticism, and within multivariate specifications, the presence of *any* female panellist increases the probability of criticism by 10%.

5.2 The Appellate Body

At the appellate level, we begin by looking at the relationship between a division's majority composition, under the assumption that when the *majority* of ABMs possess a specific identity or background characteristic, it is more likely to influence a report's legal analysis and findings, and consequently a governments' evaluation of it. Specifically, we look at whether a division was composed of a majority of members from: a civil law background; a mixed legal tradition; primary academic occupation at time of appointment; primary government occupation at time of appointment; any government trade experience; a US education. We also examine the influence of the presence of at least one female ABM on a division. We report bivariate correlations between criticism and each element of bench composition separately, and findings from a multivariate analysis that controls for other factors likely to influence the probability of criticism (see Figure 21.6 for significant multivariate findings and Table 21.2 for all multivariate results).[41]

[40] To estimate the relationship between each separate panel composition covariate and the probability of a critical statement, we first fit a logit model, with report statement as the unit of analysis. Within the multivariate analysis to estimate the probability of a critical statement, we fit a logit model and the parameter vector for the model with a pooled logistic regression, with report statement as the unit of analysis. In addition to panel characteristics, we control for the wealth and size of the government issuing the statement, whether the statement was made by the US or the EU, and whether the dispute involved either the Anti-Dumping Agreement or the issue of zeroing in anti-dumping disputes. All covariates reported in Table 21.1.

[41] To estimate the relationship between each separate AB division covariate and the probability of a critical statement, we first fit a logit model, with report statement as the unit of analysis. Within the multivariate analysis to estimate the probability of a critical statement, we fit a logit model and the parameter vector for the model with a pooled logistic regression, with report statement as the unit of analysis. In addition to AB division characteristics, we also controlled for the wealth and size of the government issuing the statement, whether the statement was made by the US or the EU, and whether the dispute involved either the Anti-Dumping Agreement or the issue of zeroing in anti-dumping disputes. All covariates reported in Table 21.1.

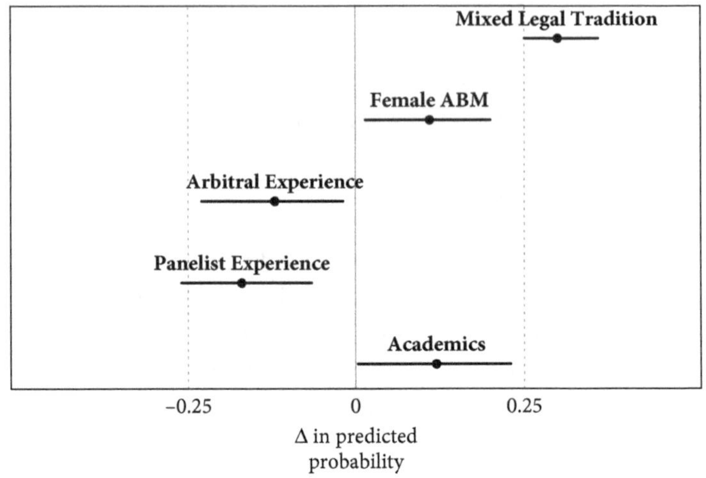

Figure 21.6 Likelihood of critical report statement*

* Simulated estimates of probability that a given report statement will be critical. Circles represent the expected effect on the probability of criticism as each composition characteristic moves from non-majority (0–1 members) to majority (2–3) members for a given division, and all other variables are held constant at their means. For female ABMs, the circle represents the expected effect on the probability of criticism as a division moves from no women to one or more women ABMs. The lines are 95% confidence intervals. When the circles and lines are solid, there is at least a 95% confidence of a positive or negative effect on the probability of criticism. See Table 21.2 for full results of the pooled logistic odds regression.

As for legal culture, there is no significant relationship between majority civil law or common law ABMs and criticism. However, when the number of ABMs with a mixed legal tradition on a division goes from zero to two, there is a 24% higher chance that the report will be criticized. In multivariate specifications, a majority mixed law division remains significantly associated with a greater likelihood of criticism. In terms of gender, no significant bivariate relationship exists, but within multivariate specifications—as with panels—the presence of any female ABM on a division increases the probability of criticism by 11%.

Turning to professional background, the only characteristics found to be significantly related to criticism are arbitral experience, experience as a WTO dispute panellist, and academic positions at the time of appointment. Within multivariate models, more ABMs with international arbitration experience reduces the likelihood of criticism by 12%, while divisions with majority WTO panellist experience reduces it by 17%. In contrast, more academic ABMs increases the probability of Members voicing criticism by 12%. While more ABMs with government trade experience is associated substantively with lower likelihood of criticism, this factor never reaches conventional significance levels in any model specification.

Table 21.2 AB division composition and critical statements

	Estimated Probability of Critical Statement
ABM Majority Mixed Law	0.431[b] (0.203)
Any Female ABM	0.474[b] (0.204)
ABM Majority Academics	0.5545[a] (0.274)
ABM Majority Arbitral Experience	−0.528[b] (0.224)
ABM Majority WTO Panellist	−0.839[c] (0.273)
ABM Majority Government Occupation	0.265 (0.306)
ABM Majority Government Trade Experience	−0.156 (0.233)
GDP per capita (logged)	−0.156[b] (0.067)
Population (logged)	0.095 (0.070)
Anti-Dumping Agreement	−0.577[b] (0.256)
Zeroing Dispute	−0.607 (0.489)
EU Statement	−0.811[b] (0.363)
US Statement	0.322 (0.303)
Constant	2.077 (1.455)
Observations	700
Log Likelihood	−423.796
Akaike Inf. Crit.	875.592

Note: [a] $p<0.1$; [b] $p<0.05$; [c] $p<0.01$

6. Conclusion

Moving beyond the judicial appointment stage, this chapter explored whether, *once on the bench*, certain identity characteristics matter for the sociological legitimacy of the WTO's dispute settlement mechanism. In terms of diversity, dispute panellists have been quite geographically representative except for the Middle East and North Africa, with only 4% of all panellists hailing from that region. In contrast to panellists, few Latin Americans and Europeans have been appointed to the AB, while nearly half of all AB members come from the East Asia and Pacific region. With only two individuals from Egypt, MENA is similarly underrepresented at the appellate level.

Panels seem to be overrepresented by individuals coming from a country with a civil law tradition. This contrasts starkly with the AB, where about half are from countries with a mixed legal tradition. Interestingly, there have been six disputes heard by an appellate division composed entirely of individuals from mixed legal traditions and none by a bench of all common law or all civil law ABMs. Gender diversity is glaringly absent from both stages of dispute settlement, with women representing only 15% of all panellists and a mere 18.5% of the twenty-seven ABMs appointed.

Turning to professional background, a majority of panels have been composed with at least two panellists who had some form of prior experience with the WTO. Moreover, a vast majority of panellists have held a political or government position while sitting on a panel, and roughly half of all panels have been composed of at least two repeat panellists.

ABMs typically possess a distinct professional profile from that of panellists in terms of professional background, although a majority have some experience in or with the WTO. Fewer ABMs, however, held government positions at the time of appointment and many have extensively more legal experience (in government or academia). In sharp contrast to panellists' prior experience, only seven AB members had previously served on a dispute panel.

When looking at the relationship between adjudicator characteristics and the sociological legitimacy of the DSM (as proxied by expressed support or criticism of reports), one identity trait that seems to matter is gender. The presence of *any* female panellist or ABM is consistently associated with a *greater* likelihood that any government will issue a critical statement on a report drafted (in part) by her. Combined with the lack of women on panels and the AB (though this has slowly improved over time), these findings do not bode well for calls to increase gender representativeness in the WTO's DSM.

Another consistent finding is that academics appointed to panels or the AB tend to spark greater criticism from governments on reports they have helped draft. This comports with the argument that academia lends itself to (the appearance of) relative insensitivity to political considerations.[42] In contrast, previous WTO panellist experience seems to slightly reduce government criticism of reports, though there is a stronger association at the appellate than panel level. We found no significant relationship between criticism and other professional background characteristics that we might expect to improve the DSM's sociological legitimacy, namely GATT/WTO delegate experience or experience in a government's trade ministry.

[42] Creamer and Godzimirska (n 17).

Our main finding is that the identity of the panellists and ABM *does not consistently or strongly* matter in any meaningful way for how WTO members evaluate the DSM's exercise of authority. This supports Baetens' claim that the 'identity (and likely the diversity) of the adjudicators is less important where adjudicatory bodies have a strong and permanent institutional framework'.[43] The role of the WTO's Legal Affairs Division and the Appellate Body Secretariat in streamlining the outcomes and procedures may very well be the best explanation behind this, as it prevents diversity from being reflected in dispute rulings. An alternative explanation may be that the bench's diversity matters more its *normative* legitimacy—and for scholars—than it does for governments.

[43] Baetens (n 16). See also, Pauwelyn (n 5).

22

Ethnicity, Religion, and Diversity at the International Criminal Court

Is More Too Much?

Solomy Balungi Bossa and Gilles Landry Dossan

1. Introduction

States' continued acceptance of and recourse to international dispute settlement, including international criminal courts and tribunals, demonstrates the central role of international judicial institutions. The thorny question of their legitimacy ultimately comes down to 'confidence in the stability and adequacy of the law, and confidence in the integrity and predictability of courts and tribunals administering the law'.[1] From this angle, confidence seems closely linked to the essence of the judicial function, and justifiably so. As international law strives to adapt to a globalized world, international courts have a structuring function: beyond the settlement of international disputes, they may contribute to the transparency, consistency, and effectiveness of the international legal order.[2] However, a discussion on public confidence in international courts ought to include an enquiry into the individuals in charge of applying the law, their integrity in the administration of justice, *in fine* their legitimacy as a full component of the international legal system. A general survey into the legitimacy of judges lies beyond the purpose of this contribution.[3] Rather, we will challenge the representativeness of the individuals populating the benches of international courts and examine whether they (should) reflect the diversity of stakeholders.

Although judges at the International Criminal Court ('the Court' or 'ICC') are elected by the States Parties to the Rome Statute, they are accountable to a

[1] Wilfried Jenks, *The prospects of international adjudication* (Stevens and Sons Ltd 1964) 101.

[2] Sandra Szurek, 'La composition des juridictions internationales permanentes: de nouvelles exigences de qualité et de représentativité' (2010) 56 Annuaire français de droit international 43.

[3] 'Even the public at large has become aware of the fact that from time to time international judges render decision which deeply affect the daily life even of ordinary citizens. As a natural consequence, selection procedures are growing in complexity, carried by the consideration that judges entrusted with such extensive and deep-going responsibilities should enjoy a maximum of legitimacy'. Quoted by Sandra Szurek, ibid.

Solomy Balungi Bossa and Gilles Landry Dossan, *Ethnicity, Religion, and Diversity at the International Criminal Court* In: *Identity and Diversity on the International Bench.* Edited by: Freya Baetens, Oxford University Press (2020). © The several contributors. DOI: 10.1093/oso/9780198870753.003.0022.

variety of actors. They handle different and even incongruous expectations from the accused (rights of the defence), and the victims (reparations for damages suffered), but also from civil society, which has an interest in ensuring that justice is delivered in accordance with universally established standards (fair and equitable process).[4] In the context of reflecting on the diversity of the Court's bench, it should be emphasized that diversity constitutes a major springboard for overcoming the uncomfortable reality that some observers have described as 'dissonance', namely the tension that may exist between the methods and concepts used by the Court and the contexts in which they are applied.[5] In other words, diversity on the bench allows the application of the law in an international context marked by a plurality of cultures.

Aspects of diversity such as religion and ethnicity may be addressed to some extent in the composition of national benches but not in international courts.[6] However, the concepts of religion and ethnicity are far from absent from the Court's Statute: quite on the contrary, they are central to the elements of the substantive crimes under the Court's jurisdiction.[7] This suggests that diversity is a virtue to be protected as a matter of substantive criminal law, indeed to the point that threats or harm thereto can be punished at the international level. Questioning their relevance as criteria for the diversification of the Court's bench is therefore not a futile undertaking. Based on this postulate, the present chapter aims to assess whether ethnicity and religion should be added to the criteria to be considered in the context of the election of ICC judges as an avenue for reinforcing its legitimacy. What space do or could they occupy in the legal framework of the Court? We will respond successively to these questions by presenting, first, the existing diversity criteria stipulated in the legal instruments governing the Court, and then by questioning the relevance of ethnicity and religion as further tools for diversifying the Court's bench.

[4] The issue of diversity of the Court does not seem to be alien to the movements that gave birth to it. An author noted that 'la Cour Pénale Internationale doit en grande partie sa naissance au travail d'impulsion qui a été mené par les organisations non gouvernementales, et notamment la coalition internationale pour la création de la Cour pénale internationale, qui ont porté la création de cette juridiction, qui ont servi de d'aiguillon et ont été extrêmement présents dans le développement du processus qui a conduit à la création de la Cour'. See Françoise Mathe, 'L'internationalisation de la justice pénale' in Jacques Krynen and Jacques Raibaut (eds), *La légitimité des juges: actes du colloque des 29-30 octobre 2003* (Presses de l'Université des sciences sociales de Toulouse 2004) 141.

[5] Brandeis Institute for International Judges, *Toward an International Rule of Law* (Brandeis Institute for international judges 2010) 1.

[6] Abhinav Chandrachud, 'Diversity and the International Criminal Court: Does Geographic Background Impact Decision Making' (2013) 38 Brooklyn Journal of International Law 487.

[7] Arts 6, 7(1)(h) and 8(2)(b)(ix) of the Rome Statute.

2. Existing Diversity Criteria in the Legal Framework of the Court

The Rome Statute does not escape the classical duality attached to the constituent treaties of international organizations: not only is it a normative instrument prescribing rights and obligations for the States that are parties to it, but it also creates a new legal order and a new subject of international law. Examples of the former include States Parties' obligations to cooperate with the organization; examples of the latter can be found in the rules relating to the functioning of and interactions between the various bodies of the institution itself. States' adherence to the Rome Statute will allow, *inter alia*, to assess the legitimacy enjoyed by the international organization.

Exploring the diversity of the ICC's bench necessarily requires a careful analysis of the Rome Statute, in order to identify the elements intended to enhance such diversity, taking into account the *droit dérivé* of the Court. A close reading shows that the Statute is far from silent on the question of diversity. While regulating the qualification, appointment, and election of judges, it does not fail to prescribe the criteria that must be met by individuals who sit on the bench of the Court (A). However, the application of these criteria is not limited to the appointment of judges, it also affects the constitution of the chambers of the Court and thus the exercise of the function of judge (B).

2.1 Diversity as Part of the Selection Criteria for ICC Judges

Article 36 of the Rome Statute, relating to the qualification, appointment, and election of judges of the Court, enumerates the criteria or conditions to be fulfilled for serving on the bench of the Court. Article 36.3 provides as follows:

> 3. (a) The judges shall be chosen from among persons of high moral character, impartiality and integrity who possess the qualifications required in their respective States for appointment to the highest judicial offices.
> (b) Every candidate for election to the Court shall:
> (i) Have established competence in criminal law and procedure, and the necessary relevant experience, whether as judge, prosecutor, advocate or in other similar capacity, in criminal proceedings; or
> (ii) Have established competence in relevant areas of international law such as international humanitarian law and the law of human rights, and extensive experience in a professional legal capacity which is of relevance to the judicial work of the Court;

(c) Every candidate for election to the Court shall have an excellent knowledge of and be fluent in at least one of the working languages of the Court.

Although this description allows to grasp the qualifications required to be a judge of the Court, not all elements mentioned necessarily contribute to the diversity of the bench. Article 36.3 (a) focuses on the qualities that each judge must possess: morality, impartiality, integrity, and qualifications required to be a judge in her or his State of origin. Because of the customary character of these criteria[8] and the functions assigned to the Court (criminal jurisdiction), it is understandable that, during the negotiations, States showed greater interest in geographic representation and diversity of experience than in the question of the judges' personal qualities and professional background.[9]

Article 36.3 (b) distinguishes between judges who have a particular expertise in criminal law and have previously served as criminal judges, prosecutors, or advocates (List A), and judges who have qualifications in international law, particularly in international humanitarian law or human rights law, with extensive legal experience relevant to the work of the Court (List B). This distinction has practical consequences for the composition of the bench since lists of persons belonging to both categories are drawn up for the election.[10] While the need for proven criminal law expertise is obvious for a Court that is called to determine the criminal responsibility of individuals appearing before it, this is less the case concerning experience in public international law. The justification for such inclusion lies in the acquis of ad hoc criminal tribunals previously established to try crimes now covered by the Rome Statute: in practice, issues of public international law are often the subject of discussion in the proceedings before the Court.[11] This is the case, for example, with the problem of

[8] Mariano J Aznar-Gomez and Eleni Methymaki, 'Article 2' in Andreas Zimmermann and Christian Tams (eds), *The Statute of the International Court of Justice: A Commentary* (3rd edn, OUP 2019) 306 (para 22).

[9] Referring to the *travaux préparatoires* of the Statute, William A Schabas noted that 'there was great concern that the Statute contain rules and mechanisms designed to ensure judges of high quality, with recognized expertise and experience. With this in mind, the United Kingdom proposed that there be a screening process subsequent to nominations and prior to the election. Although the concept received much sympathy, the concerns of most delegations were about ensuring geographic representation and experience from the major legal systems rather than the professionalism of the individuals making up the Court.' See William A Schabas, *The International Criminal Court: A commentary on the Rome Statute* (OUP 2016) 689.

[10] Art 36.5 of the Rome Statute: 'For the purposes of the election, there shall be two lists of candidates: List A containing the names of candidates with the qualifications specified in paragraph 3 (b)(i); and List B containing the names of candidates with the qualifications specified in paragraph 3 (b) (ii). A candidate with sufficient qualifications for both lists may choose on which list to appear. At the first election to the Court, at least nine judges shall be elected from list A and at least five judges from list B. Subsequent elections shall be so organized as to maintain the equivalent proportion on the Court of judges qualified on the two lists.'

[11] Zhu Wen-qi and Sureta Chana, 'Article 36' in Otto Triffterer (ed), *Commentary on the Rome Statute of the International Criminal Court: observer's notes, article by article* (München Beck 2008) 945.

reconciling the immunity of Heads of State and Government with the obligation of States Parties to cooperate with the Court in arresting individuals under arrest warrants.[12]

The requirement of fluency in one of the Court's working languages (English and French) is also critical.[13] Without entering into a detailed discussion on the working languages, it should be noted that the Court's linguistic diversity has a major influence on its functioning.[14] Setting out linguistic diversity criteria may further contribute to increasing diversity on the bench in terms of legal systems and culture.[15] Moreover, the prohibition on having two judges of the same nationality on the bench (common among international courts) is important.[16] Article 36.7 regulates instances of dual nationality by prioritizing the State in which the candidate ordinarily exercises his or her civil and political rights.

We believe that the criteria most likely to ensure the diversity of the Court's bench are found in Article 36.8, which provides as follows:

> 8.(a) The States Parties shall, in the selection of judges, take into account the need, within the membership of the Court, for:
> (i) The representation of the principal legal systems of the world;
> (ii) Equitable geographical representation; and
> (iii) A fair representation of female and male judges.
> (b) States Parties shall also take into account the need to include judges with legal expertise on specific issues, including, but not limited to, violence against women or children.

While the previous Articles focused on the quality and personal competence of judges, Article 36.8 embraces the collegial logic of the ICC bench and emphasizes the need for States Parties to ensure broad representation. As such, this college will have to represent the main legal systems of the world, so the seats available on the bench will have to be equitably distributed between the geographical regions and ensure gender representation, while making sure that it includes persons with expertise on specific issues such as violence against women or children. These criteria are based on longstanding practice established by other international (criminal)

[12] *The Prosecutor v Omar Hassan Ahmad Al-Bashir*, Decision under Article 87(7) of the Rome Statute on the non-compliance by South Africa with the request by the Court for the arrest and surrender of Omar Al-Bashir, ICC-02/05-01/09 (6 July 2017).

[13] Art 50.2 of the Statute.

[14] Leigh Swigart, 'Linguistic and Cultural Diversity in International Criminal Justice: Toward Bridging the Divide' (2016) 48 University of the Pacific Law Review 197. Leigh Swigart 'Unseen and Unsung: Language Services at the International Criminal Court and Their Impact on Institutional Legitimacy' in (F Baetens ed), *Legitimacy of Unseen Actors in International Adjudication* (Studies on International Courts and Tribunals (CUP 2019) 272–96.

[15] ibid.

[16] Art 36.7: 'No two judges may be nationals of the same State. A person who, for the purposes of membership of the Court, could be regarded as a national of more than one State shall be deemed to be a national of the State in which that person ordinarily exercises civil and political rights.'

courts and tribunals.[17] The drafters of the ICC Statute to some extent innovated existing practices by highlighting, for example, the importance of equitable representation based on gender, taking into account developments in the practice of ad hoc tribunals.[18] As the purpose of the present contribution does not allow for a detailed analysis of each criterion, we will confine ourselves to brief comments on their interdependence and effects on the diversification of the Court's bench.

The cumulative character of the criteria identified in Article 36.8 is clear from the use of the coordinating conjunction 'and', as well as from the word 'representation', linking all of them. Given that the diversity in legal cultures follows, to a large extent, the division of the world in geographical regions, the first and second criterion identified in Article 36.8 seem closely linked to each other. However, the relationship between these two criteria and the criterion of fair gender representation is not as obvious. At the same time, the three criteria must apply cumulatively: they coexist and interact with one another in the service of diversity, a fundamental basis of the Court's legitimacy. As one commentator has pointed out, 'a judicial body which is the emanation of only one social category, of one ethnic group, of a single culture, of a single gender group, loses legitimacy'.[19] Thus, particular attention should be paid to the strict observance of these criteria in the process of electing and appointing judges.

Almost two decades after the establishment of the Court, the effect of these criteria is significant as they have objectively contributed to the diversification of the ICC's bench. For example, out of twenty-seven former Members of the Court, thirteen were female.[20] The usefulness of these criteria is even more clearly illustrated by analysing the recourse of States Parties to a particularly important instrument in the selection of judges to sit on the Court: the *minimum voting requirements.* The States Parties have set up Minimum Voting Requirements (MVRs) to ensure a balanced bench of highly qualified judges. The MVRs bind the States Parties at the time of voting[21] and may change from one election to the next. States are required to vote in accordance with the requirements set out for the election year; a ballot that does not comply will be invalidated. States are required to respect three criteria for MVRs: legal expertise (list A/B), region, and gender[22]—with the latter two criteria applying only during the first four rounds of voting.[23] The gender MVRs are

[17] Ruth Mackenzie and others, *Selecting International Judges: Principle, Process, and Politics* (OUP 2010) 24.

[18] ibid 47

[19] Françoise Mathe, 'L´internationalisation de la justice pénale' in Jacques Krynen and Jacques Raibaut (eds), *La légitimité des juges* (Université de Toulouse 2003) 144.

[20] See the list of former judges on the Court's website <www.icc-cpi.int/about/judicial-divisions/biographies/Pages/former-judges.aspx>accessed on 15 August 2019

[21] See *Informal Guide and commentary to the Procedure for Nomination and Election of Judges of the International Criminal Court*, Sixteenth session, New York, 4-14 December 2017 (herein after Informal Guide). See also *Commentary-Procedure for the nomination and election of judges, the Prosecutor and Deputy Prosecutors of the International Criminal Court* (ICC-ASP/3/Res 6) within the Informal Guide.

[22] ibid 1 para A 1.

[23] ibid 2 para E 7.

designed to increase the likelihood that each gender has at least six judges on the bench.[24] During any given ballot, each State Party only has one vote per seat to be filled.[25] The applicability of each of the MVRs is determined at the outset of each ballot.[26] There should be a minimum of three judges on the Court for each of the regions, depending on the number of States Parties that have ratified the Rome Statute from a particular region.[27] Numbers may not drop beyond this minimum. MVRs require regional groups to play their part by pro-actively nominating sufficient numbers of candidates to fill the minimum numbers. For each vacancy in a region, at least two candidates have to be put forward.

MVRs apply even more strictly when there is a judicial vacancy at the Court. Only candidates who meet underrepresentation criteria, if any, may appear on the ballot paper. This approach discourages the practice of replacing an outgoing judge with another from the same country.[28] In terms of its contribution to the diversity on the ICC bench, MVRs 'make it more likely that candidates that fulfil underrepresented criteria are elected'.[29] In sum, the legal framework of the Court contains precise obligations for States Parties in determining the composition of the bench.

2.2 Diversity as Part of the Criteria Influencing the Judicial Function

The diversity criteria regulating the selection of judges have repercussions well after their appointment. Indeed, certain criteria appear to significantly influence how judges function on the Court, particularly as regards their assignment to one of the divisions of the Court. Article 39 of the Rome Statute relating to the Chambers of the Court determines the allocation of judges to divisions for the purpose of handling cases. Far from being limited to a simple statement on the number of judges in each division, this Article specifies the basis on which each division is composed. Here the diversity criteria again emerge as the Court has to take into account the 'nature of the functions' to be performed by each division, as well as the qualifications and the experience of the individual judges, before assigning a particular judge to a division. Thus, the composition of a division must lead to a specific result: an appropriate combination of judges with experience in criminal law and judges with experience in international law. On the basis of judges' qualifications and competence, Trial Divisions and Pre-Trial Divisions have to have a majority of

24 ibid 7 commentary on para 20(c).
25 ibid 6 commentary on para 20(b).
26 ibid.
27 ibid.
28 ibid 9 commentary on para 27(e).
29 ibid 9 commentary on para 22.

judges with criminal law experience. The relevance of such a composition is quite clear: the ICC is first and foremost a Court in charge of criminal cases.

The competence in international law on the basis of which some judges have been elected to the Court becomes a less operative criterion with regard to the exigencies of the Court's criminal trials. Judges with experience in international law are more present in the Appeals Division. Under Article 81 of the Statute, this Division is responsible for deciding appeals on acquittal or sentencing decisions and appeals against other types of decisions. Knowing that these decisions are likely to involve procedural errors, factual errors, errors in law, or errors affecting the fairness of the procedure or the decision, judges with more significant experience in international law are considered more qualified to answer these questions in light of the standards established by the Statute and general international law. Indeed, its case law shows that, at the appeals level, the Court deals with issues that are not only related to criminal law but also to international law.[30] The Statute's criterion relating to the judges' specializations allows the Appeals Division to be in a better position to rule on, for example, the reconciliation between States' obligations under the Statute and those arising from other international sources of international law.

Since, by virtue of the rules of the Court, the President assigns each judge to a division,[31] taking into account the provisions of Article 39, there is nothing preventing him or her from also taking into account the particular composition of a division in the process of assigning a case to it. The President might, for example, consider the representation of female judges in a division to assign a case where the crimes are gender-related, particularly given the important role that women judges have played in the development of the consideration of gender-related crimes.[32] So, the actual content of judges' office duties may be influenced by the same criteria which governed their appointment to the Court and their presence in a particular division. This influence is more noticeable in cases of disqualification or recusal of a judge:[33] here, the criterion of nationality, although not expressly mentioned by the Statute as reasons for disqualification or recusal, may be something the President considers when assigning a case to a division. A division may be seized of a case, while having on its bench a judge from the country where the crimes were committed. Due to the politically sensitive nature of some cases, a judge may have to recuse herself or himself, or be disqualified from the case. For example, in a situation such as Côte d'Ivoire, where crimes were intimately linked to electoral and

30 *The Prosecutor v Omar Hassan Ahmad Al-Bashir* (n 12).

31 Rule 4(2)bis of the Rules of Procedure and Evidence.

32 See for example in this volume: Chapter 17 by Teresa Anne Doherty, 'The Contribution of Women Judges and Prosecutors to the Development of International Criminal Law' and Chapter 18 by Juan Pablo Pérez-Léon-Acevedo, 'The Contribution of Female Judges to the Victim Jurisprudence of the International Criminal Court'.

33 Louis Savadogo, 'Incidents Affecting the Composition of International Courts and Tribunals' (2017) 55 The Canadian Yearbook of International Law 113.

power-sharing issues, it may be particularly difficult for an Ivorian judge to participate in the proceedings.

From the foregoing, it appears that the Court has not been reluctant to incorporate criteria relating to diversity in its functioning. Criteria enshrined in the Statute such as gender or geographical representation constitute the matrix principle of the Court's organization, thereby contributing to its legitimacy. The observed practice of the Court shows that these criteria are consistently observed.

3. The Relative Absence of Ethnicity and Religion Criteria in the Legal Framework of the Court

The notion of diversity covers a broad field which implies a plurality of criteria. Beyond the elements of geographical representation, legal culture, and gender, many other criteria may emerge as essential to the diversity of any given legal framework. Ethnicity and religion are two of these. At the national level, these two criteria can play a role in the appointment of judges serving on the highest judicial benches but also in the practical exercise of their judicial function. The situation of judges on the US Supreme Court bench is emblematic in that the majority decisions reflect the tension between (ultra) conservatives and progressives, or liberals. What about judges of the ICC whose mission is to judge crimes that 'deeply shock the conscience of humanity'[34] and who usually intervene in the context of tribal and/or religious armed conflicts? The legal framework of the Court makes no reference to ethnicity or religion as criteria of diversification (A), even though they are noticeable through a residual presence in the office of the judge (B).

3.1 The Quasi-absence of Ethnicity and Religion in the Legal Framework of the Court

The apparent absence of religion and ethnicity from the legal framework of the Court is surprising for two reasons. First, these two criteria are of paramount importance in the appropriation of diversity *lato sensu*. Indeed, most international instruments for the promotion and protection of human rights overwhelmingly list ethnicity and religion as prohibited grounds of discrimination, thereby affirming the value of diversity that such features bring about. The Charter of the United Nations and international human rights-related instruments, including the Universal Declaration of Human Rights (UDHR) envisage their operational relevance in the study of diversity indicators. For example, Article 16 of the UDHR

[34] Para 2 of the Preamble of the Rome Statute.

stipulates that a person has the right to marry and to found a family 'without any limitation due to race, nationality or religion'. Similarly, Article 1.3 of the UN Charter promotes respect for human rights and fundamental freedoms, all 'without distinction as to race, sex, language, or religion'. Although ethnicity is not explicitly mentioned, in contrast to the word 'religion', it can be deduced from the spirit of these instruments or be assimilated as part of the term 'origin'.

Second, the ICC was established to try and punish those found guilty of crimes under international criminal law including crimes against humanity, war crimes, and genocide. With few exceptions, these crimes have a strong ethnic and religious dimension, as they are marked by the ethnically or religiously distinctive target of their harm. A survey of the situations dealt with by the Court corroborates this finding. Whether it concerns the Central African Republic (CAR), Myanmar, or the Democratic Republic of Congo (DRC), the situations are similar. While the CAR and Myanmar cases concern religion, the Congolese and Sudanese cases are more related to ethnicity. By way of illustration, the armed conflict in CAR has opposed (or opposes) the armed groups of *Anti-balaka* (mostly Christian) and those of *Seleka* (mostly Muslim), while the armed conflict in the DRC,[35] opposed the *Hema* and *Lendu* communities in the Ituri region.

Despite this, none of the legal texts of the Court, particularly the Rome Statute, seems to take account of religion and ethnicity in the context of the bench's desired diversity. In doing so, the Court is following the long tradition of its predecessors, even while innovating on certain aspects like gender. The diversity criteria enshrined in the Statute, contrary to ethnicity and religion, represent the preferences of the States that established the Court and therefore form objective anchors of its legitimacy. These are, in fact, fundamental requirements that emerged from the experience of national courts and then gradually reached international institutions:

> there is increasing agreement in relation to most common law and civil law national courts that the judiciary needs to be broadly reflective of the make-up of society in order for it to command public confidence and maintain political legitimacy as unelected institution of power.[36]

These attempts to reflect the make-up of society are 'generally focused not on ethnicity […] but on issues of geographic representation and the representation of different legal cultures'.[37]

[35] See the different decisions of the Court in the *Prosecutor v Thomas Lubanga Dyilo* Case <www.icc-cpi.int/drc/lubanga?ln=fr> accessed on 8 August 2019.

[36] Ruth Mackenzie and others, *Selecting International Judges: Principle, Process, and Politics* (OUP 2010) 24.

[37] ibid 25.

3.2 The Residual Presence of Ethnicity and Religion in the Legal Framework of the Court

Despite the absence of ethnicity and religion from the diversity criteria, their residual presence in the Court's legal framework, especially in the exercise of the judicial function, should be noted. Religion is present in a variety of contexts ranging from the application of professional secrecy to the communications of the accused. Article 73.3 of the Rules of Procedure and Evidence, for example, provides that 'in making a decision (on privileged communications and information), the Court shall give particular regard to recognizing as privileged those communications made [...] between a person and a member of a religious clergy; and [...] the Court shall recognize as privileged those communications made in the context of a sacred confession where it is an integral part of the practice of that religion'. Article 85.b of the same instrument further incorporates religion by using it its definition of a victim: '[v]ictims may include organizations or institutions that have sustained direct harm to any of their property which is dedicated to religion, education, art or science or charitable purposes, and to their historic monuments, hospitals and other places and objects for humanitarian purposes'. This reminds judges of the need to pay particular attention to religious properties in the context of armed conflicts. The *Al Mahdi* case serves as an illustration: ICC Trial Chamber VIII recognized the accused's responsibility, beyond all reasonable doubt, as a co-author of war crimes for intentionally directing attacks on religious and historical buildings in Timbuktu (Mali), in June and July 2012.[38]

The concepts of ethnicity and religion are embedded in the Court's legal matrix, their manifestations being detectable throughout the Court's procedural and substantive legal provisions. As such, they affect the work of the judge.[39] Understanding the extent to which they should be taken into account in a particular case is part of the exercise of shedding appropriate light on the case's legal and factual specificities. While the purpose of the Court, through the work of the judge, is to try the perpetrators of serious crimes, the ultimate challenge remains the pacification of those societies where the different ethnic and religious communities need to reconnect and learn to live together in peace.[40] An appreciation of these dimensions is crucial which is why mechanisms such as recourse to experts to understand the different implications (mainly ethnic and religious) of the conflict that lies at the root of the crimes is essential for any judge. However, this residual presence should not lead to a definitive conclusion on their relevance

[38] *The Prosecutor v Ahmad Al Faqi Al Mahdi*, ICC-01/12-01/15-171 (27 September 2016).

[39] Peter Murphy and Lina Baddour, 'Evidence and Selection of Judges in International Criminal Tribunals: the need for a Harmonized Approach' in Elies Van Sliedregt and Sergey Vasiliev (eds), *Pluralism in International Criminal Law* (OUP 2014) 368.

[40] In the Preamble of the Statute, the Contracting States expressed their concern that the 'delicate mosaic' made of 'common bonds' and cultures shared among all people may be shattered at any time.

as criteria for a general assessment of the legitimacy of the Court—as will be addressed in the next section.

4. The Irrelevance of Ethnicity and Religion as Diversity Criteria

While the legitimacy of a court like the ICC might be partly informed by the diversity of its bench, it is ultimately a multifactorial construction. Ethnicity and religion are essential components of diversity, contributing to the judge's quest for a full and complete understanding of the conflict, as demonstrated above. However, the relevance of these criteria for the assessment of broader questions concerning the legitimacy of the Court is dubious because their contribution is not easily assessable. This is due to the difficult objectivization of ethnicity and religion (A), and the limited scope of their impact on the reinforcement of the legitimacy of the Court (B).

4.1 The Complex Objectivization of the Criteria of Ethnicity and Religion

The term 'objectivization' refers to an approach or a process of making objective, palpable an idea, a situation, in order to provide a real existence. From this definition, it can be deduced that objectivization refers to the idea of visibility, tangibility, and reality. As a result, it is easy to understand the near-unanimity regarding gender issues or equitable geographical representation as criteria for diversity on the bench of an international court. Questioning religion and ethnicity as diversity criteria implies, in the context of this study, determining the relevance of using such criteria in the appointment of judges of the Court. The first question that arises is the definition of these concepts for such purpose. Difficulties concerning the definitions and regulation of religion and ethnicity in the international legal order[41] complicate their incorporation as criteria for the choice of judges. Indeed, in the absence of commonly accepted definitions of what constitutes a religion or an ethnic group, it is difficult for States Parties to the Statute to reach a consensus on a list of religions or ethnicities admitted for the selection process.[42] On what basis could religious practices be considered relevant to the selection of judges? Since each State itself may comprise several ethnic groups, on what basis would it

[41] James A R Nafziger, 'The functions of Religion in the International Legal System' in Mark W Janis and Carolyn Evans (eds), *Religion and International Law* (Martinus Nijhoff Publishers 2004) 156–59; Mohammad Shahabuddin, *Ethnicity and International Law: histories, Politics and Practices* (CUP 2016) 12–22.

[42] ibid.

identify what constitutes an ethnicity or ethnic group to be considered and then allocate a candidate judge to that ethnicity group or religion? Such an undertaking calls for a real anthropological and sociological adventure which would present many difficulties in the context of multilateral negotiations for the appointment of judges to the Court. The difficulties that States have already encountered in devising a definition of these concepts in international law makes the possibility of a consensus on these issues unlikely. How will States be able to determine a formula for equitable representation of all religions and ethnicities? Recalling that the present criteria result from a long tradition of international jurisdictions in which they have proven their worth, one may question the relevance of including new criteria with such indeterminate characteristics. Beyond their mere relevance, the concepts of ethnicity and religion have generated substantial challenges in the past: the situation faced by the panels established by the UN Interim Mission in Kosovo is a clear example of how such concepts may hamper the work of judicial bodies.[43]

Moreover, while the criteria contained in the Statute of the Court are objective and relate to a candidate's public life, religion, and ethnicity are part of their private sphere. This subjectivity makes it very difficult to assess a person's religion or ethnicity, without entering into the realms of her or his private life. Concerning religion, the European Court of Human Rights ruled in the *Folgero and others v Norway* case that disclosure of information about religious beliefs relates to some of the most intimate aspects of privacy.[44] As far as ethnic identity is concerned, the same Court has held in the case of *Ciubotaru v Moldova,*[45] that this was an integral part of the protection offered by Article 8 of the European Convention on Human Rights. Consequently, the use of these criteria would form a complex precedent, in contradiction with the rights and freedoms enshrined and guaranteed by human rights instruments: the process of selection of judges would involve a judgment on their membership of an ethnic or religious group. Unlike gender, qualifications, or language proficiency, which are easily verifiable factual elements, it is more difficult to determine whether an individual belongs to a religious or ethnic group.

Similarly, to take these criteria into account in assessing the diversity of the Court's bench would be to ignore the differences between the international and the national legal sphere. Clearly, international law is above all a matter of relations between States or groups of States where each strives to assert its interests not necessarily in religious or ethnic terms (better adapted to national realities or contexts) but in terms of national and/or legal representativeness. It is effectively a question of recalling the fundamental differences between the internal order and the international order. Where the internal order has legal subjects who maintain

[43] David Turns, '"Internationalized" or Ad hoc Justice for international criminal law in a time of transition: the cases of East Timor, Kosovo, Sierra Leone and Cambodia' (2001) 6 Austrian Review of International and European Law 123

[44] ECHR, *Case of Folgero and others v Norway*, Application no. 1572/02, Judgment of 29 June 2007.

[45] ECHR, *Case of Ciubotaru v Moldova*, Application no. 27138/04, Judgment of 27 April 2010.

unequal relations according to their legal situation in domestic law (individuals facing the State, the latter organizing the lives of these individuals), the international society is marked by a primacy of actors (States) characterized by their sovereign equality.[46] The international order has the peculiarity that its primary subjects—States—are sovereign entities possessing common attributes, whether they are African, American, or European. Whether we are talking about a developed or a developing State, we focus on the existence of a population established in a territory with relatively defined boundaries, with political authority.

Seen in this light, international law and the institutions reinforcing it (e.g. international courts) represent a factor of cohesion and standardization, a common ground among States that are politically, sociologically, and culturally varied. To maintain, and indeed to promote, diversity in this common ground among widely diverse States is not only difficult but also potentially perilous an endeavour. Neo-realist and neo-liberal scholars have outlined the difficulty for States to let emerge such concepts in particular fields because 'religion and cultural (ethnic) diversity cannot be accommodated in a global multicultural international society. They must be marginalized or overcome if international cooperation is to take place'.[47] To include ethnicity and religion in the criteria is clearly an ineffective and counter-productive step, the added value to the legitimacy of the Court being far from undeniable. In fact, the States Parties might show some reluctance in considering new criteria for the election of judges, considering that 'there seems to be a consensus that the very essence of the process in which international judges are selected cannot be altered, at least while sovereign States remain the building blocks of the international community'.[48]

4.2 The Limited Contribution of Ethnicity and Religion as Diversity Criteria in Assessing the Legitimacy of the Court

In addition to being imprecise in their content, ethnicity and religion seem to be limited in their contribution to strengthening the legitimacy of the Court. Is it not generally the case that the qualifications and independence of judges are the key words that support the legitimacy of any jurisdiction? Can ethnicity and religion fit into this dynamic? Nothing is less sure. These two concepts introduce at the Court a personal and subjective dimension that irreversibly undermines its impartiality and therefore its credibility within the public opinion.

[46] Robert Kolb, *Theory of International Law* (Hart 2016) 62–64

[47] Scoot Thomas, 'The Global Resurgence of Religion, International Law and International Society' in Mark W Janis and Carolyn Evans (eds) (n 38) 329.

[48] Daniel Terris, Cesare P R Romano, and Leigh Swigart, *The International Judge: An Introduction to the Men and Women Who Decide the World's Cases* (University Press of the New England 2007) 37.

Indeed, as recalled above, ethnicity and religion affect the very person of the judge as an individual and less as a person designated by the States Parties to deliver justice in accordance with the applicable texts. Whereas in the present state of affairs the concepts of ethnicity and religion may be latent in their work and serve as a framework for reflection in their judgment in certain cases, they emerge more as elements which can be used to challenge judges' impartial or independent functioning. To choose a judge on the basis of religious or ethnic criteria is to run the risk of parties to the trial questioning the impartiality of the bench on the basis of their religious beliefs or their belonging to an ethnic group mentioned in the case. Of course, the same criticism may be levelled against existing criteria of diversity, notably that of nationality.

The criterion of nationality may raise impartiality concerns as a matter of principle. Indeed, it was transposed to international criminal courts from the context of inter-State dispute settlement, in which different considerations might apply, or indeed might have applied at the time when inter-State adjudicatory mechanisms were devised. However, in practice, the nationality criterion does not appear problematic in its application at the ICC. At any rate, these considerations would pertain in an examination as to whether retention of nationality as a criterion is desirable; they are not relevant for a discussion considering the inclusion of new criteria, such as ethnicity or religion. The established practice might mitigate in favour of retaining a criterion that is otherwise problematic as a matter of principle (such as nationality), but it does not provide a reason for introducing new problematic criteria (such as ethnicity or religion). For such reason to be provided, it should at least be demonstrated that the criterion to be introduced may not only outweigh the concerns of principle but also offer additional value as a matter of practice, to the point that it renders its introduction worthwhile.

In the present discussion, it might be worth noting the difficult relationship between the law that a judge is supposed to apply and religion, for instance. One might consider that, unless religion finds its way into the law,

> religion is private where the law is public. Religion is what we had before we had law. Religion is the domain of irrationality and charismatic authority, law is the realm of reason and the bureaucratic. International understands its birth as a flooding forth from the darkness of religious strife, antidote to the passions of faith, on guard against their re-emergence as ideology.[49]

This assumption is far from being without consequence, as the insertion of religious and ethnic criteria might induce that judges chosen on the basis of such criteria might later consider it acceptable to have recourse to these concepts in the

[49] David Kennedy, 'Losing Faith in the Secular: Law, Religion, and the Culture of International Governance' in Mark W Janis and Carolyn Evans (eds) (n 38) 313.

very application of a law whose premise is the achievement of a common ground between an infinite variety of religious beliefs and ethnic traditions in order to become a common language among nations.

5. Conclusion

Despite their potential attraction in questioning diversity on the bench of the ICC, it must be acknowledged that, as selection criteria, ethnicity and religion are not relevant. They present a subjective aspect which casts on them an anathema of irrelevance. However, such a statement cannot obscure the contribution, albeit modest, of the criteria relating to ethnicity and religion in the legal order of the Court. A complete understanding of a conflict in its ethnic and religious dimensions can strengthen the legitimacy of any Court if stakeholders acknowledge the Court's capacity to navigate through the underlying factors of a conflict. Such a perception is likely to change if these elements become a basis for the appointment of the judges to the Court. As we are clearly reminded, 'representativeness of international bodies is desirable, but if pushed too hard, it might create a trade-off with competence, since in practice only a few countries have sufficiently large pools of suitable candidates to cover all the various international judicial appointments'.[50]

[50] Daniel Terris, Cesare P R Romano, and Leigh Swigart, *The International Judge: An Introduction to the Men and Women Who Decide the World's Cases* (University Press of the New England 2007) 38.

23
The Significance of Religious Diversity in International Human Rights Adjudication

Kristen Hessler

1. Introduction

> The continuing and rising influence of cultural or religious justifications for women's inequality is one important reason why it is so significant for women's rights to be recognized as human rights.[1]

In this chapter, I explore the relevance of religious diversity in international human rights adjudication by focusing on the issue of abortion rights in the United States as a case study. Pointing out the complicated relationship between women's human rights and religion, I argue that it is a mistake to emphasize religious representation as a direct contributor to the normative legitimacy of either judicial deliberation (a matter of process) or the substantive outcomes of judicial decision-making regarding human rights, whether in domestic or international courts. I first clarify the distinction between normative and sociological legitimacy, and point out two ways in which ethnic, racial, or religious diversity on courts may matter morally. I then describe the US case study regarding reproductive rights in detail, before discussing three reasons for scepticism regarding the claim that religious diversity among judges is a component of normative legitimacy for international courts.

2. Normative and Sociological Legitimacy

Normative legitimacy concerns the right of a political or social institution to make authoritative decisions within their defined purview; as Nienke Grossman puts it,

[1] Susan Moller Okin, 'Feminism, Women's Human Rights, and Cultural Differences' (1998) 13(2) *Hypatia* 37.

Kristen Hessler, *The Significance of Religious Diversity in International Human Rights Adjudication* In: *Identity and Diversity on the International Bench*. Edited by: Freya Baetens, Oxford University Press (2020).
DOI: 10.1093/oso/9780198870753.003.0023.

'[a] court is legitimate when it possesses justified authority'.[2] Importantly, normative legitimacy is different from sociological or perceived legitimacy, which concerns the extent to which an institution is believed to be or accepted as legitimate by those for whom the institution's decisions are supposed to be authoritative. Normative and perceived legitimacy are in some ways interrelated; for example, satisfying normative requirements for legitimacy (such as fairness, transparency, representativeness, etc.) is one important way that institutions can bolster opinions about their legitimacy. Nonetheless, they are distinct notions, as can be seen by imagining a corrupt institution that might be nonetheless accepted as authoritative, or (conversely) an institution that actually satisfies the conditions of normative legitimacy which might come to be viewed as suspect, perhaps due to concerted efforts to discredit the institution as part of a partisan political agenda.

Part of the point of evaluating institutions in terms of normative legitimacy, rather than using the richer, more demanding idea of justice, is that it is unrealistic to expect social and political institutions to function in fully just ways all the time. Nonetheless, these institutions perform important functions, even when they are somewhat flawed or issue substantively unjust decisions or outcomes. It would be deeply destabilizing to insist that institutions function in a fully just way in order to maintain their authority. Therefore, the point of normative legitimacy is to establish a threshold of functioning considered (morally) good enough to justify the institution's right to make decisions which are regarded as binding. The second reason for thinking in terms of normative legitimacy rather than justice is that there exists reasonable public disagreement about what justice requires, so that the same outcome may be viewed by different groups as either confirming or undermining the institution's normative legitimacy. While a court would eventually lose its normative legitimacy if it persistently violated accepted procedural constraints or consistently issued recognizably and deeply unjust outcomes, it is important that it can retain its normative legitimacy despite sometimes functioning sub-optimally or occasionally issuing decisions that at least some people find substantively unjust.

Importantly, normative legitimacy (like sociological legitimacy) may come in degrees. For the concept of normative legitimacy to do its intended work, there must be some threshold of legitimacy below which an institution forfeits its authority.[3] However, it is certainly possible and arguably helpful to accept that

[2] Nienke Grossman, 'Sex on the Bench: Do Women Judges Matter to the Legitimacy of International Courts' (2012) 12(2) Chicago Journal of International Law 647–84, at 651.

[3] As Peter Fabienne notes in his summary of the Lockean (liberal) tradition of political authority: 'When a political authority fails to secure consent or oversteps the boundaries of the natural law, it ceases to be legitimate and, therefore, there is no longer an obligation to obey its commands.' Peter Fabienne, 'Political Legitimacy' (*The Stanford Encyclopedia of Philosophy*, Summer 2017), Edward N. Zalta (ed) <https://plato.stanford.edu/archives/sum2017/entries/legitimacy/> accessed 29 February 2020.

institutions' legitimacy may be improved above that threshold level, or, to put the point another way, an institution can tarnish or compromise its legitimacy without falling below the threshold where it loses its authority. Judgments about when a criticism of an institution becomes a stain on its legitimacy rather than a predictable imperfection require substantive argument about the standards of legitimacy appropriate for the institution in question.

3. Descriptive Representation Among Judges and the Normative Legitimacy of Courts

I begin with two familiar ways in which ethnic and religious diversity of judges on courts (international or domestic) may be morally significant. The first is that a social group's lack of representation in prestigious positions in government and other areas of social, economic, and political life is often indicative background injustice. In the United States, for example, racial and ethnic minority groups and women are underrepresented on the federal bench: '[o]f the 1,304 currently sitting judges, just 20% are racial or ethnic minorities while 27% are women... White men account for 60% of all sitting federal judges; nonwhite women account for just 7%'.[4] Underrepresentation of women is also a problem on international courts; as Nienke Grossman reported in 2012, '[t]he paucity of women sitting on the benches of many of the world's most important adjudicative bodies is striking'.[5] There is little reason to think that this situation has changed drastically in the interim. At the time Grossman was writing, there were no women on the International Tribunal for the Law of the Sea (ITLOS), for example; today, only three of the 21 ITLOS judges are women.[6] Such patterns of disproportionate representation indicate that studies are urgently needed to investigate and reform the causes of this underrepresentation, including possible bias in appointment processes. Systemic patterns of bias and privilege have real effect on who ultimately becomes a judge, and these patterns are amenable to change via social and political policy choices. Insofar as underrepresentation of non-dominant groups is a marker for substantive discrimination at multiple levels of social and political systems, therefore, it urgently needs to be rectified as a matter of basic social justice.

[4] John Gramlich, 'Trump's Appointed Judges are a Less Diverse Group than Obama's' (*Pew Research Center*, 20 March 2018) <www.pewresearch.org/fact-tank/2018/03/20/trumps-appointed-judges-are-a-less-diverse-group-than-obamas/> accessed 29 February 2020. For racial and gender disparities on State courts, see Tracey George and Albert Yoon, 'The Gavel Gap: Who Sits In Judgment on State Courts?' (*American Constitutional Society for Law and Policy*) <http://gavelgap.org>accessed 29 February 2020

[5] Nienke Grossman, 'Sex on the Bench: Do Women Judges Matter to the Legitimacy of International Courts' (2012) 12(2) Chicago Journal of International Law 647–84, at 652.

[6] International Tribunal for the Law of the Sea: Members <www.itlos.org/the-tribunal/members/> accessed 29 February 2020.

The second is primarily, though not merely, symbolic. We can call this the 'role model' model. This is the view that President Obama expressed when reflecting on his Presidency's impact on US courts:

> I think there are some particular groups that historically have been underrepresented—like Latinos and Asian-Americans—that represent a larger and larger portion of the population. And so for them to be able to see folks in robes that look like them is going to be important.[7]

The representation of women and members of underrepresented minorities in positions of authority also signals social acceptance of members of those groups as full members of society, qualified to hold political power and entitled to respect and deference regarding their expertise. This is not merely symbolic, however, because such representation informs cultural assumptions about members of social groups, eroding stereotypes and acculturating individuals from various social groups to working with others across group differences in pursuit of common goals. For example, the presence of women on the US Supreme Court is not only symbolic of the increasing social and political equality of women in the US, but is also a powerful driver of cultural change (as Americans become accustomed to seeing women treated with respect for their intellect, expertise, and formal authority at the highest levels of government), thereby contributing to the progressive evolution of gendered social norms in the process.

The assumption that the legitimacy of courts depends at least in part on the descriptive characteristics of the judiciary is stronger for national rather than international courts; nonetheless, 'there is growing awareness at the international level of the strong link between the composition of a court and its legitimacy . . . '.[8] Considerations of diversity on international courts do not, however, track the same characteristics as do national courts, where 'there is increasing agreement in relation to most common law and civil law national courts that the judiciary needs to be broadly reflective of the make-up of society in order for it to command public confidence and maintain political legitimacy as an unelected institution of power'.[9] The most salient form of 'descriptive representation' for international courts is nationality.[10] The ICJ Statute, for example, claims that 'in the body as a whole the

[7] Jeffrey Toobin, 'The Obama Brief: The President Considers His Legacy' (*The New Yorker*, 26 October 2014) <www.newyorker.com/magazine/2014/10/27/obama-brief> accessed 29 February 2020.

[8] Ruth MacKenzie and others, *Selecting International Judges: Principle, Process, and Politics* (OUP 2010) 25.

[9] ibid 24.

[10] See Abhinav Chandrachud, 'Diversity and the International Criminal Court: Does Geographic Background Impact Decision Making?' (2013) 38(2) Brooklyn Journal of International Law 487–521: '. . . international instruments require that the composition of international courts and tribunals must fairly reflect the diverse geographic realities of the geopolitical world' (488). For a critique of 'the nationalist presumption', see Tom Dannenbaum, 'Nationality and the International Judge: The Nationalist Presumption Governing the International Judiciary and Why It Must Be Reversed' (2012) 45 Cornell International Law Journal 77–184.

representation of the main forms of civilization and of the principal legal systems of the world should be assured',[11] and the Rome Statute of the International Criminal Court similarly requires 'equitable geographic representation'.[12]

The concern with national representation on international courts can be seen as having the goal of alleviating potential or perceived background injustice in cases where international courts adjudicate conflicts between States directly, or have the potential to become *de facto* forums where some States wield greater power than others internationally.[13] When either of these situations is the case, States from geographical regions that are unrepresented (or underrepresented) might be at a real or presumed disadvantage, assuming that a judge's nationality can be expected to influence his or her decisions. For example, the International Criminal Court has to date indicted only individuals from Africa, despite conducting investigations in other parts of the world (including Afghanistan and Colombia).[14] As one observer notes, '[a]gainst this backdrop, increasing numbers of judges from the African Group of States have been appointed to the ICC, perhaps on an implicit understanding that their presence on the court is essential to preserve its legitimacy'.[15]

The issues of descriptive representation of judges considered so far are primarily relevant to background injustices such as differential opportunities for individuals from minority or disadvantaged social groups to become judges, or the distribution of judicial power on international courts among States and geographical regions. However, many argue that judicial diversity matters because a judge's background may affect their decision-making on the bench. For example, it is often argued that judges bring a particular standpoint to court decisions based on their ethnicity, religion, gender, or broader cultural background. This is the view that US Supreme Court Justice Sonia Sotomayor controversially embraced when she said in a speech, ' … I would hope that a wise Latina woman with the richness of her experiences would more often than not reach a better conclusion than a white male who hasn't lived that life'.[16] Judge Patricia Wald (former judge on the US Appellate Court and International Criminal Tribunal for the Former Yugoslavia) concurs with the idea that women's gendered experiences influence their judging, arguing that '… being a woman and being treated by society as a woman can be a

[11] Ruth MacKenzie and others, *Selecting International Judges: Principle, Process, and Politics* (OUP 2010) 27.

[12] ibid 29.

[13] ibid 31–37.

[14] Carolyn Kenney and John Norris, 'International Justice on Trial?: Taking Stock of International Justice Over the Past Quarter Century,' Center for American Progress, 28 March 2018. <www.americanprogress.org/issues/security/reports/2018/03/28/448415/international-justice-trial/>accessed 29 February 2020.

[15] Abhinav Chandrachud, 'Diversity and the International Criminal Court: Does Geographic Background Impact Decision Making?' (2013) 38(2) Brooklyn Journal of International Law 487–521, at 489.

[16] 'Lecture: A Latina Judge's Voice' (*New York Times*, 14 May 2009) <www.nytimes.com/2009/05/15/us/politics/15judge.text.html?action=click&contentCollection=U.S.&module=RelatedCoverage&region=Marginalia&pgtype=article>accessed 29 February 2020..

vital element of a judge's experience. That experience in turn can subtly affect the lens through which she views issues and solutions'.[17]

These comments illustrate the idea that a judge's gender or cultural, ethnic, or religious background shapes their worldview, which in turn may affect their decisions in substantive ways. If judges with different backgrounds predictably bring different perspectives to judging, ensuring the impartiality of courts may require that a wide range of perspectives be represented among the judiciary. Echoing this idea, Sherrilyn Ifill argues that 'diversity on the bench can enrich judicial decision-making by including a variety of voices and perspectives in the deliberative process'.[18] But if this is correct, then the normative legitimacy of courts may depend at least in part on a diversity of backgrounds among judges. As Nienke Grossman has argued regarding gender, '[b]ecause impartiality is a fundamental driver of legitimacy, severe over- or under-representation of one sex detracts from a court's normative legitimacy'.[19]

Without addressing this broad question (whether normative legitimacy depends on descriptive representation of women and members of underrepresented minority groups among judges), I turn instead to a much narrower question: whether diversity of the religious backgrounds of judges contributes to the normative legitimacy of courts adjudicating human rights. I focus in particular on the question of whether the religious affiliation of judges should be expected to affect the quality of judicial deliberation or decisions regarding human rights. In order to focus the discussion, I first turn to a conflict in the United States regarding the reproductive rights of women (including the right to legal abortion).

4. Case Study on Religion and Women's Human Rights: Reproductive Rights in the US

As a globally subordinated group, women have struggled to make it the case that the reality of their lives is reflected in both domestic and international law. Even when laws formally protect women's human rights, substantive realization of those rights in everyday life has often lagged far behind. One of the reasons for this is that, in many societies, gender equality flies in the face of traditional cultural and religious norms that are deeply entrenched and therefore profoundly resistant to change.[20]

[17] Nienke Grossman, 'Sex on the Bench: Do Women Judges Matter to the Legitimacy of International Courts' (2012) 12(2) Chicago Journal of International Law 647–84, at 658.

[18] Sherrilyn Ifill, 'Racial Diversity on the Bench: Beyond Role Models and Public Confidence' 2000 57(2) Washington and Lee Law Review 405–95, at 405.

[19] Nienke Grossman, 'Sex on the Bench: Do Women Judges Matter to the Legitimacy of International Courts' (2012) 12(2) Chicago Journal of International Law 647–84, at 660.

[20] See Charles Beitz, *The Idea of Human Rights* (OUP 2009) 186–96; Martha Nussbaum, *Women and Human Development: The Capabilities Approach* (CUP 2000) 167–212; Susan Moller Okin, 'Is Multiculturalism Bad for Women?' in Joshua Cohen and Matthew Howard (eds), *Is Multiculturalism*

Often, the conflict between women's human rights and cultural, ethnic, or religious perspectives is couched in terms of a divide between Western and non-Western cultures, where Western cultures are identified with international human rights norms, and non-Western ones are associated with resistance to those norms. For example, many discussions of the perceived legitimacy of women's international human rights focus on the reservations to the Convention to Eliminate All Forms of Discrimination Against Women,[21] entered by many predominantly Muslim countries, asserting the priority of Islamic law over CEDAW's provisions wherever they conflict.[22] As another example, in a paper examining States' responsibilities under international human rights law to change religious and customary laws within their own borders, Abdullahi Ahmed An-Na'im focuses on the issue of 'changing Islamic religious laws in relation to the international human rights of women'.[23] Susan Moller Okin's famous essay, 'Is Multiculturalism Bad for Women?', locates this cultural divide within domestic politics of Western, liberal States, asking, '[w]hat should be done when the claims of minority cultures or religions clash with the norm of gender equality that is at least formally endorsed by liberal states (however much they continue to violate it in their practice)?'[24] And laws banning the wearing of Islamic headscarves or other coverings in public in France have often been justified as a way of upholding the value of gender equality, in response to the perception of the veil as a marker of the subordination of women within Muslim communities.[25]

I want to turn this framing on its head, however, and think about diversity of religious backgrounds in the adjudication of women's human rights with a focus on abortion and other reproductive rights in the United States. By problematizing the human rights situation for women within the US, a globally dominant culture and one that strongly endorses at least the idea of human rights (if not always the legitimacy of international human rights law), this framing can help clarify the morally

Bad for Women? (Princeton University Press, 1999); Cochav Elkayam-Levy, 'Women's Rights and Religion—The Missing Element in the Jurisprudence of the European Court of Human Rights' (2014) 35(4) University of Pennsylvania Journal of International Law 1175–222.

[21] Convention on the Elimination of All Forms of Discrimination Against Women (adopted 18 December 1979, entered into force 3 September 1981) 1249 UNTS 13 (CEDAW).

[22] See, for example, Michele Brandt and Jeffrey Kaplan, 'The Tension Between Women's Rights and Religious Rights: Reservations to CEDAW by Egypt, Bangladesh, and Tunisia' (1995–96) 12(1) Journal of Law and Religion 105–42.

[23] Abdullahi Ahmed An-Na'im, 'State Responsibility to Change Religious and Customary Laws' in Rebecca Cook (ed), *The Human Rights of Women: National and International Perspectives* (University of Pennsylvania Press 1994)167–88.

[24] Susan Moller Okin, 'Is Multiculturalism Bad for Women?' in Joshua Cohen and Matthew Howard (eds), *Is Multiculturalism Bad for Women?* (Princeton University Press 1999), p. 9.

[25] Eun-Jung Katherine Kim, 'On the Burka Ban' (2012) 26(4) Public Affairs Quarterly 293–312; Cochav Elkayam-Levy, 'Women's Rights and Religion—The Missing Element in the Jurisprudence of the European Court of Human Rights' (2014) 35(4) University of Pennsylvania Journal of International Law 1175–222. (I return to this question in section 5.)

complex issue of deference to religion when it seems to conflict with international human rights legal standards, and the considerations relevant to adjudicating such conflicts in international courts. I will clarify the conflict between women's human rights and religious culture in the US by focusing on the US Supreme Court, and then draw out the puzzles that this situation raises for the question of religious diversity in international human rights adjudication.

The confirmation battle in 2018 for President Donald Trump's nominee to the US Supreme Court, Brett Kavanaugh, was perceived as significant for both religious groups and women's rights in the US in part because of its potential impact on the legacy of the Supreme Court's 1973 decision, *Roe v Wade*, which recognized a Constitutional right to abortion.[26] As *The Economist* recently noted regarding *Roe*, '[c]onservative Christians were scandalized at such a decision being taken by the Supreme Court; it was this issue above all others that brought such voters to the Republican party, and this issue above all others that politicized the court'.[27]

This issue is, in turn, relevant to the question of religious diversity on courts. Against the demographic data concerning Americans' religious affiliations, the religious demographics of the current Supreme Court bench are striking: three judges are Jewish, and the other six are Catholic. Catholics first became the majority among Supreme Court judges in 2006, though historically the representation of Catholics on the Supreme Court bench has been relatively scarce compared to Protestant Christians (the dominant religious tradition in the United States).[28] Evangelical Protestants form the largest religious group in the US, at 26% of the total US population, and Catholics are another 21%.[29] Both religious groups are heavily opposed to legal abortion. The disproportionate representation of Catholics in particular on the Supreme Court raises the question: why? The answer, according to many observers, refers back to abortion rights and *Roe*. As one analysis put it:

> A defining policy agenda issue for recent Republican administrations ... has been opposition to *Roe v. Wade*, which created a constitutional right for a woman to abort a non-viable fetus. The Catholic Church has been at the forefront of opposition to abortion, and many conservative Catholic lawyers and jurists have consequently been drawn to the Republican Party and placed in the pool of potential judicial appointees.[30]

[26] 'And Brett Makes Five: How America's Supreme Court Became So Politicized' *The Economist* (15 September 2018) 25.

[27] ibid.

[28] Sheldon Goldman, 'The Politics of Appointing Catholics to the Federal Courts' (2006) 4(2) University of St. Thomas Law Journal 193–220.

[29] Becka Alper and Aleksandra Sandstrom, 'If the U.S. had 100 people: Charting Americans' religious affiliations,' Pew Research Center, 14 November 2016 <www.pewresearch.org/fact-tank/2016/11/14/if-the-u-s-had-100-people-charting-americans-religious-affiliations/>accessed 29 February 2020.

[30] Sheldon Goldman, 'The Politics of Appointing Catholics to the Federal Courts' (2006) 4 (2) University of St. Thomas Law Journal 193–220, at 217.

A recent news item about exactly this question echoes this analysis:

> Except Justice Sonia Sotomayor, all of the Catholic justices on the Supreme Court are conservatives, appointed by Republican presidents. And there's reason for that. While there is a liberal, social-justice strain in Catholicism, there is a sharp divide between them and more conservative Catholics. And their dominance on the court has to do with ideology, said Marci Hamilton, a professor at the University of Pennsylvania who once clerked for former Supreme Court Justice Sandra Day O'Connor. 'I think it's because the Catholic vote can be relatively predictable on abortion,' Hamilton said. 'Now, that doesn't fit with Justice Sotomayor, but with respect to the male Catholics that have been on the court, they have been largely devoted to decreasing the power of *Roe v. Wade*.'[31]

Finally, this issue is relevant to the status of reproductive rights in international human rights law. While the reservations to CEDAW entered by majority-Muslim countries has garnered much scholarly attention regarding religious conflicts with women's human rights, the United States, of course, is one of only two countries in the world that has signed but not yet ratified CEDAW (the other is Palau), which places it slightly ahead of the six that are not even signatories (the Holy See, Iran, Somalia, South Sudan, Sudan, and Tonga).[32] For this reason, while the US has ratified other human rights treaties and conventions that are relevant to women's human rights, the issue of reproductive rights and abortion in particular is not explicitly included in the formal obligations the United States has incurred directly as a result of ratifying those other instruments. However, in July 2017, the CEDAW Committee issued a general comment on gender-based violence against women, which includes the following assertion:

> Violations of women's sexual and reproductive health and rights, such as forced sterilization, forced abortion, forced pregnancy, criminalization of abortion, denial or delay of safe abortion and/or post-abortion care, forced continuation of pregnancy, and abuse and mistreatment of women and girls seeking sexual and reproductive health information, goods and services, are forms of gender-based violence that, depending on the circumstances, may amount to torture or cruel, inhuman or degrading treatment.[33]

[31] Sarah McCammon and Domenico Montanaro, 'Religion, the Supreme Court, and Why It Matters,' National Public Radio 7 July 2018 <www.npr.org/2018/07/07/626711777/religion-the-supreme-court-and-why-it-matters>accessed 29 February 2020.

[32] See UN Women, Convention on the Elimination of All Forms of Discrimination Against Women, States Parties <https://treaties.un.org/pages/ViewDetails.aspx?src=TREATY&mtdsg_no=IV-8&chapter=4&clang=_en>accessed 29 February 2020.

[33] UN Committee for the Elimination of All Forms of Discrimination against Women, General Recommendation No 35 on Gender-Based Violence against Women, Updating General Recommendation No 19, in 'Note by the Secretariat, Compilation of General Comments and

Since Article 7 of the International Covenant on Civil and Political Rights (ICCPR), which the US has ratified, establishes a legal human right against cruel, inhuman, or degrading treatment, the CEDAW comment can be taken to establish at least a textual basis for an obligation under international human rights law on States that they avoid criminalizing or overly restricting women's access to abortion and other reproductive services.[34]

The US, however, is moving in exactly the opposite direction. States within the US with predominantly conservative Christian majorities have been steadily scaling back women's effective access to abortion within their territories, without explicitly making it illegal in all circumstances. Human Rights Watch reports that:

> [m]any states implement regulations that, in practice, may be unduly burdensome. For example, some states require that women and girls who wish to terminate a pregnancy submit themselves to counseling, which, in addition to being unsolicited, is often manifestly biased and medically unsound.[35]

Even if *Roe* is not overturned, concerted efforts at the State level to impose more and more restrictions on clinics that provide abortion 'could still see tens of millions of women in states with conservative legislatures denied the ability to exercise in practice the right *Roe* recognized in principle'.[36]

5. Religious Representation and Normative Legitimacy of Courts

This leaves us with a puzzle. What can international human rights adjudication accomplish, assuming that women's reproductive human rights are being eroded in the United States, largely due to the efforts of a politically influential coalition of religious groups, and does religious diversity in international adjudication of human rights law play a significant role in the way forward?

General Recommendations Adopted by Human Rights Treaty Bodies' (26 July 2017) UN Doc CEDAW/C/GC/35.

[34] While the linkage of two different human rights conventions in this way is unlikely, given the separate mandates of the distinct treaty bodies, it is perhaps at least marginally encouraging that the European Court of Human Rights has determined that the prohibition of inhuman and degrading treatment (Convention for the Protection of Human Rights and Fundamental Freedoms (European Convention on Human Rights, as amended) (ECHR) art 3) is relevant to access to maternal health in at least one case (involving a pregnant woman in Poland who was 'deliberately denied timely access to the genetic test to which she was entitled by doctors opposed to abortion'). See 'Fact Sheet: Reproductive Rights,' European Court of Human Rights, June 2018 <www.echr.coe.int/Documents/FS_Reproductive_ENG.pdf>accessed 29 February 2020.

[35] Human Rights Watch, 'Abortion: United States.' <www.hrw.org/legacy/women/abortion/us.html> accessed 29 February 2020.

[36] 'And Brett Makes Five,' *The Economist* (15 September 2018) 25.

Focusing on abortion rights in the United States may not seem to set us up well to answer these questions, due to the complicated relationship between the United States and international human rights law in general. As stated above, the US is not a party to CEDAW, and it often resists oversight from international bodies, including treaty bodies, regarding its internal human rights record, even for treaties and covenants it has ratified.[37] Moreover, it is not party to a supranational court like the Inter-American Court of Human Rights.[38] However, partly because there is no obvious international legal jurisdiction in this case, the complexities of this scenario enable us to step back and consider some of the more abstract issues it raises. In this section, I discuss three such issues, each of which is (I argue) grounds for scepticism regarding the thesis that religious representation is a component of the normativity of the deliberation (process) or decisions (outputs) of international courts.

The first issue concerns the practical difficulties in achieving a salient form of religious diversity on international courts in a way that is relevant to the issue of abortion rights. Not only is achieving such a standard of diversity impractical, but also, whatever enhancement of judicial legitimacy that religious diversity could secure for national courts does not translate well to international courts.

To start with, the relevance of judicial diversity for the normative legitimacy of courts arises when the religious background of judges may affect judicial decisions and deliberations. Therefore, religious diversity among judges would seem to matter most when the religious diversity already present among the population for which the court is ruling has a deeper social or political significance relevant to a legal dispute (as is the case regarding the religious element of the debate about reproductive rights before the US Supreme Court). When that is the case, what would an adequate standard of religious diversity among judges require? As a first thought, a completely fair measure of religious diversity among judges might be that the bench should 'map' (or match) the religious make-up of the relevant population. Failing that, it might seem that key religious minorities whose rights are at stake should not be completely unrepresented on the bench. But both of these standards very quickly run into insurmountable practical challenges. Before we consider the practical challenges at the international level, consider what these standards would require for a national court like the Supreme Court. There are

[37] See, for example, Jamie Mayerfeld, *The Promise of Human Rights: Constitutional Government, Democratic Legitimacy, and International Law* (University of Pennsylvania Press 2016), for an extensive case study regarding the deliberate attempts of the US government over several administrations to marginalize international human rights law, including the Convention Against Torture, subsequent to ratifying that treaty in 1994.

[38] The IACtHR in 2012 decided a case about in vitro fertilization that many saw as relevant to abortion due to its ruling on the legal status of the embryo. *Case of Artavia Murillo et al. (In Vitro Fertilization) v. Costa Rica.* (Preliminary Objections, Merits, Reparations and Costs) Inter-American Court of Human Rights Series C No 257 (28 November 2012). See also Julieta Lemaitre and Rachel Sieder, 'The Moderating Influence of International Courts on Social Movements: Evidence from the IVF Case Against Costa Rica' (2017) 19 Health and Human Rights Journal 149–60.

nine Supreme Court judges at any one time, and more than nine religious affiliations garnering more than 1% of the population (including the second largest religious category, the 'unaffiliated'), so proportionately mapping the Supreme Court to Americans' religious affiliations seems mathematically impossible.

We might attempt the more modest goal of representing only the minority religions, on the grounds that these are voices that are less likely to be familiar in the dominant culture and therefore need more representation than the majority views. This would also be prohibitively difficult in the American context, however, as there are six religious affiliations garnering either 1% or 2% of the population, plus a basket of 'other faiths' that collectively comprise 2% of the population but likely are not even remotely interchangeable if the goal is judicial representation. Moreover, broad categories like 'Catholic' mask tremendous cultural and other differences that are relevant to the legal relevance of religious identification (e.g. liberal social justice Catholics versus conservative Catholics). A further consideration is that such differences would surely become divisive battlegrounds if judicial representation were at stake. Moreover, a judge may or may not 'represent' her social group in a way that most members of that group would endorse. For example, US Supreme Court Justice Clarence Thomas was very publicly vocal about rejecting 'the civil rights movement's focus on structural racism and its corresponding calls for structural remedies', unlike many American blacks.[39] Finally, as many feminist and other social justice theorists have recognized, all social identities consist of multiple, intersecting group memberships, each of which may have a different social and legal significance from any of the others.[40] Therefore, even if an appropriate distribution of religious affiliations were to hand, selecting judges to match it would entirely leave out other social identities that also have legal significance.

If religious diversity among judges as a standard of normative legitimacy for courts runs into this much trouble at the national level, the problems are only magnified for international adjudication. First, international adjudication should be relevant precisely where domestic remedies and processes have been exhausted and domestic law has been found out of sync with international norms. Assuming that this much is in fact the case regarding reproductive rights in the United States, it would be difficult to know what the proper standard of religious diversity among judges on an international court would be, if the legitimacy of international adjudication were linked to judicial diversity. One basic question is whether the international court should aim to represent the religious demographics of the US, or to transcend them? There are reasons for caution either way: representing domestic

[39] Kimberlé Crenshaw, 'We Still Haven't Learned from Anita Hill's Testimony' *New York Times* (27 September 2018) <www.nytimes.com/2018/09/27/opinion/anita-hill-clarence-thomas-brett-kavanaugh-christine-ford.html>accessed 29 February 2020.

[40] Trina Grillo, 'Anti-Essentialism and Intersectionality' (1995) 10 Berkeley Women's Law Journal 17–30; Audre Lorde, 'Age, Race, Class, and Sex: Women Redefining Difference' from *Sister/Outsider* (Crossing Press 1984), 114–123.

demographics risks simply reproducing the existing conflict in the international forum, while attempting to transcend them faces additional problems in justifying as legitimate whichever religious views are represented at the international level. Either path seems to only amplify the debate over legitimacy without a clear way forward in resolving the domestic tension between women's human rights and religious worldviews.

The second reason for scepticism about the contribution of religious diversity among judges to the normative legitimacy of international courts concerns the standards of normative legitimacy for international courts at a more abstract level. Nienke Grossman has argued for a 'reimagining' of standards of procedural fairness for international courts to include more than the traditional requirements of State consent and fairness to litigants.[41] International courts have significant, and growing, impacts on nonlitigants, both because 'international courts shape the obligations of states prospectively and impact both state and nonstate actors not before the court', and because 'international courts explicitly promote specific normative regimes like human rights or free trade'.[42] In various ways, however, cases before international courts may not adequately represent the interests of all relevant entitlement-holders or stakeholders; for example, '[g]overnments may be undemocratic, unrepresentative, or even if democratic, guided by a small subset of elites with unique interests far removed from those of much of the population. Also, there may be transnational groups with rights being adjudicated in a dispute who are not represented by a state'.[43] In such cases, Grossman argues that '[p]rocedural fairness requires that those whose entitlements are being adjudicated have the opportunity to advocate for their rights'.[44]

As she argues, entitlement holders who are not litigants may in some cases nonetheless have a right to an impartial hearing, or to have an opportunity to affect the cases outcomes (for example, if their 'international rights and obligations' are at stake in a dispute).[45] However, Grossman argues that procedural fairness does not require hearing separately from an entitlement holders whose 'position is being represented by a litigant': 'In other words, procedural fairness requires a third-party hearing only if the state refuses to or cannot make the entitlement holder's case in its own presentation to the international court.'[46]

Unfortunately, there is some evidence that women's rights may not be adequately addressed or protected by international courts, even when one or both sides claim to be representing women's interests. For example, Cochav Elkayam-Levy has

[41] Nienke Grossman, 'The Normative Legitimacy of International Courts' (2013) 86 Temple Law Review 61–105.

[42] ibid 68.

[43] ibid 82.

[44] ibid.

[45] ibid 81.

[46] ibid 82.

studied three separate cases (involving Switzerland, France, and Turkey) in which the European Court of Human Rights (ECtHR) upheld national bans on women or girls wearing Islamic headscarves in public schools (as teachers or as students).[47] In each decision, the Court applied the 'margin of appreciation doctrine', which allows States broad latitude to balance the free exercise of religion with the aim of promoting secularism (since all of the States in question have historically established secularism in public spaces as a State interest).[48] One of the considerations the ECtHR judges referred to in these decisions was the idea that the wearing of headscarves is a form of subordination for Muslim women, and thus is incompatible with State aims of promoting gender equality.[49] For example, in the *Dahlab* case, the Court argued that:

> ... the wearing of a headscarf might have some kind of proselytizing effect, seeing that it appears to be imposed on women by a precept which is laid down in the Koran and which, as the [Swiss] Federal Court noted, is hard to square with the principle of gender equality. It therefore appears difficult to reconcile the wearing of an Islamic headscarf with the message of tolerance, respect for others and, above all, equality and non-discrimination that all teachers in a democratic society must convey to their pupils.

Importantly, in this case, each side claimed to represent women's interests in some respect: the plaintiffs were all women making claims on their own behalf, while the States claimed to be representing the plaintiffs' interests as women by emphasizing not just their administrative duty to balance the State's pursuit of secularism with rights to free exercise of religion, but also the value of gender equality in public spaces. However, according to Elkayam-Levy:

> Characterizing the decisions is the very little discussion, if any at all, on what constitutes these 'women's rights,' how the bans are promoting gender equality, and in what manner women's rights are being protected by restrictions on their religious dress. The generality of the rulings shed light on the regrettable absence of women's human rights analysis.[50]

As a result, the human rights of women as a group seemed to get lost between the plaintiff's claims, which were interpreted by the court as claims on behalf of their

[47] Cochav Elkayam-Levy, 'Women's Rights and Religion—The Missing Element in the Jurisprudence of the European Court of Human Rights' (2014) 35 University of Pennsylvania Journal of International Law 1175–222.
[48] ibid 1182.
[49] ibid 1186, citing *Dahlab v Switzerland*, App No 42393/98, Reports of Judgments and Decisions 2001-V European Court of Human Rights 447 (15 February 2001).
[50] ibid 1182.

free exercise of religion, and the States' insistence (and the Court's apparent agreement) that gender equality weighed in favour of the bans, not against them. These cases therefore seem to indicate a problematic situation in which women's rights are not adequately represented in international courts, even while women's interests are nominally represented by not one but both parties to the dispute.

While the question of what procedural fairness requires in such cases is complicated, it nonetheless seems clear that religious diversity among judges would not be much of a bolster to the normative legitimacy of the Court in these cases, and might in fact pull in the opposite direction. While there is some evidence to suggest that part of the problem in these cases is that 'Muslim applicants are substantially less likely to receive favourable judge votes' in cases before the ECtHR,[51] the perception that women are unequal to men within Islamic communities would not be addressed and would arguably be exacerbated by greater representation for Muslim men as judges on the Court; a meaningful form of increased religious representation for Muslim judges in these cases would therefore require ensuring adequate representation of Muslim women in particular.

However, the pursuit of procedural fairness and normative legitimacy by ensuring judicial representation for specific demographic groups raises all the practical problems discussed earlier of determining what adequate representation for demographic groups would be in cases where the interests of applicants seem to be (at least in part) a function of their membership in cross-cutting and overlapping social and religious groups. More importantly, this conception of procedural fairness and normative legitimacy risks confining us to a model of judicial partiality rather than independence, insofar as it tightly links the normative legitimacy of courts to the social identities of judges. A better model would be to ensure not a descriptively representative bench, therefore, but that as many judges as possible, whatever their descriptive characteristics, are adequately receptive and responsive to women's concerns, including the concerns of women who are members of minority religious, ethnic, or racial groups.

The third reason for scepticism about the connection between religious representation among judges and the normative legitimacy of courts can be seen by examining the role of religion in the dispute about reproductive rights. As we have seen, the closest connections between descriptive representation among judges and normative legitimacy of courts obtain in situations where social groups that are not represented on the bench are also socially marginalized groups whose perspectives risk being unheard or inadequately acknowledged in judicial decision-making. However, some evidence exists that in international legal cases regarding reproductive rights, the traditional Catholic perspective tends to be represented as one side of the case. As an example, consider a study of the *Gretel Artavia Murillo et al.*

51 Dan Koev, 'Not Taking It on Faith: State and Religious Influences on European Court of Human Rights Judges in Freedom of Religion Cases' (2019) 18(2) Journal of Human Rights 184–200, at 184.

v. Costa Rica case before the Inter-American Court of Human Rights (IACtHR).[52] The authors of this case study argue that data about the amicus briefs submitted to the court justify characterizing the parties to the dispute as 'feminist' versus 'Catholic'. While the authors also use the terms 'conservative' or 'anti-abortion' to describe the Catholic side (and the term 'pro-choice' to describe the feminist side), they argue that it is illuminating to see the international network of conservative amicus brief authors as Catholic, given the backgrounds, social networks, and religious and institutional affiliations of their authors, as well as the substantive views put forth in the briefs (and to see the 'pro-choice' authors as 'feminist' based on the same considerations). As the authors note, the conservative briefs 'for the most part trace networks that adopt Catholic definitions, framing them not as religious arguments but as bioethics'.[53]

If this framing of the opposing sides in *Aravia Murillo* is apt, what does this signify for the relevance of religious diversity among judges at the IACtHR to the legitimacy of the Court's decision in this case? One salient point is that this is not a case in which the basic human rights of members of a religious group are violated or insecure due to their religious beliefs or affiliation (as might occur in cases of religious persecution), nor is it a case where religious rights themselves (such as freedom of association and free exercise of religion) are at stake for members of a particular religious group (as might be the case regarding minority religious groups in States that have an established religion). While even in these kinds of cases it might be difficult to establish that religious representation among judges on an international court is a requirement of the normative legitimacy of the court's decisions, the rationale for doing so would presumably be a concern for the human rights of members of the religious group. In *Aravia Murillo*, by contrast, the relevant religious perspective constitutes a foundational element of one view of the reproductive rights of women versus the rights to life of a fetus or embryo. The human rights of Catholics or members of other religious groups per se are not at issue.

If the conservative side of this dispute essentially represents a Catholic perspective on abortion rights for women, it's not obvious that procedural fairness in that case would require representation of that religious perspective among the judges deciding the case. Moreover, such a requirement would again seem to imply a background assumption of a problematic level of partiality among judges; for example, that Catholics will reliably vote with the orthodox Catholic view on abortion. As we noted earlier, however, there are liberal as well as conservative Catholics, and (especially in the United States) many Protestant Christians would vote in line with

[52] Julieta Lemaitre and Rachel Sieder, 'The Moderating Influence of International Courts on Social Movements: Evidence from the IVF Case Against Costa Rica' (2017) 19 Health and Human Rights Journal 149–60.

[53] ibid 153.

the 'Catholic' perspective. Just as the nationalist presumption among international judges has been challenged, the legitimacy of international courts requires an assumption that judges are applying the law to the facts of the case rather than representing their own side in a conflict.

6. Conclusion

As I argued at the start of this paper, lack of descriptive diversity among judges on international courts can indicate problematic biases against members of certain social groups in their pursuit of judicial careers. Such bias is always unjust and should be rectified as a matter of social justice. However, this claim does not support the idea that the normative (as opposed to sociological) legitimacy of international courts requires broad descriptive representation among judges. Rather than pursuing an account of normative legitimacy for international courts that includes diverse representation of religious backgrounds among judges, it seems much more to the point to work towards ensuring a culture of judicial decision making that is sensitive to the perspectives and voices of women and other right holders whose claims come before the court. In the case of women's rights, this may require explicit representation for women's voices and careful attention women's human rights claims, especially when women's rights claims diverge both from those of religious groups and the State. This conception of legitimacy also avoids creating the problematic impression that judges are excessively partial to litigants who are members of their own demographic groups.

24

Diversity on the Bench of the European Court of Human Rights

A Clash of Paradigms

*Angelika Nußberger and Freya Baetens**

1. Introduction

International courts are not only melting pots of different legal cultures, but also objects under anxious political observation. Diversity is important to international courts: it matters who is sitting on the bench. And it matters what diversity exactly means. International courts differ from national courts in terms of the perception of their diversity. Factors that constitute the identity of adjudicators and are perceived as neutral at the domestic level, such as age, former profession, and cultural background, are not necessarily considered neutral in an international court. Conversely, factors that are not seen as acceptable domestically, such as membership of a political party, may be acceptable for judges at the international level. In order to understand the role of international judges in general and those on the European Court of Human Rights (ECtHR) bench in particular, this chapter scrutinizes the factors influencing the world views and personalities of judges and their effects on the judicial process (leaning towards collective or individual decision-making) as well as the extent to which the judiciary is perceived as trustworthy. The chapter also analyses the ECtHR's continuous battle with the fundamental balancing act of dispensing individual justice while safeguarding the consistency of the system in its entirety. In the final section, the chapter examines the factors that unify the Court despite, or perhaps even because of, its diversity.

* The authors are grateful to Veronica Lavista for her assistance in preparing this chapter for publication. The views and opinions expressed in this chapter are those of the authors and do not necessarily reflect the official position of the ECtHR.

This work was partly supported by the Research Council of Norway through its Centres of Excellence funding scheme (project number 223274) and the FRIPRO Young Research Talents (project number 274946).

Angelika Nußberger and Freya Baetens, *Diversity on the Bench of the European Court of Human Rights* In: *Identity and Diversity on the International Bench.* Edited by: Freya Baetens, Oxford University Press (2020).
 DOI: 10.1093/oso/9780198870753.003.0024.

2. Input: Different Perceptions of Contextual Factors on the National and International Level

Factors that constitute the identity of adjudicators and are perceived as more or less 'neutral' (meaning they are unlikely to influence judicial appointments) at the domestic level, such as age, former profession, and cultural background, are often not considered 'neutral' in an international court.

2.1 Age

An advanced age is traditionally seen as an important advantage for any person involved in decision-making, as demonstrated by many idioms and proverbs: 'wisdom comes with age' and an 'eminence grise'. Age, however, may also indicate a more conservative outlook on life, which in turn may translate in a reluctance to adopt a more progressive stance towards legal development and an unwillingness to accept evolving interpretations of the law. Such stereotypes generally apply both to national and international courts. In the international context, age is not only related to less or more experience and less or more openness for change, but also to the fact of being witness of or involved in ground-breaking political events such as World War II, life under communism, revolutions, and upheavals such as the Hungarian Revolution in 1956, the Prague Spring in 1968, or the strikes in Poland in the 1980s, the Velvet Revolutions in Eastern Europe in the late 1980s and early 1990s, the war in Yugoslavia, to name just a few of the most important events and developments in the 20th century.

The respective life experience of the judges will inevitably shape their world view in one way or other. This is important since international and regional courts are often established or see their powers expanded in the wake and in response of radical political or social change, in the hope of preventing a similar calamity in the future. The Permanent Court of International Justice was founded after the First World War; the International Court of Justice (ICJ), the European Court of Justice, the dispute settlement system of the General Agreement on Tariffs and Trade (GATT), and the ECtHR after the Second World War.[1] At the same time, the role and tasks of regional and international courts might change over time. Even if they are set up to carry a specific historical message to future generations, this original idea might fade and make way to new challenges.

[1] Statute of the Permanent Court of International Justice (concluded 16 December 1920, entered into force 20 August 1921) 6 LNTS 379, 390; Statute of the International Court of Justice (concluded 26 June 1945, entered into force 24 October 1945) 3 Bevans 1179; EC Treaty Protocol on the Statute of the Court of Justice; General Agreement on Tariffs and Trade (signed on 30 October 1947) 61 Stat. A-11, 55 UNTS 194; Convention for the Protection of Human Rights and Fundamental Freedoms (European Convention on Human Rights, as amended) (ECHR).

Thus, the European Court of Justice, the dispute settlement system of GATT and the ECtHR all underwent significant institutional reform and expansion in the aftermath of the end of the Cold War. At the EU level, for example, the Maastricht Treaty (effective in 1992) established the three pillars of the Union: one supranational pillar created from three European Communities (which included the European Economic Community (EEC), the European Coal and Steel Community and the European Atomic Energy Community), the Common Foreign and Security Policy (CFSP) pillar, and the Justice and Home Affairs (JHA) pillar.[2] The European Court of Justice gained power with the entry into force of the Amsterdam Treaty in 1999, whereby issues from the third pillar were transferred to the first pillar.[3] In 1995, the GATT system became the World Trade Organization's (WTO) Dispute Settlement Body, which is more of a 'real' court in the sense of being able to issue binding decisions that could no longer be vetoed by the losing party, reversing the old system so that decisions were now automatically adopted unless there was a consensus not to do so.[4] In 1998, the European Commission of Human Rights, which decided on the admissibility of applications, was abolished by Protocol 11, and the European Court of Human Rights became a full-time institution.[5]

In terms of judicial outcomes, it is decisive how far the mind-sets of the adjudicators who populate the benches of these courts are open to something new even if they have been 'formed' in a different (historical) period. More generally, the impact of historical experience on decision-making is not predictable: different people will draw different conclusions. Just as a Minister of Defence who has been in active service may well be more cautious in sending soldiers to battle, so may a judge who lived through the Second World War, be far more aware of the seriousness of 'the threat or use of force' or of human rights violations in situations of extreme tension. But this is not necessarily so: having first-hand experience may also scar individuals to an extent that they are unable to see former enemies as current friends and act accordingly.

A famous example is Pierre-Henri Teitgen, a former World War II French resistance fighter, who was later appointed Minister of Justice under Charles de Gaulle in the immediate post-war period. In his biography, he describes how he was responsible for the execution of Pierre Laval on 15 October 1945 despite an unfair procedure—the jurors had insulted the accused during the jury trial and not even

[2] Treaty on European Union (Maastricht Treaty).

[3] Treaty of Amsterdam Amending the Treaty on European Union, The Treaties Establishing the European Communities and Related Acts (published on 10 November 1997, entered into force on 1 May 1999).

[4] DSU, Dispute Settlement Rules: Understanding on Rules and Procedures Governing the Settlement of Disputes, Marrakesh Agreement Establishing the World Trade Organization, Annex 2, 1869 UNTS 401, 33 ILM 1226 (1994).

[5] Council of Europe, Protocol 11 to the European Convention for the Protection of Human Rights and Fundamental Freedoms, Restructuring the Control Machinery Established Thereby (published on 11 May 1994, entered into force 1 November 1998) ETS 155.

pretended to be impartial.[6] Teitgen then became one of the authors of the European Convention on Human Rights (ECHR) in the 1950s and one of the first generation of judges at the ECtHR in 1976.[7]

Other examples can be found in the enlargement of the bench after the end of the Cold War and the implosion of the USSR when membership of the Council of Europe expanded massively.[8] Some of the older judges had made careers as eager and successful members of the Communist party, while others, who were (in some cases considerably) younger, viewed Communism as a scourge. An example of the former group was the first Russian Judge on the ECtHR bench, Vladimir Tumanov, who previously chaired the Department of State and Law in Bourgeois Countries at the Institute of State and Law of the USSR Academy of Sciences.[9] He had risen to scholarly fame in 1974 with the publication of his magnum opus '*Contemporary bourgeois legal thought. A Marxist evaluation of the basic concepts*'. At the same time, he was one of the bridge-builders in the time of perestroika. As he knew the Western legal systems well, he could recommend elements to be transferred and implemented in the USSR. Thus, he was the first one to write about the idea of constitutional justice in the famous Soviet law journal *Socialisticheskoe Gosudarstvo i Pravo*.[10] Later he was rewarded with the Chairmanship of the Constitutional Court for his loyal service as well as for his innovative ideas.

On the other side of the ideological battlefield were judges from the newly independent States such as the Baltic and the Caucasian States—some of whom had been born in the late 1960s or early 1970s (and thus only in their thirties or early forties when they arrived in Strasbourg).[11] Some had been educated in the US or at European universities and viewed the Cold War through a lens heavily determined by prevalent opinions in the West. They returned to the land of their ancestors often with an ardent desire to right historical wrongs, including via the legal systems.[12] A comparable and related situation arose with judges from the former

[6] Pierre-Henri Teitgen, *Faites entrer le témoin suivant 1940-1958* (Rennes 1988) 255et seq. The chapter on 'Laval' is introduced by the sentence: '*De tous mes souvenirs des jours tragiques, ceux de l'affaire Laval restent parmi les plus pénibles*.' ['Of all my memories of tragic days, those of the Laval case remain among the most painful'].

[7] Pierre-Henri Teitgen, *Faites entrer le témoin suivant 1940-1958* (Rennes 1988) 489 et seq; Bates (ed), *The Evolution of the European Court on Human Rights* (OUP 2010).

[8] In 1987 21 States had ratified the European Convention on Human Rights; by 1998, 40 States had done so.

[9] A Saidov, 'In Memory of Vladimir Tumanov—Patriarch of Russian Comparative Law Science' (2011) 7–8 Law of Ukraine: Legal Journal 290.

[10] V A Tumanov, ...chto ckryvaetcja za "vozrazheniem" estestvennogo prava v sovremennoj burzhuaznoj jurisprudencii' (1954) 5 Socialisticheskoe Gosudarstvo i Pravo 8.

[11] See Chapter 10 in the present book: Helen Keller, Corina Heri and Myriam Christ, 'Fifty years of women at the European Court of Human Rights: successes and failure of the Council of Europe's gender agenda'.

[12] E Voeten, 'The Impartiality of International Judges: Evidence from the European Court of Human Rights' (2008) 102 American Political Science Review 417, 423, 428, 430;

Yugoslavia after the civil war: some older nominees to the ECtHR had had distinguished careers under the old regime, while others had been on the forefront of the political fight for independence.[13]

With a different age may also come a different educational background: this holds true for former USSR nationals who studied in Communist universities, as opposed to their younger compatriots who studied in the liberal West. Legal education is generally very different, not least with a view to its focus on the respective national legal systems or on international and European law, and it is also evolving over time.

The fact that judges are, as everybody else, shaped by history, is rarely made explicit. Whenever judges themselves have, however, to 'judge history' their convictions might come to the fore. One rare example of a credo about experience and belief is the following passage of a concurring opinion to the Chamber judgment in the famous case *Kononov v Latvia*:

> Before elaborating on some of these points, I must explain that my perception is somehow tainted by my own national background. I was born in the Netherlands just after the Second World War and grew up with the perception that the Nazis and their collaborators were entirely in the wrong and those who fought against the Nazis (including members of resistance groups) were completely in the right. Whatever acts the resistance groups had committed against the occupying German forces or against Netherlands nationals who had collaborated with them, it had always been for the right cause. If resistance groups had silenced collaborators who had informed on Jews or persons in hiding, they had done the right thing. And in the event that, after the war, a person who had been a member of a resistance group was found guilty of a crime committed during the war, it certainly had nothing to do with his or her underground work, but only with the settling of personal scores or with ordinary crime.[14]

Whenever nominating a judge for the international bench, governments have to bear in mind that choosing the 'oldest' person does not only mean selecting the person with most years of experience, but also that such experience has to be viewed within the light of its particular time. Age is not neutral: it may well be indicative of a certain world view, which makes the State's nomination choice even more political than usual.

[13] Fred J Bruinsma, Matthijs de Blois 'Rules of Law from Westport to Wladistock, Separate Opinions in the European Court of Human Rights' (1997) 14 Netherlands Quarterly of Human Rights 175, 185.

[14] *Kononov v Latvia* App no 36376/04 (ECHR, 24 July 2008) Concurring opinion of Judge Myjer; analysis of further historical cases: *Janowiec v Russia* Apps no 55508/07 and 29520/09 (ECHR, 21 October 2013), *Vassiliauskas v Lithuania* App no 35343/05 (ECHR, 20 October 2015), *Drelingas v Lithuania* App no. 28859/16 (ECHR, 12 March 2019).

2.2 Former Profession

In many domestic judiciaries, judges on the highest benches have often 'risen through the ranks': starting at a court of first instance, vying for promotion to the appeal benches, with the ultimate prize being an appointment to the supreme court or court of cassation.[15] The highest domestic court benches therefore are populated with men and, to a lesser extent, women who are 'lifelong professional judges' in the sense that they already have had a twenty- or thirty-year career on the lower benches. This is, however, not true for the common law systems where judges, as a rule, have to work as counsel and be especially successful in order to be appointed to the bench. In any case, the run-up to the highest bench may be so elongated that in some cases, such as Belgium and Italy, special measures have to be put in place to avoid a 'revolving door system' whereby most judges would only be able to serve less than five years before retiring.[16] It is in most countries therefore unheard of that a 'new judge' would be appointed to the highest bench without having long-term judicial experience.

Constitutional and (the highest) administrative courts form the exception to this rule: in many countries, these courts reflect to some extent political representation in the parliament and the judges appointed to these benches often have a (distinguished) background in politics, legal practice, or academia without ever having been a judge.[17] In this regard, appointments to the benches of these national courts resemble nominations at the international level. Formally, the rules stipulate that an ECtHR judge 'shall be of high moral character and must either possess the qualifications required for appointment to high judicial office or be jurisconsults

[15] Lee Epstein, Jack Knight, and Olga Shvetsova, Comparing Judicial Selection Systems (2001) 10(1) William and Mary Bill of Rights Journal 18.

[16] In Belgium, the Judicial Code was amended, so as to require that a judge could only be elected President of the Court of Cassation, if (s)he was more than five years away from retirement (Art 259 *quinquies* of the Belgian Judicial Code, as amended by the Law of 16 December 2006). The statutory retirement age for judges in the Italian Court of Cassation was increased from 70 to 72 in 1992 (Decree Law 503-1992, Art 16), and to 75 in 2002 (Decree Law 289/2002, Art 34(12)). In 2014 both these Decrees were abrogated in Decree Law 90/2014, Art 1, however, that change was suspended in 2014–16 (Art 5(1) of Decree Law 168-2016). As explained in a complaint made before the European Parliament (Petition No 0036/2018 by Pierpaolo Volpe (Italian) on the discrimination resulting from the recent Italian decision to extend the retirement of certain categories of magistrates), exceptions to the increase in the age of retirement for magistrates of the court of cassation were reduced in the years 2014–16 as they seemed to target a more limited category of magistrates with the stated aim to serve the interest of service. In particular, it should be taken into account that the aim of the exception, as explained in the incriminated 2016 law, was to ensure continuity in senior positions given the many reforms carried out for the definition of pending litigation. These decrees (exempting those magistrates of the court of cassation up to the age of 72 or 75) were not continued beyond 31 December 2017: the current retirement age is 70.

[17] Michaela Hailbronner, 'Rethinking the Rise of the German Constitutional Court: From Anti-Nazism to Value Formalism' (2014) 12 International Journal of Constitutional Law 626, 646; John E Ferejohn, 'Constitutional Review in the Global Context' (2002) New York University Journal, Legislation and Public Policy 49.

of recognised competence'.[18] In other words: having formerly served on the bench of a high domestic court is not an absolute requirement. It is, however, remarkable that some countries have nominated to the Strasbourg Court the presidents of their highest national courts, either supreme courts or constitutional courts, sometimes even before the end of their respective mandates.[19]

Yet, as many, if not more, judges have entered the court through the second-mentioned door, as 'jurisconsults of recognised competence'. These include not only law professors but also legal practitioners, government agents, representatives of international or regional organizations, and even NGO employees. It is harder for small Member States to find enough suitable candidates since they do not have universities or large law firms which would allow them to nominate 'home grown' candidates who have earned international reputations in human rights law. Nominating domestic judges might also be difficult due to the small size of the judiciary.

The increasing mobility of scholars has led to the emergence of 'international research hubs', such as the Max Planck Institutes and specialized international law centres within top-ranking universities, that attract talented researchers from all over the world in search of funding and collaborative teams. Scholars leave their home countries in order to specialize and build their reputation internationally, resulting in a situation where few experts work within their country of nationality.[20] However, after several years or even decades of work abroad, they find that at home they are no longer 'in the running' to be nominated for international posts because they lack domestic political clout and internal 'professional socialization'. As a result, arguably the best candidates for the bench may well no longer be considered in the national nomination process.

Whatever a potential candidate's professional background—whether a judge, a lawyer, or an academic—it will have an impact on the way a Strasbourg judge assesses cases. It cannot be denied that there will be what might be called '*une deformation professionnelle*'—ex-lawyers will see the cases through the lens of the victim or the accused of a human rights violation, ex-professors will concentrate on what they consider to be the most interesting legal questions, and judges will build on their experience within the national judiciary. That does not mean that a different starting point in working on a case will necessarily lead to a different result. But

[18] Convention for the Protection of Human Rights and Fundamental Freedoms (European Convention on Human Rights, as amended) (ECHR), Art 21(1).

[19] See the nominations for Finland (Election of judges to the ECtHR List and curricula vitae of candidates submitted by the Government of Finland Doc 13729 (13 March 2015) Pauliine Koskelo) and Azerbaijan (Election of judges to the ECtHR List and curricula vitae of candidates submitted by the Government of Azerbaijan Doc 14131 (6 September 2016) Khanlar Hadzhiev).

[20] Paulette Siekierski, Manolita Correia Lima, and Felipe Mendes Borini, International Mobility of Academics: Brain Drain and Brain Gain (2018) 15(3) European Management Review 329–39; Jesus Velasco, Academic Brain Drain (2014) Americas Quarterly; Alex Nunn, The 'Brain Drain' Academic and Skilled Migration to the UK and its impacts on Africa' Report to the AUT and NATFHE (2005).

it cannot be assumed that all judges approach the cases on their desks in exactly the same way. For national courts this *déformation professionelle* is less decisive as judges have, as a rule, basically all the same formation and background. Here again, constitutional courts are the exception and resemble more international courts.

2.3 Cultural Background

The cultural background of judges is even more difficult to grasp. Religion or lack of religion, interest in arts, history, literature, politics, world view—are all relevant. Again, the diversity of international judges will be greater than the diversity of national judges. Factors such as religion might be less important where all religions are represented, such as at the Strasbourg Court, than where there are specific 'competing' religions in one country. The religious affiliation might often not be known unless the judge openly talks about it. At the same time, it might come to the fore in especially sensitive cases touching upon moral questions such as beginning and end of life.

As the Europe-wide average of domestic professional judges reaches an approximately 50–50% gender balance, gender is increasingly becoming a neutral factor insofar as domestic courts are concerned.[21] This laudable balance is, however, only achieved due to the significantly higher percentage of women judges on the benches of lower courts. Looking at the benches of the highest domestic courts (supreme courts, highest administrative courts, and constitutional courts), women judges are, in many countries, still largely absent.[22] As discussed in various other chapters in the present book, women judges are still relatively rare (approximately 17%) on the benches of international courts.[23]

At the ECtHR, the Council of Europe put a policy in place in 2004 that out of each three candidates for election, nominated by a Member States, only two can be of the same gender.[24] The Nordic countries and Switzerland started appointing

[21] European Judicial Systems, 'Efficiency and Quality of Justice' (2018) 26 Council of Europe European Commission for the Efficiency of Justice (CEPEJ) Studies 113.

[22] With men still holding a 63% share in Supreme Courts, European Judicial Systems, Efficiency and Quality of Justice (2018) 26 CEPEJ Studies 115.

[23] See eg. Chapter 2, Liesbeth Lijnzaad, 'The Smurfette Principle: Reflections about Gender and the Nomination of Women to the International Bench'; Chapter 6, Catherine Drummond, 'The Party-Appointment Process: Addressing Barriers to Equal Opportunities for Women in the Appointment of Ad Hoc Adjudicators'; Chapter 7, Rebecca Emiene Badejogbin, 'African Women's Paths to the International Bench: How to Overcome Double Discrimination'; Chapter 16, Valerie Hughes, 'Adjudicating International Trade Cases in the World Trade Organization: Does Gender Make a Difference?'; Chapter 26, Josephine Jarpa Dawuni, 'Keeping Gender on the Agenda for International Benches: a Case Study of the African Court on Human and Peoples' Rights'.

[24] Council of Europe, Parliamentary Assembly Recommendation 1649(2004) (20 Jan 2004)—See Chapter 10 in the present book: Helen Keller, Corina Heri, and Myriam Christ, 'Fifty Years of Women at the European Court of Human Rights: Successes and Failures of the Council of Europe's Gender Agenda'.

women judges early on, and the policy has now resulted in women from a variety of countries being appointed to the bench. This is not limited, as sometimes thought, to judges from small and Eastern European countries: the current Spanish, German, and Turkish ECtHR judges, for example, are female. However, France, Italy, Russia, the United Kingdom, and a number of other countries have never sent a woman to Strasbourg. Nevertheless, in 2019, only fifteen out of 47 ECtHR judges, or 31.9% are women. Gender may have become an increasingly neutral factor for the domestic bench—but this is certainly not the case yet for appointment to the international bench.

2.4 Affiliation to a political party

Conversely, factors that are not seen as 'neutral' domestically, such as political activities, may be seen differently for judges at the international level. As is the case for gender, the highest domestic courts have more in common with international courts in this regard than with lower domestic benches. For judges in a court of first instance, political activity or party membership will often be seen as undesirable or even prohibited, particularly as the bench may consist of only three judges or even one sole judge. Higher domestic courts and international courts on the other hand usually consist of larger groups of judges sitting on any given case—although the ECtHR's practice of having a sole judge perform a 'first triage', in order to alleviate the pressure of the increasing number of pending cases on the Court, deviates from this.[25] In the context of these larger benches, an approximate representation, not only of nationalities of Member States, but also of political ideologies, is sometimes seen as desirable as it may neutralize party politics. Different countries may have a different understanding of the appropriate role of political parties and the left/right-wing divide plays out in varied ways—but the key factor which will affect the perception of judges' impartiality and independence is how close they are to their respective appointing authorities after they have joined the bench. This is more of a problem in some States than in others.

3. Output: Understanding of Role Models and Functions

In order to understand the role of international judges in general and those on the ECtHR bench in particular, this section scrutinizes the effects of 'diversity' on the bench. It is argued that diversity has an impact on the different role models of judges, and different pre-conceptions of society and State.

[25] Rule 52A of the Rules of Court of the European Court of Human Rights.

3.1 Understanding the role of judges

Distinctive legal cultures approach judicial decision-making broadly speaking from two opposing angles: either as a collective or an individual process. In the tradition of the Anglo-Saxon common law systems, on the one hand, individuality is key: arriving at a judgment in the form of a compromise is arguably to be avoided. The logical line of thinking of an individual member of the bench ought not to be watered down—lest compromise be seen as weakness of convictions. In the European continental tradition, as also adopted in for example Latin America, the judge is only perceived as a judge because (s)he is part of a particular collective body. From this perspective, compromise is positive—the underlying idea being that a group of judges collaborating will arrive at a better solution than any judge acting on their own.

These domestic approaches have been extrapolated to the international level—and in some cases, have allowed for a hybrid *modus operandi*. In the ICJ, for example, the judges tend to always sit in plenary (although smaller chambers are possible) and issue a 'judgment of the court'. Rarely, however, is this a unanimous decision—often one or more dissenting and separate opinions are attached, which may well attract more following or criticism than the actual judgment. Frequently, further development of the law allows what was once a sole judge's dissent to evolve in a majority-supported judgment years later.[26] The Appellate Body of the WTO on the other hand focuses more strongly on collegiality: even though cases are heard by only three (out of seven) Appellate Body members, there is an unwritten rule that the sitting members discuss their draft report with the four non-sitting members in order to ensure optimal coherence in the jurisprudence.[27]

ECtHR judges are allowed to issue separate and dissenting opinions, but the number of dissenting opinions is relatively low. The dissents that have been issued are interesting from a scholarly perspective: they show a judge's individual approach and personal interest in shaping the 'common good'. Unlike in the foundational years of the Court,[28] dissents at the ECtHR deal only rarely with disagreement on major concepts, but rather show specific approaches towards interpreting the Convention in a particular case or applying the agreed principles to the facts at hand. Notably, there seems to be pressure on dissenting judges to 'explain themselves' to justify their deviation from the collective opinion: as a result, some

[26] See eg *Case Concerning the Gabchikovo-Nagymaros Project* (*Hungary v Slovakia*) (Separate Opinion of Vice-President Weeramantry) [1997] ICJ Rep 88, on sustainable development.

[27] A Ralph Carnegie, 'The Impact of the World Trade Organization on International Law' XXXI Course on International Law (WTO 2004) 49.

[28] See eg the dissents by the British judge Gerald Fitzmaurice, J G Merrills, 'Sir Gerald Fitzmaurice's Contribution to the Jurisprudence of the European Court of Human Rights' (1982) 53 British Yearbook of International Law 115.

dissenters find it necessary to be even longer than the actual judgment. In this respect, the legal culture in which the judge's mind was formed plays an important role: in contrast to the common law legal systems, French and Italian legal systems, for example, do not allow for dissenting opinions. The German legal culture is located in between the two as it allows dissenting opinions only for Constitutional Court judges. Even there they are used only sparingly.

Arguably, at times, the use of dissents and, more generally, the style of judicial decision-making, is as much a question of individual personality ('judicial temperament', in the words of White and Boussiakou)[29] as one of legal culture—though the two can be related. Whether judges should develop the law—and if so, the extent to which they are supposed to do so—is still a highly controversial question. Some regard the 'ideal judge' as an engaged figure, while others prefer a distanced observer. In the French tradition famously summarized by Montesquieu, the judge is the 'bouche de la loi', the mouthpiece of the law: the facts are 'inserted' and the judgment is 'produced', without any freedom to further develop basic concepts on the part of the bench. This approach is not workable in practice and—based on the idea of the Convention as a 'living instrument'—it is obvious that any form of legal progress requires continuous development.[30] The counterargument would be that judges should not be determining what progress is (and therefore not be engaged in continuous development)—this task is reserved for the legislative and executive branches.[31]

At the international level, the judiciary stands often accused of being hostile to subsidiarity in order to narrow the scope of national law and the sovereign powers of States.[32] This is arguably incorrect: legal progress does not necessarily entail pushing for increased centralism—on the contrary, as the ECtHR case law shows,[33] there is significant support for the idea that many issues are better dealt with at the local level. In this context, separate and dissenting opinions form a good opportunity for suggesting possible opportunities to further develop the law—while avoiding the criticism that the Court as such is 'going too far' in its binding opinions. In general, most would agree that judges have to rise above their personal convictions. Dissents which are seen as 'ideological' are swiftly critiqued by

[29] Robin White, Iris Boussiakou, 'Separate opinions in the European Court of Human Rights' (2009) 9(1) Human Rights Law Review 37.

[30] George Letsas, 'The ECHR as a living instrument: its meaning and legitimacy' in Andreas Føllesdal, Birgit Peters, and Geir Ulfstein (eds), *Constituting Europe* (CUP 2013) 106; Stephan Theil, 'Is the "Living Instrument" Approach of the European Court of Human Rights Compatible with ECHR and International Law?' (2017) 23(3) European Public Law 587.

[31] Jean-Paul Costa, 'On the Legitimacy of the European Court of Human Rights' Judgments' (2011) 7(2) European Constitutional Law Review 173.

[32] Paolo G Carozza, 'The Problematic Applicability of Subsidiarity to International Law and Institutions' (2016) 61(1) American Journal of Jurisprudence 51.

[33] *G.I.E.M. S.R.L. and others v Italy* Apps nos. 1828/06, 34163/07 and 19029/11(ECHR 28 June 2018); *Moreira Ferreira v Portugal (No. 2)* App no. 19867/12 (ECHR, 11 July 2017); *Garib v The Netherlands* App no. 43494/09 (ECHR, 6 November 2017); among many others.

outside observers.[34] On the contrary, there does not seem to be a common understanding on limits of critique of the majority's arguments. Some judges use very harsh words,[35] while others prefer a more diplomatic language introducing their comments with words like 'I respectfully disagree'. The latter approach takes into account the authority of the Court as an institution while the former insists on the individual judge's freedom of expression.

As stated by Stijn Smet, 'often no insight can be gleaned from the Court's judgments on the comparative strength of human rights in conflict [which] leaves a stark impression that the Court's balancing exercises are steered by subjective preferences'.[36] The dissenting opinion in the case *Fürst-Pfeifer v Austria*, might serve as an illustration to this point. The facts of the case are that a regional newspaper had published the personal health data of a psychiatrist who frequently acted as a court expert in child custody cases. Balancing Article 8 (the right to privacy) against Article 10 (the freedom of expression), the majority found that the latter prevailed. Two judges wrote a dissenting opinion, arguing that 'Article 8 is *not* analysed almost anywhere . . . Instead, the majority turns its attention to Article 10 immediately . . . the majority is of the view that the circumstances of this case call for engagement in one-sided scrutiny . . . [But there] can be no fair balancing exercise if all the weight is placed on one side of the scales while the other is left almost unloaded'.[37] They conclude—using very strong words—that '[t]his judgment has several major flaws. . . [which] have produced the most regrettable result – a one-sided, unbalanced and, it appears, fundamentally unjust judgment'.[38]

Strongly worded dissents can also be explained by reference to the subject matter. Thus, freedom of expression cases for instance seem not only to evoke deep-seated personal convictions,[39] but are also intensely embedded in cultural traditions. While the US tradition is in favour of more or less unrestricted free speech, the continental tradition tends to uphold other rights and concepts such

[34] See eg the Russian Judge Dedov's dissent in *Bayev and others v Russia* App no. 67667 (ECHR, 20 June 2017) and the ensuing debate https://strasbourgobservers.com/2017/07/13/bayev-and-others-v-russia-on-judge-dedovs-outrageously-homophobic-dissent/ accessed 23 April 2020; Kushtrim Istrefi, Emma Irving, 'Rights in the Populist Era, A Comment on Bayev v. Russia (ECtHR): More Didactic than Persuasive' (2018) 31 Harvard Human Rights Journal 159; Başak Çali and Stewart Cunningham, 'Judicial Self Government and the Sui Generis Case of the European Court of Human Rights' (2018) 19(7) German Law Journal 1977.

[35] *Lambert and others v France* App no 46043/14 (ECHR, 5 June 2015), *Fürst-Pfeifer v Austria* Apps no 33677/10 and 52340/10 (ECHR, 17 August 2016).

[36] Stijn Smet, *Resolving Conflicts between Human Rights: The Judge's Dilemma* (Routledge 2016) 106.

[37] *Fürst-Pfeifer v Austria* Apps no 33677/10 and 52340/10 (ECHR, 17 August 2016), Joint Dissenting Opinion of Judges Wojtycek and Kūris [10].

[38] *Fürst-Pfeifer v Austria* Apps no 33677/10 and 52340/10 (ECHR, 17 August 2016), Joint Dissenting Opinion of Judges Wojtycek and Kūris [1].

[39] Fred J. Bruinsma, Matthijs de Blois 'Rules of Law from Westport to Vladivostok, Separate Opinions in the European Court of Human Rights' (1997) 14 Netherlands Quarterly of Human Rights 175, 185: Stiansen, Øyvind and Voeten, Erik, Backlash and Judicial Restraint: Evidence From the European Court of Human Rights (August 17, 2018) <http://dx.doi.org/10.2139/ssrn.3166110>accessed 19 August2020.

as human dignity. The different ways in which judges use their power to issue a dissent mirror how they perceive their own role.

3.2 Focus: Individual Justice or Legal Consistency

The understanding of the role of a judge is closely linked to the perception of what is more important—individual justice or legal security linked to a consistent application of the law. This can be illustrated at the example of some recent cases the Court had to deal with. The applicant in *Béláné Nagy v Hungary* had lost her right to a disability pension in 2010 due to a change in the eligibility criteria.[40] For some time, she did not receive any disability payments, but then the applicable law was reformed in 2012, replacing the disability pension with a disability allowance for which Ms Nagy did meet the criteria. However, as she had not been in receipt of a disability pension on the relevant date and had not accumulated the requisite number of days covered by social security as stipulated in the new law, she nevertheless did not obtain the allowance. The judgment on 10 February 2015 (rendered with the narrowest majority possible: four out of seven judges) regarded the termination or reduction of rights to social security benefits as a violation of Article 1 Protocol 1 (right to property). It ruled that, notwithstanding the fact that Ms Nagy had lost her right to receive a disability pension, she had a continuing legitimate expectation to disability benefits. The fact that she did not qualify for an allowance under the new rules was deemed an unjustified interference with her property rights.

The joint dissent disputed the majority's finding that the applicant held a property right and, as a result, the Court should have refrained from reviewing the claim. Since the Court could only examine the refusal to grant benefits after the 2012 reform at which point the applicant did not meet the requisite conditions, she did not have 'possession' that could have been the subject of government interference in violation of Article 1 Protocol 1. The case was referred to the Grand Chamber, where on 13 December 2016, a slight majority of 10 (out of 17) voted in the same way as the Chamber judges. A joint dissent confirmed the prior dissent, finding that:

> We are very well aware of the applicant's difficult situation. She fell through the holes of the social-security net when it was reformed. But nevertheless we consider that hard cases do not make good law. Such cases cannot be a reason to change the Court's long-standing and well-entrenched approach to the

[40] *Béláné Nagy v Hungary* App no 53080/13 (ECHR, 13 December 2016).

> interpretation of 'possessions' and 'legitimate expectations' within the meaning of Article 1 Protocol No. 1 to the Convention.[41]

A similar discussion took place in *Károly Nagy v Hungary*, concerning a compensation claim brought by a pastor whose claims before the domestic labour courts had been rejected as unenforceable after his dismissal by the Hungarian Reformed Church, as he was considered to be employed under ecclesiastical and not civil law.[42] On 1 December 2015 the Chamber rendered its judgment, once again with the narrow majority of 4:3, but this time finding no violation of Article 6 (right to fair trial).[43] This was confirmed on the Grand Chamber level, once again with a small majority.[44] Here again, the main question was whether to accept the long-term jurisprudence of the Court and to apply it to the circumstances of the case or to make an exception in view of the individual situation of the applicant. Among all the dissenters Judge Aleš Pejchal was the most outspoken in declaring that case-law would not matter in such a case:

> There are cases before this Court which cannot be rejected only with reference to the case-law, although such a method seems to be correct in a large majority of cases. That is, with reference to already existing interpretation of the Convention and its Protocols in cases similar to, but never entirely the same as, the instant case. This is one of those exceptional cases which require consideration solely by virtue of the text of the Convention interpreted in the most restrained way.[45]

These two cases, in which opposite conclusions were reached, illustrate how a vote based on what is understood to be 'individual justice' risked affecting the consistency of the legal system in its entirety—with consequences to be felt not merely at the regional human rights law level, but also for the domestic legal systems of each of the 47 Member States. The voting records of the individual judges also show that *who* is on the bench can make a major difference, due to that individual's legal culture and resulting perception of the legal discourse.

[41] *Béláné Nagy v Hungary* App no 53080/13 (ECHR, 13 December 2016), Joint Dissenting Opinion of Judges Nussberger, Hirvelä, Bianku, Yudkivska, Møse, Lemmens and O'Leary [45].

[42] *Károly Nagy v Hungary* App no 56665/09 (ECHR, 1 December 2015).

[43] *Károly Nagy v Hungary* App no 56665/09 (ECHR, 1 December 2015), the dissent of Judges Raimondi, Keller and Kjølbro referred to rejecting the second set of procedures as being incompatible with the Convention *ratione materiae* as the claim was not based on grounds recognized under domestic law and article 6 cannot be interpreted as creating rights that are not recognized under such law; Judges Sajó, Vuchinic and Kūris dissented on the finding of no violation of article 6(1) of the Convention.

[44] *Károly Nagy v Hungary* App no 56665/09 (ECHR, 14 September 2017).

[45] *Károly Nagy v Hungary* App no 56665/09 (ECHR, 14 September 2017) Dissenting Opinion of Judge Pejchal, 64.

3.3. Basic Perceptions of State and Society

Faced with the interactions between State and individual there are two different pre-conceptions of the starting point as either trust or mistrust. This is based on experience. Someone who has lived in an authoritarian regime that neglects the views and needs of individuals will assume that an individual protesting against the State will have a good reason to do so. On the contrary, someone who has grown up in a liberal democracy where the policy is focused on the rights of the individuals will, as a rule, tend to believe that the rights of the individual have not been violated. This will, however, not be a conscious choice but rather a subconscious element in decision-making. Despite the different starting points, the result of the assessment is not necessarily different.

4. Conclusion: One Unified Court—in Spite of its Diversity

Finally, the question is: can there be a 'unified Court', if the members of the bench are so diverse, at least from the legal cultural perspective? In other words, what holds the Court together in spite of its diversity? There are several factors that do this and form the 'corporate identity' of the Court. First, the Court has done (and is doing) a lot to integrate new judges into the institution. There is a specific 'narrative' the Court has developed of what it stands for and what its philosophy is. The judges on the ECtHR bench do form a collegial body, sharing a feeling of being all 'European judges'. Second, the ECtHR has a strong back-bone: its Registry with its institutional memory. It functions like a machine capable of dealing with 70,000 decisions on an annual basis.[46] At the same time it has developed techniques for preserving the consistency of its case-law which are handed down from one generation of lawyers drafting the judgments to the next generation. Third, judges on the bench share the common aim of upholding a high standard of human rights protection in Europe. They are all devoted to what the Preamble to the Statute of the Council of Europe calls 'the spiritual and moral values which are the common heritage of their peoples and the true source of individual freedom, political liberty and the rule of law, principles which form the basis of all genuine democracy . . .'[47]

[46] Ledi Bianku, Peter Kempees, 'The European Court of Human Rights' in Freya Baetens (ed) Legitimacy of Unseen Actors in International Adjudication (CUP 2019) 108.
[47] Statute of the Council of Europe [1949] ETS No. 001.

25
Peru's 'Intercultural Law' Proposal
Promoting Ethnic Diversity in the Administration of Justice

Clara María López Rodríguez

1. Introduction

This chapter critically analyses the role of indigenous peoples in international decision-making focusing on two areas of international law: human rights law as adjudicated by the Inter-American Court of Human Rights (Inter-American Court) and investment law as applied by investment arbitration tribunals. It is submitted that participatory mechanisms are important in these cases and appointment processes need to be reformed to achieve diversity on the international bench while securing indigenous peoples' rights before international tribunals. This chapter proposes an additional but complementary way to ensure participation of indigenous peoples in international adjudication: the recognition by courts and tribunals of the role of indigenous people's jurisdiction, ie indigenous peoples' right to enact and apply their own customary norms in their territories, enforce those rules and resolve disputes based on their own legal systems.

This chapter first clarifies the definition of indigenous peoples under international law and explains the relevance of their rights in disputes decided by the Inter-American Court and investment tribunals, addressing the main criticisms that have risen regarding the lack of diversity of adjudicators. Secondly, this chapter explains the concept of indigenous peoples' jurisdiction and argues that the recognition of indigenous legal systems has been a long-standing demand of indigenous peoples. Thirdly, focusing on Peru as a case study, this chapter provides a better understanding of the concept of indigenous peoples' jurisdiction, analysing its nuances and difficulties, but also the importance of regulating such jurisdiction at the domestic level. Fourthly, this chapter analyses how indigenous peoples' jurisdiction has become relevant in disputes before the Inter-American Court and investment tribunals. The chapter concludes that achieving diversity in international courts and arbitral tribunals and enabling participatory mechanisms is an important way of increasing the legitimacy of international bodies. Moreover, in order to respect indigenous peoples' claims to self-determination

Clara María López Rodríguez, *Peru's 'Intercultural Law' Proposal* In: *Identity and Diversity on the International Bench*. Edited by: Freya Baetens, Oxford University Press (2020).
DOI: 10.1093/oso/9780198870753.003.0025.

and self-government, which include their right to adopt their own customary laws and legal systems, indigenous peoples' jurisdiction should be considered when resolving disputes that affect them.

2. Indigenous Peoples and International Adjudication

2.1 Definition of Indigenous Peoples under International Law

Article 1 of the International Labour Organization Convention 169 (ILO C169) defines indigenous peoples,[1] dividing them into 'tribal peoples' (ie groups who have their own distinct culture and traditions but who may not have existed before colonization) and 'indigenous peoples' (ie groups that existed prior to colonization and who have maintained their own institutions). ILO C169 establishes the same rights for both groups. The reference to tribal peoples was included, as distinct from indigenous peoples, to prevent specific countries from circumventing ILO C169 on the basis that, since the entire population had been subjected to colonization, ILO C169 would not be applicable.[2] Self-identification is the fundamental element to determine to which groups ILO C169 applies.

The UN Declaration on the Rights of Indigenous Peoples (UNDRIP) does not contain a definition of indigenous peoples. During its drafting, different definitions were discussed, and it was acknowledged that, historically, indigenous peoples had suffered due to definitions that were imposed on them.[3] Hence, the final draft adopted a flexible approach, including only guidelines to ascertain who could be identified as indigenous as well as emphasizing the right of indigenous peoples to self-identify as such following their own customary norms.[4] In this vein, the preamble recognizes a common characteristic of indigenous peoples: the fact that they have suffered from historic injustices through colonization and dispossession of their lands, territories, and resources, and that they have been prevented

[1] Convention concerning Indigenous and Tribal Peoples in Independent Countries (adopted on 27 June 1989, entry into force 05 September 1991) 1650 UNTS 383 (ILO C169) Art. 1. 'This Convention applies to: (a) tribal peoples in independent countries whose social, cultural and economic conditions distinguish them from other sections of the national community, and whose status is regulated wholly or partially by their own customs or traditions or by special laws or regulations; (b) peoples in independent countries who are regarded as indigenous on account of their descent from the populations which inhabited the country, or a geographical region to which the country belongs, at the time of conquest or colonization or the establishment of present state boundaries and who, irrespective of their legal status, retain some or all of their own social, economic, cultural and political institutions.'

[2] Alexandra Xanthaki, *Indigenous Rights and United Nations Standards: Self-Determination, Culture and Land* (CUP 2007) 72.

[3] Erica Irene Daes, 'Note by the Chairperson-Rapporteur of the Working Group on Indigenous Populations, Ms. Erica-Irene Daes, on Criteria Which Might Be Applied When Considering the Concept of Indigenous Peoples' (1995) E/CN.4/Sub.2/AC.4/1995/3 para 6.

[4] United Nations Declaration on the Rights of Indigenous Peoples (adopted 2 October 2007) UNGA A/RES/61/295 Art 33.

from exercising their right to development in accordance with their own needs and interests. Similarly, the American Declaration on the Rights of Indigenous Peoples (ADRIP) does not contain a definition of indigenous peoples but confirms that self-identification is essential.[5] Hence, under international law, the principle of self-identification is used to identify indigenous peoples. Other relevant factors include historic discrimination, land dispossession and the existence of distinct customs and traditions that differentiate a group from other sections of the population.

2.2 Interaction between Indigenous Peoples' Rights and the Inter-American Court of Human Rights

Several disputes involving indigenous peoples' rights have been decided by the Inter-American Court. For instance, the landmark case of *Sarayaku v Ecuador* concerned an agreement between the State and an oil company for the exploration of an oil block located in Sarayaku territory, concluded without consulting the indigenous people. The Court reiterated that the right to property under the American Convention on Human Rights (ACHR) encompassed the unique relationship between indigenous people and their lands and included a right to Free, Prior, and Informed Consent (FPIC).[6] Even though the Inter-American Court has adopted many decisions safeguarding the rights of indigenous peoples, the composition of the Court has attracted criticism due to its lack of diversity and the opacity under which States appoint the judges.[7]

Under the ACHR and the Court's Statute, seven judges are elected from lists of three candidates proposed by each State Party. This system has been criticized for two reasons: (1) the process whereby States propose candidates is unregulated and lacks publicity, resulting in political appointments rather than merit-based selections;[8] (2) this lack of transparency at the domestic level is translated into the Organization of American States (OAS), where the General Assembly elects judges by secret ballot without debate or participation from civil society.[9] As a result, the

[5] American Declaration on the Rights of Indigenous Peoples (adopted 15 June 2016) AG/RES 2888 (XLVI-O/16) Art I.2.

[6] *Kichwa Indigenous Peoples of Sarayaku v Ecuador, Merits and Reparations, Judgment* (2012) Series C No. 245 (Inter-American Court).

[7] Katya Salazar and Naomi Roht-Arriaza, 'Democracia y Transparencia En El SIDH: Una Experiencia En Marcha/Democracy and Transparency in the IAHRS: An Experience in Progress' (2017) 8 Revista Direito e Práxis; Karlos Castilla Juárez, 'Lo Bueno, Lo Malo, Lo Feo y Lo Deseable En La (s)Elección de Integrantes de La Comisión y La Corte Interamericana de Derechos Humanos' (2017) 20 Iuris Dictio 119; Center for Justice and International Law, 'Position Paper No. 10-The Selection Process of the Inter-American Commission and Court on Human Rights: Reflections on Necessary Reforms' (2014) <https://cejil.org/en/position-paper-no-10-selection-process-inter-american-commission-and-court-human-rights-reflections> accessed 29 February 2020.

[8] Castilla Juárez (n 7) 123; Katya Salazar and Naomi Roht-Arriaza, (n 7) 1652, 1662.

[9] Castilla Juárez (n 7) 123.

bench lacks diversity in terms of gender and ethnicity.[10] Throughout the existence of the Court, there has never been a judge who self-identified as indigenous.[11]

In recent years, many reforms have been suggested. In particular, non-governmental organizations such as Centro por la Justicia y el Derecho Internacional (CEJIL), Open Society Justice Initiative (OSJI), and Due Process of Law Foundation (DPLF) have proposed to increase transparency in the selection of judges.[12] These organizations advocated, *inter alia*, that a panel of independent experts within OAS be created to review the candidates' CV's and to conduct a public interview with them.[13] Perhaps in response to this, the OAS General Assembly issued a Resolution in 2016 acknowledging the importance of gender and geographic diversity in the composition of the Court.[14] This Resolution encouraged States to nominate candidates that would ensure a 'balance in terms of gender, representation of the different regions, population groups, and legal systems' and established that, prior to the election, candidates should deliver a public presentation of their 'vision, proposals, and the initiatives that they would undertake if elected'.[15]

Although the election process as stipulated in the ACHR and the Statute of the Inter-American Court has not been reformed, the 2016 Resolution shows awareness of the importance of diversity. It should be praised as a way to promote the selection of judges with an indigenous background. However, there is a complementary means to ensure indigenous peoples' participation in judicial decision-making at the international level: through the recognition of indigenous jurisdiction.

2.3 Interaction between Indigenous Peoples' Rights and Investment Arbitration

Aside from human rights litigation, indigenous peoples' rights have also become relevant in international investment law. Disputes between investors and host States have peaked in recent years after concessions were cancelled following opposition to projects by indigenous peoples.[16] In these cases, States have consistently

[10] Centro por la Justicia y el Derecho Internacional (CEJIL), *Documentos de Coyuntura: Aportes Para El Proceso de Selección de Miembros de La Comisión y La Corte Interamericanas de Derechos Humanos* (Centro por la Justicia y el Derecho Internacional 2005) 11; Castilla Juárez (n 7) 125.

[11] Castilla Juárez (n 7) 125.

[12] Salazar and Roht-Arriaza (n 7) 1669.

[13] Center for Justice and International Law (n 7) 33.

[14] Promotion and Protection of Human Rights, General Assembly Resolution AG/RES 2887 (XLVI-O/16) (Washington DC, 14 June 2016).

[15] ibid.

[16] See amongst others, *Burlington Resources Incorporated v Ecuador,* ICSID Case No ARB/08/5, Decision on Jurisdiction (2 June 2010); *Copper Mesa Mining Corporation v Ecuador,* PCA Case no 2012-2, Award (15 March 2016); *Occidental Petroleum Corporation and Occidental Exploration and Production Company v Ecuador*, ICSID Case No ARB/06/11, Award (24 September 2012); *Bear Creek*

referred to human rights to justify non-compliance with the investment treaty.[17] At the same time, States have argued that investors have breached indigenous peoples' rights.[18]

One example can be found in the case of *Bear Creek v. Peru*. In this case, the claimant brought proceedings under the Peru-Canada Free Trade Agreement (FTA) against Peru for having revoked the concession rights it had previously granted over a mining site. Bear Creek claimed that Supreme Decree 032-2011 entailed an indirect expropriation of Bear Creek's investment and that by enacting such measure Peru had treated Bear Creek unfairly and inequitably.[19] For its part, Peru argued that it had to cancel the concession to protect its citizens given that Bear Creek had failed to comply with indigenous peoples' rights, essentially the right to FPIC and citizen participation.[20] FPIC is the right of indigenous peoples to be consulted on legislative and administrative measures that may affect them directly as recognized by Article 6 of the ILO Convention 169 and domestic Peruvian law.

As a matter of jurisdiction, indigenous peoples' rights were potentially relevant in ascertaining whether Bear Creek complied with 'international standards' when engaging with indigenous peoples; if it had not, it would be barred from arbitral proceedings.[21] Indigenous peoples' rights were also relevant for the determination of several questions on the merits, namely whether the State conduct was a justified response to the 'social unrest' allegedly attributable to the investor or an exercise of regulatory power for the protection of safety and public order, and whether the investor's concession rights were conditional on its complying with obligations towards indigenous peoples.[22] Finally, indigenous peoples' rights were relevant to determining damages. In particular, the roles and obligations of Peru and of Bear Creek 'in the outreach to the local communities' was relevant to determine

Mining Corporation v Republic of Peru, ICSID Case No ARB/14/21, Award (30 November 2017); *South American Silver Limited (Bermuda) v The Plurinational State of Bolivia,* PCA Case 2013-15, Award (30 August 2018).

[17] Silvia Steininger, 'What's Human Rights Got To Do With It? An Empirical Analysis of Human Rights References in Investment Arbitration' (2018) 31 Leiden Journal of International Law 33, 42. Freya Baetens, 'Invoking human rights: A useful line of attack or a defence tool for States in investor-State dispute settlement?' in M Scheinin and others (eds), *Human Rights Norms in 'Other' International Courts and Tribunals* (CUP 2019) 227–62.

[18] *Bear Creek Mining Corporation v Republic of Peru,* ICSID Case No. ARB/14/21, Award (30 November 2017) (n 16) paras 306, 326, 328; *South American Silver Limited (Bermuda) v The Plurinational State of Bolivia,* PCA Case 2013-15, Respondent's Objections to Jurisdiction and Admissibility and Counter-Memorial on the Merits (31 March 2015) [117–120]; *SAS v Bolivia, Award (2018)* (n 16) paras 369, 372–377.

[19] *Bear Creek Mining Corporation v Republic of Peru,* ICSID Case No. ARB/14/21, Award (30 November 2017) (n 16) paras 341, 499.

[20] ibid 406, 412.

[21] ibid 306, 328.

[22] ibid 507, 508.

whether Peru's liability could be reduced or excluded due to contributory fault of Bear Creek.[23]

In 2017, the arbitral tribunal found Peru liable for indirect expropriation of Bear Creek's investment and awarded US$18 million. The arbitral tribunal reached this decision on the basis of contract law rather than human rights considerations. It held that

> all outreach activities by Claimant were known to Respondent's authorities and were conducted with their approval, support, and endorsement, and that no objections were raised by the authorities in this context. […] Respondent, after its continuous approval and support of Claimant's conduct, cannot in hindsight claim that this conduct was contrary to the ILO Convention 169 or was insufficient, and caused or contributed to the social unrest in the region.[24]

Hence, the tribunal dismissed the human rights arguments on the basis that Peru could not contradict its previous behaviour: Peru could not argue that the investor had breached human rights given that such allegations were not made during the development of the project. Since arbitral tribunals adjudicate disputes in which indigenous peoples' rights are central, the lack of diversity among investment arbitrators is especially relevant. This could be improved if arbitration institutions were to ensure that their lists of arbitrators were regionally diverse, giving parties the opportunity to appoint arbitrators from the specific regions where conflicts involving indigenous rights take place.[25] Another possibility would be to increase transparency by creating a public database showing an arbitrator's background and cases.[26]

One cause for backlash against investment arbitration is that other than the foreign investor and the host State, actors who could potentially be affected by an arbitral decision, lack standing before the arbitral tribunal. There is no guarantee that States will defend indigenous peoples' interests in this forum; in many cases the interests of the State may even conflict with indigenous peoples' interests.[27] For this reason, participatory mechanisms such as *amicus curiae* are important to enhance transparency and safeguard the position of those that may be indirectly affected by the outcome of a dispute.[28] Whether *amicus curiae* submissions

[23] ibid 565–69.
[24] ibid 412.
[25] Judith Levine, 'The Interaction of International Investment Arbitration and the Rights of Indigenous Peoples' in Freya Baetens (ed), *Investment law within international law integrationist perspectives* (CUP 2013) 128.
[26] Lucy Greenwood, 'Tipping the Balance – Diversity and Inclusion in International Arbitration' (2017) 33 Arbitration International 99, 107.
[27] William Shipley, 'What's Yours Is Mine: Conflict of Law and Conflict of Interest Regarding Indigenous Property Rights in Latin American Investment Dispute Arbitration' (2014) 1 Transnational Dispute Management.
[28] Levine (n 25) 128.

are permitted, will depend on the applicable treaty and rules of arbitration.[29] Some Bilateral Investment Treaties (BITs) and FTAs explicitly enable the arbitral tribunal to allow the participation of third parties.[30] Finally, arbitration rules such as Article 37 of the International Centre for the Settlement of Disputes (ICSID) Rules also enable arbitral tribunals to allow *amicus curiae* submissions. Notwithstanding the importance of these mechanisms, the recognition of indigenous peoples' jurisdiction is of utmost importance to enable participation of indigenous peoples in international judicial decision-making.[31]

3. Access to Justice via Indigenous Peoples' Jurisdiction

3.1 What is Indigenous People's Jurisdiction?

Indigenous peoples have a right to access justice through their domestic legal system without facing discrimination, enabling them to obtain the same 'substantive notions of justice' as the rest of the population. As provided for in ILO C169 and confirmed in UNDRIP and ADRIP, indigenous peoples also have a right to exercise their 'their own normative framework',[32] meaning their own customs, laws, and institutions.[33] The only limits are fundamental rights contained in domestic laws and internationally recognized human rights.[34] Indigenous peoples have long demanded this right to operate their own customary legal systems. Before the adoption of ILO C169, indigenous people's rights were recognized to some degree under the ILO Convention 107 (ILO C107) which aimed not only to protect their rights but also 'their progressive integration into their respective national communities', as stipulated in the preamble.[35]

The goal of integration was explicitly rejected during the reform negotiations of ILO C107 and abandoned with the adoption of ILO C169. Indigenous peoples' associations emphasized that in order to overcome the integrationist approach, 'the laws and customs of indigenous nations and peoples must be recognised by States'

[29] Mariel Dimsey, Meagan Wong, and Rebecca Hadgett, 'Article 4. Submission by a Third Person' in Dimitrij Euler, Markus Gehring, and Maxi Scherer (eds), *Transparency in International Investment Arbitration* (CUP 2015) 130, 131 <www.cambridge.org/core/product/identifier/CBO9781139939577A021/type/book_part> accessed 29 February 2020.

[30] United States-Peru Free Trade Agreement (adopted 12 April 2006, entry into force 1 February 2009) (US-Peru FTA) Art 10.20.3.

[31] ILO C169 169 Art 12.

[32] Daniel M Brinks, 'Access to What? Legal Agency and Access to Justice for Indigenous Peoples in Latin America' [2018] The Journal of Development Studies 1, 2.

[33] UNDRIP Art 34; ADRIP Art XXII.

[34] ILO C169 Art 8.1.

[35] Convention concerning the Protection and Integration of Indigenous and Other Tribal and Semi-Tribal Populations in Independent Countries (adopted 26 June 1957, entry into force 2 June 1959) 328 UNTS 247 (ILO C107) 107.

legislative, administrative and judicial institutions and, in case of conflicts with State laws, shall take precedence'.[36] Moreover, when discussing the content of the new ILO C169, a difference was pointed out between the positive laws of the State and the customary norms and procedures of indigenous peoples which should be granted 'significant weight'.[37] Domestic legal procedures would have to be established to resolve conflicts between national laws and courts, on the one hand, and indigenous customary laws and procedures, on the other.[38] The importance of indigenous customary laws and institutions was again emphasized in the UNDRIP negotiations, during which indigenous peoples proposed to include in the draft that due recognition should be given to 'the customs, traditions, rules and legal systems of the indigenous peoples concerned'.[39]

However, international instruments, such as ILO C169, UNDRIP, and ADRIP, do not use uniform language in this respect. For purposes of consistency, this chapter employs the term 'indigenous peoples' jurisdiction' to refer to the rights of indigenous peoples recognized under international and domestic law, including their right to: (1) enact their own norms through their own processes of law-making; (2) apply such customary norms in their territory; (3) to resolve disputes through their own customary processes.[40]

3.2 Indigenous peoples' participation in international judicial decision-making

While reforming appointment processes for investment arbitrators and Inter-American Court judges, as well as implementing participatory mechanisms, are important to ensure that indigenous peoples' rights are respected at the international level, the better way to enable their participation in judicial decision-making is through the recognition of indigenous peoples' jurisdiction. First, demanding that international bodies such as investment tribunals should be composed of individuals who self-identify as indigenous is not realistic. But more importantly, serving as judge at the Inter-American Court of Human Rights or as an arbitrator in an investment dispute would require assimilation of indigenous peoples into mainstream society and this has been explicitly rejected by indigenous peoples themselves.

[36] ILO, *Partial Revision of the Indigenous and Tribal Populations Convention, 1957 (No. 107)* (Geneva 1987) 14, 15, 115 <www.ilo.org/public/libdoc/ilo/1987/87B09_172_engl.pdf> accessed 29 February 2020.

[37] ibid 116.

[38] ibid.

[39] 'Joint Submission by Indigenous Organizations on "General Provisions" of the Draft U.N. Declaration on the Rights of Indigenous Peoples' (2005) E/CN.4/2005/WG.15/CRP.2 27, 28 <www.ohchr.org/EN/Issues/IPeoples/Pages/WGDraftDeclaration.aspx> accessed 29 February 2020.

[40] ILO (n 57) 169 Art 8; UNDRIP Art 2.7; ADRIP Art XXII.

This is not to say that a person who self-identifies as indigenous cannot become a judge, for instance, before the Inter-American Court. This should be a possibility opened to any individual who fulfils the requirements set out in the ACHR. In fact, some reform proposals encourage States to facilitate the appointment of indigenous candidates.[41] Although such reforms may be complementary, only the full recognition of indigenous peoples' jurisdiction by international courts and tribunals will fulfil the demands of indigenous peoples. Indigenous peoples' jurisdiction does not necessarily resemble national jurisdiction: it has been defined as the intersection between indigenous customary norms, the right to autonomy, and cultural processes.[42] Consequently, each indigenous community will have its own norms, which are usually not codified,[43] their own processes of enactment of such norms and their own dispute resolution processes.

Analysing each indigenous peoples' customary legal system falls outside the scope of this chapter—the reader is referred to various socio-legal and anthropological works which provide an in-depth analysis of indigenous peoples' legal systems.[44] The next section uses Peru as a case study in order to provide a better understanding of indigenous peoples' jurisdiction in practice and how domestic regulations can establish its limits and its relationship with the ordinary jurisdiction.

4. Indigenous Peoples' Jurisdiction, a Case Study: Peru

4.1 The Domestic Legal Framework

The Peruvian Constitution (1993) mirrors the international conventions outlined in section 3 of this chapter and expressly recognizes the right of indigenous peoples to exert a 'special jurisdiction' in their territory where they can apply customary norms,[45] as long as they respect fundamental rights.[46] The Constitution gives

[41] Salazar and Roht-Arriaza (n 7) 1670.

[42] Asier Martínez de Bringas, 'Los Sistemas Normativos Indígenas En El Marco Del Pluralismo Jurídico. Un Análisis Desde Los Derechos Indígenas = The Right to the Indigenous Legal Systems under the Legal Pluralism. An Analysis from a Right Perspective' (2013) 1 Revista de Derecho Político 422 <http://revistas.uned.es/index.php/derechopolitico/article/view/12140> accessed 29 February 2020.

[43] Brendan Tobin, *Indigenous Peoples, Customary Law and Human Rights: Why Living Law Matters* (Routledge 2016) 78.

[44] Emmanuelle Picolli, 'El Pluralismo Jurídico y Político En Perú: El Caso de Las Rondas Campesinas de Cajamarca' (2008) 31 Iconos Revista de Ciencias Sociales 27; Antonio Peña Jumpa, 'Marco Constitucional, Legal, Jurisprudencial y Consuetudinario Para La Gestión Del Agua En Las Cuencas Peruanas' (2012) 12 Círculo de Derecho Administrativo 233; Martínez de Bringas (n 42); Antonio Alfonso Peña Jumpa, 'The Constitutional Right to Communal Justice in Peru. An Approach from the Huancané (Puno) Aymaras' Experience' (2016) 47 Derecho & Sociedad 187; Tobin (n 43); Marc Simon Thomas, 'The Effects of Formal Legal Pluralism on Indigenous Authorities in the Ecuadorian Highlands: Effects of Formal Legal Pluralism' (2017) 22 The Journal of Latin American and Caribbean Anthropology 46.

[45] ibid Art 149.

[46] Constitución Política del Perú 1993 capítulo I. Fundamental rights are regulated under Chapter I of the Peruvian Constitution.

little guidance on the specific competences of this special jurisdiction but establishes that it should be coordinated with the ordinary jurisdiction through a general law.[47] This general law should establish the material, personal, and territorial scope of indigenous peoples' jurisdiction and a system to resolve any conflicts that may arise between the national and indigenous legal systems. Despite this constitutional mandate, 27 years after the enactment of the Peruvian Constitution, the Peruvian Congress has not yet approved this general law. The first proposals in this regard were submitted during the legislative period 2011–2016 and reviewed by the Commission of Andean and Amazonian Peoples of Congress ('Andean and Amazonian Commission' or 'the Commission') which recommended an alternative drafting.[48] The Commission's recommendations formed the basis for the Proposal of a Law of Intercultural Coordination of Justice 773/2016-CR ('Intercultural Law Proposal') which is currently being discussed in Congress.[49]

Other initiatives seek to regulate the interaction between the ordinary and indigenous jurisdictions, including the draft Coordination Protocol by the Executive Council of the Judicial Power,[50] which addresses both national courts and indigenous jurisdiction.[51] The Protocol mandates that courts maintain a constant dialogue with indigenous authorities and establishes guidelines to ascertain the personal, material, and territorial jurisdiction of indigenous legal systems.[52] Another initiative is the enactment of the Law of Justices of Peace which provides that Justices of Peace must act 'in coordination' with indigenous jurisdiction.[53]

In spite of the absence of a proper coordination law, indigenous jurisdiction is exercised as a matter of fact in Peru. As a result, there have been conflicts between the ordinary and the indigenous jurisdiction which have been resolved on a case-by-case basis by domestic courts, including the Peruvian Constitutional Tribunal. But the current situation is undesirable, given that there is no clarity on the scope and limits of indigenous jurisdiction, ie who can exert indigenous jurisdiction?

[47] ibid.

[48] Comisión de Pueblos Andinos, Amazónicos, Afroperuanos, Ambiente y Ecología, 'Dictamen Recaído En Los Proyectos de Ley 313/2011-PJ y 2751/2013-CR Con Un Texto Sustitutorio Por El Cual Se Propone La Ley de Coordinación Intercultural de La Justicia' (2013) Dictamen 01-2013-2014/CPAAAAE-CR.

[49] Proyecto de Ley de Desarrollo del Artículo 149 de la Constitución Política del Perú que Regula la Coordinación Intercultural de la Justicia (N° 773/2016-CR).

[50] Peruvian Constitution Art 138; Texto Único Ordenado de la Ley Orgánica del Poder Judicial 1993 (Decreto Supremo N° 017-93-JUS) 72. The Judicial Power ('Poder Judicial') refers to the organs of the state in charge of the administration of justice, which include the Supreme Court, Superior Courts of Justice, Courts of First Instance and Justices of Peace. The Executive Council is the management organ of the Judicial Power.

[51] Poder Judicial and Oficina Nacional de Justicia de Paz y Justicia Indígena, 'Protocolos Para Una Justicia Intercultural' (2015) <www.pj.gob.pe/wps/wcm/connect/935d36804343733dbb5affe2da5cdfbc/Protocolo-de-Coordinaci%C3%B3n-entre-Siste-y-Ronderos.pdf?MOD=AJPERES&CACHEID=935d36804343733dbb5affe2da5cdfbc> accessed 29 February 2020.

[52] ibid 47–50.

[53] Poder Judicial and Oficina Nacional de Justicia de Paz y Justicia Indígena (n 51); Ley de Justicia de Paz (N° 29824) Arts. 60–64.

What is the territorial, material and personal jurisdiction of indigenous legal systems? In case of conflict between domestic courts and the indigenous legal system, which prevails? Who decides conflicts between the ordinary and indigenous jurisdiction? All these questions must be addressed by a general law in order to avoid situations such as the ones described below.

4.2 The Need for a General Law of Coordination between the Ordinary and Indigenous Jurisdictions

This section presents two cases that exemplify the need for a general law of coordination between the ordinary and indigenous jurisdiction in Peru. The first shows that the competences of indigenous jurisdiction have to be clarified in order for this right to be exercised by indigenous communities with as little interference as possible. The second demonstrates that regulation is necessary to preserve the individual rights of the members of indigenous communities.

In 2012, the Constitutional Tribunal had to ascertain whether a native community could prohibit transport companies from entering its territory. The native community of Tres Islas, which includes the Ese' Eja and Shipibo people and is located in the region of Tambopata in Madre de Dios, had long suffered the effects of mining in their territory, including the loss of swamps, fisheries, and wildlife, along with deforestation and the presence of illegal miners that had led to excessive alcohol consumption and prostitution.[54] Considering this to be caused by the unlicensed activities of transport companies, the community established a control point on the main road and forbade the companies from entering its territory. Two companies filed for *habeas corpus* against the president of the community,[55] alleging that their freedom of movement had been infringed as that their activities had been approved by the regional government.

The transport companies' claim was upheld by the criminal courts in first instance and on appeal.[56] The president of the native community filed for *habeas corpus* before the Constitutional Tribunal arguing that the decision to prevent the entrance of the transport companies was lawfully adopted under indigenous jurisdiction and, therefore, did not breach any right to freedom of movement.[57] The Constitutional Tribunal found in favour of the community, concluding that

[54] *Sentencia de 11 de septiembre de 2012* Tribunal Constitucional EXP. N.° 01126-2011-HC/TC Antecedentes.

[55] The process of habeas corpus is one of the constitutional proceedings established under the Constitutional Code which aims to protect rights related to personal freedom. The process of habeas corpus may be brought against any person provided that there is a breach of the right to personal freedom and related rights. See Código Procesal Constitucional (Ley N° 28237) Art 25.

[56] Under Peruvian Law the criminal courts have competence to decide on *habeas corpus* in first instance. See Texto Único Ordenado de la Ley Orgánica del Poder Judicial Art 50.

[57] *Sentencia de 11 de septiembre de 2012* (n 54) para 37.

the two companies had not obtained the necessary licenses and permissions to cross through its territory, overturning the decisions of the lower courts, and ordering the companies to cease the breach of communal property rights.[58] The Constitutional Tribunal focused on the right to land of indigenous peoples and their right to autonomy, instead of their right to the special jurisdiction.[59] But the facts of the case and the arguments of the parties demonstrate the relevance of indigenous jurisdiction.[60]

This case supports the argument that it is urgent for Congress to enact the Intercultural Law Proposal. In the absence of a law of coordination, indigenous peoples may otherwise have to go through costly and lengthy litigation. If the scope and limits of indigenous jurisdiction were clearer, and processes to resolve conflicts were set out in the law, such litigation could be avoided and third parties would find it more difficult to build legal arguments against norms or decisions adopted under indigenous jurisdiction.

The second case, which again involved the community of Tres Islas, demonstrates that the Intercultural Law Proposal is also necessary to preserve the rights of the individual members of indigenous communities. In 2016, the Constitutional Tribunal dealt with an *habeas corpus* claim filed by the president of the community of Tres Islas on behalf of Juan Villar Vargas and Herbert Cusurichi Payaba, two members who had been prosecuted for rape. Both had maintained sexual relations with girls in the community who were 12 and 13 years of age. According to the claimant, such facts fell under the jurisdiction of the community and, under the community's customary norms, the conduct of Juan Villar Vargas and Herbert Cusurichi Payaba was not unlawful.[61] The Constitutional Tribunal concluded that the facts fell under the competence of the ordinary jurisdiction and dismissed the *habeas corpus* claim. It affirmed that indigenous jurisdiction was still subject to the Constitution which mandated that all persons and institutions had to respect fundamental rights,[62] and in this case, the right to indigenous jurisdiction had to be balanced against the rights of the child.[63] The Tribunal held that Article 149 of the Peruvian Constitution could not be interpreted as meaning that the Peruvian State has renounced its punitive power and, therefore, any crime relating to fundamental rights such as the right to life, health, physical, mental and moral integrity, and freedom could not be decided via the special jurisdiction of indigenous peoples.[64]

[58] ibid 11.
[59] ibid 40.
[60] ibid 37.
[61] *Sentencia de 3 de marzo de 2016* Tribunal Constitucional EXP N° 07009-2013-PHC/TC antecedentes.
[62] ibid 11–13.
[63] ibid 19.
[64] ibid 35.

In a separate opinion, Judge Marianella Ledesma criticized the decision of the majority, not because of its outcome but because of its lack of reasoning. She contested the legal basis of the majority ruling that no crime relating to fundamental rights could be decided by the special jurisdiction of indigenous peoples. This general rule relied on by the majority had no support in law and should be regulated by a law of coordination.[65] She emphasized the urgency of the enactment of the Intercultural Law Proposal arguing that, otherwise, cases such as this one were framed as 'conflicts of competence' and that, as a result, many grave breaches of fundamental rights could remain unpunished.[66]

Both cases show that the Intercultural Law Proposal should be enacted by Congress as soon as possible to avoid litigation that erodes indigenous jurisdiction and, at the same time, to protect the most vulnerable members of indigenous communities.

4.3 Who Can Exert Indigenous Peoples' Jurisdiction?

The Peruvian legal framework employs various terms to designate indigenous peoples including: (1) peasant communities (*comunidades campesinas*); (2) native communities (*comunidades nativas*); (3) peasant patrols (*rondas campesinas*); and (4) indigenous peoples (*pueblos indígenas u originarios*). These terms identify communities that have historically existed in Peru and that have been subject of legal recognition.[67] The Law on Peasant Communities recognizes the juridical personality of these groups and regulates their rights.[68]

Whereas the peoples identified under the first two categories—native and peasant communities—existed prior to colonization or, at least, are able to trace their origins to the peoples that inhabited Peru's territory prior to colonization, the term *rondas campesinas* refers to a more recent phenomenon.[69] *Rondas campesinas* emerged in the mid-1970s in the region of Cajamarca, located in northern Andes, as a response to crime, insecurity, and the absence of State institutions in the region.[70] Their success at conflict resolution and crime prevention

[65] ibid voto particular de Marianella Ledesma.

[66] ibid voto singular de Marianella Ledesma 31.

[67] Antonio Peña Jumpa, 'Las Comunidades Campesinas y nativas en la Constitución Política del Perú: Un Análisis Exegético del Artículo 89o de la Constitución' (2013) 40 Revista Derecho & Sociedad 195, 197.

[68] ibid.

[69] The Spanish version of the term is preferred in this article since the English term 'patrols'—though commonly used in the existing literature as the translation of *rondas campesinas*—bears a military connotation that can be misleading. In Spanish, the term *rondas* designates a group of persons that walk around something.

[70] Hans-Jürgen Brandt, 'La Justicia Comunitaria y La Lucha Por Una Ley de Coordinación de La Justicia' [2017] Derecho PUCP 215, 228; Oscar Espinosa, 'El Movimiento Indígena y La Justicia Comunitaria En El Perú' in Anibal Galvez Rivas and Cecilia Serpa Arana (eds), *Justicia Intercultural*

meant that the *rondas campesinas* expanded, as a form of communal organization, to other parts of the country. *Rondas campesinas* are also recognized and regulated by the Law and are incorporated and registered in Superintendencia Nacional de los Registros Públicos (SUNARP).[71] *Rondas campesinas*, as a form of legal organization, can emerge inside peasant or native communities or outside them. In the latter case, they are referred to as 'independent' or 'autonomous' *rondas campesinas*.[72]

Finally, the term 'indigenous peoples' is contained in the Law on Free Prior and Informed Consultation (FPIC Law),[73] which develops the right to FPIC established under Article 6 of the ILO C169. The FPIC Law does not contain a definition of indigenous peoples but establishes objective and subjective criteria for identifying them. The objective criteria are as follows:

(a) Direct descendance from original populations in the national territory;
(b) Lifestyles and spiritual and historical links with the territory that they traditionally use and occupy;
(c) Own institutions and customs; and
(d) Cultural patterns and lifestyle which are different from other sectors of the population.[74]

The subjective criterion refers to the collective consciousness of a group as having indigenous identity.[75] In addition, the FPIC Law, unlike the Laws of Peasant Communities and Native Communities, does not require incorporation before the public registry. Hence, the category of indigenous peoples acts as a fallback covering all those groups that regardless of registration are, nevertheless, indigenous.

Article 149 of the Peruvian Constitution, which regulates indigenous peoples' jurisdiction, stipulates:

> *The authorities of Peasants and Native Communities, with the support from 'Rondas Campesinas' may exercise jurisdiction within their territory, in accordance with their customary law, as long as they do not breach fundamental rights.' The law*

en los Países Andinos Contribuciones para su Estudio (Red Andina de Justicia de Paz y Comunitaria 2013) 20.

[71] Ley de Rondas Campesinas 2003 (Ley Nº 27908). The SUNARP is an autonomous decentralized body of the Justice Sector in Peru and the governing body of the National System of Public Registries.
[72] Espinosa (n 70) 20.
[73] Ley del derecho a la consulta previa a los pueblos indígenas u originarios, reconocido en el Convenio 169 de la Organización Internacional del Trabajo (OIT) 2011 (Ley Nº 29785).
[74] ibid Art 7.
[75] ibid.

establishes the means of coordination between this special jurisdiction and the Peace Judges and the rest of the Judicial Power.[76]

Given the ambiguous wording of this constitutional provision, it is unclear whether the *rondas campesinas* could exercise indigenous jurisdiction themselves. ILO C169 defines tribal peoples as those groups who 'share social, cultural and economic elements which distinguish them from other sections of the national community, and whose statute is regulated wholly or partially by their own customs or traditions or by special laws or regulations'. This is the case of *rondas campesinas*: not only is their status regulated under a special law, but they also have their own cultural identity, which builds on Andean heritance and colonial tradition.[77] Further, they require the same level of protection as indigenous peoples under international and Peruvian law so the Peruvian Supreme Court has expressly established that *rondas campesinas* should enjoy jurisdiction.[78] For these reasons, the Intercultural Law Proposal recognizes the jurisdiction of native and peasant communities, *rondas campesinas*, and indigenous peoples.

4.4 Personal and Territorial Scope of Indigenous Jurisdiction

Article 149 of the Peruvian Constitution offers little guidance as to which disputes may be submitted to indigenous peoples' jurisdiction. It merely states that indigenous peoples may exercise jurisdiction in their territory, according to their customary law, as long as they respect fundamental rights. The Intercultural Law Proposal specifies that indigenous peoples, peasant and native communities, and *rondas campesinas* exert special jurisdiction over facts occurring in their territory and that these disputes shall be decided by their authorities according to their own customary norms.[79] The definition of territory in the Intercultural Law Proposal is wide and, in line with ILO C169,[80] includes not only the lands that indigenous peoples inhabit but also lands that they occupy or use in any manner.[81]

Under the Intercultural Law Proposal, the special jurisdiction also extends to conflicts or facts which occur in their territory and involve persons that do not belong to the communities but, as will be explained in the next section, third parties may question indigenous jurisdiction.[82] In addition, the Intercultural Law

[76] Peruvian Constitution Art 149. (emphasis added)

[77] ibid; Víctor Malpartida Castillo, 'Poder judicial, justicia inclusiva y justicia intercultural' (2010) 8 Revista Oficial del Poder Judicial 65, 67; Brandt (n 70) 228.

[78] Corte Suprema de Justicia de la República, 'Acuerdo Plenario Nº 1-2009/CJ-116' (2009),7–8.

[79] Intercultural Law Proposal Art 8.

[80] ILO C169 Art 13.

[81] Intercultural Law Proposal Art 2.a.

[82] ibid Art 8.

Proposal clarifies, in relation to the limits of indigenous jurisdiction, that serious crimes such as homicide, rape, drug trafficking, terrorism, crimes against humanity, amongst others, fall under the exclusive competence of the ordinary jurisdiction.[83]

The Intercultural Law Proposal has adopted an intermediate approach.[84] Advocates of a more minimalist approach have argued that indigenous jurisdiction should only entertain interpersonal disputes, ie it should not extend to third parties outside of indigenous communities.[85] Some proposals even went as far as establishing that indigenous peoples should only enjoy interpersonal jurisdiction, excluding any dispute involving matters related to administrative, labour, environmental, agrarian, hydrocarbons, tax, mining, human rights, and public and private international law.[86] Such general and wide limitations would render indigenous jurisdiction meaningless and would leave indigenous peoples without a right to act in cases similar to those of the transportation companies and the community of Tres Islas. On the maximalist side, those who supported an expanded notion of indigenous jurisdiction argued that there should be no limits to indigenous jurisdiction inside their territory.[87] Hence, under this maximalist option cases such as the child rape case in the community of Tres Islas would remain unpunished.

The Intercultural Law Proposal's approach is preferable to both the maximalist and minimalist approaches, in so far as it ensures that serious offences would be resolved by the ordinary jurisdiction and, at the same time, indigenous peoples would be able to exert jurisdiction over matters which they have traditionally dealt with under their customary norms. Arguably, the Intercultural Law Proposal still leaves space for controversy given that it does not clarify which matters have been 'traditionally' dealt with by indigenous peoples. While there are certain issues which can be said to be commonly dealt with by all indigenous communities, such as family disputes, others will depend on the specific community. For example, indigenous peoples in Lake Titicaca as well as other communities in central and northern Andes have traditionally resolved disputes regarding water resources.[88] Hence, the current Intercultural Law Proposal

[83] ibid Art 10.

[84] Brandt (n 70) 223–33.

[85] ibid 223–26.

[86] Comisión de Justicia y Derechos Humanos, 'Predictamen Recaído En Los Proyectos de Ley 313/2011 PJ, 973/2011CR, 2751/2013CR y 2886/2013CR, Con Un Texto Sustitutorio Mediante El Cual Se Propone La Ley de Coordinación Intercultural de Justicia' (2015) <http://www2.congreso.gob.pe/sicr/comisiones/2011/com2011jusderhum.nsf/746aabb1ed76b49a05257a6900618267/46f5b67dcbf26fd705257d7a005e556d/$FILE/5.15PREDICT313.pdf> accessed 22 October 2018, Art 4.

[87] Brandt (n 70) 227–233.

[88] Jorge Armando Guevara Gil, 'Derecho de Aguas, Pluralismo Legal y Concreción Social del Derecho' in Jorge Armando Guevara Gil (ed), *Derechos y Conflictos de Agua en el Perú* (Pontificia Universidad Católica del Perú 2008); Peña Jumpa, 'Marco Constitucional, Legal, Jurisprudencial y Consuetudinario Para La Gestión Del Agua En Las Cuencas Peruanas' (n 44).

would potentially enable indigenous peoples to make decisions on land rights and natural resource governance.

4.5 Appeals and Cases of Conflict Between the Ordinary and Indigenous Jurisdictions

The Intercultural Law Proposal sets out specific grounds under which indigenous individuals may appeal to the Constitutional Tribunal and allows third parties to question indigenous jurisdiction. Individuals can appeal to the Constitutional Tribunal if they feel their fundamental rights have been breached by a decision adopted under indigenous jurisdiction.[89] However, if there is no breach of fundamental rights, the proposal does not provide a right to appeal on other grounds. Only if the individual affected by indigenous jurisdiction is a third party, does the Intercultural Law Proposal enable her or him to question the jurisdiction of indigenous peoples.[90] If third parties question indigenous jurisdiction or if there is a conflict between jurisdictions, the Intercultural Law Proposal provides that it should be solved through 'good faith dialogue' between the ordinary jurisdiction and the authorities of the peasant or native community, indigenous peoples, or *rondas campesinas*.[91]

The solutions provided by the Intercultural Law Proposal are unsatisfactory for two reasons. First, members of indigenous communities can only appeal where fundamental rights are breached; they have no right to appeal on other grounds nor to question indigenous jurisdiction. This generates an imbalance. Secondly, the Intercultural Law Proposal has not established how the questioning of jurisdiction or conflicts between the ordinary jurisdiction and indigenous peoples' jurisdiction will be resolved. The provision of 'good faith dialogue' is inoperative since the Intercultural Law Proposal does not establish what will happen if there is no agreement. The Intercultural Law Proposal could instead provide for a two-step process. In the first step, a committee composed by magistrates from the ordinary jurisdiction and representatives of native and peasant communities, *rondas campesinas* and indigenous peoples would adopt a decision by majority.[92] In a second phase, the party that disagrees with the decision of the committee could initiate a constitutional procedure to obtain a decision by the Constitutional Tribunal.[93] Whichever solution is adopted, the final draft of the Intercultural Law Proposal should undergo a process of consultation with indigenous peoples in order to comply with the ILO C169 and the FPIC Law. Only after consultations have been concluded can the Intercultural Law Proposal be enacted by Congress.

89 Intercultural Law Proposal Art 4.
90 ibid Art 9.
91 ibid Art 11.
92 Brandt (n 70) 242.
93 Comisión de Justicia y Derechos Humanos (n 86) 19.

5. Indigenous Peoples' Law and Jurisdiction in International Judicial Decision-Making

5.1 Indigenous customary law and jurisdiction and the Inter-American Court

The Inter-American Court has discussed indigenous customary law in many of its decisions. For example, in *Aloeboetoe v. Suriname*, the Court decided that Suriname had to pay damages to the ascendants and descendants of Saramaka indigenous persons who had been subjected to forced disappearances.[94] The Court then had to establish who were entitled to receive these damages. Suriname argued that its civil code was applicable,[95] but the Court decided that indigenous customary law (which was 'strongly matriarchal')[96] should be used to identify the individuals entitled to damages.[97] Customary norms could not contradict fundamental rights recognized under the American Convention, and as a consequence, the Court did not apply any distinction as to sex when establishing who the ascendants were, even though this may have been contrary to Saramaka customary law.[98] Moreover, the Saramaka had their own customary family law: they did not need to bring disputes before State courts but could submit them within their indigenous legal system.[99]

Indigenous customary norms and customary practices were also important in the case of *Awas Tingni v. Nicaragua* in which the Court established that, when defining indigenous property rights, such as the right to ancestral property, their own customary laws and practices should be taken into account.[100] The Court concluded that 'possession of the land should suffice for indigenous communities lacking real title to property of the land to obtain official recognition of that property, and for consequent registration'.[101] The State has an obligation to provide mechanisms that allow delimitation, demarcation and titling of indigenous lands 'in accordance with the customary law, values, customs' of the community.[102] This illustrates that customary indigenous law and practices are used in the jurisprudence of the Inter-American Court to require States to (1) grant title over indigenous lands without the need of prior official registration, subject only to

[94] *Case of Aloeboetoe et al v Suriname, Reparations and Costs* (1993) Series C No 15 (Inter-American Court of Human Rights).

[95] ibid 55.

[96] ibid 62.

[97] ibid 58.

[98] ibid.

[99] ibid 58.

[100] *Mayagna (Sumo) Awas Tingni Community v Nicaragua, Merits, Reparations and Costs Judgment* (2001) Series C No. 79 (Inter-American Court) para 151.

[101] ibid; Martínez de Bringas (n 42) 421.

[102] *Awas Tingni v Nicaragua* (n 100) para 138.

possession of the land; (2) delineate the borders of such land in accordance with the laws and practices of indigenous peoples.

The Inter-American Court also applied indigenous peoples' norms and practices in relation to natural resources in the case of *Saramaka v. Suriname* where the State had granted mining concessions on indigenous territory without consulting indigenous peoples. In addition, the State had breached indigenous peoples' right to land by failing to delineate and demarcate their lands. The Court established that FPIC should be carried out according to indigenous peoples' customs and institutions and that, in case the investment project was to proceed, indigenous peoples should be granted 'just compensation'.[103] All disputes concerning FPIC or compensation should be resolved 'by the Saramaka people in accordance with their traditional customs and norms'.[104] This shows how indigenous peoples' norms and practices are relevant to establishing the content of the rights recognized under the American Convention, such as the right to land.

5.2 Indigenous Peoples' Law and Jurisdiction and Investment Arbitration

Though indigenous jurisdiction has not yet formed the main focus of any investment arbitration dispute, it has played a role in some procedures. For example, in *Bear Creek v. Peru,* the expert report of Dr Antonio Alfonso Peña Jumpa submitted by Peru clearly addresses the importance of indigenous jurisdiction when resolving disputes relating to indigenous peoples' lands.[105] In order to ascertain whether a land transfer to the investor was valid, the arbitral tribunal had to look into indigenous laws and decisions adopted under customary adjudicative mechanisms. Even though the tribunal left these considerations out of its final award, the expert report demonstrates that indigenous peoples' jurisdiction may affect investment arbitration insofar as it is part of the domestic law of the host State. In Peru, domestic law sets out which indigenous groups can bring a case or serve as *amicus curiae* before arbitral tribunals dealing with property matters. While *amicus curiae* submissions may bring indigenous legal arguments to the tribunal's attention, indigenous peoples' customary laws may only be applied by the arbitral tribunal when resolving the dispute if the relevant BIT or FTA includes general domestic law or public international law in their applicable law clause. In the case of Peru, for example, 12 FTAs and BITs provide for the application of domestic law.[106] Most of

[103] *Saramaka People v Suriname Preliminary Objections, Merits, Reparations, and Costs* (2007) Series C no 172 (Inter-American Court) para 27.

[104] ibid 27.

[105] *Bear Creek Mining Corporation v Republic of Peru,* ICSID Case No ARB/14/21, Expert Report of Antonio Alfonso Peña Jumpa (6 October 2015) [77].

[106] Convenio entre el Gobierno de la República del Perú y el Gobierno de la República Argentina sobre Promoción y Protección Recíproca de Inversiones (adopted 10 November 1994, entry into force

the treaties ratified by Peru, 21 in total, contain an applicable law clause enabling the arbitral tribunal to apply public international law.[107]

In *South American Silver (SAS) v. Bolivia*, SAS sued Bolivia for unlawful expropriation and frustration of legitimate expectations following the nationalization of the Malkhu Kota Mining Project (in Potosi).[108] Bolivia argued that the investor had breached indigenous peoples' rights inciting a violent opposition that justified the nationalization of the project under the doctrine of police powers.[109] The investor knew or should have known the domestic and international legal framework applicable to extractive activities in Bolivia, obliging the State to reverse the project if the investor disrespected indigenous peoples' rights.[110] The way in which indigenous peoples were organized and self-governed was relevant to the dispute:[111]

24 October 1996) (Argentina-Peru BIT) Art 10.4; Acuerdo entre el Gobierno de la República del Perú y el Gobierno de la República de Colombia sobre Promoción y Protección Recíproca de Inversiones (adopted 11 December 2007, entry into force 30 December 2010) (Colombia-Peru BIT) Art 27.1; Convenio entre el Gobierno de la República del Perú y el Gobierno de la República de Cuba sobre la Promoción y Protección Recíproca de Inversiones (adopted 10 October 2000, entry into force 25 November 2001) (Cuba-Peru BIT) Art 2.2.2; Convenio entre la República del Perú y la República Federal de Alemania sobre Promoción y Protección Recíproca de Inversiones (adopted 30 January 1995, entry into force 1 May 1997) (Germany-Peru BIT) Art 10.5.5; Agreement Between Japan and the Republic of Peru for the Promotion, Protection and Liberalisation of Investment (adopted 21 November 2008, entry into force 10 December 2009) (Japan-Peru BIT) Art 18.15; Convenio entre la República del Perú y la República del Paraguay sobre Promoción y Protección Recíproca de Inversiones (adopted 1 February 1994, entry into force 18 December 1994) (Paraguay-Peru BIT) Art 8.5.5; Convenio entre el Gobierno de la República del Perú y el Gobierno de Rumanía para la Promoción y Protección Recíproca de Inversiones (adopted 16 May 1994, entry into force 1 January 1995) (Romania-Peru BIT) Art 8.4; Acuerdo para la Promoción y Protección Recíproca de Inversiones entre la República del Perú y el Reino de España (adopted 17 November 1994, entry into force 16 February 1996) (Spain-Peru BIT) Art 9.3.3; Agreement between the Swiss Confederation and the Republic of Peru on the Promotion and Reciprocal Protection of Investments (adopted 11 November 1991, entry into force 23 November 1993) (Switzerland-Peru BIT) Art 9.4; Tratado de Libre Comercio Perú – Panamá (adopted 15 May 2011, entry into force 1 May 2012) (Panama-Peru FTA) 12.23; Tratado de Libre Comercio Perú – Costa Rica (adopted 26 May 2011, entry into force 1 June 2013) (Costa Rica-Peru FTA); Tratado de Libre Comercio Perú – Honduras (adopted 29 May 2015, entry into force 1 January 2017) (Honduras-Peru FTA) Art 12.23.

[107] Switzerland-Peru BIT Art 9.4; Argentina-Peru BIT Art 10.4; Paraguay-Peru BIT Art 8.5.5; Romania-Peru BIT Art 8.4; Spain-Peru BIT Art 9.3.3; Agreement Between Australia and the Republic of Peru on the Promotion and Protection of Investments (adopted 7 December 1995, entry into force 2 February 1997) (Australia-Peru BIT) annex; Germany-Peru BIT Art 10.5.5; Acuerdo de Libre Comercio entre Perú y Chile (adopted 22 August 2006, entry into force 1 March 2009) (Chile-Peru FTA) Art 9.5; Cuba-Peru BIT Art 2.2.2; Chile-Peru FTA Art 11.22; Canada-Peru FTA Art 837.1; Colombia-Peru BIT Art 27.1; Free Trade Agreement between the Government of the Republic of Peru and the Government of the People's Republic of China (adopted 28 April 2009, entry into force 1 March 2010) (China-Peru FTA) Art 139.3; Free Trade Agreement between the Republic of Peru and the Republic of Korea (adopted 21 March 2011, entry into force 1 August 2011) (Korea-Peru BIT) Art 9.16; Panama-Peru FTA Art 12.23; Costa Rica-Peru FTA Art 12.23; Acuerdo de Integración Comercial Perú – México (adopted 6 April 2011, entry into force 1 February 2012) (Mexico-Peru FTA) Art 11.29; Honduras-Peru FTA Art 12.23; Comprehensive and Progressive Agreement for Trans-Pacific Partnership (adopted 23 January 2018, entry into force 30 December 2018) (CPTPP) Art 9.25.

[108] *SAS v Bolivia, Award (2018)* (n 16) paras 508, 634.

[109] ibid 523, 524.

[110] ibid 640.

[111] *SAS v Bolivia, Respondent's Objections to Jurisdiction and Admissibility and Counter-Memorial on the Merits (2015)* (n 18) para 43.

Bolivia explained how indigenous peoples' jurisdiction worked, focusing on dispute resolution mechanisms and the customary indigenous laws that applied in the area of the mining project.[112] In 2010, the communities (*ayllus*) that were affected by the project decided to suspend all mining activities in their territories alleging that the investor had breached their collective rights.[113] In order to proceed with the project nevertheless, the investor created a parallel organization of indigenous individuals that supported the project.[114] This organization did not function in accordance with the customary practices of the indigenous communities and sparked conflict in the region.[115] Bolivia claimed that the investor's employees infiltrated in community meetings wearing indigenous authorities' attire in order to influence decision-making processes.[116] This conduct led to violence and provoked the reversion of previously granted concessions.[117]

In its award, the arbitral tribunal acknowledged the conflict between indigenous communities and stated that the investor 'appears to have contributed to the escalation of the conflict and ultimate acts of violence'.[118] It concluded that the expropriation of the investment was justified on public purpose grounds and compliant with due process requirements, however, no compensation had been paid. The tribunal did not accept that the concessions had been reversed as an exercise of police powers (which would have removed the need to pay compensation).[119] As in *Bear Creek*, the reasoning was that, since Bolivia did not state at the time of the reversion that police powers were being exercised, it could not successfully argue this later on, in the arbitration.[120] Consequently the State was ordered to pay over USD 18 million to the investor (corresponding to the costs incurred in the project).[121] Given that the investor had sued Bolivia for over USD 300 million and that the arbitral tribunal accepted the amount that Bolivia had offered to the investor before the start of the arbitral proceedings, this case was perceived as a victory for Bolivia.[122]

This case shows the relevance of indigenous peoples' jurisdiction when resolving investment disputes and how indigenous customary laws and legal systems can affect the outcome, particularly in the context of land rights and access to natural resources. By considering the nuances and particularities of indigenous

[112] ibid 44–57 and 73.
[113] ibid 113.
[114] ibid 100, 122–28.
[115] ibid 100, 118, 124.
[116] ibid 168–69.
[117] ibid 176.
[118] *SAS v Bolivia, Award (2018)* (n 16) para 563.
[119] ibid 623.
[120] ibid 625.
[121] ibid 872.
[122] 'Bolivia Gana El Arbitraje Internacional a South American Silver de Canadá' *Correo del Sur Digital* (Bolivia, 22 November 2018) <https://correodelsur.com/politica/20181122_bolivia-gana-el-arbitraje-internacional-a-south-american-silver-de-canada.html> accessed 29 February 2020.

peoples' jurisdiction, instead of relying on purely contractual terms, arbitral tribunals can enhance their legitimacy by paying attention to matters of indigenous public interest.

6. Conclusion

Indigenous peoples have a right to enact and enforce their own customary laws and apply their own dispute resolution mechanisms, as established under domestic and international law. This chapter has defined these rights as indigenous peoples' jurisdiction. While acknowledging the importance of reforming the appointment system of judges at the Inter-American Court and of arbitrators in investment arbitration, as well as the relevance of enhancing participatory mechanisms for indigenous peoples in general, this chapter has argued that respect for indigenous rights in international judicial decision-making can be better facilitated through the recognition of indigenous peoples' jurisdiction. This approach responds to the demands of indigenous peoples to maintain their own customs and legal systems. Furthermore, it respects indigenous peoples' refusal to assimilate and integrate into mainstream society which would be required if indigenous individuals were to serve as adjudicators in international courts or investment tribunals.

26

Keeping Gender on the Agenda for International Benches

A Case Study of the African Court on Human and Peoples' Rights

J Jarpa Dawuni

1. Introduction

In 2012, Judge Julia Sebutinde made history as the fourth woman to be elected to the bench of the International Court of Justice (ICJ) in over 70 years of the Court's existence. Sebutinde's election was remarkable for reasons beyond her sex: she was also the first woman from the African continent (compared to 15 African male judges before her).[1] As an international judge, Sebutinde's appointment embodies the intersection of race, gender, geographical location, and other identities which women from non-western societies have to navigate.[2] Sebutinde's journey to the ICJ, like most other women judges, was largely the result of her personal agency, professional experience (having served as a judge on the bench of the Special Court for Sierra Leone), and unwavering ambition to become an international judge.[3] Sebutinde's multiple and intersecting identities are reflective of her journey to the international bench, a journey which she describes as '*different threads that were woven into a kind of cloth, the kind of cloth that I now am*'.[4]

Justice Sebutinde's journey further illustrates the experiences of an increasing number of African women judges sitting on international benches. Yet, while the ICJ is still struggling (and currently failing) to achieve an equitable representation of women judges, the ACtHPR has made much more progress in reaching a sex

[1] International Court of Justice, All Members, International Court of Justice, at www.icj-cij.org/en/all-members (accessed 29 February 2020) (listing 108 historical members). Identifying all four women judges, Rosalyn Higgins (United Kingdom), Joan Donoghue (USA), Hanqin Xue (China) Julia Sebutinde (Uganda).

[2] Josephine Dawuni, 'Introduction: Challenging Gender Universalism and Unveiling the Silenced Narratives of the African Woman Judge' in Dawuni Josephine and Akua Kuenyehia (eds), *International Courts and the African Woman Judge: Unveiled Narratives* (Routledge 2018).

[3] Nienke Grossman, 'Julia Sebutinde: An Unbreakable Cloth' in Dawuni Josephine and Akua Kuenyehia (eds), *International Courts and the African Woman Judge: Unveiled Narratives* (Routledge 2018)

[4] ibid 52

J Jarpa Dawuni, *Keeping Gender on the Agenda for International Benches* In: *Identity and Diversity on the International Bench.* Edited by: Freya Baetens, Oxford University Press (2020).
DOI: 10.1093/oso/9780198870753.003.0026.

representative bench in a relatively shorter period since coming into force in 2006. This chapter seeks to answer two questions. First, why was the ACtHPR able to achieve gender parity when other international courts that have existed for longer, have not succeeded? Second, how can the gender parity gains made at the ACtHPR be sustained at the African regional level, and replicated within other international courts? By posing these questions, I do not imply that women no longer face challenges in the nomination and election processes to international courts—or within other African regional courts. Even where women have successfully made it through these stages, women judges may still be subjected to biases and discrimination due to the gendered power structures in the professional spaces they occupy.[5] This chapter proceeds as follows: in the section that follows I briefly discuss the theoretical and methodological approaches to evaluating the position of women in international courts. The next section critically examines the factors contributing to gender parity outcomes in the African Court—namely, legal instruments, specific strategies, and vested actors. The final section presents best practices for achieving gender parity on international benches.

2. A Note on Theory and Methods

The proliferation of international courts and tribunals within the last two decades has occasioned an increase in scholarly interest in normative questions of legitimacy, representation, and the law-making powers of these institutions.[6] A parallel development to these normative questions has been the awakening of feminist legal scholars questioning the nexus between normative legitimacy and the representation of women as judges within these courts. Charlesworth, Chinkin, and Wright's, *Feminist Approaches to International Law*[7] remains a critical piece in scrutinizing the inherent patriarchal nature of international law and its effect on positioning women as objects, but not as subjects of international law capable of contributing in their own right to the discourse. Chinkin et.al paved the way for a

[5] Gabrielle Kirk McDonald, 'Reflections on my Journey for Justice' in Jeremy Levitt (ed), *Black women and International Law: Deliberate Interactions, Movements and Actions* (CUP 2015)

[6] See generally; Mackenzie and others, *Selecting International Judges: Principle, Process and Politics* (OUP 2010); Nienke Grossman, 'Shattering the Glass Ceiling in International Adjudication. Virginia Journal of International Law (2016) 56 (2), 213–82. Nienke Grossman, 'Sex on the Bench: Do Women Judges Matter to the Legitimacy of International Courts?' (2012) 12(2) Chicago Journal of International Law 648–75; William, Schabas and Shannonbrooke Murphy (eds), *Research Handbook on International Courts and Tribunals*. (Edward Elgar Publishing 2017). Erik Voeten, 'The Politics of International Judicial Appointments' (2009) 9(2) Chicago Journal of International Law 387–405; Stephanie Vauchez, 'More women—but which Women? The Rule and the Politics of Gender Balance at the European Court of Human Rights' (2015) 26(1), The European Journal of International Law 195–221; Daniel Terris, Cesare Romano and Leigh Swigart, *The International Judge: An Introduction to the men and Women who Decide the World's Cases* (OUP 2007).

[7] Hilary Charlesworth, Christine Chinkin, and Shirley Wright, 'Feminist Approaches to International Law' (1991) 85(4) American Journal of International Law 613–45.

renewed focus on the descriptive and symbolic representation of women in international courts[8] and arbitration.[9] Consequently, feminist legal scholars have examined multiple questions, including why women should be appointed and what difference they would make on the bench. More recently, the interest of scholars and policy-oriented activists has started to converge—as feminist legal and theoretical explanations have explored the myriad of challenges women face in judicial selection processes.[10]

While these theoretical discussions have implications for all women judges from the African continent, the 2018 election of two women and one man to fill three vacant positions on the bench of the African Court on Human and Peoples' Rights (ACtHPR), in particular, brought the number of women on the 11-member bench to six (55%).[11] This means that barely a decade after its establishment, the ACtHPR met the gender equity benchmarks set by the Protocol on the African Charter on Human and Peoples' Rights on the Establishment of an African Court on Human and Peoples' Rights (Court Protocol)[12] and the Protocol to the African Charter on Human and Peoples' Rights on the Rights of Women in Africa (Maputo Protocol).[13] In this regard, the ACtHPR has surpassed the achievements of other courts such as the ICJ, the European Court of Human Rights (ECtHR), and the European Court of Justice (ECJ), which have each been in existence for much longer but are still struggling to achieve gender parity.

In situating the particular outcomes of the ACtHPR within the larger discourse on women and international courts, I draw on two theoretical frameworks—critical discourse analysis[14] and postcolonial feminist theory[15]—to evaluate the gender parity outcomes in the ACtHPR. Critical discourse analysis provides the tools through which the misrepresentations or under-representations of the lived realities of specific people may be corrected, or challenged through a critical review

[8] Shashank Kumar and Cecily Rose, 'A Study of Lawyers Appearing Before the International Court of Justice 1999–2012' (2014) 25 European Journal of International Law 893, 904–17; Rosa Ehrenreich Brooks, 'Feminism and International Law: An Opportunity for Transformation' (2002) 14(2) Yale Journal of Law and Feminism; Grossman (2016)

[9] Lucy Greenwood and C Mark Baker, 'Is the Balance Getting Better? An Update on Issues of Gender Diversity in International Arbitration' (2015) 31 Arbitration International 413, 471

[10] Laura Moyer, 'Gender on the International Bench' in Susan Sterett and Lee Walker (eds), Research Handbook on Law and Courts (Edward Elgar, 2019); Vauchez (2015) n 6; Grossman (2016) n 6.

[11] African Court on Human and Peoples' Rights. Current Judges<http://en.african-court.org/index.php/judges/current-judges>accessed 29 February 2020.

[12] Full text of the Protocol establishing the court is available at <https://au.int/en/treaties/protocol-african-charter-human-and-peoples-rights-establishment-african-court-human-and>accessed 29 February 2020.

[13] Full text of the Maputo Protocol can be found at <https://au.int/en/treaties/protocol-african-charter-human-and-peoples-rights-rights-women-africa>accessed 29 February 2020.

[14] Ruth Wodak, 'What Critical Discourse Analysis is About – A summary of its History, Important Concepts and its Developments' in Ruth Wodak, Michael Meyer (eds), Methods of Critical Discourse Analysis, (Sage 2001) 1–13

[15] For a general discussion of postcolonial feminism see; Chandra Talpade Mohanty, 'Under Western Eyes: Feminist Scholarship and Colonial Discourses', (1984) 12/13 On Humanism and the University I: The Discourse of Humanism

of the existing discourse.[16] By investigating the role of power in constructing knowledge, critical discourse analyses give voice to the voiceless and provides avenues for intervention to correct perceived wrongs.[17] Within the African context, critical discourse analysis has played a central role in correcting the lack of feminist discourse on women and judging. These silences have only now begun to be corrected and the voices of women judges are being brought to the fore with the first edited anthologies on African women judges in domestic and international courts.[18]

As a theory belonging to the genre of critical studies, postcolonial feminist theory challenges the social construction of knowledge production, which often limits the personal agency of the monolithic 'third world woman or postcolonial woman' in what Mohanty refers to, when she invokes the idea of knowledge production:[19]

> [t]he definition of colonization I wish to invoke here is a predominantly discursive one, focusing on a certain mode of appropriation and codification of 'scholarship' and 'knowledge' about women in the third world by particular analytic categories employed in specific writings on the subject which take as their referent feminist interests as they have been articulated in the U.S. and Western Europe.

Postcolonial feminism questions the presumptive conclusions in the writings of liberal feminists and the tendency to treat 'non-Western' women as a homogenous group—with little to no attention given to intersecting and overlapping differences based on culture, history, imperialism, and other modes of conscious and systematic homogenization of the lives and experiences of the non-Western 'other' woman. Applying a postcolonial feminist lens to this chapter, therefore allows for a deeper and wider examination of the nuances in the experiences and positionality of continental African women. Postcolonial feminism further allows for an evaluation of how the contextual location and positioning of the woman judges' agency, the relative power of the State and the ability of women's mobilization combine to explain outcomes for women judges' ascension to international courts. Placing this chapter analyses within these two frameworks of critical discourse analysis and postcolonial feminism provides a check on critiques that are quick to evaluate the success of the African woman as owing to external (Western) influences and

[16] Critical discourse analysis is a multidisciplinary paradigmatic approach to the study of social problems such as race, sexism, and other manifestations of inequality through critical consciousness; see generally, Brian Hodges, Ayelet Kuper, and Scott Reeves, 'Qualitative Research: Discourse Analysis' (2008) British Medical Journal, 337, 570–72. Theo van Leeuwen, 'Genre and field in Critical Discourse Analysis: A Synopsis' (1993) 4(2) Discourse and Society, 193–223

[17] Jan Blommaert and Chris Bulcaen, 'Critical Discourse Analysis' (2000) 29 Annual Review of Anthropology 447–466

[18] Gretchen Bauer and Josephine Dawuni (eds), *Gender and the Judiciary in Africa: From Obscurity to Parity?* (Routledge 2016); Josephine Dawuni and Akua Kuenyehia (eds), *International Courts and the African Woman Judge: Unveiled Narratives* (Routledge 2018)

[19] Chandra Talpade Mohanty (1984) (n 15) 333–34

erasing or minimizing the personal agency and the advocacy of African women's organizations. Working with these two frameworks, the chapter engages in an analysis of current research on African women judges in international courts, drawing on the lived experiences of women judges as individual actors to evaluate how the totality of one's identity and professional experiences directs their journeys to the international bench.

As I argued previously:[20]

> [t]he experiences of women judges on international courts are different and spread along a continuum of race, class, social status and other intersecting identities, thereby requiring a more nuanced analysis of who these women are and their geographical origins. Moreover, if scholars continue to turn a blind eye to intra-group diversity, the chances are higher for reproducing scholarly discourse that does not accurately account for the voices and narratives of women from the regions of the world considered 'third world' or 'developing.' The discourse on women judges, as it currently stands, is not structured to account for such intra-group dynamics fully.

Women judges on international benches come from different geographic backgrounds and embody different lived experiences. Much of the existing scholarship on women and judging has been developed in the US and Europe, thereby driving the narrative on women judges through a western feminist lens. Most of these studies have not adopted intersectional approaches[21] to evaluate the multiplicity of identities that judges inhabit and the role of history and politics in shaping these identities. In adopting a western-dominant approach to the study of women judges, scholars risk situating the experiences of all women judges within the universalizing global discourse that omits to analyse the opportunities and challenges women judges face from an intersectional perspective.[22] By accounting for race, postcolonial feminism questions the application of methods and paradigms grounded in a universal global feminist discourse which has repeatedly omitted the voices and experiences of other women—often other racial or ethnic minorities.[23]

As a critical theory, postcolonial feminism challenges universalist knowledge production on the experiences of women, arguing instead for a contextualized analysis that takes into account the location and lived experiences of women from the

[20] Josephine Dawuni, 'Introduction: Challenging Gender Universalism and Unveiling the Silenced Narratives of the African Woman Judge' in Josephine Dawuni and Akua Kuenyehia (eds), *International Courts and the African Woman Judge: Unveiled Narratives* (Routledge 2018) 7

[21] Iyiola Solanke, Putting Race and Gender Together: A new Approach to Intersectionality (2009) 72(5) Modern Law Review 723–49; Kimberle Crenshaw, 'Demarginalizing the Intersection of Race and Sex: A Black Feminist Critique of Anti-Discrimination Doctrine, Feminist Theory and Antiracist Politics (1989) 1(8) University of Chicago Legal Forum 139–66, at 140

[22] Dawuni (2018) in Legal Narratives (n 2).

[23] Mohanty (1984) (n 15), Crenshaw (1989) (n 21).

'global South'. The purpose of centring the experiences of the non-Western woman 'other' in the hegemonic cycle of knowledge production is to disrupt the power relations embodied in the voices of western feminists—often presented as 'knowers and producers' of knowledge.[24] Invariably, in the selection of judges to international courts, the idea that meritorious selection processes aim to choose the 'best qualified candidate' demands further analysis of what these meritocratic standards are, who determines what they should be and who assesses whether or not someone meets those standards. More importantly, the question of *which* women are expected to get on the international bench has yet to be critically analysed.

3. Getting Women on the Bench: The Interplay of Legal Instruments, Specific Strategies, and Vested Actors

The work of activist feminist scholars, legal civil society organizations, and gender equality campaign groups has coalesced in recent years around a common goal: increasing the number of women judges in international courts and tribunals.[25] The lingering perception that international judicial selection processes are rooted in merit and that 'the most qualified candidate wins' has been called into question.[26] When examined against the power relations between contending countries, the role of merit in the selection of judges remains unclear, as established power structures and the 'invisible club' mostly play to the advantage of certain male nominees.[27] Different courts have had varying outcomes in achieving sex balance or near-parity and data presented in the table below shows their gender report card which shows the ACtHPR as the most sex-balanced court as of this writing.

The data presented in Figure 26.1 below shows gender representation in selected international courts and tribunals.[28]

[24] For a comprehensive critique by 'third world' feminist discourse, see works by Mohanty (1984) (n 15).

[25] Beyond the growing scholarship on the subject of women in international courts, see the work of organizations such as GQUAL Campaign aimed at increasing the number of women in international courts and tribunals <www.gqualcampaign.org/home/>accessed 29 February 2020. Similar organizations dealing with women in international arbitration include and Arbitral Women <www.arbitralwomen.org accessed 29 February 2020.

[26] Mackenzie and others (2010) n 6; Voeten (2009), n 6.

[27] Susan D. Franck and others, 'The Diversity Challenge: Exploring the Invisible College of International Arbitration' (2015) 53 Columbia Journal of Transnational Law 429–506; Mackenzie and others (2010) n 6; Romano and others (2007) n 6.

[28] The courts in this figure were selected to represent regional, geographic, and jurisdictional diversity. The data in this chart were collected from the individual websites of the courts and tribunals. The data is current as of March 2019. The institutions represented in the chart are: ACtHPR (African Court on Human and Peoples' Rights); ACHPR (African Commission on Human and Peoples' Rights); ECHR (European Court of Human Rights); ICC (International Criminal Court), UNADT (United Nations Administrative Tribunal); MICT (Mechanism for International Criminal Tribunals); ICJ (International Court of Justice): IACHR (Inter-American Court of Human Rights); ITLOS (International Tribunal of the Law of the Sea).

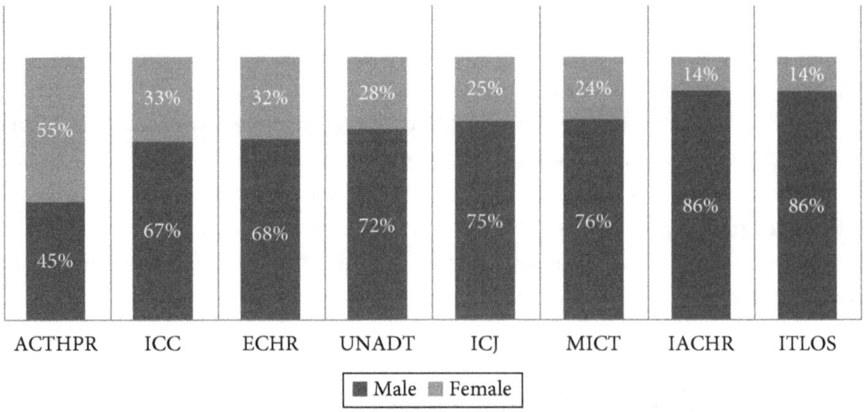

Figure 26.1 Gender diversity

With the exception of the ACtHPR, all other courts listed above have yet to reach a 40% benchmark. This suggests that the road to achieving gender balance on some international benches is still an upward battle. It is possible to learn from past mistakes, the poor gender record of the ICJ informed the negotiations leading to the Rome Statute establishing the International Criminal Court (ICC) which contains specific wording on meet gender balance.[29] Using the case of the ACtHPR, the next section presents the argument that sustaining and improving gender parity on the benches of international courts calls for the creative interplay of three factors—legal instruments, specific strategies, and vested actors.

3.1 Legal Instruments

3.1.1 Reforming judicial selection processes

Most judicial selection processes to international courts apply a two-step formal process—the first is the nomination stage and the second is the election stage. Both stages are guided by rules and procedures contained in international treaties and

[29] Louise Chappell, '"New," "Old," and "Nested" Institutions and Gender Justice Outcomes: The View from the International Criminal Court' (2014) 10 Politics and Gender 572, at 574–76.The work of advocacy groups such as the Women's Caucus for Gender Justice, and feminist legal actors played a role in negotiating for the inclusion of 'progressive gender' issues in the drafting of the Rome Statute, though Chappelle argues that the provisions were not as 'comprehensive' as feminist activists would have liked, yet they ensured that the Rome Statute would perform better than previous international courts in order to 'better recognize gender power relations, represent women's voices, and achieve a degree of redistribution of resources in post-conflict environments' p 577.

domestic policies. In between these two formal processes there are many informal and semi-formal processes which are beyond the current discussion.

3.1.1.1 The nomination stage

The nomination stage takes place within the domestic sphere where candidates perceived or assessed as meeting the judicial requirements may be nominated by their governments. National sovereignty allows for individual countries to set their own criteria for nominating qualified candidates. Complexities arise where there are no openly accessible rules and procedures for nominating candidates, thus making the process less transparent and likely to result in the selection of candidates for reasons other than merit and qualification.[30] In the case of the ACtHPR, Article 11(1) requires that judges nominated are of 'high moral character and of recognized practical, judicial or academic competence and experience in the field of human and peoples' rights'. No further guidelines are provided as to how these standards are to be assessed and weighed. Article 12 provides 'that State Parties may nominate up to three candidates, at least two of which shall be nationals of the nominating State and that due consideration shall be given to adequate gender representation'. What exactly constitutes 'adequate' gender representation is not defined, thereby leaving room for nominators to apply arbitrary and ad hoc standards in deciding the gender balance of the nomination list.

At the African Union (AU) level, the body responsible for communicating vacancies on the bench is the Office of the Legal Counsel (OLC). The OLC issues a *note verbal* to the foreign ministries in Addis Ababa for onward transmission to their respective governments in their national jurisdictions. At the domestic stage, the *note verbal* is transmitted to the Ministry of Justice and the Ministry of Foreign Affairs. Anecdotal evidence gathered through interviews with judges suggests that in the past, there were no open calls for nominations when the *note verbal* is sent to the domestic governments, thereby shrouding the nomination process in secrecy.[31] The decision on which candidate to nominate is often undertaken by key gatekeepers including the Chief Justice, the Attorney General, or the Minister of Foreign Affairs. The names of shortlisted candidates are given to the President for his approval and onward transmission to the OLC.[32]

The process of nominating candidates to international courts and tribunals has not always been transparent, open, and accessible to eligible candidates.[33] The

[30] Mackenzie and others (2010) (n 6) , Romano and others (2007) (n 6).

[31] Nienke Grossman (2016) confirms how the opacity of national nomination procedures can affect getting the best qualified candidates when available positions are not openly advertised.

[32] The wording on the process of nomination candidates can be found in the 2018 note verbal issued to the foreign ministries of Member States based in Addis Ababa <https://au.int/sites/default/files/announcements/34089-annc-502.18_bc-olc-66.5_eng_nv_for_election_for_judges_june-july_2018.pdf>accessed 29 February 2020.

[33] Grossman (2016) (n 6); Mackenzie and others (2010) (n 6).

experience of Akua Kuenyehia, who was Ghana's nominee to the ICC in 2003, is instructive:[34]

> I did not hear about the vacancy; I had a call from the Attorney-General. I went to see him, and he told me 'the President has asked us to nominate you for the ICC.' I told him I was not interested, and he said 'well, that means you are turning the President down.' That made me take the matter seriously, and I decided to accept the President's nomination.

Good networks are important avenues for hearing about judicial openings: for example, Julia Sebutinde learned about the vacancy at the ICJ while she was already working as a judge at the Special Court for Sierra Leone, as Grossman notes:

> Judge Sebutinde learned that an African judge on the Court would likely be leaving his post in the coming years because she was living in The Hague during the Taylor trial, and '[i]t's a small city and you do get to know things around.' She reached out to confirm the vacancy with the Ugandan Embassy in New York. In her words, 'I was lucky to have asked the right question at the right time.' She then traveled back to Uganda to 'discover who the national group was, talk to them, convince them that I was interested in this job,' and have them write a letter to the UN Secretary General channeled through the Ugandan Foreign Ministry. She also sought and obtained approval from the Cabinet and President. '[T]here was no way that I was going to be nominated as a Ugandan candidate without that [political] clearance'.[35]

The experience of Elsie Thompson, elected to the ACtHPR bench in 2010, further demonstrates the opacity of the nomination processes. As Rebecca Badejogbin writes:

> Thompson was recommended for nomination by someone who had known about her human rights work - Ambassador Nkoyo Toyo, Nigeria's Ambassador to Ethiopia. She was then, also the permanent representative of Nigeria to the AU, and incidentally, a woman who wanted the position to be occupied by a suitably qualified woman.[36]

These three experiences, and many others presented in *International Courts and the African Woman Judge: Unveiled Narratives*,[37] highlight that not all women had

[34] Dawuni and Kuenyehia (2018) (n 2) 63–64.
[35] Grossman (2018) (n 3) 46.
[36] Rebecca Badejogbin, Elsie Thompson: 'The Trajectory of a Noble Passion' in Dawuni and Kuenyehia (2018) (n 2) 132.
[37] ibid.

access to informal networks that supported their nomination. Even for the most qualified candidates, personal networks play a vital role at the nomination stage of international judicial appointments.[38]

Despite the presence of language aimed at achieving *adequate* gender parity in the ACtHPR Protocol, the ACtHPR had a sex-imbalanced bench in its first decade, with only two women judges sitting on the 11-member bench at any given time (18%).[39] The length of time it took for the bench to achieve gender balance indicates that the requirement to ensure *adequate* gender representation in the nomination processes was not being followed.[40] To address this issue, the 2016 Ordinary Session of the Executive Council adopted the '*Modalities on the Implementation of the Criteria of Equitable Geographical and Gender Representation in AU Organs and Institutions*'. Section III addressed the need to take the gender equity provision of the Court Protocol into account and to ensure that all nomination lists submitted by governments include the name of at least one woman.[41] Since governments have important roles in deciding who gets to represent their State, the goal of this communique was to demand reforms at the domestic level, including clear guidelines and procedures for disseminating vacancies to attract a wide pool of qualified candidates. The 2016 reform set an institutional culture-change in motion, resulting in the subsequent election of four women judges between 2017 and 2018.[42]

While governments may make political calculations to nominate women candidates, there is no guarantee, however, that the domestic internal processes will make the nomination processes open and accessible to all qualified female candidates. Consequently, efforts aimed at reforming domestic processes should broaden participation to allow qualified candidates who are nationals of the nominating State but residing outside of the State to be nominated. Allowing nationals residing abroad will increase the pool of judicial candidates beyond those currently serving in the national judiciary which has often been the practice. Broadening participation will increase the quality of judicial nominees and increase opportunities for women with diverse experiences to apply. Lastly, the lack of domestic nomination processes can be rectified if the AU adopts uniform guidelines that its Member States would be obligated to follow in their domestic nomination process. These guidelines should include timely and wide advertising of vacancies in print as well as online and creating a judicial selection committee consisting of highly reputable jurists to interview prospective candidates. This committee's decision should

[38] Mackenzie and others (2010) (n 6).
[39] Dawuni (2018) (n 2).
[40] Josephine Dawuni, 'Vive la Diversité! Roadmap to Gender Parity on African Regional Courts?' (2017) Feminist Critiques of International Law Symposium <https://voelkerrechtsblog.org/vive-la-diversite/>accessed 29 February 2020.
[41] See EX.CL/953(XXVIII), 'Modalities on the Implementation of the Criteria of Equitable Geographical and Gender Representation in AU Organs and Institutions,' <https://archives.au.int/handle/123456789/4949>accessed 29 February 2020.
[42] Dawuni (2017) (n 39)

ideally be binding on nominating States. Having a thorough application and review process at the nomination stage raises the chances of nominating the best qualified candidates.[43]

3.1.1.2 The election stage

The election of shortlisted candidates takes place at the meeting of the Assembly of Heads of State and Government. Judges are elected by secret ballot from a pool of candidates who fulfil the representation requirements in terms of geographical distribution, legal traditions, and gender. Governmental preferences play a key role in determining the outcomes and the power relations often benefit candidates from the most politically powerful States.[44] Despite attempts to minimize political horse-trading, the trading of votes continues to be a crucial determinant in judicial electoral outcomes. After electing two women at the 2016 meeting, the Assembly suspended elections for the two remaining seats because not all member states had complied with the requirement that at least one out of the three nominees must be a woman.[45] At the AU Summit held in 2017, two women, Chafika Bensaoula of Algeria and Tujilane Rose Chizumila of Malawi, were elected to fill the remaining two vacancies, bringing the number of women on the ACtHPR bench to four. In 2018, two more women were elected to the bench, Imani Aboud of Tanzania and Stella Isibhakhomen Anukam of Nigeria.[46]

Even judicial candidates who passed through the domestic nomination processes may come up against the AU's internal mechanisms aimed at achieving geographic representation,[47] sometimes at the cost of gender representation. Elsie Nwanwuri Thompson of Nigeria was one of only two female judges elected to the 11-member bench of the ACtHPR in 2010. Though nominated by her government for a second term, she was not re-elected by the Assembly of Heads of State and

[43] Ebrahim-Carstens, (2016: 100) discusses the composition of the Internal Justice Council (IJC) consisting of 'independent, gender- and geographically-diverse representative body, chaired by an eminent international jurist [. . .] It is composed of a management representative, a staff representative, and two external distinguished jurists nominated by management, and the Staff Association respectively. The IJC, at the conclusion of a rigorous selection exercise, presents a full written report to the General Assembly to which is annexed a copy of the vacancy announcement and the detailed curriculum vitae of two recommended candidates for each post. In this report, the IJC explains the method and process for selection, and makes recommendations to the General Assembly for the appointment of the candidate judges, providing guidance on the statutory requirements.'

[44] Mackenzie and others (2010) (n 6).

[45] Discussions with a lawyer at the OLC revealed this information, but I could not locate the exact communique calling for the suspension of the elections, nor did I get information in which countries did not nominate women.

[46] Josephine Dawuni, 'Beyond the Numbers: Gender Parity on the African Court on Human and Peoples' Rights – A Lesson for African Regional Courts?' (2018) <https://ilg2.org/2018/08/28/beyond-the-numbers-gender-parity-on-the-african-court-on-human-and-peoples-rights-a-lesson-for-african-regional-courts/>accessed 29 February 2020.

[47] The African Union has five distinct political regions to ensure the representation of the diversity of the continent, these are classified into the North, South, East, West, and Central regions. AU member states grouped according to regions can be found here <https://au.int/en/member_states/countryprofiles2>accessed 29 February 2020.

Government because that would have tilted the geographical representation in favour of the Western Africa region. Judge Prisca Nyambe, a former ad hoc judge on the International Criminal Court for Rwanda (ICTR) and current judge on the Mechanism for International Criminal Tribunals (MICT) also fell victim to geographical representation preferences. On two occasions, her nomination at the domestic level did not make it past the AU's internal screening processes, because she is a Zambian national, and on both occasions, the Southern Africa quota had already been met.[48]

3.2 Enforcement of Gender Parity Policies and Women's Representation

Grossman's 2015 study of twelve international courts showed that the founding documents of international organizations and tribunals sometimes provide parity policies and gender-sensitive aspirational targets for achieving sex-representative benches.[49] The 2017 and 2018 elections to fill vacant positions on the ACtHPR bench confirmed Grossman's argument that even aspirational targets contribute to increasing the number of women on the bench. Nevertheless, continuous monitoring and advocacy for adherence to these provisions remain vital for sustaining gender parity gains. But what about women's representation when the founding documents of a court do not contain any such wording? The long history of the ICJ provides the answer to this question: women have taken up only four seats (3.6%) out of 108 ICJ judges in over 70 years.[50]

The absence of gender parity policies in founding documents of courts should, however, not be a death knell for achieving gender parity. Currently, within the Africa region, the ACtHPR is the only court whose founding document specifically refers to the need to consider gender when nominating and electing judges. The Economic Community of West African States Court of Justice (ECOWAS Court) and the East African Court of Justice (EACJ) do not have provisions aimed at meeting a minimum gender threshold. Nonetheless, the ECOWAS Court has shown that the absence of parity rules should not preclude the use of other institutional mechanisms to promote gender parity. From a historical record of 29%

48 The African Union system has adopted a framework to achieve gender parity across all regional and domestic spheres by 2063. Other mechanisms include Solemn Declaration on Gender Equality in Africa (SDGEA) and the Maputo Protocol. In furtherance of these goals, 2015 was declared the 'Year of African Women's Empowerment towards Agenda 2063' and 2016 as the 'Year of African Human Rights with a focus on Women's Rights.' The outcomes of these different instruments are monitored under the yearly Gender Scorecard, the most recent version is available at <https://au.int/en/documents/20181105/african-gender-equality-and-womens-empowerment-scorecard> accessed 29 February 2020.

49 Grossman (2016) (n 6).

50 The list of past and current judges on the ICJ can be found at International Court of Justice: All Members <www.icj-cij.org/en/all-members>accessed 29 February 2020.

female judges by mid-2015, the numbers dropped to 10% by the end of 2017. With the last election held in 2018, women now make up 2 out of 5 judges, representing 40% of currently serving ECOWAS judges[51].

Thus, where founding documents do not provide for gender parity guidelines, other documents can be used to push governments in the election process. One such institutional mechanism is the Protocol to the African Charter on Human and Peoples' Rights on the Rights of Women in Africa (Maputo Protocol), which establishes a continental legal framework for promoting gender equity. Article 9 of the Protocol specifically grants women the 'right to participate in the political and decision-making process'. As a gender equalizing norm, Article 9 (2) provides that 'State Parties shall ensure increased and effective representation and participation of women at all levels of decision-making'. While there is no threshold or definition of what constitutes 'effective representation', creating favourable and transparent conditions for women to be nominated increases the chances of women being elected. To bolster the implementation of the Maputo Protocol's reporting framework, the Solemn Declaration of Gender Equality in Africa (SDGEA) was adopted in 2004 to monitor the progress of the Maputo Protocol through a national reporting mechanism.[52] The SDGEA consists of a mechanism for assessing national efforts towards achieving gender equitable representation and monitoring the rights of women across the African continent, while the representation of women in judicial appointments falls under the wider definitions of participatory governance.[53]

Furthermore, the annual reports of States at the UN Annual Meetings of the Commission on the Status of Women (CSW) can be used as a tool for naming and shaming governments who are consistently failing to nominate women candidates for judicial positions. There is currently no empirical evidence to show that this strategy has been used in the past when it comes to judicial appointments. Advocates of gender equitable judicial appointment outcomes can learn from the strategies adopted by other women's organizations in putting pressure on governments who had not yet signed the Maputo Protocol. The advocacy push for the ratification of the Maputo Protocol shows that the gender score card was an instrumental strategy in convincing Ministers of Foreign Affairs to pressure their governments to sign and ratify the Protocol.[54] Additionally, the Gender Unit of the African Union should lobby domestic governments to fulfil their treaty obligations under the gender parity provisions in the Maputo Protocol by targeting, recruiting,

[51] These data are on file with the author based on a dynamic table containing the number of judges on all African courts since their establishment.

[52] <www.mrfcj.org/pdf/Solemn_Declaration_on_Gender_Equality_in_Africa.pdf>accessed 29 February 2020.

[53] Melinda Adams, 'African Women's Movements and the African Union' in Olajumoke Yacob-Haliso and Toyin Falola (eds), The Palgrave Handbook of African Women's Studies (Palgrave Macmillan 2019)

[54] ibid.

and submitting the names of potential female candidates even if they are not nationals of the nominating State. Lastly, women's rights organizations can invoke international legal frameworks and treaty obligations to demand equal representation of women. Article 8 of the Convention on the Elimination of All Forms of Discrimination against Women (CEDAW) provides:

> States Parties shall take all appropriate measures to ensure to women, on equal terms with men and without any discrimination, the opportunity to represent their Governments at the international level and to participate in the work of international organizations.[55]

Article 8 therefore places a legal obligation on States by setting an international framework for women's participation and representation in international organizations. Governmental support is critical to the success of any international judicial campaign. Where the stakes are high, for example in terms of the perceived prestige of the court, governments attach importance to judicial elections and are willing to create teams to support their candidates during the campaign and election phases. Such domestic support mechanisms should include a recognition of the gendered aspects of negotiating election to international benches.

3.3 Specific Strategies

3.3.1 Building domestic and cross-national coalitions

The UN World Conferences on Women beginning in Mexico City (1975), Copenhagen (1980), Nairobi (1985), and Beijing (1995) and the Beijing Platform for Action led to the growth of international collaboration and coalitions aimed at strengthening solidarity among women's groups.[56] At the regional level, the appointment of women as heads of judiciaries (either as Chief Justice or President of Constitutional Courts) across Africa is indicative of regional norm diffusion and snowball effects of the growing trend of women's judicial leadership in countries across the continent.[57] Social activist movements pursuing social, economic, and political goals through coalitions with other organizations remains key to the advancement of women's rights issues across Africa.[58]

[55] Convention on the Elimination of All Forms of Discrimination Against Women (CEDAW) 1249 UNTS 13 (1979).

[56] For a fuller understanding of the work of the United Nations in promoting women's rights through conferences and women's coalition building, see UN Women <www.unwomen.org/en/how-we-work/intergovernmental-support/world-conferences-on-women>accessed 29 February 2020.

[57] Josephine Dawuni and Alice Kang, 'Her ladyship the Chief Justice: The rise of Female Leaders in the Judiciary in Africa' (2015) 62(2) Africa Today, 45–69.

[58] Adams (2019) (n 53).

Global feminist organizations spurred by the UN Women's conferences and the UN Decade for Women have produced best practices on coalition building to advance women's rights globally.[59] Building strong national and international coalitions for monitoring governments in the fulfilment of their treaty goals is central to achieving gender-balanced courts. Coalitions such as the Coalition on the International Criminal Court (CICC) and the Women's Initiative for Gender Justice were instrumental in ensuring that the Rome Statute contained quota provisions aimed at creating a gender-balanced court.[60] After achieving the incorporation of quota provisions, these coalitions and organizations have remained vigilant, through activities such as sending out questionnaires to judicial candidates to help them prepare for elections, organizing candidate panel discussions before elections are held in New York, and monitoring election cycles.

Another organization that supports women nominees during elections is the International Association of Women Judges (IAWJ). Established in 1991, the IAWJ is a voluntary organization of over 6000 women judges from around the world with the primary goal of supporting each other.[61] As part of activities to promote the election of women judges to international courts, the IAWJ created a committee focusing on judicial nominations to the ICC. Through this committee, the IAWJ has engaged in massive campaigns to notify its members of judicial vacancies and review the curricula vitae of its members who are interested in being nominated. As the executive director, Lisa Davis noted:[62]

> We sent an official letter to the Director of the Secretariat of the Assembly of State Parties and the head of the Advisory Committee on Nominations of Judges on the importance of the fair gender representation on the court [. . .] What we did learn over the last 15 months is that the process and the positioning of women candidates for the ICC needs to start years in advance. It is a very political process. We believe the IAWJ offers the platform to raise the visibility of women judges, provide the opportunity for networking and skills building, and increase women's judicial leadership. But what we might be doing more of, moving forward through our committee is to help steer our interested members to those within our membership and other organizations who can help them navigate the political path to nomination within the international bodies.

The importance of networking, agenda setting, and mentoring cannot be underestimated. Aspiring women judges will have to work through their collective

59 ibid.

60 Chapell (2014) (n 29).

61 International Association of Women Judges (IAWJ) <http://www.iawj.org/> accessed 29 February 2020.

62 Author discussion with Lisa Davis, Executive Director of the International Association of Women Judges, Washington, DC Wilson Center, June 2018

groups to build the needed critical mass and devise strategies to win international judicial elections. Women's civil society groups are crucial actors when it comes to supporting women's judicial nominations. In 1995, Justina Kelello Mafoso-Guni was appointed the first woman High Court judge in Lesotho. Having also been the first woman lawyer in the country, Mafoso-Guni spent the early part of her career working in neighbouring Zimbabwe. However, as Ellett recounts, Mafoso-Guni's appointment as a High Court judge was met with protests by members of the Law Society, because the judiciary in Lesotho, until that point, had remained men only, thereby feeding the fears that a woman could not be a High Court judge.[63] Mafoso-Guni was officially appointed to the High Court after two years of serving as an acting judge. Her appointment, it seems, would not have been possible but for the mobilization of the members of the International Federation of Women Lawyers (FIDA) who mounted a nation-wide campaign to support her in the media and among members of the Law Society.[64]

At the African Union Commission on Human and Peoples' Rights (AU Commission), women make up half of the Commissioners. NGOs are important allies in getting women elected through their persistence in holding governments accountable for nominating women for international positions.[65] Women's activist groups can play a crucial role in signalling the importance of gender balance in the nomination process and putting pressure on governments to respect and honour their commitments under regional and international gender equity frameworks.

Without sustaining such advocacy, women's nominations to international and regional courts will remain uncertain. In the case of the African regional courts, women's cross-national coalitions are important. One such organization, the Solidarity for African Women's Rights (SOAWR), an umbrella coalition of women's rights organizations which has been at the forefront in advocating for women's rights across the continent.[66] Through SOAWR, domestic coalitions can push for national governments to nominate and vote for women candidates. In a 2005 statement issued to the AU Commission, members of civil society organizations made a three-point demand, to be considered by governments in the nomination and election processes. These demands were that candidates meet the minimum standards for holding the highest judicial office in their country of origin, that States broaden

[63] Ellett (2018) (n 2) 113.

[64] Women's movements at the domestic level has been credited for the largest increase in the number of female federal judges in the United States under Jimmy Carter's presidency, see Mary Clark, 'Changing the Face of the Law: How Women's Advocacy Groups Put Women on the Federal Judicial Appointments Agenda' (2002) 14 (243) Yale Journal of Law and Feminism 244–54.

[65] Hans Viljoen, 'Promising Profiles: An Interview with the Four New Members of the African Commission on Human and Peoples' Rights' (2006) 6 African Human Rights Law Journal 237–48.

[66] Solidarity for African Women's Rights (SOAWR) <www.soawr.org/>accessed 29 February 2020.

the participation of nomination processes to allow civil society participation, and that States increase citizen trust in the legitimacy of the nomination processes by adhering to transparent selection processes.[67]

3.3.2 Preparing future judges

Feminist legal scholars had hoped that the global feminization of legal professions—measured by the increase in the number of women graduating from law schools and entering the legal professions—would translate to increased judicial appointments of women.[68] At the domestic level, the feminization of the legal profession is yet to be translated into the feminization of the upper hierarchies of the judiciary.[69] Some countries have nominated women judges for international courts, but others have consistently failed to do so.[70] Critics may argue that a growing number of women gaining access to these benches could mean that unqualified women are now being admitted too. But for all these years that men have been appointed to these courts, why has the same argument not been advanced against them? Why is it that when women gain access to historically male-dominated spaces, the onus is placed on them to show that they got there on merit? Arguments that the pool of qualified women is too limited no longer hold true as Vauchez's study of the ECtHR shows that women judges are as qualified as their male counterparts.[71] The persistence of a gender imbalance on the bench is rather indicative of continued gender hierarchies that view women as underqualified or unelectable judicial candidates.[72]

To sustain the progress made in improving the gender representation on the benches of some international courts, continuous efforts must be made to enlarge the pool of qualified applicants. Efforts should involve insider-outsider collaborations aimed at identifying strategies to train, mentor, and recruit qualified

[67] Strengthening from Within: Law and Practice in the Selection of Human Rights Judges and Commissioners (Open Society Justice Initiative and International Commission of Jurists, 2017) <www.justiceinitiative.org/publications/strengthening-within-law-and-practice-selection-human-rights-judges-and-commissioners> accessed 11 August 2020.

See also a more recent report on electing judges to the ICC, Raising the Bar: Improving the nomination and election of judges to the International Criminal Court (Open Society Justice Initiative, 2019)<www.justiceinitiative.org/uploads/7627a69c-dc69-43da-a58c-c66162f1c2b0/raising-the-bar-20191028.pdf>accessed 29 February 2020.

[68] Ethan Michelson, 'Women in the Legal Profession, 1970-2010: A Study of the Global Supply of Lawyers' (2013) 20(2) Indiana Journal of Global Legal Studies .

[69] Sally Kenney, 'Gender and Justice: Why Women in the Judiciary Really Matters' (Routledge, 2013)

[70] Grossman (2016) (n 6).

[71] Stephanie Vauchez, 'More Women—But Which Women? The Rule and the Politics of Gender Balance at the European Court of Human Rights' (2015) 26(1) The European Journal of International Law 195–221.

[72] Francois Tulkens, 'More Women – But Which Women? A Reply to Stéphanie Hennette Vauchez' (2015) 26(1) The European Journal of International Law 223–27: Tulkens observes that the Belgian nominee Eva Brems to the ECHR was considered 'underqualified' despite her long and impressive professional record.

women. Other tactics could include creating a transformative culture of women-friendly institutional mechanisms among three focal actors and gatekeepers—within judiciaries, within the national Ministries of Foreign Affairs, and among women's civil society organizations, who could serve as allies through the national nomination process. Women have the credentials to occupy top judicial positions at the domestic level, but that alone is insufficient for appointment to international courts.

Demonstrating international experience is a crucial requirement to a successful election campaign. International collaborations through global networks such as the IAWJ can provide women with the requisite international networks for building this type of social capital. Nominating bodies at the domestic level should not choose women candidates who only have experience in gender-related matters to prevent confining women judges to specific areas of international law. As some international criminal courts are winding down, the 'market' may get more restrictive, thereby increasing the competition for judicial positions. To make it past the first mark in the nomination process, women candidates will most likely have to demonstrate international judicial experiences that surpass those of their male colleagues.

4. Vested Actors

4.1 Personal Agency

Listening to the personal narratives of African women judges is important to situate the lived realities of women judges within the larger discourse on gender and judging. Employing legal narratives as a discursive analytical and critical tool allows the researcher and the reader to simultaneously see and hear the role of interlocking identities of the individual judge.[73] Feminist legal scholarship, and scholarship on international courts in particular, has tended to place a high premium on legitimacy, democracy, representation, and equality as advocacy tools for demanding gender parity.[74] A woman's agency includes the fundamental human right to choose her profession. Consequently, all qualified candidates should have an equal opportunity to contest for judicial positions without having to jump through domestic political hoops and barriers. Judge Florence Ndepele Mwachande Mumba of Zambia served as a judge on the International Criminal Tribunal for the former Yugoslavia (ICTY) and the International Criminal Tribunal for Rwanda (ICTR) and is currently serving in the Extraordinary Chambers of Cambodia

[73] Dawuni (2018) (n 2).
[74] Moyer (2019) (n 10).

(ECCC). Judge Mumba did not allow the prejudices against girls pursuing a law degree to deter her. As she recounts:[75]

> At the University, I wanted to study theology, unfortunately, it was not offered. In my search for something new to study, I came across the Law School and decided to register there. Some of my friends discouraged me saying that some male students in the Law School were failing because law studies were difficult. I challenged them that I would follow those who passed their law courses. I was fortunate in that some of the senior male students were helpful, they shared their textbooks with me. At that time, it was not easy to find law textbooks in Zambia. In my class, I was the only girl. I always faced teasing from the male students and some of our lecturers who felt that I was in the wrong class as they did not expect women to qualify as lawyers. I found out later that there was one lady who had completed her final year law studies.

Similarly, as ICJ Judge Julia Sebutinde recounts, '30 years ago, if someone had told me that a young girl from a humble family in Kiwafi Village in Entebbe would one day be the first African female judge on the World Court, I would probably think they were crazy!'[76] The political and financial support of nominating governments is vital to candidates' chances of successful election,[77] but Sebutinde had to bear the financial costs of the campaign process herself, with little to no support from her government. As Grossman notes:

> Sebutinde met with Ambassadors or embassy officials in The Hague, New York, Geneva and Brussels in order to present her candidature. In The Hague alone, she made 'no less than 200' visits to embassies. The Ugandan embassies would assist in organizing the meetings. Her trips, meetings and materials, such as a printed brochure about her candidacy in all six languages of the United Nations, were all self-funded and cost her thousands of dollars.[78]

The experiences of Judge Mumba and Judge Sebutinde are located within the larger reality of women judges, who, despite their qualifications, still have to prove again and again that they are as qualified as their male counterparts.[79] In the case of Judge Gabrielle Kirk McDonald, the first and only African American woman to serve on an international court (ICTY) as of this writing, having the backing of

[75] Florence Mumba, 'Women judges in International Courts and Tribunals: The quest for Equal Opportunities' in Josephine Dawuni and Akua Kuenyehia (eds), International Courts and the African Woman Judge: Unveiled Narratives (Routledge 2018) 29.

[76] Grossman (2018) (n 3) 37.

[77] Mackenzie and others (2010) (n 6).

[78] Grossman (2018) (n 3) 46.

[79] Vauchez (2015) (n 6).

the US government did not prevent her from facing prejudice as an international judge. As she notes in her foreword in *International Courts and the African Woman Judge: Unveiled Narratives:*[80]

> I can relate to the legal narratives of the seven African women international judges. As an African-American woman growing up in the late 1950s and 1960s in the United States, I have faced many struggles because of the happenstance of my gender and race. My passion for justice has taken me from my work as a civil rights lawyer at home in the United States, to a search for justice and human rights in my work at the international level.

For black women judges, moreover, gender and race issues intersect, affecting their experiences on the benches of international courts.[81] While the personal agency of the woman judge is critical to her surviving the shocks on the road to the international bench, we should be cognizant of the politics of judicial selection at the international levels, and how race and gender may combine to create an implicit bias in the evaluation of an individual's meritocratic qualities and abilities.[82]

4.2 Political Accountability

One cannot discuss appointments and elections to international courts without discussing the fundamental role played by governments. States continue to occupy primacy in the international sphere, thereby acting as important gatekeepers to judicial appointments. Some researchers have suggested that certain governments may deliberately nominate a weaker female candidate just so the stronger male candidate gets elected, while they still avoid criticism for not nominating women.[83] As mentioned earlier, the AU Assembly of Heads of State and Governments has pledged to achieve 50/50 gender parity. This pledge, coupled with the Maputo Protocol and women's civil society activism, has helped to propel gender parity across all institutions within the AU system.[84] As critical actors to the selection and election of international judges, the Assembly of Heads of State and Government

[80] McDonald (2018) (n 2) xiii.

[81] Most of the judges I have interviewed tend to shy away from answering the question if they have faced racism in their work as international judges. Off record conversations and anecdotal evidence gathered from conversations with other Africans working in these international courts do show there are high levels of racial bias and discrimination and the judges are not immune from such biases. Consequently, I discuss the issue of race briefly in Dawuni, Legal Narratives (2018) under the subheading 'What it ought to be' p 17.

[82] McDonald (2018) (n 2), yet the question of race remains largely unexplored in the scholarly discourse on the appointment of international judges.

[83] Vauchez (2015) (n 6) Kumar and Rose (2014) (n 8).

[84] AU 50/50 gender policy <www.un.org/en/africa/osaa/pdf/au/gender_policy_2009.pdf>accessed 29 February 2020.

has lived up to its pledge of promoting gender equality within the African Court and other mechanisms such as the African Commission on Human and Peoples' Rights. More research is needed to examine what factors influence the political calculations of governments in deciding whether to nominate a female or male candidate. While such analysis is beyond this chapter's focus, I would argue that based on current trends and patterns within the African Court, governments across Africa are living up to their political promise of gender parity as manifested by the record number of qualified women they have nominated and elected to the African Court.

5. Conclusion

As international relations and legal obligations of States get more complicated and nuanced, so is the need for understanding not only the legitimacy of international organizations, but also the actors involved. Judicial diversity remains an important variable for measuring and assessing the legitimacy of international courts, and gender diversity has been central to this ongoing analysis. My research has shown that women from the African continent have edged ahead in the global statistics concerning international women judges.[85] Nonetheless, this increase does not necessarily indicate the crystallization of gender neutrality in the institutional norms and practices of these courts. Continuous monitoring is needed to appoint more women to these courts' benches, and where progress has been made, continued vigilance is needed to safeguard the gender parity gains.

Achieving gender-balanced benches can be likened to tidal waves—the ebb and flow of the judicial selection processes are subject to international political calculations and relative power structures of States, thereby impacting the extent to which national governments can control the process of having their candidate elected. The foregoing discussion has shown that recent efforts undertaken by the AU to promote mechanisms for electing qualified women judges may have yielded results in the ACtHPR.

Recognizing the multi-layered and intersectional challenges women face in judicial selection processes requires nuanced analyses to devise a priori strategies that could lead to gender equitable outcomes. The proposals presented in this chapter could help to enhance the selection processes at domestic and international levels. For example, a panel of independent experts should review the applications for nomination at the national level to ensure that the most qualified candidates are selected. If these processes are open and accessible, qualified women candidates will be found from the three places where international judges often originate—judiciaries, academia, and the diplomatic corps.

[85] Dawuni and Kuenyehia (2018) (n 36).

In conclusion, this chapter argues that the quest for gender parity on international benches, the relative gains made, and the strategies for achieving sex-balanced benches should not be evaluated in a vacuum. Each court needs to be evaluated against the social, historical, and political context of its structure, location, and jurisdiction, as each of these factors will determine the existence and capacity of the legal instruments, the specific strategies, and the vested actors. The evidence presented here indicates that the African context provides important lessons for governments, feminist legal scholars, policy practitioners and women's organizations around the world in their quest to keep gender on the agenda of international court benches.

Epilogue

Diversity, Inclusion, and Legitimacy in International Courts and Tribunals: Insights from Within, Perspectives from the Periphery—An Island Girl Speaks

Janet M Nosworthy

1. Introduction

Discussions surrounding humanity and diversity characteristics such as gender, ethnicity, race, culture, including legal and judicial culture, and religion have the ability to make us decidedly uncomfortable. They require deep analysis of self, nation, race, religious belief, political opinion and association, cultural practice, and more. They compel intense self-critiquing as we lay our legal souls bare, subjected to the type of microscopic scrutiny which we might not be quite ready for. Complaints have been raised in some quarters that the field of international law is too much of an exclusive 'members' club', allowing limited access to only a few, while the selection process for judges to populate the benches of international courts and tribunals appears to be flawed. Additionally, the system would not provide sufficient levels of diversity and would fail to readily embrace the incorporation of judges who are members of minority groups. Arguably, judges from coveted select jurisdictions and profiles are consistently favoured whereas others appear in relatively limited numbers or not at all. This non-inclusive approach could be cause for reduced levels of confidence in international courts and tribunals, thereby tarnishing their legitimacy.

As a result of my experiences and observations in the sphere of international criminal law and having served on the bench of two international criminal tribunals (the International Criminal Tribunal for the former Yugoslavia (ICTY) and the Special Tribunal for Lebanon (STL)), I have, quite reluctantly, formed the view that, although we have made progress in structuring the composition of benches of international courts and tribunals to facilitate improved levels of diversity, a more inclusive approach to selection is required. In face of this apparent deficiency, greater effort could be made to attract and include members of minority groups among the ranks of the international judiciary.

In this Epilogue, I contemplate my own experiences with diversity and inclusion in international justice, in the context of international criminal law in particular,

Janet M Nosworthy, *Epilogue* In: *Identity and Diversity on the International Bench.* Edited by: Freya Baetens, Oxford University Press (2020). DOI: 10.1093/oso/9780198870753.003.0027.

through multi-focal minority lenses: primarily that of gender (as a female in a still substantially male dominated field) and geography (in that I am the product of a small third world, middle-income, developing island State). Jamaica is certainly not one of the first jurisdictions which spring to mind when giving thought to 'the main forms of civilization', or the '*principal* legal systems of the world'. Moreover, I am of Afro-Caribbean racial stock and before joining the international judiciary, I worked as a Prosecutor and a Defence lawyer in a common-law legal system. I start this Epilogue by looking at the concept of international justice (section 2), followed by a brief investigation into the identity crisis created by the interaction of diversity, inclusion, and legitimacy (section 3). Subsequently I discuss some judicial reflections in the mirror of international justice (section 4), the present need for action (section 5), and the meritocracy vs. diversity debate (section 6), in order to finish with an outlook on the future (section 7).

2. The Concept of International Justice

2.1 Foundations

At the heart and base of this discourse is *international justice*. Broken down in practical terms, this concerns who should be given the opportunity to sit on the benches of international courts; who should participate in and influence their judgments and decisions; who should perform the all-important judicial task of interpreting and developing international law and determining the principles of substantive and procedural law or to lay out the case law which governs and is cited and applied in international court proceedings. This issue, whilst seemingly uncomplicated, is in fact intricate and inextricably linked to the legitimacy of international law itself.

An intensified approach to diversity would strengthen international courts and tribunals as institutions. Given the strong interconnection between international and domestic law, in that the two jurisdictions operate circuitously and feed into each other, there is both a trickle-down and a filter-up effect within the two spheres of law. Prior to their appointment, international judges have worked in domestic jurisdictions, whether in a judicial, legal practice, academic, or other capacity. They bring to international benches their store of legal knowledge, culture, and experience. Some substantive and procedural rules from domestic jurisdictions can be applied in the international adjudication process, particularly in instances where there is no clear avenue for resolving such issues in international law itself.

Conversely, these same judges acquire additional knowledge and experience in international courts and build case law and jurisprudence from which legal principles will be extracted for future application whether in their particular court or tribunal or by other international courts. These principles may then be considered and, as appropriate, applied by domestic courts when they are dealing with and interpreting domestic laws in matters that overlap in international law, such as human rights, piracy, terrorism, or gender-based crimes. For example, when a domestic court decides to charge and try perpetrators for crimes over which the International Criminal Court (ICC) could have jurisdiction, it will likely look to the ICC case law as a complementary source of judicial guidance. In sum, when international judges return to practice in their domestic jurisdictions, those jurisdictions benefit from their knowledge and experience acquired internationally. Accordingly, the international community as a whole, as well as individual domestic jurisdictions, reap considerable benefits from enhanced levels of global participation and contribution to the practice and development of international law.

2.2 International Character

As a prelude to the substance of my discourse, I wish to give due emphasis and deference to the *international* character of international justice, and specifically international criminal justice. We, as international lawyers, live in an age of global justice and universal jurisdiction. The latter principle, encroaching as it does on State sovereignty, is highly controversial and has its detractors. Nonetheless, it is a feature of contemporary international law, engaging cross-territorial investigation and prosecution, which are justified, first, because of the serious and horrific nature of the crimes committed; second, due to the fact that third States and international tribunals only initiate proceedings after the State responsible for investigation and prosecution has failed to take the necessary steps to carry out its obligations (complementarity); and lastly, by virtue of the alleged obligation of States to prevent the commission of such crimes and to bring alleged perpetrators to justice. The notions of global justice and universal jurisdiction are grounded in the fact that international crimes such as genocide, enslavement, torture, crimes against humanity, war crimes, or violations of international humanitarian law, have not only domestic but also global impact. Such infractions harm the general international community and the international legal order. Equally, disputes between States are oftentimes politically polarizing. They threaten world order and peace, having a global ricocheting effect when they remain festering and unresolved.[1]

[1] Kathryn Sikkink and Hun Joon Kim, 'The Justice Cascade: The Origins and Effectiveness of Prosecutions of Human Rights Violations' (2013) 9 Annual Review of Law and Social Science 269.

The long-term object of international justice, including international criminal justice, is the achievement of *world* peace.[2] I therefore start from the premise that the stakes in international criminal law and international criminal justice belong to all of us. They are not confined to any one country, jurisdiction, race, ethnicity, religious grouping, continent, geographic region, or gender. They transcend matters of culture, whether social, civil law, common law, Islamic law, Judaic law, or otherwise. They surpass political divisions, associations, or ideology. International justice belongs to the world so both in principle and in practice, it should demonstrate this essential condition of *global* inclusion rather than exclusivity. If it lacks inclusivity then it would not be *international.* If it belonged to any one group or class of persons, then, equally it could not be *international.*

3. Diversity, Inclusion and Legitimacy: an Identity Crisis of Sorts

From my experience, an international tribunal's legitimacy is stronger when it is both diverse and inclusive. In this sense, identification of a country, region, or area with at least some members of an international tribunal helps to increase its legitimacy. When the factor of *identity* is carefully examined, it comprises a substantial and complex facet of any individual's *persona,* whichever their State or jurisdiction of origin. For the purposes of this Epilogue, I loosely describe *identity* as: a sense of self-association, of belonging to a group, organization, or entity. It imports a practical or psychological nexus by reason of ethnicity (nationality, race, tribe, language), geography (continent, country, region, north south, east, west), legal-judicial culture (common law/civil law or Islamic) as well as ideological or social culture (with whom a person, group, or nation connects or *identifies*).

This mental nexus or connection to other persons or groups or organizations with which a person identifies, exists to the extent that he or she emanates from or forms part of that group, bears characteristics, identical or similar to that group, or shares common practices, interests, or goals with them, around which they unite. This mental or psychological connection as a state of mind may be present in an individual's relationship with an international court or tribunal which dispenses international justice. The contrary also occurs: there might be disconnection from or absence of identification with the international court.

A *minority* is a relative term when applied within diverse communities globally. The Merriam Webster Dictionary defines it as: 'a group that is in some way different from the majority of a society or population or alternatively, any small group

[2] As reflected, for example, in the Preamble of the Rome Statute of the International Criminal Court, 2187 UNTS 3 [hereafter 'ICC Statute'], and Art 2(3) Charter of the United Nations, 1 UNTS XVI [hereafter 'UN Charter'].

in society which is different from the rest on grounds of their race, religion political beliefs or other reason, or the members of such a group'. Beyond this meaning, the term 'minority' is a highly charged concept, evoking notions of power and dominance, suggesting comparative imbalance by way of advantage, disadvantage, preference, prejudice, dominance, subjugation, and all that these conditions import, as indicated in the following apt description 'a culturally, ethnically or racially distinct group that co-exists with but is *subordinate* to a more dominant group'.[3] In my opinion, the concept of a minority additionally carries a hidden meaning, based on (often negative) stereotypes surrounding intellect, learning, and competence generally.

I understand striving for 'diversity' and 'inclusion' to imply a need for a wider selection range for the international bench, which will in turn enhance its balance, neutrality, and equality. These terms hold out an expectation, if not of an absolute equality of contenders, then an anticipation of equality of opportunity. It should not incorporate exclusivity. The disputes brought before international courts originate from different jurisdictions in terms of political and economic power, geography, ethnicity, religion, social culture, and international or regional stature. The actors in the international theatre (States as well as non-States) are politically and economically unequal in many respects but this should not affect how they are perceived and treated within the international justice system (equality before the law).

3.1 Averting an Identity Crisis

For international courts to be viewed as truly international, the aim for effective *inclusion* would be to increase the level of individuals' identification with those courts through the presence of a broad ranging representative selection of judges on their benches, including judges from minority groups, in addition to judges originating from traditional or 'principal' jurisdictions. Moreover, the United Nations itself practices the principle of diversity in engagement of persons for the performance of its work on behalf of the nations of the world, as an Equal Opportunity and Non-Discrimination employer.[4] Another underpinning basic principle of the UN creed

[3] Definition and facts—Britinnica.com. As the term is used in social sciences, this subordinacy is the chief defining characteristic and as such minority status does not necessarily correlate to population.

[4] See the United Nations Development Program (UNDP) website and the section entitled Gender, diversity, and inclusiveness reads as follows: 'UNDP believes that an inclusive culture attracts the best talent. Our diverse workforce delivers effectively by tapping into different perspectives, experiences, knowledge, and approaches. We are leveraging our workforce's potential and achieving greater organizational excellence.' UNDP's strategy for Gender parity includes taking measure to address challenges to achieving an equal balance between men and women at each level of posts. UNDP's strategy for advancing Diversity and Inclusiveness is to create a work environment welcoming to all, where everyone feel valued and can perform at their best regardless of age, gender, identity, disability caste, ethnicity, nationality, religion, sexual orientation, or any other status.<www.undp.org/content/undp/en/home/jobs/gender-and-diversity.html>accessed 16 August 2020. See also Sustainable Development

is the sovereign equality among Member States.[5] It would be unreasonable and inconsistent with UN policy if this principle was not enforced in relation to the selection of judges and their appointment to international benches.

The Statute of the International Court of Justice (ICJ) states that: '[a]t every election, the electors shall bear in mind not only that the persons to be elected should individually possess the qualifications required, but also that in the body as a whole the representation of the main forms of civilization and of the principal legal systems of the world should be assured'.[6] Equally, the Procedure for the Nomination and Election of Judges, the Prosecutor and Deputy Prosecutors of the International Criminal Court (ICC Procedure) provides that: 'States Parties shall, in the election of judges, take into account the need for the representation of the *principal* legal systems of the world [...]'.[7] The term 'principal' denotes those jurisdictions of greater prominence within the international community that are perhaps considered by some to have greater levels of credibility or representativeness among their judiciary and legal actors in the wider international sphere. Those legal systems are often centuries old and their laws and jurisprudence have historically formed the base of international law, including international criminal law.[8] In more recent times, it has been said they have been at the forefront of human rights, though I consider that this is debatable.

In light of the importance of these principal legal systems, it is not my intention to challenge the presence of their representatives on international benches: they bring a much-needed perspective which they have gained within those jurisdictions, whether in substantive or procedural law. I understand the intention to ensure that judges from these principal jurisdictions are always among the total slate of judges who emerge from the rounds of election, because of what they are regarded as bringing to the judicial process and for reasons of perceived credibility and legitimacy of the courts themselves. However, I believe that diversity is a result or outcome of inclusion and *vice versa*.

Goal (DG) number 5 which aims to achieve gender equality and empower all girls and women in access to employment, managerial positions, political office, and positions of empowerment. See UN SDG Knowledge Platform website <www.sustainabledevelopment.un.org/content/documents/21252030 accessed 16 August 2020.

[5] The principle of sovereign equality among Member States is recognized in Art 2(1) UN Charter.

[6] Art 9, Statute of the International Court of Justice, 33 UNTS 993 [hereafter 'ICJ Statute'].

[7] Art 19, Procedure for the Nomination and Election of Judges, the Prosecutor and Deputy Prosecutors of the International Criminal Court (ICC-ASP/3/Res 6)—*consolidated version* [emphasis added], which states in full that: 'States Parties shall, in the election of judges, take into account the need for the representation of the principal legal systems of the world, equitable geographical representation and a fair representation of female and male judges.'

[8] *Prosecutor v Lubanga*, ICC T.Ch., Decision Regarding the Practices Used to Prepare and Familiarise Witnessses for Giving Testimony, 30 November 2007, para 41; and *Prosecutor v Katanga and Ngudjolo*, ICC PT. Ch. I, Decision Revoking the Prohibition of Contact and Communication between Germain Katanga and Mathieu Ngidjolo Chui, 13 March 2008, p 12

I have seen the importance of promoting and maintaining identification and association with an *international* court and its bench: the effect of fostering feelings of inclusion is that the court becomes clothed in legitimacy in the eyes of citizens of far-flung jurisdictions. The drafters of the ICJ Statute may be said to have attempted to include these considerations by allowing States that do not have a judge of their nationality on the Court to name an ad hoc judge for their specific dispute.[9] Although this may enhance the identification of a party to a specific dispute, it does not necessarily solve the issue of the Court's legitimacy in general. The challenge is to structure composition of the bench so as to permit a selection balance so that no one group appears to dominate or stand out as preferred, or consistently unrepresented or underrepresented. Composition must be *visibly* diverse. Diversity then becomes powerful in itself and the practice of inclusion becomes demonstrative, as a neutralizer of notions of preference or prejudice toward a particular class, group (whether traditional or minority), or jurisdiction within the international community.

Legitimacy is a supremely intangible quality which should be viewed in terms of the apparent ability of an international court and its judges to deliver effective justice. This entails, as guaranteed by human rights standards, a fair and expeditious trial by a competent, independent, and impartial court established by law, both in effect and in appearance to the greater global community.[10] It also incorporates whether, and the extent to which, persons in domestic jurisdictions, including minorities, could reasonably *identify* with international judges or feel a connection with, or a stake in, the settlement of disputes by an international court.

In my opinion, where legal subjects within domestic jurisdictions do not form this necessary association, because they do not identify with any judges on the bench, this results in an aversion on the part of those jurisdictions that feel excluded from global efforts towards building an international legal system. This in turn serves to alienate governments and citizens of those jurisdictions (and possibly other States in their region) rather than encourage them to wholeheartedly join and provide logistical support for the global fight for justice and peace. This is particularly the case for international criminal prosecutions and trials of alleged perpetrators falling under the scope of domestic jurisdictions or of international courts and tribunals.

Diversity and inclusion reflected in the practice on the bench minimize the risk of any such identity crisis or deficiency and serve to solidify international courts' perception as being relevant, sustainable, and sensitive to their culture, legal systems, and moral values, and as having the ability to understand the challenges

[9] Art 31(2) and (3) ICJ Statute.

[10] Art 7, Universal Declaration of Human Rights (adopted 10 December 1948 UNGA Res 217 A(III)); Art 14, International Covenant on Civil and Political Rights, 999 U.N.T.S. 171 (entered into force 23 March 1976).

within the communities where cases before international courts originate. In sum, diversity and inclusion validate international courts and their benches, enhancing their global standing.

3.2 What Minorities Bring to the International Judicial Table

In my experience, unreservedly, building benches which are diverse and which allow a reasonable level of participation from minority groups is not only essential to the process of adjudication but reinforces legitimacy in the eyes of the world, being more consonant with the spirit and intent of global cooperation and contribution to international justice. Their inclusion serves to enhance international benches, rather than weaken or undermine them. Members that are not from countries that traditionally have had a stronger influence in the development of international law bring different, unknown insights and perspectives from their communities. When they are connected to the jurisdictions, regions, or communities where the dispute originates they also bring a deeper understanding of the socio-political dynamics, cultural norms, and behaviours within their diverse cultures as well as facilitating access to a fuller knowledge of background history and socio-political context, where procedurally and evidentially appropriate. Consequently, in my experience, they can open up, enrich, and affect judicial discourse and deliberations, permitting each individual member of the bench and the bench as a unit to be better informed and more ably approach the issues for determination before them. The debate is magnified and expanded because of this dynamic, this plurality. This allows special pockets of focus, in order to resolve factual and legal issues which should always guide judicial determination. Their presence could result in a more searching examination of the facts and a heightened application of the law, pushing law interpretation and law development.

This benefit, however, is countered by possible bias if left unchecked. In the same manner that a judge who is personally in favour of tighter gun control measures within inner city communities might be less likely to interpret a firearms law in a manner which facilitates greater public access to firearms' licences, likewise the personal experiences and opinions of international judges may affect their considerations of the issues before them. I have noted that this is particularly the case where judges hold strong personal opinions backed-up by historical, social, or religious endorsement. This applies often in situations where the subject matter of the legal issues for determination is directly or indirectly related to the minority characteristic of an international judge sitting on a case, for example, in cases concerning conflicts between different confessional groups, ethnic or political groupings. International judges who are minority members are not immune to the possibility of judicial indiscretion. Issues of bias and prejudice aside, it is a judicial predicament which all judges, domestic and international, must acknowledge where it threatens to superimpose itself onto a judicial determination. Where they are able to identify these situations, judges ought to respond by attempting to 'blinker' their personal opinions and focus on giving appropriate consideration to the evidence and the pertinent applicable and procedural laws. Injustice and unfairness is a result that each judge must jealously guard against for purposes of legality and legitimacy—and this applies as much to a minority judge as to any other.

4. Judicial Reflections in the Mirror of International Justice

I have seen that in truth, people around the world, whether for reasons of social or judicial culture, continental origin, region, ethnicity, sexual orientation, race, or religion, do not want to be excluded from the process of adjudication. They want to be represented on international benches. They want to hear people who speak the languages and dialects which they speak. They want to see, among the mix of judges, those who understand their cultural and moral values, their social interactions, and behaviour. They want recognition and validity. They crave the type of endorsement which they see being meted to seemingly select members of non-minority communities. In the quest for real rather than pretended legitimacy, inclusion and diversity walk hand in hand. This is why, when composing international benches, effort should be made to ensure that an admixture of international law professionals is brought together: domestic judges, prosecutors, defence lawyers, academics, diplomats, arbitrators, human rights advocates, and more. Each brings their unique concentrated experience, expertise, and learning as the decision, facts, or law may require during the course of adjudication. Combined, they form a formidable blend of jurists to jointly crack the judicial nutshell and deliver justice.

In my view, a more diverse international bench will also help to engender a sense that a given international court is more likely to deliver a judgment in accordance with the facts and the law, when the facts involve conflict and underlying socio-political-economic undercurrents including allegations of political divisions and perceived interference by hegemonic powers. I do not contend that current international benches are totally bereft of diversity but rather that some major (principal) actors and countries are overly recurrent. Meanwhile, certain minorities seem to fall through the election or selection cracks, obvious through their absence.

4.1 Sizing Up the Situation

Does *size* of the jurisdiction from which a judge comes matter? Here, I am compelled to answer with one loud resounding yes! When contemplating the selection of judges for the international bench, geographical size, the size of a State's economy, global financial standing and influence are a distinct advantage, a huge asset rather than a disability. This applies not only to judges, but also to support staff and other crucial players.

Subsurface, my perception is that there is a reluctance to assign what is regarded as a big *man's* job (sitting on an international bench) to 'little people' (persons coming from small, third world, apparently insignificant, jurisdictions). There appears to remain a lingering feeling that they lack the judicial skills and experience, erudition, independence from political ideology and possibly governmental control. In allowing them access to the international bench, they may bring corrupt practices from their domestic jurisdictions. Financially, their home States contribute little to the court system. They have nothing to barter or offer in return but their presence on the international bench. As a result, there is a tendency to believe that such persons are not primary candidates for selection, as they might 'dilute' the quality of the Bench. If elected nevertheless, this dilution can only be curbed by ensuring that the majority (including the president) on a given bench fits a particular (principal) mould, which is confined to certain exclusive jurisdictions in order to maintain quality control over international justice.

Indeed, even when issues of gender are considered, I am inclined to believe that the manner in which a woman of first world origin and one of third world origin (or of a smaller jurisdiction, or a member of a minority) is dealt with, may be decidedly different. Their suitability for the bench may be judged by different standards. They might be regarded as possessing different judicial capabilities and 'without more', one may be perceived as possessing greater professional and judicial credibility than the other, rendering minority access remote or extremely limited.

4.2 Lessons in Legal History

Over centuries, through its endless bloody wars, ethnic strife, unlawful imprisonments, anarchy, despotism, enslavements (including sexual enslavement), religious persecutions, autocracies, colonization, imperialism, and more, history has played an entrenched part in shaping legal principles and opinion. It has also been filled with struggles of citizens and peoples around the world for achievement of legal status, basic human rights, and recognition. In the process, it has taught us not to trust each other, to be mindful of each other's motives and actions. History has dictated the content of our laws. It has instructed how we award, deny, or qualify human rights and freedoms; how we view equality (or inequality) before the law; whose evidence we find acceptable in the absence of need for further proof; how we deal with the most heinous international crimes and infractions; the remedies and redress we offer or deny to those whose fundamental rights have been breached and the extent to which they could be described as 'just and effective', and lastly, the treatment of minorities within our communities and what protection, if any, we might offer them consistent with their guaranteed constitutional rights.

Historical grievances and wounds do not heal easily and we are only just learning to slowly put our guard down and to cooperate in order to solve the world's legal problems. It has been slow and painstaking without any certain promise of an easier road ahead. Now, maybe more than a chink is open in the window of opportunity. Sometimes the principles of international law, themselves, present a stark and telling picture of the practical historical realities. I recall my first interactions as a law student with public international law: the principles of law recognized by *civilized nations of the world.* I reflected on the concept. Which are they, these civilized jurisdictions? Conversely, which were the uncivilized jurisdictions outside of this framework of international judicial erudition and influence? Did it mean that no judge, decision, or judgment from my jurisdiction could ever participate in generating a principle that could become a source of international law, could ever form the foundation of a general principle of international law?

I learnt that this very exclusive rationale is firmly grounded in Article 38(1) of the Statute of the International Court of Justice, the 'World' Court, which decides disputes between States as well as issuing advisory opinions. The criterion was simple, yet, to me, fully loaded, given the meaning of the term *civilized* with its racial, regional, religious, and cultural connotations and delimitations. From my perspective as a student, it seemed clear that only certain exclusive jurisdictions were envisaged. Not the most inclusive approach to adjudication in its prime. However, at the time (this phrase originated in the Statute of the Permanent Court of International Justice) the view was that all nations were considered civilized 'because law implies civilization'.[11] For me, the polarizing nature of this criterion, even though it has now been firmly rejected by international courts,[12] was consistent with a mindset which splits legal systems of the world into categories and holds out the promise that only specific jurisdictions and particular judges may be counted on to deal with complex issues of law and the formulation of principles and resolutions which may be reasoned or useful. In order for us to progress mentally and symbolically, we can be encouraged by the fact that this qualification is no longer *du jour* and is discredited as an unworthy anachronism.

There are still lingering remnants of this mindset in the selection process, particularly where it is not clearly set out how to effectively and fairly manage the situation through quotas or systems that offer careful guidelines, for example,

[11] Lapradelle, Procès-Verbaux of the Proceedings of the Advisory Committee of Jurists (1920) Annex no 3 p 335.

[12] Alain Pellet, 'Article 38' in Andreas Zimmermann, Christian Tomuschat, Karin Oellers-Frahm, Christina J. Tams (eds), *The Statute of the International Court of Justice: A Commentary* (OUP 2012) 836–37.

concerning assignment of judges to panels.[13] I concede that others without minority membership might hold a more generous view of the process, but my conversations and interactions with members of other minority groups generally have not allowed me to completely and sincerely embrace a more obliging view.

5. If it Ain't Broke, Don't Fix it—Why Now?

Why entertain this conversation now? Great achievements in terms of diversity have already been made: currently, the two permanent international courts—the ICJ and the ICC—have African men at their helm (Abdulqawi Yusuf from Somalia and Chile Eboe-Osuji from Nigeria, respectively). The ICJ, moreover, has an Asian, female Vice-President (Xue Hanqin from China). Two Eastern European women are heading two international ad hoc courts: the Kosovo Court and the STL (Ekaterina Trendafilova from Bulgaria and Ivana Hrdličková from the Czech Republic, respectively).

In the past, ICC Presidents have included an Asian man (Song Sang-Hyun from South Korea) and a Latin-American woman (Silvia Fernández de Gurmendi from Argentina), while a male Caribbean national has headed the ICTY (Patrick Lipton Robinson from Jamaica—currently serving on the ICJ bench). The ICJ and the Special Court for Sierra Leone have both had a female President (Rosalyn Higgins from the UK and Shireen Avis Fisher from the USA, respectively) and the ICTY has been presided over by an African-American woman (Gabrielle Kirk McDonald). Members of minority groups have also been appointed as Vice-Presidents of international courts and tribunals. Muslims are serving on the international bench with Christians and persons of other faiths; while civil and common lawyers have been sitting together since the establishment of most international courts. Diversity has never had it so good.

So, why stir up a judicial selection hornet's nest at this time? I could not honestly advance that the selection system is completely broken. On the contrary, there is no doubt that it is working. However, it needs maintenance and upgrading to give it the necessary curb-appeal, modernity, and marketability. Times change so different responses have to be formulated to reflect this temporal reality. After the League of Nations, the forerunner to the United Nations, was established in 1920, its membership comprised only of 63 countries as of 1939. The map of the world has been re-arranged considerably since then, particularly during the last fifty years. Many new countries have been created in the post-colonial era or secured

[13] See eg Rule 4(2) of the Rules on the Assignment of Kosovo Specialist Chambers Judges from the Roster of International Judges which provides that: For the purposes of Assignment, the President shall be guided by objective criteria such as experience, expertise, seniority gender, and geographical representation.

autonomous rule. As of 2020, there are 195 countries in the world, of which 193 are Member States of the United Nations and two have non-member observer status (the Holy See and Palestine). International justice, and correspondingly, membership of and access to international benches have to be viewed against that background and contextualization.

Admittedly, the diversity in top appointments as outlined above is certainly worthy of note and encouraging. Notwithstanding, we must take care not to represent this as the rule rather than the exception. Within the last ten to five years, solid strides towards increased diversity have been made but there is still room for improvement. How we will achieve this goal is yet to be resolved. In the interim, we are celebrating cautiously, in the face of what I have witnessed as an 'unwritten rule' that there may only be one female President in the life of an international court or tribunal and that, unless mandated to the contrary, female judges should be perpetually in the minority (no more than a third or quarter of the total judicial cadre). Correspondingly, we are still seeing only a sprinkling of diversity rather than significant representation.

In international adjudication, real effort and determination is required in order to custom-build a truly inclusive system which is appropriately diverse in terms of gender and other identity elements. To this end, precise regulatory provisions are useful in ensuring a progressive approach to selection criteria and voting strategies. Article 36(8)(a) of the ICC Statute is an example:[14] State Parties should give consideration to a fair representation of male and female judges. Another illustration can be found in the Rules on Assignment of Kosovo Specialist Chambers Judges from the Roster of International Judges: for the purpose of assigning judges to panels, the President 'shall be guided by objective criteria such as experience, expertise, seniority, gender and geographical representation . . . .'[15]

This demonstrates the type of instruction and attention to necessary criteria which should be incorporated in rules governing bench composition after election. But regulatory provisions could go even further to ensure inclusive results, for example, specific requirements could be adopted to regulate the selection of candidates who are allowed to run for election in the first place. Evidently, each international court is different in terms of its jurisdiction and circumstances giving rise to its establishment. In the case of ad hoc and hybrid international courts where some judges are specifically drawn from the jurisdiction from which the matters originate or the surrounding region, special measures have to be put in place to ensure that these benches still retain a truly diverse, international character and are gender-balanced.

[14] Art 36(8)(a) ICC Statute: 'The States Parties shall, in the selection of judges, take into account the need, within the membership of the Court, for: (i) the representation of the principal legal systems of the world; (ii) equitable geographical representation; and (iii) a fair representation of female and male judges.'

[15] Rule 4(2), Rules on the Assignment of Specialist Chambers Judges from the Roster of International Judges, KSD-BD-02/1 (adopted on 14 March 2017).

6. Meritocracy vs Diversity Debate

Very often the issue of meritocracy is raised as a hurdle or reason for non-inclusion of members of certain groups, or for numerical limits being placed on their inclusion. Quite properly and reasonably, merit must always be a defining measure in selection for or appointment to the international bench, or indeed, the domestic bench. A judicial nominee or contender should possess the qualifications of a judge, whatever their jurisdiction of origin and whatever their characteristics such as gender, culture, race, ethnicity, or religious denomination. Indeed, all international courts set qualifications which their judges must possess. For example, Article 13 of the ICTY Statute stipulates that ICTY judges must be 'persons of high moral character, impartiality and integrity who possess qualifications required in their respective countries for appointment to the highest judicial offices'.[16]

Nonetheless, I have observed that inherent in the *merit* enquiry lies often a quiet and persistent resistance to bench diversification and inclusion beyond minimal levels. It is insinuated that, should we pursue diversity more extensively, selected candidates would be unable to fully meet selection and performance criteria. I entirely reject this insinuation: the role played by women judges, for example, in the development of international law over a relatively short period, not only on issues concerning gender and children, but more generally, utterly discounts this misconception. Moreover, who could properly question whether women must be involved in adjudicating serious violations of international law which affect the global communities of which they form part? They must be adequately represented when disputes between States are being determined and opinions are rendered on matters which will affect domestic jurisdictions, States, and their citizens around the world.

6.1 What's Good for the Goose is Good for the Gender!

Bringing women into the judicial process in greater numbers is essential, for many reasons. First, not including women, except in low numbers, would mean

[16] Art 13, Statute of the International Criminal Tribunal for the former Yugoslavia, Security Council Resolution 827(1993) 25 May 1993 [hereafter 'ICTY Statute']. See also Art 36(3) (a) and Art 36(3) (b)(i) and (ii) ICC Statute, which provide that: 'Every candidate for election to the Court shall (i) have established competence in criminal law and procedure and the necessary relevant experience whether as a judge Prosecutor, Advocate or other similar capacity in criminal proceedings or (ii) have established competence in relevant areas of international law such as humanitarian law or the law of human rights, and extensive experience in a professional Legal capacity which is relevant to the judicial work of the Court.' Under Art 36(3) (c) ICC Statute: '[e]very candidate for election to the Court shall have an excellent knowledge of and be fluent in at least one of the working languages of the Court'.

denying real participation in international justice to roughly one half of the world's population.[17] In fact, in many jurisdictions, women currently outnumber men. Additionally, many international crimes target women as victims: rape, sexual assault, imprisonment, sexual slavery, forced marriages, genocidal acts, and the recruitment of child soldiers. In such cases, women judges have participated in watershed decisions, which have aided the development of international criminal law, pushed the judicial agenda and helped to bring the international criminal justice into the 21st century.

The best illustration is the landmark *Akeyesu* case,[18] which was the first trial before the International Criminal Tribunal for Rwanda (ICTR). One of the trial court judges was a woman: Navanethem Pillay from South Africa, who later became the ICTR President and who has written the foreword to this book. Her critical role in this groundbreaking jurisprudence has been acknowledged,[19] when rape was defined for the first time within the context of an armed conflict as 'a physical invasion of a sexual nature, committed on a person under circumstances which are coercive'[20] and sexual violence as 'any act of a sexual nature […] under circumstances which are coercive'.[21] This is not limited to penetration of the human body. The issue of consent was not recognized as a material element of rape/sexual violence in light of the violent and oppressive context within which rapes take place during genocide, crimes against humanity, or armed conflict.[22] This allowed the victim's lack of consent to be inferred from the 'coercive' circumstances of the sexual violation rather than as an essential element which would have needed to be established through positive evidence of a clear refusal. It was held, momentously, that the act of rape itself could constitute genocide, when carried out against the adversary's female population, with the intent 'to destroy in whole or in part a national, ethnical, racial or religious group'.[23]

Another seminal demonstration of female judges' contributions is the case of *Bosco Ntaganda*,[24] before an ICC Appeals Chamber where two of the five judges were female (Sanji Monageng from Botswana and Christine Van den Wyngaert

[17] See Worldometers, population by Gender, Age, Fertility Rate, Immigration—Male Gender 50.4%, Female 49.6 of a total 7,162,119,434 world populations. Data provided by United Nations Department of Economic and Social Affairs, Population Division. World Prospects: 2017 Revision. The 7.7 billion population mark was reached in 2018.

[18] ICTR-96-4-T, *Prosecutor v Jean Paul Akeyesu* (2 Sept. 1998) Judgment [hereafter 'Akeyesu'].

[19] Catherine A. MacKinnon, 'The ICTR's Legacy on Sexual Violence' (2008) 14 (2) *New England Journal of International and Comparative Law* 101.

[20] *Akeyesu* (n 18) para 598.

[21] *Akeyesu* (n 18) para 598.

[22] *Akeyesu* (n 18) paras 497–99, 507–08, 596, and 688.

[23] Art 2 Statute of the International Criminal Tribunal for Rwanda, UN Doc No. S/RES/955(1994) [hereafter 'ICTR Statute'] reflects the Convention on the Prevention and Punishment of the Crime of Genocide, 78 UNTS 277 (9 Dec. 1948).

[24] ICC-01/04-02/06 OA5, *Prosecutor v Bosco Ntaganda* (15 Jun. 2017) Judgment on Appeal against 'Second Decision on the Defence's Challenge to the Jurisdiction of the Court in respect of Counts 6 and 9'.

from Belgium). This case arose out of a conflict situation in the Democratic Republic of Congo and concerned the alleged systematic rape and sexual slavery of child soldiers by members of their own troops (rather than perpetrators from the opposing side of the conflict). The Defence challenged the ICC's jurisdiction on the ground that the accused could not be found responsible under international criminal law for the rape of child soldiers of the *Union des Patriotes Congolais/Forces Patriotiques Pour La Liberation du Congo* given that the accused's membership of the same Forces excluded criminal liability.

The ICC held that there was no requirement that the victims of the war crimes of rape and sexual slavery should be 'protected persons in the (limited) sense of the grave breaches or Common Article 3 [of the Geneva Conventions]'.[25] Within the framework of international criminal law, subject to the acts having taken place within and being associated with an armed conflict, (whether of an international or non-international character), to satisfy the nexus requirement which delineated war crimes from ordinary crimes, 'members of an armed force or group are not categorically excluded from protection against the war crimes of rape and sexual slavery under Article 8(2)(b) (xxii) and 2(e)(vi) of the Statute when committed by members of the same armed force or group'.[26]

In dismissing the appeal, the Appeals Chamber expressly endorsed the Trial Chamber's finding that 'there is never a justification to engage in sexual violence against any person; irrespective of whether or not this person may be liable to be targeted and killed under international humanitarian law'.[27] Given the absence of any general rule excluding members of armed forces from protection against violations by members of the same armed force, there was no ground for assuming the existence of a rule specifically for the offences of rape and sexual slavery. An objective observer might properly form the view that this is a demonstration of legal development and international *justice* working at its very best to give just protection to victims of international crimes and to ensure that alleged offenders do not escape jurisdictional reach and prosecution.

So, undoubtedly, women judges bring special perspectives and insights from within the female community, allowing their judicial brothers to more readily comprehend female victims and their behaviours within the highly volatile, socially and culturally pressurized circumstances of sexual assault and rapes in times of conflict. I have observed that they can help to avert any residual cultural tendency within the male ranks of the bench to judge victims of these offences harshly on moral, social grounds such as their mode of attire, their type of employment; their marital status, and even adverse class, racial, or ethnical stereotyping.

25 ibid para 51.
26 ibid Key Finding 2, p 3.
27 ibid para 65.

6.2 Cultural Shock and Awe

Before I entered the world of international criminal law, after decades of practice in my domestic jurisdiction, I was not particularly aware that I was a 'common law' lawyer. However, I was given a rude awakening when presented with large swathes of hearsay evidence during my first week of trial in my first case as an international judge. I was in 'judicial cultural shock'. In time, I learnt to deal with the issue in terms of weight and to employ a refined evidential sifting process, *after* admission of the evidence. Within weeks of my arrival on the international bench, a civil law judicial sister confided to me that she was very confused by the fact that in these international proceedings the judges had *nothing* to do, as the common law lawyers over-ran the courtroom and wrested control of the proceedings from the judges. By way of knee-jerk reaction, the common law lawyer in me surfaced and was, at that time, deeply puzzled and concerned by her remark. I remained mute.

I was eager to work with and learn from my civil law judicial colleagues and hoped that I might have a reciprocal role to play in increasing their store of legal knowledge and experience. It was a fair exchange between the judicial sorority and fraternity on all sides of the cultural divides. In fact, a few of my new civil law colleagues initially viewed cross-examination by counsel as minimally more than an exercise in futility. Many discussions were held concerning its relative merits. With the passage of time, with greater experience, they came to comprehend and embrace it as a valid contribution to the process of judicial determination. As common law jurisdictions are not identical in every respect (and neither are all civil law jurisdictions alike), though there are common threads, there is also scope for inter-change of knowledge within those individual legal cultures themselves.

I have observed that justice is better served with this cross-cultural fertilization within the international judiciary, international judges step outside of their legal and judicial comfort zones to best perform their judicial duties. Diversity provides a platform for imparting and receiving new knowledge. It is highly transformational. Having embraced diversity in their experience in international law, judges know that they have grown in judicial cultural terms. They have learned to examine other cultures, and to critique their own judicial system and accommodate principles and practices from other cultures, in joint effort to reach a common solution to matters. Judges are then also able to inject what they have learned and integrate new principles into their own judicial systems to aid the development of international and domestic law and international justice and peace.

7. Looking to the Future

In light of the above considerations I conclude that diversity in the strategic selection of members to the international bench is an investment in the future of international law. Each judge brings with him or her 'baggage' from their own judicial culture: it is what they have practiced for decades. They carry moral values, socio-economic reference points, and legal principles and procedures from their domestic jurisdiction or the jurisdiction where they conducted their legal studies. On the international bench, they are confronted with new substantive and procedural law, as well as perspectives as opined by other judges. They must learn to re-focus and let go, where necessary and appropriate. In other words, they must shed some of that baggage, in order to navigate their way through the practice, principles, and procedures of international law.

Diversity builds bridges of understanding, judicial comity, universal fraternity, enhancing judicial knowledge, and cooperation. Very importantly, this multi-dimensional bridgework permits people in domestic jurisdictions around the world to feel a sense of association and identity with, of relevance to the international system, its courts and its judges. With ongoing developments that allow greater inclusion and participation, I remain hopeful and positive that continued improvement will be made so that steadily and incrementally, we will achieve the type of bench compositions which are more diverse and inclusive. In this way, international benches will be enhanced and international courts strengthened. If international law, justice, and peace are positively affected, this will bring huge gains globally.

My observations and opinions should not be construed as a denial of, or challenge to, the great contribution made by international judges coming from traditional or principal jurisdictions of the world, who are male, or who are not minority members. Undoubtedly, they have played an important role in building international (substantive and procedural) law from its inception. Within international law, we tend look to those jurisdictions for judicial instruction or guidance when resolving not only international disputes but additionally when adjudicating in the domestic milieu. Increasingly though, we are looking beyond the boundaries of their case law and decisions when hearing and determining legal matters, where resolution is not provided within international law itself. There will always be a place for judges, whatever their gender, from those 'principal' jurisdictions. What was advocated in this Epilogue is that the selection net be cast wider to include more 'outsider' nominees and that the system be geared more effectively to attract women and minorities of merit to ensure more diverse benches.

Index